BUTTS, R. Freeman. The education of the West; a formative chapter in the history of civilization. McGraw-Hill, 1973. 631p il map bibl 72-5118. 10.95.   ISBN 0-07-009409-8.   C.I.P.

Vastly different from Butts' previous text, *A cultural history of Western education* (1955), which was marred by the shadow of World War II and poorly contrasted totalitarian indoctrination against democratic enlightenment, the present work casts all education into a conceptual framework called "civilization building" and is very broad in scope and filled with unnecessarily complicated generalizations. It dwells at great length on prehistoric peoples, relying heavily on recent anthropological literature. In contrast to most texts, this one understates the importance of individual educators and overstates large general notions such as "modernization." The volume contains unique chapters on the "dispersion" of various educational traditions, numerous maps and charts to illustrate and delineate the schematic generalizations, and a good bibliography of standards works in English. This is a truly ambitious and energetic undertaking that attempts successfully to break with such recent traditional histories of Western education as Ralph L. Pounds, *The development of education in Western culture* (1968), and Adolphe E. Meyer, *An educational history of the Western world* (CHOICE, Sept. 1972), etc. For use in undergraduate and graduate courses.

THE EDUCATION OF THE WEST

A Formative Chapter in the History of Civilization

R. Freeman Butts

Teachers College
Columbia University

McGraw-Hill Book Company

New York   St. Louis   San Francisco   Düsseldorf   Johannesburg
Kuala Lumpur   London   Mexico   Montreal   New Delhi   Panama
Rio de Janeiro   Singapore   Sydney   Toronto

The Education of the West: A Formative Chapter in the History of Civilization

Successor to *A Cultural History of Western Education.*

1 2 3 4 5 6 7 8 9 0 DODO 7 9 8 7 6 5 4 3

Library of Congress Cataloging in Publication Data

Butts, Robert Freeman, 1910-
    The education of the West.

    Includes bibliographical references.
    1. Education—History.   I. Title.
LA11.B83   370'.9   72-5118
ISBN/0-07-009409-8

This book was set in Press Roman by Creative Book Services, division of McGregor & Werner, Incorporated. The editor was Robert C. Morgan; the designer was Creative Book Services; and the production supervisor was Sally Ellyson. The printer and binder was R. R. Donnelley & Sons Company.

CONTENTS

PART IV
THE DISPERSION OF WESTERN EDUCATION
AND THE MODERNIZATION OF TRADITIONAL SOCIETIES
(1700 A.D. - THE PRESENT)

ILLUSTRATIONS AND EXHIBITS

ABOUT THE AUTHOR

Born in Springfield, Illinois, R. Freeman Butts attended the Experimental College and the College of Letters and Science of the University of Wisconsin in Madison where he earned a B.A. in Humanities and an M.A. and a Ph.D. with concentrations in history, education, and philosophy. In 1936, after a year of post-doctoral study in the same fields at Columbia University, Professor Butts joined the full-time instructional staff of Teachers College, where he has been William F. Russell Professor in the Foundations of Education since 1958 and Director of the Institute of International Studies since 1965. He is also a member of the Faculty of International Affairs of Columbia University and Associate Dean for International Studies at Teachers College.

He was a Fulbright research scholar with the Australian Council for Educational Research in Melbourne (1954); educational adviser at the Central Institute of Education, University of Delhi in India (1959); recipient of a Carnegie Travel Grant for research in newly independent countries of Africa and Asia (1961-1962); and senior specialist at the East-West Center of the University of Hawaii (1965).

He has been president of the History of Education Society, the Comparative and International Education Society, the National Society of College Teachers of Education, and the American Educational Studies Association.

His books include:

The College Charts Its Course (1939)

A Cultural History of Western Education (1947 and 1955)

The American Tradition in Religion and Education (1950)

A History of Education in American Culture (1953) (with Lawrence A. Cremin)

Assumptions Underlying Australian Education (1955)

American Education in International Development (1963) (the sixth John Dewey Society Lecture)

PREFACE

In the early 1960s, when the writing of this book was broached, the idea was to make it a third edition of *A Cultural History of Western Education,* which was first published by McGraw-Hill in 1947 and revised in 1955. But it has turned out to be a new and different book. A momentous decade that speeded up revolutionary transformations in the world of nations as well as in the world of scholarship and education made the original plan obsolete.

True, the earlier book had ventured upon a new path for its time in its effort to view the history of education as an integral part of the history of social institutions and the history of ideas. I hoped, thereby, to remedy a defect in much of the prior writing and teaching in the history of education—namely, a tendency to look upon education as an institution isolated from the major forces at work in the surrounding society and culture. In this respect I anticipated by a decade the revisionist movement that swept American historiography in the late 1950s and early 1960s. (See Bibliographical Notes, pp. 569-570.)

The earlier book was rooted in a social concern that the study of history should be a basic resource for getting a firm grasp on the critical problems facing public policy in education as well as for gaining reliable knowledge about the educational past. In this effort to highlight those persistent political, economic, religious, and intellectual controversies of the past which would be most illuminating to the making of informed judgments about the predicament of the present, I anticipated the clamor of the 1960s that education be relevant to the great issues and human needs of our time.

In these two respects I reaffirm for this book the basic intentions of the earlier book: to provide a history of education broadly based in general history and, at the same time, to display a timely sense of the meaning of historical themes for the deepest civilizational crises of the present. But the older book did not and, in many respects, could not anticipate the range of revolutionary changes that culminated during the 1960s. While it is too soon to make definitive historical judgments, it is entirely possible that the third quarter of the twentieth century marked a distinctive turning point in the human condition, a turning point that may well be compared with one or two of the other major transformations in human history. So a new book had to be written. Although this book inevitably draws upon some of the insights and materials of *A Cultural History of Western Education,* it may be considered a successor to the earlier book rather than a revision in the usual sense. It is, however, revisionist in the most fundamental sense.

Several clusters of events in the world and of trends in scholarship have combined to require a new approach to history in general and to the history of education in particular. Leading all other events in their cumulative effects upon the vast majority of mankind is the coming to political independence of the peoples of more than half the world in less than a generation following the end of World War II. By the opening of the 1970s more than sixty of the sovereign nations of the world were less than twenty years old. They had been released from or had thrown off the colonial rule of the Western empires faster than anyone had dreamed possible before 1945. In their economic, political, and social conditions the new nations ranged from being mostly traditional to highly modernized. The gap between their state of development and that of the most modernized of the older sovereign nations constitutes one of the most portentous and dangerous facts of contemporary life. A world half poor and half rich can be no more secure than a nation half slave and half free.

What is particularly important is that this enormous disparity in the human condition is now recognized as having been caused in some measure by massive disparities in education. The rich nations are well educated; the poor nations are poorly educated. The gap between the more modern nations and the less modern nations is no less an educational gap than an economic or technological gap.[1] So, as the leaders of the new nations have launched their programs to modernize their economies, achieve a national unity and integrity, improve their rural and urban ways of life, and strengthen popular participation in their national affairs, they have turned to education as one of their chief resources for modernization. Naturally, they have turned to the more developed nations to see what lessons, both good and bad, they can learn from earlier experiences with education in the modernization process, what they can emulate and adapt, and what they should reject as harmful and alien.

No one who has not lived, worked, and grappled with the staggering problems of a people seeking to become modern while faced with the mountainous forces of tradition can appreciate the difficulty of what Lauriston Sharp, the Cornell University anthropologist, calls "a wholly new phenomenon in human history: men standing in one cultural age, demanding another."[2] This demand requires that the peoples of both cultural ages reassess the role that education has played in the building of their societies, recognizing that sometimes education enhances the forces of tradition and stability and at other times speeds the processes of social change and modernization.

A second cluster of events that requires reinterpretation in the history of education is typified by the cumulative crises that welled up in the modern societies of the 1960s. It is an irony of major proportions that just as half the world was aspiring to become modern as rapidly as possible, grave doubts were being raised in the already modern nations about the desirability of the very modernity to which the traditional societies were aspiring. The industrialization and technology that had made possible a

---

[1] For extensive documentation of the widening gap in the 1960s, see Edgar Faure et al., *Learning to Be, The World of Education Today and Tomorrow*, UNESCO, Paris and Harrap & Co., London, 1972.
[2] Lauriston Sharp, *The Role of the University in Promoting Change,* Cornell University, Ithaca, N.Y., 1962, p. 9.

high average standard of living among modern societies was found to cause dangerous pollution of the environment. This pollution is a formidable threat to living at all in an industrial and technological society.[3] The cities that had been the nucleus of modernity, indeed the very centers of all civilization for 5,000 years, were becoming the blight of modern civilization as the infectious ghettos of the inner cities exuded poverty, disease, frustration, crime, and rioting. The future of urban life itself came into question, and the flight to the "outer cities" or suburbs left the urban centers of the United States largely black and poor. The rural sectors harbored the disadvantaged poor of all ethnic stocks, especially the American Indian, Spanish speaking peoples from Mexico and the Caribbean, and poverty-stricken blacks and native whites. In all cases, a major symptom of disadvantage was the deprivation of education.

An America that had only lately taken up a posture of responsible participation in world affairs seemed to waver and pull back to an earlier stance of nonparticipation in the world as it blanched in the face of the war in Indochina from which it had great difficulty in extricating itself. For the first time in its history a majority of the American people came to oppose a war its nation was waging, a war which did not seem to have either the justification of democratic ideals or of manifest destiny.

And, above all, that cardinal principle of the American dream, a faith in massive educational endeavor, came under frontal attack. A fresh squadron of educational critics bombarded the educational system from top to bottom. Whereas the objective of critics in the 1950s had been the looseness, the laxity, and the soft pedagogy of a "mushy" system that needed greater intellectual rigor and adherence to higher academic standards, the target of the critics of the 1960s was the rigid, stultifying, and heartless pedagogy that stifled creativity, joy, and informal learning. A public school system which in the 1950s catered too much to the interests and needs of children was now suddenly pouring all children into the uniform mold dictated by the dominant establishment types that ruled an affluent society.

While the schools were dehumanizing the younger children in the view of the critics, older students began to rebel against the 500-year-old traditions of the university, an institution that had grown up with Western civilization itself. Underneath the surface violence and disruption that swept the campuses in the late 1960s was a growing disenchantment with the very purposes that had marked higher education in traditional civilizations as well as in modern societies: technical preparation for government, military, and industrial bureaucracies; specialized intellectual competence in the technologies as well as the scholarly disciplines of knowledge; and certification of competence in the public professions that served the welfare of society.

The battle cry of discontent heard "from sea to shining sea" was summed up in the plaint that higher as well as lower education was irrelevant to basic social values and had sold out to the vested interests of the established order. The lines of the argument were carried to their ultimate conclusion as the attack was launched against

---

[3]For a brilliant analysis from a global perspective, see Barbara Ward and René Dubos, *Only One Earth; the Care and Maintenance of a Small Planet,* Norton, New York, 1972.

the very idea of organized education itself: the call for deschooling society, doing away with organized schools and universities, resorting to informal or nonformal alternatives, and having a greater reliance upon television and the mass media for educational purposes, or conversely, a greater reliance upon small, personal, face-to-face groups, somehow free of bureaucratic and professional controls.

All this clamor requires a steady and hard new look at the history of education in relation to the organization and management of increasingly complex societies. If, as some social seers were predicting, the world was moving into a phase that could be described as postindustrial, posturban, postdemocratic, postmodern, or even post-civilized, was it also entering a stage when organized education was dispensable? Are we moving into a postschool civilization? Or is that a contradiction in terms? An answer to these questions requires not only a hard look but a long look at the course of education in human history.

Finally, a third cluster of changes requiring a radical reinterpretation in the history of education arose during the 1960s with new conceptual themes that marked scholarly investigations in the several humanistic studies and social sciences. Paramount among these themes was the call for history writing to drop its parochial framework and to broaden its perspective beyond the local, the provincial, and the national to embrace the larger supranational civilizations and even the world itself. Symbolic of this change were two presidential addresses at the American Historical Association, one that marked the opening and the other the closing of the decade of the 1960s.

In December 1959, C. Vann Woodward spoke of the avalanches of events since 1945 that imposed an age of reinterpretation upon American historians:

> These avalanches go under such names as the collapse of Western imperialism, the revolt of the colored peoples of Asia and Africa, the rise of Eastern nationalism, the westward advance of the frontier of Russian hegemony, and the polarization of power between the Russian and the American giants. All these developments and more have contributed to the shrinkage of Europe in power and relative importance, and thus to what is probably the greatest of all opportunities for historical reinterpretation.[4]

Whereas Woodward in 1959 stressed the relations of Russia, Europe, and America in the internationalizing of history writing, John K. Fairbank, in his address nearly a decade later, stressed the need to confront the relations of China and Asia to America as a special case of the fact "that we are all in a world crisis of growth and change, explosive 'development' and violent 'modernization,' at home and abroad."[5]

Many among us are trying to take a next step: to move from an integrated European-American history to an intercultural and interconnected world his-

---

[4] "The Age of Reinterpretation," *American Historical Review,* vol. 66, no. 1, p. 13, October 1960.
[5] John K. Fairbank, "Assignment for the '70's," *American Historical Review,* vol. 74, no. 3, p. 863, February 1969.

tory. But this is not an easy step to take. It cannot be taken merely by area specialists, intent on the uniqueness of their areas, but only by historians able to steer their way across the 360-degree ocean of human experience.[6]

This emphasis upon an interconnected world history means that a parochial view of the history of education will no longer do. The history of American education must not only be anchored in general American history but should be seen in the setting of the civilization of the West and, in so far as feasible, in relation to the world setting. I do not claim that this book is a world history of education. It is not. I have not attempted to survey, summarize, or digest the histories of education in the various countries or areas of the world. But I do hope that in focusing upon the international and intercultural origins of the education of the West and in turn upon its impact upon some other societies of the world, this book takes a step in the direction that Fairbank pictured as the historical assignment of the 1970s. The goal beyond this book is a truly international effort to produce a worldwide history of education that will view national histories of education in a global perspective and in their interrelationships, a cooperative enterprise that the fraternity of educational historians should be launching forthwith.

Not only has history writing begun to broaden its purview of the civilizations of the world, but the several social sciences have been marked by an increasing concern with comparative studies and with the interconnectedness of societies and cultures. Sociologists, anthropologists, economists, and political scientists are rediscovering the comparative and cross-national concerns of such diverse nineteenth-century synthesizers of social thought as Durkheim, Toennies, Weber, Marx, Tylor, and Morgan. They are modifying the speculative but imaginative formulations of the pathfinders with soundly based empirical investigations and with carefully drawn theoretical constructions.

The new trend toward syntheses takes the form of comparative studies of whole nations, whole societies, whole regions, and the cross-cultural analysis of such major social institutions as bureaucracy, empire, elites, families, and education. The concern now includes attention to the regularities and uniformities discernable in various societies and cultures as well as the differences among them. Thus, comparative sociology, comparative anthropology, comparative politics, comparative economics, and comparative history have joined comparative philosophy, comparative philology, comparative religion, and comparative education as subdisciplines, or at least major persistent interests, of the several social and humanistic disciplines.

One of the most significant results of the conjunction since 1950 of the revolutions in the world of nations, the crises that have faced modern civilization in all parts of the world, and the broadening perspectives of scholarship in history and the social sciences has been a revival of concern with the major directions of worldwide social change. This concern is not a return to the easy optimism about the progress of social evolution which had been a touchstone of eighteenth- and nineteenth-century Western thought. But it is a dissatisfaction with the narrow empirical studies of

[6]Ibid., p. 871.

particular times and places by historians and social scientists who are wholly engrossed in the study of the small details of closely restricted social situations.

Two aspects of this effort to study the large rather than to study the small are particularly significant for the history of education. One is the overall effort of archaeologists, anthropologists, and historians to study the regularities as well as the peculiarities in the transition from prehistoric stages of social development to the emergence of urban civilizations in various parts of the world. The other is the effort of sociologists, economists, political scientists, and historians to study the uniformities and the distinctive differences in social change as various traditional civilizations move into modern forms of society and culture. The role of education in the original civilization-building process can only be hinted at in the introductory part of this book, but the role of education in the origin of the civilization of the West and its subsequent modernization in more recent times are the main themes of the book. The interdisciplinary study of the modernization process that began in the societies of the West four to five hundred years ago and that is taking place today in so many parts of the world is a must for those who would view the history of Western education in its most fundamental social and cultural setting.

This book is an effort to take a long and comprehensive look at what the education of the West has meant for the development of its own civilization and for the development of some of the civilizations beyond the West. Despite its length it can be little more than an extended interpretive essay on the meaning of that development. It cannot be a detailed descriptive history nor an encyclopedic resource of factual information. To do justice to the theme would take a multivolume history which I hope can eventually be done. But meanwhile I believe there is great merit in the effort to survey the total development of such a major theme in a single volume.

I have tried to avoid the obvious faults of a survey that jumps lightly or superficially from one topic or place to another and crams the pages full of detailed facts. I have tried to make it truly a survey in the sense that the author and reader together will level their sights upon the general contours and boundaries of the historical terrain with a view to formulating new insights concerning the paths that education and civilization have travelled together.

This book intends to ask the question of history, "What has been the role of education in the making of the traditional civilization of the West and in transforming the civilizations of the world into modernity?" It does not expect to extract an easy answer from Clio, who has not been observed to be particularly animated in musing on this theme. But it does hope for her approving nod in the search.

R. Freeman Butts

ACKNOWLEDGMENTS

One of the warmest satisfactions an academic author derives from completing a new book (aside from the day he sends back the final page proofs to the publisher) is paying public penance and appreciation to his family for the travails he has caused them and paying tribute to his colleagues for the generous help he has received from them. In these regards I have been more than blessed—with a wife and family who have suffered more than most and with a succession of teachers and associates who have steadily tried to teach me more than I could learn.

In acknowledging my indebtedness for help in writing this particular book, however, I should like to include not only the members of my immediate family but also the collective members of the institutional families who have nurtured me so faithfully:

—To the University of Wisconsin and especially to Alexander Meiklejohn's Experimental College for initiating me into the heritage of Western civilization and for thrusting me into its thicket as a means of disciplining my search for understanding

—To Teachers College, Columbia University, for providing me with long and unflagging support in shaping a professional career dedicated to the work of education which I view as a prime maker of the conditions that enhance the quality of the human career throughout the world

—To the East-West Center of the University of Hawaii for granting me cherished time at an opportune moment for reflection and association with colleagues from both Western and Eastern civilizations

I have thus been the fortunate beneficiary of three major forms of America's vast investment in higher education: as a student in a state university in the Middle West, as a teacher in a private university in the East, and again as a student in a federally supported unit of a state university in the Far West. In my own small way I have become a personal "center" in which the variety of America's university traditions have met. This book owes much to these almae matres.

I have also been the recipient of ministrations by three of America's most solicitous cultivators in the vineyard of international education. A Fulbright award from the United States government for educational research in Australia in 1954 began the process of widening my horizons beyond Europe and America. A travel grant from the Carnegie Corporation of New York in the period 1961-1962 took me out of the West and ensnared me irretrievably in the web of international education being spun by the new nations of Africa and Asia. And a Ford Foundation grant to Columbia University in 1965 assured my future involvement in the international affairs of education through the recently established Institute of International Studies at Teachers College. It made possible a continuing and highly prized dialogue with an extraordinary company of graduate students and assistants in my doctoral seminars on the comparative history of Western education and on education in the modernization process.

Among these, pride of place belongs to Charles H. Lyons, prize graduate student and now prized colleague. I also highly appreciate the contributions of Virginia R. Arroyo, Beatrice A. Beach, Theodore Bracken, Sheffield Bunker, June Fair, Robert V. Farrell, Arden Holland, Nang Nang Kim, Richard Rubinger, Louis J. Setti, and Edwin J. Williams. I am especially indebted to Theodore Bracken for his creative work on the illustrations and to Margaret Nicholson for her assistance in preparing the bibliography and the index.

The indispensable one, of course, in making it possible for me to endure an administrative life along with teaching and writing is Myrtle Augustin, my invaluable assistant this past decade. To her, doing the impossible takes only a little longer.

How does one possibly repay such an outpouring of educational beneficence from both public and private largesse, from both institutional support and collegial stimulation? Certainly, by absolving all donors and associates from responsibility for what may have sprung from the resources they tendered and, hopefully, by somehow advancing an education devoted to freedom and equality for the peoples of this one earth.

PART I

EDUCATION AND THE CIVILIZATION-BUILDING PROCESS

CHAPTER I

A CONCEPTUAL FRAMEWORK FOR STUDYING EDUCATION IN HISTORY

A. THE DILEMMA IN HISTORY WRITING: GRAND DESIGN OR DESCRIPTIVE NARRATION

A basic dilemma faces a writer who assumes the task of dealing with the long perspective of human history. One possibility is to hit upon a grand design or theme that will give comprehensible order to the past, lead the reader through masses of apparently incoherent data, and thus help him to arrive at a meaningful understanding of man's perplexing journey on this planet. Another possibility is to concentrate upon a descriptive narration, simply to describe the past in narrative form and let the facts speak for themselves.

In general, two types of grand design have been most popular in the scholarly literature of history, the humanities, and the social sciences: one consists of recurring cycles of ups and downs, the other leads a straighter or unilinear course, usually upward.[1] For centuries it has seemed likely to many writers that the recurring life cycle they observed in nature or in the careers of individual men could well be applied to the growth, maturity, and decline of societies and of whole civilizations. Subtle and complicated variations on the cyclical theme range all the way from those of ancient Greek historians and philosophers, through that of the Italian Vico in the eighteenth century, to those of the giant system builders of recent times, Hegel, Spengler, Toynbee, and Sorokin.

The other main type of grand design explains human history as an evolutionary process of change in which all societies proceed basically through similiar stages of growth, all heading in the same general direction. The most influential of these themes of unilinear evolution has been the idea of progress which was widely publicized by

---

[1] For examples of these views, see Bibliographical Notes, pp. 572-573

3

Western European philosophes of the eighteenth century, and incorporated into nineteenth century sociological and anthropological literature by Comte, Spencer, Morgan, Tylor, and others. Variations on this theme found their way into history, literature, philosophy, and psychology, as well as into biology and the social sciences. If cyclical theories of human history have tended to express pessimism about the present and future of mankind, the theories of progress and unilinear evolution have generally been optimistic about the ultimate possibilities of human improvement.

In recent decades, however, scholars in history and the social sciences have grown increasingly wary of the grand design as an approach to the explanation of man's behavior, and have begun to rely more and more heavily upon the painstaking methods of empirical science to achieve reliable and valid descriptions of individual and social behavior. In the middle of the nineteenth century, historiography received a tremendous infusion of scientism from several German historians, notably Leopold Von Ranke, who argued persuasively that historians could describe the past as it actually was if only they faithfully adhered to rigorous scientific methods.

History is still being fought over, on one side by the humanists with their affinity for literature, religion, and philosophy, and by the social scientists on the other with their affinity for the methods of the physical and biological sciences. Historians themselves are divided as to whether history is an art or a science—or the queen of both together. The dominant scholarly atmosphere, however, in many an American academic hall of professional historians is well described by John Higham:

> To achieve a thoroughly positivistic history, the professionals put great emphasis on critical examination of original texts, on checking evidence, and on bibliographical apparatus. To penetrate as deeply as possible into past events, they welcomed specialization and wrote monographs on carefully limited subjects. To cleanse scholarship of the subjective coloration of the historian's own personality, the professionals endeavored to banish the function ... of passing moral judgments on men and movements.[2]

Doctoral research studies and textbooks especially have followed the tempting road of simply "telling the story" of the past as accurately as possible, in order to maintain the stance of objectivity.

In the effort to come to terms with the long history of mankind, this book will try to avoid the temptation, on one hand, to look for easy or neat schematic themes that do violence to empirical data and, on the other hand, simply to describe what seem to be the important facts and trends, not worrying about synthesizing generalizations or the meaning of the story. This book rests upon David Potter's conclusion that:

> ... the historian really cannot abstain from generalization and cannot escape theory. The choice before him is not between a "factual" and a "theoreti-

---

[2] John Higham (ed.), *The Reconstruction of American History,* Harper Torchbooks, New York, 1962, p. 18.

cal" approach but between, on the one hand, theoretical assumptions which have been recognized and, so far as possible, made rational and explicit and, on the other hand, unrecognized, half-hidden assumptions which remain unordered and chaotic.[3]

This book will attempt to avoid alike the cosmic overviews and grand generalizations long favored by theologians, metaphysicians, and speculative sociologists as well as the worm's eye view and the sheer empirical narrative favored by purely descriptive historians and social scientists. The descriptive materials will be based as far as possible upon the facts contained in empirical studies produced by close students of history and the social sciences whose concern has been primarily not to inspire, to bring about change, or to save souls, but to describe human events accurately. At the same time, it will rely upon a theme of explanation that will aid in the understanding of the history of Western education and its impact beyond the West. The effort will be made to organize, interpret, and give order to the materials which have been selected from an overwhelming mass of historical "stuff" by formulating what Stuart Hughes called "central grouping symbols" or conceptual schematizations that fit "the pieces of historical data into an organized form in terms of process or structure."[4]

The theme I have chosen for treating the history of Western education is the process of civilization building. It is a theme as old as written history itself but whose rationale is now deeply rooted in recent scholarly studies in history and the modern social sciences; it is as new as the contemporary confrontation between the developed and the less developed nations, the latter inhabited by people demanding an education that will bring to them a greater share in the benefits of modern civilization. It is a theme that views the history of education as an aspect of a coherent theory of social change as well as an integral part of the cross section of a particular time and place in the past. On one hand, it takes account of the long periods of social stability and cultural continuity in which education played essentially a conserving role, and, on the other hand, it takes account of the periods when fundamental social change and cultural upheaval led to the major human transformations in which education played a formative role. It is a theme which combines the interpretative values of a grand design approach to the study of history with the empirical values of sound descriptive narration.

The term *civilization* is admittedly a difficult term for those in the Western world to use, because it has acquired so many pejorative connotations of contrast between higher and lower cultures and between superior and inferior peoples. These connotations have been bequeathed to us in the West largely by the eighteenth and nineteenth centuries. The philosophes of Western Europe were at great pains to draw

---

[3] Edward N. Saveth (ed.), *American History and the Social Sciences,* Free Press, New York, 1964, p. 22.

[4] H. Stuart Hughes, "The Historian and the Social Scientist," *American Historical Review,* vol. 66, no. 1, p. 26, October 1960.

the contrasts between their own age of "enlightened" civilization and the preceding period of "barbarism" of the very dark Middle Ages in Europe. The giant founders of anthropology and sociology, Comte, Spencer, Morgan, Tylor, and, in general, the social evolutionists used the term to contrast the advanced or high cultures of the peoples of the West (themselves) with the backward or low cultures of savage and barbarian peoples of the non-West who were still assumed to be in earlier stages of human development and thus had not yet progressed to the higher stages of European civilization. For some two hundred years, popular as well as scholarly writers weighted down the term with assumptions that the civilized white peoples of the West had a mission to carry their civilization to the uncivilized peoples of the non-West who were predominantly black, brown, red, or yellow.

The word *civilization* thus has had a long, confused, and involved history, as have most important words.[5] As a result, civilization as a useful concept lost ground in the world of scholarship because of the imprecision and the nationalistic, racial, religious, or metaphysical overtones given to it, especially at the hands of the proponents of a grand design in history. A product of the eighteenth and nineteenth centuries, it was eschewed by many empirical scholars during much of the twentieth century.

In recent years, however, the term *civilization* has gradually been divested of its ethnocentric Westernism, its connotations of racial or national superiority, and its metaphysical or speculative quality. It has begun to acquire a surer foundation in empirical and substantive scholarship in the social sciences as well as in the humanities. Significant and solid contributions have been made to the concept by archeologists, ethnologists, sociologists, political scientists, and historians. Divested of its nineteenth century ethnocentric and racial connotations, the term *civilization* can now be profitably used to apply to those transforming processes of social change marked significantly by urbanization, social differentiation, political institutionalization, and written knowledge. For this reason I now believe it is particularly useful for the interpretation of education in history.

Despite the difficulties inherent in such broad generalizations and the dangers of oversimplification with respect to extremely complex matters, my preference is to say that the greatest transformations in the human career, as they involved education, have been three:

1. The evolutionary process during which prehumans came to form human folk societies. (For a summary see Section D, this chapter.)
2. The civilization process during which folk societies adopted or are still taking on the characteristics of urban literate society and culture. (For a summary see Section A, Chapter 2.)
3. The modernization process in the course of which traditional folk societies and traditional civilizations adopted or are still taking on the characteristics of modern civilization. (For a summary, see Section A, Chapter 6.)

---

[5]For the historical meanings of the term *civilization* and its newer empirical foundations, see Bibliographical Notes, pp. 573-575, 581.

Civilization is a worldwide matter; it embraces the second and third major transformations of mankind. Its major characteristics will be outlined at the beginning of Chapter 2. Just a few introductory words will be devoted here to each of these three major transformations and the resultant developmental stages that have characterized human history. This book cannot deal substantially with education in the evolutionary process, but a fuller elaboration of the role that education has played in the building of traditional civilization and modern civilization constitutes the major framework for this book.

The first great transformation in man's career, the long evolutionary process which lasted for one or two million years (some archeologists now say five million years), marked the time during which prehuman hominids became human. When *homo sapiens* appeared some 20,000 to 50,000 years ago, the biological evolutionary process of becoming human was for all practical purposes completed. The resulting general stage of human society attendant upon the appearance of *homo sapiens* consisted first of wandering ways of life based upon hunting, gathering, and collecting food and then of more settled ways of life leading to the production of food, whether in village-farming communities or by the pastoral care of animals. Archelogists have long distinguished the food gathering types of societies by calling them paleolithic and the food producing societies neolithic. For purposes of the history of education I prefer to put both types together, as Robert Redfield does, and think of both generically as *folk societies.*

Despite the undoubtedly great difference between the two forms of folk society with respect to their tools and weapons and their means of subsistence, they both apparently had in common educational processes that were structurally undifferentiated and unspecialized, and they were surely nonliterate. What these educational processes were like in prehistoric times remains largely in the realm of inference and speculation, but it seems clear that the trend of thought among prehistorians today is to give more weight to the cultural role of knowledge and education and to changes in social institutions as formative aspects of the transition from wandering folk societies to settled folk societies rather than to attribute the changes solely to technological developments.

The second great transformation in the human career was the civilization process whereby farmers, herdsmen, and warrior bands became city builders and urbanizers. In the process of building civilization, social institutions became differentiated and specialized, writing was invented, and knowledge and education were organized and formalized. This transformation, often called the urban revolution by archeologists, has by no means been completed throughout the world. Although there are relatively few isolated communities which today have had very little contact with either traditional or modern civilization, folk society's ways of life do live on, albeit to a decreasing extent. I find it useful to call the resulting second stage of human society the stage of *traditional civilization,* based as it was and is upon literate, urban ways of life which were first generated in Southwest Asia around 3500 B. C. and subsequently during the following two to three thousand years in Egypt, India, the Aegean and Greece, China, Middle America, and Peru. (See Figure 1.1–The Generative Civiliza-

Figure 1.1 The Generative Civilizations

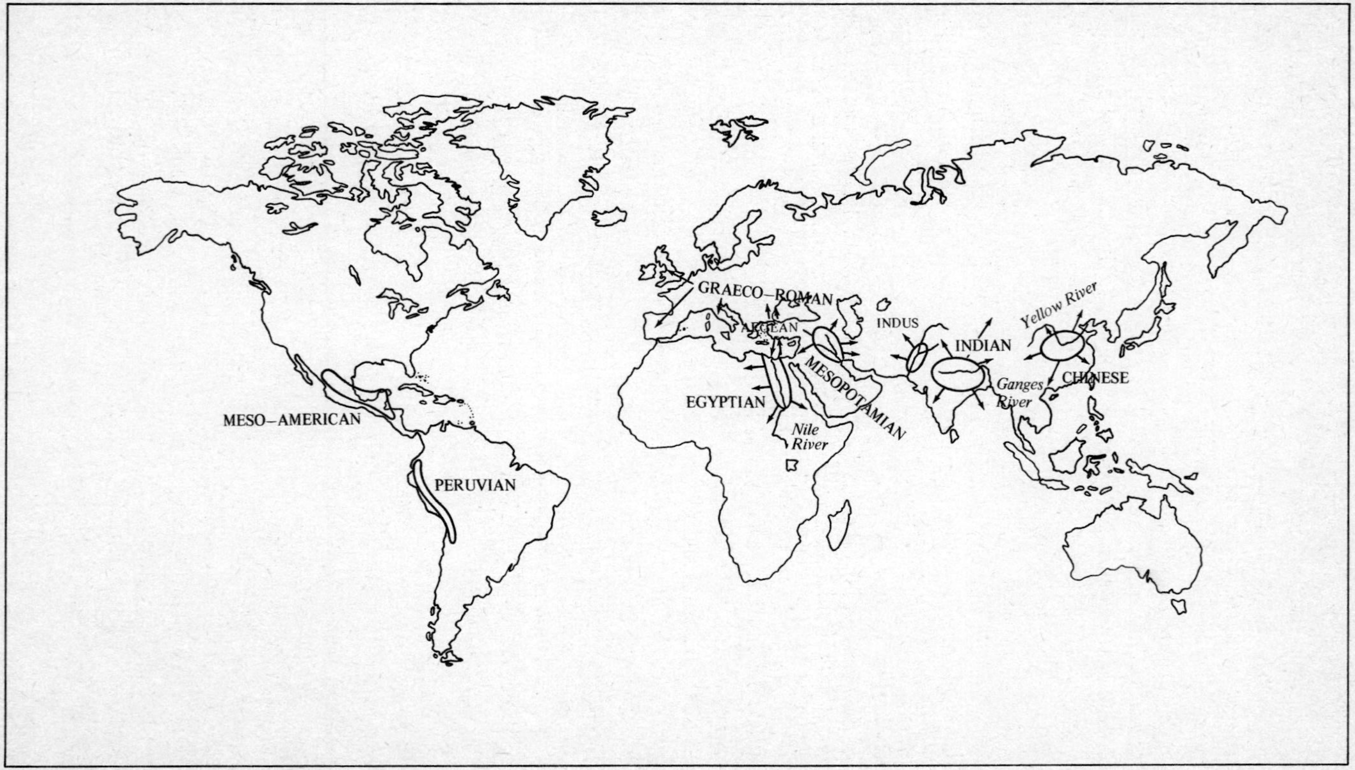
GRAECO–ROMAN
AEGEAN
INDUS
INDIAN
Yellow River
CHINESE
Ganges River
MESOPOTAMIAN
EGYPTIAN
Nile River
MESO–AMERICAN
PERUVIAN

tions.) By and large, organized institutions of education were major characteristics of traditional civilizations.

The third great transformation of man is the modernization process whereby civilized, urban builders developed new modes of production and distribution of goods based upon the use of inanimate power and more efficient tools, and new social institutions increasingly nationalized, secularized, and popularized. This modernization process began as early as 500 years ago in parts of western Europe and took the form of the industrial revolution some 200 years ago. Traditional forms of civilization in other parts of the world have been affected by the modernization process only in the past 50 to 100 years; in some parts of the world the process has only just begun. At the basis of the resulting third stage of human development, *modern civilization,* are widespread systems of organized education.

We may be at the beginning of a fourth great transformation in the human career, a process whereby modern man is becoming cosmopolitan man. This process is made possible by a technological and organizational revolution based upon universal education and upon electronic forms of information gathering, storing, retrieval, and dissemination, as well as upon electric and nuclear power, which have produced an enormous increase in the speed of transmission of energy and transportation of material things. Whatever the fourth stage in human society may come to be called, *worldwide ecumene* or postmodern civilization, it will require a suitable education to bring it into being and to sustain it.

For more than 5,000 years the process of civilization building has been appearing at different times and places in various parts of the world; and for 500 years the process of modernization has been proceeding quite unevenly around the world. As a result, some whole societies today can be characterized as predominantly modern or as predominantly traditional. At the same time, even the most traditional of contemporary civilized societies now have some modern forces or modernizing agents at work in them. At the other extreme, the most modern of contemporary societies contain pockets where traditional ways of life continue relatively untouched by the modernizing forces in the society.

The contemporary world thus witnesses the coexistence of the second, third, and possibly the fourth stage of human development. Even though there are few, if any, *pure* folk society groups left anywhere in the world, the historical process by which precivilized folk societies are touched and changed by civilization continues to operate; this modernization process not only continues but is accelerating throughout the world. The role of education in these major transformations of the human career has never had the attention it deserves. The formative influence of education in the process of civilization building in its traditional, modern, and worldwide forms deserves a hard and creative look. Unfortunately, this book cannot tell the whole story; it can only guess at it, as it some day may be told after a great deal of painstaking and imaginative research in historical, comparative, and international education has been carried forward.

B. RESOLVING THE DILEMMA: CIVILIZATION BUILDING AS THEME

What this book attempts to do is to use the theme of civilization building in the effort to give to the history of Western education a perspective and rationale that it has lacked: a sense of historical movement that incorporates both the element of continuity and the element of social change. For civilization is a process of becoming, not simply a state of existence. The moving and dynamic character of the civilization process makes it particularly illuminating as a theme for the history of education, for it is peculiarly useful in linking the past to the present. The process of making cities and creating an urban way of life not only began a long time ago in Mesopotamia, the Middle East, Africa, India, China, Greece, and pre-Hispanic America; it is still going on as it spreads to every part of the globe.

Civilization building is also appropriate as a theme for the history of education for it links together the different parts of a particular society. Since the first rise of civilization, the urban way of life has been a generative force in stimulating social change in the rural, agricultural, and nonurban sectors of a civilized society; these latter have been affected by the educational influence of the city as well as by the other cultural influences radiating out from the urban center. This relationship between urban and rural life has, of course, not always been congenial. The tension between the two is as old as the first civilizations themselves, and it is as new as the movement of rural Puerto Ricans and American blacks to New York City, or the reluctance of university students trained in Santiago, Sao Paulo, Kampala, New Delhi, or Melbourne to leave the city and go out to the villages or the bush to become teachers. The great magnet of the city has a seemingly irresistible drawing power for the educated and uneducated alike and, where it has drawn large numbers of people to the city, it has magnified the problems of society and education.

Another compelling reason why the civilization-building process is appropriate as a theme for the history of education is that it links one society with another. The interplay between civilized societies and the surrounding nomadic, warrior, or farming peoples, and the interchanges between one culture and another have been prime sources of social change since the first generative civilizations appeared. The process is thus as old as the spread of writing from Sumeria to the peoples of the Middle East. It continued as Hellenistic cities radiated out from Greece, as Islamic teachers crossed the Sahara to the African Sudan, and as monasteries, schools, and burghs spread from Rome across Western Europe. It is as new as the opening of an English-speaking university in Zambia or the sending of American teachers to East Africa.

Much has been made in recent years of the importance of the nation-building process for the newly independent countries of the world. I believe that it is even more important to recognize civilization building as an encompassing process of social change more inclusive than nation building. It went on before nations existed; its characteristics transcend and embrace individual nations. Conceivably, new forms of education could aid national states and national cultures to arrive at a genuine world civilization: a worldwide ecumene relying upon rational and scientific methods of thought, guiding urban, technological, and industrial societies toward more humane and enlightened conditions of life.

Finally, the theme of civilization building as a historical process is useful in interpreting the history of Western education, because education has been, and continues to be, one of the prime formative instruments by which civilization itself is transmitted and renewed, whether that transmittal be from one generation to the next, or from one society to another. The formative influence of education in the making of civilization is as old as the story of the temple priests of Sumer, the scribes of Egypt, the gurus of India, or the Sophists of Athens; it is as new as the opening of a village school in the Congo, the building of a secondary school in an outlying province of Afghanistan, the reform of a teacher-training college in the highest Andes of Peru, the international exchange programs of a hundred nations, or the illiteracy eradication projects of UNESCO.

Looking upon education as integral to the process of civilization building may even aid in the understanding of civilization itself, for one of the essential characteristics of civilization has been formal education. As mankind devised ways to take deliberate charge of his affairs rather than simply to conform to his surroundings, as he learned to live in cities and with cities, as he sought to organize his ideas rather than simply to repeat tales, as he began to write down his ideas as well as to pass them on orally, and as he was able successfully to direct social change in some deliberately planned direction—he became civilized. As mankind became civilized, he found that he must teach and learn more systematically, more regularly, and for longer periods of time than had been necessary in his precivilized folk way of life. Whereas precivilized societies could manage with informal educational means alone, formal education became a necessity in civilization. Formal education was first and foremost a product of an urban way of life.

In its very essence, then, the civilizing process is an educative process. Formal education arose with the first civilizations; it has flourished in traditional civilizations; it takes on special significance in the modernization of traditional societies. I believe that people cannot achieve, maintain, or improve their modern urban existence without highly developed forms of education.

In its most general terms, education is the conscious intent and deliberate effort of one person to impart knowledge to another, to influence his manner of thinking, to guide his behavior, to shape his values and attitudes, or to develop his skills. It may include these intentions and efforts in various proportions, but the expectation is that it will produce enduring and effective results in the learner. Of course, education may involve more than one person as *teacher* and more than one person as *learner.* Or it may involve the deliberate and systematic efforts of a person to educate himself. In the literature of the social sciences, informal education is often distinguished from formal.

Informal education involves teaching or instruction that is likely to be incidental or secondary to some other purpose or some other task which the "teacher" deems primary. Parents, family members, adult warriors, farmers or hunters, storytellers, priests, seers, the press, radio, television, governments, factories, businesses, churches, all may "teach" by conveying knowledge, shaping attitudes, or transmitting skills as they conduct their regular business, whether that be the never-ending activities of caring for and nurturing children, or conducting the political, economic, social, and religious affairs of a society. Informal education may be unspecialized, spasmodic, and unsystematic in its methods; yet, in its pervasive influence it may be almost coextensive with the meaning of culture itself, defined as the distinctive patterns of symbols, ideas, values, attitudes, and beliefs that are historically derived, learned, shared, and transmitted for the guidance of the behavior of the people in a particular society.

By contrast, formal education is usually defined as teaching or instruction that is regularized, systematized, and organized into programs of teaching and learning at identifiable times and places. It is normally conducted by professional teachers who specialize in the function of education or to whom the function is delegated. Formal institutions of education envisage teaching as the primary purpose of their existence rather than an incidental function designed and carried on to serve some other purpose.

The distinction between formal and informal education is, however, not always easy to make or keep clear. Schools, universities, museums, academic societies, and libraries are generally recognized as formal institutions of education. Their locale, management, and goals have varied widely in history. Schools and advanced institutions of education have been run by scribes and priests, guilds and royal courts, industries and trade unions, individuals and political parties, as well as by governments, churches, and voluntary agencies. In this book, by and large, I shall have more to say about the operation of the formal institutions of education as these interact with their societies and culture than about the total complex of informal ways in which a culture educates its people. Yet, I shall give much attention to the movements of formative ideas in the society and in the culture as these have influenced the shape and role of formal education in civilization.

The recognititon that formal education played an important role in creating the first civilizations of the Afro-Eurasian ecumene, in the development of modern civilization in the West, and in accelerating the modernization of the contemporary traditional civilizations of the non-West is justification enough for emphasizing formal education. In taking on the obligation to internationalize the history of Western education, I must leave to others the full story of the total range of informal educative processes—if indeed they can ever be meaningfully distinguished from the entire history of human culture itself.

Actually, I believe the term *organized education* is preferable to *formal education,* for it carries forward the meaning that education is not only a deliberate effort to promote teaching and learning but that the effort takes the form of a social organization. Theodore Caplow defines an organization succinctly as "a *social system* that has an *unequivocal collective identity,* an *exact roster of members,* a *program of activity,* and *procedures for replacing members.*"[6] Applying this definition to education gives a reasonable principle of limitation for determining what to include and what to exclude under the heading of organized education. Schools, academies, colleges, or universities can be viewed as social systems, each consisting of "a set of persons with an identifying characteristic plus a set of relationships established among these persons by interaction."[7] These "sets of persons" include the teacher and students who re-

---

[6]Theodore Caplow, *Principles of Organization,* Harcourt, Brace & World, New York, 1964, p. 1.
[7]Ibid., p. 1.

peatedly interact with each other in identifiable and continuing ways. The collective identity is usually the name of the school or the teacher. The exact roster of members includes both teachers and students who are recognizable by each other as such. The program of activity includes the curriculum, the plan of study, and the schedule for meeting together in an orderly and regular manner. The procedures for replacing members may apply to the admission and graduation of students as well as to the recruitment, training, appointment, promotion, and tenure of teachers.

The term *organized education* has a further advantage over *formal education.* Recent organizational theory points to this fact: "All living organizations are both formal and informal at the same time. In short, every organization exhibits some formal elements—those that are explicitly prescribed—and some informal elements— those that are not explicitly prescribed."[8]

C. MANKIND'S WORLDWIDE PASSAGE TO CIVILIZATION

In the effort to arrive at a schema for the interpretation of the history of education, I have tried to portray it against the background of the long sweep of human history, from hunting and gathering societies to farming and pastoral societies, to civilized urban societies, and to modern industrial societies.

This general direction of social change is portrayed in Figure 1.2, which attempts to show Mankind's Worldwide Passage to Civilization in the various regions of the world. It can only approach the roughest approximations of a timetable because archeological finds and interpretations continue to change. Of course, it will not satisfy an expert archeologist or anthropologist, but it is based upon recent published accounts by leading scholars in the field.[9] No matter what discrepancies of detail there may be, the direction of ten thousand years of human prehistory and history is unmistakeable.

Two other visual portrayals of the great transformations in the human career hint at the role of education in the overall process. Figure 1.3 stresses the typology of the major stages of historical development in the form of a cornucopia in which education has a key role to play in the overall civilization-building process. The narrow end of the horn represents the small-scale folk societies with their homogeneous, intimate, subsistence ways of life reflecting unspecialized and undifferentiated social institutions based upon family and kinship groups and oral language.

As the horn expands in size and shape there is room for some societies to continue in much the same folk pattern for long periods of time but for others to begin the transforming process of adopting an urban way of life marked by written language, differentiated social institutions, political and educational structures, full-time, specialized division of labor and accumulation of surplus wealth, systematization of knowledge, the appearance of ruling and teaching classes, and territorial organiza-

[8]Ibid., p. 22.
[9]See Bibliographical Notes, pp. 573-575.

Figure 1.2 Mankind's Worldwide Passage to Civilization

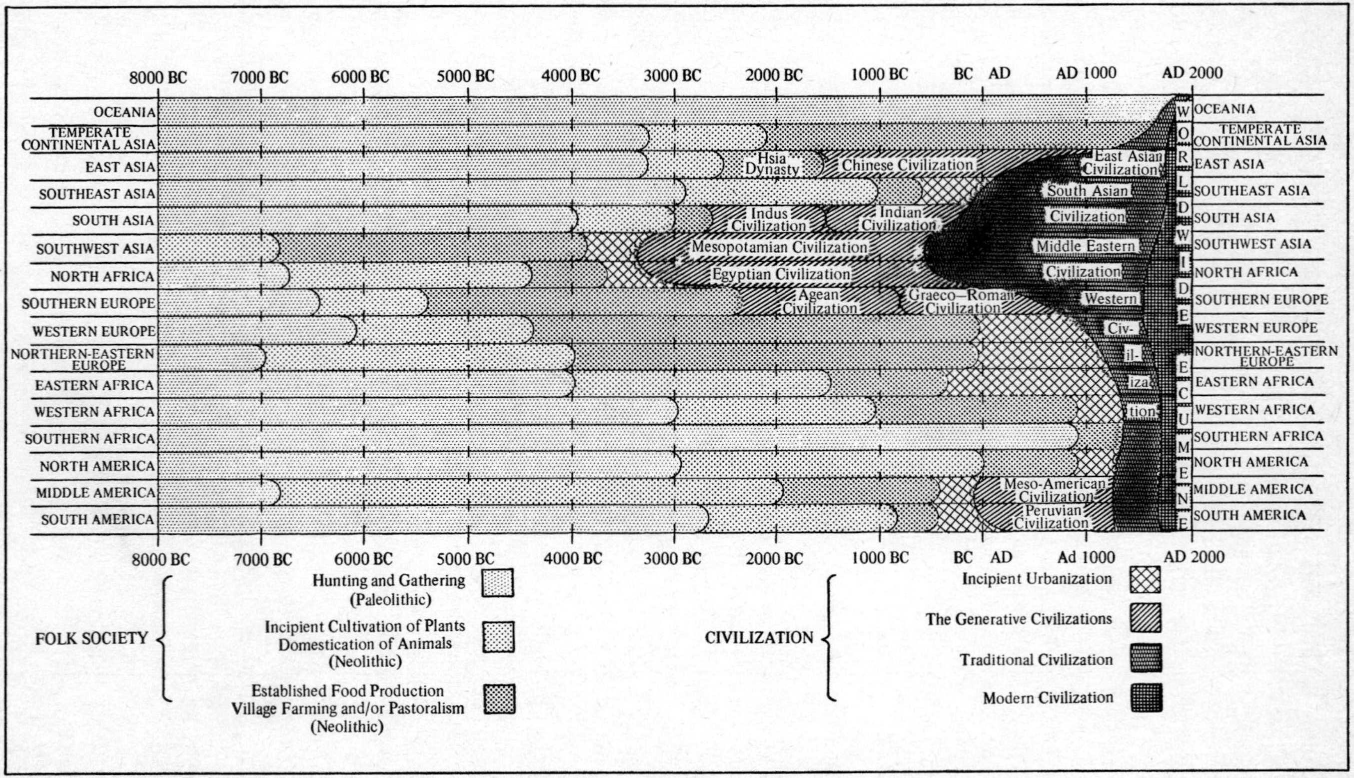

Figure 1.3   Education in the Cornucopia of Civilization

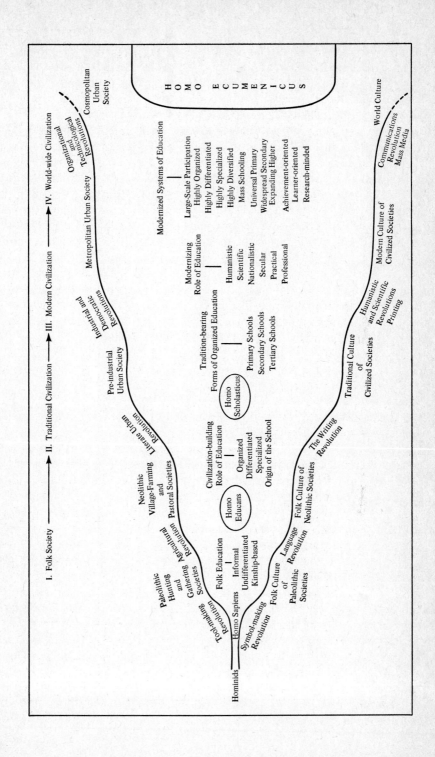

tion of political affairs. As we approach the open end of the horn of plenty, the radical increase in size reflects the whole complex of modern revolutions embraced by such unlovely but pregnant process terms as urbanization, industrialization, nationalization, internationalization, intellectual specialization, scientification, technicalization, secularization, mass communication, and, inevitably, "educationalization."

The cornucopia of civilization symbolizes that human societies in fact have vastly increased their culture content and knowledge, produced more of the goods of life, and supported larger populations in the later stages than was possible in the earlier stages. This is not to say that the large-scale, modern end of the horn of plenty is necessarily better than the small-scale, traditional end. But the difference in scale is there, it is vastly important, and education has had much to do with it. Whether the open end of the cornucopia, now representing the potential plenty of modern civilization, will eventually enlarge to embrace a worldwide civilization will rest, in part at least, in the hands of the world's educators.

Figure 1.4 combines the typological portrayal of the cornucopia with the chronological dimensions of Figure 1.2, thus to give a time perspective on education in the human career. It illustrates the approximate dates of the major transformations when they first appeared in some parts of the world, while at the same time it stresses the continuing coexistence of folk society, traditional civilization, and modern civilization.

The Delicate Matter of Terminology

What to call the people who lived in the long periods of time before the appearance of the first civilizations of the world is not an easy or simple matter. The terms used in scholarly as well as in popular discourse with respect to group characteristics always require care and precision, especially so at the present time when national, ethnic, and racial feelings are so volatile. Resentments are particularly deep over the names people have been called which seem to carry derogatory connotations because of generations of servitude, colonial subjection, or social, political, or economic inferiority. These have left their marks on peoples who are now in a position to express openly their pent-up resentments and elicit from their former masters the expressions of respect which they feel are long overdue.

Yet, the facts of variation in cultural and social development among different peoples, as determined by the soundest and most careful scholarship, cannot properly be covered up or denied solely in the effort to avoid hurt feelings. Somehow, the realities of social, cultural, and technological differences both in the past and present must be faced, if rationality and human welfare are to be served.

One set of particularly offensive terms in wide use in Europe and America in the nineteenth and twentieth centuries was derived from early ethnologists who applied their evolutionary assumptions to successive stages of man's development and came up with the terms *savage, barbarian,* and *civilized.* The first two quickly became highly colored terms of reproach or disdain, and the latter, of course, became the one to describe the highest and best levels of human accomplishment. It was all too easy to imply that some contemporary societies were still in a savage or a barbarian stage. Also

Figure 1.4 Pathways of Education in the Human Career

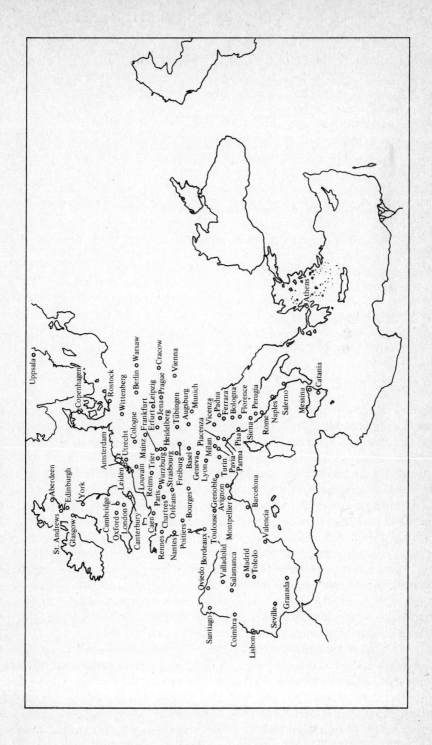

objectionable to many is the word *primitive* when used to apply to peoples who have been scarcely affected by the civilization process. *Primitive* often carries a connotation of backwardness or inferiority much as the use of the term *native* in colonial areas carried a stigma of inferiority as compared with the terms of respect applied to colonial rulers, traders, or settlers. Scholarly discourse has largely dropped the terms *savage* and *barbarian*, except to apply to peoples who lived long, long ago. In general, *savage* was applied to early stone age hunting peoples who lived prior to any civilization or who remained untouched by it; *barbarian*, to later stone age peoples who lived before the first civilizations or outside the early civilizations.

At the opposite terminological extreme are the nineteenth century archeologists' terms which took their cue not from traits of character, race, or personality (as the terms *savage, barbarian*, and *primitive* seemed to do), but from the tools made by groups of men in their various stages of development. Thus, the early archeologists classified the principal "ages of man" according to the kind of materials from which their tools were made:

Paleolithic Age	Early or Old Stone Age
Neolithic Age	Later or New Stone Age
Bronze Age	Early Metal Age
Iron Age	Early Iron Age
Industrial Age	Late Iron Age

The terms *paleolithic* and *neolithic* are neutral enough to avoid ruffling national or ethnic or racial sensibilities; but by themselves, they do not reveal a great deal about the social, or cultural, or educational processes whose remains provide the raw material for reconstructing a prehistory of man's cultures.

There are other terms that do highlight the development of human culture by stressing the presence or absence of written language. For example, *preliterate* and *prehistoric* apply to those peoples who lived before writing was invented anywhere in the world. The term *nonliterate* is sometimes applied to those peoples who lived any time after 3500 B. C. when writing was invented, but who still did not develop or adopt a written language of their own. I need not call attention to the obvious difficulties of using the term *illiterate,* which carries the connotation of inability or incapacity to become literate. But useful as these terms are in pointing to social and educational implications, they do not aid very much in calling attention to the overall way of life of the society to which they refer. They are useful terms for the history of education, but not the most useful.

More recent archeological terminology has concentrated not so much upon the toolmaking process as upon the way of life that must have provided the total context within which the tools were made and used. Braidwood and Howe, for example, describe the sequence of general cultural developments of Southwest Asia in several stages: food-gathering, food-collecting, food-producing, "village-farming community way of life," "incipient urbanization," and eventually an "urban way of life" which, for short, we have called civilization.[10] The more recent terminology from archeology and anthropology seems to be more appropriate for the history of education than the earlier terms, but since both are widely used today in the scholarly literature, I have continued to use both in Figures 1.2, 1.3, and 1.4.

Comparable Terms for Stages of Human Development

Paleolithic Age	Food-gathering societies ⎱	Folk societies
Neolithic Age	Food-producing societies ⎰	
Bronze Age ⎱	Literate urban societies	Traditional civilization
Early Iron Age ⎰		
Late Iron Age	Industrial society	Modern civilization

It is next to impossible to use technical terms with which all scholars will agree, so complicated is this whole field. It is virtually impossible to use any popular terms which will not ruffle some racial or ethnic sensibilities. But *some* terms must be used, and the problems must be faced. This book therefore follows Robert Redfield's use of the term *folk society* as most acceptably meeting the scholarly evidence concerning objective differences among societies, both past and present, and yet is most free from objectionable connotations that will arouse sensitive feelings.[11] It carries positive connotations conducive to discussion of culture and education. All races and ethnic groups have had their share of folk societies; all still display today some elements that can fairly be described as typical of folk society wherever it appeared.

The term *folk society* is thus used in this book to include both paleolithic and neolithic societies, both food-gathering and food-producing ways of life. It embraces the "precivilized," "preliterate" or "prehistoric" peoples who lived prior to 3500 B. C., before the rise of the first cities, or the first written language, or the first systematizing of written knowledge anywhere in the world; and it embraces those societies that have continued to exist alongside of or relatively untouched by the civilized societies that have developed in all parts of the world at different times since 3500 B. C. Since the sequence of historical development of precivilized societies and cultures during the first 99 percent of the human career is so hazy and is based upon so little direct cultural evidence, I shall not try to reconstruct an educational history of prehistoric times. I shall simply try to summarize some of the characteristics that seem to apply to education in folk societies in general.

A defect of the cornucopia schema protrayed in Figure 1.3 is the possible impression that a regular succession of "ages" took place at the same time in all parts of the world. Quite the contrary. *Homo sapiens* probably overlapped in time with

[10] Robert J. Braidwood and Gordon R. Willey (eds.), *Courses Toward Urban Life: Archeological Consideration of Some Cultural Alternates,* Aldine, Chicago, 1962, pp. 132-146.
[11] Robert Redfield, *The Primitive World and Its Transformation,* Cornell University Press, Ithaca, N. Y., 1953; and Margaret Redfield (ed.), *Human Nature and the Study of Society: The Papers of Robert Redfield,* vol. 1, University of Chicago Press, Chicago, 1962.

other species of *Homo* and migrated to different parts of the world at different times. Paleolithic societies did the same. Neolithic societies certainly overlapped in time with paleolithic societies, and both with urban civilizations. Humankind's passage to civilization began at different times in different parts of the world, as illustrated in Figure 1.1. Similarly, Figure 1.3 tries to make it clear that while some societies and cultures have succeeded one another in the order indicated, folk societies, traditional civilization, and modern civilization all coexist today.

Ten thousand years ago all of the ten million human beings on earth were hunters and gatherers. Today there exist only a few, perhaps a quarter of a million people, who live substantially as the original hunting peoples did.[12] During the past five thousand years the vast majority of mankind came to live in some form of pastoral, peasant farming, or preindustrial urban society. Today, perhaps two-thirds of mankind's 3½ billion people (predominantly in Asia, Africa, and Latin America) still live in societies that have been shaped by the traditional forms of agrarianate civilization that stemmed from the original agricultural and urban revolutions. Perhaps a third of mankind (predominantly in Europe, North America, Russia, and Japan) now live in societies that have been fundamentally affected by the modern forms of civilization that arose in connection with the scientific, industrial, and democratic revolutions following the sixteenth and seventeenth centuries. The disparities among and within these coexisting types of traditional and modern societies have deep and pervasive historical roots closely interwined with the development of education.

D. THE FIRST TRANSFORMATION OF MAN: FROM HOMINID TO *HOMO EDUCANS*

It took manlike creatures from a million to two million years to become human, that is, to acquire the physical structure of *Homo sapiens* and the ability to develop a human society and human culture. For most of that time the way of life of protohuman groups was based upon the gathering of food by means of free-wandering, collecting, and gathering. It can only be assumed that their very existence must have depended in large measure upon their ability to learn from one another and to teach their children how to find food and survive. For 99 per cent of man's time on earth, we can only infer or guess at how, why, and what it was he taught or learned.

In general, the presumed age of man has increased as new discoveries have been made, and Africa and Asia are now competing for the honor of being regarded as the birthplace of mankind. At this writing East Africa seems to be ahead in the "age race." Some scholars think that *Pithecanthropus* had essentially human characteristics as long as 500,000 to 600,000 years ago; or it may be that "man" will eventually embrace *Australopithecine* forms which seem to include *Homo habilis* of the Olduvai Gorge in Tanzania (1,750,000 years old) and possibly *Kanapoi hominid* from the Rift Valley in Kenya (4,000,000 years old), or even the Lothagam specimen of Northern Kenya

---

[12] See Carlton S. Coon, *The Hunting Peoples,* Little, Brown, Boston, 1971, p. xvii. Examples are pygmies, bushmen, hill tribes of India, Andaman Islanders, Australian aborigines, Ainus of Japan, Eskimos, and some Indians of North and South America.

(5,300,000 years old). For how much of this time prehuman men made and used wooden or stone tools to aid them in maintaining their existence is still uncertain, but the time probably lies somewhere between *Pithecanthropus* and *Australopithecus*.

The story of the social life and cultural works of prehuman man during his toolmaking existence is even more uncertain than that of his physical evolution, and the place of education can only be inferred or assumed. The evolutionary process, once thought to be purely biological, is now generally conceived to be social and cultural as well, and where social and cultural development is involved, some sort of education is involved. The very process of biological evolution from *Australopithecus* to *Homo sapiens* was probably influenced by the social interaction in which the making and using of tools, the creation of language and conceptual thought, and the development of cooperative group habits helped to shape man's morphology over the million or two million years of his evolution. During that time, it was not the individual with the mightiest jaws, or the sharpest teeth, or the largest frame who became the prototype of humankind. It was the one who could shape and use to advantage the most effective tools or artifacts and engage most effectively in the developing arts of communication and social action. Without these contrived arts and skills which we call culture, man was a puny animal indeed. The first fundamental transformation by which man became human resulted from the interactive and reciprocal influences of biological, social, and cultural development. In its very essence, the process of evolution included the process of education.

Without acquiring the capability to teach to oncoming generations the social and cultural arts and skills that had been learned, the race would not have become human— and it possibly would not have survived. The development of language itself (that most distinctive of all human tools) may have been related to the prolonged period of infant helplessness (that most distinctive biological characteristic of *Homo*), as parents nurtured, cared for, and transmitted through incipient words the experience, behavior patterns, beliefs, and ways of life which they in turn had learned. It is even possible that the interactive processes of language and physical nurture played a part in developing the brain and central nervous system to the place where coordination of hand and conceptual thought not only made human culture possible but helped to mold the human species itself. The biological and cultural development of man went hand in hand during the first great transformation in which manlike creatures gradually became human. The biological result, *Homo sapiens* (man the wise), had a capable assist from his social and cultural self, *Homo educans* (man the nourisher).

Homo sapiens has been variously described as a symbol-making animal. a toolmaking animal, a social animal, a political animal, a rational animal, and a spiritual animal. Each of these characteristics has been identified as the basic element which distinguishes *Homo* from the rest of animal nature and gives him his distinctively human characteristics. It may now be that *Homo* should not only be described biologically as *Homo sapiens* but socially and culturally as *Homo educans.* It may well be that the most apt way to describe the process of man's becoming human is to say that he became a *teaching and learning* animal. The role of education in this first and longest process of transformation in the human career is one of the greatest stories that has never been told. It may be that it can never be told because of the difficulty of inferring a social or a cultural process from the archeological evidence. It is a suggestive hypothesis, however, to argue that prehuman man became human as he learned how to transmit his cultural traditions more and more effectively; in a word, by learning how to educate himself and others.

Folk Society: Food-gathering and Food-producing Ways of Life

Virtually all we know about the earliest forms of human culture must be inferred from examination of the things men made that have been preserved in the earth. The oldest of these are stone tools and weapons; hence the term paleolithic has been applied to this stage of man's development. The problem of reconstructing man's society and culture in early paleolithic times is even more difficult than reconstructing his biological characteristics from his skeletal remains. But we do know that from about 500,000 years ago until about 100,000 years ago the tools showed little change over long periods of time. The inference is that man's conditions of life and his methods of teaching toolmaking skills were relatively rudimentary and unchanging. Paleolithic man subsisted in small bands by means of collecting or hunting food.

Sometime between 100,000 and 75,000 years ago, paleolithic men somewhere in Southwest Asia began to make and use standard tools as they adopted improved patterns of restricted wandering, selective hunting, and intensified collecting methods for the gathering of their food. They no longer wandered aimlessly; they organized themselves and the making of their tools, no matter how crudely or how simply. As they did these things, they began to improve their communication through meaningful speech, and they began to create social institutions for governing the conduct of their groups. In all these ways prehuman men were learning how to teach their acquired culture to their young.

Signs of the greater cultural skill among later paleolithic men were many: their stone blades showed greater refinement in design and sharpness; bone tools appeared; fire was employed; bows, spear throwers, and harpoons were fashioned; skins of animals were shaped and sewn for use as clothing; vessels were made to contain food and liquids; caves and huts were used for habitation; and artistic expression took the form of line drawings, paintings, carvings, and decorations. As population increased, it seems likely that cooperative, organized efforts aided in the search for food and in the organization of war and defense. Ceremonies and rites were held either for burial or perhaps for magical propitiation of the forces that were believed to rule life after death. Startling testimony to the remarkable intellectual skills of prehistoric man is set forth by Alexander Marshack, whose studies of record-keeping notations on hundreds of bones of later paleolithic times led him to say:

> Apparently as far back as 30,000 B. C. the Ice Age hunter of western Europe was using a system of notations that was already evolved, complex, and sophisticated, a tradition that would seem to have been thousands of years old by this point . . . this notation was a cognitive, time-factored, and time-factoring technique . . . the notations we have analyzed are not yet writing as we know it.

Nevertheless, the roots of science and of writing seem to be here. Apparently we have archaeological evidence for use of the same basic *cognitive processes* that appear later in science and writing.[13]

The major point here is that man's development must be considered as a total intellectual, social, and cultural evolution, not simply an improved physical ability to fashion and use more complicated tools: "the tool was only one aspect of a wider, cognitive, cultural evolution."[14]

Similarly with language and communication: "The word . . . like the stone tool and fire, was an adjunct and a product of the increasingly complex, widening, time-factored, time-factoring capacity and potential of the hominine brain and its culture."[15]

There must have been an accompanying process of teaching and learning of considerable refinement and sophistication to match the knowledge represented by the complicated arithmetical and calendrical notations that Marshack has studied.

Then, some 10,000 to 12,000 years ago, *Homo sapiens* learned how to produce his food rather than simply to hunt for it. In the course of this transformation mankind's social and cultural development changed radically. Not only did neolithic man greatly improve his stone and bone tools and weapons by polishing and refining them (hence the term New Stone Age or Neolithic Age), he also designed and built more complicated dwellings; developed pottery manufacture to a high state; produced a more stable food supply by cultivating a variety of grain crops and domesticating animals; made clothes by sewing, spinning, and weaving; built canoes and boats for travel and trade; developed an organized social life based upon village farming and relatively settled communities of family, clans, and tribes; and devised more complicated forms of ceremonies, rites, and religious beliefs.

The importance of the neolithic or agricultural revolution is not disputed as a major transformation in the human career (some believe it was the greatest of all); but its relationship to what went before and what came afterwards is viewed differently by various archeologists. V. Gordon Childe sees the change to a neolithic culture as the first great revolution after the appearance of *Homo sapiens,* and the rise of cities and of civilization as the second; Robert J. Braidwood sees them both as integral parts of one great process of change from a life of food gathering to a life of urban civilization. Whichever view is taken, the distinctive role of education in the transition from paleolithic to neolithic cultures remains so obscure that I have lumped together the paleolithic and neolithic stages under the general term *folk society.*

The neolithic phase of folk society's development was not a chronological period to which absolute dates applying to all parts of the world can be assigned. It is rather a

---

[13] Alexander Marshack, *The Roots of Civilization; The Cognitive Beginnings of Man's First Art, Symbol and Notation,* McGraw-Hill, New York, 1972, pp. 57-58.

[14] Ibid., p. 110.

[15] Ibid., p. 110.

way of life, centering on food-producing activities which appeared in different parts of the world at different times. (See Figure 1.2—Mankind's Worldwide Passage to Civilization.) It is a stage of social and cultural development that generally came after the paleolithic stage based upon food gathering and collecting and before the rise of cities and an urban way of life. Neolithic society was marked by two principal kinds of food production and therefore two ways of life. One was based upon agriculture and cultivation of grains; the other was based upon the the breeding and herding of animals. The former began with incipient cultivation and "vegeculture" and then developed effective cultivation of field grain and the planting of seed by turning the soil with stone hoes or by the gardening of root crops. Hoe agriculture was typical of Middle Eastern and European neolithic societies; root garden agriculture developed in monsoon Asia, Southeast Asia, and southern China. The evidence seems to be that the first food production may have begun sometime during the period 10,000 to 12,000 years ago in the region of Mesopotamia; it appeared later than that in other parts of the world.

There has been debate as to whether or not neolithic cultivation preceded neolithic pastoralism; by and large most of the evidence seems to indicate that it did in most regions of the World. But in general when farming and pastoral husbandry came together in various mixed forms the result was the neolithic village type of community, apparently appearing in embryonic form for the first time in the hill country of Mesopotamia sometime after 7000 B. C. and becoming so well formed and diffused between 6000 B. C. and 4000 B. C. that the village farming type of community life became, so to speak, the model or basic type of society in which most of the people of the world have lived for most of the time since then.

The prototypes from which the first Afro-Eurasian civilization developed were the neolithic villages of the Mesopotamian high country to the east, north, and west of the Tigris and Euphrates rivers. The neolithic farmers cultivated such grains as wheat and barley, and they domesticated cattle, sheep, goats, and swine. They could become economically self-sufficient without being constantly on the move to find their food; their children could be more productive in helping with cultivation and herding; and the people could have more children. So population increased. A surplus of food and goods even made possible an incipient trade with other villages, for the neolithic villages in Mesopotamia were not completely isolated. Herdsmen would run into each other; migrants would go from place to place throughout the region which eventually became something like a continuous agricultural area. Nevertheless, trade was not the principal basis or ingredient in a village's economic affairs.

As the neolithic way of life spread to other parts of the world or grew up independently of outside influence, an almost infinite cultural variety developed in tools, weapons, ornaments, art, and pottery; there was probably a similar variety in ideas, beliefs, and customs. In fact, the development of oral language may have been the most transforming cultural change of all. In any case, neolithic refinement in tools and artifacts is clearly evident. Their inventiveness and creativity were also remarkable, as neolithic villagers discovered, developed, or domesticated nearly all of the food plants and animals still known today.

In social and cultural affairs there seemed to be some major differences between those peoples who became dominantly villagers and those who became dominantly pastoralists. In the neolithic villages the women became more important than they were in the hunting or fishing societies. Women wielded the hoe in field or garden; they made pottery for the storing and cooking of cereal foods; and they spun and wove textiles. No wonder that matrilineal relationships dominated the kinship patterns of many neolithic societies, that fertility rites became common, and that mother goddesses dominated the religious and ritual scenes. A close connection between the fertility of earth, so important for the production of food from the land, and the fertility of woman, so important for the production of human offspring, was too obvious to be missed. The village with its enclosures, its stress on stability, security, and fecundity gave women—and children—a higher priority than they had had in the hunting and gathering ways of life. Village life must have been less adventuresome and less exciting than the hunting life, but the human family evidently came to prefer it. Informal education in the villages surely took its cues from the household arts and crafts. The need to measure lands, reckon accurately the best time for planting, cultivating, and reaping crops led to a stress upon measurement and calculation that eventually found its way into the intellectual concerns and formal education of urban civilization.

In contrast, the dominantly pastoral societies required a kind of social discipline, a physical prowess more suitable to the male, and a style of life that depended on scouting, exploring, possibly attacking, and surely defending against the predators, animal or human, who would threaten the flock or herd. Thus pastoral societies seemed to stress the patrilineal side of kinship relationships and to stress the need for unquestioning obedience to the chieftain. The gods of the nomad on the open steppe were more likely to be male gods. The education of the pastoralist youth was likely to stress the active concerns of the moving herds, the social obligation of being a loyal member of the team in time of danger or crisis, the prowess of riding and searching, the physical dexterity connected with the life cycle of animals and seasons, rather than the requirements of a more closely contained and settled, if not more secure, community life.

Education in Folk Societies

As we try to sum up the general characteristics of folk society and folk education, what shall we say? First of all, it is the kind of society in which all men lived for more than 99 percent of the time mankind has inhabited planet Earth. It is the kind of society in which most men lived for much of the time even after the first civilization appeared. And it is the kind of society in which a few still live today. Beyond these facts, each observer of a folk society will tend to emphasize what his background, training, and interests lead him to see. It is generally agreed, however, that folk societies were intimate groups of people organized either in roving bands or in small settlements; they were relatively isolated from contact with other groups; they displayed unspecialized and undifferentiated social institutions based largely upon the pervasive web of tribal, clan, family, and kinship relationships; and they generally functioned by means of oral communication and informal education, without a written language or systematic bodies of organized knowledge. The functions of political control, economic activity, religious ritual, and education were not regularly assigned to specialized institutions to carry out these particular functions.

The political scientist finds few overt signs of the formal political institutions he is accustomed to studying: no full-time rulers, executives, or legislative assemblies, no political parties, no full-time judges, no policemen or bureaucracies of government officials. A deliberate legislative function is seldom typical; custom rather than law controls conduct. The headman, chief, or council of elders performs intermittently the different political functions of making rules, applying rules, and judging infractions of rules. Most of the time such headmen or chiefs are absorbed in the activities of hunting, fishing, or farming which occupy everyone else in the community or the band. The controls of action for the individual are the deeply ingrained customs or obligations that he has learned informally in the course of his daily life with family and kinfolk. There is little deliberate effort to modify or change the rules. The political scientist would thus say that the political functions in a folk society are diffuse, undifferentiated, and intermittent.

The economist finds a folk society to be largely self-contained and based on subsistence needs with little or nothing to spare beyond what was needed for immediate consumption. In general, neolithic tools were an improvement upon paleolithic implements, but tools were relatively few, tools to make tools were rare, and power other than human or animal was unknown. Each group was relatively self-contained with little or no economic dependence upon any outside group. Each supported itself from the land, the forests, the rivers, or the sea.

Food and goods were often allocated, however, according to customary obligations to family members or other persons holding some special social status in the group. These transactions might involve nonreciprocal giving or reciprocal exchange, but in general they did not involve a regular institution like a market for exchange of goods; also absent were money, trade, and a spirit of economic or commercial gain. There seemed to be few or no full-time specialists. Typically, every member of the society helped in gathering or producing food and engaged in the sustaining activities required for survival. Division of labor applied only to sex and age groups. As in politics, the folk society's economy could not be unraveled from the web of familial relationships that made up the basic structure of the social system.

Anthropologists and sociologists have found that face-to-face primary relationships dominate the whole of folk society. In social terms it is intimate, particularistic, homogeneous, and ascriptive. Because a folk society may have been as small as a few dozen or a few hundred people, everyone could know everyone else rather intimately. Because the group was relatively isolated and may have remained so for scores or even hundreds of years, a strong sense of group solidarity was likely to develop. The people may actually have grown to *be* alike physically as well as socially and culturally. What one man did and thought, another man did and thought; and so for women and children from generation to generation. Within a particular folk society customs remained relatively stable and fixed over long periods. Ties of family (nuclear or extended), of clan (the symbolic family), and of tribe dominated all others as one's status in the hierarchy of kinship determined one's obligations, duties, and prerogatives. Rights and responsibilities were ascribed according to the status and the role one was expected to play rather than on the basis of one's achievements or useful contribution to the group's activities.

The isolation, the homogeneity, the intimacy of folk life meant that people seldom thought critically about what they did or what they believed. What they did and what they believed were right, for who did differently? Without comparison with other ways of life, without disruptive contact from the outside, the age-old patterns according to which everyone acts seemed unquestionably to be the ways that everyone should act. Somehow the unconscious inculcation of normal sentiments developing from infancy in talk, gesture, and custom acted as the basic controls for action, rather than explicit, organized, formalized rules or precepts. Without written language, without written records, without books, the rules were embodied more in conventional tacit patterns of behavior than in explicit or formal codes of ethics or in systematic regulations to be memorized and recited on demand. This is not to say that morality was not learned nor that moral precepts were not memorized from the myths, the stories of ancient heroes, the exploits of superhuman but personal deities. How else could they be retained except by memory, and how else could they be transmitted explicitly except by word of mouth? These myths certainly were to be cherished and emulated, but they were not to be analyzed or made objects of critical scrutiny.

No wonder, then, that in small, isolated, intimate, unspecialized, and nonliterate societies education should be an integral part of the undifferentiated, face-to-face, personalized social and cultural process. Where no one specialized in governing or administering, where no one specialized in a particular type of labor or work, where no one specialized in the transmission of ideas or knowledge, it was natural that no one specialized in teaching or in learning. All adults were teachers; we can never know how deliberate or self-conscious some may have become in inducting their children into family, tribal, or village tasks. Undoubtedly some were more effective than others, just as some children undoubtedly learned more rapidly and more effectively than others. But with no written language and with full dependence upon an oral tradition which may or may not have had special custodians or "rememberers," there was seldom an organized school. It was inevitable that an accomplished paleolithic man must have taught more than one boy at a time to throw a weapon, or skin an animal, or make a tool. Surely the neolithic village women most skilled at making pottery or weaving cloth must have attracted more than one girl at a time to watch and to learn. But the evidence for the existence of schools is scarce.

Without writing, a stable and consistent basis for organized knowledge was difficult to come by, despite the evidence of rudimentary notation systems. There was accumulated practical wisdom, valuable technical lore, traditional ways of making, doing, and drawing; but systematic, sequential sets of ideas that could be regarded as a body of organized knowledge or predictive science were absent. This meant that most folk societies were largely cut off from accurate and reliable knowledge of other societies and even of their own past. Any time farther back than the memory of the oldest persons was subject to the inaccuracies of untrained oral transmission and the haziness of dimming memories, unless special training in accurate remembering or notation was learned and practiced. Even more than lacking a sense of history, the absence of writing prevented access to the thought or ways of other peoples in places beyond the normal range of a particular folk society. What was happening in the other valley, or beyond the mountain, or across the plains was likely to be unknown except as personal contact was made and as oral reports filtered in from the outside. So in a folk society there was little to study, but much to do and learn. As the main controls of conduct were informal, so was education informal. As everything else was conducted by nonspecialists, so was education conducted by nonspecialists. As kinship bonds were strong, so education consisted largely of acquiring the beliefs, behavior, attitudes, and moral convictions appropriate to one's age, sex, status, and role in the society.

All this may sound as though all folk societies, both past and present, were very much alike. This is the exact opposite of the truth, for anthropologists and ethnologists have emphasized over and over again how vastly varied are the practices of the peoples they have studied. By inference, there must have been a similar variety in the social systems, the cultural patterns, and the educational practices of the innumerable precivilized societies that dotted the earth before historical times. In some folk societies, certain persons came to be recognized as having particular functions in the formulation of customs and ideals. These elders, medicine men, seers, or storytellers constituted something of a priestly and teaching class. There is evidence that special training may have been given to those who were to be inducted into the priestly class. This consisted of special transmission of the peculiar skills of the class, including special knowledge of certain magical formulas, certain songs, or the ability to conduct certain rites and ceremonies. Where secret fraternities existed, they developed their own special initiation processes. In addition, some societies apparently had certain handicraft or occupational groups that specialized in house building, metalworking, toolmaking, garment making, or tattooing. These groups would then initiate young people into the skills and secrets of the group.

Folk societies also conducted special initiatory or puberty rites for the adolescent or older youth who were to be inducted into full adult membership. Although puberty rites were not characteristic of all groups, they represent a kind of educational agency that was commonly controlled by the elders. In general, we may say that folk education was carried on, not by separate schools or formal educational institutions, but by the adult members of the society as they performed their regular activities. The teaching function was not normally delegated to specialized teaching groups. It may be that reliance upon formal schools and specialized teaching in prehistoric societies was greater than we now believe; the absence of written records makes certainty impossible. We can only infer that each group tried to bring up its children in the image of its elders.

In any case, it is clear that precivilized folk education knew nothing of books and schools. It was undoubtedly motivated by the needs of self-preservation. It was probably carried on by the active participation of the learner as he imitated adult activities or was shown how to make tools, engage in the hunt, and fight in the wars. The children absorbed the qualities in action that the culture recognized as good; they were punished for actions that the group considered inimical to its welfare. They heard the myths, the folklore, and the songs that made up the approved tradition, and they felt the pressures of group approval and disapproval.

At the time of puberty, boys and girls probably went through more or less elaborate ceremonies and initiation rites which served to impress upon them their obligations and duties as accepted members of the society in good standing. All sorts of variations were probably found in these rites. Physical suffering may have been a feature, to test the stamina and endurance of the initiate. Direct moral precepts may have been preached to the young so that they might learn and emulate the qualities of character deemed desirable by the society. Various features may have symbolized the new status: a change of name, the conferring of magical powers, the imposing of long periods of silence, purification of the body, circumcision, tattooing, drinking each other's blood, and other possible tests and rites.

But beneath the obvious differences in cultural content among present day folk societies, and probably among prehistoric societies, there are the common qualities that grow out of isolation, intimacy, homogeneity, undifferentiated institutions, strong kinship relationships, and lack of written language and organized knowledge. Folk societies in the past seemed to have these characteristics in common and thus to differ from the civilized societies that began to appear some 5,000 to 6,000 years ago. In these major respects the remaining folk societies of the twentieth century A. D. seem to differ as a type from the major contemporary civilizations, both traditional and modern. Yet most societies today have become so culturally mixed that, as Redfield says, in every primitive band or tribe there is civilization, and in every city there is the folk society. To paraphrase Redfield we might go on to say that in every urban way of life today there is informal education, and into most present-day folk societies there has come the school. That is one reason why contemporary folk societies are changing so much more rapidly than did the prehistoric folk societies which persisted for so long with so little change before there were any literate urban societies. The school has played a major part in the civilizing of folk societies ever since the first civilization arose; it is playing a still larger part in the modernization of peoples all over the world today.

CHAPTER II

MANKIND'S PASSAGE TO CIVILIZATION— AND TO SCHOOL
(3500 B.C.-500 B.C.)

A. THE SECOND TRANSFORMATION OF MAN: FROM FOLK SOCIETY TO TRADITIONAL CIVILIZATION

About 3500 B.C. in the Mesopotamian region of Southwest Asia, the second great transformation in the human career was getting under way as some of the neolithic village-farming communities began to organize themselves into larger towns which eventually became centers for a literate, urban way of life and which in turn began to exert greater or lesser influence over a number of smaller, ancillary village and farming settlements. By 3000 B.C., fully developed urbanization had appeared in the Middle East, and at various times thereafter in India, the Aegean, China, and pre-Columbian America. (See Figure 1.2.) Meanwhile, however, throughout much of the world, paleolithic and neolithic folk societies continued to adhere to their traditional pre-urban or pre-civilized ways of life centering upon hunting, pastoralism, or village-farming communities.

With the rise of the first civilization in Mesopotamia, education embarked on a radically new kind of relationship to the development of human society and culture. It began to have a special function and identity of its own along with other institutions which came to be identified as temple, city, and state. As an introduction to this new role for education, I shall cite several recent statements which will serve to highlight the social and cultural ingredients whose interaction characterized the birth of human civilization on earth.

In a classic formulation about the original urbanization process as it took place in various parts of the world, V. Gordon Childe identified ten characteristics that distinguished civilized life from precivilized folk life: the art of writing; the beginnings of exact and predictive science leading to reflective, systematic, and critical thought; an enlarged size and growing interdependence of settlements; surplus of food leading to the central accumulation of capital and the large-scale planning and management of human afairs; full-time technical specialists and improved tools; a greatly expanded foreign trade; a ruling class differentiated from the ruled; social organization based upon a territorial state and impersonal relationships rather than kinship and upon political structures somewhat differentiated according to function; the building of monumental public works ranging from irrigation and storage facilities to ceremonial temples or centers; and the creation of highly developed art forms.[1]

In a later comment, Childe attributed the main element in the rise of cities to the accretion of an economic surplus that could support specialized classes of professionals:

> I have taken this as the essential character of a city: *a community that comprises a substantial proportion of professional rulers, officials, clergy, artisans and merchants who do not catch or grow their own food*, but live on the surplus produced by farmers or fishermen who may dwell within the city or in villages outside its walls. These professionals and full-time specialists represent a new class of persons, an absolute addition to the population that could be included in, or supported by, any barbarian community.[2]

Childe's formulation of the essential elements in the origins of civilization deeply affected the thought and rationale of two decades of scholarship in archeology, ethnology, and the social sciences. A symposium volume edited by Braidwood and Willey in 1962 revealed the wide influence of his hypotheses upon modern archeologists whose recent work has covered nearly every part of the earth.[3] Their symposium also revealed how rapidly new archeological findings lead to revisions in generalizations concerning the origin of civilization. In the past decade the influence of changes in irrigation, climate, tools, or economic surplus in bringing about the "urban revolution," as Childe called it, is being downgraded as new discoveries or interpretations are made. Such influences as cumulative patterns of social organization, the interchange of things and ideas, and the growth of systematic written knowledge are being upgraded as explanations for the appearance of civilization in one place and time or its lack of appearance in another place and time.

Technological achievements have long been recognized as ingredients of civilized as contrasted with precivilized societies, but changes in patterns of social organization are receiving greatly increased attention from scholars who represent different fields of study and different social orientations. Stuart Piggott, of the University of Edinburgh, puts it this way:

[1]V. Gordon Childe, "The Urban Revolution," *Town Planning Review*, vol. 21, pp. 3-17, April 1950.

[2]V. Gordon Childe, "Civilization, Cities and Towns," *Antiquity*, vol. 21, no. 121, p. 37, March 1957. Italics added.

[3]Robert J. Braidwood and Gordon R. Willey, *Courses Toward Urban Life; Archeological Considerations of Some Cultural Alternates*, Viking Fund Publications in *Anthropology*, no. 32, Aldine, Chicago, 1962.

"Civilization" is used to mean a society which has worked out a solution to the problem of living in a relatively large permanent community, at a level of technological and social development above that of the hunting band, the family farmstead, the rustic, self-sufficient village or the pastoral tribe. Civilization is something artificial and man-made, the result of making tools of increasing complexity in response to the *enlarging concepts of community life evolving in men's minds.*[4]

Identifying this element of increasing social differentiation in civilization building, as being even more important than the strictly economic element, is of great significance for the history of education. The "enlarging concepts of community life evolving in men's minds" are the products, in part at least, of possibilities opened up by organized education. It profits little to argue whether more complex tools led to more complex social organization or whether increasing social differentiation led to the development of more complex technology. The important thing is that when both were present in an interacting way, civilization appeared—and with civilization appeared the organized school, a particularly potent form of social differentiation.

Another type of analysis adds to urbanization and social differentiation a third ingredient for special emphasis in the meaning of civilization, namely, the institutionalization of political authority based on territorial residence rather than upon kinship. Robert McC. Adams defines state societies as those "hierarchically organized on political and territorial lines rather than on kinship or other ascriptive groups and relationships."[5] He agrees with his fellow anthropologist, Morton H. Fried, that there were only six "pristine" states that "developed *sui generis* out of purely local conditions" and that all other states are "secondary." The six are exactly what most anthropologists and historians refer to as the primary civilizations, namely, Mesopotamia, Egypt, Indus Valley, North China, Mesoamerica, and Peru.

Fried's definition of the state closely approximates that of Adams: "the complex of institutions by which the power of society is organized on a basis superior to kinship."[6] Fried goes further than Adams in stressing the coercive character of the state as a means of maintaining an established social order of stratification. Fried also goes much further than Adams in identifying education as one of those "specialized institutions" designed to indoctrinate the members of the state with the values of the stratified social order:

> There can be little argument with the observation that in all societies the single most significant complex of social-control apparatuses is to be found in the system of education, including both formal and informal means.[7]

---

[4] Stuart Piggot (ed.), *The Dawn of Civilization; The First World Survey of Human Cultures in Early Times,* McGraw-Hill, New York, 1961, p. 11. Italics added.

[5] Robert McC. Adams, *The Evolution of Urban Society; Early Mesopotamia and Prehispanic Mexico,* Aldine, Chicago, 1966, p. 14.

[6] Morton H. Fried, *The Evolution of Political Society; an Essay in Political Anthropology,* Random House, New York, 1967, p. 229.

[7] Ibid., p. 9.

Other scholars emphasize the culturally liberating role of education in the civilization process:

It was during the Bronze Age that . . . we can for the first time speak of civilization. Now, in certain areas of the earth, men were living not in groups or hordes but in organized communities, submitting to the disciplines and profiting by the opportunities of the city, intent upon the quality of living rather than upon mere existence, enjoying (some of them) that degree of leisure and wealth that makes possible *the pursuit of learning* and the cult of art, and stabilized by the possession of *the written word* which could enlarge the individual horizon by the experience of the past and preserve for the future whatever of value man might invent.[8]

In this definition note especially the phrases "pursuit of learning" and "the written word." They point to the most widely agreed upon characteristic that distinguishes civilization from folk society: the presence of a written language. Sir Leonard Woolley puts it this way: "the most convenient and easily recognizable criterion of civilization is the knowledge of the art of writing."[9] In fact, Sir Leonard goes so far as to say:

The art of writing seems to arise naturally and almost inevitably from the condition of urbanization and also to be essential to its maintenance. In no part of the world has civilization at any time advanced to any considerable heights or achieved any permanence unless by the aid of writing; but just as civilization generally implies the development of city life so writing has never been introduced in any other than an urban society.[10]

The interlocking character of these four ingredients of civilization (urbanization, social differentiation, political institutionalization, and writing) is evident in all of the approaches cited here, but for the origins of organized education the greatest of these may well be the invention of writing. Woolley begins with urbanization, refers to organized communities, and ends up with writing. Piggott begins with the urban community resulting from technological and social development and concludes by saying:

Amongst these basic skills and inventions . . . perhaps the greatest invention of all was that of writing, the discovery that a set of conventional symbols could be constructed whereby human speech could be recorded in permanent form.[11]

---

[8] Jacquetta Hawkes and Sir Leonard Woolley, *Prehistory and the Beginnings of Civilization*, vol. 1, *History of Mankind, Cultural and Scientific Development*, Harper & Row, New York, 1963, p. 360. Italics added.

[9] Ibid., p. 359.

[10] Ibid., p. 631.

[11] Piggott, op. cit., p. 14.

And Childe, too, ends with writing:

> [Writing] not only represents a new instrument for the transmission of human experience and the accumulation of knowledge, but is also symptomatic of a quite novel socio-economic structure—the city.
> Of course this Urban Revolution, just like the Neolithic Revolution, was a gradual cumulative process. There are intermediate stages between self-sufficing, i.e., neolithic, food-producing communities and "cathedral cities." It may be arbitrary to choose writing as marking the critical point. But what is the alternative?[12]

I think there *is* an alternative and that is to follow through on what is implied by the social invention of writing itself, namely, that fully developed writing must have been created by a literate class of people who received a formal education in an institution organized for that purpose. Gideon Sjoberg puts it succinctly:

> The existence of writing implies a literati, which in turn requires for its propagation some method of formal education, a supporting political apparatus to ensure its hegemony and continued sustenance, and merchants, artisans, and a variety of servants to provide needed goods and services.[13]

His statement provides a useful antidote for the usual assumption by many sociologists, anthropologists, economists, and political scientists that education simply reflects the society in which it exists and responds more or less passively to the impact of other more active social institutions upon it. Sjoberg at least hints at the notion that education is not simply a social instrument for doing the bidding of the dominant classes of the state, but that education in an urban society may be supported by the political and economic institutions because of the very power of leadership that education and an educated class exert in shaping the society itself.

So perhaps we should not be content to characterize civilization primarily in terms of writing but should link with it the urban social institution that made writing possible, namely, the school. Indeed what product of civilization can better be characterized as an *urban-generated, socially differentiated, politically institutionalized organization based on and devoted to written knowledge?* How better to define a school throughout most of its history? No other historical institution has been so intimately or predominantly concerned with the creation and transmission of written knowledge—which several of our definers of civilization put at the heart of the rise of civilization itself. And few other institutions have provided the social and cultural glue which has helped to mold the characteristic forms of civilization out of diverse peoples. In a real sense organized education has helped to produce and maintain those forms of historical societies characterized by McNeill as civilizations, to wit, "unusu-

---

[12]Childe, "Civilization, Cities, and Towns," p. 37.

[13] Gideon Sjoberg, *The Preindustrial City; Past and Present,* Free Press, New York, 1960, p. 33.

ally massive societies, weaving the lives of millions of persons into a loose yet coherent life style across hundreds or even thousands of miles and for periods of time that are very long when measured by the span of an individual human life."[14]

The intimate connection between the art of writing and the appearance of formal schools has long been recognized in histories of education, for it can easily be demonstrated that early schools in most societies were writing schools. It has not, however, been so explicitly recognized that organized education was not simply a device for teaching writing, enormously important as that is, but was an integral part of the total civilizational process itself, sometimes helping a society to adapt to change or fundamentally transform itself, sometimes helping it to maintain its social stability, and sometimes even contributing to a process of retrogression.

The burden of this chapter is to discuss the role of education in the building of the world's first civilizations. This was an enormously complex process, not yet fully understood, but at least some of the components of the process are widely agreed upon. I have referred to them as urbanization, social differentiation, political institutionalization, and written knowledge. I shall not try to assign priorities or claim causal connections among the four, but I shall try to indicate how organized education was intimately related to and possibly had a formative role to play in all four.

B. MESOPOTAMIAN CIVILIZATION: PROTOTYPE FOR THE WORLD

It is now generally agreed that human civilization first appeared in the river valleys of the Tigris-Euphrates in the course of the fourth millenium B.C. Mesopotamian civilization, the prototype of all other civilizations, was not only the first, it was one of the longest-lived, covering more than 3,000 years. Many scholars now believe that it influenced the other major Afro-Eurasian civilizations of its time; it led to the West through Egypt, the Aegean, Greece, and the Mediterranean; and it led to the East through Iran and India, and possibly as far as China. Drawing upon the Greek word for it I refer to these interconnected civilized areas of the world as the Afro-Eurasian ecumene. (See Figure 2.1.)

Fortunately, our knowledge of the Sumerians who accomplished the original feat of civilization has been vastly increased by archeological and linguistic studies of recent decades. In fact, the existence of such a people was not even known a hundred years ago when European archeologists were adding to the world's knowledge of the Middle East by busily turning up hundreds of Babylonian and Assyrian as well as Egyptian inscriptions. At first, Egypt was thought to be the cradle of civilization, and then Babylonia and Assyria came to the fore. Fortunately for the history of education, the new knowledge of the transition from neolithic folk society to literate urban

[14] William H. McNeill, *A World History*, 2d ed., Oxford University Press, New York, 1971, p. v.

society in Mesopotamia has considerably enhanced the role of education in the original civilization-building process.

One of the world's foremost authorities on the Sumerians puts it this way:

> From the point of view of the history of civilization, Sumer's supreme achievements were the development of the cuneiform system of writing and the *formal system of education* which was its direct outgrowth. It is no exaggeration to say that had it not been for the inventiveness and perseverance of the anonymous, practically oriented Sumerian pundits and *teachers* who lived in the early third millenium B.C., it is hardly likely that the intellectual and scientific achievements of modern days would have been possible; it was from Sumer that writing and learning spread the world over.[15]

Even allowing for the pardonable enthusiasm of a scholar as he describes the achievements of "his" people, this is an extraordinary salute to the role of teachers and of organized education in helping to bring about one of the great transformations in the human career.

We cannot, of course, trace in any detail the fortunes of education during the 3,000 years of the Sumerians and their successor societies in Mesopotamia. Still less can we follow education through Anatolia (Asia Minor), the Levant, or Iran. All we can do here is to suggest some general trends and conclusions that might be drawn for the major generative civilizations of the Afro-Eurasian world. On the basis of present knowledge, a chronology that usefully illuminates the history of education in Mesopotamian civilization is as follows:

3500 B.C. - 2500 B.C. The Formative Period
    A. Sumerian Temple Communities (3500 B.C. - 3000 B.C.)
        1. Pictographic writing appears
        2. Protoliterate schools appear
    B. Sumerian City-States (3000 B.C. - 2500 B.C.)
        1. Invention of fully developed cuneiform writing
        2. Appearance of fully developed schools for scribes—the *edubba*

2500 B.C. - 1500 B.C. Florescence and Diffusion
        1. Akkadians adopt Sumerian writing and education
        2. Babylonians adopt Sumerian-Akkadian education and spread it throughout lower Mesopotamia

1500 B.C. - 500 B.C. Congealing and Dispersion
        1. Assyrians assimilate Sumerian-Akkadian-Babylonian education and spread it throughout upper Mesopotamia
        2. Organized education becomes increasingly formalistic in the heartland of Mesopotamia while fundamental change begins in the Levant to the west

[15] Samuel Noah Kramer, *The Sumerians; Their History, Culture, and Character*, University of Chicago Press, Chicago, 1963, p. 229. Italics added.

Figure 2.1   The Afro-Asian Ecumene of the Ancient Middle East

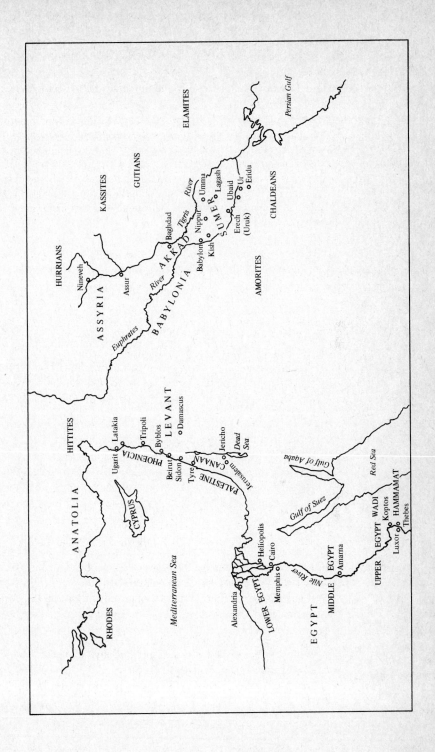

Only the specialist could follow the intricacies of the story, but the accumulated archeological data point unmistakeably to three or four millenia of lively interconnections and interactions among the neolithic peoples of the whole region formerly known as the Near East (Mesopotamia, Anatolia, the Levant, and Persia) and now consisting of the national states of Iraq, Jordan, Syria, Israel, Lebanon, Turkey, and Iran. Between 4500 and 3500 B.C. agricultural settlements, like those which had formed earlier in the hill regions north and east of Mesopotamia, began to appear in the lower valley regions. The flourishing settlements of these river valley people, known archeologically as the Ubaid people, were probably soon penetrated by Semitic nomads from the west. This cultural mixture produced a fertile ground for the arrival of the Sumerians who possibly came southward from the region of the Caspian Sea around 3500 B.C.

The Formative Period (3500 B.C.-2500 B.C.)

Sumerian Temple Communities: Protoliterate Education (3500 - 3000 B.C.).   The protoliterate or protohistorical period in Mesopotamian history, marked by the arrival of the Sumerians in Lower Mesopotamia, produced rapid changes in technology, genuinely new forms of social organization, and a system of pictographic writing which began to lay the basis for fundamental changes in the character of society, culture, and education. The fusion or mixture of the already flourishing neolithic societies with incoming peoples of different tongues seemed to ignite the florescence of life which led to the first civilized forms of society and culture. Active intersocial and intercultural contacts prepared the ground for the "breakthrough" to civilization.

A remarkable series of technological developments having to do with irrigation systems, sailing boats, wheeled vehicles, metallurgy in copper, bronze, and gold, and extraordinary skill in the major art forms accompanied increasing specialization in craftsmanship and increasing social differentiation in the management and administration of human affairs. Something approaching a professional ruling class appeared in the form of temple communities or theocratic polities whose chief managers were priests who administered public affairs in the name of and on behalf of the gods.

The early Sumerian political-religious-economic rationale went something like this: All of the land of a certain territory and its produce belonged to the gods. The priests, dedicated to serving the gods, assigned landholdings to be worked by groups and by individuals, organized the great work forces required for large-scale irrigation, collected the surplus from crops for storage and redistribution, levied taxes, supervised the massive temples which were presumed to house the gods, stimulated long-distance trade, and kept the records required for the orderly conduct of large-scale affairs. As stewards for the gods, the priests were at once political rulers and administrators, religious leaders, and economic planners and managers. Not only did the population increase significantly in the temple community and its surrounding territory, but full-time specialists and full-time officials, including a literate group, or literati, began to form a class of persons theretofore never known in the world, namely, urbanites who were distinguished by the fact that they did not produce their own food. For the first time in human history an urban form of community life replaced the typical folk society village based on kinship ties and a subsistence economy.

During the protoliterate period one critical element in the ability to organize large numbers of people for large-scale enterprises was the ability to keep accurate records of an increasing number of dealings in property, trade, and ownership. Thus, in a very real sense, the invention of an effective system of written symbols and notation made complex social organization feasible and city-state life possible.

Another critical element in this whole process seemed to be that the priests organized themselves into colleges or "corporations" explicitly for carrying out their political, religious, economic, and their educational functions. Both terms carry the connotation that the priests were full-time professionals performing functionally specific duties in a clearly defined social organization for which special admission, selection, and training came to be necessary. In the course of their duties the priests apparently hit upon the device of systematic written records to make their tasks more efficient and successful.

The earliest pictographs so far discovered in Mesopotamia are inscribed on clay tablets found at Erech (Uruk) and at Jamdat Nasr. They are records concerning property and business dealings of the temples dating back to about 3500 B.C. These pictographic signs or symbols representing things (a sheep, a cow, a fish, an ear of corn) seem to be the first steps toward writing, but they were records, not true writing. By 3250 B.C., however, clay tablets found at Ur reveal that some of the signs were being used to signify spoken syllables as a means of indicating the case of nouns and the inflexion of verbs. This is the beginning of true writing. By 2900 B.C. tablets from Erech show signs representing syllables that stand for sounds in a conventionalized way. So it is usually argued that by 3100 or 3000 B.C. fully developed writing had appeared in the Sumerian temple communities or city-states of Lower Mesopotamia.

This portentous development around the beginning of the third millenium B.C. in the cities of Mesopotamia eventually affected all human civilization. It meant that communication through a conventional system of audible symbols, which has become a distinctive characteristic of human beings as distinguished from all other animal beings, could now become in written form a basis for building civilized human societies. Gelb defines writing as a "system of human intercommunication by means of conventional visible marks." He goes on to say, "writing began at the time when man learned how to communicate his thoughts and feelings by means of visible signs, understandable not only to himself but also to all other persons more or less initiated into the particular system."[16] While many peoples in various parts of the world developed systems of pictorial devices to convey meanings from one person to another, it was the Sumerians who first developed a system whereby the visible signs

---

[16] I. J. Gelb, *A Study of Writing,* University of Chicago Press, Chicago, 1952. (Phoenix edition, 1963), p. 11.

stood for the sounds of oral language. The protoliterate period in Mesopotamia marked the transition from pictographic writing and opened the era of logographic systems of word writing in what came to be called cuneiform. The Sumerian system may have stimulated the creation of all the other logographic systems.[17]

The educational significance of the Sumerian protoliterate period may be stated this way: It seems fair to assume that the priestly colleges or corporations found that they needed to simplify and conventionalize the writing that aided them in their social and cultural functions. They began to delegate some of their members to specialize still more in the affairs of writing, and these persons came to be known as scribes. As the priests and priestly scribes worked in concert to arrive at common phonetic meanings for the signs that originally represented things, they produced true writing. And induction into the skills and knowledge necessary to understand several hundred written signs must have been a long, arduous, and organized process.

It may or may not be the case that formal schools were organized as early as the protoliterate period in Mesopotamia. It is easily possible that scribes connected with an *edubba* (tablet house) became teachers as such. Certain it is that some of the oldest known pictographic clay tablets from Erech contain word lists deliberately intended for study and practice, " . . . that is, as early as 3000 B.C., some scribes were already thinking in terms of teaching and learning."[18]

Without pressing the question as to which came first, it is reasonable to assume that organized schools were in the process of formation along with the process of urbanization, social differentiation, political institutionalization, and the creation of writing. It is wholly possible that organized education was an integral and necessary part of the corporate and collegial life of the priestly and scribal class. The formal school may even have helped to create true writing and push forward the transition from pictogram to phonogram. The school may have had a more positive role than simply to become a means of transmitting writing after it had been created. The *edubba* may have been a socially organized means of welding the priestly colleges together and spreading their influence among the villages and other Sumerian cities, not simply a passive instrument for perpetuating the knowledge of writing among an already organized class.

[17] Ibid., chap. 6. Gelb argues that the evolution of writing in general followed several stages which I have simplified somewhat as follows:

 Forerunners of writing included pictographs (pictorial representations) and mnemonic devices (like the notations on bones or the knots of ropes) which conveyed meaning without using a language form.

 Full writing includes phoneticization in which the visible sign comes to stand for a linguistic sound. Full writing is thus phonographic, i.e., the written symbol expresses oral language. Phonography moved through three historical stages: *logographic systems* in which the signs principally stood for words and occasionally for syllables (Sumerian, Proto-Elamite, Proto-Indic, Egyptian, Hittite, Cretan, and Chinese); *syllabic systems* in which the written signs came principally to represent syllables and in which both the signs and the syllables they represented were greatly simplified (Phoenician, Hebrew, and Aramaic): and *alphabetic systems* in which the written sign stood for a single sound of a language (Greek, Aramaic, Hebrew, Latin, Indic, etc.) (See Figure 2.2, p. 41.)

[18] Kramer, op. cit., p. 229.

Figure 2.2   From Pictograph to Alphabet: the diagram shows how *aleph,* an ox, *beth,* a house, and *nun* or *nakas,* a snake, evolved into the letters A, B, N of our alphabet.

egyptian hieroglyph	semitic proto sinaitic 1600 - 1400 b.c.	early canaanite 1400 - 1300 b.c.	canaanite c. 1200 b.c.	early phoenician 1100 - 1000 b.c.	archaic greek forms 850 - 700 b.c.	latin alphabet

Stuart Piggott (ed.), *The Dawn of Civilization,* McGraw-Hill, New York, 1961, p. 160.

These comments are, of course, highly speculative and go well beyond the limits of historical precision with respect to the protoliterate period for which the historical record is so limited. But they are clearly grounded in the empirical evidence that has been dated as belonging to the later city-state period of Sumerian history for which we now have considerable written documentation. The only question is the matter of precise timing, a question that continues to be uncertain so long as unmistakable, written records are unavailable.

Sumerian City-States: The Rise of the School (3000 B.C.-2500 B.C.). Building upon the half millenium of achievement by the temple communities, a still more complicated form of social organization, the city-states of Sumer, produced a remarkable level of civilization in Lower Mesopotamia which not only influenced the neighboring folk societies to the north, east, and west, but undoubtedly affected the rise of civilization in Egypt, and possibly radiated as far as the civilization of the Indus Valley. It was during this period in Sumer that the appearance of a formal system of organized education became unmistakable. The city was in essence an association of free groups of men who, though they consisted of differentiated classes, organized themselves for common political and military purposes based upon territorial residence rather than upon kinship or religion. Thus they were citizens of a city-type political organization embracing one or more of the temple communities which had been organized for predominantly religious and economic purposes. Each citizen apparently belonged to one of the temples as well as to the city.

How all this came about is still far from clear, but apparently in the period between 3000 and 2700 B.C. an occasional strong-man or war leader rose to power on the basis of his military superiority. This semisecular king, together with his aristocratic council of elders or nobles and his popular assembly of "men" or commoners, constituted the earliest form of secular political structure that can be called a state. As the kings came to exercise increasing political authority, they deliberately enlisted the loyalties of the people or the citizens of the city-states who in turn developed a consciousness of themselves as belonging to the city and as having an affinity in common with their fellow citizens. The development of the king's palace as a social institution requiring military as well as civil administration made of it a rival to the priestly temples, both of which needed a corps of literate, educated managers. Skilled craftsmen, entrepreneurial merchants, and trained professionals mingled with farmers and peasants in the active marketplaces of the cities where ideas as well as goods were briskly exchanged.

It was in this setting of social heterogeneity and busy vitality that the Sumerian cities became intellectual and cultural centers as well as political, economic, and religious centers. Not only did the cities consist of large numbers of persons who did not produce their own food, but they also began to develop a peculiarly urban or civilized outlook on the possibilities of social change. They developed a new confidence in their ability to control the rivers by irrigation or drainage, to produce better crops, to build more imposing temples or palaces, and to spread their ideas to the countryside or to other cities. Apparently they felt it was their destiny to do all these things.

In sum, the Sumerian cities began to influence strongly, if not transform, the folk societies with which they came in contact. The peasant villager who experienced for the first time the vast monumental temples or the palaces of the kings or the markets could not help but feel the force of change that the city displayed. And the warrior bands that swooped down from the mountains or in from the deserts to plunder and depart or to conquer and stay were also transformed to a greater or lesser extent by the city life they encountered. As they did this, they became civilized by the ways of the city. They were never again quite so isolated, or quite so homogeneous, or quite so unspecialized as were the folk societies who never had the encounter.

What held the civilized way of life together, what enabled it to spread during the formative period and to maintain itself through all sorts of political storms were not only the technological achievements of the Bronze Age but a central cultural corpus of knowledge and ideas developed by and handed on by that remarkable institution known to us as a school and to the Sumerians, who invented it, as an *edubba.* The neolithic farmers could adopt better tools from the city craftsmen and thus become better farmers or peasants, and the nomadic warrior bands could borrow bronze weapons or make better chariots and thus become superior warriors, but neither the farmers nor the nomads could become truly civilized until they borrowed the literate means of education which the Sumerian cities had created and which in turn helped to shape the character of the first exemplars of urban, civilized life.

We do not possess many details concerning the exact character of the earliest schools of the formative period, but we do have the competent judgment of scholars that "by the middle of the third millenium B.C., there must have been a number of schools throughout Sumer where writing was taught formally."[19] From the large number of school textbooks in the form of clay tablets that have been turned up in

[19] Kramer, op. cit., p. 229.

excavations of cities dating back to 2500 B.C., Kramer describes the earliest known schools as follows:

> The Sumerian school was known as *edubba*, "tablet house." Its original goal was what we would term "professional," that is, it was first established for the purpose of training the scribes necessary to satisfy the economic and administrative needs of the land, primarily, of course, those of the temple and palace. This continued to be the major aim of the Sumerian school throughout its existence. However, in the course of its growth and development, and particularly as a result of the ever widening curriculum, it came to be the center of culture and learning in Sumer. Within its walls flourished the scholar-scientist, the man who studied whatever theological, botanical, zoological, geographical, mathematical, grammatical, and linguistic knowledge was current in his day and who in some cases added to this knowledge.[20]

This then is a brief characterization of the earliest schools known to have been created by man. They were a constituent element in the origin of a literate, urban way of life. They were professional in purpose rather than religious, or arcane, or mystical, i.e., they prepared persons to engage in the most important tasks of the society and at the highest levels required to plan, manage, and administer the increasingly complex affairs of society. The schools produced scribes who became administrators and leading officials, not simply "writers," for "scribe" became the shorthand way of saying that a person who could read and write was automatically one who could administer or manage something beyond his own personal efforts to produce food or the material necessities of life.

As centers of professional scholarship which enabled the educated elite to apply their knowledge to practical affairs, as moulders of the written language itself, and eventually as fountainheads for the production of creative writing which ranged across religious, artistic, or scientific themes, the Sumerian schools played a genuine formative role in shaping the society and the culture which in turn had produced them. As the potentiality of schooling became more evident, the necessity and desirability for some persons to specialize in the teaching function of society became clear, and the original corporations of priests became a kind of model for creating the corporations of scribes who formed the original teaching profession. The school was a major element in the stupendous feat of civilizational breakthrough achieved by the Sumerians in the formative period of their history. A people who created the urban way of life itself created an educational institution to match.

Florescence and Diffusion (2500 B.C. - 1500 B.C.)
Scarcely less impressive than the Sumerians' achievement in creating the school was the widespread diffusion of their culture and education. To put it another way, the educational system created by the Sumerians during the first millenium of their history helped to civilize the successive waves of peoples who extended their rule over

[20] Ibid., pp. 230-231

Mesopotamia during the following 2000 years. As the center of political power moved from the southern cities of Sumer northward and upriver, so the Sumerian educational institutions, literary traditions, and bodies of knowledge were adopted by those to the north, first by the Akkadians, then by the Babylonians, and finally by the Assyrians, to say nothing of many other peoples of lesser political importance (Gutians, Elamites, Amorites, Hurrians, and Kassites). The diffusion of the Sumerian cultural tradition by means of a systematic educational system makes it possible to speak of a massive Mesopotamian civilization which embraced the enormous mixtures of peoples who flowed into and through the Tigris and Euphrates river region for some 2000 years following 2500 B.C.

The cultural achievement and educational system which characterized such city-states as Erech, Ur, Lagash, Eridu, and Nippur were displaying a high point of vitality and creativity at the time when Sargon of Akkad (2370-2315 B.C.) conquered them in the twenty-fourth century B.C. The Semitic-speaking Akkadian invaders, duly impressed by the cuneiform writing, the schools, and the literary and scientific achievements of the Sumerians, adapted the Sumerian written language to their spoken tongue. Sargon was able to exert widespread political authority over the Sumerian cities not only because he built a large and effective standing army, but also because he built a strong centralized and complex hierarchy of officialdom that amounted to the incipient bureaucracy of empire. (See Exhibit 15.1—Imperialism at a Glance, pp. 518-519.)

Thereupon followed a period of nearly 300 years (2000 to 1700 B.C.) of territorial contention among states with the pendulum swinging between rival groups of oligarchies on one side and strong-man kings or tyrants on the other. Throughout this period, the Akkadian language gained in strength until it eventually became the official language of the entire region, while Sumerian gradually disappeared from current usage, becoming a classical language confined largely to the scribal schools of the temples and palaces.

The period of Sumerian history came to a close with the winning of military and political power over Mesopotamia from still further upstream by the kings of Babylon, the most notable being Hammurabi (1792-1750 B.C.). By 1700 B.C. the Babylonians had spread their influence over the whole of civilized Mesopotamia, and the Sumerians disappeared as a political entity. But their cultural and educational influence by no means ended at that point. Just as the Akkadians had taken over Sumerian culture and education, so did the Babylonians take over the Sumerian-Akkadian language, culture, and education. This meant a vast expansion of influence for Sumerian education. The spread of scribal schools not only accompanied the spread of empire but made possible its very realization.

Despite the trend toward imperial centralization of political authority and the disruptions caused by the Indo-European charioteer invaders beginning around 1700 B.C., there is evidence of continuing vitality and flexibility in the social organization of the cities. Of particular interest to the history of education is the fact that professional associations (not primarily political or economic) provided a kind of mutual protection and status for highly trained and educated persons. There seemed to be genuinely independent associations of diviners, priests, physicians, or scribes, all of whom required extensive education.[21] The strength of such professional organizations enabled them to survive the rise and fall of empires for nearly 2,000 years.

For several hundred years the educated classes of Mesopotamia were of necessity bilingual. Even though Akkadian replaced Sumerian as the spoken language of the people, the literary output in the Sumerian language continued until around 1500 B.C. The scribes of the *edubbas* not only wrote in Sumerian, they began to translate the Sumerian works of all kinds into Akkadian. First, law codes, royal inscriptions, and legal decisions began to appear in Akkadian, and then the Sumerian myths and epics. Around 1700 B.C. the translation of Sumerian texts into Akkadian apparently stopped, but the scribes maintained their bilinguality for centuries. Sumerian texts, preserved in classical form, became a model for style and content not only to Akkadians, but also to the Babylonians and Assyrians, as well as to the Hittites and other peripheral civilizations. Even the Akkadian-speaking scribes in the *edubbas* of the Babylonian period could write new works in Sumerian, much as the Italian-, French-, and English-speaking scholars of the Renaissance in Europe could compose in classical Greek and Latin.

The *edubbas* at their best were quite versatile institutions. As the story unfolds, the description by Kramer is extraordinarily illuminating:

> It was in the course of the last half of the third millenium that the Sumerian school system matured and flourished. . . . The number of scribes who practiced their craft throughout those years ran into the thousands; there were junior scribes and "high" scribes, royal and temple scribes, scribes who were highly specialized for particular categories of administrative activities, and scribes who became leading officials in state and government. There is every reason to assume, therefore, that numerous scribal schools of considerable size and importance flourished throughout the land. . . .
>
> Moreover, rather unlike present-day institutions of learning, the Sumerian school was also the center of what might be termed creative writing. It was here that the literary creations of the past were studied and copied; it was here, too, that new ones were composed. While it is true, therefore, that the large majority of graduates from the Sumerian schools became scribes in the service of the temple and palace and among the rich and powerful of the land, there were some who devoted their lives to teaching and learning. Like the university professor of today, many of these ancient scholars depended for their livelihood on their teaching salaries and devoted themselves to research and writing in their spare time. The Sumerian school, which probably began as a temple appendage, became in time a secular institution; the teachers were paid, as far as we can see, out of the tuition fees collected from the students. The curriculum, too, was largely secular in character.[22]

---

[21] A. Leo Oppenheim, *Ancient Mesopotamia; Portrait of a Dead Civilization,* University of Chicago Press, Chicago, 1964, chap. 2.

[22] Kramer, op. cit., pp. 230-231.

As might be expected, the major pedagogical goal of the schools was to teach the aspiring scribe how to read and write the cuneiform language. So the teachers drew up hundreds of textbooks, or rather a systematic series of wax tablets which classified the syllables, words, and phrases the students were to copy and memorize. Such texts thus amounted to lists of elementary syllables (*tu-ta-ti; bu-ba-bi,* etc.) and classified lists of signs that stood for related words or phrases (animals, trees, cities, and the like). These lists of signs, syllables, and words became almost wholly standardized for all the schools of Sumer by 2000 B.C., and as Akkadian came into use from 2000 B.C., onward, many of the texts were written in the form of dictionaries or encyclopedias in both languages. It is the recovery of such bilingual texts that has made the task of comparative linguistic analysis so rewarding in tracing the sequences of language development from Sumerian to Akkadian to Babylonian and to Assyrian.

The linguistic continuity over three thousand years also reflected an educational continuity. In some cases a new linguistic group of people who came in contact with the Sumerian-Akkadian school system would send their young men to the established schools of Mesopotamia to acquire the knowledge needed to set up schools in their own lands upon their return. In other cases the alien peoples would import Sumerian-Akkadian scribes to teach their own young men. The practice of foreign exchange among students, scholars, and teachers seems to indicate that international education has nearly five thousand years of history behind it. All signs pointed to a continuum of wide-ranging contacts with peoples and civilizations at great distances from the Tigris-Euphrates Valley.

Although the curriculum of the *edubba* was apparently dominated by language and literary studies, the pattern of archeological discoveries points also to secular studies. Students copied legal contracts and records, codified laws, royal edicts, all kinds of letters, inscriptions, reports, dictionaries, and magical receipts. The elementary study of mathematics took the form of computation tables and measurement tables of length, area, capacity, and weight as well as the more advanced study of practical mathematical problems related to irrigation, canals, and the like. Babylonian mathematics achieved something of a florescence in the eighteenth century B.C. around Hammurabi's time. A sexagesimal system of notation and fractional quantities with theoretical attention to algebraic and even quadratic equations was the result of intense efforts by Babylonian scribes whose accomplishments were not matched for another thousand years. Their successors apparently were satisfied to copy endlessly their computations.

Discovery of a few medical texts implies that some Sumerian schools taught some medical lore, and at least one farm manual (from about 2000 B.C.) has come to light which makes it appear that some *edubba* teachers had painstakingly compiled detailed instructions on irrigation, weeding, plowing, sowing, harvesting, threshing, and winnowing. Kramer believes it is clear that this was a textbook for training scribes in the skills of managing an efficient and successful farm estate—obviously a professional career of enormous importance throughout Mesopotamian history.[23] This is further substantiation that in the florescent days of Sumerian education the schools had a vital

[23] Kramer, op. cit., pp. 105-111.

and functional relationship to the principal social concerns of the society—economic as well as political and administrative.

This point is still further borne out by a study of the occupations of the fathers of about 500 individuals who identified themselves as scribes around 2000 B.C.

> The fathers of the scribes, that is, of the school graduates, were governors, "city fathers," ambassadors, temple administrators, military officers, sea captains, high tax officials, priests of various sorts, managers, supervisors, foremen, scribes, archivists, and accountants—in short, all the wealthier citizens of an urban community. Only one single woman is listed as a scribe in these documents, and the likelihood is, therefore, that the student body of the Sumerian school consisted of males only.[24]

In short, the *edubbas* gave a literate education and training to those persons who were required to plan, manage, and administer the affairs of a civilized society based upon a large-scale polity, an urban way of life, and extensive social and economic differentiation.

All in all, the florescent period of Mesopotamian education was marked by a great stream of intellectual continuity and literary assimilation. Each age and each people reworked the received tradition to accord with its own characteristics. And the schools apparently responded to outsiders with considerable effectiveness, helping to acculturate the aliens and the strangers who kept coming from the surrounding regions, coming either to conquer and settle, or to trade and return home, or to learn and be taught. In general, Mesopotamia gave more than it received during this period, and its educational system was one of the principal instrumentalities. When it began to lose the power to influence others, to teach them its accumulated knowledge, to share its intellectual treasure, and to adapt itself to the needs of others, its creativity as a civilized core area began to weaken. A deadening formalistic education was one of the signs of decline.

Congealing and Dispersion (1500 B.C.-500 B.C.)

During the last third of Mesopotamia's three thousand years of life as a distinctive civilization two major trends marked the history of education, each denoted by a different meaning of the term dispersion.

In the first sense of dispersion, the Sumerian-Akkadian-Babylonian tradition of scribal education was diffused or disseminated through much of the Middle East, far beyond the confines of the Tigris-Euphrates Valley. The principal political carrier of the Mesopotamian educational tradition was the Assyrian Empire which at its height included most of Western Asia from Iran to the Mediterranean and Egypt. Furthermore, the Hittites who dominated Anatolia for several centuries and the sea peoples of the Levant who traversed the Mediterranean Sea were also affected by the Mesopotamian cultural and educational tradition. Altogether the new cosmopolitan form of civilization that was emerging in the Middle East rested in large part upon organized

---

[24] Ibid., pp. 231-232.

groups of literate, trained professionals who administered governments, managed armies and estates, conducted trade, formulated laws, and taught schools.

The second trend in Mesopotamian education was its increasing formalism and narrowing of purpose and content. The congealing and constriction were particularly evident in the citadels of conservative literary tradition in the heartland of Mesopotamia, while the centers of change and innovation in language, literature, and education began to move toward the West, first to the cities of the Levant and then to the cities of the Aegean and Greece. This second meaning of dispersion involved a dissipation or breaking apart of the coherent and creative elements which had given Mesopotamian education so much of its vitality and social and intellectual leadership during its formative and florescent periods.

The reasons for these two trends, both dispersive in character but quite divergent in effect, are difficult to sort out and complex to analyze. But they set a pattern for development which seems to show up in other civilizations. The dispersions of Greek education in Hellenistic times, of Latin education in the late days of the Roman Empire, of Christian education in Medieval Europe, and of Western education in modern times come readily to mind.

The basic elements of Sumerian-Akkadian-Babylonian civilization were adopted largely unchanged by the Assyrians during their rule of Mesopotamia from the fourteenth century to the sixth century B.C. Reaching the height of their power in the eight and seventh centuries B.C., the Assyrians found it their turn to be overthrown by Chaldean conquerors, often known as the Neo-Babylonian dynasty, of whom Nebuchadnezzar II was the most famous ruler in the sixth century B.C. Finally, the political independence of Mesopotamia came to an end under the double blows of the Medes who conquered Nineveh in 612 B.C. and the Persians who conquered Babylon in 539 B.C. In the fifth century, B.C., the great temple of Marduk at Babylon was destroyed and the priesthood dispersed. For all practical purposes the influence of the central core of the Mesopotamian intellectual, religious, and educational tradition had come to an end even though cuneiform writing survived for another 500 years.

Despite the recurring episodes of chaotic dynastic rivalry alternating with expanding imperial rule, an ever-growing urban way of life persisted throughout this cosmopolitan period of Mesopotamian history. In fact, many rulers deliberately stimulated urbanization. And where the cities went there also went the schools. In the heartland of Mesopotamia, the great cities continued to be Babylon, Damascus, Nineveh, Assur, and Susa; but by the first millenium B.C. they were being rivalled by new cities in the Levant to the West.

As early as the fourteenth century B.C., one of the most famous of these was Ugarit, an international concourse of spoken tongues, scribes, and ideas as well as goods and merchants, where revolutionary experiments with written languages were being carried out. From 1000 B.C. onward, Phoenician cities like Tyre and Sidon became important commercial, intellectual, and colonizing centers for much of the Mediterranean; and from 900 B.C. onward the cities on the coast of Anatolia began to trade with the Greek cities in the Aegean and eventually developed flourishing trade with the cities of the Greek mainland by the middle of the eight century B.C. Significantly enough, this period from 1200 B.C. to 700 B.C. was not only a period of rapid spreading of city life and founding of colonial cities, but an exceedingly formative period in the development of new styles of written languages and educational institutions whose generative centers were the cities of the eastern Mediterranean and the Aegean Sea.

Meanwhile the ancient centers of the traditional culture tended to turn in upon themselves and perpetuate the literary and linguistic forms of the classical languages of Sumer and its Akkadian variations. As so often happened in later civilizations, the high prestige schools became the citadels of traditional learning, glorifying the purity and the sanctity of the Great Tradition of culture and proclaiming themselves as the defenders of the true knowledge against those who would neglect or corrupt it. The mathematical, the scientific, and the practical components of the earlier scribal schools declined in favor of the purely literary and linguistic. The original, generous professional purpose of the Sumerian *edubba*—designed to train scribes for the major public affairs of the city, the state, the temple, and the economy—became a narrow, technical purpose: to train experts adept in writing the cuneiform language, which itself was losing ground to the more simplified languages of the West Semites and the Greeks. This constricted view of Mesopotamian education narrowed the meaning of the profession of scribe.

This archaism, this looking to the past, tended to happen over and over again when a great civilization found itself under attack, losing its political power, or being bypassed by newer and more energetic societies. The defenders of the Great Tradition tend to glorify its classic, golden era and to argue that the language and literature, the religion, the culture, the systems of thought, the moral and aesthetic virtues of the earlier days must be preserved and transmitted unchanged to successive generations if the civilization itself is to survive. So perhaps for the first time, the basic ingredients of a so-called classical education were formulated and defended. This theme, with appropriate variations, can be heard in Hellenistic times, in late Roman times, in late medieval times, and in late Renaissance times. It can even be heard in late modern times as the Western colonial powers extolled their own classical forms of education as prime agencies for "civilizing" the less advanced peoples of Asia, Africa, and the Americas.

Meanwhile, the newer and more aggressive peoples with less refined cultures were often eager to accept the higher, classic culture of the older civilization as a means of learning the lessons and of entering the charmed precincts of civilization itself. Some new societies might borrow or assimilate the old without making basic changes of their own. This is largely what the Babylonians and Assyrians did during the three thousand years of Mesopotamian civilization.

But other peoples not only learn the lessons of the old and emulate or assimilate much of it, but also basically reassess and modify it on their own terms and in light of their own characteristics and aspirations. In the process they develop a distinctive civilization of their own. This is what the peoples of the Levant and the Aegean did in the first millenium B.C. when they came in contact with the great variety of languages, ideas, and customs that flowed through the Eastern Mediterranean region from Mesopotamia to the east, Egypt to the south, and Anatolia and Greece to the north.

Thus it was that the scribes of the coastal cities of the Levant not only found themselves in another Babel of spoken tongues, but also in a labyrinth of written languages, each with hundreds of signs and symbols to master. These included the cuneiform of the Sumerians, Akkadians, Hittites, and Hurrians, and the hieroglyphics of the Egyptians and the Cypriote-Minoans. Beginning as early as the seventeenth or sixteenth century B.C., the scribes of Palestine and Syria began the experiment of simplifying the several systems of logographic writing, an experiment that eventually resulted in a variety of syllabic scripts. From the eleventh century on, these syllabic forms of writing were still further simplified to the point where the number of written symbols was reduced to the signs needed to represent the relatively few sounds that are used in a spoken language. These thirty or so signs came to make up the alphabets of the major languages. The Phoenicians are usually given credit for the feat of inventing an alphabet. However, Gelb argues persuasively that the West Semitic scripts were really syllabic and not fully alphabetic, because they did not have signs for the vowels, and that the Greeks created the first true alphabet by inventing signs for the vowels as well as for the consonants.[25] (See Figure 2.2, p. 41.)

The point here is twofold: the new creativeness in language development arose in international centers where the mingling of peoples led to new intellectual and educational forms; whereas the ancient centers made a virtue of maintaining the old forms of writing (and of education) despite their complexity and inability to respond easily to social and intellectual change. The scribes who had mastered the difficult cuneiform language after many years of hard work had a vested interest. They were not likely to admit that easier and simpler methods of writing and of education, which could be mastered in a shorter time by larger (and thus less able) numbers of people, could be better than the old.

The professional purpose of the original Mesopotamian schools was eventually lost, but the organizational framework, that enabled the schools to develop in the first place by achieving a corporate life for scribes and teachers became ossified into a protectionist cult that sought to resist change. At that point Mesopotamian education became so congealed that it was susceptible to the disintegrative forms of dispersion rather than its disseminative qualities. It no longer had the power to share its ancient abundance through the disseminating powers of dispersion. The peoples with alphabetic languages, who could realize their promise of wider literacy through broader access to schools, created the newer and more dynamic centers of civilization which successive societies and cultures would come to emulate.

Meanwhile, the Old Babylonian literary tradition, which had been formulated between 1750 and 1600 B.C., began to be standardized and canonized from about 1500 B.C. onward. Eventually the whole literary tradition was pressed into compendia that formed the prescribed curriculum of the schools. Whatever was not in the curriculum was not worth knowing. Literature lost its creative force and began to be frozen into stereotyped forms, the pedagogical goal for scribe and student stressed slavish copying, even to the specific form of wording that had to be followed in edition after edition so that the original would be preserved without change. This

---

[25] See I. J. Gelb, *A Study of Writing*, University of Chicago Press, Chicago, 1952. (Phoenix edition, 1963), chaps. 5 and 6.

formalistic transmission of the corpus of the literary tradition became the principal task and goal of the scribal schools.

Indeed, it could be argued that in this case educational practice was a formative influence in the more general constriction and fossilization of Mesopotamian civilization itself. For example, the virtual absence in the curriculum of a whole genre of literature later made famous by the Greeks–history, social and political criticism, philosophy, logic, and moral or ethical analysis–meant that the Mesopotamian schools and their teachers were not really engaged in educating youth for citizenship, for their social roles, or for intellectual challenge. Mesopotamian education thus weakened the texture of a civilization which needed to face momentous social changes but was not able to rise to the challenge.

Instead, Mesopotamian education was content to rehearse and rehash the lessons of a purely literary scholarship husbanded by successive generations of increasingly cloistered academic scribes. Above all, they cherished the complex and difficult cuneiform literature which also was becoming more and more remote from the spoken language of the times. The scribes seemed to glory in the obscurity of their classical language. There is even evidence that they not only did not try to compete with the newer and more efficent scripts by simplifying the cuneiform, but even added to the number of logograms in use during the first half of the first millenium. The classical language of the schools could compete with the new vernaculars and the new scripts only on the basis that it bestowed exclusive powers of intellectual achievement and prestige upon those who were admitted to the academic elite and who acted as its self-appointed custodians.

Conclusion: The Curve of Educational Development

It is, of course, difficult to generalize about the complicated web of history spun out over three thousand years, encompassing a large region of the world and involving millions of people. Yet the institutions of human civilization have great ingredients of continuity, stability, and uniformity which give common characteristics to diverse peoples over long periods of time. It is this persisting character of social organization which gives some validity to the effort to generalize despite the exceptions, the differences, and the contradictions.

In the process of generalization I have found what seem to be three major periods in the three thousand years of Mesopotamian educational history, each roughly a millenium in length. The first third (from 3500-2500 B.C.) I have called the *formative period.* During this time the Sumerians created organized and formal schools to go along with their creation of written language, temple communities, city-states, and an urban way of life based upon social differentiation and specialization of political and economic tasks. If this be called the original urban revolution, it may also be called the original educational revolution. The schools helped to produce the trained people who transformed folk societies into human civilization.

The second third of Mesopotamian educational history (from 2500 to 1500 B.C.) I have called the *florescent period.* During this time the Sumerian educational system became a flourishing institution of remarkable scope and vitality. As it was extended, systematized, and adopted by Akkadians and Babylonians, the schools were turned into creative centers of literary, scientific, and practical achievement. They helped to make possible the elaborate institutions of bureaucratic and imperial government, international trade, and intellectual perspectives that marked a cosmopolitan civilization of enormous scope and vitality.

The final third of a distinctively Mesopotamian educational history (from 1500 to 500 B.C.) I have called the *dispersive period*. The educational system slowed down, lost its creative and innovative style, and became much more formalistic and repetitious in character. But nevertheless it continued to be disseminated over still wider areas of the Middle East by the Assyrian Empire, and for much of the period it continued to influence the successive waves of pastoral folk peoples and the satellite civilizations of the region. It also began to contract and congeal as it became less responsive to the new currents of ideas, languages, and peoples who were on the move in its domain and on its peripheries. Dispersion came to mean dissipation, decay, and eventually disappearance in the face of new and more viable forms of civilization and education. This benchmark curve of educational development may oversimplify the story, but may also be useful as a conceptual tool with which to look at successive civilizations for the sake of possible comparisons. The pattern is schematized in Figure 2.3.

In succeeding chapters we shall try to see if the rhythm from formative through florescent to dispersive stages of development is unique to Mesopotamian education or whether it reflects a general pattern that applies in some useful respects to educational developments in other major civilizations.

Persisting questions that deserve particular attention have to do with the innovative versus the conservative role of education in society. Under what social and cultural conditions does education contribute to social change, as it did in Mesopotamia in the formative and florescent periods; and under what conditions does education contribute to the conservation and maintenance of traditional ways of life as it did in the dispersive period? Do the content and character of education have any particular formative influence on the direction that civilization itself takes in different periods of time?

We are not ready to answer these questions in detail, and perhaps we shall never be able to do so with great assurance or certainty, but the analysis of Mesopotamian education leads me to these propositions:

1. When organized education is deliberately designed to prepare persons directly for a fairly wide range of the key roles required for the conduct of public affairs in a society (political, economic, professional, and technical), it is likely to be more innovative than when its purpose is to prepare persons for a limited occupation or a particular class in society. For example, the early scribal schools of Mesopotamia trained young men for all the major tasks of managing and administering an increasingly complex society, whereas the later schools focused more exclusively upon the tasks of preparing a limited scribal class whose major purpose was to copy and preserve the literary and religious tradition of the past.
2. When the literary studies help to widen the perspectives of the mind of the student and try to make him self-objective towards himself and his society and

Figure 2.3   The Curves of Educational Development in Mesopotamian and Egyptian Civilizations

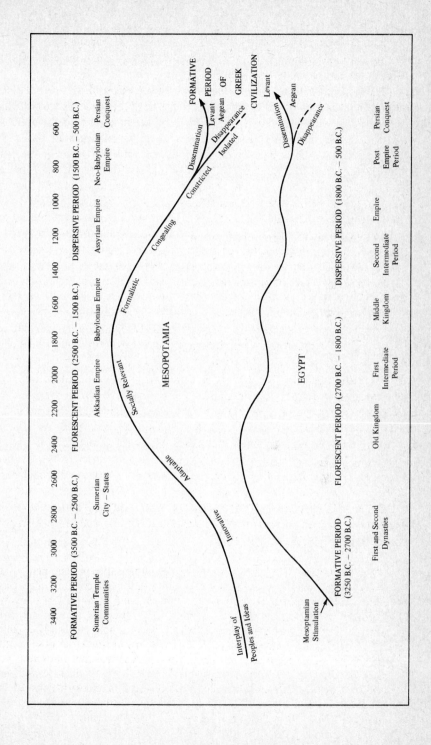

its role in relation to other peoples, education is likely to be more innovative than when the literary studies concentrate upon the wisdom literature of the past and serve primarily to narrow one's intellectual horizons or divert attention from the social or cultural problems of the contemporary civilization.

3. When the sciences and applied sciences are taught with concern for understanding the general principles involved as well as for the application to technical and practical problems, the education is likely to be more innovative than when they are taught primarily as rules of thumb contained in "how-to-do-it" manuals.

4. When the attitudes inculcated in students stress an achievement motivation directed at public service for the wider society as well as individual excellence of work, the education is likely to be more innovative than when it concentrates on developing the feelings appropriate to the ascribed status or particularistic loyalties of an ethnic, religious, kinship, or intellectual elite.

5. When the teaching profession is so organized that its priorities include continuing efforts to promote the society's powers of adaptability and its ability to deal with an increasing complexity of social institutions and when the profession enables its members themselves to become creative producers in the arts and sciences, education will be more innovative and liberating than when the organized profession concentrates primarily on protecting the selection, standards, qualifications, and welfare of its own members.

6. When education becomes predominantly formalistic and uncreative, divorced from the major practical affairs of society, and closely held by a privileged academic elite, it helps to promote social rigidity and general decline of vitality in the civilization itself.

I believe that the history of Mesopotamian education illustrates these generalizations. At least, they may serve as hypotheses to be tested when we come to the civilizations and to the eras when the written historical records permit considerably more confidence in making general propositions.

C. THE WIDENING ORBIT OF CIVILIZATION

We now double back in time to discuss very briefly the history of education in the other major civilizations that marked the Afro-Eurasian ecumene in ancient times. (See Figures 1.1 and 1.2.) The second major center of civilizational development was in the Nile Valley of northern African; the third in the river valleys of northern India; the fourth on the islands and shores of the Aegean Sea; and the fifth in the river valleys of northern China.[26] We shall deal first with Egypt, and then very briefly with India and China before moving to the Aegean which led directly to Greece and to the West.

Education in Egyptian Civilization
We begin this essay on the role of education in Egyptian civilization by asking the question, "Does the curve of educational development as outlined for Mesopotamia

[26] Archeological finds in 1970 point to a flourishing civilization lying about equidistant between Sumer and the Indus valley in southeastern Iran.

apply to Egypt?" The answer in all candor must be, "It does, and it doesn't." The chronology of 3000 years of Egyptian history is, of course, a complicated and specialized matter upon which the experts disagree. For purposes of this discussion I have adapted the periodization and chronology given by John A. Wilson[27] and applied it to the educational development as follows:

3200-2700 B.C. *Formative Period*
    A. Mesopotamian Stimulation (3250 B.C. ± 150 years)
    B. First and Second Dynasties (3100-2700 B.C.)

2700-1800 B.C. *Florescence and Revival*
    A. Old Kingdom (2700-2200 B.C.)
        1. Third through Sixth Dynasties
    B. First Intermediate Period (2200-2050 B.C.)
        1. Seventh through Eleventh Dynasties
    C. Middle Kingdom (2050-1800 B.C.)
        1. Twelfth Dynasty

1800-500 B.C. *Repetition and Dispersion*
    A. Second Intermediate Period (1800-1500 B.C.)
        1. Thirteenth through Seventeenth Dynasties
        2. Hyksos Rule
        3. Eighteenth Dynasty
    B. Empire (1500-1100 B.C.)
        1. Eighteenth through Twentieth Dynasties
    C. Post-Empire Period (1100-500 B.C.)
        1. Twenty-first through Twenty-sixth Dynasties
    D. Persian Conquest (525 B.C.)

If we superimpose this outline of Egyptian education upon the curve that represents the rhythm of organized education in Mesopotamia, we get Figure 2.2. The answer to our question is that that in its most general terms the Egyptian experience does seem to follow a rhythm or curve that begins with an external stimulation and proceeds through formative and florescent stages that ultimately give way to a period of formalism, constriction, congealing, and repetition. To be sure, the various periods are different in length and intensity; the ups and downs should not be taken too literally; and the absence of definitive historical records makes close comparison difficult.

Formative Period (c. 3250 B.C.-2700 B.C.). In contrast to the widespread intercultural contact among the neolithic societies of Mesopotamia, the folk societies of Egypt clustering around the Nile Valley apparently had relatively little contact with outside cultures until the latter part of the fourth millenium. Then, sometime between 3400 and 3100 B.C., it seems clear that the transition from neolithic folk society to civilization took a sudden leap forward. The major catalyst in this abrupt development

[27] John A. Wilson, *The Culture of Ancient Egypt*, Phoenix Books, University of Chicago Press, Chicago, 1965, pp. 319-320.

seems to have been the stimulation received from the Sumerian protoliterate civiliza-tion of Mesopotamia[28] in the form of art motifs, architectural use of bricks, cylinder seals, potter's wheel, metallurgy, and above all, the idea of written language. The theory is that whereas the Egyptians did not borrow the cuneiform characters of Sumerian script, they did borrow the *idea* that written symbols could convey spoken words. The theory is further supported by the fact that Sumerian influence seemed to be localized in Upper Egypt rather than in the Delta. This meant that the contact with Sumeria was probably by sea via the Gulf of Persia and the Red Sea and then overland across the Wadi Hammamat to Koptos on the Nile, just below ancient Karnak and Thebes. (See Figure 2.1.)

We do not know, of course, who did the travelling to make the contacts with Sumeria. The fact that the influence seemed to be all one way—from Sumeria to Egypt—would seem to indicate that it was the Sumerians or some intermediary peoples who did the travelling. Wilson argues that the influence was effected not by conquest, nor by colonization or immigration, nor by commerce alone, but somehow the influence was exerted through "cultural conquest without physical conquest." Since no one knows for sure, the presumption could be that the traveller most likely to pass on the idea of writing without conquest or commerce as prime motives might indeed be a scribe or teacher, or at least a literate person; and if he was not fully literate, at least he had to be familiar enough with writing to convey the idea that written signs could convey the meaning of words. Whoever it was, the point is that the stimulus quickly energized Egyptians to produce a literate class of scribes who could create their own system of writing and thus catapulted Egypt into civilization. At the very least, the intellectual and educational achievement symbolized by Sumerian writing apparently had a formative influence in producing a similar civilizational achievement in Egypt.

It is even more interesting to note that within a very short time—and contem-poraneous with the appearance of writing—Egypt was unified into a single political entity around 3100 B.C. by a dynasty from the south, traditionally attributed to Menes. It is, of course, wildly speculative, but it is nevertheless fascinating to contem-plate that the contact with Sumeria had helped the rulers from the south to develop new techniques of social organization that enabled them to unify Egypt from within. If so, it would not be the last time that one element in a society gained strength over its rivals by virtue of its contact with the educational and intellectual achievements of outsiders. This process was to be repeated over and over in centuries to come—in Europe, in Asia, in Africa, and in America. Education proved early in man's career to be a powerful political instrument.

While much of the foregoing is speculative, none of it is impossible. What is closer to verification, however, is the fact that Egyptian education in the early phases of its formative period seemed to be much more explicitly shaped by political purposes than was the case in the temple communities of Sumer. This leads us to a brief comparison between the formative periods of Mesopotamian and Egyptian civilizations. What took a thousand years in Mesopotamia took five hundred years in

---

[28] Ibid., pp. 36-42.

Egypt. This was partly because Egypt had the advantage of borrowing what Sumer had painstakingly developed over a long period of time and partly because Egypt's geographic isolation led to the very early development of a highly centralized political state which in turn speeded up the building of civilization—but at enormous cultural cost to its creativity. In contrast, the independent city-states of Sumer laboriously built up a common cultural and educational network *before* they developed a political unity which was eventually imposed upon them by outsiders.

Remember that the three characteristics of the civilizational process in Sumer, in addition to the invention of writing and schools, were urbanization, social differentiation, and political institutionalization. While all three were interrelated, urbanization and social differentiation played especially significant roles in the formation of the Sumerian temple communities while political institutionalization under the war leaders came later with the rise of the city-states.

In contrast, the formative period in Egypt took place primarily under the political stimulus and leadership of the pharaoh-king, who made the entire land of Egypt into a kind of enormous personal estate ruled by him from his elaborate household or court-city. Cities were never as important in Egypt as they were in Sumer or later in Greece, and the cities of Egypt never achieved the fairly large measure of autonomy that they did in the Mesopotamian empires or in the Hellenistic or Roman empires. Another way to put it is that Egypt "never reached the full urban stage."[29]

Similarly, even though Egypt did display the growth of social differentiation and specialization of economic and political functions characteristic of civilization elsewhere, it did not produce the strong, wealthy, self-conscious organizations of a professional kind that characterized the city-states of Sumer. The agricultural villages remained the dominant economic unit; the cities never became independent intellectual or cultural centers. The king's royal household played the role of the city, and the king's family of officials and retainers was the civil bureaucracy. This meant less autonomy and less flexibility in Egyptian civilization from the very beginning, a circumstance that earlier produced less creativity in Egyptian education and a longer period of constricted repetition.

Indeed, the development of writing itself may have had an even more important political ingredient in Egypt that it had in Mesopotamia. The usual assumption is that writing was developed in Egypt primarily for the economic advantage accruing from the need to keep an accurate calendar to predict the rise and fall of the Nile and for the religious purposes of assuring the god-kings' happiness in the next world. The very term *hieroglyphic* reveals the religious and magical character of the wall writings designed to decorate the tombs, temples, and monuments of the kings. But the political purpose of Egyptian writing is revealed by the early development of a more simplified script called *hieratic,* a kind of shorthand to be used for all the practical purposes of state, economy, and science for which the hieroglyphic script was too cumbersome and esoteric. Its political purpose is stated succinctly by Professor Jean Lelant of Strassbourg University, who says that "in Egypt writing is contemporaneous with the creation of the single state, and with the systematic organization of irrigation.

[29] Ibid., p. 35.

Writing was, in effect, originally an instrument for the communication of orders, rather than for a registration of ideas. It is absolutely essential for organization and command."[30]

Unfortunately, we know even less about the role of education than we know about cultural development in general during the formative period of the first few dynasties. Whether or not there were any formal schools cannot be affirmed for certain. Some scholars claim that all education prior to 2000 B.C. (i.e., prior to the Middle Kingdom) was conducted by fathers for their sons or by officials and priests for their apprentices. Other scholars argue that the rapidly expanding bureaucracy in the formative period required more scribes than the priesthoods could produce, and so a special class of scribes with a special education had to be created to supply the needs of the state as well as the priesthoods.

In light of such disparity of views we can only say that some formal group collaboration must have attended the rapid invention of such a complicated writing system, as indeed it did in Mesopotamia, and some formal instruction or schooling must have been the means of initiating newcomers into its mysteries. If this could have been achieved primarily in the informal atmosphere of private homes or households or by an apprenticeship system in court or temple, it was only because the numbers were few and the more intimate circle of the king's household or court made regular instruction available and effective. It is entirely possible that the style of life in the Egyptian king's court, in contrast to that of a Sumerian type of urban life, could have resulted in a tutorial form of education, such as that which characterized the manors of England and of the southern United States in contrast to the formal schools of the more urbanized communities of old England or New England. But, again, there is so little evidence for the earliest period that we shall turn to the florescent period where the evidence for schooling is unmistakeable and its general characteristics clearer.

Florescence and Revival (2700 B.C.-1800 B.C.). The 500 years of the Old Kingdom are considered to be the great creative period in Egyptian civilization. This is the period of the finest workmanship on the pyramids, the classics of art, sculpture, and literature, and innovations in science, mathematics, and speculative thought. The invention of the 365-day calendar is widely recognized as a remarkable feat of precise observation and record-keeping; a compilation of medical knowledge known as the Edwin Smith Surgical Papyrus reveals considerable scientific objectivity and relatively little reliance upon magical lore; and the Memphite Theology reflects a nearly rationalistic effort to arrive at a basic theory explaining the creation of the world and the intelligible laws of the universe rather than a recital of purely customary mythology.

All three of these latter instances were products of the literate scribes. Their education enabled them to create and transmit a growing body of systematic knowledge and rational thought, much of which had a highly practical purpose. There was little intent to speculate for purely intellectual purposes or to produce art for art's sake. Politico-religious practicality seemed to be the dominant rule.

[30] Jacquetta Hawkes and Sir Leonard Woolley, *Prehistory and the Beginnings of Civilization*, Harper & Row, New York, 1963, p. 664, n. 13.

Writing became more widespread by the middle of the Old Kingdom as the demand for more literate officals increased. I can only assume that this meant that schools and the means of formal instruction also increased in order to train the members of an expanding bureaucracy. It is entirely possible that the first, or at least the most important, schools were established by the kings at their courts in order to train scribes. As a member of the royal retinue and official family of the king, the scribe's role ranged from that of the lowly but essential clerk or secretary to the highest type of responsible administrator.

In addition to the court schools for scribes, there were undoubtedly temple schools whose tasks were twofold, to replenish the supply of priests for the ever-growing priesthoods charged with eternal care of the pharaoh-god's tombs, and to act as training schools for the civil bureaucracy. Actually, these two functions may have been scarcely distinguishable inasmuch as the king was a god-king and inasmuch as the high priests served basically as public officials.

Finally, there is evidence that the various government bureaus of the expanding bureaucracy eventually established "department schools" as a means of training their own employees. Schools for the horse cavalry were run by the "Stable Scribe", for the treasury by the "Silver Scribe", for agriculture by the "Grain Scribe", and so on for architecture, engineering, vineyards, library, and the like.

We cannot trace the ups and downs of educational organization through the various phases of the florescent period. The best we can do is to identify some of the major outlooks and attitudes inculcated in students by the educational system as these are revealed in those typical literary forms of Egyptian civilization, the "Manuals of Instruction." These books of advice on what every aspiring boy should know were written as a kind of wisdom literature by fathers for the edification of their sons. What makes the books of instruction doubly interesting is that they were apparently not only originally written as teaching devices for one's own family or friends, but they eventually became textbooks in the schools. As such, they were copied endlessly as untold generations of schoolboys over several centuries used them as models in learning to read and write the Egyptian language. This wisdom literature glorifies the goals of success, material wealth, efficient and obedient achievement, and confidence that knowledge and hard work will pave the way for the student to become the "compleat bureaucrat."

The busy activism, the practical optimism, and the self-confident aggressiveness of the Old Kingdom were rudely shattered after some 500 years by an intermediate period of civil strife and breakdown in the central authority of the kings, marked by widespread political decentralization, economic decline, and loss of confidence in the future. Despite the political and economic difficulties of this First Intermediate Period, the scribes and their schools apparently continued to function more or less effectively under the tutelage of nobles and priesthoods. They even managed to produce some of the most creative pieces of Egyptian literature, ranging from counsels of despair or indulgence to moral crusades for greater social justice.

The promise of social justice, however, was overwhelmed by a resurgence of centralizing power by the pharaohs of the Middle Kingdom. With the reunification of

Egypt by a king from the south, Egypt embarked upon two-and-a-half centuries of renewed expansion, power, and self-confidence. One of the goals was a deliberate renaissance to emulate the achievements of the Old Kingdom. The centripetal power of the pharaohs was reasserted over the provincial nobles and the corporate priest-hoods, a new capital was established at Thebes, and the extraordinary temple to the new god Amon was built at Karnak. As cultural affairs and classical literature flourished at home, the influence of Egyptian language and culture spread to the Aegean, the Levant, and Anatolia. This outward thrust of Egyptian culture and commerce after a thousand years of internal civilizational development was a bit "Unegyptian," but it is characteristic of a florescent, aggressive, self-confident civiliza-tion that it should try to disseminate its intellectual wares to other peoples.

The expansionism of the Middle Kingdom undoubtedly affected education. The profession of scribes and the schools that produced them were actively "going" concerns. Perhaps the best expression of the self-importance in which the scribes held themselves is the famous *Satire on the Trades* which sets forth a classic pattern of outlook toward the superiority of the "white collared" professions over the lower, menial, and manual trades. Thus spoke one Khety as he travelled up the Nile to place his son in the school for scribes of the capital city:

> I shall make thee love writing more than thy [own] mother. . . . Moreover, it is greater than any [other] office; there is not its like in the land. . . .
> I have seen the metalworker at his work at the mouth of his furnace. His fingers were somewhat like crocodiles; he stank more than fish-roe.
> Every craftsman that wields the adze, he is wearier than a hoeman. . . . When [the stonecutter] . . . sits down at the going in of Re [sunset?], his thighs and his back are cramped.
> The barber is (still) shaving at the end of dusk. . . .[31]

After paying his respects in similar fashion to the lot of the merchant, builder, gardener, farmer, weaver, courier, embalmer, cobbler, laundryman, and fisherman, Khety concludes by praising the rewards of the scribe:

> Behold, there is no profession free of a boss—except for the scribe: he is the boss.
> But if thou knowest writing, then it will go better with thee than [in] these professions which I have set before thee. . . .[32]

What started out as a satire composed by a literate father for the edification of his son eventually became a popular textbook of accepted truth in the required curriculum of the scribal schools of the Empire. Instead of *A Satire on the Trades* it might better have been called *The Gospel According to the Sainted Scribe.*

[31] James B. Pritchard (ed.), *Ancient Near Eastern Texts Relating to the Old Testament,* 3rd. rev. ed., Princeton University Press, Princeton, N. J. 1969, pp. 432-434.

[32] Ibid., p. 434.

Repetition and Dispersion (1800 B.C.-500 B.C.). For a second time the seemingly sturdy structure of Egyptian political power was shaken to its foundations by civil wars among competing dynasties and by the Hyksos invaders from the north, who conquered Egypt and ruled it for 200 years from within their walled and armed camps. As before, however, this Second Intermediate Period (1800-1500 B.C.) retained enough stability and continuity for the priesthoods to survive and for the intellectual and literary corpus to be handed down by the educational system. So few writings have been preserved that little is known with accuracy. After the Hyksos were expelled in 1570 by a Thebean dynasty from the south, a new and imperialistic Egypt emerged which had strongly nationalistic overtones but which basically embodied the forms and content of the culture and education of the florescent period. What impresses most historians is the imitative and repetitive character of the culture in the thousand years embraced by the Empire and the Post-Empire period from roughly 1500 to 500 B.C.

True, there were signs of change. The foreign conquests of the Empire, which took its borders as far north as Syria and east to the Euphrates, brought Egypt into contact and competition with the Hittite and Assyrian Empires. This meant the literature of the schools came to be flecked with foreign phrases and content. But the flirtation with the cultures of other peoples had more effect on the outsiders than it did on Egypt. The Canaanites of Palestine borrowed the Egyptian language signs and simplified them on their road to creating an alphabet, whereas Egyptian literature rejected outside influence, re-copying its own classical forms even as it adopted colloquialisms and relegated classical Egyptian to the dead language of religious ritual.

So there was no innovative break in the educational tradition. Repetition was the essence; and repetition led eventually to dispersion in the sense that education became congealed, constricted, dissipated much as it did in Mesopotamia. But there was a major difference: dispersion meant disintegration rather more than dissemination. As Wilson puts it, the Egyptians were not the "cultural missionaries" that the Mesopotamians were before them, and the Greeks, the Romans, the Arabs, and the Westerners after them. Perhaps it is just as well.

While Egyptian education under the Empire was able to respond to the bureaucratic needs of a reinforced and strengthened central government, it did not seem to be able to produce any new ideas. This was the heyday of the departmental or governmental bureau schools (mentioned earlier) in which specialized career training was the order of the day. The goals of training the efficient bureaucrat seemed to overshadow all others. No significant new achievements were made by the scribes or scholars in the fields of science, mathematics, engineering, architecture, medicine, or literature. They seemed to be focusing their attention on strengthening the specialized hierarchies of the civil bureaucracy and of the ecclesiastical bureaucracy. After all, Wilson estimates that the priestly brotherhoods owned one person in ten and one-eighth of all the arable land of Egypt. If the temple priesthoods were this powerful, their temple schools must also have been a power.

No wonder that the ideals expressed in the wisdom literature of the Middle Kingdom became so popular in the Empire. But there was a difference. Khety had extolled the life of the scribe as a life of greater ease than the manual trades could provide, but he also extolled the ideal of public service. Now, however, the life of the secretarial profession was extolled as a privileged good in itself and even a haven of retreat from public life. What had been a goal to be achieved by the upward-mobile Khety for his son had apparently become a vested interest to be preserved at all costs by the scribal schools of the Empire. Not only was the *Satire on the Trades* required in the schools of the Empire, but the imperial scribes produced their own variations on the same theme. One was known as *In Praise of the Learned Scribes:*

> They did not make for themselves pyramids of metal, with the tombstones thereof of iron. They were not able to leave heirs in children, . . . but they made heirs for themselves in the writings and in the [books of] wisdom which they composed . . . their names are [still] pronounced because of their books which they made, since they were good and the memory of him who made them [lasts] to the limits of eternity.
>
> Be a scribe, put it in thy heart, that thy name may fare similarly. More effective is a book than a decorated tombstone or an established tomb-wall. . . . It is better than a [well-] founded castle or a stele in a temple.[33]

This theme on the values of the life of a scribe and the value of knowledge transmitted in writing was repeated over and over in the copy books of the schools of the period. "Be diligent", is the most common exhortation to the students; constant praise of the values of patience, reticence, piety, humility, and abstention from the vices of drink and women. Warnings against choosing various careers are also common: the worst calamities seem to befall those who become farmers, soldiers, charioteers, priests, and bakers. The remedy, of course, is to become a scribe and an official to whom all good things will come. When the school texts were not being directly moralistic, they often contained models of letter-writing to be copied; and when all else was said and done, the Egyptian scribal teacher could fall back, as teachers in all literate societies may do, on requiring the pupils to copy straight word-lists. No matter what the moral ideal might be, the pedestrian aim of learning how to write words correctly was ever present, especially in a language whose orthography was as difficult as it was in ancient Egyptian.

As far as we can tell, the curriculum of the beginning scribal schools thus consisted of the wisdom manuals, model letters (either actual or imaginary), and word-lists. The more advanced instruction must have been more specialized according to the kind of career the student was hoping to follow. The manuals or copy books in mathematics, science, and medicine give virtually no explanation of rules or principles. They give the impression that they are notes made by a master craftsman for his oral use in teaching an apprentice.[34] They seem to be oblivious to the problems of pedagogy or teaching method. Indeed, the most commendable "advertisement" an

---

[33] Ibid., pp. 431-432.

[34] V. Gordon Childe, *Man Makes Himself*, New American Library, New York, 1951, p. 153.

author could give his text was that it followed faithfully a text that had been written several centuries earlier.

Little can be said of education in the post-Empire period except that formalism and conservatism and repetition seemed never-ending in the schools. Just as the art forms deliberately sought to copy the remote past, so did the schools repeat the literary formulas of the past. But the lively, spirited, confident assurance of the Old and Middle Kingdoms seemed to be gone. The qualities of withdrawal and quiet piety seemed to be most in favor. The ritualistic preoccupation with the hereafter, a characteristic so fully reflected in *The Book of the Dead,* finally became a reality in the late Empire and post-Empire.

The dispersive period of Egyptian education epitomized the conservative, uncreative, and traditionalistic school systems of the civilized world, slavishly passing on maxims and word lists of an eminently "practical" but somehow curiously irrevelant nature. The literary education which once prepared men for active leadership in the bureaucracy that created the high civilization of the Old and Middle Kingdoms somehow no longer prepared the scribal elite to direct or stimulate national development. Even the wider extension of literacy beyond the few top officials did not lead to imaginative drive and creativity. The steady decline of the civilization seemed to be reflected in the formalistic and highly conventionalized type of education that characterized the post-Empire period. And this was the kind of education that Egypt possessed when she was in closest touch with neighboring peoples and societies in Phoenicia, in Palestine, in Syria, and in the Aegean. Her colonies abroad might have taught her much; the colonies of foreigners inside Egypt might have learned much. But the Egyptian power to educate had been dissipated; only the power to repeat the lessons of the past remained.

Whatever the differences the civilizations of Egypt and Mesopotamia displayed in their rhythms of educational development, I find a basic similarity in the general movement from formative to florescent to formalistic stages. Egyptian education generally played an innovative role as it prepared young men for the wide range of civil, military, and religious careers demanded by the burgeoning society of the formative and florescent years. Then, by and large, the career opportunities in government were restricted as the temple priesthoods tended to overshadow the disrupted civil establishment of the dispersive period. Much of the energy of the temples and the priestly foundations was devoted to the unproductive yet perpetual ritual care of the tombs of kings and nobility. So literary training was narrowed by the demands of religious ritual. It thus became more and more repetitive and conservative. But even the government service lost much of its devotion to developmental and productive enterprises. Sheer maintenance of the political and economic system was hard enough, without developing it.

I would say therefore that it is not only the preparation of young people for a wider *range* of social roles that enables education to be innovative; it is also the *kind* of role which they are being prepared to play in public affairs that counts. Preparing people for a large number of specialized roles can be as stultifying as preparing them for a few, if the roles themselves are merely to be those of mechanically following orders, and the preparation is for operating as a small cog in a large bureaucratic machine. Preparation for administrative and policy roles devoted to improving the society's productive life and the welfare of its people is more likely to lead to an innovative and liberating function for education. This function occurred more in the formative and florescent periods; less in the dispersive period.

I have the impression that literary studies in the schools concentrated upon wisdom literature far more extensively and for a much longer time in Egypt than in Mesopotamia. Therefore, Egyptian education gives a more conservative and conventional impression, even in its florescent period, than does Mesopotamian. At least the Mesopotamian experience passed through the successive Akkadian, Babylonian, and Assyrian adaptations of the Sumerian literary heritage, each adding its own modifications. To be sure, the Egyptian scribes began to widen their perceptions in the florescent intimations of social justice doctrines, and even in the religious explorations of Antonism in the Empire, but both movements seemed to be relatively short-lived and of little lasting influence. Conservatism, tradition, and the conventional wisdom seemed to dominate Egyptian education throughout most of its long history. This produced a remarkable social stability—and a remarkable cultural sameness.

I find little difference between the two civilizations in their handling of the sciences in schools. Neither Mesopotamia nor Egypt seemed to put much stress on theory or general principles. The pyramids seemed to represent a technical engineering skill not matched by the Mesopotamians, but the level of scientific knowledge does not seem to be as important in this achievement as the administrative management and logistic marshalling of masses of stone and masses of men. Artistic skill and technical craftsmanship were not a matter of priority in the schools of either civilization. The scientific progress of the formative and florescent periods did not lead to an intellectual breakthrough. The schools were preoccupied with bureaucratic concerns in the early periods and ultimately with priestly rituals in the later periods.

There seems little doubt that the achievement motivation was strong in the Egyptian scribal schools of the formative and florescent eras when preparation for civil service seemed to be the prime goal. There was even a great deal of emphasis upon studying hard and learning well so that one could "do a good job" in the various lines of work for which the skills of literacy were required. When this was the case the schools were responding to pressing social needs, and the scribes as state officials were putting their learning and their experience to use in the schools. But when the achievement motive tended to be narrowed into formulas for gaining the favor of the "great man" in order to get ahead, the schools were in danger of becoming training grounds for sycophants, even in the florescent period. When the schools of the dispersive period began to preach quiescence and silence as the goals of the scribe, the apex (or rather depths) of conventionality had been reached.

The generalization that inculcation of achievement attitudes is more likely to be an innovative factor than training for ascriptive status, must therefore be modified in the case of Egypt. If achievement relates to preparation for a government service that is "on the move" to develop the country, that tendency is favorable to educational innovation as a means of political and economic development. If, however, achievement simply means learning how to get into and get along with a privileged elite that is under the personal thumb of an all-powerful ruler, the achievement motive to success can be as stultifying as the particularistic motives connected with playing out an ascribed status. In fact, the two become virtually indistinguishable—and they both tend to conservatism and traditionalism in education.

Finally, the role of the organized teaching profession in Egyptian education is difficult to estimate, but one thing is clear. The Egyptian scribes did not seem to have as much independent corporate life in the formative and florescent periods as their counterparts in Mesopotamia did. The overweening power of the god-kings and the lack of an autonomous urban community life contributed to this difference. Yet the centralized power of the pharaoh did mobilize from above the scribal energies and focus them upon the national developmental process. As a result, the scribal schools of the formative and florescent periods had a fairly close relationship with the dynamics of social change despite the less vital urban character of Egyptian civilization. In the dispersive period, however, the protectionist and elitist temper of the powerful priesthoods effectively joined with the disintegration of royal power to fasten a conservative, not to say a reactionary, mold upon Egyptian education from which it did not recover under internal auspices. Educational revival had to await the arrival of a succession of outsiders, over the ensuing centuries, notably the Greeks, the Romans, and the Arabs. And then the interplay and stimulation of external ideas and peoples produced a new kind of civilization arising after three thousand years of the old.

Education in South Asian and East Asian Civilizations

At this point a full-scale world history of education might well turn to consider the other generative civilizations that arose in the third or second millenia, B.C., eventually to form the connecting tissues of the Afro-Eurasian ecumene that extended from the Pacific to the Atlantic. Both India and China display two to three thousand years of civilizational development (usually designated as their ancient periods of history) which reveal formative, florescent, and dispersive stages in the civilization-building process. (See Figure 2.4) They arose somewhat later than the Mesopotamian and Egyptian civilizations, their ancient periods continued roughly a thousand years longer to around 500 A.D., and their vitality was such that they have persisted as recognizable civilizational forms down to the present time, constituting essential cores of a South Asian civilization and an East Asian civilization. (See Figure 1.2, p. 14.) Similarly, the Graeco-Roman civilization that arose in the Aegean and the Mediterranean regions displayed roughly parallel periods of formation, florescence, and dispersion before flowing into the formation of Western civilization, the newest and latest of the world's major civilizations. (See Figure 3.2, p. 81.)

Fascinating and important as such broad-scale analyses and comparisons would be, the scope of such a story is far too great for a single volume; even the outlines of the development would need to be filled in by much more substantial scholarly work oriented deliberately to the conceptual framework of comparative civilization building. Scholarship available in the English language is particularly weak in bringing together authentic archeological data and modern empirical historiography. Complicat-

Figure 2.4   The Curves of Educational Development in the Ancient Civilizations of India and China

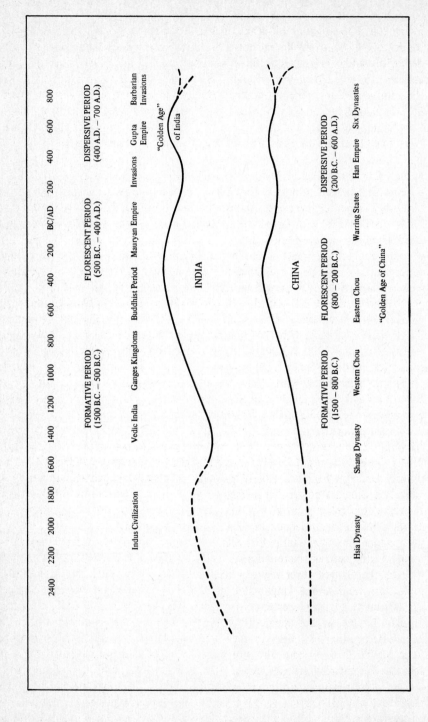

ing all else is the absence of clear evidence for the detailed, chronological analysis of the history of education in ancient India and China, much of our present knowledge depending upon traditional accounts written down centuries after the events. All that can be attempted here is a reminder to the reader that there *was* a contemporary civilization-building process going on in South Asia and in East Asia from around 2500 B.C. to 500 A.D. and that its educational aspects need much more systematic study for publication in the English language. We shall then return to the principal theme of Western education with its wellsprings deep in Graeco-Roman civilization.

India   The chronological history of India between 2500 B.C. and 500 B.C. is so obscure that its educational history may never become usefully comparable to that of the other major civilizations. Archeological findings make it clear that an urban, literate civilization, with large-scale organization of society and of government, flourished sometime between 2500 B.C. and 1500 B.C. in the Indus River Valley. Until the written script of the Indus or Harappa civilization is deciphered, however, the role of education can only be conjectured to be somewhat like that in the Sumerian cities from which the idea of writing may have flowed to the Indus as it did to the Nile.

Between 1500 B.C. and 500 B.C. (sometimes called the Protohistoric or Vedic period) the *role* of education in Indian civilization becomes somewhat clearer, if not its sequential history. The Aryan-speaking peoples, who invaded India from the northwest from 1500 B.C. onward, developed an oral cultural tradition of great sophistication in the Sanscrit language, epitomized in the verses and hymns designed to placate the gods, known as the Rig Veda. The formulation of this oral tradition and its cultivation and transmission were the special province of a priestly class of Brahmins who must have systematically taught the verses and the rites they prescribed to oncoming generations of priests. Prodigious feats of memorizing were obviously accomplished in this process. In this early Vedic period of Indian history, before Sanscrit was committed to writing, when town life was only rudimentary, and when priestly prerogatives were closely guarded by the Brahmins, the oral tradition in education gained a power that seemed to be one of the significant differences between India and the other great civilizations in their formative periods, a difference whose lasting educational consequences need much investigation.

Some time after 900 or 800 B.C. Vedic society in northern India began to reveal some of the basic characteristics of civilization building: town and city life spread through the Ganges River region, specialized occupations including merchant classes took form, and several kingdoms began to establish political rule and rudimentary administrative systems over extensive territories. The hierarchy of class distinctions brought by the Aryans apparently hardened into a more rigid caste system, which encouraged primary loyalties to the caste transcending those of the territorial state. Recognized castes besides the Brahmins were the warrior-rulers (Kshatriya), the gainfully employed (Vaishya), and the serfs and servants (Sudra). The caste system was a factor in Indian society which undoubtedly had vast significance for education. Organized schools seemed to be more exclusively devoted to religious and priestly purposes in preference to governmental or commercial purposes than was the case in any of the other major civilizations.

The formative period of organized education in India may have culminated in the period between the eighth and sixth centuries B.C. when more or less formal schools took shape for priestly and religious purposes. The earliest such institutions were probably the schools established by learned Brahmins in their homes to teach a few students the sacrificial rites and priestly rituals along with the exact verses of the Rig Veda. Such schools probably produced the elaborate commentaries known as the Brahmanas, which compositions spelled out in minute detail the rituals prescribed by the Brahmins.

Rival schools began to appear, perhaps in the seventh century B.C., as a reaction against the excessive ritualism, the claimed prerogatives, and the arrogance of the Brahminical schools as well as against the urbanization of life and the secularization embodied in the growing bureaucratic pretensions of the Gangetic kingdoms. Protesting holy men, who preached the values of asceticism, mystical ecstasy, and the enlightenment that comes from retreat to the woods, gathered adherents about them in their forest schools. These were the sources of another major aspect of the elaborate Indian oral literature, the Upanishads.

A third type of school was eventually established in the midst of the great intellectual and religious ferment that gave rise to Buddhism and Jainism in the sixth century B.C. Just when this happened is not clear, but education took on a more highly institutionalized form as it was promoted by monasteries where the Buddhist or Jainist monks, living a corporate life, exerted the group control characteristic of a collective body of teachers or a priestly college rather than the domestic schools taught to a few followers in the homes of individual Brahmin priests. This corporate approach, along with its more generous attitude toward caste, gave Buddhist education a special power for several centuries.

Just when schools in India began to concentrate on written language rather than oral communication is also not clear. Possibly Buddha himself learned to write, but scholars are still debating how and when written language appeared in India. In any case writing in a vernacular script known as Brahmi was clearly present in the third century B.C. during the rule of Asoka (273-232 B.C.). Whether Brahmi grew out of the undeciphered Indus script or whether it had originated in a Semitic script brought from the West in the eighth century B.C. is much debated. But it had obviously been shaped phonetically by scholars over a long period of time to adapt it to various Indian dialects (known as Prakrits).

With the rise of the Mauryan Empire in the late fourth century B.C. the florescent period of Indian education was well underway. Even before that time, perhaps as early as the sixth century B.C., some of the cities of India became well known for the large numbers of students and teachers who had gathered there. Outstanding were Benares in eastern India, Taxila in the northwest, and, some centuries later, Kanchi in the south. Even during the 500 years of invasions and general political instability between 200 B.C. and 300 A.D., the Brahminical schools must have given a kind of social and cultural unity to the small educated class throughout the various parts of India by virtue of their common learning and participation in the Sanscrit themes. These were also the periods of the greatest influence of Buddhism which also acted as a kind of cultural unifier among the disparate peoples of India. Thousands of students are reputed to have flocked to the schools of the Buddhist monastery at Nalanda in the fifth century A.D.

In any case, the role of education must have been especially significant in the florescent period which roughly spanned the more than one thousand years between the sixth century B.C. and the sixth century A.D. By common consent ancient Indian culture is considered to have reached its peak during the Golden Age of the Gupta Empire from 320 A.D. to 570 A.D. During this period Buddhism receded within India but expanded to Central Asia and East Asia. In contrast Sanscrit went through a remarkable revival in a manner somewhat similar to the renaissance of Latin and Greek literature in Europe a thousand years later, becoming a common language of administration as well as culture and religion. The Brahminical schools must have had a key role in this revival and in the formulation of Hinduism, which took its definitive form at this time, as did the great epics, the Mahabharata and the Ramayana. In addition, secular knowledge in grammar, astronomy, mathematics (the decimal system), and medicine were pursued rigorously for a time. The creativity and power of Indian culture carried it northward to the Himalayas and southward through Southeast Asia.

Just what role education played in this expansive florescence and then in the dispersion and dissipation of the Gupta Empire and the subsequent "medieval" period of Indian history is far from clear. What is clear is that recurring warfare between rival dynasties seemed to be the rule until the invading Moguls once again established a kind of centralized control over much of India in the sixteenth century and inaugurated a new, if not a modern, era in India.

It may be that the overweening religious orientation of Indian education, its stress on the inner life of meditation or outward ritual, its persistent preferences for oral rather than written knowledge, for literary themes rather than for the scientific or practical, its relative neglect of training for bureaucratic and administrative competence in the arts of governing and of social organization, and its ascriptive insistence upon caste loyalties and prerogatives rather than upon achievement by merit all had their part to play in the relative instability of Indian political life in the ancient period. On the other hand, some scholars argue that literacy was obviously universal among the upper Brahmin and Kshatriya castes and possibly widespread among the middle-level Vaishyas in the Mauryan and Gupta Empires.[35] So education must have had an enormous role in the cultural commonality that makes it possible to speak of an Indian civilization persisting through the complexities of seemingly endless foreign conquests, persisting yes, but somehow far less successful than the Chinese in absorbing and assimilating the folk societies that constantly beat on its frontiers or doggedly maintained their separate identities within the encompassing civilization.

China   Just as the oral tradition pervaded Indian education, so the strength of the written tradition indelibly shaped Chinese education. The ramifications of this basic

---

[35] Kathleen Gough, "Implications of Literacy in Traditional China and India" in Jack Goody (ed.) *Literacy in Traditional Societies,* Cambridge University Press, London, 1968. pp. 69-84.

difference run through their respective educational establishments from top to bottom. For centuries the power of the Brahmin in India rested on his mastery of Sanskrit verses along with the religious and spiritual prerogatives they conveyed; in China the power of the scholar-administrator rested upon his mastery of the revered Chinese books which contained the maxims to guide his personal and public conduct and attested to his right to rule.

The Chinese written characters, representing words and ideas rather more than the phonetic sounds of oral speech, enabled all who learned the characters to read the same books and develop a commonality or cohesiveness that tended to overcome the disparateness of local tongues. Much of this accomplishment resulted from the high priority given to book learning as the essence of formal education, and to formal education as the high road to governmental as well as scholarly preferment. All told, these were monumental advantages in building and maintaining successive large-scale political empires over long periods of time, despite the pressures to particularism that constantly beset the vast Chinese mainland. India, meanwhile, was laying the groundwork for an almost insurmountable linguistic particularism during the many centuries that it refrained from developing Sanscrit into a common written language.

The dawn of authenticated historical civilization in China is usually assigned to the Shang Dynasty who ruled in the eastern reaches of the Yellow River Valley in northern China roughly from 1700 or 1500 B.C. to 1100 or 1000 B.C. Possibly stimulated by cultural influences from West Asia, including the idea of writing, the peoples of this region developed city-states, social stratification of classes, rudimentary political institutions under kingships, a bronze technology, incipient Chinese writing—and possibly schools to teach the system of writing. The formative period of Chinese education continued uninterruptedly under the early Chou Dynasty (1122 or 1027 B.C. to 770 B.C.) who came from the west to conquer the Shang peoples and adopt their culture. The Chou built walled towns and developed a somewhat feudal system of vassal states, with schools established in the capital cities to teach the boys archery and charioteering as well as writing and artithmetic. The earliest extant books in Chinese date from this era.

The florescent period of ancient Chinese education lasted approximately for 1,000 years, beginning with the rise of the eastern Chou Dynasty in the early eighth century B.C. and lasting roughly to the decline of the first Chinese Empire under the Later Han Dynasty around 200 A.D. During the 400 years of the Eastern Chou, China achieved its Golden Age in thought and culture. Despite a cross-hatching of rival states, there was a discernible growth of centralization of political power, with some ten states gradually emerging by the sixth century B.C., marked by written codes of law and increasingly effective bureaucratic and administrative systems based on the spread of literacy and formal schools. Technologically, China started the period well behind the Middle East but gradually caught up in a burst of commercial, urban, and expansionist activity in north China which led to the gradual incorporation of central and southern China into the orbit of Chinese civilization. Philosophically, this was China's greatest creative age, when its traditional systems of thought crystallized around Confucius and Mencius, Taoism, Legalism, and numerous other schools of thought which influenced Chinese culture and education for centuries.

Politically, the florescent period was slowed during 200 years of the Warring States (roughly 400 B.C. to 200 B.C.), while a gentry class of officialdom and a bureaucratic class of administrators rose to power. Then, with astonishing suddenness, China was unified into a huge territorial empire towards the end of the third century B.C. by the Ch'in rulers, who created a centralized bureaucracy for civil and military administration on a uniform basis and stifled the creativity of the hundred schools of thought by clamping down on the educational process and burning the books.

When the Han rulers took over around 200 B.C., they softened the militarism of the Ch'in by installing the Confucian ideal of the enlightened scholar-administrator as the official policy of the imperial court. Under Emperor Wu Ti a court school, sometimes called a university, was created in 124 B.C. to signalize the importance of education based on the Confucian classics as the necessary preparation to develop the morally superior man to serve in the civil bureaucracy. Significantly, the selection of such men, it was decided, should be based upon written examinations as a test of merit.

The examination system remained a staple to which Chinese schooling was oriented for the next 2,000 years. Together, the examinations and the system of schools that prepared for them provided an educational glue that gave a stability and cohesiveness that few if any other civilizations have had. They also eventually produced a conservatism and a traditionalism that inhibited social change. But in the early Han empire there was a cultural interaction, a dynamism, and a creativity in technological invention that far surpassed the West in textiles, iron casting, porcelain, and the use of paper, draft horses, water mills, and crossbows. Close investigation should be made of the role education may have played in this florescence. It is estimated that literacy among the ruling class in China may have matched that of florescent India and Greece.[36]

With the advent of the Later Han Dynasty in the first two centuries A.D. the disintegration of the empire began to set in, somewhat paralleling the decline of the Roman Empire in the West. The merit system of the earlier Han examination system was dissipated by a nine-grade ranking system that virtually gave preferences to the great privileged families and ruling cliques. How much this change resulted from or caused a weakening in the schooling system is hard to estimate, but in any case the succeeding four centuries of the Six Dynasties, from 200 A.D. to 600 A.D., saw an inability of the Chinese intellectual system to assimilate the series of invaders from the steppes with enough success to maintain the vitality of the ancient imperial civilization. Eventually, however, under the T'ang Dynasty beginning in 600 A. D., the dispersive period of ancient Chinese education gave way to a new grouping of forces in the north of China that amalgamated the folk invaders with the civilized Chinese, thus regenerating the Chinese imperial system for another 1300 years until its demise in 1912 A.D.

In is generally agreed that Chinese education played a stabilizing role in the greater ability of Chinese civilization to surmount the kind of warrior onslaughts that brought down the Roman Empire by 500 A.D. and reduced India to a state of political

[36]Ibid., p. 71.

impotence. It is less certain what part education played in the period between 600 A.D. and 1600 A.D., during which time China was vastly superior to the West in most realms of science and applied technology.

The consensus concerning the modern period since 1600 A.D. points to such deficiencies in the traditional educational system of China as its fixation upon the wisdom literature of the past, its idealization of formalism and ceremonialism in behavior and orthodoxy in thought, its reliance upon private educational auspices for the few rather than upon public provision for the many, its shunning of the goal of practicality and progress in the satisfying of human wants, its narrowing of the achievement motivation from public service to personal prestige and preferment, its stodgy reluctance to adapt the examination system to the kind of scientific and secular knowledge that blossomed in the West from 1500 A.D. onwards, and the gradual erosion of the ideal of genuine educational and moral merit as the basis for governance in favor of cramming for the passing of examinations and the formal prerogatives they bestowed.

All civilizations have had their share of such ingredients of educational conservatism, China perhaps more than most, the West perhaps somewhat less. We now turn to the role of education in the civilization-building process of the Graeco-Roman world.

CHAPTER III

GREEK CIVILIZATION: WELLSPRING OF WESTERN EDUCATION

As the interplay of societies and cultures worked its remarkable way across the face of the eastern Mediterranean world during the thousand years between 500 B.C. and 500 A.D., the civilization process gradually moved westward as well as eastward. Before the Greeks descended on Egypt bearing their civilizational gifts under the banners of Alexander of Macedon in the fourth century B.C., they developed their own distinctive style of civilization. In doing this, they borrowed much from the civilization of the Aegean as well as from the Levant, from Mesopotamia, and from Egypt itself. At first the borrowers and emulators, the Greeks eventually became the conquerers, the bestowers, and the emulated. The age-old enactment of intercivilizational influence was played out with particular vigor and vitality on the shorelands and the islands west of Asia and east of Europe in the Aegean Sea.

It is not the intention here to embrace an extreme diffusionist explanation for the spread of the civilization-building process and education, particularly not to subscribe to the idea of one-way diffusion from Mesopotamia or Egypt to Europe. As modern scholarship unfolds, it is probably best to speak, as I have tried to do, about intercivilizational contact rather than unilinear influence as a prime means of educational and social change. The recent revision of dating methods based on carbon 14 and tree-ring calibration to establish absolute chronology in *prehistory* has raised serious doubts about the old diffusionist assumptions in archeology.[1] Specifically, Colin Renfrew argues that megalithic monuments in Europe and Malta date back to 4000 B.C. and thus are *earlier* than those in the Aegean and Egypt. So they could not have been the result of colonization from the Eastern Mediterranean to Western Europe.

This evidence, however, does not disturb the prehistory chronology relating Mesopotamia and Egypt to the Aegean and Greece. Nor does it weaken the importance

[1] See, for example, Colin Renfrew, "Carbon 14 and the Prehistory of Europe," *Scientific American*, vol. 225, no. 4, pp. 63-72, October 1971.

of intercivilizational contact documented by historical records after the creation of writing. What it does do, in Renfrew's words, is to reinforce the current archeological thinking which I have stressed in Chapters 1 and 2. "Today social and economic processes are increasingly seen as more important subjects for study than the similarities among artifacts."[2]

A. AEGEAN CIVILIZATION (1900 B.C.-800 B.C.)

Minoan Crete (1900 B.C.-1400 B.C.)

We can say little from direct evidence about the influence of Egypt upon the development of Greek education, nor of its influence upon the education of the lively island civilization centering upon Crete in the second millenium B.C., commonly named after its kingship title Minoa. Probably settled by peoples from Asia Minor, Crete possessed neolithic settlements by 4000 B.C.; there possibly was commerce between Crete and Egypt as early as 3000 B.C.; and between 2100 B.C. and 1900 B.C., a distinctive Minoan civilization arose on Crete replete with bronze tools, potters' wheels, and pictographic writing. The acme of Minoan civilization, with its nerve center in the palace at Knossos, is usually placed sometime between 1700 and 1400 B.C. By 1700 B.C. the Cretans had developed a partly pictographic and partly syllabic script that has come to be known as Linear A, but has not yet been fully deciphered. Sir Arthur Evans assumed it was a special "Minoan" language, but some scholars now believe it was an adaptation of some Middle Eastern script possibly related to Luvian (an Anatolian tongue of Indo-European origin) or to the Semitic Akkadian tongue which was the lingua franca of the whole Mediterranean world in the first half of the second millenium B.C.[3]

Mycenaean Greece (1400 B.C.-1100 B.C.)

Meanwhile a Greek-speaking people (sometimes known as Achaeans) who had arrived on the mainland of Greece sometime between 2500 and 1900 B.C. had developed a palace civilization centering at Mycenae somewhat like that of Minoan Crete and probably influenced by it. Their written language (first discovered on Crete and then later on the mainland) is known as Linear B. It has affinities with Linear A but is now

---

[2] Ibid., p. 72.

[3] Sir Arthur Evans, *The Palace of Minos*, 4 vols., Macmillan, London, 1921-1935. However, Leonard R. Palmer, *Mycenaeans and Minoans*, 2d. rev. ed., Faber, London, 1965, works out a somewhat different chronology. Palmer argues for Luvian, p. 332. The relationship to Akkadian is argued by Cyrus H. Gordon, "Notes on Minoan Linear A," *Antiquity*, no. 123, pp. 124-130, September 1957; and "Akkadian Tablets in Minoan Dress," *Antiquity*, no. 124, pp. 237-240, December 1957. For the relationship between Linear A and B, see Michael Ventris and John Chadwick, *Documents in Mycenaean Greek*, Cambridge University Press, London, 1956; and John Chadwick, *The Decipherment of Linear B*, Cambridge University Press, London, 1958.

A case for the independent origin of Minoan-Mycenaean civilization is made by Colin Renfrew, *The Emergence of Civilization; The Cyclades and the Aegean in the Third Millenium B.C.*, Methuen and Co., London, 1972, but he recognizes the likely external influences on Aegean writing.

widely recognized to be a written form of an archaic Greek tongue. At some time, either 1600, 1500, or 1450 B.C., the Mycenaean Greeks apparently captured Knossos and ruled it for a period, either from 1600 to 1150, or from 1450 to 1400 B.C., during which time they either brought their Linear B script with them or adapted the Linear A of the Cretans to their own Greek language. All these matters have been the subject of intense scholarly controversy for nearly fifty years. In any case the Mycenaeans are believed to have given the major form to a civilization that dominated the Aegean area from around 1400 to 1100 B.C.

Unfortunately, little light has been thrown on the role of education in either Minoan Crete or Mycenaean Greece. About all we can do is assume that the commercial interests of both Cretans and Mycenaeans brought them in touch with the literate world of the Eastern Mediterranean and that their writing developed out of their seagoing contacts and mercantile interests. The vast majority of documents so far deciphered from Linear B consists of records, inventories of goods, accounts, ritual lists, names of towns, and historical figures. So far, no extensive poetry, literature, science, religion, or wisdom literature has come to light.

We are thus left with the assumption that the written languages of Linear A and B were a result of the same general sort of development whereby the scribes of Mesopotamia, Egypt, the Levant, and Asia Minor produced their respective written languages. This process entailed long and arduous training to learn to read and write the scripts through some form of formally organized schools. We can only infer that the Cretan and Mycenaean societies also had scribes and thus had schools of some kind. This is the assumption made by H. I. Marrou, the foremost historian of ancient education.[4]

At the moment we can go little further, except to say that the Cretan and Mycenaean experience was part of the widening orbit of civilization which now began to embrace parts of southeastern Europe and Asia Minor as well as the Middle Eastern core area in the second millenium B.C. Their language efforts may have been a part of that ferment of experimentation which the scribes of the Levant were beginning to undertake as early as the seventeenth or sixteenth centuries B.C.

What the Aegean heritage might have bequeathed to the later Greeks, if the Mycenaeans had not been driven out of Crete around 1400 B.C. (or 1150 B.C. according to Palmer) when Knossos was finally destroyed, or if the Mycenaean Greeks had not been driven from their homeland by the invasions of the Dorian Greeks between 1200 and 1000 B.C., one cannot say. There is some evidence that the Minoans were a more peaceful lot, for the Knossos palace was not fortified; presumably, therefore, the Cretan scribes played a prominent administrative role in their government. On the other hand, the warrior class of charioteers and nobles in Mycenae may have given the military an early primacy over the scribes in their governmental and cultural affairs.

As it is, there seems to have been a great decline if not a complete disruption of the literate tradition on both Crete and mainland Greece following the destruction of

---

[4]H. I. Marrou, *A History of Education in Antiquity*, Mentor Books, New York, 1964, p. xix.

Knossos around 1400 and of Mycenae around 1100 B.C. The presumption, further, is that the literate sector of the Cretans and Mycenaeans must have been very small and limited indeed, perhaps even more restricted than those in Egypt and Mesopotamia, for literacy might not have disappeared so completely if it had been fairly widely dispersed among the population. Repeated invasions of Mesopotamia, Egypt, and the Levant had never completely wiped out all literacy in those areas. We can only infer, therefore, that both Crete and Mycenae were "oligoliterate" societies, a term used to signify that literacy was restricted to a relatively small proportion of the total population.[5] Other terms have been used for this phenomenon, such as "stunted literacy," "special literacy," and "conditional literacy."

Since none of these quite applies, as Goody and Watt say, to societies where there is a fully developed but socially restricted phonetic system of writing, I suggest that a useful contrast could be signified by using the terms "elitoliterate" and "demoliterate." "Elitoliterate" could refer to the restriction of literacy to a social elite which is small and is highly trained for specific purposes, somewhat as the term "elite troops" is used to signify those selected for special training. "Demoliterate" obviously refers to the dissemination of literacy more widely if not universally among the population. The former term links the Cretan and Mycenaean civilizations (and probably their education) to the Mesopotamian and Egyptian style of scribal culture; the latter term signifies one of the crowning achievements of the Ionian Greeks, who thereby affected fundamentally the course of human civilization from their time onward.

The Homeric Age (1100 B.C.-800 B.C.)

Following or during the Dorian invasions of the Greek mainland from 1200 to 1000 B.C., the Mycenaean Greeks dispersed from the centers of their civilization on the Peloponnesus, as did other Greeks who found themselves threatened by the Dorian invaders who seemed to be headed for the rich agricultural lands of the Peloponnesus. Many of the Greeks who had been living in Attica apparently fled across the Aegean to that part of the coast of Asia Minor which came to be called Ionia. For some 300 years the Greeks who dispersed around the Aegean Sea developed an aristocratic form of folk society combining an agricultural and commercial base with a warrior nobility recognized as the ruling class. Some call this period a "dark age"; others a feudal period that represented a retrogression from the height of the Mycenaean civilization.

The epic poems of Homer, the *Iliad* and the *Odyssey*, describe this and the Mycenaean period of Greek culture; thus these eras are sometimes referred to as the Homeric Age. Economic and social institutions were based upon an agrarian way of life, but gradually specialized skills of artisanship grew up in connection with ship-building, public defense, weapon-making, and the commerce that was increasingly carried on by the seagoing traders with Egypt, Phoenicia, and the Middle East.

[5] Jack Goody and Ian Watt, "The Consequences of Literacy" in *Comparative Studies in Society and History,* vol. 5, no. 3, p. 313, April 1963; reprinted in Jack Goody (ed.), *Literacy in Traditional Societies,* Cambridge University Press, London, 1968, p. 36.

Homeric society was thus apparently not the typical form of folk society based solely upon village farming communities or pastoralism. It was rather more like the "feudal" society of Medieval Europe with an aristocratic court life marked by courtly manners and a code of chivalry that combined the arts of war with the arts of oratory and polite conversation.[6] The analogy with medieval Europe is apparently justified insofar as feudalism may be defined as "a very important political device for the revival of a declining civilization and for the extension of civilization to new peoples not formerly civilized."[7]

But another important ingredient went into the make-up of the Homeric poems: They were written down sometime between 850 and 750 B.C. with an eye for their appeal to the emerging upper classes of the dawning city-states of Ionia in the late ninth and early eighth centuries B.C. This view is succinctly stated by R. R. Bolgar as follows:

> We know that these epics were composed originally to amuse the great men of the post-tribal period, and that they were not given their final form until the recension of Peisistratus, by which time the city-state was a social reality. Consequently, they lay an understandable emphasis on those traits which the pictured past shared with the emergent civilisation of the *polis,* on the popular assembly, the interplay of prestige and eloquence, and the reasoned exploitation of practical possibilities. . . . Culturally speaking, the Homeric poems belong rather to the beginnings of the city-state than to the heroic period of Mycenae and Troy. Moreover, throughout Greek history, but in particular during the golden age of Athens, they played the same role as the Authorised Version later did in England. They formed the source-book of the educated imagination. . . .[8]

The Homeric epics thus provide a link between the heroic and aristocratic ideals of the Mycenaean civilization and the more democratic ideals of the rising city-state civilization of Ionia. The practices of education they reveal concerning the Heroic Age are probably not so important as the continuing impact they had upon the centuries of Greek education to follow. But perhaps these two must go together: (1) The Homeric poems idealized the court life of knightly culture with its round of physical sports and games, and its cultural achievements in music, dancing, singing, games, poetry, and eloquence. Underlying these skills, however, was an ethical or ideal value often summed up in the term *arete,* perhaps translatable best as a combination of valor, honor, and glory to be achieved by the Great and Noble Deed.[9] Presumably these skills and values were taught by tutors to individual boys during the Heroic Age. Later,

---

[6] Marrou, op. cit., pp. 23-26, makes this point; as does Werner Jaeger, *Paideia, The Ideals of Greek Culture,* Oxford University Press, New York, 1965, vol. 1, Book 1, chap. 3, pp. 35-56.

[7] Rushton Coulbourn (ed.), *Feudalism in History* (c. 1956), Archon Books, Hamden, Conn., 1965, p. 383.

[8] R. R. Bolgar, *The Classical Heritage and Its Beneficiaries from the Carolingian Age to the End of the Renaissance,* Harper Torchbooks, New York, 1964, pp. 16-17.

[9] For details of education in Homeric times, see Marrou, op. cit., chap. 1.

when the city-states institutionalized education, they established music schools, *palaestras,* and gymnasiums to perpetuate the chivalric ideals of culture and education as described by Homer. (2) Then literacy required its own kind of school. After the epics were written down in Greek texts, probably in Ionia between 850-750 B.C., eventually one text was brought to Athens (probably in the sixth century) and officially adopted as the result of public competition. When this was done, the written texts became the textbooks for generations of schoolboys to read, memorize, and recite, if not emulate, in all parts of the world where Greek was taught or learned in schools.

In this effort to combine literacy with *arete* the Greeks created new forms of organized education, different in goal, in organization, in substance, and in spirit from the organized schools known to any other civilization up to that time. The goal was something new under the sun, but literacy and *arete* were not always easy bedfellows.

B. THE FORMATIVE PERIOD OF GREEK EDUCATION
(800 B.C.-500 B.C.)

The rhythm of educational development operating in the cases of Mesopotamia and Egypt seems to apply with particular usefulness to the course of Greek education. What seems to be the most striking difference is that the formative and florescent periods of organized education in Greece were of relatively short duration as contrasted with the length of the dispersive period. Schools were organized fairly quickly in the matter of two or three centuries, and their most creative period was a burst of activity that lasted less than two centuries (from 500 B.C. to 300 B.C.). The dissemination of Greek educational ideas and practices continued, however, in much of the Middle East (to 200 A.D.), in the Roman Empire (to 500 A.D.), in the Byzantine Empire (to 1500 A.D.), and in medieval and Renaissance Europe (to 1700 A.D.). All in all, the dispersion of Greek education has continued for more than 2,000 years. It is still much alive wherever traditional Western education has penetrated.

Figure 3.2 encompasses the entire development of Greek education down to the formative period of Western education. This chapter concentrates on the formative and florescent periods of Hellenic education. The next three chapters deal with the continuing and the recurring influence of Hellenism upon the Roman, the Christian, the Byzantine, the medieval and the Renaissance education to come. These testify to the characterization of Greek civilization as an ever-flowing wellspring for the sustenance of Western education.

The Rise of the Polis and "Demoliterate" Society
In describing the origins of schooling in the Sumerian cities and Egypt in the fourth millenium B.C., we called attention to four interrelated ingredients of the civilizing process: urbanization, social differentiation, political institutionalization, and written language. In this process priests and kings organized schools for the training of the

scribes deemed necessary to perform the administrative and leadership functions of the small ruling class in what I have dubbed an elitoliterate society. Now the Minoans on Crete and the Mycenaeans on the mainland of Greece were possibly developing a similar type of scribal education down to the middle half of the second millenium B.C., a time when the Middle Eastern educational systems were entering their dispersive phases. If the Aegean civilization had not been destroyed in the latter half of that millenium, we can only guess what the character of the subsequent Greek civilization would have been. As it was, life on the Greek mainland reverted to a more rural, feudal kind of dark age following the Dorian invasions, and the distinctive formulation of Greek civilization took place first on the western coast of Asia Minor from 800 to 500 B.C.

All of our four ingredients were involved in the rise of Hellenic civilization, but they took on quite different characteristics when they appeared first in such Ionian cities as Miletus and Ephesus and later on the Greek mainland. After all, the Greeks were not starting from scratch. As the Ionian Greeks fled eastward across the Aegean and came into still closer contact with the Middle Eastern civilizations than formerly, they were able to sluff off more rapidly the remnants of tribal folk society that had marked the rule of their "primitive" kingships and warrior aristocracies during the Mycenaean age and the succeeding dark age.

The first thing to note about the formative period of Greek education is that it came on the heels of a long period of intercivilizational contact and in the midst of the social and cultural ferment of the first millenium B.C., a ferment that had shifted from the heartlands of Mesopotamia and Egypt to the eastern shores of the Mediterranean where the interplay of ideas and of peoples had been heightening from the twelfth and tenth centuries B.C. onward. The Ionic Greeks added to this ferment their own distinctive heritage which included the Mycenaean courtly and aristocratic culture as well as the poetic and epic traditions passed down by generations of bards. But as they fled the invasions of the aggressive Dorians, they settled in compact groups on the alien if not hostile shores of Asia Minor where their own differing traditions had to be reconciled in the face of the strangers they confronted. This phenomenon produced a cohesiveness of social organization—partly for protection and partly to preserve their familiar and cherished heritage—and stimulated them to devise new forms of political organization more quickly than they might otherwise have done. The result, in brief, was the creation of the Greek polis, the city-state that had some characteristics in common with its predecessors in Sumer but which developed a style and genre all its own.

While some of the outward forms of tribe and clan were kept, the Greek polis moved rapidly to drop the essentially ascriptive characteristics of kinship ties typical of folk societies and established citizenship in the polis as the overriding tie that bound the community together. The bonds of the territorial state became the primary form of social cohesion, superior to family or kin, class or caste, or any kind of voluntary association. The rules for governing the polis were not to be the arbitrary will of gods, or priests, or kings, or god-kings, but the rules drawn up in the form of laws

Figure 3.1   The Graeco-Roman World of Education

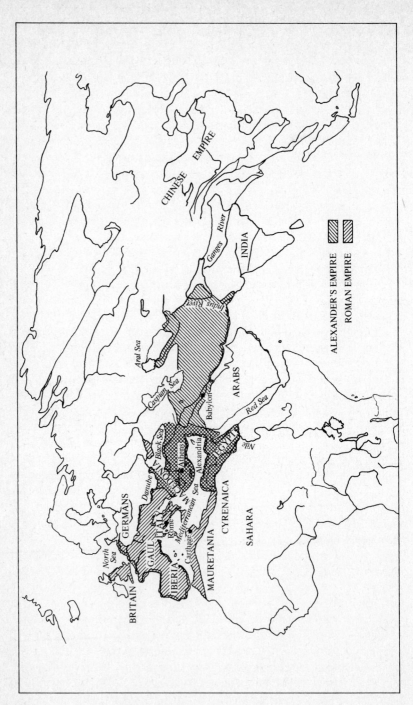

Figure 3.2 The Curve of Educational Development in Graeco-Roman Civilization

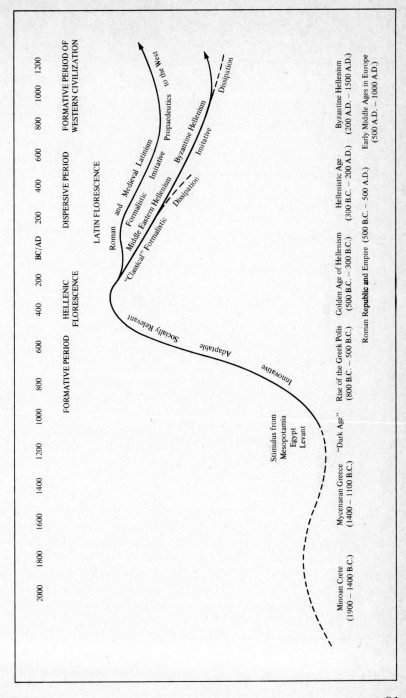

administered by magistrates on behalf of those who had the largest stake in the city, its "citizens." To be sure, the early Greek city-states were aristocratic in form, with the large landowners exercising the dominant voice through the councils of elders or councils of nobles who by the eighth century B.C. had even taken over power from the hereditary kings.

In the course of the seventh century, however, a far more democratic development took place: independent farmers were drawn into the ranks of the city-state army as infantrymen or hoplites. The power of massed, coordinated, and disciplined bodies of soldiers organized into the phalanx proved far superior to the cavalrymen of the nobles; the hoplites thus became an egalitarian bulwark of the citizenry in the sixth century B.C. It was not exactly "one man-one vote," for aliens and slaves and the propertyless were not yet admitted to membership in the popular assembly or courts, but the base of political participation went far beyond anything that had ever been known before. Democracy was thenceforth a political form to be reckoned with. And when the propertyless men of the city of Athens were admitted to citizenship by the end of the sixth century, the franchise was broadened still further. Athens had become a mercantile as well as an agricultural state, relying heavily upon the rowers of its navy and the artisans who produced the commercial goods for trade abroad as well as at home.

It is true that some of the Greek city-states did not choose to develop commerce or seagoing trade nor to extend citizenship beyond the independent farmer. Sparta was the prime example on one side, holding back from the brink of democracy; Athens was the prime example on the other side, diving into the democratic waters. Even Athens, however, never opened up its citizenship privileges to women, to aliens, or to slaves. The estimate is made that the total population of Attica in the late fifth century B.C. numbered between 250,000 to 350,000 persons; of these, adult male citizens probably reached only 35,000 to 50,000. The total citizen class, including women and children, thus amounted to somewhat over half of the total population, with possibly something less than a fourth being aliens and a fourth slaves.[10]

The point, then, is that many of the Ionian city-states in Asia Minor and the city-states of mainland Greece produced a style of social and cultural life which uniquely wove together urbanization and political institutionalization in ways that enormously broadened the scope of social and cultural participation among a higher proportion of the population than had been true of any other civilization. While social differentiation was obviously present too, it did not take the rigid form of social stratification of caste in India or the hardening of class lines that characterized most of Mesopotamian and Egyptian history.

Specialization in the economic and commercial spheres was obviously highly developed, but in political and cultural affairs the ideal of the generalist was another of the unique contributions of the polis: every citizen, no matter how exalted or how lowly, should take his part in the public affairs of law court and assembly, of games

---

[10] See A. W. Gomme, *The Population of Athens in the Fifth and Fourth Centuries, B.C.*, Blackwell, Oxford, 1957, Appendix.

and music and theater, of military service, and of religious festivals. The citizen as "free man" should do all these things—and he therefore needed a "liberal education" appropriate to the competence expected of a free man. This could not be the narrow or technical education required of the specialist; it must be the broad, generous, and general education befitting the wide varieties of active participation expected of the citizen who would serve the common good of his city and in turn be served by it.

Before we turn to the new forms of education that the Greek polis devised in order to train the new kind of citizen, we must mention the fourth ingredient in the origin of civilization—which may indeed have been the most influential of all—the Greeks' contribution to written language and organized knowledge. We have noted how the origin of written language itself was a creation of the temple communities and city-states of Sumer, and how the scribes of the commercial cities of the Levant from Ugarit in the north, southward to Byblos, Sidon, and Tyre had been simplifying the scripts of the Middle East and developing alphabetic forms of writing during the second and first milleniums, B.C. The Mycenaeans and the Greek city-states were in close commercial and cultural touch with these developments.

The Phoenicians are usually given credit for inventing the alphabet which made writing so much easier and therefore available to so many more people. Some scholars believe, however, that this was only the next to the last step in inventing a true alphabet, inasmuch as the Phoenicians devised letters for the consonants but not for the vowels in their spoken language. It was the Greeks of Ionia, they argue, who took the final step by devising a written letter for each vowel sound as well as for each consonantal sound. It was this achievement which really "democratized" literacy and made it possible for the knowledge of reading and writing to be learned by virtually every person in a society during a relatively short period of schooling.[11] The Greeks made a demoliterate society possible and created the schools to go with it.

The best evidence seems to be that fully alphabetic writing in Greek was introduced into the Ionian city-states sometime in the ninth century B.C. Since their language did not have so many consonants as the Semitic language of the Phoenicians, the Ionian Greeks had five signs left over, so they applied these signs to their five vowels. Every basic sound now had a written letter. This meant that reading and writing could be learned in something like three years instead of ten. Since writing could spread so rapidly through the population, a special class of scribes whose secret mysteries gave them a monopoly of the power of writing was not necessary. The estimate is made that it took only 100 years from the introduction of the alphabet to its widespread use; some say from 850 to 750 B.C., others say from 750 to 650 B.C. This was the time when the Greek oral tradition was written down, when the poems of Homer and Hesiod were transcribed, probably in Ionia. Just how and when and who learned the new Greek writing well enough to perform this magnificently creative task may never be known. But it is clear that the city life made it possible, and we can only assume that some kind of corporate life or continuing contact among the writers was

---

[11] I. J. Gelb, *A Study of Writing,* rev. ed., University of Chicago Press, Chicago, 1952. (Phoenix edition, 1963), pp. 176-205.

sustained. What is also clear is that a fairly high degree of literacy was evident in the cities of mainland Greece as well as in Ionia by the end of the seventh century or the beginning of the sixth century B.C.

We can further assume that some form of organized educational effort, at least for a few, was in existence during this formative period of Greek writing. Education may have been largely in the form of individual tutoring among the well-to-do classes. Or, indeed, there may have been some kind of priestly or professional class of poets and bards who frequented the temples of the early city-states and who may have systematically inducted novitiates into the art of reading and writing. This would have clearly been in line with developments in the earlier civilizations, but our evidence is weak on this score. We do know, however, that a peculiarly vital form of intellectual life developed first in the Ionian cities and then on the Greek mainland. This took on religious and philosophical characteristics of major significance.

In the early Aegean period Greek religious beliefs were akin to those of other folk societies in assuming that anthropomorphic gods inhabited the heavens and earth, directing the destinies of man. The Homeric epics give a clear picture of the family of Greek gods who helped to bring about a common feeling of identity among the various Greek cities as the celebration of religion was transferred from the king's palaces to the public temples of the city-states. One reason a tightly organized priestly class with a special authority did not gain great power in Greece, outside of a few temples such as that at Delphi, was the fact that much of Greek religion was a public affair in the hands of magistrates.

Religious institutions thus had two educational faces: an open "daylight" aspect connected with the worship of the gods of the cities, and a secret aspect associated with the mysteries and cults open only to the initiates. The civic religion was celebrated in public ceremonies, song, dance, drama, athletic games, and city shrines by means of which the individual citizen achieved social identification with his group. The secret societies emphasized the selective character of their membership and special interests devoted to specific gods or rites.

Eventually, however, it was the Greeks' approach to critical thought and the systematization of knowledge that was to change the character of education more than any other thing they did. And this achievement may well have been made possible by their creation of fully-developed alphabetic writing.[12] When the custody of a sacred tradition is entrusted to a highly trained few, as in the elitoliterate societies of Mesopotamia or Egypt, it is difficult for criticism or dissent to arise, but when literacy becomes widely prevalent, as in the demoliterate city-states of Greece, it is easier for skepticism and criticism to be expressed. At least this happened in some of the Ionian and mainland cities.

When the Homeric epics were written down, they began to be treated as myths rather than as received truth. Some of the Greek thinkers began to try to devise more logical and rational explanations for the phenomena of the natural world. The sheer effort to classify and categorize physical phenomena was made easier by the use of the

[12] See especially, Goody and Watt, op. cit., pp. 34-68.

more flexible and simplified Greek writing system. What remained simply word lists to be memorized among the Mesopotamians and Egyptians became the categories for classifying distinctive bodies of knowledge and the systematic analysis of logical thought by the Greek philosophers. The important thing for the history of thought and education is that an intellectual revolution was taking place along with the political and economic revolutions of the sixth century B.C. No longer content to accept mythological explanations of the observed regularity of physical phenomena, some men began to devise rational explanations in the form of natural laws, often concentrating upon a single fundamental element.

For example, Thales, who may have been familiar with the geometry of the Egyptians and the cosmology of the Babylonians, came to the conclusion that water was the essential characteristic of all matter. Pythagoras, who may have been familiar with the Indian philosophy of withdrawal from the everyday world of affairs, found mathematical consistencies in the movement of the stars as well as in musical tones. Anaximander estimated that the universe was infinite in size and that man was a higher form in the long process of evolution. Xenophanes believed that reality was guided by a single god or directing force. Anaximenes found the essence of things in air, and Heraclitus found it in fire. Empedocles suggested a theory of evolution. Leucippus and Democritus formulated an atomic theory of the construction of the universe. Hippocrates developed the study of medicine. Anaxagoras located permanence in the realm of mind (*nous*) that lies behind change and gives order to it.

Whatever else the pre-Socratic philosophers did, they created new versions of the way to think about the world and the universe. They turned away from anthropomorphic explanations in favor of the impersonal laws of nature not subject to individual whim; indeed, this was the way the polis was intended to operate in the human sphere. If the universe was basically rational, then obviously rationality is the proper way of life for man. Or perhaps it was the other way round: if man could organize a rational way of life in the polis, could nature do less when it came to organizing the world and the cosmos?

Goody and Watt argue not only that the flexibility and simplicity of alphabetic writing made it possible for the Greek city-states to become essentially literate societies as a whole, but that they established many of the institutions that became characteristic of all later literate societies.[13] Among these were new forms of organized schooling that increasingly became available to a large part of the population.

Education in the Open Polis of Athens

The political, intellectual, and demoliterate character of the Greek city-states proved to be fertile ground for the creation of three types of organized schools. It is fruitless to try to determine where and when the first Greek schools appeared, but by the seventh century B.C. most city-states had not only developed highly disciplined forms of military training but had organized formal schools devoted principally to physical education. Called the gymnasium or *palaestra*, these institutions kept alive the warrior

[13] Ibid., p. 67.

or feudal ideal of the heroic age but translated it into the form of athletics and sports which could be practiced by most of the young men and boys of the citizen class in the polis. Marrou believes that the *palaestra* was the earliest of the three types of schools to become popular in the city-states—well before the end of the seventh century.[14]

The second type to appear, some time in the sixth century B.C., was the music school, which also embodied a continuation of the courtly ideal of the aristocratic heroic age. In this school the boy learned to sing, to play a musical instrument, and, above all, to recite the epic poetry of Homer and the lyric poetry of Hesiod, Theognis, and Tyrtaeus. Together, these two poetic traditions provided the vehicle for much of the moral training that bound the Greeks to their polis and helped them achieve their identity as Greek citizens, whether the ideal be the noble deed of the Homeric hero-warrior type or the steadfast loyalty and hard-working farmer-rural type glorified by Hesiod. The Greeks designed these two types of schools very largely in the oral tradition, but before the end of the sixth century B.C. a third type appeared, the literacy school, or, to point the contrast with the others, a reading school. Of the three, it came latest on the scene, but it outlasted the others to the extent that eventually the very name *school* came to mean the literacy or reading school.

We cannot possibly elaborate on the varieties, the likenesses, or the differences found in the three kinds of schools in the different city-states of Greece. They have been described in great detail by Marrou, Jaeger, Freeman, and other authors; they are best represented by those of Athens whose reputation and influence in the long run outdid all others. For a time it looked as though Sparta might become the model for Greek cultural development, but Sparta's bid for leadership in Greece ended rather abruptly around 500 B.C. when slave rebellions prompted the Spartans to try to maintain the status quo rather than to innovate and experiment with new forms of social organization. From that time on, Sparta became petrified culturally, socially, and educationally. Sparta's "great refusal" in effect handed over the cultural and social leadership of Greek civilization to Athens, which continued to grow and to change as it moved from the sixth century into the fifth. At the time when Sparta was deciding to become a "closed" polis and to make its education almost exclusively para-military, Athens was expanding the idea of education to make it broadly "civil"—or better "civilizing"—in the sense that it would form the citizen for a life of full participation in the wide range of activities worthy of the city. This was the meaning of *paideia* in the open polis.

One of the crucial developmental differences between Sparta and Athens was the fact that the unification of the surrounding territory of Attica by Athens took place more by gradual political consolidation than by harsh military conquest. As a result, the base of citizenship in Athens came to be much broader than in Sparta. At the beginning of the seventh century B.C. the rulers of the Athenian state consisted of a king as military leader and magistrates as civil officials. Thereafter, the king's military and political power began to decline, whereas that of the civil officials increased. This

---

[14] Marrou, op. cit., chaps. 2 and 4.

process of widening the base of Athenian citizenship went on more or less successfully through the seventh and sixth centuries B.C.

The key step in political institutionalization was taken by Cleisthenes in 502 B.C. when citizenship and the political basis of suffrage were changed from kinship to territorial groupings. On a basis of almost complete democracy the citizens elected the various branches of government: the popular assembly (legislative); the law court (judicial); and the Council of Five Hundred and the magistrates who carried out the desires of the Council (executive). These came to be the basic forms of Athenian political democracy. Indeed, they characterized the differentiated political institutions which marked the Greek city wherever it was transplanted in succeeding centuries. Their presence, along with Greek educational institutions. signified the presence of Greek civilization.

In the eighth and the seventh centuries B.C. profound economic as well as political changes took place in the Greek world. As the Greeks found that their olive oil and wine were products that the Eastern societies desired, an active foreign trade grew up that began to convert the Greek countryside from farming and raising livestock to the cultivation of vineyards and olive trees. A corollary of these economic changes was the drive for colonies to produce the foodstuffs and textiles that were no longer being produced in sufficient quantities at home. The struggle for markets led to an active period of colonization that spread Greek settlements to almost all parts of the Mediterranean world, east to the Levant, south to Egypt and North Africa, and west to Sicily, Italy, Spain, and France. Urban life became much more important than ever before, as dispossessed persons sought a new living in the cities and as others tried to improve their economic status. The urban character of life, with its attendant commercial class, gave Athenian education a cosmopolitan and varied scope that was never reached by the dominantly rural and agricultural society of Sparta.

Just when the first formal schools appeared in Athens is not certain, but we do know that several educational laws have been attributed to Solon in the early part of the sixth century B.C. The presumption is that schools of some sort (probably *palaestras*) existed as early as the seventh century and that music and literary schools were widespread by the end of the Persian Wars in 480 B.C. It is probably true that before Solon's time some schools already existed concerning which he made the regulations attributed to him. Whether he formulated the laws or not, the state by his time had begun the practice of paying school tuitions for boys whose fathers had been killed in the armies. These were probably among the first educational benefits for families of veterans. Other state regulations concerning education apparently compelled parents to see that their sons learned their letters and acquired the ability to swim. The state also appointed a public supervisor for education, and eventually the law required parents to see that their sons were given an elementary education that included gymnastics, music, and letters.

In contrast to the basically military-elitist bias of Spartan education, the aims and content of Athenian education tended toward the democratic ideal. Reflecting a far broader conception of citizenship, Athenian education set out to provide youth with an intellectual and aesthetic, as well as a physical and military foundation for citizenship. In the Athenian educational ideal, these four aspects were expected to be brought into a well-rounded whole in which all reached a perfect balance or harmony. The ultimate goal was the achievement of those qualities of character that would enable the individual to become an effectively functioning member of the democratic city-state. Although the Athenian ideal of education called for harmonious development of the intellectual, aesthetic, physical, and military powers of the individual, different teachers were assigned the task of nourishing the several aspects of the citizen's character. Differentiated educational institutions were in the making.

The development of physical ability was placed in the hands of the gymnastic teacher (*paedotribe*), whose task was to develop physical stamina, grace, and health through exercises in the *palaestra*. The boys were taught how to run, jump, swim, throw the javelin, and wrestle. Considerable emphasis was put upon the ability to control one's body easily and gracefully as well as skillfully. The boys exercised individually or in pairs, and careful supervision was exerted to see that the boys were matched evenly and played the game in a sportsmanlike fashion. Individual instruction rather than a class or graded method of teaching seems to have been characteristic of elementary education.

The teacher of music (*citharist*) was given the specialized function of developing a sense of rhythm and melody. The boys learned to play the seven-stringed lyre, to sing, to chant, and to dance. These abilities not only developed the individual's aesthetic senses but also prepared him to take part in the civic and religious festivals of his city. He could thus participate in the instrumental, poetic, and singing contests, in the war dances, in the rites to the gods, and in family celebrations connected with birth, marriage, and death. Most of the direct training for dancing was accomplished, not in the schools, but in connection with the Greek chorus that was so important a feature of the dramatic and religious festivals. A *choregos* (chorus master) was appointed to choose and train the members of the chorus for the various public occasions.

The teacher of letters (*grammatist*) concentrated on linguistic and intellectual development. He taught the boys to read, to write, and to count. They learned to read by memorizing the alphabet, learning rhymes and songs about the various letters, and eventually reading from such books as the *Iliad, Odyssey*, Hesiod's *Works and Days*, and Aesop's *Fables*. They practiced oral speaking freely in order to learn correct pronunciation. They learned to write on wax tablets or papyrus as the teacher dictated materials to them to copy. Counting was usually done on the fingers or with stones. Sometimes the teaching of letters and of music went hand in hand, instruction in both being given by the same teacher or by two teachers in the same school.

Beyond the three forms of elementary education just described, the Athenians put considerable emphasis upon physical education and military training. State gymnasiums provided physical education of an advanced type, where youths from fifteen or sixteen years of age concentrated upon achieving excellence in the sports of the pentathlon, running, jumping, discus throwing, javelin throwing, and wrestling. Military training was emphasized for Athenian youth from the age of eighteen to twenty during a two-year period of cadet training. At this time the boys learned the methods of defensive and offensive tactics, studied the topographical features of the country, and began to specialize in cavalry, infantry, or naval maneuvers. At the age of twenty the young man was ready to take his place as a full citizen and as a full-fledged member of the armed forces. Physical education and military training thus comprised nearly the whole of advanced education in Athens prior to the fifth century B.C.

All in all, this formative period in Athenian education reflected a combining of the heroic aristocratic tradition with the new forces of urbanization, social diffentiation, political institutionalization, and literacy. The aristocratic tradition was carried on in the gymnasium and music school, which made available to the whole citizenry what had formerly been the exclusive domain of the nobility. The urban life made it desirable and possible to replace the individual tutors for this training with organized schools, specific teachers in charge, and definite places and times for instruction. The development of writing, of course, led to the popularization of literacy among the whole citizen class. Athens could have stopped short of making these adaptations, as indeed Sparta did. She could have remained an aristocratic, conservative, rural-oriented society, as Sparta did. If she had done so, there might not have been a florescent period in Greek civilization, or it might have fallen to another city to cultivate. But Athens did respond and in doing so created a brilliant civilization in what, up to that point in history, was a spectacularly short period of time.

C. THE FLORESCENT PERIOD: THE GOLDEN AGE OF HELLENISM (500 B.C.-300 B.C.)

During the burst of cultural creativity that marked the golden age of Athens in the fifth century B.C. and the period of ferment that followed in the fourth century, the principal agencies of Greek education took on their major institutional forms, and the range of fundamental theories about the role of education found notable expression in a galaxy of writers on education. Few major innovations in Greek educational institutions or educational theories took place after the fourth century. For 500 years after 300 B.C., or indeed for 1500 years, the dispersion and dissemination of Hellenic education was more important than its creativity. But in the process the education of half the world had been fundamentally changed.

The Glory—and the Flaw— in the Ideal of the Polis
The height of the political and military power of Athens was reached in the fifth century B.C. along with the greatest effectiveness of Athenian democracy, soon after Athens made so bold as to send aid to the Greek cities of Asia Minor in their revolt against Persia. When the Greek city-states, with Athens at the head, emerged victorious from the Persian Wars, the Delian Confederacy, formed to ward off further invasions from Persia, was gradually transformed by Athens from a league of independent states into an Athenian Empire.

Democratic and imperial Athens was bound to come into conflict with the other major military state in Greece, aristocratic and conservative Sparta. Athens as leader of the "free world" of her day, was trying to unite all Greece under her leadership and her control. Sparta, as modern totalitarian states have done, upheld the right of self-determination of small states, except for those under *her* control. The long rivalry for power and for markets led eventually to the disastrous series of military campaigns known as the Peloponnesian War from 431 to 404 B.C. This was largely a struggle between Athenian sea power and Spartan land power, between a political democracy and a military dictatorship. It was not until Athenian sea power was destroyed by a series of disastrous and traitorous actions that Sparta finally was able to impose terms of peace upon Athens. Democracy, discredited in the eyes of many and overthrown in a reactionary backlash engineered by the oligarchs between 411 and 404 B.C., was able to restore itself for a time after the war was over.

For several decades the political situation in Greece was chaotic, not to say anarchic, as each city-state fought against others. The desire for autonomy was so deeply rooted in Greek political traditions that the cities could not unite voluntarily, and no one city-state could impose its military power long enough to bring about a consolidated empire. A strong polis-centered isolationism prevented the building of a sense of community that might have made for real inter-city cooperation and peace.

Within each polis the Greeks, curiously, failed to develop the administrative and professional organizations that might have nourished a social stability and a political sturdiness to match the freedoms they cherished. If Mesopotamians and Egyptians relied too heavily upon stultifying bureaucracies, the Greeks did not sufficiently recognize the managerial advantages of well-organized bureaucracies and educational systems:

> Their freedoms were protected by no professional jurists, no professional public servants of any kind. There was no system of public schools in Athens to prepare the young for life in a democracy, no higher education at all until the Sophists came along. There were no organized political parties to formulate policy, channel differences of opinion, or effect compromise by alternate rule. The Greeks had especial need of wise statesmen, and produced some notable ones; but they did not produce enough of them, or have any reliable means of keeping them in power.[15]

As the fourth century wore on, it produced an increasingly wide gap between the economic fortunes of the lower classes and the wealthy upper classes. This led to constant conflicts that weakened the attempts to achieve international unity or cooperation. When oligarchs were in power, they sought to consolidate their own interests. When popular movements gave power to tyrants, the attempt was to "soak the rich." Citizens began to lose interest in politics and to resist the burdens of military life, so that irresponsible politicians and mercenary soldiers took over the field. The ground was prepared for the loss of political independence as the number of citizens decreased, the class of noncitizens increased, slavery became much more common, patriotic zeal weakened, and military preparedness rested with an army of hired mercenaries.

The time was thus ripe for the conquest of Greece in 338 B.C. by King Philip of

[15] Herbert Muller, *Freedom in the Ancient World,* Harper, New York, 1961, pp. 201-202.

Macedonia, who had been able to solidify all Macedonia under his power. Alexander the Great, following in his father's footsteps, not only ruled Greece, but conquered Asia Minor, Syria, Egypt, and Persia as far east as the Indus. As monarchy was imposed once again in Greece, a long political process was consummated, a process that had started in kingly rule, shifted to aristocracy, then to tyranny, then to democracy, and finally back to monarchy again. But now the kingship was imperial in scope, not local nor tribal nor limited to the confines of a single city-state.

When Alexander died in 323 B.C., a series of wars ensued and three large units emerged, Macedonia, Syria, and Egypt, each under its own Hellenistic ruler and each carrying on wars against the others, until all were finally brought under the sway of Rome by 30 B.C. The ruling classes in the Hellenistic empires of the Middle East were largely Greeks and Macedonians who brought their Greek culture and education with them. Athens maintained a democratic form of constituion and a cultural aura, but the vitality of democracy was smothered with the loss of political independence.

Contrasting Educational Roads to Citizenship in the Polis

One of the most persuasive ideas that guided the conduct of generations of Greek citizens was the belief that the polis provided the best means by which the individual could come to the complete realization of himself. When the conception of the state focused upon military dictatorship, as in Sparta, the individual was expected to accept the discipline of becoming a superb soldier. When the conception of the state was democratic, flexible, and generous, as in Athens at its best, then the individual was expected to develop his humane capacities to their fullest extent in order to be a citizen worthy of his state. When the two ideals came into mortal conflict in the fifth century B.C., thoughtful men of different political, economic, and intellectual persuasions tried to formulate what mental and moral habits should be developed by citizens of the polis to enable them to cope with the rapidly changing social and cultural conditions of the florescent period. In this process educational theory was born. For the first time in history men began to give special thought and attention to the role of education in building and maintaining their civilization.

It was in this period of brilliant but tense social change that the Sophists appeared on the scene in Athens as an educational phenomenon of the golden age. The Sophists were mainly itinerant teachers who came from Asia Minor and the Aegean Islands, attracted by the active life of Athens. They reflected both the glory of the ideal of democratic citizenship and also the flaw in its practice. On the positive side, the Sophists heralded a wholly new form of political education based on development of the skills and knowledge needed by the citizen to undertake his varied roles in the new democratic polis.

What made the educational approach of the Sophists so new was that it appealed directly to the aspirations of the individual citizen, not as a means of inducting him into a privileged association or corporate body of scribes or of training him for a specialized occupation or vocation. What the Sophists did was to stress the need for education in the use of verbal and written language as a competence that all citizens should have for the performance of their private and public activities. The earlier speculations of the philosophers of Asia Minor had been devoted to scientific explanations concerning nature and the cosmos; in this sense they were the originators of *science*, not philosophy. But when the Sophists, who were basically teachers, began to apply the methods of rational thought developed by the natural philosophers to matters of human conduct, they were creating the broader traditions of philosophy which originated in the *educational* problems that faced Athenians in the fifth century B.C. They taught youth about virtue (ethics), the management of cities (politics), the management of households (economics), the art of thinking (logic), and the art of persuasion (rhetoric).

They gave prime importance to rhetoric. So many persons needed to make speeches in the assembly and in the courts and so many were becoming good at it that individuals could no longer rely on extemporaneous speaking but had to resort to careful composition of written speeches in advance of oral delivery. The Sophists were ready and willing to help out the novices for a fee and to explicate the elaborate rules of rhetoric for the inexperienced. The point is that between 450 and 350 B.C. the Sophists as teachers helped to spread knowledge based upon reading and writing as necessary accomplishments for the successful performance of the everyday duties and tasks of the adult citizen of the Greek polis.

Gradually, the Athenian Fathers began to be prejudiced against the Sophists, to think of them as superficial, shallow, and overdialectical, and as sellers of tricks of the trade instead of as seekers after the truth. So long as Athens rode the crest of prosperity and power prior to the Peloponnesian War, the Sophists were not only tolerated but greeted with enthusiasm, especially by the young men; but when Athens began to shake and crumble under the impact of war, the conservative fathers began to be suspicious of these newfangled teachers who, in their view, were doubtless corrupting the youth of the city. Worst of all, they seemed to be questioning the old customs, political traditions, the state gods, and religious beliefs. In time of war such skepticism could not be tolerated. The urge to reaffirm the ancient loyalties led to attacks upon the Sophists. Many of them had to leave Athens, and the most famous of all, Socrates, was tried and condemned to death for his allegedly impious teaching.

Against the opportunistic practices of the Sophists, Socrates arose to do combat in the latter half of the fifth century as he sought to define generalized principles of conduct that would be binding upon all men. The measure of all things ethical was not to be any man, but only the *good* man. Universal principles of morality could be discovered if men would only discuss their conceptions and, by mutual agreement, arrive at general ideas. His belief that universal ideas emerge from the common social life of man seems to embrace the basic democratic tenet of consent, but it is not so clear that Socrates in his old age remained so staunchly an adherent of democracy. In any case, the question is still paramount today-how far a democracy can go in allowing itself to be undermined by those who demand the freedom to criticize it but exercise no basic loyalty to democratic institutions or to the democratic procedures of due process. It may ultimately be decided that the greatest weakness of Socrates was his failure to stress a positive education for citizenship that would develop the basic loyalties to the common values of democracy at the same time that it developed the ability to criticize, which was Socrates' chief glory.

Socrates quickly gained great popularity among the young men of Athens because of his keen analytical powers, his ability to puncture the pompous and boastful, and his constant interest in a broad range of subjects. He asked the profound questions concerning the future of Athens and the general nature of justice, truth, good, and beauty. He was at once a typical Athenian citizen and yet, through the magic of his tongue, the force of his personality, and the weight of his ideas, he was the outstanding intellectual figure and teacher of his time.

Of all that might be said about Socrates, perhaps his most important educational contributions were his methods of teaching and his conception of the role of knowledge in conduct. The "Socratic method," as it has been known ever since, is essentially the method of question and answer. Socrates always insisted upon rigid and strict definition of the terms and subject under discussion. In his conversations and dialogues he assumed the role of the humble seeker after truth. He would challenge someone's statement, refute and confute it with adroit questioning, bring his opponent from "unconscious ignorance" to "conscious ignorance," lead him to a blank wall, and then begin to build up his own account of the problem. His questions, usually to be answered by "yes" or "no," were intended to serve as a guide to a general proposition to which the group would agree.

Socrates always came back to the primary role of knowledge in the solving of ethical and moral problems. The pursuit of knowledge through the oral but disciplined dialogue is the high road to good conduct. He heard some of the Sophists preaching that the individual man was the measure of all things and that therefore each man can decide for himself what is right or wrong. This has been translated lately as "each person doing his own thing." Socrates set himself against such excessive individualism by insisting that true knowledge transcends individual perceptions and determines what is right or wrong for all.

When it came time for Plato to formulate his conceptions of the state and of citizenship, which were to be so enormously influential for centuries to come, he did it out of an aristocratic and conservative background at a time when democracy was on the defensive in Athens. Plato was even more impressed than was Socrates by the excessive individualism of Athenian democracy as well as by the apparent military superiority of the well-disciplined aristocracy of Sparta. He grew up in the chaotic period when the great struggle between Athens and Sparta was dividing the loyalties of men and creating partisan conflicts throughout the Greek world. He took the search for truth away from the marketplace of ideas which Socrates relished so much and lodged it with a highly trained intellectual elite.

In his *Republic* Plato dreamed hopefully of an ideal state which would do away with factional conflict, which would give the ruling power to an aristocratic class of the wise and just, and in which all individuals would be strictly subordinated to the good of the state. He felt that justice would be achieved if each person did the job he was best fitted by nature to do. The masses of people would do the work of the world; the courageous and physically fit would do the fighting and protecting; and the most intellectual would be the philosopher-kings to do the ruling. Good citizenship, thus, was a matter of serving the state, whether to work, or to fight, or to rule.

Needless to say, this was a denial of the historic Athenian democracy, which had been built upon the democratic principle that all citizens should be obliged to work, and protect, and rule the state. It is useless, but nonetheless interesting, to speculate what the history of civilization would have been if Plato's genius had been exerted on the side of democracy rather than of aristocracy. The "classical tradition," which he helped so much to formulate, might thus have given countless generations of men a predilection for democracy rather than a justification for a state in which an aristocratic, intellectual elite was believed to be the only appropriate ruling class.

Plato paid little attention to education for the masses of people who were to do the work of the city; he was interested primarily in the education of the warrior and ruling classes. Education is designed not only to form the character appropriate to the ideal society but also to act as a selective agency by means of which the most able are brought to light. Children should be reared in state nurseries before the age of six, and during this time they should be taught fairy tales, nursery rhymes, and stories of the gods, with emphasis upon the virtuous gods and omission of immoral stories. From the ages of six to eighteen the main ingredients of education should be music, dancing, gymnastics, and reading, all to create the proper moral spirit. The object of early education is to blend these elements into harmonious proportions. From eighteen to twenty, further physical training, and especially military training, should occupy the time of the men. At the age of twenty those who are to become warriors should begin their assigned tasks, whereas those destined to become guardians or philosopher-kings should continue a course of higher study for ten years, this course to consist primarily of mathematics (arithmetic, geometry, astronomy, and musical harmony).

At the age of thirty, the less brilliant of the ruling class should go into the lower civil offices of the state, and the more brilliant should continue their studies for another five years. After a regimen of philosophy (dialectics and metaphysics), which makes up the highest study of all, dealing as it does with pure reality and pure knowledge, the true philosopher-kings will have finished their preparation for ruling at the age of thirty-five. They then are to go out for fifteen years into the actual world of practical experience and take part in the military and political affairs of the state. At the age of fifty they are ready to become "elder statesmen," spending most of their time in philosophical pursuits but taking their unavoidable turns in office as a matter of public duty. Their main task, however, is to contemplate and think about the essence of the good life by which the state should be regulated.

Plato's predilection for the intellectual discipline of mathematics and philosophy is clearly revealed in this plan. He believed that such mental training was the best preparation for the conduct of public affairs. Once the philosopher-kings are trained in the pursuit of knowledge, they are ready to solve problems of all kinds. Thus Plato not only helped to shape the content of higher education of the Western world to come but also set the pattern of mental discipline that has been so much a part of European and American education almost to the present time.

Another voice that spoke with tremendous authority for later ages was that of Aristotle, who, together with Plato, exerted a greater influence upon the philosophy and educational ideals of Western civilization than that of any other ancient figure. Aristotle's conception of leisure as superior to trade or manual work helped to substantiate the dualism between knowledge and action that Plato had formulated.

Accepting as right and natural that the weight of a few free citizens should rest upon the backs of the great mass of workers and slaves who did the actual labor of mining, manufacturing, agriculture, and commerce, Aristotle insisted that a liberal education was appropriate only to the free citizens who had the leisure to engage in intellectual affairs. The liberal man must be one who is not only politically and intellectually free but also economically free; he had to be wealthy enough to escape the drudgery of actual work in making a living. Liberal studies could thus easily become identified with those intellectual activities with which a leisure class found pleasure in passing the time. For many centuries the more directly "practical" studies were largely excluded from the education that was called liberal.

Aristotle's intellectualistic and aristocratic bias showed clearly in his *Politics*. He granted that farmers, artisans, and tradesmen may be necessary for the economic well-being of a state, but he argued that they should not be regarded as free citizens or as free men. These manual and lower occupations, with their degrading effect upon the souls and minds of men, make them unfit for the practice of virtue and thus of freedom. In the best type of state (aristocracy) free citizens would not engage in such occupations. One of the weaknesses of a democracy was that farmers, tradesmen, and artisans were admitted to the fold of citizenship despite the fact that they were not capable of achieving a liberal education. Liberal studies develop the intellectual virtues of free men; illiberal studies are those that give direct vocational preparation for degrading occupations.

In his *Ethics* Aristotle argued that the highest form of virtue was pure speculation and contemplation. Man as knower is higher in the scale of human than man as doer or citizen. Man's rational nature has two major aspects: the moral virtues which make up the character of a man are the outcome of habit formation; and the intellectual virtues which seek knowledge and truth are the outcome of teaching. At the earlier stages of education the goal may well be character-formation and the inculcation of the moral virtues, but as the youth grow older the goal of liberal education at the higher levels is unmistakably the cultivation of the intellectual virtues.

The intellectual faculties of man are of two major types. The more noble is the theoretical reason which aims at knowledge for its own sake, determines the truth or falsity of conclusions concerning the permanent and unchanging aspects of existence, and formulates the first principles that describe and explain the eternal world of man, of nature, and the universe. The liberal studies which best aid the intellectual faculties to discover these first principles are, from lower to higher, logic, mathematics, biology, psychology, astronomy, physics, cosmology, ontology, metaphysics, and theology. These scientific or speculative branches of knowledge constitute the highest liberal studies because they are expressions of the theoretical or contemplative faculties of reason.

The less noble kind of intellectual faculty is the *practical* reason which aims at knowledge having to do with action and conduct (prudence) or the making and producing of things (art). The practical reason which deals with the changeable and the variable in things and events seeks knowledge that will guide human conduct and formulate rules for action. The liberal studies that aid the practical reason in this process are what today would be called the social sciences and fine arts. Aristotle himself gave a good deal of attention to these "less noble" studies in his *Politics, Ethics, Economics, Rhetoric,* and *Poetics* as well as to the higher theoretical studies of pure science and philosophy.

Aristotle's enormous influence upon the Western European intellectual tradition helped to fix for centuries the ideal that truth-seeking was a higher goal for man's rational nature than was character formation, that the acquisition of organized knowledge was superior to moral guidance as an aim of higher education, and that theory was more to be valued than practice as the end of a liberal education. Yet the victory of "intellectualists" in favor of cultivating the mind as the chief goal of education was never fully won, for "practicalists" were constantly returning to the struggle to assert and reassert the claims that education should be devoted to improving the conduct, the attitudes, and the behavior of man as well as his mind.

The overall effect of both Plato's and Aristotle's teachings has been to emphasize the cultivation of the intellect as an educational goal rather than dealing with the practical problems of contemporary politics. Some educators of today would term such intellectualism a dangerous retreat to the ivory tower of academic isolation at a critical time when an education devoted to social responsibility is the best hope of an enduring civilization. Other contemporary educators would hail Plato and Aristotle as the surest guides through our chaotic world of unrest and change.

We have mentioned three educational roads to the ideal of citizenship for the polis: the development of practical political skills with the Sophists, the arrival at consensus of the right and the just through dialogue with Socrates, and the attainment of pure knowledge of the good and the true through the discipline of philosophy with Plato and Aristotle. There remains yet another road to good citizenship: the achievement of right moral judgment through the discipline of rhetoric and humanistic literature. This is the view of the long-lived teacher of rhetoric, Isocrates, who carried on several decades of running battle with the opportunistic and narrow technicalism of the Sophists on one hand and with the abstract philosophy of Plato on the other. Isocrates expressed disdain for both approaches to solving the fateful problems facing the polis following the Peloponnesian War.

Isocrates' formula for remedying the ills of Athens was neither to concentrate on individual success with the Sophists nor to escape into philosophic lament with Plato. It was to face frontally and plunge into remedying the problems resulting from poverty, factionalism, excessive individualism, overpopulation, and the despair of military defeat. His major social program centered upon an "international" solution: the creation of a Pan-Hellenic union under Athenian leadership to establish colonies on the coast of Persia. Isocrates argued in essence that the highest human good being happiness, and the chief forms of human excellence lying in service to the city, the chief means to this *arete* is man's faculty of *logos,* the ability to conduct discourse which can lead him to sound practical judgments. The public form of *logos* in action is rhetoric; the private form of discourse is internal thought itself. In a sense then, man is a persuading animal who by means of communication with others has been able to found cities under the rule of law and thus to establish civilization itself.

The ideal citizen is thus the *rhetor,* or orator. He is a man who is devoted to public affairs, accepts the responsibilities of citizenship, informs himself thoroughly by a broad range of studies, bases his social principles upon reason, and develops a sense of good judgment about the problems facing the city. Then and only then is the orator ready to try to persuade his fellows of policies he has been trained to think about and to pursue. Of course, he should also develop high standards of style and taste in his compositions and in his speeches.

Isocrates heaped scorn upon the idea that the good citizen could be formed by long years of immersion in purely abstract academic studies like mathematics or dialectics or science. These may be subjects appropriate for boys or callow youth but not for grown men. The philosophers may end up being teachers of what they have learned, but they will have no practical knowledge useful to their times or relevant for the lives of their students. Isocrates took the Sophists' image of rhetoric as a narrow technical training for public speaking and transformed it into an ideal for the highest type of public service to the city and to mankind.

Isocrates saw clearly that the genuine orator must be primarily a man of good character, devoted to the public good. Rhetoric is not merely a means of persuading people to action; it lays upon the rhetorician the obligation to work for the welfare of the state. Thus an orator must be a good statesman if he is to be a good orator. The preparation for such an ideal, therefore, not only must include a study of the principles and techniques of rhetoric but also must emphasize a broad background of liberal arts, including literature, logic, history, political science, ethics, art, and music, as a basis for forming good judgments of public policy.

Of major importance, also, is the emphasis Isocrates put upon the practicality of knowledge. Philosophy to him was the means by which knowledge is used for the practical business of making judgments and decisions concerning proposed courses of action. Knowledge for its own sake and without relation to action is not properly to be called knowledge. Isocrates realized the necessity of education as a process of building a sense of community responsibility. He worked long and arduously for Panhellenic unity, but his efforts were never crowned with genuine success before Greece fell to the Macedonian conquerers.

In general, it may be said that, despite the influence of Isocrates upon Cicero and Quintilian in Roman times, his ideals were never as fully accepted by the educational theorists of the Western world as have been those of Plato and Aristotle. One of the reasons may be that the democratic ideal which produced Isocrates' conception of the relation of knowledge to action was to go into an eclipse from which it did not emerge for some 2,000 years.

Another reason may be that Isocrates made it plain that man cannot achieve certainty in matters of moral conduct and practical judgment. Moral principles must be worked out in a painfully slow process of discussion, dialogue, and discourse, and they must be tested by their success in guiding human conduct. Man can arrive at accurate and valid judgments only by persistent study of relevant facts, analysis of relationships, and rational inference free from emotional bias. Man cannot achieve irrefutable, certain knowledge in human affairs. Yet, as the polis declined, men *wanted* certainty. They sought it in philosophy and religion. Then, when hope for better times returned—as it did recurringly during the next 2,000 years—they would perennially return to rhetoric to aid them to improve themselves and their civilizations.

Scholars have long debated whether Plato or Isocrates "won" the debate they started 2,400 years ago on the relative virtues of philosophy versus the humanities in the formation of the good citizen and in the conduct of a just social order.[16] This is the kind of debate that has no definitive winner. Plato has had the advantage that his prose is far more captivating and his arguments lend themselves to generalization and speculation in endless ways. In that sense he is far more a "classic" writer than Isocrates, whose writings seem much more pedestrian and bound to the confines of his local Greek world. He had no corporate organization that carried on his teachings in a formal "school of philosophy" over the centuries.

Yet, Isocrates' emphasis on literature rather than on philosophy as the subject matter of the schools has given him the nod with millions of teachers in thousands upon thousands of classrooms since his day. For the literary curriculum has surely predominated over the philosophic or the scientific, as the humanist culture has overshadowed the scientific culture until recent centuries. So I would opine that Plato has won in the minds and outlook of the world's highly educated communities, especially the aristocratic elite of such communities; and Isocrates has won among the teachers who shape the curriculum in the day-to-day classrooms of the world's literary schools.

The Major Institutions of Florescent Greek Education

By the end of the florescent period (say, during the last quarter of the fourth century B.C.), the basic forms of Greek education had taken shape. A discernible system of schools was beginning to appear with something approaching elementary, secondary, and higher institutions of education, although we must be careful not to impose our modern conceptions of these terms upon the ancient Greeks. These levels were not articulated systems with easily recognized grades or forms or classes or required courses or degrees or diplomas. Where the teacher was, there was the school. Parents selected a teacher, agreed to a contract, paid the fees, and sent their sons to him. The notion of a curriculum or a course to be run was not yet common practice, although proposals concerning such requirements were beginning to be made as we shall soon see. But the functions of the teachers were clearly differentiated. Three types of first-level schools for boys aged six or eight to twelve or fourteen were conducted by three kinds of teachers: the *palaestra* taught by a teacher of gymnastics (*paedotribe*); the music school taught by the *citharist;* and the reading school taught by the teacher of letters (*grammatist*). Sometimes a teacher of letters and a teacher of music would set up an establishment together so that boys could acquire both kinds of instruction at the same time.

At the beginning of the period the *grammatist* and the *paedotribe* were the most

---

[16] See, e.g., Jaeger, op. cit., vols. 2 and 3; Marrou, op. cit, chaps. 6 and 7; and Frederick A. G. Beck, *Greek Education, 450-350 B.C.,* Methuen, London, 1964, chaps. 5, 7, and 8.

popular teachers; often a boy would spend part of the day with the literary teacher and part of the day with the gymnastic teacher in the *palaestra*. The school day was long, lasting from sunrise to sunset. Public opinion was the most potent force impelling parents to have their sons educated. By the end of the period, however, the popularity of the gymnastic training and music for young boys began to decline in favor of the literary school, as courtly ideals of the aristocratic tradition gave way to the literate skills of urban life.

The character of second-level education changed more radically during the florescent period than did elementary education. At the beginning of the period the dominant form of education for boys beyond fourteen or sixteen years was provided in the public gymnasiums. Athens, for example, provided three gymnasiums at public expense. The Academy was the oldest and most sought after by the aristocratic elements in Athens; the Lyceum, founded by Pericles in the fifth century in response to the popular movements of the day, catered particularly to the newly enfranchised citizens from the commercial and artisan classes; and the Cynosarges catered to aliens, traders, and residents who had not achieved full rights of citizenship. Each gymnasium was under the direction of a public official known as the *gymnasiarch*.

Then, as the political, economic, and intellectual ferment of the second half of the fifth century turned the attention of young men to the teaching of the Sophists, a whole new exciting world of intellectual and political training opened up. By and large, the Sophists did not establish fully organized schools with special buildings or regularized courses of instruction. Rather, they travelled about gathering such students as they could and making contractual arrangements to teach particular skills for specified fees and periods of time (anywhere up to three or four years). Their methods have been described by Marrou as "collective tutoring."[17]

The principal skills the Sophists taught turned out to be rhetoric, dialectic, and grammar. We have already mentioned the early popularity of rhetoric and public speaking as a means to political prowess. Empedocles is credited with being the founder of rhetoric and Gorgias its master exponent and practitioner. The art of dialectic also came to be very popular for its value in the courts and the public debates that embellished the Greek city, its markets, and its assemblies. Protagoras was the epitome of the art of winning an argument by debate and disputation. The techniques ranged all the way from carefully constructed logical inferences and systematic reasoning to the cunning or cynical spinning out of verbal tricks and paradoxes. The use of the latter resulted in the Sophists' bequest of the word *sophistry* to the languages of the West. The widespread interest in epic poetry, drama, and literature also led to an increasing interest in analyzing language itself, its structure and forms, its sound and etymology, its rhythm and metre. Protagoras, Hippias, and Prodicus were chief formulators of what came to be known as grammar.

The Sophists as a total group did not limit themselves to these fields of inquiry and teaching. The intellectual ferment included attention to mathematics (especially arithmetic, geometry, astronomy, and musical acoustics), geography, history, and the

[17] Marrou, op. cit., p. 80.

like. By and large, the Sophists did not pursue the natural science and cosmological interests that had intrigued the Ionian philosophers of the sixth century. The Sophists devoted themselves to man and his works, particularly his practical, political, and intellectual pursuits.

It is of little moment to argue whether the Sophists were working at the secondary level of education or higher education level. The point, I believe, is that their influence as teachers and as spadeworkers in a variety of intellectual fields was more important than the institutional forms they created. By the end of the fifth century they had turned up so many ideas and elicited such enthusiasm for intellectual affairs that a wave of educational institutionalization followed in the course of the fourth century B.C. I count this as part of the florescence of educational development. If the enthusiasm stimulated by the Sophists had not been put into organized form, their civilizing effect might have been dissipated.

As it was, their rhetorical interest was captured in the establishment of rhetorical schools, the most famous being founded in 392 B.C. by Isocrates. Similarly, the Sophists' interest in dialectics, flowing through the work of Socrates, combined with the streams of interest in logic and mathematics to produce schools of philosophy, notably the Academy of Plato in 387 B.C. and the Lyceum of Aristotle in 335 B.C. Somewhat later and heralding a new direction for philosophy were the Garden of Epicurus in 306 B.C., and the Stoa of Zeno in 301-300 B.C. These latter will be dealt with in discussion of the dispersive period. As these schools of rhetoric and schools of philosophy took organizational form in the fourth century B.C., they unmistakably began to display what can reasonably be called "higher education." The more or less intermittent and informal methods of the Sophists had given way to regular institutions of advanced education.

Thereupon a great tradition was launched that eventually swept into Western civilization. In Plato's Academy and Aristotle's Lyceum the works of these philosophers were handed down from generation to generation, and their teachings imprinted on the mind of the Western world. The very names of these schools have been preserved in the academies of France, England, and the United States and the *lycées* of France, the *Lyzeum* of Germany, and the lyceums of the United States.

Plato's Academy gave itself largely to the study of philosophy (dialectics, physics, metaphysics, ethics, politics, law, and literature) and of mathematics (arithmetic, geometry, music, and astronomy). The Lyceum carried on the tradition of Aristotle's wide-ranging interests, including metaphysics, logic, aesthetics, ethics, politics, and rhetoric, but also a great emphasis upon the natural sciences (physics, mechanics, meteorology, botany, zoology, anatomy, geography, geology, and medicine.) Aristotle's work in the Lyceum led to the classifying and organizing of the major disciplines of knowledge. Alexander the Great subsidized Aristotle's researches with large grants of money, and many men were commissioned to gather scientific data for Aristotle as they marched with Alexander's armies on their extensive campaigns in all parts of his empire.

The schools of philosophy, more than the schools of rhetoric, began to take the form of fraternal brotherhoods or teaching orders involving careful selection of initiates, explicit regulations for a communal life, regular times and places for meeting and teaching, prescribed courses of study and lectures, and identifiable rosters of membership for teachers and students. They became full-fledged educational organizations. In fact the Academy and the Lyceum recaptured something of the semireligious brotherhoods of the earlier Pythagorean and Orphic cults, while the Epicureans and the Stoics foreshadowed something of the monastic ideal of the Christian era.

Military training was a third kind of advanced or higher education commonly expected of the youth of the citizen class. Whether or not this type of training was compulsory before the fourth century B.C. is a matter of debate. Growing out of the gymnasial training, a youth would normally engage in two years of service as a cadet (*ephebos*) in the army; at the end of this time he would enter into full citizenship at a public ceremony. Even during the Persian and Peloponnesian Wars, the individualistic nature of Athenian democracy apparently had relied heavily upon voluntary service in the armed forces of the city. During most of the 5th century B.C., this arrangement seems to have worked well enough because of the common expectation that a responsible citizen would engage in military defense of the city-state.

In the fourth century B.C., however, when recurring defeats caused democracy to waver under attacks from without and individualistic excesses to spring up from within, state control of education was expanded. The Ephebic College was established in 335 B.C. by the Athenian assembly, and military training was made compulsory for all citizen youth between the ages of 18 and 20. At the age of 18 each youth had to prove his legitimate birth as a citizen, have his hair cut, don a uniform, and be inducted into the Ephebic College. The establishment of compulsory military training grew out of the recommendations of Plato and Xenophon, who had been impressed by the effectiveness of the armies of Sparta, where military training had long been required of all citizens. The movement was brought to a head by the Battle of Chaeronea in 338 B.C. when Philip of Macedonia utterly defeated a combined force of Athenian and Theban armies.

As the rhetorical and dialectical interests of the Sophists took organized form in the institutions of higher education in the fourth century so did their grammatical and literary interests flow downward into the second level institutions. For reasons that are not wholly clear, a new type of secondary school began to emerge, a grammar school taught by a grammarian (*grammaticos*). Such teachers appeared on the scene before 300 B.C. At least three factors seem to have been involved: the decline of the aristocratic and courtly traditions centering around gymnastics and sports, the upsurge of interest in intellectual and political affairs stimulated by the Sophists, and the need for extended linguistic and grammatical training for the pursuit of the higher education becoming available in the schools of rhetoric and philosophy. As so often happened in the course of civilization building, the expansion of knowledge led to the necessity for more extended formal educational training at the preparatory level; and as educational preparation became more extensive, the possibility of increased specialization heightened. This specialization began to take the form of specific subjects or fields of knowledge identifiable not just as wisdom in general, but as rhetoric, logic, grammar, mathematics, history, and the several branches of natural philosophy or natural science (particularly as classified by Aristotle).

Thus, as the florescent period slipped into the dispersive period, between the close of the fourth century and the opening of the third century B.C., the major forms of Greek education had taken shape: The reading school had become the chief means of elementary education with the gradual decline of gymnastics and music for the younger boys. The grammar school was about to become the major form of secondary education in place of the gymnasium, which became increasingly a social and recreational center for the urban life of aristocratic male citizens. The schools of rhetoric and philosophy replaced military training as the preferred type of higher education; even the Ephebic College itself took on something of the character of a fashionable finishing school for upper class youth, combining military with intellectual studies.

The shift from the rural tradition of a warrior folk society to the urban political climate of a civilized society was epitomized in the institutional transformation of the schools.

CHAPTER IV

THE DISPERSION OF HELLENISTIC EDUCATION IN THE GRAECO-ROMAN WORLD
(300 B.C.-1500 A.D.)

"The most significant characteristic of the Greeks is that no group of them settled anywhere without at once establishing a school, and organized education was the most important single factor in the process of hellenization and also in the resistance to that process."[1] This is a remarkable generalization concerning the importance of organized education and its central role in the spread of Greek civilization. Moses Hadas points out that "the basic meaning of *hellenizein* (to hellenize) is to *speak* Greek and its proper use is with reference to people who would not normally be expected to do so. In its wider sense hellenization is the adoption of Greek modes of behavior in general by people not themselves Greek."[2] The significance of the generalization that organized education was the chief factor in teaching non-Greeks not only to speak Greek but to adopt Greek modes of behavior cannot be over emphasized.

Not only did the Greeks rely heavily upon organized education to perpetuate their civilization at home (as did the Mesopotamians and the Egyptians before them), but Greeks moved restlessly outward from their homeland until they eventually spread their culture over vast parts of the civilized world in the course of the thousand years that can be identified as Hellenic and Hellenistic (roughly 800 B.C. to 200 A.D.). The

[1] Moses Hadas, *Hellenistic Culture; Fusion and Diffusion*, Columbia University Press, New York, 1959, p. 59.
[2] Ibid., p. 45.

Greeks diffused their civilization as far east as India and through the Roman Empire as far west as Britain. (See Figure 3.1—The Graeco-Roman World of Education.) In comparison with the Greeks, the Mesopotamians and Egyptians were stay-at-homes (unless indeed the Egyptians sailed to America). But still more important, there was something about Greek civilization that was apparently more acceptable or more attractive to alien peoples than even was the case with the massive cultural achievements of Middle Eastern civilization. The impact stemmed not only from their political, military, and economic prowess but from the character of their language and literature, their thought and knowledge, their art and style of life, and, as Moses Hadas says, their penchant for spreading the education they developed during their formative and florescent eras. Without the school as a civilizer the influence of Greek civilization would have been far less than it was.

The transition from the florescent to the dispersive period in Greek education is symbolized by the two generations coming at the end of the fourth and beginning of the third century B.C. Isocrates died in 338 B.C., within a week of the defeat of the Greeks by Philip of Macedon at the Battle of Chaeronea. The Pan-Hellenic union of the city-states for which Isocrates had argued all his life was now to be achieved only at the cost of losing independence to the Macedonians. Aristotle died in 322 B.C., a year after Alexander's own death which put to an early end the remarkable fifteen years of conquest whereby Alexander extended the sway of Macedonian rule and Hellenic culture east to the Indus and south to Egypt. Within the generation that marked the turn of the new century, the last of the major schools of philosophy were established at Athens (the Epicurean in 306 B.C. and the Stoic in 301-300 B.C.), and the first and foremost of the Hellenistic institutions of higher education was established outside Athens (the Museum at Alexandria, *ca.* 290 or 280 B.C.).

These events symbolize why I have chosen the date 300 B.C. as a convenient hook upon which to hang the end of the creative educational period of Hellenism and the beginning of the Hellenization of the peoples to the east and to the west, to the north and to the south of Athens. Just when to date the close of the Hellenizing period is a matter of choice. If political rule is the criterion, some use the date when Rome completed the conquest of Macedonia and Greece (146 B.C.); others when Egypt, the last of the major Hellenistic kingdoms, was conquered by Rome (30 B.C.). Either of these dates could justifiably be used to mark the end of the Hellenistic period.

If, however, cultural and educational "rule" is the criterion to be used, the problem is much more difficult. The Hellenistic period in the Middle East could well be said to extend to 200 A.D. Greek educational institutions were carried by Alexander wherever he went and were established in turn by the Hellenistic successors to Alexander in the major kingdoms that followed the breakup of Alexander's Empire: the Ptolemaic dynasty which ruled in Egypt for 300 years from 323 B.C. to 30 B.C.; and the Seleucid Empire which extended from Asia Minor to India. By the end of the third century B.C. political disintegration was already bedevilling Egypt, and the Seleucid Kingdom was breaking into sections, with major centers at Pergamum in Asia Minor, Parthia southeast of the Caspian Sea, and Bactria embracing the Hindu Kush in the northeast. But despite these political changes, the influence of Greek styles of life and educational institutions remained strong, especially in key cities, until as late as 200 A.D. For example, Plutarch (d. 120 A.D.) did much of his scholarly writing in Greece itself; the scientist Ptolemy (d. 161 A.D.), who marked the culmination of Greek astronomy and geography, worked at Alexandria; whereas Galen (d. *ca.* 200 A.D.), who did the same for Greek medicine, did most of his work in Rome.

In Eastern Europe and Asia Minor the Hellenistic educational tradition continued almost without a break throughout the thousand years of the Byzantine Empire. This may be dated from the removal of the capital of the Roman Empire from Rome to Constantinople by Constantine in 300 A.D., or from the designation of Zeno as Byzantine Emperor in 474 A.D., or from Justinian's rule in 527-565 A.D. The Greek cultural predominance is, however, generally conceded to have lasted until the overthrow of Byzantium by the Ottoman Turks in 1453. So the Hellenization of Eastern Europe can be said to extend virtually to 1500 A.D., and through the Greek Orthodox Church and related institutions down to the present.

Hellenization of the West took place largely through the political instrumentality of the Roman Empire and thus might be said to close with the end of the Western Empire around 500 A.D.; but the influence of Hellenistic education on Western Europe was carried on through Latin education during the Middle Ages until explicit Greek models again came to the fore in the humanistic education of the European Renaissance. In this sense, Hellenism is embedded in much of Western education to the present time.

For purposes of this chapter, however, I believe a convenient date to use for the close of the dispersive period of Greek education east of Athens is 200 A.D. By this time the aggressive expansionism of Hellenism begun by Alexander had ended, and the beginnings of a distinctive Christian-Byzantine culture were forming. For most of this 500-year period, Greek civilization and Greek education were the models most eagerly emulated by the intellectual and educated classes of Western Asia and the Middle East. In the Mediterranean world west of Athens, Greek culture had to compete with Carthaginian and Etruscan cultures until the dominance of Rome around 300 B.C. From that time forward, Greek education was emulated or assimilated for nearly 800 years so that we can properly speak of Graeco-Roman education as a prime agency in the civilizing of the entire Roman world to the end of the Empire around 500 B.C.

A. HELLENIZING EDUCATION IN THE EAST (300 B.C.-200 A.D.)

Hard upon the heels of Alexander's conquests, hundreds of thousands of Greeks moved eastward to escape the depressed conditions at home and to better themselves economically. Naturally, as they clustered in newly built Greek cities, they carried with them their Greek institutions. They took their gymnasiums and their primary schools wherever they went, and in certain key cities they also established, with the help or stimulus of Hellenistic rulers, grammar schools, rhetorical schools, and philosophical schools. The Hellenistic rulers, needing administrators, physicians, and professionals to manage their cities and kingdoms, encouraged teachers and scholars to aid in spreading Greek education. Indeed, a "Greek" came to be identified almost as much by his acquisition of Greek education as by his ethnic background. Entrance into the upper classes of intellectual, political, and economic power very often rested upon acquiring the fundamentals of a Greek education, much as was the case in modern colonial empires when a French or an English education proved to be the road to preferment by the ruling estate. In fact, a Greek education was the principal means of distinguishing between the "civilized" and "non-civilized" sectors in the population. In former days, the "barbarian" was viewed by the Greeks as anyone who did not live in a Greek city. Now that Greek cities existed over much of the civilized world, the distinction became educational rather than geographical.

Even after the military expansion of Hellenism began to decline and emigration from the Greek homeland similarly declined after 200 B.C., Greek cultural and educational forms continued to prevail in most of western Asia and the eastern Mediterranean for another 400 years. The Greek language was the lingua franca of the region and the young man who aspired to "higher" pursuits found it desirable to have a higher Greek education. This remained substantially true in the Parthian kingdom and in the Bactrian kingdom as well as in Egypt until around 200 A.D. The entire Afro-Eurasian ecumene was connected from the Atlantic to the Pacific when the Kushan Empire in the first century A.D. linked the Parthian and the Roman Empires on the west with India on the east. We know that Hellenic art styles influenced both China and India, with the fulcrum of contact for interchange between Greek, Iranian, Indian, and Chinese forms of civilization being Bactria and the Hindu Kush. Possibly there was literary and educational interchange too, but the evidence is too thin to say.

It seems clear, however, that by the end of the second century A.D. the Hellenic inroads had spent themselves, either being absorbed or put on the defensive. Thereafter, the creative energies of the intellectual classes began to move toward new philosophical formulations which subordinated the inherited Greek patterns of rational thought to religious formulations in both eastern and western garb. These semi-religious philosophies embodied the search for salvation and happiness in a spiritual world beyond the reach of the Greek polis and its human citizenry.

Generalizations are not easy, but it seems possible that the shift from a "daylight" religion of interest in this world to a spiritual interest in the future life reflected the change from a free and vigorous social life to a restricted political life that occurred when the Greek cities lost their independence under Macedonian, Hellenistic, and Roman rule. When the civic ideal of the city-state no longer had a vital meaning for the Greek mind, many intellectuals sought refuge in religious contemplation and mysticism. This change tended to diminish the civic, practical, and moral character of education and to emphasize its more narrowly intellectual and academic character.

Another side of the picture was that the social gap between the Greek educated upper classes and the uneducated lower classes began to widen in Hellenistic times. The large landowner became more powerful whereas the formerly independent farmer lapsed into peasantry or slavery while his counterpart in the cities became more dispossessed than ever. So it was, first in the greek cities of the East and then later in the Latin cities of the West, that the poor and alienated masses of people became potent candidates for the new Christian religion that began to take form in the Levant.

Christianity appealed to the downtrodden of the cities of Asia Minor, Syria, and Palestine much as Mahayana Buddhism did in northwest India and Hinduism in southern India. All three great religions emerged in social conditions characterized by large clumps of underprivileged persons huddled in cities marked by heterogeneous groups of peoples who had been cast adrift from the moorings of their traditional cultures. Then, as now, poverty, hopelessness, and alienation in an urban setting proved to be a combustible mixture.

Educational forms, which had been hammered out under the conditions of a free polis in florescent days and which had appealed to the upper classes of a privileged Greek estate in the flourishing urban environment of Hellenistic cities, no longer seemed relevant either to the upper classes or to the lower classes. The upper classes from 200 A.D. onward increasingly turned to mystery philosophies; the lower classes to the hope of salvation in popular religion.

As the Hellenistic period wore on, larger areas of land came under cultivation, the slave class became ever more numerous, and conflicts raged between lower and upper classes, between urban and rural factions, and between agrarian and commercial interests. As the number of free citizens became smaller, the concept of leisure appealed more and more to the philosophers of the upper classes. As the number of unfree workers increased, their *manual* labor came to be looked down upon as *menial* labor by the leisure classes whose wealth and status freed them from work with their hands. Thus, the social and economic conditions seemingly began to justify more than ever the distinction Aristotle had made between the *liberal* arts suitable to a *free* man as opposed to the practical arts suitable to an unfree man.

From Polis to Paideia

In the course of the dispersive period the spirit of Greek education changed in a fundamental way as it responded to the political, economic, and religious tenor of Hellenistic times. Greek education was most vital and creative when the democracy of the polis was at its height or still seemed capable of coping with the critical social and intellectual problems of the florescent period. Education became more sterile and narrowly academic when political demoracy was lost or discredited and the purposes for which education had originally been designed could no longer find fruitful outlet in society.

Conversely, education itself proved to be a formative element in helping to bring about this social decline. The changes that the educators themselves made in the schools of the dispersive period served to create habits of mind among Hellenistic gentlemen that led them to prefer an intellectualistic education, which looked to the past, rather than a political or practical education oriented to the crises in the civilization of their day.

Whereas education had been oriented in the florescent period to the political ideal of the polis, it reoriented itself in the dispersive period to the cultural ideal of *paideia*. The fifth century goal of the all-around development of an individual's body, mind, and character as the road to good citizenship began to give way to a greater emphasis upon training of the individual's intellectual and spiritual faculties, principally by means of literary and philosophical studies and a corresponding de-emphasis upon civic, artistic, and physical development. In general, this was a reflection of the decline of the democratic and activist model of the polis and the rise of the humanistic and contemplative model of *paideia*. What had been a broadly political and social setting for education now became an individualistic concern for "cultural development" achieved most effectively through acquaintance with the classical literature of the florescent period. Rather than looking to the solution of the broad-ranging and cultural problems of the polis, education began to look to the literary creations and culture of the past as the prime means of forming the mind and character of the future. This was *paideia*.[3]

This basic transformation of the meaning and purpose of education was reflected in part in a change in the institutional forms of education. The most obvious outward change was the decline and eventual disappearance of the music school and gymnastic training for the boys and the rising to preeminence of the literary school at all levels of education. The institutional framework for education, however, continued to be the polis. During the third and second centuries B.C. education became more systematized than ever before, state or civil control exerted itself more forcefully, and the three distinct levels of education, elementary, secondary, and higher, began to take more definite shape. These were the educational institutions that were carried over into the Roman Empire and passed on to Western Europe.

As less and less attention was given to gymnastics and music for younger boys, the school of the *grammatist* became the common type of elementary school. With the development of the science of grammar, the school of the *grammaticos* came to be recognized as the accepted second-level or secondary school for boys from about thirteen or fourteen to sixteen or eighteen years of age. Noteworthy, too, was the decline of military education and the growing popularity of the various schools of philosophy and rhetoric as the chief forms of higher education.

Even the Ephebic College, which had been set up primarily for military and physical training, took on a more intellectual content around 300 B.C. In the third century B.C., the requirement for military training was reduced to one year and then made voluntary, and in the second century B.C. requirements in philosophical and rhetorical studies were made part of the curriculum along with physical education. The Ephebic College in Athens thus lost much of its democratic and civic quality and became more nearly like a fashionable semi-military academy for well-bred young aristocratic gentlemen. A hundred Greek cities in all parts of the Hellenistic world generally repeated this trend. The gymnasium became the "clubhouse" for the *ephebia*.

To broaden our view now to include the whole Hellenistic world beyond Athens, the evidence seems clear that public support and control of education were on the increase. Many cities chose a supervisor or inspector of schools, either appointed or elected. The *paidonomous* took part in the appointment of teachers and exercised

---

[3]For a brief and illuminating discussion of the concept of *paideia*, see H. I. Marrou, *A History of Education in Antiquity*, Mentor, New York, 1964, pp. 137-147 and pp. 296-308; for an exhaustive and aristocratic treatment, see Werner Jaeger, *Paideia, The Ideals of Greek Culture*, Oxford University Press, New York, 1965, vol. 1, Book 1, chap. 3, pp. 35-56.

general supervision over the curriculum of the schools. Teachers' salaries were some-times paid out of public funds or from the income of private endowments as in Miletus, Rhodes, and Delphi.

Higher education also took definite institutional form during Hellenistic times. Athens remained a great intellectual center. In addition to the Academy, Lyceum, Cynosarges, and the rhetorical schools founded there in the fourth century, two new schools had been founded as the century closed. Epicurus opened his school in a garden, from which the Epicurean school derived its name, the Gardens. Zeno opened his school in the portico of a building, from which his school became known as the Stoa (from the Greek word meaning porch) and his philosophy as Stoicism. Collec-tively, these schools were quite influential in attracting thousands of young men to Athens over the centuries. Some modern historians have applied the term "University of Athens" to this collection of schools, but this is a misnomer, for few of the institutional forms associated with modern universities were present. The univeristy organization as we know it is essentially Western in origin, stemming from thirteenth-century Europe.

In Hellenistic times the other cities that arose to compete with Athens as cosmopolitan intellectual centers not only included Alexandria in Egypt, where the Hellenistic kings established a great library and museum for the carrying on of advanced study and research, but several other cities that became famous for their libraries, museums, and schools of philosophy and rhetoric, notably, Pergamum, Antioch, Rhodes, Ephesus, Smyrna, and Halicarnassus. Most of these institutions were founded and supported by Hellenistic kings, mainly to glorify themselves, but the effect was to stimulate a state interest in higher education which was carried still further by the Roman emperors. Often the presiding officials and teachers were appointed, paid, and controlled by the Hellenistic kings. By the end of the Hellenistic period, schools and higher institutions were so widespread that a quite considerable reading and educated public existed. Hellenistic education laid the groundwork in content and organization for the Roman educational system, which was patterned upon it and which in turn laid the foundations for the educational institutions of the West.

The shift from polis to *paideia* as the lodestar for education was reflected not only in a change of institutional forms but even more in the transformation of the content and spirit of the educational program at various levels of the system. The fifth-century conception of education as primarily the shaping of character for moral and social purposes faded before the conception that the best educated person is the one who has developed his intellectual capacities to the highest point. The free man became identified with the man of culture rather than with the man of action.

In the course of the Hellenistic period the dominant elementary school teacher came to be the *grammatist,* who concentrated on the teaching of reading, writing, and counting. The teacher of music (*citharist*) and the teacher of gymnastics (*paedotribe*) began to play a smaller and smaller part in the elementary education of young Greek boys. The "school" became the *reading* school. An education for literacy replaced an education for well-rounded development. This was a most important change in emphasis, for it was the school of the *grammatist* that set the educational pattern for the Romans and thus was carried to western Europe and eventually wherever the Westerners went. The discipline was strict, even harsh and brutal. There was no nonsense preached about attending to the nature of the child or his development or his needs or interests in learning.

Just as the *grammatist* became the typical teacher of a primary school in Hellenistic times, so did the *grammaticos,* or grammarian, become the typical teacher at the secondary level. Since that time the major secondary schools of the entire Western world—and wherever Westerners carried their educational institutions—have been generically thought of as, and even called, grammar schools. As Marrou points out in his excellent description of the Hellenistic secondary school there were often studies of science as well as of letters, but letters by all odds came to dominate the field.[4] The teaching of grammar comprised four types of study: literature, theory of grammar, morphology, and composition. In literature the pride of place went to Homer's *Iliad,* but attention was also given to other epic poets like Hesiod, to lyric poets (principally Sappho and Pindar), to dramatic poets (above all Euripides and Menander), and in last place to such prose authors as Demosthenes and Isocrates.

The Hellenistic scholars and teachers were not themselves the creators of great classics of Greek literature, but they did create the "classical tradition" in the sense that they drew up lists of the great books and the great authors worthy of being studied. They codified, classified, and canonized the works of literature which they considered to be the masterpieces of the first class or first rank, namely, the "classics." Marrou puts it this way:

> As something essentially *classical,* Hellenistic civilization was the opposite of those revolutionary, innovating cultures that are propelled forward by a great creative drive. It rested essentially upon the peaceful possession of an already acquired capital. . . . A classical culture can be defined as a unified collection of great masterpieces existing as the recognized basis of its scale of values.[5]

Paideia came to be the education whereby the mind and spirit of man were formed by the values to be imbibed from study of the classical culture. In this way he was to become truly civilized. So in its broadest sense—and one might say in the hands of the broadly visioned grammar teacher—grammar included the great Greek literature. In its narrower sense grammar came to mean the formal analysis of language into its basic structural parts, the inflection of words, and composition.

For a time, teachers of mathematical science, especially geometry and arithmetic, were considered to be a part of secondary education. Apparently their concern was not in computation or in the application of mathematics to practical problems. They viewed geometry as an abstract sequence of theorems, *a la* Euclid, not a matter for engineers and surveyors; and arithmetic was the theory of numbers, *a la* Pythagoras, not a matter for accountants or statisticians.

For reasons not easily ascertainable the grammarians were able to eliminate the

[4]See Marrou, op. cit., pp. 223-250.

[5]Ibid., pp. 224-225.

mathematical sciences from the secondary schools. In effect Plato and Aristotle were repudiated in this process. Education was not to be a matter of training the theoretical reason by means of scientific or mathematical study as Plato and Aristotle had proposed, nor was it to become the arena for a training in practical affairs as Isocrates had proposed. Rather, it took on the characteristic Hellenistic form of *paideia,* a forming of the character and mind by literary studies rather than by the sciences or by the social and political studies. As a result, one of the most fundamental transformations in the whole history of education may have taken place.

Who could claim after such a development as this, a development shaped by the countless decisions, deliberate or semideliberate, of generations of teachers who found the literary culture more satisfying than the scientific culture, that education does not have a formative influence on civilization? Who can say but that this trend within Hellenistic education did not help to delay the beginnings of modern science and thus the onset of modern civilization itself for a thousand years?

Mathematics and science, however, did not disappear from the educational scene; they continued to be cultivated at the level of higher education. Their absence from secondary education meant that they did not form part of the core of common culture for successive generations of secondary school students; only those who took up the subjects in a specialized way at a few advanced centers kept the studies alive. The principal means to this was the Museum founded at Alexandria shortly after 300 B.C. and lasting until nearly 400 A.D. Its 700-year existence nearly matched that of the rhetorical and philosophical schools of Athens. Similar institutions were established at a few other key Hellenistic cities in the Aegean and eastern Mediterranean, notably, at Rhodes, Pergamum, Ephesus, Smyrna, and Beirut.

The institution at Alexandria was made up of a collection of research institutes to which scholars came from all over the Hellenistic world to pursue their studies and to which younger men came to work as disciples of the older masters. A definite corporate and community life grew up around common meeting and dining rooms, attractive promenades, and an extraordinary library in the sciences as well as in letters. While teaching was not the primary interest, it is obvious that much learning went on in the association between older and younger men, as well as among colleagues. It was in a sense a forerunner of the modern research institute or think tank where scholars gathered to advance knowledge or to synthesize it. They approached the creative literary works of others in the analytical and critical mood that might be called the first Ph.D. approach to literature.

The range of studies at Alexandria included astronomy, geometry, trigonometry, physics, geography, and medicine as well as language, literature, rhetoric, and philosophy. There was little in the way of training for technology or for the professions, except for medicine; no law; no engineering; no agriculture; no administration; no professional education. The accumulation of knowledge at Alexandria gave it such stature that *Alexandrian* became almost synonomous with *Hellenistic.* The scholars there and elsewhere not only regarded themselves as guardians of the florescent literary tradition, they worked it over so systematically and thoroughly that it was largely through their efforts that the classical tradition was preserved at all. If they had not been so zealous with their grammars, word lists, commentaries, lexicons, and transcriptions, the extant written record would have been immeasurably depleted.

As it is, the florescent period of Greek civilization is one of the best and most fully reported periods of any ancient civilization. By preserving and selecting the best in the tradition, the Alexandrians helped to create that tradition for all its successors. And the origins of the tradition that was trasmitted were not solely Greek. The process of translating the Old Testament from Hebrew into Greek, resulting in the Septuagint (because it entailed seventy scholars), was undertaken at Alexandria beginning in the third century B.C

Aside from the institutions of higher education at Alexandria and the other museums, the mathematical and physical sciences were scarcely to be reckoned with, so predominant were the rhetorical and philosophical schools.[6] And in the rivalry between them, rhetoric was the clear winner in the minds of most Hellenistic Greeks. Rhetoric was the queen of the liberal arts, eloquence the chief goal of the educated man; indeed, it became the very mark of the civilized man in contrast to the barbarian.

The original purpose of rhetoric, of course, had been the highly practical one of improving the effectiveness and the wisdom of the orator as he took part in the democratic political process of the polis. But from the third century B.C. onward the interest became not so much political as cultural. Persuasion gave way to elegance, the policy plea to an oration or declamation. As the rhetorical schools found less and less practical political outlet for their teachings and as young men could no longer find genuine use for their oratorical talents in the absence of a vital democratic society, they began to emphasize the delights of rhetorical style for its own sake. The turning of a nice phrase, a witty saying, an appropriate allusion became more important than convincing the popular assembly or the courts.

Philosophy, too, changed its character. It no longer could pose as the prime study to train the guardians who would be the wise rulers of the state. The kings would now rule by authority of arms, not knowledge. So philosophers turned to becoming the moral guardians of the society, not its political guardians, or they turned to the life of asceticism and retreat from the society altogether. They adopted a distinctive dress and style of life. A few dropped out entirely to signal their protest against the dominant establishment of their day. "The Cynics pushed this break with society to such a point that it became self-contradictory and scandalous: They never washed, never had their hair cut, wrapped themselves in rags and lived on alms like beggars, claiming to be outside ordinary polite society."[7] Setting a pattern of dissent and dissidence, the Cynics wandered from city to city, giving no regular instruction, and often tangling with the police.

In contrast, the four major schools of philosophy in Athens (the Platonists, the Aristotelians, the Stoics, and the Epicureans) maintained a regular corporate and communal life. When Zeno set up his school, he followed generally the tradition of Socrates and Plato. The Stoics preached that, since nature is inherently reasonable, conformity to the natural order of things is living according to the dictates of reason. Nature is rational because it is directed by a single, omnipotent, and rational God.

[6]Ibid., pp. 267-295.

[7]Ibid., p. 282.

They taught that tranquil acceptance of what life brings and calm indifference to painful circumstances are the highest goods in life. The moral life is to find reason in nature and to live resolutely in the light of these findings. Hence, Stoicism came to imply an imperturbable acceptance of the difficulties of life. Through its doctrines and its semireligious nature, Stoicism was a forerunner of Christianity, and indeed helped to shape much of Christian thought and practice.

The Epicurean school operated from a quite different philosophical orientation. Epicurus had been influenced by Democritus, a traveling Thracian philosopher, who had taught that matter was eternal, indestructible, and uncreated, and that the universe was merely infinite space filled with material atoms, operating by chance rather than by a creative intelligence or reason. Thus Epicurus did not believe in a divinely inspired natural world but in a mechanistic universe. Happiness consists in avoiding pain of the body and anguish of soul and in seeking pleasure. The good life is found in achieving freedom from the evils of pain, useless desires, and obstructing fears; the highest good is the pleasure of intellectual pursuits. Epicurus specifically stated that sensual pleasures did not constitute happiness, but nevertheless successive generations insisted upon believing that Epicureanism meant "Eat, drink, and be merry, for tomorrow we die."

Both the Stoics and Epicureans resembled evangelical religious orders; they sought converts to their ideas, and they held fraternal festivals, took care of their sick, and provided burials for their dead. But they did not become churches; they remained primarily schools of thought. They had no creeds or dogma, no priests, no public worship, and no ecclesiastical organization. The major Athenian schools continued to be favorite places to send Roman youth during the height of the Roman Empire. They even outlasted the fall of the Western Roman Empire, finally being closed by Justinian in 529 A.D. because they were pagan. The other Hellenistic centers of learning continued more or less active under the Roman Empire and then received another stimulus from Arab and Jewish scholars between the eighth and thirteenth centuries.

It is difficult to assess the contributions of Hellenistic higher education. It might be put this way: In respect to the accumulation of knowledge through systematic classification and investigation, the Hellenistic scholars took enormous strides. They made knowledge of the Greek classical tradition more easily available to scholars of the civilized world from that time forward. But in respect to the *aim* of education, Hellenistic higher education exalted the intellectual ideal of knowledge for its own sake to the extent that the welfare of the student and of society was largely overlooked. Hellenistic education lost the earlier Greek fervor for creating good citizens in a free and democratic state, and it lost concern for the development of the physical, aesthetic, and moral qualities of the well-rounded individual.

In modern terminology, Hellenistic education embraced the graduate school ideal of research but neglected the undergraduate ideal of teaching for general understanding and social participation. Its dominant concern was the pursuit of organized knowledge for the perfecting of the individual in the image of the literary classics. The culture of *paideia* became above all the culture of literary humanism. In fact, when Varro and Cicero came to translate the Greek term *paideia,* they turned it into the Latin term *humanitas.* It was not the creative education of the democratic polis in its florescent period that the Romans borrowed; it was the literary education of the Hellenistic *paideia* that they finally came to emulate.

B.   LATINIZING EDUCATION IN THE WEST (300 B.C.-500 A.D.)

In the long view of the history of education, the Roman experience may well be viewed as a major phase of the dispersive period of Greek education in the course of which Hellenism and Latinism were amalgamated to form the Graeco-Roman education which had a recognizable life in Europe until around 500 A.D. As Alexander's empire provided the political framework within which the civilized peoples of the Middle East were Hellenized, so did the Roman Empire act as an instrument whereby the diverse folk peoples of Western and Southern Europe were both Hellenized and Latinized. The Goths were quick to accept the Graeco-Roman civilization; the Franks considerably slower, but the Germanic-Roman fusion was well on its way by the end of the sixth century A.D.

The massive scope of this Graeco-Roman education and its importance for the later development of Western civilization warrant special attention to Roman education. But it can well be looked at in two perspectives. One perspective sees it as an integral part of the larger history of Hellenic civilization which constituted, along with that of the Middle East, India, and China, one of the four ancient civilizations of the Afro-Eurasian ecumene. In this larger sense Roman education was a phase of the dispersive period of Hellenic education. (See Figure 3.2, page 81.)

The other and shorter perspective views Roman education as having an identity of its own which paralleled Roman political and institutional life and which acted as a link between the decaying Hellenic civilization and the rising civilization of the West. As such, it displayed its own curve of educational development which follows the familiar formative-florescent-dispersive pattern. Its formative period was generally that of the Roman Republic, roughly from the fifth to the first centuries B.C. During this time the Hellenistic phase of Greek education led to the spread of organized schools in Rome. The florescent period extended from the first century B.C. to the end of the second century A.D., i.e., from the end of the Republic through the early centuries of the regnant Empire. During this time the characteristic institutions of Roman education were fully developed. The dispersive period included not only the later centuries of the declining Empire from the third through the fifth centuries A.D., but also the early centuries of the Middle Ages in Europe (500 A.D. - 1000 A.D.). As the Empire disintegrated so did Roman education disintegrate. But a thin lifeline of Roman educational thought and practice continued to exist and managed to disseminate a modicum of Latin learning through much of the early medieval period, sometimes known as the prodromal or gestatory period of Western civilization.

Thus the larger dispersive period of Greek education not only includes its initial and continuing impact upon Rome, but also the narrower dispersive period of Roman education itself which furnished the lessons which the peoples of Western Europe learned as they prepared to develop their own distinctive form of civilization. These common Latin lessons learned by diverse peoples speaking many different languages proved to be exceedingly useful in spreading a common culture in Europe at a time when the cosmopolitan culture of the Middle East was losing its Hellenistic veneer and beginning to break apart. The latter-day Roman schools Latinized the West (taught it to speak Latin) as the earlier Greek schools Hellenized the East.

The Formative Period of Roman Education Under the Republic (Fifth Century B.C.-First Century B.C.)

The prehistory of the Italian peninsula is clouded with the uncertainties arising from successive migrations from Europe and Asia Minor. By the eighth century B.C. the Etruscans dominated the west coast of Italy above the Tiber River, the Latins dominated the central portion of the west coast, and other Italian tribes elsewhere. The culture of the Latins, presumably much like that of other agricultual folk societies, came to focus upon the city of Rome, whose legendary founding is usually put at 753 B.C. Between the eighth and sixth centuries B.C. the rural Latin tribal life was transformed by kings and aristocratic families into political institutions similar to those of the early Greek city-states. The rural aristocracy, however, was deeply attached to the land and thus much different from the warrior aristocrats of the Greek heroic age. The virtues of hard work, loyalty to the community, and piety were to be honored more than the noble deed or individual competition of arms or sports.

From Virtus to Paideia   Before 500 B.C., Roman education, like that of all peasant folk societies, was directed by the family and guided by the aim to induct the children into the customs of the group in order to preserve its folkways. The Romans summed it up as *virtus.* Ideals of high moral character, integrity, courage, and prudence were inculcated as the children imitated their parents going about the ordinary business of living. The general aim of family education was to instill in the boy reverence for the gods, piety towards his parents, respect for the laws, and the skills of war and peacetime occupation.

The legendary founding of the Roman Republic is usually given as 509 B.C., the time when the Romans threw off the rule of the Etruscans and at the same time did away with their kings. The aristocratic patricians continued to be the dominant political power in Rome during the fifth and fourth centuries B.C., expressing their power through the Senate. The rural attachment of the aristocratic class possibly delayed for a long time the urbanizing and Hellenizing trends which the Etruscans had earlier and more quickly adopted. Despite their contact with the Greek colonial cities in Italy during the fifth and fourth centuries B.C., the Romans were more deeply affected by the Greek culture of the later Hellenistic dispersion than the contemporary florescence on the Greek mainland.

It is possible that formal schools may have existed in Rome as early as 500 B.C., but if so, they did not play a very large part in comparison with the family type of education provided by the well-to-do. The elementary school in Rome, known as the *ludus* (originally meaning "an activity that has no practical end"), was presided over by the *ludi magister,* or *litterator,* who was the Latin equivalent of the *grammatist* in the Greek schools of the East.

Children from the ages of seven to eleven or twelve, often girls as well as boys, were taught to read and write Latin and to count on their fingers, with pebbles, or with an abacus. In comparison with Greek schools of the time, instruction in music and gymnastics seems to have been lacking in Roman schools. These schools were private and voluntary, with little supervision by the state. The pedagogue who took the boys to school and acted as guardian was prominent in Roman education as well as in Greek. He sometimes even acted as tutor or teacher, for in an upper-class household he was often a Greek slave who was quite equal to such a role. Inasmuch as elementary education was a private affair, it is clear that Roman education was designed principally for the upper classes who could afford to buy their children an education.

Marrou believes that the earliest Roman elementary schools date as far back as the seventh or sixth century B.C. to the Etruscan period of Rome antedating the Republic. The Etruscans had a written language related to Greek and thus presumably had literary schools to teach the language as early as 600 B.C. Since the Latins took their alphabet from the Etruscans, they may have adopted their primary school education too.[8]

By the fifth century B.C. class distinctions in Rome were fairly well established. At the top were the patricians who were principally the large landowners, traders, and stock raisers. Then came the plebs, or plebeian classes, composed of the free persons who owned their own small plots of land. Finally, there were the slaves, who had no political or economic rights. The most significant development in the fourth century B.C. was the growth of the *free* plebs made up of new urbanites—shopkeepers, tradesmen, and skilled workers. Guilds, or associations of workmen (*collegia*), were formed to establish standards of workmanship and to give certain privileges to the guild members. The political power of the plebs, channeled through the popular Assembly and the citizen army, grew at the expense of the Senate.

The boy of a patrician family during the republic was taught to ride, box, swim, and use the spear. Girls were taught by their mothers the details of managing a home and were trained in the conduct becoming to a Roman woman who held a relatively high position in Roman homes and society. At the age of sixteen or eighteen the Roman youth put on the dress of a citizen and accompanied his father to the Forum and to the public religious ceremonies. He thus learned the ideals and duties of a citizen, set forth not as theoretical abstractions but as matters of everyday practice and action. This type of education applied only to the upper-class families associated with the senatorial class. Children of the plebs and slaves received only enough instruction to enable them to fulfill whatever economic, religious, and military duties might be required of them. The failure to provide widespread educational opportunity for the plebeian during the heyday of Rome's economic and political power may have been one of the most costly mistakes the Romans ever made.

The consequences began to show up during the second century B.C. when the class of free plebs declined rapidly from casualties of the Punic and eastern wars. Returning veterans could not keep their lands in cultivation. As they fell into debt or lost their lands, they stayed on as tenants or hired hands. Or they migrated to the cities, swelling the urban classes of unemployed, alienated, and uneducated plebeians.

[8]Ibid., pp. 333-334.

This meant that the chances for lasting political democracy were reduced and the prospects of the Republic dimmed.

The weaknesses at home, however, were overshadowed as the military power of Rome was rapidly being extended abroad. By 275 B.C. Rome had united all Italy under its control. Then, by 200 B.C. the Punic Wars with Carthage gave Rome control of Sicily, Corsica, Sardinia, and Spain. Turning their attention to the East, the Roman legions warred against the Hellenistic kingdoms until Macedonia, Greece, Asia Minor, the Levant, Egypt, and the entire Mediterranean world came under their sway by 30 B.C. Until the middle of the second century B.C. Rome had been on the fringes of world affairs and international relations. From then on, Rome dominated the Western world for several centuries.

At home, the second and first centuries B.C. saw a long-continuing struggle between factions which professed to represent the common people and those which represented the Senate. On the whole, the Senate emerged victorious over the Assembly in the series of civil wars that lasted intermittently for a century, until such time as Octavian emerged victorious over both. When he became Emperor Augustus in 27 B.C. much of the Middle East and most of Europe came under his rule. The ideal of a city-state republic had given way to the grandeur of Afro-Eurasian Empire.

As Rome pushed ever outward during the third, second, and first centuries B.C., Roman intellectual life received tremendous stimulus from the introduction of Hellenistic thought, literature, philosophy, science, and religion. Beginning as a result of the very practical need to meet Greek traders on even terms, the desire to learn the Greek language grew apace, until at length Greek scholars and teachers began to pour into Rome. Of course, there was opposition to the Greek influence by such men as Cato the Elder, who saw nothing but evil for sturdy Rome in effete Greek culture; but even he capitulated finally. In general, most Roman intellectuals of the later Republic and early Empire were nourished on Greek thought.

In the first century B.C. a distinctive Latin literature expressing the national spirit of Rome ushered in what is usually called the golden age of Latin thought. In the days of Cicero, Lucretius, Catullus, Vergil, Horace, and Ovid, Latin literature for the first time rivaled in style and form the classical literature of Greece, and the purely imitative phase of Latin literature had passed. With regard to intellectual patterns, however, most of Latin thought was fundamentally Greek in origin and content.

In fact, R. R. Bolgar makes the point that Latin literature basically looked to the past and never dealt with the reality of the times in which it was written. "Thus, Roman literature started at the point which Greek literature reached only with the Hellenistic Age. Traditional in spirit and imitative in technique, it was never a direct expression of contemporary experience. Its language was from the first an artistic confection ordered by scholarship and remote from ordinary speech."[9]

Roman elementary schools, making paramount the aim of literacy in Latin, paid little attention to the florescent Greek ideal of a well-rounded individual, versed in music and physically well developed. Roman elementary schooling simply stressed the

[9]R. R. Bolgar, *The Classical Heritage and Its Beneficiaries from the Carolingian Age to the End of the Renaissance,* Harper Torchbooks, New York, 1964, p. 22.

ability to read and to write and to count. Just why the Roman accent should have been put upon the three R's to the exclusion of music and gymnastics is not clear, but some reasons may be advanced. The fact that the Latin language was just taking literary form during the early Republican period made it natural that the new language should be stressed in the elementary schools for patriotic reasons. Another factor may be that when Rome did develop a full-fledged interest in Greek education in the third and second centuries B.C., the Hellenistic schools of Greece and of the Middle East had already begun to drop their attention to music and gymnastics and to stress the purely literary even at the lowest levels of education. It has further been claimed that the hard-working Romans were cold to the values of music and physical development in much the same way that American pioneers found little time for such accomplishments when a wilderness continent was to be won by much hard physical labor. The moralistic rural Roman parents could not indulge athletic sports in the nude in the Greek manner.

In any case, the lot of the elementary pupil in Roman schools was apparently much like that in Hellenistic elementary schools. Most of the extant references attest to strenuous discipline and corporal punishment as integral parts of the learning process. Learning to read was a matter of memorizing the letters of the Latin alphabet, constructing syllables, learning the meanings of individual words, and studying sentence structure. Writing was a matter of copying down the dictated statements of the teacher into copybooks or on wax tablets. Counting, whether on fingers, on the abacus, or with bags of pebbles, was an important part of the three R's; arithmetic was probably emphasized because of the necessity of keeping business and houshold accounts in the growing complexities of a commercial and mercantile society. Memorizing, drill, and discipline seem to have been the major features of the Roman educational methods.

When the secondary school was first developed in Rome sometime in the third century B.C., it was imported from Hellenistic Greece and was thoroughly Greek in character. Taking as its model the *paideia* of the times, it was basically a grammer school, taught, as in Greece, by a teacher known as a *grammaticus*. The earliest Greek teacher was Livius Adronicus, brought as a slave to Rome after Tarentum had been conquered in 272 B.C. Many other Greeks poured into Rome in the following two centuries to act as teachers. They were an integral part of the general Hellenizing of the West brought about by Roman economic, political, and cultural contact with Greece. In the school of the *grammaticus*, boys from the age of eleven or twelve to fifteen or sixteen were taught Greek grammar and literature, again with little or no attention to music or gymnastics, for Rome was copying the intellectualistic pattern of education that characterized the Hellenistic East. The *grammaticus* either conducted a private school or he acted as family tutor supported by fees or by a patron; for the most part during Republican times he was not controlled or supervised by the state.

Responding, however, to the growing desire to make Latin the national language of Republican Rome, a second type of secondary school also appeared in the third century B.C., this time a grammar school for teaching Latin. In fact, Marrou points out that the very creation of Latin poetry was caused by the demand to have something for a Latin secondary school to teach that would be of comparable standard to the

Greek poets taught in the Greek secondary schools. "Latin poetry came into existence so that teachers should have something to argue about, probably as a result of national pride, for Rome would not have gone on being satisfied for long with an education that was given solely in Greek."[10] Livius Andronicus translated the *Odyssey* into Latin and composed poetic works in Latin at the request of the Roman Senate to help develop patriotism during the Second Punic War. Shortly thereafter Ennius was creating instant classics to be studied in the schools, an interesting footnote on how the schools shape a culture.

By the end of the Republican period the growth of a genuinely creative Latin literature made it possible for the Latin grammar school to hold up its head alongside the Greek grammar school. For many generations Rome had both kinds of grammar schools, one taught in Greek and one in Latin, the favored boy perhaps attending both in order to achieve the best all-around education. These schools became the means by which the patrician boy was prepared for a life of activity suitable to his class in Republican Rome. They were the roads to attainment and preferment in the realm of public office, whether in the Senate or in the army.

An interesting sidelight on the formative period of Roman education is the fact that the first secondary schools in Rome were foreign-language schools. The native Latin had a long struggle before it could pretend to provide as valuable an educational experience for Latin youth as was claimed for Greek. Then later the tables were turned. From imperial Roman times to the present nearly every European people has gone through the experience in which their vernacular had to struggle against Latin for pride of place in secondary education. And the idea spread around the world: the first secondary schools among English-speaking peoples in the American colonies were Latin grammar schools. The belief that someone else's language is better than one's own for educative purposes has had a long tradition. It is especially characteristic of a formative period of education. Once a people arrives at the florescent stage, they feel at home with their own language; in fact they begin to feel that they should disseminate it to others.

In its best days, the school of the *grammaticus* in Rome was a liberating and effective instrument of education, conceiving of grammar so broadly that it included study of the great literature of Greece and Rome. Eventually, the educated Roman knew his Vergil as well as the educated Greek knew his Homer. Under farseeing teachers the study of literature could include much of what we today would call history, ethics, and the social studies as well as poetry, grammar, composition, and literary criticism. More often, however, it became a routine study of words, phonetics, conjugations and declensions, paraphrasing, memorizing, repetition, dictation of sentences, and explanation of allusions.

For the very best education during Republican times it was considered desirable for an upper-class Roman youth of age sixteen or so to supplement his secondary grammar schooling with three or four years of study at the rhetorical or philosophical schools in Athens or at other Hellenistic centers of the East. Especially did the Romans appreciate the values of training in Greek rhetoric. Greek was useful as the

[10]Marrou, op. cit., p. 336.

international language of diplomacy, and rhetoric was useful to the politician at home in the Senate or Assembly and to the army officer in haranguing his men. Most Romans found far less value in the Greek philosophical schools, no counterparts of which were ever founded in Rome that could rival the Athenian schools of philosophy.

The earliest Latin orators who had a rhetorical education in Greek apparently arrived on the scene in Rome in the latter part of the third century B.C. Ennius came to Rome from Sardinia in 204 B.C. It is not wholly clear when Greek language rhetorical schools were first established in Rome, but it is clear that Senate decrees in the middle of the second century B.C. were intended to expel Greek philosophers and rhetoricians as inimical to Roman traditions of morality. Crates had come to Rome from Pergamum in 168 B.C., and three noted Greek philosophers came as ambassadors from Athens in 155 B.C. Cato could rage about these invasions, but his efforts to prevent the inroads of Hellenism were a losing battle as the admiration for Greek culture grew to enormous proportions in the second and first centuries B.C. In fact the victory of Greek culture among Roman aristocrats was so complete that when a rhetorical school in Latin was opened in 93 B.C. by Plotius Gallus, a partisan of the populist leader Marius, it was soon closed by the patricians on the grounds that it was too progressive in its efforts to deal with the controversial social issues of the day. Besides, the longer, more demanding, and more expensive course of Greek oratorical training would make it more difficult for other upstart plebeians to acquire and thus grow powerful in the forum or in the army.

Nevertheless, Latin rhetorical schools came on strong from the time of Cicero and the beginning of the Empire, soon rivaling the rhetoric taught in Greek. In fact, rhetoric dominated Roman higher education to the extent that neither Greek philosophy nor Greek science was ever pursued wholeheartedly by Romans at home. They did, however, avidly adopt Greek medicine and even continued to teach it in Greek until the fourth or fifth century A.D., long after rhetoric and the other liberal arts had become wholly Latinized.

Florescence Under the Early Empire
(First Century A.D.-Second Century A.D.)

During the first and second centuries A.D. the Roman Empire was at its peak. Commerce and trade prospered under relatively peaceful conditions, and the magnificent systems of roads vied with the seas as arteries of trade. Urban life became common, as cities founded throughout the empire developed in imitation of the glory of Rome itself. The provincial cities came to have a large measure of local autonomy and legal rights under the authority of the central government at Rome, which kept control of the armies, finances and taxes through central agents and secret police. The immediate successors of Augustus ruled merely because they were related to Augustus, but every now and then strong and capable emperors ruled with a sense of their obligation to the people. Such were Vespasian, Trajan, Hadrian, Antoninus Pius, and Marcus Aurelius. It is probably no accident that these were the emperors who were most interested in fostering education in various ways.

During the early Empire the basic pattern of schools did not change radically from that of the Republic. The major characteristic throughout the period was the presence of a bilingual system of education which was intended to insure that a well-educated Roman knew both Greek and Latin well. The outstanding institutional developments were in matters of emphasis and support. The chief theoretical contributions were in the form of systematic statements of educational policy, principally by Cicero and Quintilian, which were to influence succeeding centuries even more than their own day. They became the main channels whereby the rhetorical education of florescent Greece and the literary tradition of Hellenistic Greece flowed into western Europe.

Throughout the Empire the school of the *litterator* remained the common elementary school, designed principally to teach reading in Latin. Obviously the‘ quality of the teaching varied enormously from teacher to teacher and from place to place, but the long-term failure of Rome to provide effective and widespread elementary education must have been a contributing cause of the decline of the Empire. In describing the primary schools of the first and second centuries A.D., Carcopino has this gloomy judgment to make, sounding startlingly like twentieth century critics of American schools:

> On the whole we are compelled to admit that at the most glorious period of the empire the schools entirely failed to fulfill the duties which we expect of our schools today. They undermined instead of strengthened the children's morals; they mishandled the children's bodies instead of developing them; and if they succeeded in furnishing their minds with a certain amount of information, they were not calculated to perform any loftier or nobler task. The pupils left school with the heavy luggage of a few practical and commonplace notions laboriously acquired and of so little value that in the fourth century Vegetius could not take for granted that new recruits for the army would be literate enough to keep the books of their corps. Instead of happy memories, serious and fruitful ideas, any sort of intellectual curiosity vital to later life, school children carried away the gloomy recollection of years wasted in senseless, stumbling repetitions punctuated by savage punishments. Popular education then in Rome was a failure. . . .[11]

The schools of the Greek and the Latin *grammaticus* continued to be the principal secondary schools under the early empire. Eventually, the separate Greek grammar school virtually disappeared from the West although Carcopino argues that the "Roman grammarians never ceased to subordinate the study of Latin literature to that of Greek literature—much in the same way as under the *ancien régime* in France the study of French was always subsidiary to Latin."[12] Since the Latin grammar school had never been widely established in the East outside Constantinople, the Empire increasingly was divided into the Latin-speaking West and the Greek-speaking East from the third century on. Political unity of the Empire did not long survive linguistic divisiveness.

[11] Jerome Carcopino, *Daily Life in Ancient Rome; the People and the City at the Height of the Empire*, Henry T. Rowell (ed.), Yale University Press, New Haven, 1940, pp. 106-107.
[12] Ibid., p. 111.

The best grammar schools in the early Empire of the West included in their curriculum the whole round of liberal arts imported from Greece. But as time passed they dropped this wide range of studies and narrowed down to a preparatory course for later study of rhetoric. Indeed, in the hands of competent teachers the opportunity to compare Latin and Greek could have had great value in teaching and learning grammar. Some historians believe that after Cicero the knowledge of Greek began to fall away in both quantity and quality. As the essence of Greek culture began to be available in accomplished Latin poetry and prose, typified by Cicero himself and by Vergil, why study the Greek too? But Carcopino argues that the grammar schools "remained bilingual till the end of the empire."[13] Whatever may be the truth here, it is generally agreed that the secondary schools came to be constricted to technical grammar and were content to repeat the rules of the professional grammarians, to emphasize quotations and selections from the great authors instead of the literary works themselves, and to hand down allegorical and intellectualized digests of the liberal arts.

The most important of the higher schools in Imperial Rome were the rhetorical schools established for the wellborn Roman youth who was destined for a career in politics and public service. Interestingly enough, the rhetorical schools emphasizing Latin were not very common until after the Republic had died and the real professional outlet for the schools had largely vanished. Few were actually patterned on the ideals of Cicero as promulgated by Quintilian in the first century A.D. In their view the rhetorical school should be the culmination of training for the all-around development of the public orator or statesman. But by the time the rhetorical schools were well established the opportunity for guiding the destinies of the state through public oratory had practically disappeared with the passing of the Republic; their usefulness had virtually been outlived before they began to function.

In the hands of Quintilian the rhetorical school offered much more than simply the study and practice of rhetoric. He designed its course of study to include all the major fields of knowledge as a means of developing a person of broad understanding and good practical judgment. As Donald Clark puts it, "training in rhetoric can and does contribute to civilizing young men."[14] Under lackluster rhetoricians, unfortunately the majority who did not listen to Isocrates or Cicero or Quintilian, the study of rhetoric became an end in itself, living in the dead past and out of touch with contemporary currents of life. The study of oratory, when there was no longer an outlet for it in practical life, turned its attention from subject matter to correct and elegant expression. Still more often the schools patterned their procedures after the textbook themes, the effects of which were far from elegant, as described by Bolgar:

> Their schematic analyses of style and their interminable lists of figures of speech and forms of argument, considered without any reference to their

---

[13] Ibid., p. 109.

[14] Donald Lemen Clark *Rhetoric in Greco-Roman Education,* Columbia University Press, New York, 1957, p. 264.

context, were typical products of the first century B.C. and reflected the aridity and purely technical preoccupations which characterised the rhetorical schools of the period.[15]

In addition to the rhetorical schools, several other types of institutions provided opportunity for advanced education in Rome. The Athenaeum and various technical institutes and libraries became centers of medicine, architecture, engineering, and law. In the East the Athenian schools of philosophy maintained themselves over the centuries, but they were never imported to Rome. A certain proportion of Roman youth continued to attend the Athenian schools of philosophy and rhetoric as well as the Hellenistic institutions at Alexandria, Pergamum, Antioch, and Rhodes where scholars and students could gather to explore a wide range of studies, including law, medicine, architecture, engineering, mathematics, language, literature, and religion. In these institutions, however, the creative character of education was diminishing in ways that have already been described.

The most important administrative change in imperial schools was the increasing patronage and support given to teachers by several of the emperors and by some municipal authorities. In this way, the civil government came to play a larger role in the organization of Roman schools. Imperial patronage was more or less haphazard, depending upon the personal interests of individual emperors in promoting learning or upon their desire to gain support from certain sections of the population. Even before imperial days, Julius Caesar had given the rights of citizenship to certain foreign teachers and physicians who had come to Rome. Augustus also gave such favors when he allowed foreign teachers and physicians to remain in Rome when all other foreigners were being banished because of widespread famine.

In the first century A.D., the Emperor Vespasian established considerable library facilities in Rome and endowed chairs of rhetoric in Greek and Latin, paying the rhetoricians' salaries out of the public treasury. He also granted extensive exemptions from certain civic obligations to grammarians, rhetoricians, physicians, and philosophers, removing the burdens of taxes, service in the army, and the obligation to quarter soldiers. How effective or how widespread were these attempts to broaden the base of educational opportunity is not known, but the surface could only have been scratched under the best of conditions. Nevertheless, the eagerness for education seems to have been very widespread in this period, and thousands of schools in the East and the West taught children to read Greek or Latin or both.

In the second century A.D. even greater advances were made in extending schools at all levels throughout the Empire. Most of this activity was undertaken by the cities and municipal authorities, especially in the East, with occasional help and stimulation by the emperors when financial depressions affected the towns. Schools, however, were largely confined to the urban centers and restricted to children of the upper social classes.

Antoninus Pius laid upon the cities the obligation of paying the salaries of

---

[15]Bolgar, op. cit., p. 37.

teachers and of giving them exemptions; this had the effect of stimulating the already established custom of municipal support of education. Capital cities had to support up to ten physicians, five rhetoricians, and five grammarians; small cities, five physicians, three rhetoricians, and three grammarians; and others in proportion to their size. In general, the cities were to pay these salaries at public expense, and if the cities could not do so, the emperor to pay the salaries from the imperial treasury. In the fifth century A.D. Theodosius II authorized a state university in Constantinople consisting of public professors of grammar, rhetoric, philosophy, and law. The allocation was as follows: twenty grammarians (ten in Greek and ten in Latin), eight *rhetors* (five in Greek and three in Latin), two in law, and one in philosophy. This institution was perhaps the high point of interest in and support of higher education by Roman emperors.

Just as Roman civilization came to be largely aristocratic in character, so was Roman education confined in large measure to the privileged and wealthy classes. In the days of the Republic when the basis of economic and political life was fairly broad, an elementary education in schools was a common expectation for large numbers of people; but as the economic and political life became more restricted in the Empire, education was virtually limited to the aristocratic senatorial and knightly classes. Even though some remarkable advances were made in respect to the public support of teachers and a few gestures were made toward scholarships for the poor, there was little chance that the children of the lower classes could take advantage of such schooling. In general, the opportunity to rise from the lower classes was a fairly small one and became smaller and smaller as serfdom and despotism increased after the third century A.D.

From Paideia to Humanitas During the waning days of the Republic the chief formulation of the role of education in human affairs was made by Cicero, who represents the culmination of Roman accomplishments in assimilating the culture and educational theory of florescent Hellenism. Following the lead of Isocrates, Cicero centered his interest on the orator as the highest type of public figure, maintaining that the good orator must have a broad general education in the whole range of liberal arts in order to make sound decisions and to guide others in arriving at wise practical judgements. Knowledge was not to be sought simply for its own sake but as a practical guide to action in public and private life. The more humane letters were viewed not as a frosting of culture but as a means of putting intelligence to work at the job of solving the problems of this world. In his book entitled *De Oratore* Cicero outlined his conception of the art of rhetoric, indicating the kind of education he felt appropriate for the development of the public leader. Anything short of a broad liberal education in the studies proper to man (*humanitas*) would leave the orator narrow, mean, and warped in his judgments.

A word may be useful here in sorting out the terms that helped to define the attitudes of Romans toward education as they assimilated Hellenistic ideas. We have seen how *paideia* came to be used by the Greeks to mean the cultivation of all the individual's powers to their highest perfection through literature. By Hellenistic times this had come to center upon the intellectual powers above all else. Although Latin writers often used the term *humanitas* as virtually equivalent to *paideia* Cicero gave it a moral and emotional tone evocative of humane attitudes towards others, a tone that went well beyond the purely intellectual development of individuals. *Humanitas* included much more than school instruction, for which Romans used the term *institutio*; and it was more than the moral training of family life for which they used the term *educatio.*

In the characteristic manner of many accomplished scholars Cicero did not bother to discuss the principles of elementary education in his *De Oratore.* He left *educatio* to the fathers of families, and he did not direct particular attention to ordinary school instruction, or *institutio.* With respect to the latter Cicero simply described the customary round of studies being offered in the contemporary secondary schools of Rome. He called these the *artes liberales*; the Greeks had used the term *enkuklios paideia* (the education in common or general use). Cicero identified these as literature (grammar), rhetoric, philosophy (dialectics), mathematics (arithmetic), geometry, astronomy, and music. The basic ingredients of what eventually came to be known as the seven liberal arts of medieval times are here present.

What Cicero was really interested in was the range of advanced studies necessary for the formation of the *doctus orator* (the cultivated orator); and he was particularly critical of the rhetorical schools of his day because of their narrow emphasis upon the tricks of the rhetorical trade. In contrast, Cicero argued that the orator or statesman must receive the broad and cultivated education to be obtained through the *politior humanitas* (the more polished humanities). This refinement of human excellence, good taste, good breeding, and intellectual discipline is to be achieved by "knowledge of all the sciences and all the great problems of life."[16] Cicero's list of such studies is not too explicit, but he clearly included not only rhetoric and literature in their fullest senses, but also he laid great stress on history, on law or jurisprudence, and on philosophy. These seem to gain his highest priority, but he also mentions psychology, ethics, politics, military and naval science, medicine, and such sciences as geography and astronomy.

The important thing here is Cicero's concern for what we would call the "social sciences" and their relation to "all the great problems of life." This was a trend in his thinking that recalls the thought of Isocrates, although Cicero attributed his ideas to the influence of the philsophers of the New Academy in Athens. Cicero constantly stressed that the aim of the *"politior humanitas"* was not simply for intellectual or spiritual discipline but for the art of leadership in public affairs. Ironically, Cicero's stress on the role of the orator as public administrator or political leader came too late for it to be influential in preserving the Republic. So it was his fate to be remembered more for his polished style of writing than for his call to serve the public weal. His phrase, the *doctus orator,* cultivated by the more polite humanities, overshadowed the other term he used, *politicos philosophos,* to define his ideal. His "cultivated orator" came more to be emulated than his "philosophic statesman." The florescent Greek ideal of the public citizen gave way to the Hellenistic ideal of the public lecturer.

[16] Aubrey Gwynn, *Roman Education from Cicero to Quintilian,* Teachers College Press, New York, 1966, p. 101.

Education became more polite than political. A civilized man was one who was conversant with the knowledge of past civilizations, not educated to cope with the deepest crises of his own civilization.

In practice, the Romans did not listen to Cicero's plea for a broad humane education dedicated to public life. They preferred the technical study of rhetoric—or at least the teachers of rhetoric did—as a means of training for law or bureaucratic administration. They followed not his preachments in the *De Oratore*, but rather they made a textbook out of the techniques he set forth in his *De Inventione*, written as schoolboy notes to aid his own study of rhetoric as a youth.

In early imperial times the most important treatise on education was written by Quintilian who followed in the footsteps of Isocrates and Cicero. In the preface to his *Institutio Oratoria (The Schooling of the Orator)* Quintilian gave a general picture of the character of the orator who must be not merely an accomplished speaker but a well-rounded man of affairs. The orator's role of leadership in the formulation of public policy should be based upon a broad background of knowledge and sound character. The line of argument from Isocrates through Cicero to Quintilian is clear and distinct: the goal of education for the orator is the formation of a governing class whose role as citizens and managers of public affairs is based upon the finely tuned practical judgments required for the executive, legislative, and judicial functions of a complex civilization. All education from the elementary school forward must therefore be policy-oriented as well as intellectually-oriented.[17]

In Book I of the *Institutio* Quintilian described the kind of education that should be given to children prior to the study of rhetoric itself; in this respect his treatise put considerable emphasis upon the educational method and procedures appropriate to the elementary school child. Although he felt somewhat apologetic about dealing with the education of small children, Quintilian stoutly maintained its importance in the total development of the man of public affairs. Quintilian stressed the fact that boys differ in their individual capacities and that teachers should take account of these individual differences.

The good teacher will ascertain the disposition and abilities of his pupils so as to adapt his methods to each individual. Play, games, and amusements should be used for relaxation and increased efficiency as well as to stimulate interest through competition and rewards, rather than through corporal punishment. Quintilian believed that instruction in reading and writing can be given to very young children, especially if it can be made pleasurable. In learning to read, the Roman child should start with Greek first, on the theory that he would learn his native Latin anyway; since Greek was the linguistic foundation for Latin, it was only natural to learn Greek first. Quintilian set a pattern in this respect that generations of educators in following centuries would use to support their arguments for study of a foreign language as the best way to learn one's own language.

Quintilian insisted that "public" education in the school of the *litterator* was much to be preferred to private education at home with a tutor. He stressed the values

---

[17] Marcus Fabius Quintilian, *Institutio Oratoria*, H. H. Butler (trans.), Harvard University Press, Cambridge, Mass., 1921, vol 1, pp. 9-11, et passim.

of the group life that comes when boys learn together in classes; the emulation, friendships, and incitements to success thus experienced by peers in school are superior to the advantages of private teaching at home. The orator will engage in public life as an adult; he should learn how to conduct himself in groups early in life. Beyond the elementary instruction just described, the boys should have a complete grammar school training which should lay great emphasis upon grammar, composition, correct speech, and extensive reading of all kinds of authors, including the tragic, comic, and lyric poets. In addition, Quintilian mentioned music to help train the voice, mathematics and logic for the methods of proof, training in elocution, and a certain amount of framatics and gymnastics to promote the graceful use of the body and effective use of gestures.

Quintilian then devoted Books II-XII of the *Institutio* to the advanced training of the orator in the ideal rhetorical school. He prescribed in minute detail a thorough study of written composition and oral declamation, reading of the prose authors, and the formal theory and practice of rhetoric, including the various types of oratorical style, delivery, figures of speech, allusions, and analogies. Reading in law, jurisprudence, and philosophy was also deemed desirable along with the writing of themes that were to be as true to life as possible, but his enthusiasm for Cicero's social sciences was never so great as for grammar and literature.

Like Isocrates, Quintilian was distrustful of the philosophers. He was never so enamored of Greek philosophy as was Cicero, because he felt philosophy neglected the study of important everyday concerns for flights into the nonpractical world of spiritual affairs. The sweep of political, economic, and religious events in the empire was, however, against Quintilian. His voice was less and less heeded in dispersive Rome, but his views on education are important not only for what they reveal concerning the highest ideal of florescent Roman education but also because, when the *Institutio* was rediscovered during the Renaissance, it became virtually the educational bible for generations of humanist educators. Particularly influential was his Book X in which he set forth his list of great books of the Graeco-Roman world. Either Quintilian's judgment was pretty good, or he persuaded posterity to agree with him.

No other writer of the imperial period approached Qunitilian in the scope or detail of his proposals for education, but the trend after his time was to view rhetoric less as a practical or administrative art designed to be a guide to action than a decorative art to be enjoyed. Quintilian had defined three types of rhetoric. He obviously favored the deliberative type leading to public decision and the forensic or debating type involved in the adjudication of court cases, but successive ages settled for the panegyric type, devoted to laudatory or celebrational occasions.

Dispersion and Imitation under the Later Empire
(Third Century A.D.-Sixth Century A.D.)

From the third century on, the weaknesses of the Roman Empire became ever more evident. After Marcus Aurelius, the army began to play the major role in raising and overthrowing emperors; intrigue and counterintrigue on the part of the army and of the Senate produced a chaotic political situation. The autonomy of local governments vitually disappeared as the emperors took more and more power into their own hands. The Senate had little political outlet for its energies, and the aristocracy became a pampered leisure class depending for preferment upon the fancy of the emperor. If a purely literary education could do them little good, at least it could do little harm.

In the fourth century the authority of the Empire was increasingly divided between the eastern and the western parts. Diocletian began this process, which became even more pronounced under Constantine, who founded Constantinople on the site of ancient Byzantium in 330 B.C. as the capital of the Empire. From that time on, virtually two empires existed, one with a capital and senate at Rome and the other with a capital and senate at Constantinople, although for many years many emperors tried to keep alive the legal fiction on one unified empire. The theory became even more fictional as the Germanic tribes invaded its provinces during the fourth, fifth, and sixth centuries.

In the sixth century, Justinian, as emperor of the Eastern Empire, made considerable gains in reasserting his rule to the West by conquering southern Italy, Sicily, and much of the western areas of the Empire in northern Africa and southern Spain, but his successors were unable to maintain them. The Eastern Empire, virtually confined to the eastern Mediterranean, became identified more than ever with Greek and Byzantine culture. Its powers of resistance proved to be remarkably strong as it tenaciously held on to some sort of order and continuity down to the fifteenth century. (Byzantine education will be briefly discussed in the next section of this chapter, pages 137-141.)

In the western part of the Empire, society took the form of a great pyramid, with the emperor, his family, followers, army officers, and high ecclesiastics at the top, catered to by merchants and speculators, and all resting upon the work of the masses in the cities, the serfs on the land, and the slaves who rendered personal service in the houses of the well-to-do. When the Germanic tribes invaded the Empire, the emperors could not summon up enough enthusiasm or support to stave off conquest and disaster. A heavy attitude of psychological weariness and loss of nerve had so weakened the mental and moral fiber of the people that they could not respond with the courage, devotion, or loyalty that were needed to face the invader. The upper classes turned to whatever immediate pleasures they could find in such a life, and the urban lower classes turned to faith and hope in a better life to come in the next world. The ideal of a good life on this earth was apparently impossible of realization, and thus more and more people began to seek salvation in the other world after death. Such an intellectual climate was fertile soil for the spread of emotional religious faith. The failure to establish and maintain a broadly based economy and a polity devoted to the welfare of the many was basically responsible for the decline of Roman civilization, as had been true in Greece.

All these developments had significance for education, which became increasingly exclusive and aristocratic. It is possible that a more generous conception of the importance of widespread education would have played a part in maintaining a healthy political and economic condition and would have provided a bulwark against the aristocratic exclusiveness that was at the root of cultural decay. However, the past-oriented literary education of the rhetorical schools was scarcely the kind of education that would equip the ruling classes of Rome to surmount the monumental problems facing their civilization. Nor did the competing schools of philosophy do much to enable them to grapple with the harsh realities of the day.

The principal formulations concerning the relation of man to the world about him revealed a continuing opposition between otherworldly and this-worldly outlooks. The dominant otherworldly trends in Roman thought were shot through with Stoicism and the idealism of Plato. They stressed the permanent and absolute reality of the spiritual realm as against the transitory appearances of everyday life. Whereas the florescent Greeks had looked upon the dualism between the body and the soul as an opportunity to develop both harmoniously, the tendency of dispersive Roman times was to exalt one or the other to the extreme. Stoicists and Neoplatonists glorified the soul and the ecstasies of the other world, whereas Epicureans glorified the body and the pleasure of this world, even to the extent of denying the existence of the soul. The philosophical problem thus posed was of little help in the mundane tasks of saving a civilization.

Not much more helpful were the bodies of organized knowledge that were formulated in the later Empire and dispersed from Roman schools to the European Middle Ages. Scholarship in both the Greek and the Latin worlds lost its creativity in nearly all fields of knowledge, turning almost wholly to editing and digesting the works that had been codified and systematized in the earlier periods. It was almost as though the later imperial scholars saw hard times ahead and frantically sought to reduce knowledge to the compact form of small compendiums, so that they might weather the rigors of the intellectual depressions to come. Only in the field of religious thought was the creative spirit alive in the Eastern and Western world as the Fathers of the Christian church sought to reconcile Greek philosophy with the doctrines of Christianity.

From Humanitas to Scholasticus   One of the best illustrations of the course of Roman intellectual thought is the development of the liberal arts as they were drawn from Greek sources, modified by Latin authors, and made ready to be passed on to the Middle Ages. As we have seen, the arts appropriate to the free man of florescent Greece were more or less commonly agreed to be grammar, gymnastics, music, and sometimes drawing, and, on the advanced level, logic, rhetoric, dialectics, arithmetic, geometry, astronomy, and musical harmony. These were known as the *enkuklios paideia,* the elements of a common or widespread education.

The Latin scholars of the formative and florescent periods in Rome had drawn upon these Greek studies as possessing fundamental values for their own set of liberal arts. In addition to Cicero, the work of Varro in the first century B.C. was outstanding. He sought to establish nine Greek studies as the necessary equipment of the liberally educated Roman: grammar, rhetoric, logic, arithmetic, geometry, astronomy, music, architecture, and medicine. Interestingly enough, he had dropped gymnastics and drawing from the usual Greek currimulum and had added architecture and medicine. Apparently he could find no *science* in the fine arts of painting, drawing, and sculpture or in gymnastics, but he could justify architecture and medicine, as well as the other seven, on the basis that they had been developed so systematically by the Greeks that they were classified as sciences, i.e., they were based on coherent general principles and they were so well organized for teaching purposes that they could be taught as explicit arts or techniques.

In the dispersive period of the later Empire the liberal arts were narrowed to seven by excluding the two practical or applied arts so much admired by the Romans, architecture and medicine. This was done by Martianus Capella. It is interesting to note, as revealing the intellectual temper of the times, why it was that Capella in the late fourth century A.D. turned to Varro's list of nine liberal arts and then cut them down to seven. In his influential allegorical compendium called the *Marriage of Philology and Mercury,* Capella described a heavenly wedding in which the seven liberal arts acted as bridesmaids: grammar, rhetoric, logic, (later known as the trivium); and arithmetic, geometry, astronomy, and music (quadrivium). His justification for reducing the number to seven was that he wanted to keep only those arts that would interest a group of celestial, spiritual beings. He left out medicine because celestial beings had no earthly ills, and he left out architecture because spiritual beings needed no physical habitation. Music could stay because of its supermundane interest.

Here, then, by the end of the fourth century was a compendium of knowledge that did not comprise the entire range of subjects known to Greece or Rome but that did eventually fix the boundaries of western Europe's medieval curriculum in the liberal arts. They had been formalized and condensed from the Greek heritage into small literary packets of knowledge. They had come to be identified with those systematic studies of Greece which had been translated into Latin and which were thought to be suitable to spiritual and intellectual matters rather than to practical affairs. Once again, the scholars and teachers shaped a powerful educational tradition in the form of a liberal education which in turn moulded the attitudes of generations of educated Europeans to look down upon a useful or practical education as inferior to a linguistic or literary education.

In the Hellenistic Republican period the term *grammar* included not only the study of syntax, syllables, parts of speech, declensions, and conjugations but also the study of poetry. At first, successful Latin poets were quickly added to the curriculum of the schools, but once the educators had decided which were the classics, the list narrowed down to Vergil, Terence, and Horace. Following the work of Dionysius Thrax countless Hellenistic grammarians in the third and second centuries B.C. had made of Greek grammar a logical and systematic body of knowledge through their work in compiling word lists, dictionaries, and reference books. Latin grammarians of the dispersive period then began to assimilate and copy into Latin the work of the Greek grammarians in order to build up an organized study of Latin grammar. Latin grammars were basically translations of Greek grammars.

Perhaps the most influential grammar of all time was the *Ars grammatica minor* written by Aelius Donatus in the fourth century A.D. It was a short description of the eight parts of speech, elaborating the definition and characteristics of each in question-and-answer form. Another influential grammar, that of Priscian in the sixth century, was a much longer, infinitely detailed, and pedantic work containing more than 250 quotations from many Greek and Latin authors, as well as voluminous material on syntax, conjugations, and declensions. The grammars of these men and of others went through many editions. They were copied, edited, and commented upon in turn by generations of other grammarians.

Samples of Latin literature were compiled also into textbooks, digests, and collections of quotations that were used as aids in the learning of Latin. Perhaps the most famous and influential of these little readers was the book of rhymed couplets written by the fourth-century Stoic, Cato. His *Distichs* was studied for centuries down to the eighteenth century dispensing Franklin-like maxims concerning morality, caution, self-control, courage, moderation, and shrewd adaptation to the fortunes of life. Such textbooks became the provender on which the Middle Ages were nourished. They contained much of the heritage of Greek and Latin literature in a predigested form. Although they sustained life, they provided scant nourishment.

Rhetoric, as one of the language arts dealing principally with the study of expressive speech, both oral and written, went through a characteristic course of development which we have already noted. In Hellenistic Republican times it was looked upon as the highest of the studies that the aspiring Roman youth could follow, but as the imperial period progressed, public discussion no longer had the determining effect upon public policy that it had in the Senate and Assembly of Republican Rome. Rhetoric therefore came to be increasingly a dilettante exercise in formal language for the benefit of a wealthy, leisured, and sophisticated class. Whereas hundreds of textbook editions were being prepared in grammar, there were relatively few such books on rhetoric written in the later imperial period. The best known were those of Capella and St. Augustine. Cicero and Quintilian were always the models, but their original works were seldom used in full. These small handbooks and manuals illustrate the way in which the creative literary heritage of Hellenistic Rome was wrapped up in small packages for the use of scholars and students in the Middle Ages.

Logic became firmly established as one of the seven liberal arts, gradually losing its identification with philosophy as a whole. Among those who helped to pass on Aristotle's logic was Porphyry, a Neoplatonist of the third century A.D., who wrote a textbook in which he edited Aristotle's logical works and added an introduction of his own. This book was handed down through many commentaries and editions for centuries. Although Porphyry was interested in the whole range of metaphysical and philosophical thought, he specifically ruled out such problems as beyond the scope of logic. This distinction apparently suited Capella and St. Augustine, who wrote the other two notable texts on logic, both of which became important handbooks during the Middle Ages. These books dealt with the definitions of words and propositions and the use of the syllogism.

The quadrivium, or four higher liberal arts, consisting of arithmetic, geometry, astronomy, and music, were all conceived as basically mathematical studies. Despite the advances made in arithmetic by Hellenistic scholars at Alexandria, little evidence of these developments appeared in the handbooks on the liberal arts. Capella's very brief chapter on arithmetic made much of the mystical significance and properties of numbers but gave virtually no attention to the problems of computation. Arithmetic was no longer a practical means for solving useful problems as it had been among Egyptians and early Greeks, but an intellectualized and theoretical exercise in mysticism.

Despite the progress in geometry achieved in Hellenistic-Republican times by Euclid, geometry reverted more or less to the literal meaning of the word, measurement of the earth, becoming more geographic than mathematical in character. The story of astronomy was similar. The earlier observations of the Greek scientists seem to have escaped the attention of the imperial astronomers, who adopted Aristotle's work *On the Heavens* with its assumption that the earth was the center of the universe. Ptolemy in the second century A.D. brought together much of the current information on astronomy in a book that turned out to be enormously influential in all of Western Europe, for its geocentric principles were passed on to the Middle Ages through the medium of Capella. These Ptolemaic doctrines prevailed until the reassertion of the heliocentric theory by Copernicus in the sixteenth century.

Although music in florescent Greece had played its part with poetry and dancing in the aesthetic and civic celebrations of the polis, in Hellenistic Republican times music consisted of theoretical and mathematical exercises. Pythagoras and Plato had emphasized the mathematical properties of music, and Plato had disparaged the musician as a mere practitioner. It was this latter conception of music that was exalted by Roman writers as early as the time of Cicero. It is little wonder that Capella followed their mathematical and theoretical interests when he came to define music as one of the liberal arts.

The science of medicine was advanced considerably during the Hellenistic Republican period both in the East and in the West. At Alexandria and other Hellenistic centers, Greek physicians continued their investigations in anatomy, physiology, and dissection to the extent that some fundamental conceptions were established concerning the brain's relationship to the nervous system, the character of veins and arteries, and the processes of digestion and reproduction. The fact that Varro included medicine as one of the liberal arts indicates that he believed that the Greek science of medicine was worthy of a high place in Roman estimation. The most famous physician of them all was Galen, whose books written in the second century A.D. were used extensively throughout the Middle Ages.

Much more portentous for the future of the Empire was the deterioration in agriculture. Despite the deep roots of Roman society in rural and agrarian life, agriculture was not made a field of serious and sustained study or training, at least, not enough to satisfy Columella in the first century A.D. whose poignant yet indignant analysis went unheeded:

> We are men of strange habits. When we want to learn oratory, we are careful to imitate the best orator. We go to school to learn our weights and measures. We study music, song, dance, and gesture. When we want to build, we call in mason and architect. We have skilled captains for our ships, trained soldiers for our armies. We have specialists for every useful science, and we have philosophers to form our characters. Agriculture is the only science for which we

have neither pupils nor masters; yet agriculture is the science next in dignity to philosophy, almost its sister-science. We have schools of rhetoric, schools of geometry, schools of music; trained cooks and trained barbers. But I never yet heard of men who call themselves students or professors of agriculture.[18]

Schools of agriculture? Nothing could be more preposterous to the Hellenistic or Roman gentleman whose image of the educated man was epitomized in his ability to quote Vergil. Columella went unheeded. Schools concentrated on rhetoric and literature. Agricultural and technical expertise continued to decline. The Empire fell. It was to be many centuries before agriculture was to be considered a subject worthy of systematic education. Modernizing societies as late as the twentieth century still found it a difficult idea for them to accept.

Among the contributions made by Rome to the West and to the world, Roman law stands high. The judicial system, the codifying of the civil law, and the imperial system of governmental administration proved to be working models for later times and places. In the process of codifying the law the formal schools of law played a key role as centers where jurists like Ulpian and Papinian worked and taught. The most influential of such schools was that at Beirut from the third century to the fifth, whereupon Constantinople took first place. Until then the codifications were undertaken primarily to facilitate the teaching of law. Not only does the law shape education; education shapes the law.

It may not be too much of an exaggeration to date the beginning and the end of the secular aspects of Graeco-Roman thought with reference to the growth and decline of the idea of natural law. In the sixth century B.C. the Ionian philosophers of the Greek polis were attempting to fathom the essence of the cosmos by appeal to orderly laws of nature and thus to surmount the customary assumptions of folk religion. In the sixth century A.D. the jurists who codified Justinian's *Corpus Juris Civilis* attempted to construct the canons of legal procedure that govern a human society based upon orderly laws of reason. They, too, were attempting to go beyond the customary folk reliance upon family, class, and arbitrary rule. But it was to be almost another twelve centuries before the civilized laws of nations and the scientific laws of nature were to be given high priority in the education of the West. In the meantime, the laws of God and the divine rights of priests and kings were to dominate education as well as politics.

So what shall we say of the role of education in the disintegration or dispersion of the civilization of the Roman Empire? Whereas elementary schools were widely dispersed through the Empire at its height, the privilege of attending was always limited by the ability to pay the fees. Grammar and rhetorical schools, also available only to those who could afford an extended period of education, were confined to the cities and towns. Their availability was therefore doubly limited. And when urban life declined sharply throughout the Empire from the third century onward, the secondary and higher schools declined with the urban decay. Few cities were able to maintain the schools which could provide the educated leadership so desperately required to

[18]Quoted in Gwynn, op. cit., pp. 150-151.

administer a large-scale, literate, urban society. When such schools were in short supply, the educated manpower could not be produced in the numbers or in the quality necessary to enable Rome to maintain or rebuild a viable civilization, let alone to defend it. This task had to await the rise of new societies ready and able to provide the education appropriate to the arduous task of civilization-building. The Romans not only failed to make education available to their common people, they also failed to design an education for their elite that would serve them well in the task of civilization-building.

R. R. Bolgar blames the decline of the Empire upon the education that the privileged classes provided for themselves:

> Among the reasons why the Empire failed we ought probably to number the intellectual failure of the educated classes. Hampered by their traditionalism and by the strict linguistic discipline which they imposed upon their minds, the members of that class could not solve their immediate problems.[19]

When Bolgar speaks of the "strict linguistic discipline," he really means the everlasting imitation of the classic authors required by the schools:

> The techniques of imitation, the habit of reading notebook in hand to collect telling words and phrases, metaphors, parts of speech and arguments and the desirability of memorizing this material until it became part of the natural furniture of one's mind were all regularly taught in the rhetorical schools.
>
> Thus, during the last centuries of the Empire, the imitative tendency which had characterized all literature since the death of Alexander was sharply intensified. The well-organized educational system of the Empire had for its main aim to teach the two literary languages and to inculcate in the minds of all its pupils the established methods and desirability of imitation.[20]

The decline of vitality in secular thought certainly contributed to the disintegration and demise of the Empire. It was not only that the religious message and the new thought of Christianity captured the imagination of the people and the intellectual energies of able minds. These were powerful persuaders indeed. But the decline was also a result of an education increasingly irrelevant to the requirements of the age. This is not to say that a more vital, socially oriented, and widespread system of public education could have prevented the fall of the Roman Empire single-handedly, but it *is* true that the one institution that did address itself to the plight and needs of the deprived masses of the Roman cities was the Christian church. It went from victory to victory. The people had to have hope—either that men could transform their world by their own efforts, or that God would care for them through the sacrifice of his Son. The predominating choice of intellectuals and populace alike during the coming ten centuries was an overwhelming vote of confidence in God rather than in man.

---

[19] Bolgar, op. cit., p. 24.

[20] Ibid., pp. 23-24.

C. HELLENISTIC EDUCATION AND CHRISTENDOM

In the first two centuries of the Roman Empire, Christianity was viewed as simply one Eastern religion among many. Beginning as a local Jewish sect in Palestine, the Christian message gradually gained adherents throughout the Empire, especially among the underprivileged masses of the towns and cities. St. Paul was especially instrumental in universalizing Christianity among the peoples of the Eastern Empire. As the Christian sects and congregations gained followers, they came into conflict with the other Eastern religions and eventually with the Roman emperors themselves.

With the increasing trials of the Empire in the third century and the ever-increasing strength of the Christians, the emperors felt that the time had come to call a halt. Under Decius and Diocletian systematic attempts were made to reassert the absolute power of the emperors and to wipe out the Christian congregations as a means to this end, but the Christians could not be stopped. As the Empire emerged from the third century weakened and shaken, the church emerged stronger than ever. It had won the first of its many centuries of battles with the state.

Finally, in the fourth century, the attitude of the emperors changed; they found that it was the better part of wisdom to gain the support of such a powerful institution. An edict of Galerius in 311 A.D. granted to Christians the legal right to worship their god. In 313 Constantine gave Christians full legal rights, and in 325 he recognized Christianity as the official state religion, encouraging Christians to teach in the schools. From this time on, church Fathers began to argue that the state and the church should cooperate. Ambrose, Bishop Gelasius I, and St. Augustine claimed that the state should protect and support the church, and in points of conflict the church should be supreme. Here are early expressions of the idea of an establishment of religion. The triumph of Christianity was further signallized when Theodosius set out to suppress the worship of the old Roman gods as a crime against the state and to give legal protection *only* to Christians and when Justinian tried to stamp out educational paganism in 529 A.D. by closing the doors of the philosophical schools of Athens.

The Patristic Age (200 A.D.-500 A.D.)

In its long and complicated process of transformation from a local Jewish sect to a world power, Christianity relied heavily upon religious instruction but relatively less upon religious schools in the usual formal sense. This was largely due to the assumption by most of the early church fathers that Christian children would naturally attend the regular Hellenistic-Roman schools for their normal literary training. They would then receive special training in Christian morality and behavior at the hands of the family and special training in Christian doctrine as a means to salvation at the hands of the clergy.

As time pased, the attitude of the church fathers began to be less and less hospitable and more and more opposed to the pagan outlooks purveyed by the traditional Greek and Latin schools. Curiously enough, during the patristic age few church leaders ever tried to prevent parents from sending their children to the Roman schools, and few ever suggested that the church itself set up its own schools for the literary as well as the religious education of Christian children. This was done only when the long established Hellenistic or Roman schools began to disappear. The church did, however, reduce the vernaculars to written form and establish general religious schools in those parts of the Eastern Empire where there was no tradition of Hellenistic or Roman education or where there was no written language. This was done in Coptic, Syriac, Ethiopian, Armenian, Georgian, Hunnish, Germanic, and Slavic.

The great question facing Christian educators was what attitude to take concerning the pagan learning of secular schools. The answer to this question varied so much from time to time and from place to place that authority could be found for almost any position. Some Fathers, like Tertullian and the later Jerome, stood out strongly against secular schools and secular learning, urging Christian parents to have nothing to do with such sources of evil and paganism. Others, like Augustine, preached moderation, telling parents that children could be sent to secular schools if care were taken that they were not corrupted by the religious mythology and pagan morality contained in secular literature. Still others, like Origen and Chrysostom, were not at all fearful of secular learning but included in their schools the round of liberal arts and philosophy as preparatory to the highest study of Christian doctrine and theology.

In general, the church eventually assimilated most of the noncontroversial elements of the secular liberal arts if stripped of their pagan excesses. After all, grammar, rhetoric, and logic could be taught in such a way as not to corrupt the morals of youth but even to contribute to the intellectual discipline necessary for the Christian scholar. The study of Plato's philosophy and the mathematical elements of arithmetic, geometry, astronomy, and music would not be morally harmful if employed as purely intellectual exercises or as instruments for the delineation of human reason as subservient to faith.

Two large areas of human knowledge, however, were considered to be irrevelant, or even harmful, to the dominantly religous concern of Christian schools. One was the field of such practical sciences as architecture, engineering, mechanics, medicine, and law. These subjects dealt with the means of controlling the physical or human environment for the betterment of life on this earth; therefore, they were, in religious terms, of much less significance than the more spiritually inclined liberal arts. They consequently declined from neglect at the hands of the Western church during the later Empire, despite the occasional books on these subjects found in church libraries and schools.

The other field was that of the natural sciences and materialistic philosophies, which were deemed definitely harmful to the developing theology of the church. Thus the natural philosophy of Aristotle and of Hellenistic scientists was not assimilated into Latin Christian learning at this time. It was therefore not passed on to Western Europe through the Latin church and its schools. Rather, it remained in the Eastern Hellenistic centers where it was later reworked and finally introduced into Western Europe by Arabic and Hebrew scholars in the eleventh, twelfth, and thirteenth centuries. The point is that even though the church schools selected, reconciled, and assimilated some of the secular learning of Graeco-Roman civilization, they also rejected much of it, thereby virtually sentencing it to exile from the West for several centuries.

The Byzantine Taming of Hellenism (500 A.D.-1500 A.D.)

Meanwhile, Byzantium kept alive the Hellenistic traditions in education and literature for 1000 years during which time it transmitted these traditions northward to much of Eastern Europe and to Russia, southward to the Arabic Moslems of the Middle East and North Africa, as well as westward where its educational influences directly touched many parts of Europe at critical times in its history. Justinian's reconquest of southern Italy and Spain and North Africa left a bequest of imperial schools and Greek scholarship which served as reservoirs of classical learning throughout the Middle Ages. Irish monasticism drew on these resources in the sixth century, as did the English church and learning in the seventh century, the Carolingian educational movements of the eighth and ninth centuries, and above all the Italian Renaissance of the fourteenth and fifteenth centuries.

Prime agencies in the civilizing process were the Byzantine schools, whether promoted by church or by state or by both. From the seventh and eighth centuries through the eleventh and twelfth, Moslem scholars borrowed Greek science and philosophy from Byzantine sources, translated the works into Arabic,and thus eventually made available a vast store of knowledge to the West when it was finally ready to capitalize upon it from the eleventh century on. Such knowledge was a major element in the formative period of education in Western civilization during the later Middle Ages.

More direct in its influence was the Byzantine effort to Christianize and Hellenize the Slavic peoples of Eastern Europe. In the ninth and tenth centuries, the oral languages of Serbs, Bulgarians, and Russians were written down in the form of translations of the Bible, eastern Fathers' writings, and other religious works. Along with this went the conversion of Slavic leaders and their peoples to Christianity. Missionaries and monastaries began the process of spreading education through the vast land regions to the north of Byzantium.

Great though this influence was upon political leaders and within the church, the educational veneer, relatively thin on the surface, did not penetrate very deeply into the lower layers of society nor into the rural regions. In this respect, Eastern Europe followed a much more conservative educational as well as religious tradition for nearly a thousand years after its incorporation into eastern Christendom. It did not change in essence until the upsurge of contact with Western education took place in the seventeenth and eighteenth centuries.

By and large, the thousand years between 500 and 1500 A.D. showed a remarkable difference in the end points between the two halves of Christendom. At the beginning of the period the Eastern realm was at its height in power and influence under Justinian. This was followed by a recession or decline during the seventh, eighth, and ninth centuries, especially marked by the bitter struggles of the iconoclastic controversies. A second major florescence of Byzantine culture took place in the later tenth and early eleventh centuries, once again followed by a recession occasioned by the conquests of the Latin crusaders. A final renaissance appeared in the fourteenth century only to be followed by the destruction of the Empire with the fall of Constantinople to the Ottoman Turks in 1453.

Despite the ups and downs of this 1,000 years the general trend in Byzantium revealed "the shrinking nucleus of a superior civilization, fearful of loss, constantly on the defensive, stereotyped in its institutions and culture. In the West we shall see by contrast evidences not of atrophy but of growth."[21]

The contrast Bolgar refers to began with Western Christendom in a state of general disarray in the fifth and sixth centuries, a condition that did not turn for the better until the Carolingian Empire of the ninth century. From then on, a vital and aggressive civilization began to take shape which, despite its ups and downs, despite the imminent breakup of the unity of Latin Christendom, was on the verge of leaping into world prominence in 1500 rather than retiring to past glories. As one views this millenium it seems clear that the differences in direction taken by the Eastern and the Western inheritors of the Graeco-Roman civilization had something to do with the educational uses made of the classical tradition and the educational institutions that were devised to carry on the civilizing function of that tradition. Despite the greater rejection of the classics by the early Latin Fathers, the Latin Church turned out to be more hospitable to using the classics in creative ways and more flexible in designing or permitting educational institutions to be designed that promoted change rather than retarded it.

In general, the Hellenistic-style elementary schools and grammar schools continued to serve the Byzantine Empire throughout its history. The Eastern Church Fathers assumed that such schools would continue to provide the basic secular literary education required by those who would serve both church and state. Inasmuch as the imperial bureaucracy continued to be much more important and influential in the East than it did in the West, it was considered essential that elementary education continue to provide the essentials of literacy in the Greek language for boys from six or eight to ten or twelve years of age, and secondary education to concentrate from twelve to sixteen years upon advanced competence in the use of Greek by means of intensive study of Greek grammar and literature. When the government bureaucracy and the church hierarchy agreed so fully, the future of an education that served both was secure—but unexciting. Lower schools and the courses they taught did not change substantially through the long centuries of the Byzantine Empire.[22] They continued to serve the professional classes in the major urban centers, seldom reaching out to the rural or village hinterlands and thus severely limiting access to the advantages of education. In this respect the civilizing effect of the cities upon the rural regions was critically less in the East than it came to be in the West.

Another crucial difference was the inability of Byzantine higher education to break its bonds with the Orthodox Church. The great patriarch, Photius, led an intellectual revival that rested upon wide knowledge of science, history, geography, and information about other lands as well as theology and familiarity with the church

---

[21] Ibid., p. 91.

[22] See, for example, the chapter on Byzantine education by Georgina Buckler in N. H. Baynes and H. St. L. B. Moss (eds.), *Byzantium; an Introduction to East Roman Civilization*, Clarendon Press, Oxford, 1948, pp. 200-220.

Fathers. In 863, Bardas, the real power behind a weak emperor, founded a new university type of institution in which the sciences were given priority over the traditional grammar, rhetoric, and dialectic. This institution might have made a breakthrough in modern forms of knowledge comparable to that of seventeenth century Europe if the commercial classes could have broken loose from the confining power of the church and if the scholarly classes could have overcome their fondness for grammar and rhetoric, but neither could happen.[23]

Instead, when the eleventh century renaissance of interest in all things Greek (aided by the emergence of a new Greek-speaking landowning class with strongly nationalist proclivities) came along, it turned out that the literary and philosophical rather than the scientific side of Hellenism was the victor. When Emperor Constantine IX (Monomachos) established a new university consisting of a school of philosophy and a school of law, Michael Psellus, Byzantium's candidate for the "Renaissance Man," was put in charge of the faculty of philosophy. However, he interpreted philosophy to be basically a study of literature, and the sciences could not even muster a full complement of teachers.

In the mid-eleventh century, the church broke its alliance with Hellenism and reduced the influence of the secular institutions of higher education by establishing two Patriarchal Schools which set the pace for Byzantine higher education for the next centuries. These schools reflected the church's victory over Hellenism, not by rooting it out, but by shaping it to the church's ends, or, as Bolgar puts it, by "taming Hellenism:"

> The method of instruction was in every case calculated to diminish the influence of the pagan authors whose works ostensibly formed the subject-matter of the course ... the reading of texts whose plain meaning is always twisted to suit the Christian moralist, the uninspired copying of model passages ... the neglect of serious science for dilettante chatter were not likely to promote a deep understanding of the Greek tradition.[24]

No wonder that Byzantine scholarship lit no intellectual fires; that liberal education did not liberate; that the civilizing force of education did not quicken the intellectual life. The church in the East was able to confine the secular studies to a narrow range, and to keep them harnessed to the ecclesiastical aims of the church, whereas the Western church, reeling under the blows of nationalism and rationalism, was more willing, albeit reluctantly, to give greater scope to the secular studies, more autonomy to the range of human reason, and more access to education for the layman. This greater flexibility did not happen quickly or easily, but by 1500 the difference was all-important.

The massive weight of the literary side of Hellenistic education in the East diverted attention from the sciences, whereas the West eventually turned to the

---

[23] Bolgar, op. cit., p. 70.
[24] Ibid., p. 81.

scientific materials of Hellenism with avid interest. Possibly the sheer novelty of the intrusive Greek knowledge brought out intellectual reactions from the West, whereas knowledge of the same materials in the East could be seen as nothing more than repetition of the same old story that had been told with "lakes of ink" for nearly 2,000 years. Indeed, the scholarly mind-set of the Byzantine teachers, generation after generation, was strong enough to offset the efforts of emperors, of bureaucrats, and even of forward looking patriarchs who sought periodically to reform Byzantine education.

Ernest Barker suggests a fundamental reason for the lack of originality in Byzantine thought:

> The reason why so little of it was original was not the poverty of Byzantine intelligence, which had a subtle and probing power: it was rather the riches and oppressive weight of the Byzantine inheritance from ancient Greece. The more Byzantium shed the Roman or Latin tradition, which was still vigorous in the age of Justinian, and the more it became specifically and particularly Greek, the more dependent did it become on the classical models and the general literature of ancient Greece. . . . the scholars of Byzantium were content to be the disciples and copyists of the ancient masters. Classically educated, they succumbed to a . . . tendency to think that the whole of wisdom is to be found in the past, and that the duty of the present is to recapitulate and restate "the wisdom of the ancients."[25]

The point here is not only the looking to the past but the lack of a mixing of ideas and the absence of external influences that would prompt reexamination or the emergence of fresh outlooks. We have seen many times how important such interchanges were in social and educational invention. We see in Byzantium the reverse: the sterility that comes from preoccupation with a single tradition. The scholars and the teachers kept their eyes so glued on the past that they could not learn from the movements of people and ideas that flowed through their magnificent city. An urban way of life was not alone enough for intellectual creativity; it needed a vital educational way of life:

> There was no continuous and continuously organized system of university instruction in Constantinople, even though the city was the centre and focus of Byzantine life. .. [Byzantine scholars] suffered from the absence of a continuous university which could steadily uphold a permanent tradition of scholarly inquiry and the abiding standards of truth and exact science.[26]

By contrast, the cathedral schools of Western Europe were beginning to flourish as early as the eleventh century, to be followed by the university form of organization, a genuinely new type of educational institution. The West learned a great deal from

[25] Ernest Barker, *Social and Political Thought in Byzantium from Justinian I to the Last Palaeologus,* Clarendon Press, Oxford, 1957, p. 2.
[26] Ibid., pp. 49-50.

Byzantium; but eventually it struck out on its own. During the early Middle Ages, the West was almost as fascinated by the encyclopedism, the compendia, and the abridgements in Latin as the Byzantines were in the Greek. But then from the eleventh century on, the West avidly turned to the whole range of classical heritage, not just to annotate it, but to absorb and assimilate and eventually to criticize and rework it. Above all, they grasped at the science, the philosophy, the logic, the mathematics of the classical tradition. They were not to be satisfied with simply imitating the classical literature of poets and prose writers. While the Byzantine educators were dotting the "i's" and crossing the "t's" in their epilogue to Graeco-Roman civilization, the Western educators began to write the preface to Western civilization. But first they had to learn the language and the basic forms of thought of the Graeco-Roman heritage. This they did in the propaedeutic studies of the early Middle Ages.

PART II

EDUCATION IN THE BUILDING OF WESTERN CIVILIZATION
(500 A.D.-1700 A.D.)

CHAPTER V

THE FORMATIVE PERIOD OF WESTERN EDUCATION
(500 A.D.-1400 A.D.)

A. PROPAEDEUTICS TO THE RISE OF WESTERN CIVILIZATION (500 A.D.–1000 A.D.)

The term *propaedeutic* has a formidable and antiquarian ring to modern ears. Yet it almost exactly describes the educational characteristics of the 500 years between the "fall" of the Roman Empire and the "rise" of Western civilization. It means literally "to teach beforehand" (*pro-paideuein*), and in the English plural it has come to mean the preliminary learning or preparatory instruction connected with any art or science. The education of the West in the 500 years of the early Middle Ages was preparing the ground for the emergence of Western civilization.

We can say this with the advantage of historical hindsight. The men of the European Middle Ages would not have put it that way. They thought of themselves as a part of the ancient world. The men of the Byzantine ages also thought of themselves as part of the ancient world. The difference was that the Byzantines remained ancients, while the western Europeans did not. They were laying the groundwork for something quite different from the ancient Graeco-Roman civilization, a Western civilization which their successors in another 500 years were to transform once again into a modern civilization.

Herein lies a problem for the history of education. If Graeco-Roman civilization generally disintegrated, as it did, around 500 A.D., and if Western civilization began to take characteristic form, as it did, around 1000 A.D., what shall we say of education in the intervening half millenium between 500 and 1000 A.D.? Shall we simply say that those unfortunate years, loosely referred to as the early Middle Ages, were educational "Dark Ages," or that they were just in the "middle" between two really important eras? Conceptually, either is unsatisfying and overlooks recent scholarship in European history.

Or, shall we look upon this period as "a long chapter of later antiquity?"[1] In this case, we would view early medieval education as a continuation of the dispersion of Hellenistic education. There is considerable merit in this approach, especially if one's primary interest is in tracing forward the long-range influences of Graeco-Roman civilization.

Or, shall we push back the origins of Western civilization to the destruction of the Roman political and economic system around 500 A.D. and view the early Middle Ages as a prodromal or gestatory beginning of Western civilization? In this case, early medieval education becomes a propaedeutic to the rise of Western civilization, that is, it provided the preparatory courses of study and the preliminary lessons in the Latin language that western Europeans had to learn before they could build their own distinctive forms of Western education. There is also considerable merit in this view, especially if one is interested in tracing backward to its roots the origins of Western civilization. Although these two views are not entirely inconsistent, I believe the latter more nearly fits the requirements of scholarship as it bears upon the history of education. (See Figure 3.2—The Curve of Educational Development in Graeco-Roman Civilization.)

The Survival of Graeco—Roman Education

The emphasis that many historians have put upon the decline and fall of the Roman Empire gives the impression that everything went to pieces in the fourth, fifth, and sixth centuries in the West and that there was nothing but anarchy, confusion, and hopelessness for several centuries thereafter; hence, the persistence of the term *Dark Ages*. Although the Middle Ages had its share of cultural dislocation, political, economic, and religious institutions did survive and adapt to the barbarian invasions of the sixth to the eighth centuries.

In the course of the Germanic invasions by Ostrogoths, Lombards, and Franks, the center of political authority began to move from Italy northward to the Frankish kingdoms in France and Germany which were gradually consolidated under the leadership of the Merovingian kings. On Christmas day in 800 A.D. when Charlemagne was crowned emperor of the Romans by the Pope, he became in theory the legitimate successor to the emperors of the ancient Roman Empire. As such, Charlemagne was the towering political figure of the early Middle Ages, reestablishing the authority of a strong central government over much of western Europe, improving economic and agricultural life, and instituting religious and educational reforms. It was a period of considerable intellectual and educational ferment.

In the ninth century the successors of Charlemagne in state, church, and family, quarreling among themselves for control of the Empire, gradually split it into three large parts: the western Frankish kingdom ultimately becoming France, the eastern Frankish kindom, Germany, and the rest, Italy. The central administration could not be maintained in the face of the growing strength of local aristocracies and the new

[1]Frederick B. Artz, *The Mind of the Middle Ages; an Historical Survey: A.D. 200-1500,* Knopf, New York, 1953, p. 3.

series of barbarian invasions in the ninth and tenth centuries. As a result, lawlessness, insecurity, and warfare became ever more common. Safety and political authority were to be found increasingly in the hands of local strong-men who had land, a well-fortified castle, and subordinates who would fight for them. Political authority devolved into the hands of decentralized feudal lords who could promise some protection against marauders, although the kings continued to exercise a nominal control. By 962 Otto I (the Great) was strong enough to conquer Italy and establish himself as emperor, reviving the theory that he was the successor of Charlemagne and thus the legitimate heir of the Roman Empire. In theory he ruled a Latin Christendom along with a Roman Pope, the division of powers being a matter of almost constant dispute and controversy for several centuries.

Meanwhile, the rise of Islam in the Middle East was eventually to exert great influence upon Europe, Africa, and much of western and southern Asia. After the death of Mohammed, who had been able to conquer most of Arabia by 632, a series of successors, or caliphs, strove to take his place as the political and religious leader of the Arabs. Because of the military weakness of the Byzantine Empire and the superior fighting qualities of the Arab horsemen, the caliphs were rapidly able to spread their power beyond the borders of Arabia to Central Asia in the north, to India in the east, and across northern Africa to Italy and Spain in the west.

From the eighth to the twelfth centuries Islamic civilization displayed a vitality and a creativeness that radiated out from the Middle East in all directions. Learning quickly from the Byzantines, from the Persians, from the Jews, and from the Hindus, Moslem scholars turned eagerly to the task of absorbing the Greek philosophy and science and reconciling it with the tenets of Islam. Whereas Byzantine scholars seemed to prefer Greek literature above all else in Hellenism, many of the Arab scholars seemed to prefer Greek science and philosophy. They borrowed this legacy not only from Persia, which had welcomed the Greek philosophers who had been driven out of the Byzantine Empire for their paganism, but also from the Hellenistic cities which they conquered in Syria, Palestine, and Egypt. Islam added to these its own great centers for the cultivation of scholarship as well as religion.

Elementary schools were established in connection with the mosques in order to teach Arabic reading and writing as a means of learning the Koran thoroughly. Secondary schools for the study of grammar, poetry, the sciences, law, and history were set up in the more important mosques for the young of the upper classes. Theological centers were also available for the most advanced learning in the chief mosques of such principal cities as Medina, Bagdad, Damascus, Jerusalem, Alexandria, Cairo, and Cordoba. Several of these rivaled the Hellenistic museums and research institutes of earlier centuries.

The peak of intellectual vigor was reached in the tenth and eleventh centuries, after which time religious reactionaries gained control of some of the centers and drove out those scholars interested in rationalistic and scientific studies. The latter went west to North Africa and Spain where they found refuge for a time until the conservative influences won out in all directions from approximately the fourteenth century onward. The florescence of Islamic scholarship came at just the time when the

West Europeans had learned their preliminary lessons and were beginning to seek eagerly for all they could find out about the Hellenic past. They found it translated from the Greek into the Arabic and added to by the Arab scientists and philosophers themselves. The Westerners pounced upon the findings (transmitted and original) in astronomy, physics, mathematics (algebra and trigonometry), medicine, chemistry, biology, and geography. Fortunately for the West, they appropriated this knowledge while the Arabs were at their peak of flexibility, adaptability, and tolerance and before the Seljuk Turks and subsequently the Mongols clamped down on such free-ranging intellectual activity.

But we are ahead of the story, and the story of education in the West is not altogether clear. What seems to have happened in general is that the Germanic folk invasions of the fifth century swept away Roman schools as they swept away the Roman political and economic system, first in the outlying provinces and later in the center. So, as Britain fell, and Spain, and the Danubian provinces, so did their education decline. Then Gaul and Africa and, finally, most of Italy succumbed toward the end of the sixth centry. But still the educational process went on—sometimes in schools, sometimes in monasteries, and sometimes in the homes of urban professionals or country gentlemen.

In Italy the currents of Roman life continued without complete interruption despite the long period of invasions and disasters that beset the Empire from the fifth to the seventh or eighth century. Especially important for education was the fact that town life remained stronger in Italy than in any other part of western Europe. The process of Latinizing the Germanic peoples who swept into Italy continued apace, slower in some periods and swifter in others. One of the principal means of assimilation of the Germanic tribes was the existence of the secular schools that had been sponsored by the later Roman emperors and the Roman towns. The Ostrogothic king, Theodoric, even took steps to reestablish the town schools during his reign in the early sixth century, and the Lombard kings and nobles did likewise as soon as conditions were a little more settled after the disruptions caused by their coming in the later sixth century.

Although the level of instruction in Italian schools was doubtless low in the seventh and eighth centuries, some secular schools continued to function in several of the principal towns of Italy, especially in the south, where Byzantine influence remained strong and Lombard rule only nominal. Naples, Ravenna, Salerno, and Rome could boast of classical literary education throughout the early Middle Ages. These secular schools, conducted both by private teachers and by public teachers supported by the towns, did not give religious instruction but emphasized grammar (including classical literature), rhetoric, law, and medicine. The fact that such scholars as Paul the Deacon and Peter of Pisa could be called from Italy to the court of Charlemagne in the ninth century shows that instruction in the classics had persisted. Salerno was mentioned as a center of medical study as early as the ninth century, and in 825 the Emperor Lothaire I published a decree naming eight or nine Italian cities as places eligible for the establishment of higher schools to which scholars from their surrounding districts could go.

Although the evidence is sparse, there is reason for believing that some secular schools also continued to exist during the early Middle Ages in northern Europe and in North Africa. Certainly the druid schools of Ireland were for long maintained alongside the Christian monasteries. In France the schools at Chartres probably had their origins in druid schools which had been established by the Celts and had persisted until refounded and stimulated by Charlemagne in the late eighth and early ninth centuries. Not only were the lines of scholarly communication kept open to Byzantium from Italy but also to North Africa where Carthage was able to continue its Latin scholarship under the Vandals, Byzantine rule, and the Arabs down to the eleventh century.

Dispersion of Latin Education by Royal Initiative

Not only did Roman education collapse from the periphery of the empire toward the center as the Germans rolled back Roman authority, but, curiously enough, the revivals of education under religious and kingly auspices also took place from the periphery inwards: first in Ireland, which was conquered by Christianity but not by Rome; then in Britain; and finally in Gaul and Germany. After Christianity was brought to Ireland in the late fifth century, literary education followed in the wake of the establishment of monasteries. Some Irish monks not only learned Latin, but also Greek and Hebrew. Having had no direct contact with Latin as a living language, the Irish became acquainted with classical civilization solely through the study of books, word lists, digests, dictionaries, encyclopedias, and compendia. They did remarkably well, but their learning was bound to possess more than a touch of the second hand and the artificial. The Irish monks carried their classical learning and their Christianity to northern Scotland in the sixth century, then southward to England, and to the continent as far south as Italy.

By the seventh century the English had picked up the task begun by the Irish and redoubled the mission of spreading Latin education through their monastic schools. The British scholars, practical-minded from the outset, were able to simplify the teaching of Latin grammar, verse, and prose and adapt it to a people to whom it was a wholly alien tongue. Donatus, Cato, and Priscian could all assume that *their* students were little Latins living in a Latin culture, but Bede and Alcuin knew that their little Britons and Anglo-Saxons had to learn Latin in a different way, as a second language.

The revival of British education in the seventh and eighth centuries was a remarkably international phenomenon. The Anglo-Saxons had come as conquerors from the east; Irish monks came in from the west; Scottish monks came down from the north, and Italian missionaries sent by the Pope came up from the south. When Pope Gregory the Great commissioned Augustine to be bishop of Canterbury Cathedral in 597, it was the beginning of a fairly continuous exchange between Italy and Britain that lasted for centuries down to the time of the Renaissance. Not only Italians came. Theodore of Tarsus who presided as archbishop of Canterbury in the late seventh century was a Byzantine who had studied at Athens. The flow of scholars, priests, monks, and manuscripts speeded enormously the early Latin education of the British. A notable company learned their lessons well: Bede, Aldheim, Boniface, Egbert, Elbert, Alcuin. Thus, when Charlemagne was ready to concentrate on education as a foundation for the development of his new empire, he turned to Alcuin of York to be the head of his palace school and his special adviser on imperial educational affairs.

The most notable of the efforts by kings and emperors to establish schools under their jurisdiction was that of Charlemagne, whose political attempts to establish a strong centralized government were paralleled by his interest in extending education. He required the clergy to improve their ability to read and write and to raise the level of their scholarship in general so that they could write good letters, be able to calculate the date of Easter, and know the grounds of their faith. He thus required schools for teaching reading to be established where they were absent. Abbots and priests were to be examined about their educational attainments by their bishops, and corrupt manuscripts were to be corrected in monastery scriptoria. In response to this stimulus, Bishop Theodolphus of Orléans ordered his priests to see that schools were provided in every town or on every feudal manor where children might learn to read and write without payment of a fee.

In addition to this general stimulation of education for the sake of improving the religious scholarship of the clergy, Charlemagne recognized that he needed a steady supply of trained personnel for the administration of his empire. To this end he revived the palace school at his court in Aachen, which apparently had been established as early as the sixth century as a training ground for the priesthood. But now Charlemagne wanted a different kind of school, one that would train civil servants as well as church administrators.[2]

Charlemagne chose Peter of Pisa from north Italy to be the head of his palace school, but he learned to his chagrin what technical assistance advisers have often discovered since: Peter was not interested in or capable of doing the job that Charlemagne wanted done. Peter was interested in teaching the fine points of Latin composition and literary appreciation, not in training high-level manpower. Charemagne kept Peter on as an adornment to the intellectual life of his court, but he called in Alcuin in 782 to run his school and to be his adviser on educational development.

Alcuin proved to be as happy a choice as a technical adviser as Peter had been unfortunate. Education was finally recognized as being too important to be left to the odd moments of a preoccupied clergyman beset by all the tasks of running a church. It had to be turned over to a full-time professional. Alcuin, working at the task for fourteen years, was able to make considerable headway in developing a priesthood that had practical competence in using Latin. He wrote textbooks that stressed the reading of Latin for practical as well as religious purposes, not as an exercise in the literary appreciation of the ancients. He wrote dialogues in question and answer form that pupils could memorize as conversation pieces. He did not launch a revival of learning in the humanistic sense. Instead he launched an organized program of fundamental educational development upon which Western Christendom could build a sound superstructure of Latin scholarship in the coming centuries.

As the revival of education in England had been an international mix, the

[2]R. R. Bolgar, *The Classical Heritage and Its Beneficiaries from the Carolingian Age to the End of the Renaissance,* Harper Torchbooks, New York, 1964, p. 109.

Carolingian Renaissance was even more the result of an intermingling of peoples and ideas deliberately sought and managed by Charlemagne and his educational adviser. Charlemagne summoned scholars from Ireland, Spain, and Italy, as well as from England, to aid in preparing a learned clergy and officialdom for church and state. In general, the efforts of Charlemagne and Alcuin loom large when compared with those of earlier and later times. Despite weak successors, civil war, and invasion, learning and schools never sank as low after the time of Charlemagne as they had before his time.

Under Louis the Pious, the Irish scholar Clement was called to head the palace school. Under Charles the Bald, who ruled the western part of the Empire, the greatest scholar of his time, Johannes Scotus Erigena, conducted the palace school. Under this stimulus a provincial church council meeting in Paris in 824 decreed that bishops should foster schools in their dioceses so that church scholars might know better the grounds of their faith. At the same time Lothaire I, who ruled the central and Italian part of the Empire, issued a decree directing the establishment of higher schools in several Italian cities. Pope Eugenius II saw to it that a church council translated Lothaire's decree into practice by directing his bishops to establish schools in their parishes and dioceses for the teaching of grammar, the liberal arts, and religious doctrine.

Meanwhile, in the German part of the Empire, the scholar Rabanus Maurus was establishing monasteries and schools so extensively that he has been called the "preceptor of Germany." When Otto the Great revived the concept of a unified Roman Empire in the late tenth century, he installed his younger brother Bruno as virtual head of all the schools in the Empire. Bruno made the palace the intellectual center, much as Alcuin had done for Charlemagne. He stimulated learning in the monasteries, gathered together the best scholars, and collected the finest manuscripts he could find.

In England, royal interest in education was spasmodic, but considerable progress was made by Alfred the Great in the latter part of the ninth century. He established a palace school at his court for the sons of the nobility, decreed that sons of the wealthy should attend school until they were fifteen years of age, and brought to England many scholars from the Continent. Under the leadership of St. Dunstan schools were established in the churches, as well as in monasteries, in order to foster and improve learning among the priesthood.

The Clerical Guardians of the Schools When secular authorities actively sponsored education, they operated through the clergy. When kings gathered scholars about them, the scholars were clerics; and when kings ordered schools to be established, the schools were established in monasteries, churches, or cathedrals (with the exception of the palace schools themselves). Thus did kings and emperors occasionally prod the clergy and stimulate educational activity in the church. However, the direct control of most schools was in the hands of the clergy. As the political power of the Carolingian emperors declined in the ninth and tenth centuries, the Pope and the church councils began to take more and more independent action toward the encouragement of schools and education.

For example, the Second Council of Toledo in Visigoth Spain in 527 prescribed that boys destined for the clergy should be instructed in the cathedral schools under the supervision of the bishop. A hundred years later the fourth council at Toledo repeated the injunction. As a result of these and many other efforts the bishops themselves began to teach the elements of literacy in their cathedrals. With the disappearance of the traditional Roman schools the bishops had to give the fundamentals of education to prospective priests as well as theological instruction. The cathedral school (or episcopal school) was the result. In its beginnings in the sixth century and for several centuries thereafter, the cathedral school was basically an elementary school for teaching the literacy and music required for conducting church services (hence the term "song school").

Then, as Christianity spread to the countryside and as the urban basis of Roman society began to disintegrate, the church devised the parish system to cover the rural regions and the villages. This, of course, meant that more and more priests were needed for the ever growing web of parish churches. Obviously the bishop in his cathedral school could not supply the number needed, so parish priests would have to provide education for their own localities. The second Council of Vaison (529) urged parish priests to assume responsibility for educating their successors. The Council of Merida (666) applied the same principle to Spain. The obligation of parish churches, as well as cathedral churches, to maintain schools was set forth time after time by church councils and by various popes. A council held in Rome in 853 decreed that elementary instruction should be given in all parishes and that schools for instruction in the liberal arts should be established in all cathedrals. In 855 a council at Valens supported this view. In 908 the Bishop of Modena, in appointing a new priest, put as his first duty the task of maintaining a school and educating the boys under his jurisdiction.

While the spread of parish schools did not provide anything like a universal system of education, they did eventually make education more available to a wider spectrum of social classes than the Eastern Church had done. They even reached the rural regions in ways that the urbanized Greek and Roman schools had not done. To be sure, the fact that so many church councils, popes, and bishops on so many different occasions issued orders for increased attention to schools doubtless meant that the earlier injunctions had been neglected and that new pressure had to be exerted upon a reluctant or indifferent clergy. Nevertheless, the evidence of the *intent* of the church is clear, and eventually the network of schools made a Latin education more and more accessible to those who were destined for a civil career, as well as those headed for the clergy.

Even more important than the parish and cathedral schools during the early Middle Ages, the monastic schools dominated the educational scene of Europe from the sixth to the tenth or eleventh century. From the ninth century on, many monastic schools included instruction for boys going into the secular priesthood or into secular life (*externi*) as well as for those who were to become monks (*oblati*). The most influential of the monastic groups was that of St. Benedict, an Italian monk of the sixth century, who developed at Monte Cassino an elaborate scheme of regulations for the conduct of his followers. Benedictine monasticism spread over all of Italy by the seventh century and over most of Europe by the ninth century. At its peak the

Benedictines maintained several thousand monasteries, from which came a great number of bishops, popes, scholars, and teachers.

Of necessity, the manual and agricultural arts were often highly developed, for monasteries were essentially rural institutions that had to be largely self-supporting in the subsistence economy of the early Middle Ages. At a time when the secular branch of the church was not yet highly organized, the monasteries did much to convert Western Europe by spreading the gospel through their missionaries. They were also the principal literary, artistic, intellectual, and educational centers of Europe in the early Middle Ages. The preservation and copying of ancient manuscripts became one of their important functions, promoted under the rule of constant industry.

The Primacy of Transmission

In essence, the propaedeutic for the early Middle Ages was learning Latin in schools with materials produced in the Hellenistic-Roman genre but shaped to the purposes of teaching nonliterate Western Europeans a written language and a culture that would enable them to function as Christian clerics in both church and state. The dispersion of Graeco-Roman education may have been a phase in the disintegration of Rome, but it also exercised a fundamental formative influence upon the West. Westerners did not at this time fundamentally change or revise the classical heritage; they simply used its basic Latin ingredients to enable a small class of educated elite to be able to read the Scriptures and religious commentaries and administer the business of the church.[3] From the sixth to the tenth centuries "transmission" was the prime order of the day.

Some of the writers of the early medieval period who transmitted the classical tradition to the West were competent and careful; others were dry and lifeless. Usually considered to be the last of the succession of classical writers that began with Homer, Boethius translated much of the best Greek science and philosophy into Latin. His *Consolation of Philosophy* provided most of what Western Europe knew of Greek thought for several centuries. Some historians consider the Roman Boethius of the early sixth century A.D. to be the "schoolmaster to the Middle Ages," as Homer was considered to be schoolmaster to the Greeks.

Another of the intermediaries between classical and medieval scholarship was Cassiodorus, a Christian scholar and monk who contributed to the preservation of classical and patristic writings by his inauguration of manuscript copying in the monasteries in special rooms known as *scriptoria.* In his own work, Cassiodorus wrote extensively on religious topics, history, and the various liberal arts. He was not the scholar that Boethius was, but he put much material, both secular and religious, into a form that was usable by the church. Both Boethius and Cassiodorus played important roles in Latinizing the Ostrogoths who ruled Italy. Perhaps even more influential for the future of education, they adopted the seven liberal arts as defined by Martianus Capella in the fifth century but rejected his paganism. Cassiodorus quoted to such good effect the scriptural text, "Wisdom hath builded her house, she hath hewn out her seven pillars" (Proverbs, 9:1), that church educators eventually accepted all seven

[3]Ibid., p. 127.

liberal arts for use in the monastic and cathedral schools. When Capella's seven bridesmaids were finally given house by Cassiodorus' seven pillars, the medieval definition of the liberal arts was established in sturdy form as early as the beginning of the seventh century.

A third transmitter was Isidore of Seville, a Spanish bishop, who compiled an encyclopedia called the *Etymologies* which, according to modern standards, is lifeless and dull, containing hundreds of excerpts, terms, and definitions arranged according to no particular order or system. To the naïve and uninstructed the *Etymologies* must have been welcome; but far from being a creative reworking of classical thought, its barrenness reflects the decline in scholarship that had taken place by the seventh century in Spain. In contrast, an outstanding scholarly performance in England was that of St. Bede, often called the "father of English learning," who knew Greek and Hebrew as well as Latin. He wrote on music, history, biography, science, theology, pedagogy, and the liberal arts.

Prior to the eleventh century little original work was done in any of the liberal arts, yet their main task was no less than the Latinizing of Western Europe. By and large these formidable propaedeutic goals were achieved as Latin gradually became the universal medium of communication and discourse among educated persons. Grammar was consequently the most important of the liberal arts taught in the schools during the early Middle Ages, for the non-Latin peoples had to be taught the rudiments of Latin in order to be able to take part in the religious and intellectual life of the times. The grammars by Donatus and Priscian and the reader by Cato remained the influential texts.

Rhetoric, on the other hand, was largely in eclipse during the early Middle Ages. Although it maintained its place as one of the recognized seven liberal arts, rhetoric lost the predominantly oratorical and practical character it had achieved as the highest of the liberal arts under the Roman Empire. In the popular medieval manuals material was condensed from Cicero and Quintilian, but their emphasis upon the public uses of rhetoric was reduced. Rhetoric, logic, and the mathematical arts of the quadrivium had to wait until the later Middle Ages for their real influence to be felt again. In the early Middle Ages the all-inclusive work on music was that of Boethius, which was known nearly everywhere that music was taught as a liberal art.

Naturally, propaedeutical education was highly bookish in character. In an age when books were so scarce, they were regarded with great respect and even reverence, for the written word was viewed as the essence of authority. Submissiveness and obedience were qualities which the schools set out to instill in the pupils. Although many advanced scholars showed critical abilities, initiative, and originality, these were not qualities to be encouraged in young students. The propaedeutics of the Middle Ages epitomized reliance upon the textbook. If a teacher had one, he was lucky; perhaps he knew little more than was in it. Indeed, it might almost be said that a person could be identified as a teacher by the fact that he owned a textbook or had memorized one. The principal practical goal of education was the ability to read Latin, and the principal method used was memorizing the content of the required books to the accompaniment of strict discipline and corporal punishment.

Latin syllables, Latin words, and the rules of Latin grammar were read by the teacher and dictated to the pupil from Donatus, Cato, or the Latin psalter or prayer book. Often, no doubt, the material was committed to memory by the boys without their understanding the meaning of the words. Writing may sometimes have been learned too, but it was not universally taught. Music took the form of instruction in the accents of words and training in singing and chanting the phrases. The finger elements of arithmetic and some simple fundamental operations may also have been taught.

When there was little or no literature or fund of knowledge written in the European vernaculars, and when all knowledge handed down by the church was in Latin, learning to read and write Latin had a most practical value. Without it one could not broaden his horizon beyond his own little niche. Nevertheless, the Latin of the church was a foreign language to the Germanic and Celtic peoples of Western Europe. It was therefore an astonishing achievement to whip into shape countless generations of youths who must have found the learning of Latin in the schools always a difficult and sometimes a distasteful task:

> The road to the classical heritage has always lain through the schools. . . . So we find that at all periods the majority of those who came to know something about the classics started young and, even if they later became great scholars through their private efforts, acquired the beginnings of their competence through the daily routine of the classroom: which makes the routine of primary importance.[4]

By the end of the tenth century the Latinizing of the West was completed. The educated class of Western Europe had learned its preparatory lessons and was now ready to start out on its own. Mere repetition and imitation were no longer satisfying. Strict limitations confining study solely to those parts of the classical literature that bolstered church doctrine or the training of clerics were no longer so easily acceptable. Secular studies in law, medicine, natural science, mathematics, philosophy, logic, and rhetoric were to become more attractive than the literature of the Church Fathers. Genuine assimilation and adaptation and reworking of the knowledge of the past became the new order of the day. Boethius, Cassiodorus, Isidore, Bede, and Alcuin gave way to Gerbert, John of Salisbury, Peter Abelard, Roger Bacon, and Thomas Aquinas. From the eleventh century onward, the cathedral school and then the university replaced the monastery as the chief citadel of higher learning. The propaedeutics were completed; the education of the West was ready to begin. (See Figure 5.1—the Curve of Educational Development in Western Civilization.)

B. CIVILIZATION BUILDING IN THE WEST (1000 A.D.-1400 A.D.)

In discussing the origins of the Mesopotamian, Egyptian, and Hellenic civilizations we identified four major factors at work: urbanization, social differentiation, political

[4]Ibid., pp. 26-27.

Figure 5.1   The Curve of Educational Development in Western Civilization

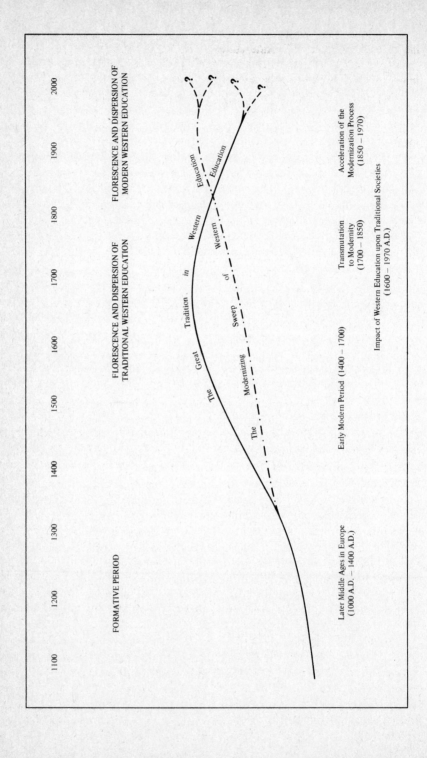

institutionalization, and literate education. It will come as no surprise, then, to find the same general factors at work in the formative period of Western civilization as it began to take shape in the eleventh to fifteenth centuries, although there were obviously deep-seated differences as well as similarities. Western civilization grew up in the later Middle Ages on the ground of an extraordinarily powerful and long-lived civilization whose forms had disintegrated but whose influence never entirely disappeared.

Graeco-Roman cities and towns were widely destroyed in northern Europe, but an urban way of life was never wholly snuffed out, especially in Italy. The specialization inherent in the differentiated occupations of town and country declined markedly in the early Middle Ages, but traffic in goods and ideas with the East never entirely stopped. The political institutions of the Empire disintegrated, but the ideal of a central political authority was kept alive, however faintly, in the Roman church and in Charlemagne's empire, as well as in Byzantium. And though many educational institutions disappeared as cities, specialization, and political authority crumbled, the means of schooling continued to be nourished by urban remnants, by persisting political authorities, and by the church itself. Indeed, as Christendom embraced the Graeco-Roman corpus of knowledge for its own purposes, it handed down educational traditions which eventually broke the strings that bound them to the church and struck out on their own.

In general, then, the formation of Western civilization was characterized by (1) a revival of urbanization as cities and commerce grew; (2) a growing social differentiation that ranged across all levels of society and was especially colored by the guild type of corporate association; (3) a political institutionalization that saw a four-way tug of war between feudalism, universal Christendom, national monarchies, and city-states; and (4) a systematizing of educational institutions that began to serve secular, professional, and religious clienteles that proved to be larger and more varied than those of any prior civilization.

Urbanization and Social Differentiation

In general, European trade and commerce had been local affairs in the early Middle Ages, but as early as the tenth century the Italian cities of Venice, Genoa, and Pisa took the lead in reviving an East-West trade which was given further stimulus by the Crusaders who relied upon their fleets, sea routes, and knowledge. In the twelfth and thirteenth centuries a great upswing in commerce carried wares from the East to the Italian cities and then by caravan on river routes into the rest of Europe for distribution at local fairs and marketplaces.

From the twelfth century on, towns grew rapidly in number, importance, and size in all parts of Western Europe, creating greater demand for agricultural products. So forests were cut, swamps drained, and agricultural techniques improved through the use of fertilizer and crop rotation. As a result, the population of Europe increased so rapidly that it is estimated that by 1350 it was greater than it had been under the Roman Empire. Freedom was enhanced, for if a serf could get to a town and stay for a year and a day, he became legally, as well as practically, free. All in all, an astonishing energy, versatility, and vitality went into the constitution of towns and cities in the thirteenth century. Cities were a major source of increasing secularization and interest in the everyday affairs of this world.

One of the most pervasive features of medieval urbanization was the forming of specialized associations for the mutual protection and welfare of persons who had common interests. This social grouping for differentiated purposes characterized nearly all aspects of Western life, from church choirs, clergymen, scholars, knights, and soldiers to merchants and artisans of all types. Particularly important in the urbanization process was the formation of merchant and craft guilds. Merchant guilds originated as traders banded together for their travels from market to market. As these guilds garnered a monopoly on foreign trade and obtained the legal right to such monopoly from the feudal lords, they in turn influenced the development of municipal governments. From these beginnings the merchants rapidly grew in wealth and power until, as the middle class, they made their way into the privileged company of the leading aristocracy and clergy. The winning of power by the merchant class was a notable step in the process of political participation which marked the later Middle Ages.

The craft guilds arose somewhat later for the purpose of regulating the manufacture of goods. By the thirteenth century they had appeared in almost every city of northern Europe. Artisans organized themselves into distinctive groups according to their craft specialties in order to protect themselves from shoddy work, low prices, and inferior workmanship and to gain a monopoly of production. Within the circle, however, the effort was made to provide equality for all members and to achieve stability to such an extent that advertising, cutting prices, and instituting technical improvements were considered disloyal and were thus prohibited. The guilds also had a religious and fraternal aspect. They often maintained altars in the churches or supported priests of their own. They helped the poor, the sick, and the aged; they built roads and schools; and they even organized military defenses.

From Feudalism to National State

From the middle of the tenth century onward the recurrent invasions and migrations of warlike folk-society peoples in western Europe began to taper off, and a greater measure of internal security and peace began to seem possible, not so much by the reestablishment of a single imperial rule over all Europe as by particularized local efforts. Thus arose feudalism in the wake of Charlemagne's faltering empire. From the tenth to the thirteenth centuries an enormously complex and variegated skein of personal and political relationships was worked out by medieval kings, nobles, and lawyers. Joseph R. Strayer and Rushton Coulborn describe feudalism in general as follows:

> Feudalism is primarily a method of government, not an economic or a social system, though it obviously modifies and is modified by the social and economic environment. It is a method of government in which the essential relation is not that between ruler and subject, nor state and citizen, but between

lord and vassal. This means that the performance of political functions depends on personal agreements between a limited number of individuals, and that political authority is treated as a private possession. Since personal contacts are so important in feudal government, it tends to be most effective at the local level where such contacts are easy and frequent. Since political power is personal rather than institutional, there is relatively little separation of functions; the military leader is usually an administrator and the administrator is usually a judge. Military functions are prominent in most feudal societies, especially in their beginnings.[5]

The system of class stratification that grew up in Europe as a result of feudal ties bound nobles together as vassal to lord and bound unfree serfs to work the land for nobles. Churchmen and nobility made up the two aristocratic upper classes, often referred to as the first and second estates, and the lower classes made up all the rest of the people, most of whom were unfree serfs. In the later Middle Ages the growth of commerce and the rise of towns made possible the appearance of a middle class with rights above those of the unfree serfs but below those of the aristocracy. The middle classes of merchants, traders, and craftsmen became the nucleus of the third estate.

On its positive side, feudalism bequeathed to modern Europe a tradition of political contract and reciprocity of obligations. The king was entitled to command obedience only so long as he fulfilled his side of the contract. On the negative side, Europe was saddled with an entrenched and hereditary aristocratic class set apart from the common people by distinctions that marked all aspects of life, including educational opportunity. After comparing the role of feudalism in the major civilizations of the world, Coulborn came to this conclusion: "The place of feudalism in history . . . is that of a very important political device for the revival of a declining civilization, and for the extension of civilization to new peoples not formerly civilized."[6]

The idea of a universal political authority would not die. Innocent III, exerting more secular power than any other pope before or after his time, believed that Christendom should be a great unified commonwealth with the pope at the head, inspiring governments everywhere to righteousness. In his view, the pope was clearly superior to secular authorities; he was successor of Peter and feudal overlord of all kings. Innocent III joined with the Lombard cities of northern Italy against Emperor Frederick II in a struggle that weakened the Empire and kept Germany and Italy so divided within themselves that strong centralized governments could not be established in those countries until the nineteenth century.

In contrast, the national monarchies in France and England became ever more powerful in their contests with the feudal nobility on the one side and the papacy on the other. Outstanding among the French kings who made such gains were Philip II (Augustus), who conquered many of the lands in France still claimed by the Norman kings of England; Louis IX (St. Louis), who gave France a long period of peace and

---

[5]Rushton Coulborn (ed.), *Feudalism in History,* Archon Books, Hamden, Conn., 1965, pp. 4-5.

[6]Ibid., p. 383.

improved the courts of law throughout the country; and Philip IV (the Fair), under whose rule the Estates-General began to take shape.

The kings of England likewise made headway in unifying their country. Beginning with William the Conqueror, the Norman rule established a highly centralized and effective central government; yet when King John was forced to sign the Magna Charta in 1215, the English nobility gave notice that they did not intend to be brought under the king's rule without a struggle. Under Henry III the great council was expanded to include representatives from the principal towns as well as members of the nobility. At the end of the thirteenth century, under Edward I, representatives of the middle classes were admitted and shape was being given to English parliamentary government. The House of Commons, made up of middle-class representatives from the cities and the landowning gentry from the rural sections, became more representative of the whole country at an earlier date than did the Estates-General in France. Furthermore, a spirit of national consciousness was heightened as the common man felt himself an integral part of the nation because he had fought in the Hundred Years War as a foot soldier.

Attacks upon the papacy by the kings grew in intensity during the fourteenth century. The principal contest involved Pope Boniface VIII and King Philip IV of France. Boniface issued a series of papal bulls in which he exhorted his clergy not to pay taxes to the kings, denied the right of secular courts to try the clergy, asserted his complete sovereignty over all secular rulers, and specifically declared Philip IV deposed. Philip IV in turn sent his agents to Italy to capture Boniface and demand that he quit the papacy. The result of the whole episode was a terrible fall in the prestige of the papacy.

Movements for Reform of the Church.   By the beginning of the fifteenth century attacks upon the church were being delivered from still other directions. Not only were secular rulers, kings, and emperors trying to extend their political authority at the expense of the church, but peasants were seething with discontent, and the middle classes were restless under the taxes and tithes that were expected by the church. Moreover, from within the church itself came the cry that clergymen were so incredibly worldly and rich that their neglect of religious duties required radical reform.

John Wycliffe, a teacher of theology and philosophy at Oxford in the fourteenth century, attacked papal authority, urged the direct responsibility of the individual to God, and sponsored the translation of the Bible into English so that all could read it. His followers, known as Lollards, followed his ideas with a petition to Parliament in 1395 to enact a series of church reforms. Parliament not only paid no attention to the petition but was induced to pass a law in 1401 for the burning of heretics. In 1408 the Archbishop of Canterbury issued a series of decrees prohibiting the publication of Lollard books and the English translation of the Bible without the license of the bishop concerned. Wycliffe was born a century too soon.

The church also came under attack in the fourteenth century from the proponents of the rising national states. One of the outstanding exponents was Pierre

Dubois, royal advocate to Philip IV of France, whose chief work, *The Recovery of the Holy Land,* argued that the church should give up its secular ambitions and leave all matters of secular authority to the state. Interestingly, Dubois proposed an elaborate plan to educate a carefully selected group of young people to be educational emissaries to the Holy Land.[7] After studying Latin grammar intensively from the age of four to twelve, they were to go to a secondary school to study Greek, Arabic, and logic. At age fourteen they were to be introduced to natural philosophy, moral philosophy, and even medicine, law, and theology. Dubois must have been one of the first to believe that an encyclopedic education was necessary for a well-prepared technical adviser, colonial administrator, or missionary.

While the church and the state quarreled about whose authority should be supreme in the lives of men, some men began to assert the right of the individual to throw off the unwarranted restraints of both in order to develop his own personality in all its aspects—creative, artistic, emotional, and physical, as well as intellectual.

Despite his deeply grounded Christianity, Francis Petrarch preeminently reflected the secular temper of individualism in his expression of the intense emotions of poet and writer struggling with the loves and hates, the successes and frustrations, the attractions of the natural and supernatural which welled up in the personal lives of people. Seeking to free human individuality from the restricting demands of church, guild, manor, and monastery, Petrarch claimed that the best portrayal of the perfection and development of human nature was to be found in the classical literature of Greece and Rome. As the initiator of a specialized interest in the Latin classics, Petrarch despised the principal medieval instruments of knowledge. He passed over logic, philosophy, science, law, and medicine and turned to emulate the Latin style of the ancient writers, especially Vergil and Cicero. In his desire to reestablish the glory of the Roman Empire, he was indefatigable in his search for classical manuscripts; he edited many of them, using only pagan sources as his authority; and he became acquainted with nearly all the accessible Latin authors. Petrarch was a forerunner of the humanists of the fifteenth century, as Wycliffe was of the Protestant reformers of the sixteenth century, and Dubois of the partisans of the nation-state in the seventeenth century.

Despite restlessness with the role of the church in medieval life stemming from kings, emperors, reformers, and assorted protesters, the church's resources and appeal to the faithful were enormous. This appeal was by no means simply political, intellectual, or doctrinal. It was the appeal of a religion of the heart, as well as one of authority and obedience. The retreat of the Benedictine monks to their monasteries in the eleventh century, and the decline of other monastic orders in the face of urbanization left the way open for a new kind of ministering to the needs of the people. This need was met by the mendicant friars, especially the Franciscans and Dominicans.

St. Francis of Assisi, responding to the demands of the time, determined to go

---

[7]Lynn Thorndike, "Elementary and Secondary Education in the Middle Ages," in *Speculum,* vol 15, pp. 404-405, October 1940.

abroad among the people as Jesus had done, helping the poor, healing the sick, and preaching the gospel of love. Soon after the year 1200, St. Francis gathered about him a few apostolic followers, and in a few years he had organized several thousand members into the Friars Minor, or Minorites. The ruling ideas of St. Francis included the determination to imitate the life of Jesus as closely as possible; a belief in the latent goodness of all men to be developed through the power of Christian love; a life of poverty as the best way to serve God; an acknowledgment of the duty of joyfulness; and love of all the beings of nature as creatures of God. In general, the Franciscans did great service to the church by reconciling the masses of the people through the example they set of returning to the humble and simple spirit of ancient Christianity.

St. Dominic, on the other hand, was a severe ascetic, noted for the rigor of his life and for his administrative activities in organizing the Dominican friars. Like the Franciscans, the Dominicans abandoned the idea of monastic seclusion and went among the people to live in poverty, especially in the cities. Profiting from St. Dominic's genius for organization, the Dominicans soon became a powerful and centralized agency of the church. They began to flood into the universities in the belief that an educated clergy was necessary if they were to fulfill their spiritual and educative mission. The mendicant orders to whom the mantle of innovation within the church had fallen eventually became the principal instruments for the spread of Latin Catholic education not only throughout Europe but to Africa, Asia, and America.

C. THE EMERGENT FORMS OF WESTERN SCHOOLING

The ferment that characterized Western civilization building in the later Middle Ages was reenacted in the field of education. Popes, bishops, priests, and monks continued to exercise control over schools, but kings, nobles, merchants, artisans, town governments, and mendicant friars got into the educational act with increasing relish and fervor.

Church Schools

The basic character of instruction for learning Latin in the elementary schools of cathedral and parish churches did not change radically in this period. The new factor arose as the political quarrels between kings, church, and cities spilled over into struggles for the control of schools. Just as modern nations have realized that economic and political development rests in large part upon the power of education, so the early rulers of the West began to realize, however dimly, the importance of this relationship. Although the church maintained its strong position in the face of protest and dissent, definite gains were made by kings and towns in establishing and maintaining schools. This was not a time when comprehensive state school systems were set up, but the groundwork was being laid for national systems which would eventually consist of vernacular, or elementary, schools for the ordinary people and classical, or secondary, schools for the upper classes.

The medieval pattern of school control centered in the church with the pope in supreme authority but with local administration of education in the hands of the bishop for his diocese or delegated by him to his *scholasticus*. The licensing of teachers came from these officials, who exerted general supervision over the schools in their jurisdiction. The Third Lateran Council in 1179 decreed that every cathedral church should have a master not only assigned to teach boys who wished to become clerics but also to teach without fee poor children whose parents could not afford to pay for the instruction. Free schools were also to be maintained in other churches and monasteries. Licenses to teach should be granted only on the basis of proper qualifications and should not be for sale.

As cities grew, it became necessary to locate schools in outlying parishes and in different parts of town, because it was difficult for children to travel from the outskirts to the central church. Conflicts over the management of new schools arose between church officials, who felt that the control of education was properly theirs, and secular agencies, which began to lay claim to the right to establish and maintain schools. Among these agencies were town governments, secular rulers, private teachers, and voluntary associations of persons who wished to endow schools for charitable purposes.

Town Schools

Italian towns continued to maintain their schools throughout the Middle Ages, some of them exhibiting more or less continuity with their original foundations in the days of the Roman Empire. With the acceleration of trade in the tenth and eleventh centuries, attention to secular learning increased. Villani's *Chronicle* estimates that by the middle of the thirteenth century there were between 8,000 and 10,000 children learning to read in the schools of Florence; there were also six schools in which 1,000 to 1,200 children were learning arithmetic; and there were four advanced schools were 550 or 600 children were learning grammar and rhetoric. Likewise, in Siena before 1250 several masters were employed by the republic to give instruction in grammar, medicine, and law in an effort to reval the schools at Bologna and Padua. The estimate has also been made that in this period there were some seventy theachers of reading in Milan, along with eight teachers of grammar. One can infer from this that many of the Italian cities were rivaling each other in providing schools under the control of the city authorities.

The movement for town control of schools also took place in northern Europe. In Germany during the thirteenth century, for example, many towns were taking steps to establish schools under the control of municipal authorities; similar steps were being taken in the Netherlands and to a lesser degree in France. In general, these schools were religious in aim and Latin in content, representing not so much an effort to establish secular instruction as simply to exert civil control over religious schools. The continuity of secular schools was not nearly so clear in northern Europe as it was in Italy, but nevertheless the growth of interest in town control of education reflected the growing economic and political power of the middle classes in medieval life.

In Germany severe struggles arose between the church officials and the town authorities concerning whether or not the towns could set up schools under their own jurisdiction. Gradually, the towns won the right to establish schools by appealing for support either to the local ruler or to the pope over the head of the local bishop. The foundations of Germany's characteristic public-parochial system were being laid as the town and church reached agreements for joint operation of the schools. Often the priest would do the teaching, but the town would pay his salary and looked upon him as a public official. As many of the Netherlands towns won freedom from the control of the feudal nobility, they also began to assert their rights to build schools and to choose and pay teachers.

Private Schools

In the later Middle Ages there is evidence that individuals and groups began to establish schools that were not directly responsible either to public authorities or to the church. The most important of these were the chantry schools and the guild schools. A chantry school was most likely to be established by a wealthy person who wished to endow a foundation to support a priest to chant masses for the salvation of his soul after death. At first, the teaching function of the chantry foundation may have been more or less incidental to the work of the priest, who usually gathered some boys together to form a choir for the Latin services. Later, the school often became an integral or even principal part of the original foundation in which education was the prime motive, not simply incidental to the religious function of the chantry. Likewise, as the guilds became important factors in town life, they often appointed a priest to teach the children of the guild members in a Latin school. These guild schools, sponsored primarily by the merchant guilds, were regular Latin grammar schools, not to be confused with the vocational preparation provided in the apprenticeship system of the craft guilds. These chantry and guild schools founded in the later Middle Ages began the pattern of private control of education that was later to become so important in England during the Renaissance and Reformation periods. The first of the English public schools, founded by William of Wykeham at Winchester in 1382, had its origins in a chantry foundation.

As the clientele available for school instruction grew larger and as the lucrative possibilities in school teaching were realized, the private teacher began to appear on the scene with a view to making his living from the fees and tuition he could obtain. In general, the private, unauthorized teacher met with resistance both from the church and from civil authorities. In 1253 the town of Ypres ruled that the three already established schools should be the only ones to give instruction outside of individual homes; private tutors could be employed in the home if they gave instruction only to the children of the family and admitted no others. The Duke of Brabant established his own schools in Brussels to settle a quarrel that arose when certain private teachers kept on teaching without the approval of the *scholasticus*. In Gloucester, England, the masters of the established grammar school brought court action to restrain an unauthorized teacher from operating in the locality, but the court decided that there could be no private monopoly in the right to conduct grammar schools.

As time went on, private teachers began to organize themselves into guilds in order to protect themselves and to gain the right to teach. For example, in Germany the teachers of writing, commercial arithmetic, and bookkeeping organized themselves into the guild of *rechenmeisters.* They took an apprentice for several years, at the end of which he became a journeyman, known as *schreiber,* until he became a full-fledged master in the guild.

Apprenticeship Education

In the early Middle Ages, as in most preindustrial societies, the most common methods of occupational education had been direct imitation and handing down of skills from father to son. With the rise of towns and the acceleration of trade in the eleventh and twelfth centuries the skills of urban artisans improved noticeably, and by the time of the emergence of the craft guilds in the twelfth and thirteenth centuries the methods of vocational education were also being refined. Since the primary purpose of the guilds was to protect the quality of products and to keep down overproduction, many rules developed concerning entrance into the craft, including the system of apprenticeship as a means of preparing youth for a skilled occupation.

The training of the artisan had three distinct stages: apprentice, journeyman, and master. As an apprentice the boy was assigned to a master craftsman, often on the basis of a written contract, or indenture, which bound both parties to keep certain obligations. The master promised to teach the boy the skills of the trade, look after his morals and religion, give him his keep and perhaps a small stipend, and teach him whatever reading and writing might be needed to carry on the trade. In most cases the reading and writing were probably negligible. In return, the boy promised to work hard and faithfully, keep the secrets of the trade, and not cause the master too much trouble. The period of apprenticeship might last anywhere from three to eleven years. The boys might start any time after seven or eight years of age.

The next stage was that of training as a journeyman, during which time the young man might travel about, working as a day laborer for different masters in their shops, or might work in a larger shop for a continuous period of time for a wage to be set by the guild. Then, if he proved his worth and could present a "masterpiece" showing that he had mastered the skills of the trade, he would be admitted, with appropriate ceremony, to the guild as a full-fledged member. As a master craftsman, he could set up his own shop, hire journeymen, take on apprentices, and become an instructor in the art of the craft.

Courtly Education

As a part of the general assertion of political authority, whether feudal or national, secular rulers began to lay greater claim to the control of education. The dukes and princely rulers of Italian cities often set up schools for the education of noble children and for the greater glorification of their court. In the thirteenth century Emperor Frederick II made his court in Sicily an international center where scholars in the liberal arts and medicine brought together streams of influence from Arabic, Byzantine, Roman, and Italian sources. In Brussels the Duke of Brabant established several elementary schools for both boys and girls in the early fourteenth century.

In England the kings increasingly asserted control of education. In the eleventh century William the Conqueror appointed Lanfranc Archbishop of Canterbury, and St. Anselm became his successor. As patrons of learning in the monasteries and cathedral schools both men helped to consolidate Norman institutions in England. In the twelfth century the court of Henry II sponsored schools in literature, science, and medicine. In 1391 Richard II denied a petition from the House of Commons that children of villeins should be prevented from attending schools. It was later decided through legislation and court decisions that all parents could freely send their children to any school in England, provided, of course, that they could afford to do so. Thus arose one element in the idea of a public school.

In response to the complicated system of personal relationships associated with feudalism, methods of educating the young noble for assuming his obligations were devised outside the regular literary schools. The ideals of chivalry which guided this education stressed the rites of warfare, religion, and courtesy. Warfare demanded training for strength, courage, endurance, and skill in fighting on horseback. The church asked ideals of mercy, honor, generosity to the fallen foe, protection for the weak, and loyalty to the Christian religion. The social graces and manners developed at the courts of the nobles added the notion of *courtoisie*. The ideal knight was thus a man of action, a soldier, courtier, and Christian gentleman, who had reverence for the church as well as loyalty to his overlord.

Although there were no separate schools for training knights, chivalric education, usually conducted at the court of the overlord, included three fairly well-defined stages of training, roughly comparable to the apprenticeship system. The first was designed for the younger boy from the age of seven to fifteen; during this time he acted as page or valet at the court of his father's overlord. As a page, he was attached particularly to the ladies of the court, whom he served and from whom he might learn how to practice the courtly graces and manners, how to sing and play a musical instrument, how to take part in religious ceremonies, and perhaps how to read and write in the vernacular.

From the age of fifteen to about twenty-one the boy acted as a squire, or attendant, for the overlord or one of the knights of the court, helping with the armor and arms, ready to assist in war, tournament, or chase. He learned to ride, hunt, and fight. He perhaps improved his social accomplishments by singing, playing reciting and composing verses, dancing, and entering into the games and storytelling activities of the times. He learned also about the coats of arms and devices of heraldry.

At about age twenty-one the young man was ceremonially inducted into knighthood by the overlord and church officials upon proof of his worth on the field of battle or tournament. As he was dubbed knight, he dedicated himself to service to his overlord and to the church, taking oaths of allegiance to both. The ritual might include a symbolic bath, prayer, or vigorous exercise as a ceremonial means of purifying himself of sins.

The young knight was now ready to enter upon his duties at the court and to undertake his obligations as a vassal, in return for which he might receive some land or other means of subsistence as a fief. His training had possibly included some instruction concerning feudal laws and how to manage a manor and estate, or perhaps he had simply gained experience by watching others deal with the workmen and serfs. In any case, he was sure to acquire the accepted attitudes of superiority toward the common people and the art of commanding others of lower station. The whole training was a class education for entrance into the aristocracy.

Girls of the noble class were also inducted into adult life by learning the religious faith and ceremonies, the social accomplishments of dancing, singing, and instrumental music, and the accepted practices of courtesy. A young girl might also receive instruction in sewing, weaving, and handicrafts, and might learn how to manage household servants. She perhaps also learned to read and write in order to be able to conduct her correspondence and to keep books if occasion required. She was trained in these duties either at home or in a convent, and then in her teens she was likely to be assigned to the overlord's court to learn the social graces of the chivalrous life and to act as a lady in waiting or attendant upon the mistress of the court until marriage. In contrast to the bookish character of the Latin schools, the education of youth of the noble classes was a direct and practical induction through experience.

In general, the provision of organized education in the thirteenth and fourteenth centuries was far more widespread in Western Europe than has hitherto been realized and probably more so than in any other civilization up to that time. This fact made possible one of the basic characteristics of Western civilization: extensive popular participation in political, economic, and cultural life.[8] Without a relatively accessible system of education, such participation would scarcely have been likely. It seems clear that large numbers of children were attending school in the towns of Italy, France, Germany, the Low Countries, and England before the end of the thirteenth century. Even though there were declines in the fourteenth century, a general momentum had begun that did not wholly stop until universal elementary education became the goal of most Western nations.

Another characteristic that Western civilization displayed before the end of the Middle Ages was the relatively quick assimilation of the ideas and knowledge of alien cultures. Here again the flexibility and vigor of the higher educational institutions of the West played a major role in welcoming the learning of other civilizations of the world. We have identified the intermingling of peoples and ideas as a major factor in the building of all the civilizations of the Afro-Eurasian ecumene. The international character of Western civilization in its origin was, if anything, more prominent than in any of the others, and much of this could be attributed to the vitality of the higher educational institutions of the recipient civilization of the West.

D. THE TRANSCENDENT IMPORTANCE OF HIGHER EDUCATION

The central intellectual problem in the formation of Western civilization was the attempt to reconcile the religious values of Christendom with the burgeoning secular growths that sprouted from new political, economic, and educational institutions. The ideal of a universal Christian commonwealth had to defend itself by force, by threat,

[8]William H. McNeill, *The Rise of the West*, University of Chicago Press, Chicago, 1963, pp. 558-559.

by argument, and by compromise against the secular challenges of feudalism, urbanization, commerce, national sovereignty, and the demands for autonomy streaming from emperors, kings, towns, guilds, and universities.

The defenders of the faith stood forth as *reconcilers*, those who attempted to keep the course of thought to what they believed were the main highways of Christian orthodoxy; but there were also the *recalcitrants*, those who kept tugging at the leashes, trying to pull away in one direction or another. For four hundred years the capacity of the reconcilers to assimilate and harness these different secular elements within the church's educational institutions was enormous, but in the end insufficient. While the church was not altogether successful, it is also true that it came closer to achieving this ideal during the later Middle Ages than at any time before or after. Perhaps this is the essence of medievalism.

The intellectual efforts to reconcile the claims of human reason as against the claims of faith led to the gigantic confrontations of the later Middle Ages, an enterprise generally referred to as scholasticism. Here we find such men as St. Anselm and St. Bernard of Clairvaux swinging far toward faith, emotion, and mysticism, whereas Roscellinus, Abelard, and Roger Bacon were tugging at the leash by exalting the claims of reason, intellect, and dialectics. The balance was then struck between faith and reason in the thirteenth century in the synthesis of St. Thomas Aquinas, the greatest of all the reconcilers.

In general, it was as though young and immature peoples were attempting to learn the lessons transmitted from the past in order to be able to solve their own problems in their own way. In this process there were two great lessons to be learned: the whole thought of the pagan world of Greece and Rome, found in the writings of the ancient Greek and Latin writers; and second, the religious thought of the patristic age, contained in the writings of the church Fathers. To these two lessons the people of Western Europe brought their own energies, capacities, and qualities. The Italians, the Spaniards, the Gauls, the Germans, the Anglo-Saxons, and the Northmen all had to learn their hard lessons from the beginning before they could make both the classical and the Christian traditions their own. It had taken some five centuries of propaedeutics simply to acquire the substance of these lessons, to become Latinized. By the eleventh and twelfth centuries the assimilation had become more vital, and by the thirteenth and fourteenth centuries the whole intellectual fabric was ready to be restated in distinctive, but not entirely new, terms.

Scholasticism

The task of assimilating, reconciling, and redirecting Graeco-Roman knowledge to make it conform with Christian doctrine enlisted the best minds of the later Middle Ages. Scholasticism was a method of selecting and classifying general statements taken from religious and classical authorities, comparing the authorities, commenting upon the statements in systematic order, examining the arguments on both sides, drawing conclusions, and refuting the arguments of the other side in detail by marshaling evidence in support of the conclusions accepted. Commentary, argumentation, disputation, and dialectical analysis played key roles in the process.

In the eleventh and twelfth centuries the scholastic orientation known as *realism* was the dominant position of the church establishment of the day. Exhibiting strong affinities with Platonic idealism, it was elaborated by such scholars as St. Anselm, St. Bernard of Clairvaux, and St. Guillaume de Champeaux. St. Anselm affirmed with St. Augustine that all reasoning and discussion about religious affairs must be preceded by faith in revealed truth. In order to arrive at valid knowledge we must first believe the authoritative doctrines of the church stated as universal propositions; only the universal proposition is real.

A dissident position, known as *nominalism,* drew support from the scientific outlook of Aristotle rather than from the idealism of Plato. The most real thing is the individual object; the universal has no independent validity, it is simply a name or a generalization applied for convenience to a category of individual things that are discovered to have similar characteristics. To arrive at truth we must start with individual objects, see how they operate, and then arrive inductively at generalizations useful in classifying their characteristics. Thus the test for reality is not faith or authority but the effort of human reason to find the reality of things.

The secular temper of nominalism was tugging at the leash of religious orthodoxy. In its reliance upon logic and dialectics as the supreme instrumentalities for arriving at knowledge, nominalism elevated human reason above faith. The cause of nominalism was aggressively promoted by Abelard in the twelfth century. More important than his specific doctrine of universals (nominalist in a way) was his attitude of questioning, criticism, and attack upon the conventional tenets of faith and authority. Finding himself successful in confounding the realist doctrines of his teacher, Guillaume de Champeaux, in the realm of dialectics and logic, Abelard turned with gusto to apply the same critical approach to theological questions.

Whereas St. Anselm had said that we must believe in order to understand, Abelard was saying that we must understand in order to believe. Abelard's book entitled *Sic et non (Yes and No)* illustrated his critical method. He listed some 150 specific religious theses and then quoted authorities from the Scriptures and Fathers to support both sides of the questions. In this way he argued that if the authorities contradicted one another it was the business of the Christian scholar to arrive at the truth by the use of human reason. His attitude of protest was probably more significant than his thought or his systematic theology. In the twelfth century Abelard was the greatest of the recalcitrants; he stimulated St. Thomas Aquinas to become the greatest of the reconcilers in the thirteenth.

On top of Abelard's critical methods of logical analysis Aquinas also had to reckon with the whole range of Aristotelian science, now translated directly from the Greek through the help of Byzantine scholarship. This included Aristotle's scientific works on biology, physics, astronomy, metaphysics, ethics, politics, and poetics. With this enormous mass of "new" material to digest, absorb, and argue over, the dialectical arguments became ever more complicated and abstruse. St. Thomas achieved reconciliation by sharply distinguishing between natural philosophy and supernatural theology. Philosophy deals with the individual phenomena of the natural world, where things are created, change,and decay; it includes everything that is open to argument or that can be demonstrated by human reason. Theology, on the other hand, deals with revealed truth, which involves the supernatural world of changeless, uncreated, eternal, and ultimate reality. These truths, the universals that make up the content of faith, are not subject to change by human reason. There can be no contradiction between theology and philosophy, no contradiction between revealed truth and scientific truth, for God is the author of both. Faith may be reasoned about as far as reason can go, but some articles of faith are beyond finite human reason. They are not "unreasonable"; they are simply not open to rational demonstration. By his elevation of faith above reason St. Thomas aided the realist cause by bringing logic and science into the service of Christian theology. At the same time, he gave greater autonomy to the workings of human reason within the bounds of the natural world of science. Science and religion may handle the same facts or ideas, but they look at them from different sides. Science and human reason start from the individual and particular thing and work up to the more general, whereas religion starts with God, the most universal of all, and works down to the individual.

Augustinian theology had not assigned philosophy and theology to different realms in this way but had asserted the identity of the two, whereas St. Thomas Aquinas gave science free rein over natural phenomena within its own restricted province. This illustrated the adaptability of the church, but also showed how Aristotle could be used to circumscribe the ranges within which human reason could work. If left to itself, reason's tug at the leash would threaten to cause trouble, but when codified and formalized by the authority of Aristotle, it could be so disciplined that it served the higher ends of theology.

The attack upon Thomism, however, was not long in coming; it was spearheaded in the thirteenth century by such dissidents as Friar Roger Bacon. He raised his voice, often querulous and rasping, in criticism of the reliance upon Aristotle as the supreme authority in scientific matters. He went far in arguing that conclusions concerning the operation of the natural world should be verified by actual experiences. He was perhaps the first to urge the use of experimentation as a check on the abstract results of theorizing and as a means of reconstructing the past and estimating the future. According to Friar Bacon, the education of his day had four great defects: its utter dependence upon the authority of Aristotle; its reliance upon established custom; its undue reliance upon popular opinion; and its concealment of real ignorance by its pretensions to knowledge. His remedies were a more thorough study of languages and literature, science, mathematics, and the methods of experimental inquiry. Bacon's recalcitrance caused him to be imprisoned as a disturber of the peace and a causer of disharmony.

Whatever the differences in point of view may have been, the dominant outlook of the great majority of the educated class was that somehow the vast treasures of classical learning being made available to Europe should be brought into line with and incorporated into the prevailing intellectual order of Western Christendom. The scholastics did not reject the classical tradition as pagan. They tried to find in it those elements that would increase the stability, the welfare, and the general sets of beliefs upon which Christian Europe had been built. Not only did the best minds find their intellectual outlets through scholasticism, they found their institutional homes in the cathedral schools and universities of the later Middle Ages. Their very name came from the *scholasticus* who ran the schools in the cathedrals on behalf of the bishop.

Cathedral Schools: The Apogee of the Scholasticus

Perhaps the most important thing about Western higher education was that it responded with alacrity to the growing urbanization, social differentiation, political and economic struggles, and recovery of the written science and philosophy of the classical tradition of Graeco-Roman civilization. Institutionally, this response was symbolized in the eleventh and twelfth centuries by the rise and spread of the cathedral schools, which were basically oriented to urban life and to professional competence rather than to purely sacred purposes:

> The most significant development from our point of view was the emergence of specialist groups in the legal, medical and philosophical fields. These subjects had been brilliantly studied during the Carolingian period and even earlier; but knowledge of them had been confined to a few remarkable individuals. With the tenth century, however, the number of these individuals had increased, and by the eleventh, they were sufficiently numerous and sufficiently organized to constitute professional groups recognisably similar to their modern counterparts.[9]

Once again, as in Sumerian, Egyptian, and Graeco-Roman civilizations, we find that the stress on professional purpose and on the social organization of professional groups was an essential factor in the creation of new and innovative educational institutions. Bolgar makes this point exceptionally clear with respect to the spectacular growth of cathedral schools between 1050 and 1150:

> They all served professional rather than strictly religious aims. Even the education they offered to those whose careers were to lie within the Church was primarily technical in character. For theology, especially the philosophical theology of the twelfth century, Canon Law, and the niceties of ecclesiastical administration must in the last analysis be regarded as professional interests. And in addition they seem to have drawn into their classrooms an appreciable number of those who intended to spend their lives in definitely lay pursuits, in legal work, medicine, or municipal and feudal business. Their fundamentally non-religious character was long masked, however, by the fact that their students were all supposed to be clerics.[10]

So these institutions, these cathedral schools, which had long been primarily devoted to elementary training in Latin, as befitted the propaedeutic purposes of earlier centuries, now became advanced professional schools in the formative period of Western civilization. Some even went further and specialized in particular professions as the teachers themselves developed particular professional specialties.

The Professional Disciplines

In the early Middle Ages some of the monastic and cathedral schools had taught elements of law, medicine, and theology along with the liberal arts, without much

---

[9]Bolgar op. cit., p. 132.
[10]Ibid., pp. 194-195.

differentiation. For example, at Chartres before the twelfth century, law and theology were taught incidentally whenever material on these subjects was found in the writings of the various church Fathers or in the various compendia of knowledge. However, from the eleventh and twelfth centuries on, the study of law, medicine, and theology gradually became recognized as separate, advanced professional disciplines; the liberal arts came to be looked upon as preparatory to these more advanced studies. With the development of a full-fledged university organization, separate faculties of law, medicine, and theology were created as well as faculties of the arts.

In Italy grammar was taught not so much as a literary study as at Chartres, nor was logic taught as a dialectical exercise as at Paris. Rather, they were looked upon as a practical preparation for the study of law, medicine, or *dictamen* (letter writing). The reasons for this doubtless lay in the laicized social development characterizing Italy: municipal life instead of feudalism, the struggles of the cities for independence, and the investiture struggles between pope and emperor. All these prompted the urban classes to seek enlightenment and support in the past political experience of the city-states of Greece and Rome.

The Roman law had remained strong in the educational tradition of the Lombard towns of northern Italy from the later days of the Roman Empire when Justinian's *Corpus Juris Civilis* had been handed down by the secular teaching class. Schools at Rome, Pavia, and Ravenna were known for the study of law in the eleventh century even before Bologna gained preeminence as a *studium generale* for the arts. Its reputation for legal studies overshadowed all others at the time of the investiture struggle in the twelfth century when the fame of Irnerius attracted students to Bologna, much as Abelard's attracted them to Paris. Under the stimulus of Irnerius and his exceedingly detailed and coherent glosses, an organized and systematic study of the whole *Corpus* constituted the required curriculum of practical legal education. The differentiation of the law from a general education in the liberal arts accompanied the growth of a new class of professional students who were older and more independent than elsewhere.

Since those who favored the emperor's side in the investiture struggle found support in the Roman civil law, the supporters of the papacy had to look for better justification of the pope's claims. This they found in 1142 in the great work of Gratian, who did for canon law almost what Justinian's code had done for civil law. He codified and systematized authorities from the Bible, writings of the church Fathers, canons of the church councils, letters and decrees of the popes, edicts of the Roman emperors, Justinian's laws, capitularies of the Frankish and Lombard kings, and the customs of the church. Gratian arrived at the position that ecclesiastical law was superior to secular law and that therefore the authority of the church was paramount. Naturally, Gratian's *Decretum* had a wide vogue as a textbook in medieval law schools until it became the fundamental authority for the study of canon law, and it has never been entirely superseded. From this time on, Bologna became famous for its canon law as well as for its civil law, and the way was paved for the rise of the University of Bologna.

During the eleventh and twelfth centuries the revival in medicine was fully as marked as that in law. For more than two centuries Salerno as a school of medicine in southern Italy rivaled in academic fame the cathedral schools at Chartres, Paris, and Bologna. The origins of the school at Salerno are obscure, but there are traces of the study and practice of medicine there as far back as the ninth century. By the tenth century it was famous for the skill of its physicians, and by the middle of the eleventh century its celebrity in Europe was established. Since Salerno was purely a medical school, it never developed other faculties and did not arrive at the completed university type of organization. It was, nevertheless, important for revealing how the medical traditions of Greece and Rome had continued in southern Italy much as the legal tradition had persisted in northern Italy.

In the eleventh century the courts of Salerno which acknowledged the authority of the eastern emperors were in constant communication with Byzantium. The concentration of medical science and its revival at Salerno were counterparts of the perpetuation of the Greek language in southern Italy. In addition to the Greek and Latin medical science of Hippocrates, Galen, and others, Arabic science began to influence Salerno through the efforts of such scholars as Constantinus Africanus, who translated Greek, Arabic, and Hebrew medical books into Latin.

But far more than medical information was thus transmitted to the cathedral schools of Europe: the whole range of Greek natural philosophy was opened up to the West by the Arabs, who had absorbed a great deal of Greek science, especially that of Aristotle, and had carried much of it to Sicily and Spain as their empire expanded across North Africa. A key center for the translating into Latin was Toledo in Spain, and the most active period was in the middle of the twelfth century. In the process of translating Greek materials into Arabic, the Arabs assimilated Greek ideas along with Hindu, Islamic, and Christian thought. Thus, as the Christian scholars of the eleventh and twelfth centuries came into contact with Arabic civilization in Spain, Sicily, and Syria, a great interest arose in translating these materials from the Arabic into Latin. The Jewish scholar Maimonides reconciled Aristotle with the Jewish religion, and Avicenna and Averroës reconciled Aristotle with Islam. As these writings flooded into Europe in the later half of the twelfth century, Aristotle and Greek natural philosophy now had to be reconciled with Christianity.

In pursuance of this task were Alexander of Hales, Albertus Magnus, and St. Thomas Aquinas, all of whom taught at one time or another at the University of Paris. By the time St. Thomas had completed his work and the Dominicans had taken up the cudgels for Thomism, Aristotle was installed permanently within Catholic doctrine. Theology had become the keystone of all university study, the highest of the high, with all other studies subordinate to it. The faculty of theology at the University of Paris ultimately became virtually an arbiter in matters theological, deciding disputes, defining heresy, and on occasion even correcting the theology of the pope himself.

The Liberal Arts

Even though professional studies had pride of place in the hierarchy of intellectual concerns in the later Middle Ages, the liberal arts were long cultivated both as preparatory studies and, in a few cathedral schools, as the prime objects of intellectual concern. They too reflected the quickening of interest in higher education as a professional preparation for the ever larger numbers of students who were headed for civil and professional employments in cities and courts and in the secular administration of the church.

The highest point in the medieval teaching of grammar and classical literature was reached at the cathedral school of Chartres during the twelfth century. While the textbooks of Donatus and Priscian were still the basis for the study of elementary grammar, students and masters alike studied the writings of the classical authors themselves. John of Salisbury, the Englishman who was Bishop of Chartres when he died in 1180, wrote a pure, gracious Latin. Cicero especially influenced his style and attitude toward life. While John also knew the Bible and the Fathers, he believed the classics were worthy of study for their own sake. Seeing no essential antagonism between the secular Romans and religious Christians, he fused them into a rounded Christian humanism. He bitterly attacked those whom he termed "Cornificians," who would offer students a "get-learning-quick" method of study so that they could cut their academic course short and proceed to the practical business of living.

John advanced nearly all the arguments that have since been made in favor of humanistic training as opposed to practical or vocational education. True education, he considered, required a thorough grounding in the classics in order to develop critical judgment and discriminating taste and to acquire the mature understanding necessary to the contemplative mind. Rhetoric or logic he thought to be of little value and even harmful unless based on wisdom gained through patient study of the literary humanities. John of Salisbury's own writings give evidence of an amazingly wide but fragmentary knowledge of classical authors. While John battled against the inroads being made by logic and philosophy upon the literary studies of grammar and style, his was a losing battle. The professional studies and Aristotelian science captured the major intellectual energies of the thirteenth century, and the study of Latin grammar drifted off into the routine details of analysis of language divorced from classical literature.

As Chartres was famous for its teaching of grammar in the twelfth century, so was Paris famous for its teaching of logic, and preeminent among the teachers at Paris was Abelard, who was instrumental in turning the attention of students from the literary humanities to the delights of dialectics. Although logic was often looked upon simply as the rules of deductive thinking designed as a preparatory study to be undertaken before advancing to the higher studies of the quadrivium and theology, Abelard was able to make logic come alive as the key instrument for probing the theological relations between man and God and the metaphysical problems dealing with the origin and nature of the universe.

A brilliant lecturer, a skillful dialectician, a witty classroom entertainer, Abelard was bold, lucid, original, and sharply controversial. He was always fresh and stimulating, and therefore he was just the sort of teacher to attract attention at a time when the usual method of teaching was dry lecturing, eternal glossing of materials, reciting of propositions and counterpropositions, citing of authorities, and abstruse disputation. His remarkable range of reading permitted him to enliven his lectures with concrete examples. By his brilliance, criticism, and pugnacity Abelard fired the interest and enthusiasm of students who flocked to his schools in Paris by the hundreds and thousands. When he was forced to leave Paris, his hold upon his students was so great that they followed him wherever he went, seeking him out in the woods and repeatedly forcing him to return to teaching to the end of his life.

Rhetoric stood low in the academic hierarchy of the Middle Ages, well below grammar and logic. By the thirteenth and fourteenth centuries it had become preoccupied with formal details of classification, types of speech, endless lists of examples, figures of speech, ways to describe an event, or a person, and on and on. One aspect of rhetoric did attract a good deal of attention from practical-minded scholars. That was the study of letter writing and the drawing up of such legal and feudal documents as contracts, wills, immunities, and appointments to office. The *ars dictandi,* or *dictamen,* had a direct utilitarian value at a time when the economic, political, and legal affairs of the church, the courts, and the cities were expanding at such a rate that record keeping was of the utmost importance. The investiture struggles and the consequent delving into legal and historical documents particularly stimulated attention to *dictamen* in the towns and schools of northern Italy.

Aside from the development of Latin for scholarly, religious, and administrative purposes, the later Middle Ages produced a vital and original literature in the vernaculars of Italian, Spanish, French, German, and English. Taking form as early as the tenth and eleventh centuries, oral vernacular literature proliferated from the twelfth century on. It included love lyrics, songs of war, romances, fables, animal stories, sermon stories, and mystery plays, all of which became enormously popular among the unschooled people of the upper as well as the lower classes. What had emerged as an oral folk literature of wide appeal developed into written forms that began to enlist the efforts of first-rate writers like Dante, Petrarch, Boccaccio, and Chaucer.

The development of this vernacular literature was of enormous importance for education, because it foreshadowed the eventual demand that schools should teach in the vernacular as well as in Latin. When this happened and vernacular schools appeared on a massive scale, Western education was ready to take what amounted to a quantum jump toward universal education—and toward the building of a modern civilization. So long as elementary schools remained in a foreign classical language there was little likelihood that mass education could develop.

Equally important advances were being made in mathematics during the Middle Ages that helped to lay the groundwork for scientific and mathematical investigations of later centuries. In the early Middle Ages the primary consideration of arithmetic had been the computation of the date of Easter with some attention to the theory of numbers, but as early as the eleventh century Gerbert, the *scholasticus* at the cathedral school of Reims, developed a better method of columnar computation and reconstructed the abacus so that it could be used more easily for the four fundamental processes. The most important change in arithmetic came in the thirteenth century, when the importation of Arabic numerals including the zero made possible the use of the decimal system. Thus an enormously simplified computation began to replace the cumbersome Latin numerals, the duodecimal system, and the Roman abacus. Such advances were indispensable to the development of modern mathematics and science.

Around the year 1000 Gerbert had been able to bring together virtually all that the Western world knew of Euclid's definitions and geometry in general. Then, in the twelfth and thirteenth centuries, the whole of Euclid's geometry, along with other mathematical works of the Greeks, Arabs, and Hindus, was translated into Latin. Similarly in astronomy, Gerbert devised ingenious models of terrestrial and celestial spheres to illustrate the motions of the earth and heavens as he understood them. In the twelfth century much more of Greek astronomy was translated from the Arabic into Latin, and in the thirteenth century Aristotle's work *On the Heavens* was also made available. Of the seven liberal arts, music continued to be almost exclusively theoretical and speculative in nature. Indeed, the applied side, playing and singing songs, was not properly considered a liberal art; it was thought appropriate only to the wandering minstrel or jester.

In general, the eleventh and twelfth centuries were a time of probing for the wellsprings of Hellenic-Roman scholarship that were waiting to be tapped by eager Western scholars thirsting for new knowledge of the past to apply to the present. From Gerbert to John of Salisbury and Abelard, new reservoirs of ideas were being discovered as the trickle of classical materials became a flood. The overwhelming mass of classical knowledge that poured into western Europe between 1000 and 1150 made the task of absorption both exhilarating and onerous. A tremendous task of educational development had to be undertaken.

So John of Salisbury and the other humanists lost the battle to the professional studies in the twelfth century, but the victory of the professional studies did not lead immediately to modernity, for they themselves were soon brought under the reins of conservatism and caution by the reconcilers of medieval scholasticism and theology, led by St. Thomas Aquinas. The thirteenth and fourteenth centuries were a time when the classical flood was dammed, tamed, and brought under the careful direction of Christian authority. Classical thought was Christianized as it never had been before, only to see the literary humanists once more take over the educational reins in the Renaissance of the fifteenth and sixteenth centuries. The scientific specialisms that had gained such a start in the cathedral schools of the twelfth century were kept pretty well under wraps, first by the scholastics and then by the Renaissance humanists, until they finally began in the sixteenth and seventeenth centuries their remarkable advance that swept all before them and helped to transform traditional Western civilization into a modern civilization.

Europeans in the twelfth century were a little like the underdeveloped peoples of the twentieth century who discovered that their advancement could be hastened by borrowing knowledge and expertise from a more advanced society. The difference was that the more advanced society for twelfth-century Europe was not a contemporary one; it had existed some 1000 to 1500 years in the past. It was the professional, specialized, technical knowledge of the more advanced Graeco-Roman civilization that initially appealed to the West, instead of its broadly literary or purely humanistic tradition. In this respect, the western Europeans departed radically from their Byzantine cousins who were favoring the literary studies of the Greeks over their scientific and technical accomplishments. This fact may reveal a fateful difference, a basic reason why the West more quickly developed a modern form of civilization while the East continued in its traditional ways.

The Origin of Universities:
From Scholasticus to Professor

As the numbers of students in the European cathedral schools increased in the eleventh century, direct management was often delegated by the bishop to a church official known as the chancellor. The chain of authority was from pope to bishop to chancellor or *scholasticus.* One of the most important powers delegated to the chancellor was the right to issue to qualified students a license to teach (*licentia docendi*) within the diocese. As certain of the cathedral schools grew to still greater prominence, the pope gave them the right to issue a license to teach anywhere (*licentia docendi ubique*), a much sought after credential.

Certain cathedral schools acquired the title *studium generale,* a place of general study, so called because they attracted students from a wide area and their license to teach was recognized beyond their own jurisdiction. By 1100 the most flourishing *studia* were those in northern France at Chartres, Orléans, Reims, Laon, and Paris; in England at Canterbury; in Spain at Toledo; in Italy at Salerno and Bologna.

In the twelfth century the growing number of teachers and students began to follow a typical medieval pattern of group action: they organized themselves into a guild, or *universitas.* The term *universitas* was originally applied to any group of people who formed a guild for common purposes, but gradually it was limited to universities of faculties and students. As this kind of corporate organization took place, cathedral schools became universities. The process of transformation was gradual, and no exact date can be given for this transition in the case of the universities that appeared in the later twelfth and early thirteenth centuries. The university of teachers was designed to protect their rights against the chancellor, the bishop, the king, the town, or anyone else who tried to bring them under control. Likewise, the students often organized themselves into guilds for protection against the teachers, the townspeople, and each other. These early student universities usually followed nationality lines according to the region or country from which the students came.

In the eleventh century large numbers of students were flocking to Paris, attracted by Abelard and his colleagues to the schools of the cathedral of Notre Dame, the collegiate church of St. Geneviève, and the abbey of St Victor. Before the end of the twelfth century the masters of these schools had organized themselves into guilds of liberal arts, law, medicine, and theology, because they felt themselves fettered by the control of the chancellors of Notre Dame and St. Geneviève. The masters, wanting to control their own affairs, appoint new members to their group as other guilds did, and issue licenses to teach, turned to anyone who would give them help in their struggles to achieve greater autonomy. On occasion, they turned to the king for help against the townspeople; Louis VII gave them the right to strike whenever they were molested by the town, and students and faculty gained the right to be tried by ecclesiastical or university courts rather than in the civil courts. If the king then began to issue too many orders to the university, as Philip Augustus did, the faculty turned to the pope for help. If the chancellor tried to require obedience of them, as the chancellor of Notre Dame did, they again turned to the pope, or they struck.

Whenever the faculty felt that restraints were intolerable, they would leave the city or threaten to do so; and as the students often joined with the faculty, the university could on occasion bring the king, the town, or the church to their terms. In their disputes with the chancellor, the faculty won from Pope Innocent III in 1212 a vital recognition of their association; Innocent ordered the chancellor to wait for recommendations from the faculty before appointing new professors. Again in 1229 the faculty appealed to the pope over the chancellor's head, and in 1231 the papal bull of Pope Gregory IX became the main fortification of the autonomy of the university faculty. Thus the papacy showed itself willing to overrule its own appointed officials and to protect the university in order to gain more direct control over it. In general, the faculty was willing to accept this help, for the pope was far away, whereas the chancellor was on the grounds and was therefore thought to be a more immediate threat.

However, the faculty also had its troubles with the pope. When the Dominican friars began to teach in the University of Paris, they often came into conflict with the other professors, refusing to walk out when the rest of the professors went on strike. The pope supported the Dominicans, and the strike was broken, but the university had shown that it was hard to control from outside and hard to govern from within.

One of the significant outcomes of the struggle for autonomy at the University of Paris was the idea that the faculty was a corporate body that had full legal power to set the curriculum, issue the license to teach, confer degrees, appoint its own members, and otherwise run its affairs without responsibility to administrative officers or a board of control outside its membership. The idea that the faculty *was* the university has had intellectual and educational repercussions ever since its origin, recurringly disputed by church, state, special interest groups, and students.

Increasingly, Paris was regarded as *the* great medieval university of Europe. The saying was "Italy has the Papacy; Germany has the Empire; and France has the University of Paris; all is well." The estimate is made that there were between 5,000 and 7,000 students at Paris in the middle of the thirteenth century. They came from all parts of western Europe. Its international makeup was even more characteristic of a university than of a *studium generale*.

In Italy the most famous university of the thirteenth century was at Bologna, where the university developed out of a cathedral school of arts, a monastic school of law, and a municipal school of rhetoric. An interesting characteristic of Bologna was the original power of the student guilds in controlling the affairs of the university. In fact, the impulse to university organization arose among students (who were much older than those in northern Europe) as they sought to achieve protection against the hostile town community and against the professors. For several decades the rector of the student guilds was recognized as the head of the university; the professors were obliged to take an oath of obedience to the student rector and abide by the regulations of the student guilds concerning the content of lectures and the length of the academic term. Other universities that achieved some status in Italy during the thirteenth century were at Siena, Padua, Naples (founded by Frederick II), and Rome (founded by the pope). By the sixteenth century student control in Italian universities was disappearing, and the towns were taking over basic control.

The universities at Oxford and Cambridge were the only universities in England for several centuries. Having achieved the faculty organization of a university by 1167 or 1168, Oxford was modeled in large part upon the faculties of Paris but was not so closely supervised by the papacy or by the local bishop. Cambridge was established later, when a group of masters moved in dissatisfaction from Oxford in 1209. This practice of secession from one university to another accounts for the establishment of many universities throughout Europe.

By the end of the thirteenth century the only universities in France, outside of Paris, were those at Montpellier and Toulouse. Montpellier was especially noted for its work in medicine. Toulouse was founded by the papacy in the 1230s as a means of combating heresy in southern France. Universities appeared in Spain at Salamanca and Seville, and in Portugal at Lisbon before the end of the thirteenth century. In the fourteenth and fifteenth centuries the university movement spread throughout north and central Europe. More than seventy-five universities were known by the end of the fifteenth century. Nothing like this diffusion of higher education occurred in any other civilization until modern times. (See Figure 5.2—The Heartland of Western Education c. 1500 A.D.)

The Idea of Licenses and Degrees

With the rise of the university system, an expansion of the liberal arts curriculum followed. Whereas the faculty of theology at the University of Paris was slow to accept the newly imported philosophical work of Aristotle, the arts faculty was much more receptive in its efforts to digest and assimilate them. In this way, the arts faculty made itself more vital and relevant to students. As Aristotle gradually became "respectable" and his philosophical and scientific studies reconciled with church doctrine, they came to be prescribed by the arts faculty along with the traditional seven liberal arts.

Whence came the power to require these studies as the heart of a liberal education? The origin of prescription seems to rest in the church's practice of licensing its teachers. Since most teachers in the Middle Ages were minor clerics and since it was felt that all clerics should be trained properly in religious orthodoxy as well as in the tools of scholarship, the church found it expedient to control entrance into the teaching profession. So a condition for granting the *licentia docendi* was the successful completion of the course in the liberal arts. With the spread of university organization, the *licentia* turned into the arts degree and was granted by the faculty of arts rather than by the bishop or the chancellor. The first complete prescribed curriculum in arts seems to have been laid down at the University of Paris in 1215.

In general, when the student had finished three or four years of study of the elementary liberal arts (trivium), he was granted the baccalaureate degree in arts,

Figure 5.2   The Heartland of Western Education (c. 1500)

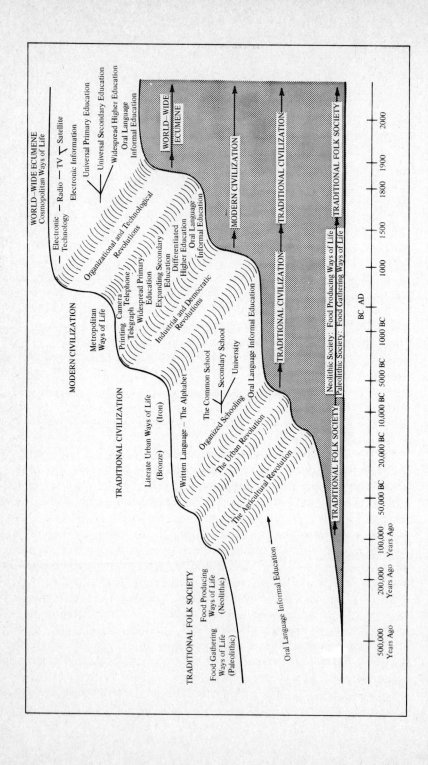

which indicated that he was ready to be an assistant teacher. He then studied the higher liberal arts (quadrivium) and Aristotelian philosophy for some three years more, at the conclusion of which he was granted the final license to teach and was entitled to become a master teacher of arts. To win the master's degree, the student usually was required to prepare a thesis and defend it against disputants in much the same manner that a journeyman presented his masterpiece to the guild members as proof of his qualification to become a master workman.

When a boy or a young man went to a university in the Middle Ages, he simply sought out the master under whom he wished to study, signed his name on that master's roll, and paid him his fees. The student then lodged where he could and acquired the clerical gown as a sign that he was a student. Since many of the students were quite young, the question of lodging became a problem, especially for the poorer students. Philanthropy came to their rescue, as rich benefactors provided buildings where they could live or the friars opened their houses to take them in. A *college* in its origin was thus simply a rooming and boarding house for young and indigent scholars. As would be natural, discipline soon became a problem, and some universities began to assign masters to these colleges to maintain discipline.

The methods of instruction at the medieval universities were principally lectures, repetitions, and disputations. The lecture was a reading aloud from the textbook by the master and then his commenting upon the material line by line. These commentaries when written out were called *glosses*. The lecturing might be very complicated as one master elaborated upon certain passages by referring to the glosses of a whole series of scholars who had commented upon each other. The repetition was basically a review of the materials of the lectures and textbooks. The disputation was a formal occasion when students defended or attacked certain theses according to established rules for argumentation.

The extracurricular side of the student's life was doubtless exhilarating. As antidotes for wordy lectures and texts, students engaged in all sorts of activities that were frowned upon by the university authorities, who made little or no effort to provide facilities for acceptable physical or social activities. The regulations listing prohibited pastimes reveal what the students most enjoyed doing. Fighting and brawling were perhaps most popular. Regulations were also issued against cock fighting; tennis; gambling; singing and playing musical instruments; and the keeping of such pets as parrots, hawks, monkeys, bears, wolves, and dogs. Apparently, students spent a great deal of time singing, telling stories, and drinking. These were activities to be expected in institutions where organized sports and physical education, scientific investigations of nature, and easy social intercourse were not admitted to standing alongside lectures, note taking, and the study of prescribed books.

Whatever may have been the attractions of student life in the thirteenth century, a career in university teaching began to challenge a career in church or state as an outlet for the energies of able young men. We have noted that virtually all the important thinkers, writers, and intellectual leaders in the thirteenth century were university-trained men or professors. As the principal molders of the intellectual life of the times, the status of the teaching profession in the universities was very high, surrounded with privileges, exemptions, and immunities. University professors did not acquire the wealth of noblemen or high churchmen, but they enjoyed much better than average living and held an enviable place in public respect and social esteem. At Oxford and Cambridge they gained special representation in Parliament, and as a group they were often sought out to decide important questions of heresy or theology or even political disputes. The cathedral schools and universities were key agencies in the formation of a distinctive Western civilization in the late Middle Ages. The university's role in shaping the culture and thought of Western civilization did not reach such a zenith again until the spurt to modernization in the late nineteenth and early twentieth centuries.

CHAPTER VI

THE FLORESCENCE
OF THE WESTERN
EDUCATIONAL TRADITION—
WITH INTIMATIONS
OF MODERNITY
(1400 A.D.-1700 A.D.)

A. THE THIRD TRANSFORMATION OF MAN:
FROM TRADITIONAL CIVILIZATION
TO MODERN CIVILIZATION

In the remaining chapters of this book we approach the third major transformation in the human career as outlined in Chapter 1. The first was the million-year evolutionary process during which prehuman men became human and formed folk societies that fanned out from Africa across the world. The second, beginning about 3,500 B.C., was the civilization process during which an increasing number of folk societies became civilized, a process that eventually resulted in the spread of traditional civilizations across the land masses of the Afro-Eurasian ecumene.

Then, beginning about 1400 or 1500 A.D. traditional civilization in the West began to be affected by the third great human transformation, the modernization process. For about 300 years the intimations of modernity gained strength, but only with difficulty against the forces of tradition which continued to dominate education. Thereafter, with accelerating speed, the transmutation to modernity spread for some 200 years through much of Western civilization from approximately 1650 to 1850 A.D. Finally, from the mid-nineteenth century onward, modernization and modern civilization began to encompass the entire world.

While the modern and the premodern societies continue to exist side by side and while they sometimes fuse into a variety of mixed forms, the overall trend toward the modern has been unmistakable for some 500 years. The principal ingredients of the early modernization process as they applied to education are discussed here, while those of the later modernization process will be discussed in Chapter 9.

Every historian has his favorite dates for marking the dawn of modern times. For a long time the Italian Renaissance of the fourteenth century was considered to be the first act of modernity, and Petrarch the first modern man; so this would put the date at roughly 1300 A.D. Or the Age of Discovery of the fifteenth century may be taken as the opening of modern times; the date would thus become roughly 1500, soon after Portuguese, Spanish, and Italian captains crossed all the ocean seas. Or, the scientific revolution of the sixteenth and seventeenth centuries may be regarded as marking the major break between medieval and modern styles of thought; in this case the key dates would become 1543 (for Copernicus), 1600 (for Galileo), or 1687 (for Newton). Or, indeed, the Industrial Revolution of the eighteenth and nineteenth centuries may be viewed as the really significant process that distinguishes modern civilization from all prior human societies; the opening date of modernity would thus become 1750 (for power machinery in the textile industry), 1776 (for Watt's steam engine), or 1830 (for the application of steam to transportation and manufacturing.

These four sets of events and their respective dates all have their merits in pointing to essential historical ingredients of modernity, but they range over a period of at least 500 years; and they do not define very precisely the major changes that marked Western education as it began to play its role in the development of modern civilization.

My own view is that the most convenient general date for marking the onset of modern education is the year 1400 A.D. I do this because it seems to me that the historical intimations of modern Western education can best be understood if the three centuries from 1400 to 1700 are viewed as something of a unit. (See Figure 5.1—the Curve of Educational Development in Western Civilization, p. 156)

This early modern period in Western education begins around the year 1400 with a series of important proposals made by humanist scholars for the reform of medieval education. These were touched off by the visit of the Greek Chrysoloras to Italy from Byzantium and a return visit by the Italian Guarino. It culminates around the year 1650 with a series of important proposals made by English Puritans and their Protestant co-workers from the continent of Europe. These proposals in turn looked to the reform of humanist education. In between, the face of European education was substantially changed, but it had by no means become entirely "modern." In fact, the period ends with the slowing down of the English revolution at mid-seventeenth century and the failure of the English reformers to modernize the mainstream of English education. This fact, along with the general inability of the modernizing leadership to consolidate the gains of the English revolution, probably delayed the full transformation of Western civilization for a century or so.

But basic changes in education had been made in the three centuries from 1400 to 1700, some traditionalizing in their effects and some modernizing. With the benefit of historical perspective the period begins the florescence of the traditional education of the West. I refer to intimations of modernity to call attention to the relatively modest steps taken toward modernity.

On the whole, the institutionalizing of the national state systems, the broadening structure of social participation, the awakening of Europe to the world overseas and an intellectual trend toward scientific realism had a generally modernizing influence on education, while the emergence of Renaissance Humanism, the Protestant Reformation, and the establishment of national state churches had a general traditionalizing effect. So while the intimations of modernity were appearing in this period, the weight of influence was on the side of establishing and maintaining a powerful educational tradition that turned out to be curiously resistant to further change. In themselves, change and innovation are not necessarily modernizing.

The Political Institutionalization of the Nation-State

The striking thing about political development in the early part of our period was the growth of the centralized political authority of the monarchies in France and England. In this process the medieval political traditions of feudalism gave way to the modern institutions of the nation-state. The trend to put more political power in the hands of the kings progressed to such an extent that the seventeenth century has often been called the age of absolutism. The medieval conception of a universal Christendom with the Pope as head received increasingly sharp blows, and constant difficulties beset the long-lived Holy Roman Empire. The time seemed ripe for a coalition of kings, merchants, gentry, religious reformers, and professional intellectuals within the various national states to break the political, economic, and religious control of the Catholic church in Europe.

Yet, the states most successful in their early efforts to centralize royal power were Catholic Spain, Catholic France, and Protestant England. They were first able to build superior royal power and centralized territorial authority by developing professional bureaucracies, strengthening loyal military forces and courts, harnessing or hobbling the upper aristocracy, and reducing the autonomy of cities and towns. Under Ferdinand and Isabella (1479-1516) and Charles I (1516-1556) who was also Emperor Charles V of the Holy Roman Empire, Spain emerged as one of the strongest national states and colonial empires in the sixteenth century. In France the trend toward royal supremacy proceeded apace. With the reign of Francis I (1515-1547) and Henry IV (1589-1610) France became one of the great centralized powers of Europe. The process reached its epitome in the hands of the supreme absolutist of all, Louis XIV who began his long reign in 1643.

In England, Henry VIII hastened the process of consolidating royal authority as he built up the navy, took over the Catholic monasteries, disestablished the Catholic church in favor of the Church of England, and won over many nobles and gentry as well as merchants to his side. The long reign of Queen Elizabeth further strengthened the power of the monarchy. When the Stuart kings, James I and Charles I, came to the throne, they forcefully asserted the doctrine of the divine right of kings, only to be set back by the revolution led by Parliament, gentry, and Puritans during the civil war in the middle decades of the seventeenth century. With the restoration of the Stuarts in 1660, Charles II and James II again claimed rule by divine right. The English people, however, soon reestablished constitutionalism by bringing in William of Orange and Mary to be rulers of a limited monarchy in the Glorious Revolution of 1688. From then on, the partnership of crown and Parliament, largely controlled by the upper classes, gave stability and power to the English nation-state.

In contrast to the growing consolidation of political authority of the nation in France and England, the German, Slavic, and Magyar states of Central and Eastern Europe were marked by confusion, rivalry, and constant change of boundaries. Much of this region of Europe was nominally a part of the Holy Roman Empire, but it displayed little of the authority usually associated with the word *empire.* Dozens of states, large and small, were ruled by family dynasties, joined together only by more or less loosely held loyalties and responsibilities, all supposedly owing allegiance to the emperor. The crown was bandied from family to family and contended for by those princes who could get the necessary political or military support. During most of the period the forces of particularism were able to hold out against the dynastic ambitions of the Hohenstaufen and Hapsburg families.

Politically, Italy was made up of a number of independent city-states, duchies, and kingdoms. No central political authority was strong enough to weld the various sovereignties of cities and states into a nation as was being done in France, England, and Spain. In those cities where the merchant guilds were strongest, republican forms of government prevailed, as in Venice and Florence. In other cases the nobles were able to maintain power, as in the duchies of Milan and Mantua and the kingdoms of Naples and Sicily. For much of the fifteenth century the Italian cities set the pace for Europe in political, economic, and cultural affairs, but their decline was signaled by the invasion from France in 1494, after which Italy became a recurring battleground for the French, the Spanish, and the Germans. Because of the strength of local rulers, particularistic loyalties, and the fortunes of war, national unity was delayed for generations in Italy as well as in Germany.

The revolt of the Netherlands against Spain and the setting up of the Dutch Republic, along with the establishment of the English Commonwealth, heralded the growth of constitutional government, in which the civil rights of merchants, gentry, and free men were proclaimed against autocratic usurpation by an absolute monarch. The documents on civil and economic freedom by John Milton, the Petition of Right in 1628, the Bill of Rights, and Act of Toleration in 1689 laid the foundations for the civil liberties that have been written into most democratic constitutions since that time.

One of the far-reaching corollaries of the consolidation of the national states was the growth of a spirit of nationalism and the accentuation of national differences. The constant wars, the growing use of vernacular languages, and a mounting sense that one's own nationality was different from (and better than) all other nationalities gave rise to strong feelings of national importance and patriotism. Schools and education have played an enormous part in the process of building up a spirit of nationalism. The inculcation of national loyalties through the schools and the teaching of the vernacular language eventually became a primary task of the national school systems. State control of educational institutions was principally promoted, however, through the agency of state-supported national churches.

From Universal Church to Nation-Churches

One of the most pregnant events for the future of Western education was the disintegration of the Roman Catholic church and the formation of a number of national churches. In 1400 the Catholic church was still the universal church of Europe in fact as well as in name, despite the growth of the conciliar movement which promulgated the theory that church government should be in the hands of a league of national churches. By the beginning of the sixteenth century the Protestant Reformation had gained enough strength to weld a series of alliances between dissident reformers and nationalizing rulers. These resulted in successful breakaway movements in Germany, Switzerland, the Netherlands, England, and Scotland. Some of these revolutions were relatively peaceful, others were particularly bloody. By the end of the Thirty Years' War at the Treaty of Westphalia in 1648, the worst of the violence, if not the passions, of religious warfare had subsided. The result in most of Western Europe was the institution of a variety of state establishments of religion each determined that education should be a major instrument of its politicoreligious policy. (See Figure 6.1)

Following Martin Luther's break with the Catholic church in 1520, Lutheranism became ever more closely allied with the civil authority. This principle of alliance between church and state was formally recognized at the Diet of Spires in 1526, when rival Catholic and Lutheran rulers met to prevent further revolts of the peasants. In the face of the common enemy the rulers decided to declare an armistice on religious warfare, announcing that each ruler should decide for himself *and for his subjects* which religion should be established in his state; a doctrine summed up in the words, *cuius regio eius religio* (whose rule, his religion). During the religious wars of the next hundred years the right of the state to determine the religion of its subjects was generally accepted; but the right of the individual person to choose his own religion was not part of the bargain. The individual could legally be only a Catholic or a Lutheran, this decision resting in the hands of his ruler.

At the end of the Thirty Years' War (1618 to 1648) Germany was exhausted, and Protestantism triumphant in the states of northen Germany. The efforts of Protestant rulers to break with the Roman church and the Holy Roman Empire were crowned with success. At the Peace of Westphalia (1648) the foundations of the present nation-states of Europe were laid, each state recognized to be completely sovereign and no longer subject to the Empire. In the eyes of some historians the Peace of Westphalia is one of the most important treaties ever signed. It put the seal upon the nation-state as the principal political form of Western civilization.

Whereas Luther's reliance upon the state had resulted in the church virtually becoming an arm of the state, John Calvin argued that the state should be considered the political and civil arm of the church, to do its bidding and carry out its injunctions. In ruling on behalf of God, Calvinist leaders asserted their right to exert strict control over all the affairs of men, economic, political, and social as well as religious. Education, of course, was one of the facets of institutional life to be included in this range of control. Calvinists played key roles in the Bohemian revolt, the Huguenot wars in France, the Dutch revolt against Philip of Spain, the Presbyterian revolt against the monarchy in Scotland, the Puritan revolution in England, and later in the American Revolution. Integral to their success was a profound belief in the value of education and an insistence that education be made available to all.

The Reformation in England produced no single dominating religious or evangelical reformer to match Luther or Calvin. Rather it took place from the top down as successive kings and queens took the initiative in overthrowing or restoring the power of the Catholic church. In these efforts Parliament sometimes supported the king and sometimes opposed him. In 1534 Henry VIII caused Parliament to pass the Act of Supremacy, which recognized the crown as the sole head of the church in England. After Henry VIII, Protestantism had varying fortunes in England. It continued to grow strong under Henry's son, Edward VI, whose affairs were run largely by Cranmer, Archbishop of Canterbury. It received a setback under Mary who restored Catholicism and Roman control of the church and forced many Protestant churchmen to flee from England. These Marian exiles were welcomed by the Calvinists of the Netherlands and Switzerland, and when they returned under Elizabeth, they brought Calvinism back to England with them, laying the foundation for Puritanism.

Under Elizabeth's long reign from 1558 to 1603 the so-called Elizabethan settlement was achieved, whereby the Church of England was established, and enough reforms were made to satisfy large numbers of Englishmen. Under the Stuart kings, James I and Charles I, the Puritans increased their demands for religious liberty, but many fled from England to America. Turning the tables under the Commonwealth, the Puritans were not sorry to see many Anglicans emigrate to America. Soon after the Stuart Restoration the Act of Uniformity of 1662 required all teachers to take an oath subscribing to the Anglican religion and to acquire a license from church officials. A few years later the Five Mile Act levied fines upon any nonconformist who taught in defiance of these regulations. The Puritans defied these laws by setting up covert schools, known as Dissenters' Academies, for their congregations. With the Act of Toleration of 1689 under William and Mary the dissident Puritans were free to teach openly once more, but the Church of England was now firmly implanted in the dominant tradition of English education. The successes of Calvinist Presbyterianism in Scotland left only Ireland as a stronghold of Catholicism in the British Isles.

Despite the inroads made by the Protestant reformations, the Catholic church remained by far the strongest single church in Europe. Italy, Spain, Portugal, France, and southern Germany continued basically loyal to the Catholic establishment, which had many advantages in addition to the custom and tradition that kept people in the centuries-old fold of their fathers. The Catholic organization, with a single head in the person of the Pope and a well-organized hierarchy of officials who looked to the head for authority, aided the church immensely when it faced the often scattered efforts of several dissident Protestant groups. Furthermore, the church made strenuous doctrinal as well as military efforts to stem the tide of Protestantism through the Inquisition, the Index, and the Council of Trent.

Perhaps the most effective counterreformation measure, from the point of view of education, was the organization in 1540 of the Society of Jesus under the leadership of Ignatius Loyola. Rejecting the monastic and mendicant type of church order the Jesuits became a militant force to war against heresy and win back ground, both geographical and doctrinal, lost to the Protestants. Loyola knit his organization into a highly centralized agency with strict eligibility tests enforced for new members. The Jesuits produced eloquent preachers, well-trained teachers, and untiring missionaries for Asia and the Americas as well as for Europe. They established an extremely efficient system of schools for training future leaders to carry on the work of the church. From the beginning, Loyola was convinced of the necessity of superior educational training as an effective weapon against Protestantism.

As a result of the Catholic Counter-Reformation in the later sixteenth and early seventeenth centuries, the Protestants gained no new victories and captured no new territory. In fact, the Catholics won back Bohemia, and the church was successfully reorganized without surrender and without compromise. A quickened interest in education was expressed through several newer teaching orders, such as the Fathers of the Oratory and the Institute of the Brothers of the Christian Schools, in addition to the older Franciscan and Dominican orders. Such orders were extremely influential in carrying the religious doctrines of Catholicism and the ideals of Catholic education to all the continents of the world.

The basic point is this: the long-established principle of the Roman Catholic church that education is properly a function of the church and should therefore be basically a Christian education was embedded ever more firmly in Western education by the Protestant Reformation and the Catholic Counter-Reformation. The vast majority of Christians between 1400 and 1700 agreed that education should be religious; they disagreed only as to the specific doctrines of the religion to be taught and as to the relative role to be played by church and state in education. The details of these differences cannot be followed here, but the general views may be hinted at in the accompanying Figure 6.1.

The Catholic view placed the church in charge of a spiritual realm superior to the temporal realm presided over by the state. Education was primarily a concern of the superior realm and only secondarily of the inferior. Luther turned this order upside down when he insisted that the Christian ruler had the right to reform the church and direct it to do the state's bidding in all areas, including education in schools and universities. Calvin veered toward the Catholic view by insisting that the state must do the church's bidding and conduct state schools according to the precepts of the true church. Richard Hooker, apologist for the Crown and the Church of England, formulated a third order whereby the state and the church are distinct corporations both of which are subordinate to the crown and thus entitled to the educative function.

Whatever the variations in their views, the majority of European Christians during the period up to 1700 accepted the idea of an establishment of religion, i.e. a close alliance between church and state. Only a few minority voices, principally those of Protestant separatists, held out against religion being established by law and enforced by the power of the state. Socinians, Anabaptists, Mennonites, and Quakers began to talk about genuine freedom of religious belief, the rights of individual conscience, and the separation between church and state as a necessary correlate of the free exercise of religion. But the ideal of religious freedom and the separation of church and state as its political embodiment were far from realization in this period. The best that was achieved was a limited toleration of minority religious groups and a

Figure 6.1   Relations of Church, State, and Education

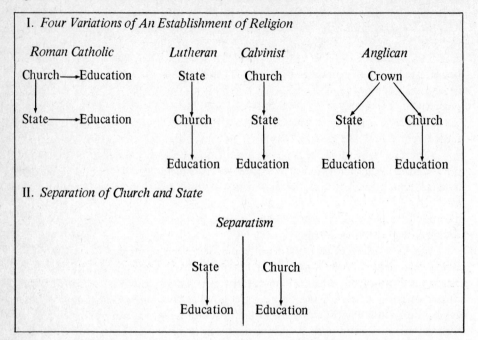

certain freedom from persecution such as was granted to French Huguenots by Henry IV in the Edict of Nantes in 1598 (but later revoked by Louis XIV in 1685), or to English Puritans by the Toleration Act of 1689. The achievement of a more complete religious freedom had to await the acceleration of modernization in Western civilization which accompanied the eighteenth century Enlightenment.

The Broadening Structure of Social Participation

The early modern period can certainly not be termed a time of democratic revolution in the sense that the eighteenth and nineteenth centuries were, but it was a time when a wider spectrum of social groups began to gain considerably more voice in the political and economic affairs of some of the nation-states. The upswing in European commerce and trade that had begun as far back as the twelfth and thirteenth centuries literally changed the map of the world during the sixteenth and seventeenth centuries. In general, the free cities of Italy and northern Germany took the lead, but by the sixteenth century the axis of commercial enterprise began to shift to the shores of the Atlantic as the explorations of Vasco da Gama, Columbus, and Magellan opened up new trade routes across the ocean seas rather than simply across the Mediterranean, the Baltic, and the North Seas.

Eventually, the growing economic power of the middle classes led to a greater political power in the major nations of Europe. Just when and how the middle classes began to exert significant political strength has become a matter of extensive, and sometimes heated, historical debate in recent years. The tendency has been to downgrade the political prowess of the urban middle classes and to upgrade the importance of the landed gentry in Tudor and early Stuart England.[1] The result of the historiographical storm over the gentry, in any case, has been to underline a greatly expanded role for the nobility and gentry in the field of education, a role which in turn strengthened the upper classes so that they were able to retain their place in the power structure of England long after their counterparts in France were able to do so. Indeed, the gentry were key allies of the Tudor kings in their drive to centralized power, and then became key participants in the revolution that enabled the House of Commons to challenge the power of the Stuart monarchy and even to overthrow it during the mid-decades of the seventeenth century.

The crucial point to make here is that facilities for organized education from lower school to university became more available to and were more heavily relied upon by a wider range of social classes, both upper and middle, both rural and urban, than ever before. This was generally the case in most of western Europe, but is perhaps best illustrated by England, which played such a key role in the modernization of the West and its expansion in the world.

Just as the political changes of the early modern period were profoundly interrelated with education, so were its economic and social developments. The primary effect of both was to create for the schools a new group of students from the rural gentry and urban middle classes, and, to a lesser extent, from lower classes. Giving their children the advantage of an education was one of the ways that the newly rich could achieve respectability. Therefore the merchant classes poured money into schools of all kinds. One way was to give money to schools already established or to help found new academic schools. Another was to demand schools of greater practical and vocational use for a life of business, commerce, and agriculture. In some countries this end was achieved through voluntary gifts and subscriptions to private schools. In other countries the middle class used its newly won political power to pass laws creating state and city schools supported at public expense for the benefit of all children. The extremes at each end of the social scale were also not overlooked. At the upper end, the nobility on the Continent were interested in setting up special academies to train their children in the proper courtly ways, while in England aristocratic youth went to grammar schools and the universities. At the lower end, religious and philanthropic agencies set about giving free or charity education to children of unemployed or pauper parents who could not afford to have them educated. In any case, the religious motive was nearly always combined with the political and economic in the efforts to provide education.

Along with the growing urbanization and commercial activity that created a network of trading cities across the face of Europe went a series of technological inventions that further accelerated trade in goods and ideas and even boosted them into global dimensions. The fifteenth and sixteenth centuries refined and enlarged the scope of technology in fortification, farming, mining, manufacturing, and precision

---

[1] For a handy summary of the main points in the controversy and excerpts from key references, see Lawrence Stone, *Social Change and Revolution in England, 1540-1640*, Longmans, Green, London, 1965.

instruments. Above all, they perfected two revolutionary inventions created in China that were especially significant for long-distance communication, commerce, and conquest: gunpowder and printing.[2] The one made mass warfare possible, the other mass education.

If Europeans had confined themselves to land warfare among themselves, it would have been one thing, but the early modern period produced technological improvements that were to affect the entire world through the arts of navigation. The Italian and Portuguese cities took the lead in this process. The development of the magnetic compass, accurate charts, measurement of latitude, the stern-post rudder, and more sturdy and responsive sailing ships enabled the Europeans to sail to all parts of the world, carrying their guns, their cannons, their goods, their books, and their ideas and institutions. Even though Western technology was still a matter for craftsmen rather than for scientists and still relied on small scale ingenuity and apprenticeship rather than upon large scale research and development, it helped to start the process which soon fundamentally changed the equilibrium among the Afro-Eurasian civilizations which had been more or less in balance for some 2,000 years.

The Awakening of Europe to the World Overseas

European historians speak of the fifteenth and sixteenth centuries as the Age of Discovery or the Age of Exploration without realizing that such terms reveal a European ethnocentrism. It may be true that Europeans "discovered" many parts of the world they had not been aware of, but from the point of view of the people, the cultures, and the civilizations "discovered" it was not a matter of "discovery." They were *there*—ever since their own great ages of exploration centuries earlier when Indians and Chinese "discovered" Southeast Asia; when Polynesians "explored" eastward to the far islands of the Pacific and westward to Africa; when Middle Eastern Moslems penetrated India, Indonesia, and Africa. In addition to these few examples of seaborne movements, countless migrations crisscrossed the land masses of all the major continents, including the treks from Asia to the Americas.

So while it was discovery time for the Europeans, they were relative latecomers to the process. In fact, for 1,000 years the flow of people and goods and possibly ideas and inventions had been mainly from the East to the West. Until 1500, Europe lagged behind the Levant and far behind China in technology and inventiveness. It is possible that Europeans learned about gunpowder, cannons, the magnetic compass, printing, and even canal lock-gates and the wheelbarrow from the Chinese. It is clear that silk and paper were carried from China to Europe. Not nearly so clear is whether *systematic* efforts to convey or to borrow scientific ideas and organized knowledge were carried on prior to 1500 in either direction.[3] It is true that Genoese merchants traversed the silk road to Cathay or sailed across the Indian Ocean, and a few Franciscan friars established missions in China in the mid-fourteenth century. It is also

[2] See Melvin Kranzberg and Carroll W. Pursell, Jr. (eds.), *Technology in Western Civilization*, vol. 1, *The Emergence of Modern Industrial Society, Earliest Times to 1900*, Oxford University Press, New York, 1967, chap. 6.

[3] Donald F. Lach, *Asia in the Making of Europe*, vol. 1, *The Century of Discovery*, University of Chicago Press, Chicago, 1965, chaps. 1 and 2.

true that Marco Polo's *Description of the World* gave an even earlier and remarkably comprehensive account of the East at the end of the thirteenth century. So Europe had really "discovered" the "far" East long before the Age of Discovery. Yet the general impact of accurate knowledge had been relatively slight in comparison with the fabulous tales of Cathay or of India, which remained for centuries the generalized name for the East.

Besides, there came a serious interruption in the free intercourse that had been established between Europe and East Asia in the thirteenth and early fourteenth centuries. The fairly friendly Mongol rulers of China were replaced by the somewhat more hostile Ming dynasty, and the Moslem Turks, after conquering the whole of the Middle East including Byzantium by the mid-fifteenth century, cut off East-West trade through the Mediterranean. A new momentum for exploration by western Europeans was stimulated by their desire to reestablish contact with the East. The search was on to outflank the Moslems and find a way around Africa to the Indies. The lead was taken in this effort by Portugal, which stood not only at the western gateway to the Mediterranean but also the west coasts of Europe and Africa. In the 1490s both India and the Americas were thus discovered by the Europeans, first by the Portuguese and the Spaniards (with able assists from Italian sea captains) and then by the English, the Dutch, and the French.

When relations between Europe and the East were renewed around 1500, it was now the Europeans rather than the Asians who were on the move. It was the Europeans who took the initiative, who sent the explorers, the merchants, the missionaries, the soldiers, and the governors. In the two centuries from 1500 to 1700 the Europeans encircled the world with trading posts, with military outposts, and with Christian missions. In the "East" the conditions of their arrival and the conduct of their business were determined in large part by the highly sophisticated Asian nations. As it happened, neither China nor Japan had very strong central governments in the sixteenth century, so the Europeans initially had relatively easy access for trade and proselytizing, even though many Chinese and Indians tended to look down upon the intrusive Europeans, tolerating them in greater or lesser degree, but seldom sending return missions to Europe.

Events of enormous significance to the entire future of the world, however, took place within Japan and China as strong rulers came to power who decided to reject the Europeans and erect a self-imposed isolation. From the mid-seventeenth century both Japan and China deliberately withdrew from contact with the West and indeed from the rest of the world for about two centuries. As a result, Europe moved more rapidly into a more modern form of civilization than did the great traditional civilizations of East Asia which not only removed themselves from the intermingling of ideas and forces that hatched the modern world, but left open the rest of Asia to the exploitation of the aggressive and competitive Westerners. India did not reject the Europeans so completely as did Japan and China; indeed the Moguls were extending their rule in northern India in the seventeenth and eighteenth centuries at the same time as the Europeans, especially the British, were building up trade on the eastern and western sea coasts of India. Not until the nineteenth century were the Westerners able to open up the civilizations of East Asia to their penetration. By that time the scramble for

Asian and African colonies that marked the later imperial age of the West was reaching its crest.

The influence of Western Europe upon Russia came sooner than that. Indeed there was considerable traffic between Western European merchants and Muscovite Russia in the sixteenth century. Italian architects and English, German, and Dutch traders were active, while Boris Godunov even contemplated establishing a university on European lines. But during the reign of the first Romanov, Michael I, in the early seventeenth century (following Jesuit successes in the Ukraine and the Polish invasion of Moscow, a reaction against the intrusion of the West set in. The tendency to withdraw, to hold off Western and Latin influence in education and religion, and to reassert the distinctive values of Russian Orthodoxy kept the West at bay for a century. By 1700, however, Peter the Great was ready to launch major efforts to come to terms with the education and culture of modernizing Europe.

Meanwhile, to the west of Europe the story was quite different. The fundamental transformation of the New World began almost immediately upon the arrival of the Europeans. In North and South America the Europeans established themselves rather quickly upon their own terms. Not only explorers, traders, missionaries, and armies arrived, but, even more important, European colonists transplanted themselves across the seas. The great civilizations of the Aztecs and Incas fell with amazing suddenness to the conquests of a few Spaniards, and the Amerindian folk societies elsewhere were pushed back before the advances of European colonists who brought their institutions, their cultures, and their whole ways of life with them.

The New World rapidly became an outpost of Western civilization which was either imposed as a cultural layer on top of the settled civilizations already there, or was established alongside the hunting or farming folk societies that had preceded the Westerners to America by many centuries but still maintained their paleolithic or neolithic characteristics. Whereas the Europeans could only make slight footholds on the edges of traditional Asian civilizations, they brought the full panoply of Western civilization as they knew it to the New World. They brought their own differing varieties of Western civilization with them: the semi-feudalism of Spain and Portugal to Central and South America, the liberal constitutionalism of the English and Dutch revolutions to the Atlantic seaboard, and the conservative, royal absolutism of the Bourbons to French Canada. These varieties or fragments of Western civilization transplanted to different grounds of the New World eventually brought forth new growths that differed substantially among themselves as well as from the original cultures and societies that sent them out.[4]

The purpose at this point is not to try to detail the transfer of Western institutions from Europe to the other parts of the world. That will be done in later chapters of this book. Our concern here is to remind that Europe's passage from traditional forms of civilization to modernity was deeply affected by its awareness of the overseas world, an awareness that developed in a significant way in the period from

---

[4]See, for example, Louis Hartz, *The Founding of New Societies*, Harcourt, Brace & World, New York, 1964.

1400-1700 and was deeply affected by the first large-scale dispersion of European peoples and institutions to other parts of the world. This dispersion resulted from a mixture of political, religious, and commercial motivations that reflected the conditions and the development of Western civilization between the fifteenth and the seventeenth centuries.

Western Europe in this period literally came to be the meeting and market place of the world, its cities the centers to which and from which flowed people, goods, and ideas in intoxicating profusion. The crossroads of world movement were no longer located in the cities of the Middle East, but rather on the edges of the vast Afro-Eurasian land ecumene in the Atlantic coast cities of Western Europe, which became the centers of a still vaster, ocean-based ecumene that circled the entire globe from 1500 onwards. Change, invention, novelty, activity became the everyday characteristics of the bustling cities and the ambitious courts. The overseas colonies were in effect offshoots of the metropoles of Europe; no matter how remote from the cities they might be, the colonies carried the European urban civilization halfway around the world in each direction.

Stimulated by the desire for economic gain among the merchant classes and among the national rulers, the initial period of Western exploration and dispersion beginning in the late fifteenth century continued into the sixteenth and seventeenth centuries. Because they first had emerged as strong consolidated national states, Spain, Portugal, France, and England were the first to establish supremacy over the trade routes of the world and thus to launch the age of early modern imperialism. As the Netherlands became a powerful and effective merchant state, it not only competed with England and France for commercial supremacy but joined them in replacing Portugal and Spain in the seventeenth century. Men's imaginations and economic desires were stimulated by the visions of conquest and wealth thus opened up by the New World to the west and the ancient world to the east. Religious, nationalistic, and commercial motives were closely interlocked with the scientific and technological advances in navigation, shipbuilding, and warfare which made the explorations and conquests possible and effective.

As the European nations began to reach out to the rest of the world from the fifteenth and sixteenth centuries onward, they began one of the most momentous movements in all human history. They began to lay the groundwork for the increasing political domination of the West over much of the rest of the world, a movement that reached a crescendo in the nineteenth and early twentieth centuries. From the mid-fifteenth century onwards the modern age has been marked by a shift in the balance of power from the traditional civilizations cradled in the land masses of the Afro-Eurasian continents to the newer ocean-centered civilization that grew up in Western Europe and America.

The expansion of man's horizons made possible by the exploration of the ocean seas laid the geographical groundwork for the appearance of a modern type of society much as the new scientific view of the universe formed the intellectual framework of modernity. The results of the accelerating flow of ideas into and out from Western Europe, the increasing movements of peoples from one place to another, the confrontation of conflicting customs, institutions, and values all led to a quickening of social change and a hospitality to innovation that helped to transform the traditional societies of Western Europe into modern societies earlier than similar changes took place elsewhere. But that was not all.

Not content to stay at home, the ever-restless bearers of Western civilization transferred their institutions and their culture to nearly every other part of the world. Sometimes westernization was rejected, sometimes accepted more or less willingly by the peoples to whom it was introduced or upon whom it was imposed. But, willing or not, for good or ill, sooner or later, the diffusion of the civilization of the West during the past 500 years has irrevocably stimulated the process of modernization in much of the world. It was not merely an accident of history nor was it by fiat of some overall cosmic design that Western Europe should initiate the modernization process. To be sure, many Westerners have spoken of their "civilizing mission" as though they were anointed to rule the world, but the manifest destiny, or superiority of peoples in their own minds, had been expressed by Sumerians, Egyptians, Greeks, Romans, Chinese, and Russians as well as by Westerners; by Jews, Moslems, Hindus, Buddhists, and Confucianists as well as by Christians. Indeed, in 1500 one might have expected the "asianization" of Europe to have taken place rather than the westernization of Asia.[5] In fact both tendencies were at work, but the weight of influence was increasingly with the West, and one of the important factors in the process was the kind of education that the Europeans were developing in the early modern period. For when they carried their education to North and South America, it became a potent builder of Western civilization, and when they carried it to the East, it acted as a westernizing and eventually as a modernizing influence. The education they carried in both directions before 1700 was an amalgam of humanistic, Christian, and to a much lesser degree scientific knowledge. By and large, Western education in its organized forms up to 1700 responded more quickly to the political, social, and cultural developments of the Mediterranean and European world than it did to the world overseas. Perhaps, however, the influence from the Old World was not as long delayed as hitherto supposed.[6]

In any case European education was enormously and directly affected by international movements of men and ideas within Europe, if not by intercontinental movements. The East in the form of Byzantine civilization played a significant role in the educational wakening of Europe until the Turks shut down cultural contacts with Western Europe after 1453. From then on, the impact of literary knowledge about the nearby "East" as derived from the ancient classics of Greece and Rome played a far larger part in the forming of the Western educational tradition than did the firsthand knowledge of a still more ancient and more remote "East" as told by contemporary merchants and missionaries. Current events have had a way of receiving less attention in educational curricula than have the traditional disciplines of knowledge.

[5] See John K. Fairbank, Edwin O. Reischauer, and Albert M. Craig, *East Asia: The Modern Transformation,* Houghton Mifflin, Boston, 1965, p. 10.

[6] Donald F. Lach's projected six volumes, *Asia in the Making of Europe,* now being published by the University of Chicago Press, throw considerable light on this question.

The Scientific Revolution

The schools are also sometimes slow to adopt the ideas being created by new fields of knowledge that have not yet attained the authority or status of disciplines. Often, this is not because the schools are indifferent or complacent, but rather because competing authorities actively prevent the schools from adapting themselves to the new knowledge. This was largely the case with the scientific revolution. It had its advocates, but during the period from 1400 to 1700 the more voluble and persuasive advocates for educational reform came from the humanist reformers and the religious reformers. The schools were not quiescent; they were often the battleground for competing ideologies. The realist reformers, despite their looking to the modern future, were bested by the humanists and religionists who were basically looking to the traditional past. Nevertheless, the realistic spokesmen's words were taken ever more seriously from 1700 on. During the period we are considering, educational realism was a small current of modernity in an ocean of tradition, but it began to run stronger and stronger as one of the major forces leading to the modernization of the West and eventually of the world.

Although victory was not in sight, the skeptic, the scientist, the rationalist, and the heretic were freer and safer in 1700 than they had been a hundred years earlier in spite of continuing intolerance, antagonism, and persecution. A growing reliance upon human reason as defined by science eventually had tremendous implications for education from the lowest to the highest levels. The main momentum for organized attention to scientific knowledge came in the seventeenth century principally from scientific societies. The Academy of Florence (1661), the Royal Society of London (1662), and the Academy of Sciences in Paris (1666) enabled men from many walks of life to associate themselves in the effort to apply scientific knowledge to social affairs, until the universities began to dominate the field in the nineteenth century.

The outstanding propagandist for science in the seventeenth century was, of course, Francis Bacon, not a scientist himself but a master of popularizing the value of science through his writings and his influential political position as lord chancellor in England. Bacon's real influence lay largely in his ability to set forth the claims of the scientific method in an eloquent, persuasive, and effective style. Bacon felt that men were too enslaved by superstition and tradition, devoted too exclusively to Aristotle and scholastic philosophy, and engrossed too much in the niceties of words and language. His remedy for these defects of thought and education was a thoroughgoing attention to the study of nature by the scientific method. In his *Dignity and Advancement of Learning* Bacon surveyed and defended science as a new method of inquiry and the experimental method as the chief basis for acquiring knowledge that would be exact, reliable, and useful. In his *New Atlantis* he let his imagination revel in describing a Utopia on an imaginary South Sea island where scientific research had developed unbelievable machines that flew in the sky, skimmed under the water, kept perpetual time, and conveyed music afar.

In his *Novum Organum (New Method)* Bacon described in detail the inductive method whereby authentic knowledge could be obtained. The scientist should observe nature, collect a wide range of facts, generalize from these individual facts to their common qualities, and express these likenesses in general formulas. Today Bacon would be criticized for merely recording masses of empirical data just because he observed them and for neglecting the strategic role of mathematics in science. Nevertheless, his insistence that knowledge arises out of experience rather than through traditional authority, and his perception of the use of a controlled method of investigation were of supreme importance. He was not the first to urge these procedures but he helped enormously to make them respectable, despite jibes and sneers for trying to extract sunshine from cucumbers and build houses from the roof down when any sensible person knew these were impossible.

The scientific revolution included not only a new method of inquiry and a new role of knowledge in human affairs but also a fundamental change in the cosmic view that gradually emerged from the scientific investigations. It took a long time for the implications to be felt; but when they were, the whole fabric of human thought was altered by the heliocentric theory of the universe. The Christian tradition had conceived of the universe as centering in the earth, with the stars and sun surrounding it, all originally created by God for His own purposes. However, when Copernicus, Kepler, Galileo, Bruno, and others had completed their scientific investigations, the outlines of a limitless universe with the sun at the center and with the earth as merely one of many satellites burst upon the consciousness of men with terrific force.

Catholic and Protestant churches alike viewed such a conception with alarm and took active steps to combat it, for they saw the world made especially for man paling into insignificance before the immensity of the universe. Copernicus died before his views were published; Kepler was denied hospitality by Lutheran theologians; Galileo was forced by the Catholic church to abjure his writings; and Bruno was burned at the stake for his.

Nevertheless, the scientific revolution proceeded against all odds, aided by the tremendous advances in mathematics, so essential for scientific measurement and computation: decimals and logarithms, the calculus, the theory of probabilities, trigonometry, and analytical geometry. The epitome of the seventeenth century scientific achievement came with the scientific world view of Sir Isaac Newton, whose epoch-making *Mathematical Principles of Natural Philosophy* was published in 1687. Building upon the prior century and a half, Newton's laws of nature remained scientific gospel until the late nineteenth century. As a result of the elaboration of the law of gravitation and the law of cause and effect, the universe came to be viewed as an orderly system of atoms moving in absolute space and time, essentially simple in structure, obeying fixed laws, and operating in a causal and uniform way. The universe was a great machine, not subject to caprice, novelty, or divine intervention, but operating according to mathematical laws.

Theories of human nature also underwent a profound change under the influence of scientific investigation. In anatomy and medicine, William Harvey was making enormous strides in discovering what the structure of the human body was like and how it functioned. Others like Hobbes and Gassendi were applying their doctrines of materialism to human nature, saying that the body, being matter, worked exactly like a machine according to mechanical laws and that mind or consciousness was not a different sort of element but merely another, more refined case of matter in motion. Such materialists were attacked as being atheists in league with the devil, for they denied the existence of an immortal soul.

In this dispute, Descartes came to the rescue with the doctrine of dualism. He asserted that, like the universe, human nature is made up of both mind (or soul) and matter (or body). Man's mind partakes of the mental substance and thus can think and exert free will whereas the body partakes of the material substance and thus is a machine obeying scientific and mechanical laws. The dualistic conception of human nature conceded that the human body is a proper object of scientific study but reserved the human mind or soul for spiritual and intellectual scrutiny alone.

With regard to the learning process a similar development took place. Empiricists were inclined to say that man learns about the external world primarily through his senses of seeing, tasting, touching, hearing, and smelling. Knowledge is built up through experience coming to the body through the senses. In contrast, rationalists were inclined to say that man learns best through his mind because sense experience is limited to the world of physical objects whereas reason can achieve permanent and absolute truth in the realm of intellect and values. This conception assigned to human reason a more important place than that of the senses in getting at the knowledge that lies behind everyday experience. Because of his great reliance upon mathematics as one of the best examples of achieving universal and certain knowledge, Descartes tended to support rationalism, but the weight of his influence fell on the side of realistic studies because of his attacks upon rhetoric and his advocacy of the study of science in the schools.

Rationalists in education tend to stress the importance of mathematics, language, and literature because these studies, they said, develop the reason more effectively than does empirical science, which, after all, depends upon the vagaries of sense experience. Until the latter part of the seventeenth century, rationalism was often closely allied with religion, but Hobbes and Bacon had fired the opening guns for empiricism, soon to be supported by Locke and by Hume and by the eighteenth-century *philosophes*. In any case, the claim of experimental science to be the chief exponent of human reason was being staked out in the early modern period; it was to be developed with great enthusiasm during the eighteenth-century Enlightenment. Meanwhile, the main line of educational development in the West was to be shaped by other, more powerful forces.

B. THE THREE R's OF WESTERN EDUCATION

The three major movements of thought that enlisted the intellectual energies and loyalties of Western educators are well-known to the readers of European history under the familiar headings of the Renaissance, the Reformation, and Realism (the scientific revolution). In the schools of the West these three R's took the form of Renaissance studies of classical humanism, religious studies appropriate to the Protestant or Catholic creeds, and realistic studies based upon the method of science and its application to human welfare.

In the period from 1400 to 1700 all three R's took the mantle of educational reform movements. Humanists set out to reform the medieval curriculum by ousting the "blotterature" of scholastic and Aristotelian studies in favor of genuine classical literature. Protestants set out to reform the medieval Catholic curriculum in favor of the original Christine doctrines as they viewed them. Realists set out to reform the predominantly "talkative arts" of humanists and credal religionists by substituting studies attuned to the realities of nature as the surest road to the betterment of man and society.

By and large, the three reform movements affected education in the chronological order in which they have been listed here, but with considerable intermingling and overlapping. The Renaissance humanists got a jump on the others by virtue of the fourteenth-century revivals of classical learning in the Italian cities, but humanism did not begin to affect education in trans-Alpine Europe until well along in the fifteenth and early sixteenth centuries. By that time the Protestant Reformation was beginning to bubble up and boil over into the schools. In the works of key humanists and key religious reformers the classical studies did double education duty: they were expected to civilize students as well as to Christianize them. This double-teaming did not always work out so well, for, as McNeill so neatly puts it, the Renaissance and the Reformation were "incompatible inseparables." Nevertheless, they came to constitute the two most pervasive R's in Western education during the three centuries under consideration. Realism was a poor third throughout this period, although it began to attract some educational attention in the late sixteenth century and increasingly so in the seventeenth.

Renaissance: From Scholasticus to Humanista

In European history, the Renaissance was long looked upon as a time of sudden and spectacular cultural flowering whose prime mover was a revival of interest in classical Greek and Latin learning. More recently, it is generally agreed that there was much more to the Renaissance than a sudden rebirth of classical literature and that many of its institutional and intellectual trends had their origins deep in the Middle Ages. The Renaissance, however, did reveal a general efflorescence of life and a speeding up of social as well as intellectual and artistic change which may be epitomized in the growing secularism of the times. Secular trends had already become strong in the Middle Ages, but during the Renaissance secularism began to permeate Western culture to an ever greater degree, until the religious struggles of the sixteenth and seventeenth centuries slowed down the secular tide temporarily. Thereafter, the secularization of life eventually became one of the distinctive ingredients of modern in contrast to traditional civilization.

The Renaissance has the same kind of peculiar fascination for Westerners that the classical age of Greece has had—a special burst of vitality and élan that ripped the seams of the medieval tradition with an extraordinary outpouring of cultural energy. It stands along with the florescent ages of Greece and Rome as one of the high spots of creativity in Western history. Having said this, most historians of education have proceeded to argue or to imply that education was an integral part of the revitalizing social and cultural trends of the Renaissance. Most would agree that the movement known as humanism was that part of the Renaissance which most directly affected the spirit and content of organized education. Many assume with the humanists themselves that such reform was wholly desirable in sweeping the musty cobwebs of medievalism out of the classrooms and flooding the schools and universities with the bright light of classical learning.[7] There is undoubtedly a good deal of truth in this picture, but it should not be accepted uncritically.

Our first task is to clarify the meaning of "humanism.' In this respect I believe that Paul Oskar Kristeller. professor of philosophy at Columbia University, has injected a note of clarity in a field that has become cluttered with a conglomeration of philosophical, intellectual, and educational preconceptions. In the first place, Kristeller defines humanism primarily as a cultural and educational movement devoted to promoting the study of Latin and Greek classics, *not* as a philosophical system or distinctive school of thought. He states that "by humanism we mean merely the general tendency of the age to attach the greatest importance to classical studies, and to consider classical antiquity as the common standard and model by which to guide all cultural activities."[8] The name itself was not coined until the nineteenth century when *Humanismus* was used by a German educator, F. J. Niethammer, to refer to the educational point of view that favored the study of Greek and Latin classics in opposition to the demands for more practical and scientific studies in the secondary school curriculum of his day.[9] This coinage is a direct descendant from the term *humanist* which had *its* origin in the Renaissance itself. Kristeller's analysis is lucid and persuasive:

> *Humanista* in Latin, and its vernacular equivalents in Italian, French, English, and other languages, were terms commonly used in the sixteenth century for the professor or teacher or student of the humanities, and this usage remained alive and was well understood until the eighteenth century. The word, to judge from its earliest appearance known so far, seems to have originated in the student slang of the Italian universities, where the professor of the humanities came to be called *umanista*, after the analogy of his colleagues in the older disciplines, to whom the terms *legista, jurista, canonista,* and *artista* had been applied for several centuries. The term *humanista*, coined at the height of the Renaissance period, was in turn derived from an older term; that is, from the "humanities" or *studia humanitatis.* This term was apparently used in the general sense of a liberal or literary education by such ancient Roman authors as Cicero and Gellius, and this use was resumed by the Italian scholars of the late fourteenth century. By the first half of the fifteenth century, the *studia humanitatis* came to stand for a clearly defined cycle of scholarly disciplines, namely grammar, rhetoric, history, poetry, and moral philosophy, and the study of each of these subjects was understood to include the reading and interpretation of its standard ancient writers in Latin and, to a lesser extent, in Greek. This meaning of the *studia humanitatis* remained in general use through the sixteenth

[7]See, for example, the classic studies made by William Harrison Woodward in the early nineteenth century, *Vittorino da Feltre and Other Humanist Educators,* Teachers College Press, New York, 1963; *Studies in Education during the Age of the Renaissance 1400-1600,* Teachers College Press, New York, 1967; and *Desiderius Erasmus Concerning the Aim and Method of Education,* Teachers College Press, New York, 1964.

[8]Paul Oskar Kristeller, *Renaissance Thought, The Classic, Scholastic, and Humanist Strains,* Harper Torchbooks, New York, 1961, p. 95.

[9]Ibid., pp. 9, 111.

century and later, and we may still find an echo of it in our use of the term "humanities."[10]

There are several points worth underlining here. From its beginning in the fourteenth century humanism was closely identified with *professional educators* and did *not* originate outside organized education as is so often asserted by European historians.[11] Its prime purpose was to promote the study of the ancient classics in schools and universities, *not* to formulate a whole new Renaissance philosophy based on man and human nature in order to replace the medieval philosophy based on God and the spiritual world. It stood in a direct line from Cicero and his conception of *humanitas* and the studies proper to humanity. What the Renaissance humanists did, however, was to narrow Cicero's rather broad panorama of *studia humanitatis* and limit them virtually to the *literary* subjects of the classical tradition.

Humanism did *not* embrace the whole range of Renaissance learning by any means. Note the emphasis upon grammar, rhetoric, poetry, and history. Note the exclusion of or deemphasis upon logic, arithmetic, geometry, astronomy, music, natural philosophy (science), metaphysics, medicine, law, and theology. The humanities did include that part of moral philosophy which was largely contained in literary rather than strictly philosophical writings, e.g., Plutarch rather than Plato, and Cicero rather than Aristotle. The *humanista* thus reemphasized the long rhetorical and literary tradition that stemmed from the Greek sophists and Isocrates through Cicero and Quintilian to the *ars dictamen* of the Middle Ages as over against the philosphical and scientific tradition that flowed from Plato and Aristotle to Abelard, Aquinas, and the scholastics of the Middle Ages.

In sum, the humanists were *professionals,* devoted to promoting classical learning in schools, universities, and the public service:

> The vast majority of humanists exercised either of two professions, and sometimes both of them. They were either secretaries of princes or cities, or they were teachers of grammar and rhetoric at universities or at secondary schools. The opinion so often repeated by historians that the humanistic movement originated outside the schools and universities is a myth which cannot be supported by factual evidence. Moreover, as chancellors and as teachers, the humanists, far from representing a new class, were the professional heirs and successors of the medieval rhetoricians, the so-called *dictatores,* who also made their career exactly in these same two professions.[12]

The humanist movement within the universities was thus basically an effort of educational reformers to inject classical models into the several academic departments of study. The humanists were most successful in capturing the chairs of grammar,

---

[10] Ibid., pp. 9-10.

[11] See, for example, Lawrence Stone in his *Foreword* to Woodward, *Studies in Education during the Age of the Renaissance,* p. ix.

[12] Kristeller, op. cit., pp. 102-103.

rhetoric, poetry, history, and moral philosophy. They were much less successful in the professional disciplines or specialties of philosophy, medicine, and law. And they were not much interested in the mathematical or scientific fields. This meant that the humanists came to dominate most of the nonspecialized departments of knowledge which have since come largely to be the provinces of the liberal arts or general education.

Bolgar points to the fact that because of the undifferentiated character of literary studies, they encompassed not only what we would call the humanities but also the social sciences:

> This lack of differentiation must be kept in mind if we are to understand how Humanism came to exercise such a profound influence. For it explains why the specific Humanist techniques of analysis and synthesis for the purposes of imitation were applied to so vast a sector of human knowledge, and why within that sector their supremacy as instruments of intellectual organisation was virtually unchallenged. If such subjects as history and political thought had possessed their own methods of study, the impact of the Humanist techniques would have been notably less since they would have been counterbalanced by alternative forms of interpretation. But as things were, they had a clear field. In the absence of other disciplines, their power to mould and fashion was for all intents and purposes absolute.[13]

The humanists were the aggressive reformers in the universities of the day, criticizing their colleagues in the other departments as irrelevant old fogies bound to the medieval past but blind to the glories of the ancient past. Humanists were the academic gadflies and progressives, as the physical scientists were to become in the nineteenth century. They criticized the scholastics, to be sure, but not primarily because of the religious or philosophical topics they dealt with but because the scholastics used medieval texts and glosses rather than the original classical and patristic authors who had written in a fine Greek and Latin style. Kristeller reminds us that humanism was not a rival philosophy to scholasticism but that it was a parallel department of knowledge.

Scholastics held the chairs of logic, natural philosophy, and metaphysics, while humanists held the chairs of grammar, rhetoric, and moral philosophy. Their rivalry was that of rival departments, not rival points of view within the same discipline. As academic rivals, the humanists criticized the scholastics for not imitating the classical authors in their writing, but the humanists did *not* drive the scholastics or Aristotle out of philosophy or theology. These latter subjects continued to be dominated by Catholic scholastics or by Protestant theologians for two more centuries. In fact it was the humanists in the literary fields and the scholastics and religionists in the philosophical fields who cooperated to hold off or delay the inroads of the scientists and realists

---

[13] R. R. Bolgar, *The Classical Heritage and Its Beneficiaries*, Harper Torchbooks, New York, 1964, pp. 295-296.

during the seventeenth and eighteenth centuries in most of the universities of Europe and America.

Although the humanists were the innovators of the day, propagandizing first in Italy and then the length and breadth of Europe for greater attention to the ancient classical studies, their innovations did not necessarily lead to the modernizing of Western education. There were two key elements in the humanist program for a revitalized education. (1) All educated men of the sixteenth and seventeenth centuries should be trained to imitate the classical language and style in their own writing and speaking. This, of course, meant training in Latin and to a lesser extent in Greek. (2) All educated men should achieve an understanding and appreciation of ancient Graeco-Roman civilization as the best means of preparing them to deal with their own life and times. When these elements went together under the tutelage of a vital and creative teacher, the learning could be both innovative and modernizing: the intellectual means were at hand to broaden perspective, sharpen insights, and acquaint the learner with the problems and solutions reached by keen observers and analysts of the past. These could illuminate the understanding and increase the options and possibilities for problem solving in extremely useful ways. They could, and in important ways did, help to spread the Graeco-Roman belief in the value of rationality as a way of life and the power of ideas to shape human affairs.

What happened, however, was that it was extremely difficult to keep the two parts of the humanist cultural and educational program going along together. The easiest part to do was, of course, the first, but this could quickly become a routine matter of rote memorizing and imitation of phrases and verses of the great authors and the not-so-great textbook writers. It was far more difficult to bring to life and keep alive in a foreign tongue a realizing appreciation of an alien and ancient civilization for generations of boys and young men who found the burgeoning life of their own day intriguing and demanding. It was still more difficult for a teacher to assist in applying the knowledge of the past to the problems of his present.

Yet the humanist spokesmen insisted that the classics did contain the keys to the educational kingdom. They put it in many different ways. Erasmus put first things first—and very succinctly—in his *De Ratione Studii:*

> Language thus claims the first place in the order of studies and from the outset should include both Greek and Latin . . . . within these two literatures are contained all the knowledge which we recognize as of vital importance to mankind.[14]

Vergerius put the matter somewhat more elegantly but to the same point:

> We call those studies *liberal* which are worthy of a free man; those studies by which we attain and practise virtue and wisdom; that education which calls forth, trains and develops those highest gifts of body and of mind which ennoble men, and which are rightly judged to rank next in dignity to virtue only.[15]

[14] Woodward, *Desiderius Erasmus,* p. 163.

[15] Woodward, *Vittorino da Feltre and Other Humanist Educators,* p. 102.

He then defined the prime liberal studies in the order of their importance: history, moral philosophy, eloquence (based on grammar, rhetoric, and logic); followed by poetry, music, arithmetic, geometry, astronomy, and natural philosophy. But the final message was the predominant theme to which the humanists regularly returned: "Literature surpasses every other form of record."[16] And Bruni spelled out the message in explicit detail:

> This leads me to press home this truth . . . that the foundations of all true learning must be laid in the sound and thorough knowledge of Latin: which implies study marked by a broad spirit, accurate scholarship, and careful attention to details. . . . To attain this essential knowledge we must never relax our careful attention to the grammar of the language . . . we must note attentively vocabulary and inflexions, figures of speech and metaphors, and all the devices of style, such as rhythm, or antithesis, by which fine taste is exhibited . . . bringing a keen, critical sense to bear upon select works, observing the sense of each passage, the structure of the sentence, the force of every word down to the least important particle. In this way our reading reacts directly upon our style.[17]

Whatever else the humanist "reform" turned out to be, the pedagogical heart of the matter was here.

Bolgar explains in detail the new pedagogical method which characterized the humanists' stock-in-trade. This was in essence to try to imitate the style of classic writers by keeping careful and detailed notebooks in which words, phrases, metaphors, anecdotes, allusions, and epigrams are classified according to subject headings on topics which could be useful in one's own writing efforts. Beginning with Chrysoloras, who brought these pedagogical instruments from Byzantium to Florence in 1396, and propounded by such humanist giants as Guarino, Bruni, Vergerius, Valla, Agricola, and Vives, the method reached its apex in Erasmus and in his *De Copia:*

> The whole purpose of the Humanists in transmogrifying Greek and Latin literature into a series of notes was to produce a body of material which could be easily retained and repeated. They made titanic efforts to remember the contents of the notebooks they compiled. The Renaissance was the age of memorizing.[18]

The humanists, of course, did not confine themselves to the narrow pedagogical matters just described. They ranged over a vast number of broader themes in their efforts to reform Western education. Some proposed greater attention to public service and civic education for the ruling classes of the Italian city states and the aristocratic classes of France and Germany and England. Some proposed boarding schools in the cities, others preferred private tutors. Some favored study of the vernaculars along with the classics, others were contemptuous of the vernaculars. Some concentrated on

[16] Ibid., p. 105.
[17] Ibid., p. 124.
[18] Bolgar, op. cit., p. 274.

Christian writers, some on pagan, some on both. Some stressed Greek as well as Latin, others only Latin. Some were hostile to science and practical arts, others simply indifferent or tolerant. But whatever they proposed and whatever differences they displayed in general orientation, the basic educational means to the broader goals was nearly always the task of writing well, and the best way to learn how to write well was to imitate the great classical writers of Latin and Greek.

Many practicing educators echoed the cry of the humanists that classical Latin should be substituted for medieval Latin in the schools and universities of the day, but others did not. The movement for educational reform, which started in Italy in the fifteenth century and soon spread to Germany, the Low Countries, England, and France, met with a good deal of resistance from the established church schools. But by dint of much writing, speaking, and traveling, the humanists made good their claims, either winning over the church schools, refounding them, or setting up new schools.

Bolgar sums up two centuries of humanist education in Europe as follows:

> At the end of the fourteenth century, the cultural tradition of the West bore the recognisable imprint of the Middle Ages. By the end of the sixteenth, the medieval elements had been replaced by others drawn from the Graeco-Roman heritage; and in between these two limits of time, we find that the method of study in general use is based on the analysis of the classical texts and the memorisation of linguistic and illustrative detail. That these Humanist studies subserved certain wide aims characteristic of the period as a whole seems almost irrelevant in view of the thoroughness of the methods employed. Admittedly there was some degree of selection, certain aspects of ancient life received more emphasis than others; but once a student had embarked upon the recommended course, once he had started analysing and memorising, the techniques he employed acquired, like some powerful engine, an impetus of their own and took in everything irrespective of its interest, so that the whole or nearly the whole of the classical heritage passed into the common stock of European thought.[19]

What Bolgar makes explicit (and is sometimes neglected by humanist enthusiasts) is that the classical heritage passed into the stock of European thought not only by direct incorporation into the curriculum of classical secondary schools of Europe but also by its transfusion into the vernacular languages of the people and even into the elementary schools. This was one of the transforming achievements of the sixteenth century. The main body of classical literature was not only directly translated into Italian, German, French, Spanish, and English so that it became available in printed form to a vast new audience which had hitherto had no access to it; but also the principal vernacular writers embodied much of the tone, the substance, the style, and the allusions of the classics in their own writings. The French of Rabelais and Montaigne and the English of Bacon and Shakespeare are but prime examples.

By the end of the seventeenth century the assimilation of the classical heritage into Western education had been achieved in obvious form in the classical secondary schools, in less obvious form in the burgeoning vernacular literature that proclaimed

[19] Ibid., p. 301.

the arrival of cultural nationalisms that would eventually burst asunder the international medium of discourse that had been based upon Latin and Greek. In the face of such developments, some educators could begin to argue that the exclusive study of Latin and Greek was no longer necessary in order to be able to absorb the classical heritage. It could be acquired through the vernacular. The reply, of course, was that the vernacular could never take the place of the real thing; only the classics could properly discipline the mind. But this was not the main argument that won the day in the heat of the religious Reformation.

Reformation: From Humanista to Pietas Litterata

The second R that permeated Western education from the early sixteenth century onward was the use of education as an instrument of religious ideology. It was, of course, nothing new that education had been a prime formative factor in the building of Christendom both in the East and the West (as we saw in Chapters 4 and 5). What was new was that education became a weapon for the warring creeds within Christianity itself. Religious sectarianism was imbedded in Western education from the elementary schools to the universities. When the sectarian creeds were at their most virulent, the schools became pawns in the struggles.

Yet, education in the Reformation was not simply a weapon in ideological combat. It in turn injected a leaven of scholarship into the religious debates that gave them peculiar relevance to the Renaissance. The linkage between scholarship and the Christian religion was fashioned in a way that made education a potent force in religion comparable to faith and ritual. E. Harris Harbison of Princeton has stressed this emergence of "scholarship as a Christian calling" in the following terms:

> The Protestant Reformation began in a scholar's insight into the meaning of Scripture. It was to a large extent a learned movement, a thing of professors and students, a scholar's revolution. ... The Catholic response to the challenge, particularly in the Council of Trent, partook of the same nature. The prestige and influence of Christian scholars probably never stood higher in all of Western history than during the two generations which embraced the lifetimes of Erasmus, Luther, and Calvin. In no other period is there anything quite like the zest for learning, the respect for scholarship, the confidence in what scholarship might accomplish—and the revolution it did accomplish—of the age of the Reformation.[20]

It was not only that the classics were needed as intellectual armament by Protestant scholars in order to combat successfully the Catholic theologians by studying the real sources of Christianity in their original languages, Greek, Hebrew, and Latin. At the same time, the Protestants argued that vernacular translations of the Bible were necessary if the common people were to be able to read the Bible for themselves. In such circumstances, the Reformation served to entrench the classics in the secondary education for at least another three centuries, but at the same time

---

[20] E. Harris Harbison, *The Christian Scholar in the Age of the Reformation*, Scribners, New York, 1956, p. vi.

eventually to undermine the classics by extending ever outward and upward the vernacular systems of education.

This link between the Renaissance and the Reformation embedded them both in Western education in a peculiarly persistent way. Not only were many of the humanists fervent reformers and many of the reformers competent scholars, the curriculum of the schools was infused with a subject matter that was at once classical and Christian, the *pietas litterata*.[21] Whereas Christianity and early Italian humanism were not particularly compatible during the fifteenth century, the two came much closer together in the sixteenth century. Erasmus was the chief spokesman for the view that classical literature could promote piety. After all, Christian culture had been based upon Greek culture, and the best of the classical writers expressed moral values that supported Christian ethics (for example, Homer, Herodotus, Lucian, and Demosthenes in Greek; and Terence, Vergil, Cicero, Caesar, and Sallust in Latin).

Notwithstanding the scholarly underpinnings of Reformation ideology, one cannot but be impressed with the tremendous importance of religious creeds. They acted as rallying centers for the loyalties of men. They gave people prime motives for living, fighting, and dying. From the educational viewpoint, one of the most striking aspects of the several religious faiths was their authoritative character. They were held so confidently because it was widely believed that the religious leaders of each sect had special insight into the supernatural, beyond which there was no appeal; consequently, the word of the religious leaders was often taken to be the word of God. From Sumerian times to the present day the ruler who wished his word to be law has proclaimed that he ruled by divine right. Another factor was the belief that moral conduct depended upon religion; a man could not be morally good unless he held orthodox religious beliefs. Thus it was argued that the moral basis of civilization itself would crumble if religious dissidents were allowed to argue as they pleased. Most religious sects were reluctant to tolerate what they considered to be heresy. In these respects the religious creeds of the Reformation exerted a powerful traditionalizing impact upon Western education.

At the same time, the Protestant stress on literacy as a means of reading the Bible led to increased availability of education—a significant aspect of the modernizing of Western civilization. Along with their insistence upon the Bible as the rule of faith, Protestants emphasized the necessity for each person to establish the grounds of his belief by reading the Bible for himself. This meant that all true believers must know how to read the Bible. The demand for a widespread education thus arose in the early modern period from religious as well as from political and economic motives. The conjunction of these motives in the national states of Western Europe and America gave rise to the conditions out of which a popular education appeared. When this happened, something new under the sun had been created. Popular education proved to be an essential ingredient in modern civilization.

It remains true, however, that the fundamental values upon which Reformation education rested, the dominating conception of the world and of man's destiny in it, remained closely identified with traditional Christianity. Despite the quarrels between Protestants and Catholics, neither departed substantially from the medieval conception

---

[21] For an excellent discussion of the *pietas litterata*, see Bolgar, op. cit., pp. 329-369.

of God and the universe. A basic agreement among Christian Catholics and Christian Protestants linked them closely together against the world view of empirical science. Both accepted a universe created by God in which man played a role assigned to him by God. Both accepted the distinction between a supernatural world and a natural world, of which the supernatural was by far the more important.

Both Catholics and Protestants believed that man's nature consisted of a spiritual soul and a material body, and man's chief end is, of course, the salvation of his immortal soul. Calvinists and Jansenists tended to dwell upon the doctrine of original sin, but this was largely a matter of emphasis, for most Christians of the day would have denied a suggestion that man is inherently good or that he is born neither good nor bad. Both Catholics and Protestants agreed that the ultimate judgment of man's success upon this earth does not come until the next world. Both would have joined against a doctrine that preached that man's ultimate justification comes from the social good that he is able to accomplish on earth.

Both Catholics and Protestants agreed that man's primary aim in education was to arrive at a true knowledge of God's laws and commandments. If the Protestants objected to the educational system of the Catholics, their remedy was primarily to set up a system of language study whereby they could read the word of God for themselves in the *pietas litterata,* unfettered by the commentaries and interpretations of Catholic scholars. Knowledge of the physical world was considered by both as far less important than knowledge of the spiritual and moral world. The learning process was conceived by both Catholics and Protestants to be most effectively conducted by a kind of mental and moral discipline, achieved principally through the study of language and literature in which reading and memorizing were paramount. Both Catholics and Protestants were in large part opposed to the implications of much of the new science.

In their ambivalence toward the works of Dame Reason, favoring her when she spoke through virtuous classical literature but condemning her when she spoke through empirical science, the Protestant reformers were scarcely promoting the modern. Rather, they were maintaining strong conserving links with the medieval tradition. Franklin Le Van Baumer summarizes the case very nicely:

> The Protestants believed firmly in all the general features of the Christian Epic. In their world, as in the Middle Ages, supernatural revelation, miracles, and witches were taken for granted. In the sixteenth century, the majority stressed faith rather than reason, opposed religious toleration, and were indifferent, and sometimes hostile, to natural science and free inquiry.
>
> Clearly, Protestantism belonged to the same genus of thought as medieval Catholicism. ... as Troeltsch has pointed out, sixteenth-century Protestantism stood for a "church civilization," i.e., a civilization in which an infallible and historic church claims the right to regulate society (either directly, or indirectly through the state) from the standpoint of supernatural revelation. ... And from the title to save souls followed logically the claim to discipline men in all their wordly activities, whether in education or politics and business.[22]

[22] Franklin LeVan Baumer, *Main Currents of Western Thought,* Knopf, New York, 1970, p. 168.

In these respects, the Protestant Reformation was not "modern" and did not promote the modernizing of Western education which eventually came to emphasize rationality over revelation, and secular over otherworldly interests. But, by allying themselves with political movements and economic trends that were to overturn the old order and thus pave the way to modernity, the Protestant reformers did hasten the appearance of the modern world:

> Protestantism was primarily and fundamentally a religious reform, but it owed its popularity and growth in large part to powerful lay movements which ran parallel with it. There can be no doubt that something *in* Protestant thought itself appealed to the most progressive elements of Western society. The Reformation was a primitivist movement which preached a return to the simple standards of the Bible and the early Christian community. But not infrequently in history primitivism serves as a lever for dislodging traditional forces and allowing others to take over. This is what the Reformation accomplished, and there is considerable irony in the situation. The reformers contributed to individualism, although none of them were individualists in the modern sense; to nationalism, although they hoped to restore Christian unity; to democracy, although hardly any of them were democrats; to the "capitalistic spirit," although they were extremely suspicious of capitalists; indeed, to the secularization of society. although their aim was exactly the reverse.[23]

Realism: From Pietas Litterata to Realia

The English word *realism* is used here as a general term to refer not only to the new philosophy of empirical science that was emerging in the sixteenth and seventeenth centuries but also to a variety of related educational theories. Some began to stress learning through sense experience and contact with actual things rather than through books and verbal symbols. Others argued that the fulfillment of school learning was to be found in the application of knowledge to the practical affairs of life rather than in elegance of speech or in religious devotion.

The three-cornered debate among the three R's of Western education that arose in the early modern period has continued in various ways to the present time. John Colet's devotion to the clarity, the eloquence, and the moral virtues of classical literature led him to scoff at medieval scholastic learning as "blotterature." Martin Luther roared condemnation of science as "That silly little fool, that Devil's bride, Dame Reason, God's worst enemy." Bishop Thomas Sprat haughtily replied to critics of science that the art of experiment was the only proper subject for mature *men* while the traditional "talkative arts" were fit only for young learners and children. And Sir William Petty heaped scorn upon the "grammaticasters" of the country schools in contrast to the useful urban arts he proposed for his College of Tradesmen.

The educational debates between humanists and realists were part of a larger cultural and intellectual conflict between the Ancients and the Moderns which marked the latter part of the seventeenth century. Fontenelle's book of 1668 symbolized the prime differences between those who believed that the mainsprings of human excel-

---

[23] Ibid., p. 169.

lence lay in classic times and those who believed the modern exponents of science were just as remarkable in their achievements as were the ancients.[24]

Such attacks and counterattacks revealed a growing sense of doubt, skepticism, and inquiry concerning the structure of ideas that men should live by. The mere fact that the leaders of each religious sect battled so vigorously against unorthodox beliefs showed that doubters and unbelievers had to be worsted. By the end of the Reformation the sheer physical destruction of the religous wars had led many to wonder whether perhaps all religious doctrines were wrong and whether a new way to truth could be found. The impact of new geographic discoveries and knowledge concerning how other people lived led many to reexamine the established social forms of their own societies and cultures and to open new horizons through which the study of nature might reveal the fundamental characteristics of man as well as of things. Acquaintance with the hunting and gathering folk societies to be found in the Americas prompted belief that the natural man and the unspoiled noble savage could be morally good without the benefits of civilization or religion. Montaigne was struck by the fact that untutored peoples with no "civilized" heritage could show such high qualities of courage, honor, and integrity. The feeling even grew that nature could produce purer and better models of moral conduct than the oversophisticated civilizations of the past could provide.

If models for man's behavior and his education could not be found in the past, either in the classical humanities of the Renaissance or in the religious creeds of the Reformation, where then? The answer obviously lay in the natural and human interests of this world as portrayed by the underlying concepts of modern science: a certainty that the secrets of nature could be revealed to man through the progressive accumulation of scientific knowledge; a belief that scientific knowledge obtained from the direct study of nature is superior to that obtained by reading a body of written knowledge inherited from the past; and confidence that the most reliable and valid knowledge rests upon the painstaking collection of empirical facts, the objective verification of those facts, and the use of mathematical formulas in their analysis.

The realistic reform of education frontally attacked the tradition that success in school should be determined mainly by the ability to memorize quantities of bookish material and to recite to the teacher what was in the book. Ever since the widespread use of written language, the most obvious method of school learning had been memorizing. When English grammars were written, they followed the grammatical rules found in Latin grammars. As rules for logic, rhetoric, and mathematics were developed, the learning of those subjects was based on memorizing the rules. The disputation required students to argue according to the rules of formal logic. Likewise, the declamation gave students the opportunity to recite excerpts from the classic writers or from pieces they had composed according to the rules of rhetoric. Some of the more advanced secondary schools stressed the reciting of lines from ancient plays in order to develop a sense of the style and usage of the classic authors. When the imitation of classic authors was so pronounced as to be slavish, the method was derided as Ciceronianism.

[24] Ibid., pp. 351-354.

Educators who were imbued with an empirical point of view began to react against the rationalistic formalism of Ciceronianism and the irrational excesses of a brutal or vindictive discipline. In general, the realists urged that learning through the senses by acquaintance with actual things (*realia*) was far more effective than merely learning words and rules from books. The inductive method of science whereby the learner begins with actual and simple observations of objects around him and proceeds to more complex and unfamiliar things was proposed as the best basis for educational method. Efforts to arouse the interest of students in what they were learning and to adapt the materials to their abilities were praised as an improvement over traditional formalism and mere bookishness.

In such ways as these the realists insisted that school methods and curriculums should be revised to fit the social and intellectual changes that were beginning to characterize modern Western civilization. In fact when the Utopians looked into the future and tried to visualize what was to be or what ought to be, they often described the ideal education in technical, scientific, and practical terms in contrast to the useless gentlemanly education they were so familiar with. Thus did Thomas More, Rabelais, Campanella, and Bacon stress the transforming role of realistic education.

Many of the doctrines of realism stemmed from an empirical philosophy which insisted that education should cultivate the scientific spirit and method. Francis Bacon attacked the "contentious" learning of scholastic dialectics and theology, the "delicate" learning of Ciceronian humanism, and the "fantastic" learning of superstition and witchcraft. He argued that all these neglected the study of nature and depended upon mere speculation or authority. Instead, education should encourage original investigation, should cultivate the habit of suspending judgment until the facts were in, and should foster a critical attitude that would free the individual from the shackles of preconceived prejudices and fixed ideas.

If Bacon was the high priest of realistic educational theory, the eminent Moravian Brethren bishop, Johann Amos Comenius, was the outstanding educationist who applied the doctrines of sense realism to pedagogical methods and content in the schools. All instruction should be carefully graded and arranged to follow the order of nature as revealed in the child's development. This meant proceeding from the simple to the complex, from the known to the unknown. Throughout all teaching, the understanding of the child should be approached through appeals to his sense experience. Comenius urged that the child learn by acquaintance with actual objects (*realia*) wherever possible and in any case through pictures and representations of things. Of his many profusely illustrated textbooks which popularized the idea of picture books for school children, his *Orbis Pictus* is perhaps the best known. He improved language teaching by giving simple descriptions of the pictures, with the vernacular and the Latin sentences written side by side.

In *Didactica Magna* Comenius set forth his educational theory and his plans for reforming the curriculum and organization of schools. In general, he was impressed with the possibilities of social reform through pansophism, that is, teaching all knowledge to all children. He neatly divided the educational career up to age 24 into four periods of six years each. His 6-6-6-6 plan provided special schools for each period: infancy, childhood, boyhood, and youth. In the school for infants up to the age of six (School of the Mother's Knee), Comenius would train the senses and bring about moral, religious, and physical development through play and games, fairy tales, rhymes, music, and manual activity.In his vernacular school for children ages six to twelve, he would teach reading, writing, arithmetic, singing, religion, morals, economics and politics, history, and the mechanical arts. The classical school for adolescent ages twelve to eighteen would teach German, Latin, Greek, Hebrew, grammar, rhetoric, logic, mathematics, science, and art. The university for youth, ages eighteen to twenty-four, would be the top rung of this ladder system.

At all levels, the subject matter would be carefully organized into classes and graded to the pupil's ability. The school year would be carefully determined, as well as hours for specific activities during the school day. Classes would be taught as groups for the social advantages thus to be gained, and the various subject matters would be correlated as far as possible. In all activities the school would be made practical for life and pertinent to an upright religious life.

Although his technical assistance was sought in Poland, Sweden, Germany, Holland, Hungary, and England (and even some mention was made of inviting him to be president of Harvard College in Massachusetts Bay Colony), Comenius suffered successive defeats and failures in his homeland because of the ravages of the Thirty Years' War. His religious sect was so generally persecuted that his influence was doubtless much less than it would have been if he had belonged to a majority group.

Jerome K. Clausen argues that Comenius' genius lay not in his originality nor in the eloquence of his writings, which were often tedious and labored, but in his eclecticism. More than any other personality of his day he was able to "combine religious, scientific, encyclopedic, and Humanistic points of view into one comprehensive scheme."[25] He was able to see the merits in all of the three R's of the early modern period and to try to design a universal system of education that would embrace the key elements in Renaissance humanism, Reformation religion, and realistic science.

Not surprisingly, his works contained some contradictions. He applauded the idea of following the interests of the child but he stressed obedience and imitation. He stressed the role of sense experience, but his textbooks centered on teaching language. He advocated universal knowledge of languages and arts, but first must come faith and piety and uprightness in morals. Nevertheless, his conception that erudition, virtue, and piety should go together formed the basis of a belief that education ought to link knowledge, conduct, and religion into a mutually supporting triad. What made Comenius more modern than many others of his day was his belief that knowledge should include *both* the humanities and the sciences.[26]

Still more modern, if anything, was Comenius' belief that universal education could be a means to universal peace in a war-torn world. Two of his writings carry

---

[25] Jerome K. Clausen, "The Pansophist: Comenius" in Paul Nash, Andreas M. Kazamias, and Henry J. Perkinson (eds.), *The Educated Man,* Wiley, New York, 1965, p. 168.

[26] For short but significant selections by Comenius, see Paul Nash (ed.), *Models of Man,* Wiley, New York, 1968, chap. 8; for longer selections, see *John Amos Comenius on Education* with an introduction by Jean Piaget, Teachers College Press, New York, 1967.

forward this idea. They are remarkable testaments to a faith still far from realized. In the *Pampaedia* Comenius put it this way:

> *Pampaedia* is universal education for the whole of the human race; for among the Greeks παιδεια means both teaching itself and the discipline by which men acquire education, while παν means universal. Therefore our goal is to be: learning παντες, παντα, παντως (for all men, about all things, in all ways).

> . . . so that at last the whole of the human race may become educated, men of all ages, all conditions, both sexes and all nations.[27]

This is an extraordinary vision, well before the Enlightenment, of the possibility of improving the welfare of all the nations of the earth on a level of equality. Indeed Comenius stated succinctly the aspirations of mankind which have in the twentieth century been called the revolution of rising aspirations. Indeed these tenets come close to the demands for national development and for modernization that have marked the independence movements of the 1960s and 1970s. Comenius anticipated them by 300 years:

> Finally then, if we consider the innate desires of man altogether, education for humanity falls into twelve parts; for everyone born man, by reason of the most intimate impulses of his nature, longs:
> (i) To be, i.e., to live;
> (ii) To live unshakeably, i.e., to be worth;
> (iii) To live observantly, i.e., to know what he has around him;
> (iv) To live by light, i.e., to understand what he knows;
> (v) To live in freedom, i.e., to desire and choose what he knows to be good, not to wish but to refuse what is bad, and to act in all things according to his own judgment, if possible;
> (vi) To live actively, i.e., to perform that which he understands and chooses, so as not to understand and choose in vain;
> (vii) To have or to possess much;
> (viii) To enjoy all he has in security;
> (ix) To be eminent and held in honour;
> (x) To be as eloquent as possible in order to convey his knowledge and his will to others promptly and clearly;
> (xi) To enjoy the favour and grace of men, so that they do not envy him, but wish him as quiet, happy and untroubled life as possible;
> (xii) Finally to enjoy the favour of God, for joy of heart and for the assurance of his happiness in God.[28]

To enable the peoples of the world to develop themselves in dignity and in freedom, Comenius proposed a system of universal schools, universal books, and universal teachers.[29] He argued that since all men of whatever station in life can

[27] *Comenius on Education*, op. cit., pp. 116-117.
[28] Ibid., p. 143.
[29] Ibid., pp. 183-199.

become literate, public schools should be set up in every village, every town, every kingdom or province, throughout the whole world. Comenius did not explain just *how* public schools could be established in all lands throughout the world, but he had a vision concerning the way they should be supervised once they had been set up. He explains this in his *Panorthosia*.[30] He proposed three worldwide institutions: a College of Light to supervise the schools of the world, a Dicastery of Peace to supervise the governmental institutions of the world, and a Universal Consistory to supervise the churches of the world. The College of Light would act as the teacher of the human race to see that the world's schools functioned in an orderly way and were supplied with books of universal knowledge written in a universal language, taught by competent well-trained teachers, with the most up-to-date and realistic methods of teaching.

The crucible of the wars of the seventeenth century and the persecutions of religious and ethnic minorities formed Comenius' deep feelings about the need for international institutions that would establish and enforce the peace of the world. While his proposals sound at once modern and utopian they were born at least 300 years too soon. They flew in the face of the rampant nationalisms that had by no means reached their zeniths. Their words carried a note of authoritarianism in his efforts to direct universal "right thinking," but they must have seemed only reasonable to a dedicated Christian like Comenius. In the perspective of the late twentieth century Comenius did not reckon on the fact that most of the world was not to become Christian despite the vast missionary efforts of 300 years. But what Comenius did envisage was the power of education to mobilize the energies and loyalties of men. This power, however, for most of the 300 years following Comenius was to be harnessed by the *nations*, not by international or world institutions.

The most popular realist in France was Rabelais, who set the people laughing at the schools in his *Gargantua* and *Pantagruel*. Writing in French and reaching a popular audience, Rabelais ridiculed the dry formalism of the humanist schools as well as other social excesses of his time. He depicted his own ideas of educational reform in exaggerated terms, caricaturing the older methods as compared with newer and more realistic methods. He advocated the classics, to be sure, but he insisted that they should give real and useful guidance to conduct rather than simply represent bookish, linguistic, and literary values. His proposed curriculum included heavy emphasis on the sciences and social studies.

Another scholar who perhaps had even more direct influence upon educational content was Petrus Ramus, who went even further than Rabelais in his adherence to the naturalistic interest in science and mathematics. Ramus lashed both the Aristotelian scholastics and the Ciceronian humanists, and the word *Ramism* was coined to represent his attack upon these twin scourges of education. He set out to reform each of the liberal arts by improving the material studied and by making the methods of acquisition simpler and easier. His efforts were directed toward a careful systematizing and simplifying of the knowledge of the ancient authors and eliminating the superfluities and intricacies of medieval commentaries. In this way he helped to make

[30] Ibid., pp. 200-230.

knowledge more applicable to actual social conditions, to free it from ecclesiastical control, and ultimately to clear the way for the new mathematics and science. His textbooks on the subjects of the seven liberal arts, as well as on physics, ethics, metaphysics, and theology, gained wide vogue in Germany, Switzerland, at Cambridge in England, and later in colonial America.

Still more modern-sounding in tone were some of the schemes proposed in England in the mid-seventeenth century. The Puritan modernizers who controlled Parliament for a decade beginning in 1649 sought a variety of proposals for the advancement of learning which in turn would help to bring about the changes in society they so earnestly desired. Their educational advisers included not only foreigners like Comenius and Samuel Hartlib from Germany and John Dury from Holland but many of their own sympathizers. Richard Mulcaster urged that instruction should be adapted to the pupil's interests and capacities and that great use should be made of physical activity, music, drawing, and games in the development of sense experience. Edmund Coote, John Brinsley,and Charles Hoole put emphasis upon actual perception of things rather than the mere study of words, the use of English in the study of all school subjects, the grading of subject matter, and the division of pupils into classes so that their abilities might be more appropriately considered, and the lightening of discipline so that learning might become more pleasant and thus more effective.

Other proposals were far more radical. These included plans for the establishment of an academy in every city to serve as a secondary school and university (John Milton), the creation of pansophic colleges in every county or town to teach all arts and sciences useful to rural life, including health and husbandry (George Snell), the establishment of a new university in London that would emphasize the scientific principles of various trades (Samuel Hartlib), and the founding of a tax-supported college to train teachers and supervise all the free schools of England (John Bathhurst).

Particularly visionary (and modern-sounding) were proposals by Samuel Hartlib, Sir William Petty, and John Dury. Hartlib's scheme for "literary workhouses" for the poor children of London included the following:

> The children were to be taught reading and writing for two hours in the day, one in the morning and one in the afternoon, so that by the age of 12, 14, or 16, they would be able to read and write and be fit in the case of boys to become apprentices or, if quickwitted, to become scholars or accountants. For the rest of the day they were to work at spinning, knitting, sewing and the making of their own clothes, their women teachers in these subjects getting a penny out of every shilling earned by the children, the rest of the earnings going towards the children's keep.[31]

Petty was one of the earliest political economists to view education as a major means of producing the human capital which would in turn provide the basis for building economic power and promoting national development. Not only should literary workhouses contribute to the useful life, but advanced educational institutions

---

[31] G. H. Turnbull, *Hartlib, Dury and Comenius.* University Press of Liverpool, Hodder & Stoughton, London, 1947, pp. 65-66.

in the form of Colleges for Tradesmen should promote the mechanical arts and manufactures:

> From this institution we may clearly hope . . . that all trades will miraculously prosper, and new inventions would be more frequent than new fashions of clothes and household-stuff. Here would be the best and most effectual opportunities and means for writing a History of Trades in perfection and exactness, and what experiments and stuff would all those shops and operations afford to active and philosophical heads, out of which to extract that interpretation of nature whereof there is so little, and that so bad as yet extant in the world?
>
> . . . There would not then be so many fustian and unworthy preachers in divinity, so many pettifoggers in the law, so many quacks in physic, so many grammaticasters in country schools, and so many lazy serving men in gentlemen's houses, when every man might learn to live otherwise in more plenty and honor. For all men desirous to take pains might by this book survey all the ways of subsistence, and choose out of them all, one that best suits his own genius and abilities.[32]

One of the most interesting and farsighted schemes, prepared for the Puritan parliamentary committee on education and written by John Dury or possibly George Snell, put stress on realistic method, common schools for all, vocational schools for prospective craftsmen, "noble schools" for those who will engage in the public service, and university education for prospective teachers, all to be supported and controlled by Parliament:

> Schools for gentlewomen should also be looked into and reformed in accordance with the advice of virtuous matrons who know what training will produce modest, discreet and industrious housekeepers. Academies may also be set up to train for public employment the sons of the chief gentry and noblemen. The monkish constitutions and customs of the Universities should be reformed, and the "noble" schools established mainly in them. The fellows of colleges should be set to elaborate such useful parts of learning as are wanting in the schools, but the chief use of the Universities should be to train the teachers of all sciences and thereby supply the schools, churches and public societies with able men, fit to teach others.[33]

If these proposals or others like them had been effectively put into practice in the seventeenth century, the industrialization and modernization of England might have been speeded by a century or more. As it was, a conservative reaction began to set in even before the Stuart Restoration in 1660. The modernizing function of education was therefore not promoted by the full force of a national state system of public education but was left largely to private and individual efforts for nearly 200 years. Even so, the momentum generated by realist educators, some of whom had

---

[32] Franklin Le Van Baumer, *Main Currents of Western Thought*, Knopf, New York, 1970, pp. 301-303.

[33] Turnbull, op. cit., p. 53.

strong religious as well as political motivations, helped England to become the only industrially modernizing nation before the end of the eighteenth century.

C. THE INTERPLAY OF TRADITION AND MODERNITY

To say that Western education was fundamentally transformed between 1400 and 1700 would probably be to put the matter too strongly, for the traditionalizing elements continued to play a predominant role. But it is fair to say that some of the schools and universities of 1700 had a much different look to them when compared with the dominant tone and character of the educational institutions of 1400. The medieval aura had been greatly modified by the classical Graeco-Roman cast of Renaissance humanism; the dialectic of scholasticism had been muted by the shrill rhetoric of religious sectarianism; and the first signs of realistic practicality were beginning to broaden educational sights, widening their upper-class literary bent to include the grubbier tasks of commercial, scientific, and practical arts.

We have been using the term *early modern* to refer to this period between the high Middle Ages and the burst of modernity that accompanied the Enlightenment to follow. Perhaps the term *protomodern* would be better. We can see some signs of the national control and orientation of education, the urban-centrism of educational effort, the opening up of educational opportunity to wider elements of the population, and the beginning of the spread of Western education to the far reaches of the world. All of these trends foreshadowed the bolder shape of things that were to come with the full onset of modernity. But to the end of the seventeenth century they were still largely foreshadowings, not the bright glare of the real thing.

Perhaps the best way to put the net effect of this period in the history of education is to say that it was producing the great tradition in Western education at the same time that it was creating the conditions that were eventually to undermine that tradition. On one hand, the coalescence of the humanist and the religious components that came to dominate secondary and higher education, bulwarked by the strong support of the ruling groups in the national states and urban centers, served to fix the classical humanities firmly at the top of the educational hierarchy of values. On the other hand, the stirring of popular feelings and aspirations attendant upon the rise of vernacular languages, of economic and political participation, and glimpses, though still faintly seen, of a possible better life on this earth through the spread of scientific knowledge, tended to undermine the statuesque image of the classical tradition.

These traditionalizing and modernizing elements in the Western education of this period did not follow one another in a straight line from traditional to modern. The early phases of humanist thought might have led to more radical reform and earlier transformation of society if their educational practice had lived up to their goals of civic activism and freedom; and realistic education might have contributed more directly to economic development if it could have been applied more rigorously, say, by the English revolutionaries. But by 1700 humanism had reverted to pedagogical sterility, and the Stuart restoration had returned England to conservative policies that played down an education in the practical arts. So the promise of modernity visualized by early humanism and realism alike was being throttled at the close of the period by the victories of a more stodgy and pedantic humanism surrounded by religious orthodoxy. Reassertion of traditionalizing forces delayed the onset of an irreversible modernization until the eighteenth and nineteenth centuries. Our present period of educational development was thus protomodern, not fully modern.

In the terms we have been using to describe the educational system of earlier civilizations we may say that 1400 to 1700 was the florescent period of the Great Tradition in Western education, but at the same time it was the formative period of the modernizing mood in Western education. (See Figure 5.1. or p. 156.) Our task or interpretation now becomes more complex than ever. For the first time, we not only need to try to indicate the general movement of Western education from formation to florescence to dispersion, but we also need to sort out those aspects of educational enterprise which served to maintain a basically traditional stance as well as those modernizing trends which were leading to fundamental change and innovation.

The ambivalence and interplay of the traditional and the potentially modern were present in profusion as the outlines of the European national systems of education began to take shape. The traditional class system of society meant that the upper classes would have the largest share of, if not the complete monopoly on, educational opportunity. The principal effort of humanists was to reform the content and orientation of an aristocratic education, not to develop a popular education for the vast majority. On the other hand, much of the effort of the Protestant reformers was devoted to providing wider opportunities for education among the lower classes, an effort based on the need for common men to be literate enough to read the Bible for themselves. But because an aristocratic class structure was so deeply ingrained in all the countries of Europe, what was more natural than to arrive at a solution which would give more education to the lower classes by making a sharp distinction between the kind of education that should be made available to the two classes?

The result was a two-track system of education: a vernacular elementary education for the lower classes, and a humanistic secondary education for the upper classes, both heavily religious in orientation. Up to 1700 the two-track system was thus basically traditional in holding to an aristocratic framework rather than developing a democratic social structure in education, but as it expanded during the eighteenth and nineteenth centuries, it became more universal in extent and moved toward the mass educational systems of modernity. The cultural nationalism which became so characteristic of modern civilization had its first great foreshadowing in the sixtenth century; thereafter it was progressively heightened by the expanding vernacular school systems of the European nation-states.

The demand for common schools for the masses of the people met with little response from the upper classes; some of the Protestant reformers occasionally seemed lukewarm. At times both Luther and Calvin seemed to be more interested in a classical secondary education than they were in vernacular education, despite their appeals for the latter type of school. Anglican leaders in England and Catholic leaders in France were generally more willing to expand and reform secondary education than they were to provide common education for the lower classes. Even where great strides were made toward providing a widespread education in which almost everyone was given some schooling, the lower classes were channeled into an inferior educational system that could not lead to higher education or to a higher status in society. Achievement of a democratic education in which everyone is looked upon as equally entitled to the kind of education which would best develop his talents was only occasionally contemplated, even on paper. State control of schools to provide a two-track system of universal education became a typical European product, but state control of schools to provide democratic as well as universal education was not strenuously attempted until the United States did so in the nineteenth century.

Another ambivalence between traditional and modern forms of education reflected itself in the conjoining of the religious and the secular in the Western education of this period. The aims of education were widened to include the modernizing secular side of life along with the traditionalizing religious side. Economic and political reformers called for vocational education and the teaching of trades to poor children. Middle classes tried to broaden the scope of vernacular and technical education so that it would meet their commercial needs more adequately. The upper classes were impelled to establish new courtly academies that would meet their desires for military and social accomplishments. Realist reformers argued for a wider curriculum that would include the sciences and practical mathematics. In all these ways the secular ingredients were mixed in with the religious. To the extent that the secular studies expanded, Western education took on a modern character.

We turn now to describe something of the institutional arrangements for the conduct of education as they arose in the protomodern period of Western European education. A striking thing is that even though the consolidation of national states was the prominent political feature of the time there was constant interplay, borrowing, emulating, and propagandizing concerning education among nations. This process of transfusion transferred the lifeblood of educational ideas and practices from one country to another and from one institution to another. The three R's of Renaissance humanism, Reformation religion, and Realistic studies tended to produce something like a common corpus of Western education that extended across national boundaries, especially at the secondary and university levels. Even the three R's of reading, writing, and arithmetic at the elementary school level showed international likenesses despite the variety of national languages in which they began to be taught.

We are so accustomed to pointing out national differences for comparison and contrast that it is well to be alert to the other side of the coin, the common and the supranational characteristics that helped to define the rise of a distinctive Western education. Not only did the new nations of Europe engage in three centuries of educational transfusions among themselves, but before the protomodern period was over they were transplanting major elements of their educational systems to their new outposts in America, in Asia, and in Africa. The process of Westernizing large parts of the world which was eventually to be so fateful for all mankind was now beginning, and though education was overshadowed at first by the national rivalries in war, commerce, and religion, it played a fundamental role from the outset, especially as the handmaiden of religion.

CHAPTER VII

THE DISPERSION
OF LATIN-CATHOLIC
EDUCATION
(1400 A.D.-1700 A.D.)

A. EDUCATION IN LATIN EUROPE

Italy

The most effective translators of humanist theory into pedagogical practice were Vittorino da Feltre who established a school in Mantua and Guarino da Verona who established a school at Ferrara. Vittorino's effort was far more liberal than that of Guarino who stressed classical scholarship to the virtual neglect of science and mathematics. Called in by the Duke of Mantua to establish a school for his children, Vittorino set out to create a school according to the ideas of Cicero and Quintilian as he interpreted them. He accepted in his school not only the children of the nobility but a few lower-class boys as well. The aims of the school were couched in terms of the Roman ideal: a wellborn youth with a broad background of knowledge, the manners and social graces suitable to the ruling classes, and loyalty to basic Christian principles. The chief means to this end were the study of the classics and mathematics.

Vittorino's course of study included all the seven liberal arts except logic. This omission represented the humanist's distaste for medieval scholasticism. Instead, major attention was given to the study of Latin and Greek grammar, to declamation, composition, and the elegances of style to be achieved through rhetoric. Much stress was put upon imitating and memorizing long passages from Cicero, Vergil, Ovid, Horace, Homer, and Demosthenes as well as other standard Latin and Greek authors. Arithmetic, geometry, astronomy, and a little music were also studied.

The significant thing is that the basic medieval liberal arts continued to be taught, with the reinterpretation given to them by the humanist emphasis upon classical literature. This could mean a revitalizing and stimulating experience for those fifteenth-century youths who caught the civic enthusiasms of the early humanist educators. Vittorino even went beyond the literary arts to try to recapture the Greek ideal of well-rounded development by making use of physical training: games, sports, athletic contests, and exercise. This whole experience was doubtless refreshing and exhilarating to many students in comparison with what was to be found in the private or church schools of the day. The fact is, however, that by the end of the sixteenth century the humanists' supreme interest in style and composition had come to overshadow the classical ideal of full personal development. It was not long before slavish attention to grammar and rhetoric led to the charges of Ciceronianism, from which humanist schools never completely recovered. By 1600 the educational revival of the humanists had fallen from Cicero's vision of broad and vital preparation for the public service to a slavish imitation of Cicero's style.

It was one of the great ironies of the history of education that *Ciceronianism* became a term of reproach. It took the humanists about a century (the fifteenth) to replace medievalism in the schools of Italy. Then, by the end of another century (the sixteenth) the vitalizing verve of the humanist revival had ended. The civic humanism had given way to literary humanism, much as the florescent Hellenic education of the active polis had given way to the Hellenistic education of literary *paideia*.

Yet the classical curriculum in the hands of well organized and dedicated teachers was extraordinarily influential. The most effective secondary schools of the Latin countries in the sixteenth and seventeenth centuries were the colleges of the Jesuits (*collège* in French, *colegio* in Spanish). They began by teaching lay youth in the major Italian cities and became so popular that by mid-sixteenth century there were over 150 schools operating in Catholic countries and requests were in for 60 more. These schools were often well equipped physically, and characteristic Jesuit thoroughness led to the systematizing and standardizing of the curriculum into what was called the *ratio studiorum*.

The Jesuit college consisted of a five- to eight-year course, taking a boy to eighteen years of age and concentrating on Latin, Greek, religion, and religious history. The Latin authors most commonly read were Cicero, Ovid, Vergil, Catullus, and Horace; Greek authors were Chrysostom, Aesop, Isocrates, Basil, Plato, Aristotle, Plutarch, Demosthenes, Thucydides, Homer, Hesiod, and Pindar. The religious writings of the church Fathers were mingled with secular prose, poetry, rhetoric, and philosophy (the latter carefully selected for moral and religious purposes so as not to conflict with Catholic doctrine).

Beyond this standard course the Jesuits instituted a three-year course in which more classical grammar and literature were studied as well as rhetoric, logic, mathematics, ethics, metaphysics, and natural philosophy. During the last year of the philosophy course, instruction was given in the theory and practice of teaching. The Fathers of the Oratory also developed successful secondary schools, deviating from the Jesuit schools somewhat in their attempt to incorporate some of Descartes' philosophy, science, and mathematics and utilizing the vernacular to a greater extent.

The teaching orders of the Catholic church also developed vernacular schools, perhaps in response to the Protestant efforts in this area. The Port Royalists and the Institute of the Brothers of the Christian Schools taught in French, as did several of the women's teaching orders. Even the Fathers of the Oratory, who were interested primarily in secondary education, developed a good deal of teaching for the early school years in the vernacular.

During the early Renaissance the freest of European universities were in Italy. The University of Padua, under the protection of the free city of Venice, had become the great scientific university, particularly in mathematics, medicine, and anatomy.

Copernicus, Vesalius, and others did outstanding work there as students and professors. However, the growing rigor of censorship instituted by the Catholic Counter-Reformation in the later sixteenth and seventeenth centuries served to reduce the Italian universities to impotence. Much the same sort of thing happened in Spain, where the universities had prospered under Charles V and Philip II. The University of Salamanca, for example, in 1561 provided that the books of Copernicus be taught in astronomy and those of Vesalius in anatomy, the first such provision in any European university. But, again, the decline of Spain as a first-rate power in the seventeenth century and the force of the Spanish Inquisition brought about a corresponding decline in Spanish universities.

France
Although France had been the cultural leader of the high Middle Ages and Italy had lagged behind, their roles were reversed in the fourteenth and fifteenth centuries as the city-states of Italy fostered the flowering of the Renaissance. By the end of the fifteenth century, however, the major thrust of creativity was weakening in Italy and new centers were forming in Northern Europe, first in the Low Countries and Germany, then in France. The key scholar in the humanist reform in France was Guillaume Budé whose career virtually spanned the first half of the sixteenth century. The key French rulers were Charles VIII, whose invasion of Italy in 1494 opened the floodgates for the Italian Renaissance to invade France, and Francis I who, failing in his attempt to reform the University of Paris, established with the aid of Budé the *Collège de France* in 1530 to embrace special royal readerships in Greek and Latin as well as humanist studies in Hebrew, French, law, philosophy, mathematics, and medicine.

From then on, French humanism could match the scholarship of Guarino in Italy or Erasmus in Germany. It also shared the same enthusiasm for detailed textual criticism linked with *pietas litterata*. Outstanding in his influence upon practical educators, even above that of Erasmus and Sturm, was Mathurin Cordier. His texts on Latin grammar, composition, and phrase-making helped to put into practice in schools the detailed and imitative methods for teaching correct Latin style that had been preached so eloquently by humanist scholars like Bruni, Vergerius, Melancthon, and Erasmus. "It is Cordier whom we must see as the real representative of the Humanism that eventually won itself a place in the educational system of Europe."[1]

This process, whereby the liberalizing goals of the original humanism were transformed into an all-absorbing pedagogical devotion to training in Latin style, is particularly evident in France during this period. At the outset, the courts had led the way in the acceptance of humanism, whereas the church and the universities had given little but opposition. The University of Paris kept aloof from the movement, which it rightly considered as a reform that would threaten its scholastic interests in theology, Aristotelian philosophy, and canon law. Humanism did gain entrance into some of the higher schools, however, in the case of the *Collège de France* and in such institutions as those set up by municipal governments at Bordeaux, Lyons, Orléans, Reims, and Montpellier.

[1] R. R. Bolgar, *The Classical Heritage and Its Beneficiaries from the Carolingian Age to the End of the Renaissance,* Harper Torchbooks, New York, 1964, p. 356.

Perhaps more important than the change from medieval to humanist content in subject matter was the rise of a new institutional form of education which was eventually to spread its influence wherever French culture was disseminated around the world. This new institution which took its form in the sixteenth and seventeenth centuries was the *collège*.[2] It signalled a basic shift from the greater freedom of medieval education to the greater supervised discipline of the early modern period, a shift which paralleled a basic change in the attitude toward children. This is the main theme of Philippe Ariès who describes at length the way the medieval view of the child as a small adult was replaced by the view that the child must be treated differently from adults, either as weaker and thus needing severe discipline, or as purer and thus needing greater freedom. The *collège* reflected the view that the child needed greater discipline and supervision.

It may be remembered that the original colleges, in the thirteenth and fourteenth centuries, were simply hostels or lodging houses for poor boys who were granted scholarships to support them while they attended the schools of the cathedrals and universities. The medieval college was thus a small, largely self-governing, communal hall of residence, giving no instruction. Gradually, in the course of the fifteenth and sixteenth centuries, the burden of instruction began to shift from the lecture halls of the cathedral schools to the colleges. This transfer was signallized in the 1452 regulations at the University of Paris, the last reform to be undertaken by the papal legate. This meant that greater discipline and control were to be exerted over the intellectual and educational lives of students as well as over their conduct. Greater stress was put upon learning of the rudiments of Latin grammar, to which were added logic and natural philosophy; and greater authority was given to the masters over the social life of students.

From the end of the fifteenth century on, the colleges began to accept a wider spectrum of students, no longer confined to prospective clerics. While the boarding school element did not disappear, the colleges became large day schools in which eventually the course was regularized and graded according to difficulty; the subjects were taught in sequence rather than simultaneously as in the Middle Ages; the students were classified and separated according to age, not mixed in together as in the Middle Ages; and the curriculum was shortened to a course of six or seven years aimed at boys from the ages of eight or nine to fifteen.

It was in the midst of this transforming process that the Jesuits, founded in 1534, began to apply their remarkable organizing as well as teaching talents. During the last half of the sixteenth century, the Jesuits began to establish their *collèges* in all parts of the Latin countries of Europe. They became extremely successful, as we have noted, largely because of the orderly and strict rules of study and of discipline reflected in their *ratio studiorum*. They began to appeal to upper class, middle class, and even lower class families. Their success in Latin countries helped to stave off the growth of state or public schools which sprang up in Lutheran and Calvinist bonds.

It was to meet the competition of the Jesuit *collèges* that the University of Paris once more underwent reform. This time the reform, let it be noted, was *not* undertaken by the papal legate but by King Henry IV, a sign of the growing national control

[2]For an interesting, though somewhat diffuse, disscussion of this development. see Philippe Ariès *Centuries of Childhood, A Social History of Family Life,* Knopf, New York, 1962, part II, chap. 2.

over education that was characteristic of the times. The goal of the reform of 1598 was to transform the colleges of the university into the Jesuit *Collèges* which had become so popular with parents, if not with students, because of the careful supervision of students, insistence upon attendance, the logical order of studies, and the examination system that checked on attendance. Henry IV's rules regulated minutely the order of studies and exercises in the faculty of arts; but the classical study was largely dry and formal, and the science and mathematics depended upon Aristotle while the new science of Copernicus and Descartes was rejected or overlooked. A new and even less fruitful scholasticism was being handed down, having little life, vitality, or connection with the new cultural trends of the day.

As the French *collège* began to take its traditional form in the sixteenth and early seventeenth centuries, a distinctive characteristic was the organization of the students into *classes*, a word picked up by the humanists from Quintilian and used influentially by Erasmus in describing the reformed school of St. Paul's in London. Since that time *class* in education has come to imply one or all of the following meanings: a place of meeting for teacher and students (a classroom), a length of time for lecture or recitation (a class period), a subject to be studied (a Latin class), or a group of students progressing through school together (the sophomore class). In all these cases, the meaning centers on some kind of orderly arrangement for teaching and learning, the ultimate in organized or formal schooling. In France the *collège* typically was organized into six to eight classes, numbered from the beginning sixth class to the upper first class which was normally topped with the logic class and the natural philosophy class.

In general, then, the secondary schools of Europe came to be carefully graded and divided into classes, with regularly prescribed books to be read in each year. This process of standardizing the curriculum met the need for a discipline that sprang out of the humanist desire for meticulous study of the classics and the need for regularizing the conduct of education as it expanded, but it has provided educational reformers ever since with ammunition with which to criticize traditional methods. As far as the secondary schools were concerned, the age-old struggle of rigidity versus flexibility in the curriculum was being won during the early modern period by advocates of rigidity.

Thus, the emergence of the classical secondary school, which crystallized in the seventeenth century as a training ground for the university, tended to thwart the modernizing role for Western education. The upper track of the two-track system fastened upon Western education the classical humanities as the principal badge of religious scholarship, political superiority, and good breeding and manners. Gentility could be won indeed by financial success but even more so by the accomplishments bestowed by a classical education, despite the claims of educational reformers that modernization rested with scientific studies and vernacular education. Ironically, the humanist secondary schools which had held out such great promise for reform in the florescent Renaissance came to be the most traditionalizing of educational forces as the West struggled to move into the modern world. Their hallmarks were the *gymnasium* in Germany, the *lycée* and *collège* in France, and the grammar school in England.

The flexible character of the wandering students of the Middle Ages gave way to order, discipline, regular attendance, a prescribed curriculum, and regular classification and promotion from one grade to the next. Constant attempts were made to make students "toe the mark." Innumerable rules were passed to prevent fighting, carrying weapons, lying, cheating, drinking, gambling, swearing, card playing, dicing, and even swimming, skating, fishing, and birdcatching. Severe punishments were meted out in the attempt to enforce discipline. Part of the necessity for discipline was doubtless the fact that the secondary schools, especially in Germany and France, began to take over many of the subjects of the traditional liberal arts that had formerly been taught in the medieval university.

The effort to teach difficult classical studies to young boys, who began the course anywhere from the age of seven to ten and finished at from fourteen to seventeen years of age, must certainly have taxed the ingenuity of the masters in matters of discipline. They therefore reacted by relying upon constant surveillance and supervision, rewards for the informer, and increasingly brutal and humiliating corporal punishment. These school tactics were among the reasons why the attitude toward children began to change with the Enlightenment toward a more humane and liberal view of the nature of children. Children could simply not be so bad as to deserve the excessively severe punishment meted out to them.

In the predominantly Latin countries the teaching orders of the Catholic church maintained a firm hold on the control of education in contrast to the Protestant and civil control in the countries of Northern Europe. It is true that in the seventeenth century the French Estates-General clearly called upon the church to establish schools in all towns and villages and to institute compulsory education. France, however, had followed the line of allowing the church to conduct schools without much civil control. In the wars between Catholics and Huguenots it was, among other things, the zeal of the Huguenots to establish schools and colleges along Calvinist models that aroused the ire of the Catholics. After the Edict of Nantes in 1598 one of the civil liberties that the Huguenots gained was the right to conduct their own schools and universities in their free cities and towns.

After Louis XIV came into power, however, education was largely turned over to the Catholic church while civil control was exerted primarily over universities in a series of edicts about what university professors could and could not teach. Louis XIV required universities to teach the French civil law as well as canon law, and several edicts were issued to prevent instruction on the works of Descartes and other modernists. The French universities thus tended to decline into impotency under the oppression of religious fanaticism and state absolutism. The Huguenots had established eight or nine higher institutions during the period of toleration, but they were effectively wiped out when the Edict of Nantes was revoked by Louis XIV in 1685 and the Huguenots were driven under cover or into exile.

At the lower levels of education, however, the stimulus of the Counter-Reformation decrees of the Council of Trent bore fruit in the establishment of many schools by church teaching orders in the Catholic countries. Among the most energetic bishoprics was the diocese of Paris, where schools were organized for the poor and laboring classes and where by 1675 some 5,000 pupils were being taught by 300 teachers. The Jesuit secondary schools were doubtless the most numerous and influential of those established by the church orders. Their efficient system resulted in several hundred institutions, attended by some 200,000 students, toward the end of the seventeenth century. The Fathers of the Oratory became another very influential teaching order in Italy and France, concentrating primarily on secondary education and going further than most teaching orders in using the vernacular language for some of their courses and adopting realistic studies in mathematics, mechanics, and geography.

Before the end of the Counter-Reformation some ten or twelve church orders were also at work in elementary education, the most important of which were the Ursulines, Sisters of Notre Dame, Piarists, Port Royalists, and Institute of the Brothers of the Christian Schools. The purpose in founding many of these was to provide free schools for poor children of the working classes, in many cases for girls as well as for boys. The number and success of the schools of these orders should caution against the belief that the Protestants alone were interested in elementary education for the masses.

It should be noted, however, that almost until the mid-seventeenth century nearly all schools in France were Latin schools. By and large the French did not begin to teach in French until Jean Baptiste de la Salle began to organize vernacular elementary schools under the auspices of the Institute of the Brothers of the Christian Schools. The Jansenists had used French in their Port Royal schools, but their influence was not widespread. Indeed, the French did not even have a term for an elementary school until the seventeenth century. In this respect the Protestant nations forged ahead of the Latin countries in providing vernacular education.

As a result of Reformation rivalries both Protestants and Catholics began to stress the training of teachers to insure orthodoxy and to make the schools more effective agencies of religious proselytizing. The Catholic teaching orders which set up teacher-training programs to ensure the better preparation of teachers included the Jesuits, Fathers of the Oratory, Port Royalists, and Institute of the Brothers of the Christian Schools. The work of La Salle and his institute was of particular significance in transforming teaching in the lower schools from a haphazard occupation to a vocation worthy to be called a profession. Whereas elementary teachers had typically received little or no specialized preparation, the institute's normal schools gave theoretical, religious, and practical training to lay persons who were not destined for the priesthood but who were to make a profession of teaching itself. In addition to religion, prospective teachers gave attention to the three R's and practical and vocational training as basic ingredients for the teaching of young children and juvenile delinquents.

In addition to the use of the vernacular language rather than Latin as the medium of instruction, the institute's humane methods of teaching created an orderly and effective school atmosphere in which children were taught in graded classes rather than exclusively by individualized instruction. Special attention was given to a secondary school program of modern subjects to meet the needs of the new middle classes and continuation schools on Sundays for those who worked throughout the other days of the week. In these ways La Salle's institute was performing modernizing functions within the overwhelmingly traditional Catholic outlook.

B. THE LATINIZING MISSIONS IN THE
OLD WORLD AND NEW

One of the most significant educational residues of the protomodern period was the transplantation of Western education to the far corners of the Old World and the New World. The European nations that led in the Western exploration of the vast ocean seas also led in the transfer of their particular forms of Western education. So it was that the stream of education spread by Catholic missionary teaching orders with the aid of the Portuguese and Spanish crowns was the first form of Western education to spread around the world. A curious historical by-product was that even though these countries by 1700 had lost their political hegemony in Europe to France and their commercial leadership overseas to the Dutch and the English, their educational implantations in the New World meant that most of Middle and South America was to become indelibly Latin and Catholic, while most of North America was to become largely "Anglo" and Protestant. These fragments of Western civilization as they were spun off from Europe to the New World in the sixteenth and seventeenth centuries were to have a profound effect not only upon the future of those parts but of the entire world itself.[3]

Another important aspect of the transplantation of Western education around the world is that while the Latin and Catholic educational missions in Asia and the Pacific had almost no competition from the Protestant north of Europe during the sixteenth and seventeenth centuries, the closing of much of East Asia to the West for 200 years meant that when the East was again reopened to Europe in the nineteenth century it was the more modernized nations of North Europe that transferred their forms of Western education to Asia and Africa. This too had fateful consequences for those parts of the world as well as for the whole world itself.

The Portuguese Thrust to the East

Located at the strategic westernmost point of Europe and the gate to and from the Mediterranean, Portugal first led in the tentative European explorations of the West Coast of Africa as early as the thirteenth and fourteenth centuries and then under the stimulus of Prince Henry the Navigator stepped up their outward thrusts to the South and East throughout the fifteenth century. Their efforts were crowned during the final decade of the fifteenth century by the voyages of Bartholomeu Dias who rounded the Cape of Good Hope and sailed up the east coast of Africa (1488), of Vasco da Gama who made it all the way to the Malabar Coast of India (1498), and of Pedro Cabral who touched on the shores of Brazil on his way to India (1501). Meanwhile, Columbus was making his voyages to the West for Spain in the 1490s, followed by Amerigo Vespucci, and by the circumnavigations of the globe in the westward direction by Magellan's fleet (1519-1522).

After Columbus' first voyage in 1492 made it clear that the Spanish and Portuguese rivalry was on in full cry, a line of demarcation in the Western Atlantic Ocean was established by Pope Alexander VI in 1493, a line which in effect divided up the entire non-European world between Portugal and Spain. Confirmed and moved

---

[3]For a fascinating theory of the role of cultural fragments in tradition and change, see Louis Hartz (ed.) *The Founding of New Societies; Studies in the History of the United States, Latin America, South Africa, Canada, and Australia*, Harcourt Brace & World, New York, 1964

still further west by the Treaty of Tordesillas (1494) between Portugal and Spain, the line gave to Portugal the exclusive right to possess all non-Christian lands halfway around the world to the east of the line, and to Spain all such lands halfway around the world to the west. While there remained much uncertainty and dispute concerning the point where halfway around the world really was, Portugal claimed religious monopoly in Brazil, Africa, and Asia, while Spain claimed the rest of the Americas and the Pacific, at least to the Philippines and the Molucca Islands (Spiceries).

This presumptuous division of the world between the Catholic Iberian countries in the late fifteenth century was aimed primarily at the Moslems who had finally been driven out of Europe but who had to be pursued to the ends of the world and punished for their eighth century conquest of the Iberian peninsula. Reconquest became a fanatical mission of both the Portuguese and Spanish conquerors and Catholic missionaries. Furthermore, the Christianizing and civilizing mission was aimed at all unenlightened heathens, those innocent of all religion as the natives of Africa, Asia, and America were believed to be, as well as those perverted by the sinister and evil doctrines of Islam. So even before the bitter family disputes and Reformation wars broke out within European Christianity during the sixteenth century, the Catholic cross was accompanying the Portuguese and Spanish swords around the world. With the explorers and the conquerors went the missionaries. By 1700 Latin missions and schools literally encircled the world.

In general, Portugal's dispersion of its Catholic missions in the fifteenth and sixteenth centuries was undertaken under the doctrine of patronage (*padroado*), whereby the Papacy granted to the Portuguese crown income from ecclesiastical properties in Portugal and the right to nominate candidates for appointment to the bishoprics in lands that were yet to be Christianized, in return for which the crown would provide the missionaries and support for the churches established in the lands eventually conquered by Portugal. In filling this responsibility of patronage the Portuguese rulers relied in the first instance upon the mendicant friars of the Franciscan and Dominican orders and then increasingly turned to the Jesuits as their principal missionizing and educational arm.

In the course of a century and a half of commercial leadership in the East (1420 to 1580) Portugal established footholds in Africa, India, Malaya, the Moluccas, Japan, and China. By the time the Spanish crown took control of Portugal in 1580 the Portuguese expansionist thrust had been blunted, and by the time Portugal was again independent in 1640 the Dutch and the British were beginning to dominate European trade in the East. From then on, Portugal's overseas domain shrank to the enclaves in Goa and Macao, but held firm in vast uncharted territories of Africa and Brazil. The religious proselytizing of the Portuguese *padroado* was often uncompromising and even fanatic, involving mass conversions forced at gunpoint by the governors and the military. In many respects the missionaries found themselves at odds with the harsh and ruthless military governors over the methods of conversion and the necessity to respect the rights and sensibilities of the people they conquered or traded with.

Franciscan missionaries accompanied da Gama and Cabral to South India, and Dominicans came in soon after. When Goa was captured in 1510 by Alfonso de Albuquerque he declared unceasing war against the Moslems but friendship for the "heathens." Schools were established straight away by Franciscans who worked especially with lower-caste Indians to prepare them to become Christian clergymen. Bishop

Joao de Albuquerque was trying to stress education, friendship, and tolerance in the Christianizing mission rather than the impatient insistence upon religious uniformity pursued by the governors who set out to destroy Moslem mosques and Hindu temples. Western plenipotentiaries have insisted on quick results in pacifying alien peoples for nearly 500 years. The lessons of technical assistance have been difficult to learn. The Portuguese missionaries as well as Christian Indians eventually became the subjects of violent retaliation as a result of forced intrusions upon the indigenous ways of life.

Two years after the Society of Jesus was made official by the Pope in 1540 the noted Spanish missionary, Francis Xavier, arrived in Goa, signallizing that from then on the Jesuits would be the principal missionary arm of the Portuguese *padroado.* Their organizing ability, the quality of their leadership, and the international character of their membership made the Jesuits an extremely effective political as well as religious and educational force. Xavier followed Bishop Albuquerque in stressing the education of children, the need to learn the languages and become sympathetically familiar with the customs of the people, and the desirability of converting the rulers and the leading classes of society rather than using mass, forced conversions. Above all, it was important to train native boys as Christians so that they could communicate with their own people. The College of St. Paul in Goa became the chief training center for the Eastern missionary effort. By 1577 its students numbered 134 boys with about half from Goa and other parts of India and the other half from Europe, South East Asia, Africa, and the Far East. The curriculum was very much a standard Jesuit program stressing Latin, Portuguese, mathematics, and music, topped off with philosophy and theology.

Following Xavier's death in 1552 the Jesuit mission in India began to assist in the mass conversion policies of the Viceroy, and the Inquisition was instituted in Goa in 1560. Another strong Jesuit leader, this time an Italian, arrived on the scene in 1574 to try to redirect the Jesuit enterprise. Alessandro Valignano dominated the scene until he died in 1606. His policies were enlightened in that he was adamant about the necessity of learning the mother tongues of the people, and he organized language seminars for this purpose. But he also believed in a curious hierarchy of white superemacy by which he classified Africans and Indians as blacks, and Chinese and Japanese as whites. He thus believed that the greatest hope for Christianizing and civilizing the heathen would lie in China and Japan rather than in the generally barbarous lands of Africa or the servile lands of India. Despite this haughty estimate, the Jesuits and Franciscans and Dominicans established numerous schools along the east and west coasts of India as well as north into the Punjab.

In general, the Christian missionaries in India had only small success. They never fathomed the complexity of Indian religion or high culture. Franciscans did not study the local languages, while the Jesuits who did learn the local languages never studied the closely held literary classics in Sanskrit. They thus never really understood Hindu civilization. They did, however, leave a residue of Christian following and a tradition for education that resulted in the state of Travancore having the highest literary rate in India even in the twentieth century.

The Jesuit missions to the east of India followed the Portuguese interest in cultivating Japan and China. They thus gave relatively little attention to the Malay Peninsula or islands of South East Asia. They did found a college in Malacca on the Malay Peninsula, the chief Portuguese administrative and trading center east of Goa, but this was primarily to train Portuguese boys for the mission priesthood. Malacca always remained a small Christian beachhead in the strongly India-oriented Buddhist culture of the region.

In contrast, great attention was given first to Japan and then to China. Both Xavier and Valignano saw in Japan the greatest hope for a Christian East Asia. After Xavier's arrival in 1549 apparently rapid success attended his efforts. His policy of sympathetic understanding of Japanese culture, training of Japanese for an indigenous priesthood, adaptation to the customs of Japan, and reliance upon education marked the early Jesuits as good "technical assistants." Thousands of converts were made (150,000 by 1582), but when Xavier was eventually frustrated by the strong hold of Buddhism upon the Japanese people, he turned hopefully to China.

Valignano found the Jesuit mission in Japan displaying particularly arrogant and contemptuous treatment of Japanese when he arrived there in 1579. He too became convinced that China was the "great white hope" for Christianity in the Far East as the Jesuits gradually came to be looked upon by the Japanese rulers as threats to their authority. Also, the rivalry between the Spanish and mendicant friars coming in from the Philippines and the Portuguese and Jesuits coming in from Malacca and Goa seriously hurt the Westerner's role in Japan. Massacres of Christian martyrs in the late sixteenth century reflected the growing Japanese hostility, but even so there were 116 Jesuits and 300,000 converts in Japan as late as 1614. Another few decades and the mission was nearly over as the Tokugawa rulers entered upon a policy of deliberate withdrawal, turned to agriculture rather than commerce, drove out the Europeans, forbade Japanese to go abroad, and killed Japanese Christians by the thousands.

While the Jesuits made early and rapid gains in Japan, their entrance to China was more tortuous and slow. But they had learned from their experience in India and Japan that to deal with the high cultures of ancient and proud civilizations they must work more slowly, sympathetically, intellectually, and educationally. They realized that they must adapt themselves to the traditional civilization they encountered. This was especially true with regard to the ethnocentric Chinese culture which looked upon all other cultures as inferior.

The Jesuits were extremely fortunate in the high quality, intellectual prowess, and scholarly attainment of their leadership in China from the late sixteenth to the late seventeenth century. Symbolically, the leaders represented the international profile of the Jesuit order; they came in succession from Italy, from Germany, and from Belgium. When Matteo Ricci arrived in China in 1582 he was accomplished in the classical humanities, law, and theology as one might expect, but also in science, mathematics, mechanics and geography. He learned Chinese and set the pattern by which the Jesuits were viewed by the Chinese more as Western scholars than as Christian missionaries. Johannes Adam Schall von Bell who succeeded Ricci in 1622 was well-versed in the modern astronomy of Copernicus and Galileo even though his church was attacking their heliocentric views. Ricci, Schall, and his successor, Ferdinand Verbiest all played the role of high court technical adviser to the emperor, assisting with calendar reforms and making known a large library of Western scholarly works in astronomy, mathematics, biology, medicine, mechanics, politics, and ethics as well as Christian philosophy and theology. They adopted the status, the dress, and the customs of Confucian scholars.

In outward respects this long tolerance of Jesuits in very high circles, even after most Europeans had been shut out of China in the eighteenth and nineteenth centuries, made the Jesuit mission in China appear to be successful. Yet, the impact was uncertain. By the eighteenth century there were few Christian converts, the influence of Western knowledge upon Chinese scholarship seemed imperceptible, and the Catholic Jesuits seemed to have accommodated themselves more to Confucianism than the other way around. In any case the Jesuits were heavily criticized in the West for the lengths to which their accommodation and compromises took them in theology and in doctrine. More easily discernible was the impact upon Europe of knowledge about China which was relayed back to Europe by the letters and information conveyed to the Jesuit colleges by their missionaries. All this helped to build a glowing picture of China which captivated the intellectuals and led to the *chinoiserie* of the West in the middle of the eighteenth century.

The net result of the missionary and educational effort of Westerners in Asia up to 1700 is far too complicated to assess with full confidence. Curiously enough, the Dutch and the British who took the lead in commercial enterprise away from the Portuguese in the seventeenth century did not stress either the Christianizing or the educating of the local populations. Their trading efforts were more highly organized as a result of their effective East India companies, but they tended to pay strict attention to the profits and little to the souls of their customers. An exception was Ceylon where the Portuguese had established many village schools, produced a catechism in Singhalese, and built colleges to train priests and teachers. In this case the Dutch continued the Portuguese policy when they came into Ceylon in the seventeenth century in contrast to their general neglect of education in Indonesia; and the British did the same when they entered Ceylon in the eighteenth century.

From the perspective of the twentieth century the mission efforts of the Catholic countries were a mixture of nationalistic, commercial, and religious aggression characteristic of the early imperialism of the major nations of the day. Viewed from the side of the Christian faithful the enterprise was an extraordinary outpouring of human energy, drive, and endurance against all but overwhelming odds in the service of the truth. Viewed from the side of many of the Asian peoples the enterprise was an unwarranted intrusion upon their traditional ways of life, but also to many of the downtrodden lower classes it offered a hope and a promise of a better life than they could possibly expect from that tradition. Viewed objectively as an exercise in international educational relations, the missionary effort was most successful where the *educational* effort surpassed the evangelical.

One could hazard the guess that the greatest gains in the art of educational impact were to be made when the outsider adapted himself to the insider and did not try to force his views with violence or punishment upon unwilling or unreceptive peoples. Long-run impact is made only when receptivity is engendered within the ruling and leadership levels as well as at the grass roots. Mass conversions among the common people of Japan and India did not seem to be greatly effective without the active support of the rulers and a widespread educational effort, but neither did the high-level advice to the Chinese emperor at his court seem to change materially the fundamental educational or scholarly system of China. The importation of unmodified alien educational institutions into a civilization where the formal educational systems were already mature and complex as in Japan and China did not provide the means for major educational, or civilizational, transformations.

The Spanish Intrusion to the West

Quite a different set of circumstances faced the Portuguese and the Spanish in the New World where they found societies that ranged all the way from the most primitive gatherers and hunters to the highly complex civilizations of the Incas in Peru and the Aztecs in Mexico. The Portuguese were far slower to exploit their newly won territories in Brazil than were the Spanish in their aggressive efforts to Latinize much of the rest of the Americas.

For some thirty years after Cabral touched on the north east coast of Brazil in 1500 and claimed it for Portugal, the Portuguese crown did not pay much attention to the new territory. Finally, the king tried the expediency of granting vast territories to military or noble proprietors in a kind of feudal arrangement whereby they were authorized to rule, colonize, and force the Amerindians who were largely hunters and gatherers to work the land. But this did not work very well, so in mid-century the king sent a royal governor to administer the colony directly for the king. Tomé de Souza, the first governor-general, took with him six Jesuit priests as well as bureaucrats, skilled craftsmen, and military supporters. The Jesuits set up "reductions" or settlements for the Amerindians, wherein they taught them how to farm and live a settled agricultural existence. They engaged in some schooling for the Indians, but it was almost entirely confined to reading and writing as the basis of religious instruction and later some Latin to prepare priests.[4]

However, Brazil remained for nearly four centuries far more rural and less urbanized than the Spanish colonies did. Also, the semifeudal arrangements that persisted led to much looser forms of social organization than in New Spain. Indians resisted slave labor, so Africans were brought in. When land wore out there was always more than enough elsewhere. The prime Portuguese motive was to profit from the land rather than to establish a new society. The Portuguese concern to Christianize and civilize the Amerindians and the Africans seemed relatively mild compared to the zeal of the Spaniards in the New World or indeed the zeal of the Portuguese themselves as they confronted the well-developed civilizations of India, China, and Japan.

For all these reasons the educational mission of the Portuguse in Brazil was not particularly effective beyond the religious instruction aimed at the conversion of the Indians. In the seventeenth century the Jesuits introduced the humanistic curriculum of the *ratio studiorum* into their colleges, which fact made them quickly attractive to the plantation owners as a symbol of an upper-class culture which would distinguish them from all the rest of the inhabitants of Brazil and provide a link with the upper-class culture of Western Europe. The Jesuit *collège* thus abandoned its exclusive goal of training religious leaders to include the secular and rural upper-classes as well. The Amerindians got fairly well lost in the process, except as young creole men who

---

[4]Robert J. Havighurst and J. Roberto Moreira, *Society and Education in Brazil*, University of Pittsburgh Press, Pittsburgh, 1965, chap. 2.

finished the college would spend some time teaching young children on the plantations, sometimes including mestizo and black as well as white.[5] By and large, however, organized education was not a very influential force in early colonial Brazil. This fact could be counted as another reason why Brazil remained so much less developed for so much longer than much of the rest of South America.

In contrast, the Spanish displayed enormous educational zeal in America during the same period, and the results were correspondingly great. Indeed, formal education was a major component of the massive transfer of Spanish culture and institutions to the New World, with portentous results for the peoples of the entire Western Hemisphere for half a millenium to come. From the point of view of the indigenous inhabitants, the Amerindians whose ancestors had come to the New World some 20,000 to 30,000 years before, the transfer was a matter of imposition of European civilization upon their own cultures, often with the intent to destroy or relegate those cultures to an inferior position. From the point of view of the Spaniards, the phenomenon was not so much a simple matter of transfer or transplantation as it was an incorporation of the territories and peoples of the New World into the Hispanic-Christian forms of Western civilization which they believed to be superior to all others. By incorporating these vast non-Christian lands into their empire they believed they were simply doing the will of God and of the Crown.

Their mission was threefold: to conquer, to Christianize, and to civilize; and education was to be an essential element in the Christianizing and civilizing mission. Reformation and Renaissance ingredients were the obvious educational tools to be used in the sixteenth and seventeenth centuries. Their impact was potentially modernizing with respect to the Amerindians but actually traditionalizing for the Spaniards who migrated as colonists and constituted a fragment of Western civilization spun off from the Iberian peninsula to Middle and South America. The contrasts between the Spanish-Indian-Catholic forms of Western civilization and the Anglo-Protestant forms that developed in North America became increasingly marked during the ensuing five hundred years. Yet the events of the sixteenth and seventeenth centuries meant that both South and North America would become basic elements of an embracing Western civilization, despite their differences. The five-century period of the impact of Western education upon the rest of the world began with peculiar suddenness and vigor in Spanish America.

When the Portuguese and their allied missionaries tried to convert the ancient traditional civilizations of India, China, and Japan they faced highly organized and highly literate urban ways of life that did not readily accept or adapt their Western Christian outlook. When the Spanish *conquistadores* and their allied mendicant missionaries invaded the traditional civilizations of Mexico and Peru, they found them much easier to dominate. The reasons for this difference are difficult and complicated. Not only was there superiority in military technology but there was a great gap between the social and political organization and the sophistication of the educated elite of the New World civilizations and those of the Spaniards, while there was no

[5]Ibid., p. 55.

such marked disparity between these latter elements in the Old World civilization and those of the Westerners.

Perhaps less obvious, but possibly as important, was the basic fact that the civilizations of the East had long and well-established systems of organized education that had helped to create a stable and durable sense of civilizational identity not easily shaken by alien intruding ideologies. The educational systems of the Amerindian civilizations, while recognizably organized, were less complicated and less reliant upon literate, coherent, and systematic bodies of knowledge deeply rooted in the intellectual traditions of the people. The Graeco-Roman-Christian-Western forms of education were more attractive and persuasive to the few Amerindians who were exposed to them than they were to Indian, Chinese, and Japanese intellectuals.

More obvious reasons for the quick and decisive conquest of Amerindians by the Spaniards were the use of firearms, horse-mounted soldiers, the agressive determination, not to say the ruthless cruelty, of the *conquistadores* and the evangelical zeal of the Christian missionaries, along with weaknesses within the Amerindian societies themselves. The Aztecs in Mexico and the Incas in Peru had only had a century or two of experience in conquering and ruling subject tribes as they forged their empires. Each was having trouble in maintaining control over dissident peoples who were restless under their rule by the early sixteenth century. In contrast, the Spanish rulers, warriors, and missionaries were riding the crest of a wave of militant political and religious reconquest, an 800-year-old process of driving the Moslem Moors out of Spain that culminated in 1492. The last Moslem stronghold in Granada was captured by Ferdinand and Isabella in the same year that Columbus discovered America. All this came as the various Spanish regions and states were being welded into a strong and centralized monarchy headed by Isabella of Castille and Ferdinand of Aragon.

The goal of spiritual reconquest was thus transferred to the New World by the missionaries who accompanied the *conquistadores* just as the goal of physical and material conquest motivated the latter. In its crassest form conquest meant to the Spaniards power and wealth; in its humanitarian form the Spaniards couched conquest in terms of Christianizing and civilizing the Amerindians. What Christianizing meant was clear enough: teach the Amerindians the forms of Christian worship, baptise them, induct them into the rituals and formulas of the Roman Catholic Church, and induce them to abandon their traditional religious rites, which sometimes involved human sacrifice. What *civilizing* meant was less easily determined, but it usually meant adoption of the forms of moral conduct, customs, and manners of Spanish Europe. These usually included adoption of Western forms of dress, language, and speech, monogamous marriage, and the use of metal tools for agriculture, mining, and building construction that had long been a part of the urban civilizations of the Middle East, Asia, and Europe. Accompanying the idea of settled agricultural cultivation of the land (where it was not already practiced) went the notion of orderly and disciplined habits of work (under the direction of the Spaniards).

Most Spaniards of the sixteenth and seventeenth centuries assumed that peoples who did not have their forms of civilization were uncivilized, and therefore needed to be subjected to their civilizing process. What they did not realize or did not take the trouble to understand was that the Amerindians in at least two major regions of the New World had developed over several centuries distinctive traditional civilizations of their own. Some missionaries did realize this and did embark on notable studies of the languages, customs, and institutions of the Amerindians, but their voices turned out to be largely ignored by the Spanish-type society that was eventually built on top of the indigenous civilization.

The Disruption of Education in the Amerindian
Civilizations of Mexico and Peru

In more recent times, however, the interests and techniques of modern scholarship in archaeology, linguistics, and history have concluded that the civilizations of Middle America and of Peru rank with the other major but older generative civilizations of the Afro-Eurasian ecumene. These civilizations are inherently fascinating for comparative study as examples of the emergence of human civilization in relative isolation from the other major civilizational centers, each of which was influenced in greater or lesser degree by one or more of the others. In fact, this relative isolation may have been one of the most fundamental reasons for the later emergence and the relatively less-advanced character of their social and intellectual forms.

The historical tragedy is that when the civilizational contact *was* made the power of the Western civilization and its aggressive self-interest left no room for genuine interaction. The influence was almost all one-way. This result may have been partially a result of a declining or dispersive stage of development within the Amerindian civilizations themselves; or it may simply have been that they had not yet reached a stage of political, economic, technological, or intellectual florescence that would have enabled them to hold out against or genuinely to assimilate the Western ways within their own. In any case, the gap between the more developed and the less developed civilizations, between the more traditional Amerindian and the protomodern Western civilization was too great for genuine interaction. The Amerindian civilizations were largely destroyed or made impotent. The impact of their educational traditions upon the future of the New World remained relatively slight. Organized education in South and Middle America became basically Latin Western, relatively unmodified by the educational forms it displaced.

Comparatively, the general archaeological judgment is that the course of development in pre-Columbian America from hunting and gathering societies to neolithic agricultural settlements and then to urban complexes paralleled the development of civilization elsewhere.[6] During the first centuries A.D. those characteristics attendant upon the earlier civilizational process in the Middle East, Asia, and Europe included a growing social stratification, economic specialization, urbanization, and political differentiation. First, among the Mayas in Guatemala, then the Toltecs and Aztecs in central Mexico, and finally among the Quechuas and Incas in Andean Peru, priestly societies arose around ceremonial centers, labor was organized by the priests, and

---

[6]See, especially, Robert McC. Adams *The Evolution of Urban Society; Early Mesopotamia and Prehispanic Mexico,* Aldine, Chicago, 1966; and Robert J. Braidwood and Gordon R. Willey (eds.) *Courses Toward Urban Life,* Aldine, Chicago, 1962.

urban elites appeared. The Mayan and Mexican civilizations developed elaborate calendars, astronomical and mathematical calculations, and pictographic writing of a hieroglyphic type. Peru did not develop a written language, for reasons that remain unclear. McNeill estimates that by 600 A.D. the Amerindian civilizations were roughly comparable to those of Mesopotamia, Egypt, and the Indus Valley in 3000 B.C.[7] He argues that this lag of 3500 years left the Amerindians at a permanent disadvantage.

During the 1,000 years from the fifth century to fifteenth century A.D. the Amerindian civilizations went through remarkable but familiar developments both socially and politically. For some reason the Mayan civilization declined and virtually disappeared by the tenth century, while Mexico developed military city-states to replace the priestly states, and Peru created a centralized political empire out of the large number of city-states. Adams finds a close parallel in stages of development that proceeded from theocratic or priestly polities to military polities to conquest states in both Mesopotamia and Mexico despite the 4,000 years difference in time. He finds the Aztec polity of 1500 A.D. similar to that of Sargon of Akkad in 2300 B.C. Others find that the Inca empire of Peru in 1500 closely resembles that of Pharoah Egypt. One of the major differences, however, seems to be in the systems of education developed in the civilizations of the Old World and the New World. We have discussed at some length the elaborate and highly structured systems of education that depended heavily if not exclusively upon the corpus of written knowledge that characterized intellectual life in Mesopotamia and Egypt from their early priestly days.

In contrast, the formal education in both Aztec and Incan civilizations seems to have developed fairly late and possibly arose as they became expansionist military states during which time the priestly authority receded before the military and political. It is, of course, entirely possible that the priests who developed the calendars and the writings of Middle America also developed formal schools, as we argued with respect to the Aegean civilization about which we have so little definite knowledge. In any case, the evidence seems to indicate that formal schools were clearly present by the time the military rulers of Mexico and Peru needed more administrators, officials, and intellectuals to maintain and extend their political power over subject peoples. This bureaucratic need for formal education we have seen before, but we do not find in America that the priestly class was so evidently professional and administrative in its organization for promoting education as was so clear in Mesopotamia and Egypt.

Aztec civilization in the fifteenth century A.D. had obviously inherited much from the successive peoples who had already inhabited the central Mexican plateau. Despite the warlike political domination of their subject peoples they apparently did little to impose their culture or religion upon them. They seemed rather more intent upon stressing and strengthening their own society and culture and religion which required the live sacrifice of human captives in honor of their pantheon of gods. Their lack of cultural imperialism apparently stemmed from no humanitarian belief in cultural relativism or the sanctity of other peoples' cultures. In fact this lack of interest in converting others proved to be an essential weakness when suddenly faced

---

[7] William H. McNeill, *The Rise of the West, A History of the Human Community*, University of Chicago Press Chicago, 1963, p. 416.

by the Spanish conquerors, for their Amerindian subject peoples seemed only too glad to help the alien Spaniards overwhelm their consanguine oppressors.

Within their own society, however, the Aztecs seemed to possess a kind of social mobility based on merit and achievement that belied their attitudes toward conquered or subject peoples. Within the Aztec community there seemed to be considerable stress upon providing some education for all Aztec children and even to make it compulsory.[8] One of the laws in the legal code of Montezuma I (1436-1464) declared with respect to the splendid Aztec capital city of Tenochtitlán: "All the wards will possess schools or monasteries for young men where they will learn religion and good manners."[9] The evident concern was to develop the character, the drive, and the discipline necessary to mold the people into a unified society that could achieve and maintain its destiny.

The Aztecs developed two types of schools, each having separate provisions for girls as well as for boys. The larger number, possibly one or more for each class, stressed physical and military training; they were taught by experienced warriors. These schools, known as Telpochalli, seemed to appeal to the ordinary people and their children. The more academic type of school, known as Calmeac, apparently was fewer in number and appealed more directly to the intellectual, upper, and priestly classes. The graduates of the Calmeac became high officials in government or priests. The teachers were priests, and the curriculum stressed discipline, manners, the Nahuatl language both oral and written, history, and the calendrical and astronomical sciences. This school sounds much like the scribal schools of Mesopotamia and Egypt. Its professional and elitist character sound familiar indeed. We can only guess that the apparently stagnant character of Aztec art, technology, and literature between 1000-1500 A.D. in the face of great emphasis upon the military must have found Aztec education possessing little hold on the masses of people.

True, the graduates of the Calmeac were well educated informants for the early Spanish monasteries but their quick acceptance of their new masters must have meant that the intellectual loyalties, or indeed political loyalties to the traditional Aztec priesthood, could not have been overwhelmingly strong. The humanistic and religious literature, the science, the mathematics, and the technology of the Western missionaries must have been far more attractive than their own abstruse hieroglyphic symbols which seemed to concentrate on recording specific events, genealogies, tribute accounts, and the like.

The most obvious, and probably the most important, difference between Aztec schools and Inca schools was that Inca schools were conducted orally for the perfectly clear reason that Incas had no written language. When the Incas conquered their neighbors over a thousand mile area of the Andes, they could not destroy their books, but they could and did enter upon a campaign of disremembering the history and culture of their subjects. Developing a highly centralized and autocratic government, heading up in the Inca who assumed godlike as well as hereditary human qualities, the

[8]Spanish clerics were apprently impressed by the notion of compulsory education. See Miguel Leon-Portilla. *Aztec Thought and Culture: A study of the Ancient Nahuatl Mind,* University of Oklahoma Press. Norman, 1963, p. 138.

[9]Fray Diego Duran, *The Aztecs: The History of the Indies of New Spain,* Orion Press New York, 1964, p. 132.

Incas were able to organize and administer a vast empire in Western South America with the capital city at Cuzco. Their society was probably more stratified and more aristocratic internally than that of the Aztecs. Certainly it was more aggressive culturally. They required their subject city-states and tribes to worship the Inca and accept their religion as well as their political rule. They sent out an official class who exacted food and tribute from the conquered peoples and redistributed produce as compensation for obedience, loyalty, and service. Thus neither a merchant class nor a market mechanism developed. They were able, without wheel and without writing, to communicate with remarkable rapidity the length of their empire by building a remarkable series of roads and training professional runners. They, too, developed a calendar, arithmetical notations, medical knowledge, irrigation systems, and a complete bureaucracy—without writing. They did develop an organized method of remembering on the basis of a complicated system of knots on cords or ropes (quipu), but no written, symbolic language. In Chapter 2 written language and formal schools were identified as basic ingredients of a civilized as distinguished from a folk society. Now, here is evidence of a civilization without a written language, and yet it did develop formal schools.

The Inca schools were of two types, one for boys and one for girls, both limited to the upper aristocratic classes. Whereas the Aztecs spread their military education fairly widely among their own people and ignored their subject peoples, the Incas aimed their schooling at the upper classes of their subject peoples as well as their own. In practicing their aggressive cultural imperialism, the Incas brought the sons of conquered chieftains to Cuzco to get them to disremember their own culture by learning the Quechua language and adopting the religion, the customs, and the institutions of the Incas. They used their school for the elite to socialize the subject peoples to Inca civilization.

The school for boys (knows as Yachahuasi) was founded by Inca Roca in the fourteenth century and expanded in the fifteenth century by Inca Pachacutec who was determined to make Quechua the common language of the empire. The school took boys between ages twelve and thirteen to fifteen or sixteen and trained them to become officials, administrators, governors, military officers, engineers, historians, poets, and bards; in fact, the school had four sections corresponding to the four provinces of the empire. All the boys learned the Quechua language, the Incan religion, songs, rites and rituals, the use of the quipu and calculations for tribute, and the history, glory, and military skills appropriate to the ruling Inca. The school for girls (Acclahuasi) stressed the domestic arts appropriate to the wives of nobility, concubines, and court attendants as well as religion and music.

So now we return to the question of the relation between written language, formal education, and Incan civilization. Much depends on the judgment as to the stage of development in Peru in 1500. It is possible, of course, that the Incas might still have developed a written language as they came into closer contact with the civilizations of the north, or if their contact with the Westerners had been more gradual and peaceable. I am not inclined to deny civilization to the Incas simply on the grounds that they did not have a written language. They did have formal schools. This could argue for the fact that organized education may be a more universal characteristic of a civilized form of society than written language is.

It could also argue for the fact that both the Aztec and Incan civilizations might better be called protocivilizations than fully developed civilizations on the ground that they would have developed full-fledged writing systems if they had had the long term intercultural contacts of the kind that characterized the Middle East from the fourth millenium B.C. onward. It could also mean that formal schools may have preceded, rather than followed, the appearance of fully developed written language and may have had a part in creating it. It might be assumed that the Incas would have proceeded to produce a written language of their own if they had not been overwhelmed by the Spanish conquest, and if instead their educational and intellectual resources had been preserved, nurtured, and transformed rather than effectively destroyed.

We can certainly say that even though organized education may be necessary for the rise of civilization, it is not sufficient to prevent its destruction in the face of massive and overwhelming physical power, disease, and depopulation. Still, a stronger, more disciplined, literate educational tradition based upon a persuasive literary, philosophical, and scientific body of knowledge might have enabled the Amerindian civilizations to preserve themselves or at least to maintain a basic identity, as the educational systems of the Middle East, India, and China did for centuries in the face of successive invasions and conquerors. However, the story in Middle and South America was far different from that of the East. The Aztecs succumbed to Cortes with the help of their subject peoples, and the Incas succumbed to Pizarro with the help of a dynastic conflict within the Incan succession—and possibly a devastating small pox epidemic. Within half a century Middle and South American education became Spanish, Christian, and Western with scarcely a trace of Amerindian education, except in the historical accounts written by a few Spaniards with the help of their Amerindian students, mates, and progeny.

C. THE FORMATION OF A LATIN EDUCATIONAL TRADITION

In Spanish America

Following the collapse of the indigenous Amerindian civilizations an Hispano-Indian civilization arose in the New World in which the intellectual and cultural characteristics of Spanish Western civilization came to dominate the Amerindian, strongly aided and abetted by Christian education. And it was not long before a third major racial ingredient was added, importation of blacks from Africa. Sixteenth-century Spanish America thus became a meeting ground for peoples whose racial backgrounds were Mongoloid from Asia (many millenia earlier), Caucasoid from Europe, and Negroid from Africa. This was one of the few times in recorded human history, if not the only time, when the three major races of mankind intermingled on so massive a scale. Not even the Middle East, where Africa, Asia, and Europe meet physically, and where cultural contact had been so significant for the origins of three major civilizations, had seen such a mixture of races.

The point of time in human history when this happened was vastly significant for the whole world. Because it was the sixteenth century and because the contact was initiated by an especially aggressive branch of Western European civilization, the intermingling had the fateful consequences of establishing a society in which the white Spanish European Westerners became the dominant element in a pyramidical society, with the Mongoloid Amerindians and the Negroid Africans at the bottom and the mixed racial products in the middle. The groundwork was thus laid for some of the portentous and explosive revolutions of the nineteenth and twentieth centuries.

Most of the whites came from Spain, ranging from the younger sons of the Spanish nobility to the servant classes. They came as conquerors, adventurers, owners, managers, and colonizers, almost 90 percent being male, and seldom if ever in groups or communities of like-minded persons (except for the missionary orders of the church). They headed primarily for the heavily populated centers of Amerindian civilization where masses of laborers were available who could do the manual work on farms, mines, and haciendas. When the Amerindian population died out, as in the Caribbean regions, blacks were brought from Africa to do the work. The setting was thus ripe for large-scale racial interbreeding, especially in the urban centers which the Spaniards built on and around the Amerindian cities.

In the course of the intermixing and the subjection of both Amerindian and African populations, a hierarchy of prestige and social status emerged with a high correlation between color and class. In general, the lighter the skin the higher the status. While population figures for Spanish America are subject to widely varying estimates, the general trend of three centuries was clear. From a wholly Amerindian population (some say as many as 50,000,000) in 1500, the incoming of 100,000 whites by the middle of the sixteenth century and the importation of African blacks resulted in a rapid and wholesale decline in Amerindians and the appearance of large numbers of mestizos (white and Amerindian) and mulattoes (white and black). Amerindians died out almost entirely in the West Indies within fifty years; on the mainland they shrank from 50,000,000 to 4,000,000 within a century of the coming of the Spaniards. Gibson estimates the racial proportions of the population of Spanish America by the end of the colonial period in the early nineteenth century to be approximately as follows:[10]

Whites	3,200,000
Mixtures	5,500,000
Amerindians	7,500,000
Blacks	750,000
Total for Spanish America	16,950,000

Of this total about 7,000,000 were in Mexico (which accounted for about half the Indians and a third of the whites), and the other four major areas had about two to two and a half million each (Peru, New Granada, La Plata, and Central America and the islands).

This transformation of society and of civilization in Spanish America was accomplished in the sixteenth and seventeeth centuries following the military con-

[10] Charles Gibson, *Spain in America,* Harper Torchbooks, New York, 1966, p. 117.

quests by three main agencies of Spanish imperialism, the state, the church, and landed gentry (an aristocratic class of colonists, owners, and managers). The prime agency foi education of the Amerindians and mestizos was, of course, the church, encouraged by the state, but largely ignored or opposed by the gentry class. When the state and the church lessened their drive for educating the Amerindians and turned toward education for whites, as they did in the late sixteenth and seventeenth centuries, the gentry gave more encouragement to education for themselves. Nobody paid very much attention to education for blacks or mulattos.

This change in educational effort over the 250 to 300 years of Spanish dominance in America roughly paralleled the social changes in political, economic, and ecclesiastical control of the three major regions. Politically and economically, the Spanish crown began its imperial invasion of America by delegating a considerable amount of its power to the private effort of individuals, explorers, *conquistadores*, and their successor colonialists called *encomenderos*, who possessed a certain similarity to the proprietaries of other European imperial powers: the captains of the Portuguese, the *seigneurs* of the French, the patroons of the Dutch, and the proprietors of the English. The Spanish term derived from the official grant of power to an individual Spaniard, called *encomienda*, by which a group of Amerindians, often a village or town, was commended to the authority and care of the Spaniard, in return for which he was to keep order, render military service to the Crown, and see to the Christianization of the Amerindians.

Encomienda was a kind of license to govern, to exploit the natural resources, and to exact labor service from Amerindians as well as collect tribute in commodities. A major difference in this practice of imperialism was that the French, Dutch, and English proprietaries all had to ship colonists from the homelands to do the work whereas the Spanish found massive, highly organized Amerindian societies available to do the work. *Encomienda* gave a legal justification for putting them to work for the Spanish *encomendero* class. The Spanish thus transferred to America the aristocratic patterns of a landed gentry who came not to work or establish a new society but to acquire wealth and maintain a gentlemanly way of life.

Whereas some of the English colonies in Anglo-America to the North turned their proprietorships into virtual self-governing polities early in the seventeenth and eighteenth centuries, the Spanish crown soon began the process of taking back political authority from the private *encomenderos* and centralizing power in the hands of the monarchy and its official agents. Two viceroyalties (technically deemed to be kingdoms under the Crown) were created in the middle of the sixteenth century: New Spain (Mexico, Central America, and the West Indies) in 1535; and Peru (virtually the entire western half of South America) in 1542. These kingdoms were ruled under the authority of Spain by a viceroy and an advisory and judicial council known as an *audiencia*. These were by no means democratic bodies, but agencies for introducing Hispanic central authority into the New World. In the eighteenth century two new viceroyalties were created: New Granada (northern South America) in 1717 and 1739, and La Plata (southern and southeastern South America) in 1776. La Plata was in great preponderance Caucasian and European with Spanish culture scarcely modified at all by Amerindians or Africans. Thus, Wagley calls this third cultural region (including northern Brazil) Ibero-America to distinguish it from Afro-America (the West Indies and the rim of the Caribbean) and Indo-America (the highlands from Mexico to Peru).[11]

In general, Europeans settled first in Afro-America. The crown and the church made least effort for education in Afro-America; they made massive attempts to educate the Amerindians of Indo-America in the early sixteenth century; but they then turned primarily to education for the Spanish descendants born in America (creoles) in the seventeenth and eighteenth centuries.

The crown found the *encomenderos* reluctant to give up their privileges of rule and exploitation of Amerindians; the missionaries found them indifferent to educating their workers. Together they tried to forge an educational policy much more humanitarian than the *encomenderos* desired or would enforce. As early as 1493 when Pope Alexander VI gave Ferdinand and Isabella exclusive rights to colonize their part of the New World he enjoined them to appoint experienced men to *instruct* the inhabitants and residents in the *Catholic faith and train them* in good morals."[12] In 1503 Ferdinand and Isabella instructed the *encomenderos* of Hispaniola to build schoolhouses and to teach the children reading, writing, and Christian doctrine, but when Dominican monks arrived in 1510 they were horrified at the deplorable slave-like conditions besetting the Amerindians. Their outcry induced Ferdinand to issue the Laws of Burgos in 1512 to 1513 prohibiting mistreatment or enslavement of Amerindians and again specifying that *encomenderos* holding fifty or more Amerindians must see that they were instructed in reading and writing and genuinely Christianized. In addition the sons of *caciques* (chiefs or nobles) were to be educated at least for four years before being returned to their *encomendero*. There was, however, no means of enforcement.

Before long the ethical issues of conquest and of *encomiendia* began to be debated vigorously in Spain. Fundamental questions were raised concerning the rights of the Pope to authorize forcible Christianization of heathens, the meaning of a just conquest, the inherent rationality and humanity of Amerindians vis-à-vis the Spaniards, the rights to property, and the like. On one side stood such humanitarians as Bartolomé de Las Casas, eventually known as "Protector of the Indians," a Dominican who condemned the whole imperial enterprise of conquest as unjust, illegal, and inhumane. On the other were such defenders of just conquest as Juan Gines de Sepúlveda who argued that the end of the Christianizing mission justified the means of armed conquest and that the barbaric Amerindian practices of torture, human sacrifice, and cannibalism justified the civilizing mission.

Impressed by the argument of Las Casas Charles V decreed in 1520 that *encomienda* had to come to an end. In the ensuing twenty years he tried to reinforce the humanitarian and religious aspects rather than the subjugation of conquest. In 1536 he instructed the viceroy of New Spain to see that *encomenderos* fulfill their

---

[11] Charles Wagley, *The Latin American Tradition*, Columbia University Press, New York, 1968, chaps. 1 and 2.

[12] Translated in J. Fred Rippy and Jean Thomas Nelson, *Crusades of the Jungle,* University of North Carolina Press, Chapel Hill, 1936, p. 5.

duties in education, the Amerindians must attend daily classes, free, and that friars who spoke in native languages should be favored. Finally, in the New Laws of 1542 to 1543 Charles V again stressed conversion and education as he restated the humanitarian principles that slavery was prohibited and that *encomienda* was not to be extended or become hereditary.

Of course, the *encomenderos* rejected the rules, and in spite of the monarchy's moderate position from the 1540s on, ways were found to continue forced labor in the form of peonage. By this means a Spaniard who loaned a small sum to an Indian was entitled to exact repayment through work which somehow led to more loans and more work until the loan never seemed to be paid back. Peonage proved to be the most persistent of all the forms of forced labor. It was incorporated in the hacienda system of land ownership which endured to the twentieth century. Despite the system of *encomienda* and the obstacles produced by the *encomenderos,* the Spanish missionaries were able to make enormous gains not only for mass conversion but what promised to be widespread educational opportunities for Amerindians during the first half of the sixteenth century. Their zeal, their dedication, and their hard work helped to produce what Wagley calls "one of the miracles of history," the strength of the impact of Spain on the New World and the speed with which Spanish culture was imposed upon Indians and Negro slaves.[13]

By the end of the sixteenth century, however, the era of mass conversion and of dedicated reform-minded mendicant clergy working within the major centers of Amerindian civilization began to fade. The mendicant friars began to quarrel among themselves and with the secular clergy of the established ecclesiastical hierarchy. The mendicants had sided with Charles V against the *encomenderos* in treating the Indians with compassion and generosity, but when Phillip II became king in 1556 he began to side with the secular clergy against the mendicants and to subject the activities of the latter to the control of the former. Worst of all, the drastic depopulation of Amerindians began to leave the mendicants with less and less reason for their real mission of Christianizing and civilizing the indigenous population.

Conversely, the creole population of Spanish-descended whites began to multiply and to assert themselves against both the lower orders of forced laborers and against their superior whites, the Spanish-born peninsulars who held all the plums of officialdom and churchdom. The creoles thus wanted more and better education for themselves in order to be able to compete with the peninsulars. The Jesuits who came onto the missionary and educational scene long after the Franciscans and Dominicans had pioneered, as they had done in Asia, began to turn their educational efforts away from the Amerindians and toward the creoles. The Francisans, the Dominicans, and the Augustinians who had concentrated upon teaching the Amerindians in their own mother tongues were left further behind as the crown began to stress the teaching of Spanish and the Hispanization of the New World as further means of strengthening the royal authority from Europe.

In both New Spain and in Peru the mendicant friars prodigiously established schools in connection with their friaries, convents, and the village and city churches.

---

[13] Wagley, op.cit., p. 5.

The Franciscans were the most energetic and effective in this educational mission during the first half of the sixteenth century. Three Flemish Franciscans began the first concentrated educational effort in New Spain when they arrived in 1522 shortly after Cortes had conquered the Aztecs. Peter of **Ghent** established the first school for Indian children, concentrating upon the sons of *caciques* but admitting lower class Indian boys as well. The most famous of the early schools was the *Colegio de San Francisco* in Mexico City which taught Latin, religion, music, painting, and sculpture, and some vocational arts and crafts.

The next year, 1523, twelve Spanish Franciscans arrived in Mexico, fresh from the humanist training they had received in Spain which was then imbued with the spirit of Renaissance reform being preached by Erasmus in the name of Christian humanism. These reforms, promoted by Cardinal Jiménez de Cisneros, were sweeping through the Universities of Salamanca, Valladolid, and the new University of Alcalá de Henares. They included the Erasmian doctrine that just as the pagans of classical Rome achieved greatness without Christianity the Europe of his day could be so much greater if it really lived up to its Christian ideals. The Franciscans in their reform applied the same line of thinking to the Amerindians whose capability for greatness, they said, could only be genuinely realized through the civilizing influence of a purified and reformed Christianity. It was something of this Renaissance spirit of classical humanist Christianity that imbued the reformed branches of Franciscan friars, the Observants or Friars Minor. Their university study of the classical languages as well as Spanish gave them a mind-set of interest in the Amerindian languages and cultures which they began to study and compile into grammars, dictionaries, and histories after their arrival in America. One of the principal promoters of Erasmian humanism was the Franciscan bishop of Mexico, Juan de Zumarraga, who naturally enough encouraged humanistic education for Amerindians as well as for Spaniards.

One of the principal beneficiaries of Zumarraga's interest was the *Colegio de Santa Cruz* founded in Mexico City under Franciscan auspices in 1535-1536. More humanistic and academic and less vocationally oriented than Peter of Ghent's school, the *Colegio de Santa Cruz* stressed Latin grammar, logic, rhetoric, and philosophy as well as music and religion. Designed primarily to produce a mature elite for church and state, its graduates, who could converse in Latin, assisted in translating the Christian scriptures into Amerindian languages.

Other mendicant friars appeared on the scene in Mexico, Dominicans in 1526, Augustinians in 1533. By 1559 there were some eighty Franciscan friaries with 380 members, forty Dominican with 210 members, and forty Augustinian with like membership. They all regularly conducted primary schools for Indian children in or near their friaries, some of these schools dealing with 300 or 400 to 1,000 pupils. A third major secondary school was established in 1548 by the Franciscans, the *Colegio de San Juan de Letran,* aimed primarily at mestizo boys. The crowning educational achievement in New Spain was the establishment of the University of Mexico in 1551 (operational in 1553) which took the University of Salamanca as its model; it even blazed new paths by opening its doors to mestizos and offering courses in Amerindian languages and culture.

Christian humanism, however, suffered major setbacks in Spain, where it soon was identified with Protestantism. Erasmus' writings were condemned, the Counter-Reformation began to pick up momentum, the Inquisition was formed, and Spain took over the mantle of Catholic absolutism. The Jesuits, arriving in New Spain in 1572, had over 300 members by 1600. Their chief educational institution was the *Colegio de San Ildefonso.* The mendicant orders lost their reform ardor in trying to compete among themselves or with the Jesuits, or they betook themselves to the frontiers of New Spain, which meant the borderlands to the north in what eventually was to become the southwest of the United States. There they established frontier mission societies combining religious education with teaching of the ways of life required to change from hunting and gathering to sedentary agriculture as basic to their continuing civilizing mission. The Jesuits joined the mendicants on the frontiers of Northern Mexico and in the interior of Paraguay, displaying the advantages of disciplined and orderly work habits under the strictly organized authority of a highly stratified society. In these ways the Amerindians were induced or forced to change their folk society ways to civilized ways.

In Peru the Dominicans accompanied Pizarro on his second intrusion, and the Franciscans arrived soon after, but education progressed more slowly in Peru than in New Spain as a result of continuing Inca resistance and civil wars among the factions of *conquistadores* themselves. It was mid-century before schools really began to spread. The Dominicans, more favored by the *conquistadores* than the Franciscans, had established about sixty schools by 1551; the Franciscans had fifty-five parishes by 1600; the Augustinians arrived in 1551. Soon after the Jesuits arrived in 1569 they began to establish their colleges, secondary level institutions with a heavily humanistic content aimed largely at the white creole population. The most noteworthy of these was the *Colegio de San Pablo* in Lima which prepared students for the University of San Marcos and even competed with it in the field of philosophy and theology. Peru had formally moved to establish a university-level institution as early as 1551, but San Marcos University was not operational until the 1580's. In general, education for Amerindians in Peru lagged behind that of Mexico, in part because of the later start and the shorter time before the decline of interest in Amerindian education that set in during the latter half of the sixteenth century.

In the period from the beginning of the sixteenth to the end of the eighteenth century the basic framework—primary, secondary, and university—of traditional humanistic and literary forms of Western education was transferred to Latin America. There were signs that a distinctive variation on primary education for the conquered peoples was being worked out in the first half of the sixteenth century, but this declined in the seventeenth and eighteenth centuries except in the missions of the frontiers, in the isolated inland or upland regions, or in the borderlands to the North.

Primary schools for the Amerindian elite were widespread throughout Spanish America in the sixteenth century. Typically they were boarding schools for children between the ages of seven and twelve, during which time the boys or girls would be separated from their families, villages, or *encomiendas* for from three to five years. They were often built next to monasteries or churches, virtually as appendages to the Christianizing mission of the mendicants. The curriculum typically centered on reading and writing (Latin at first, but the Amerindian languages after about 1530), catechism and prayers, and religious music or chanting. The discipline was strict, as befitted the authoritarian paternal role that the friars adopted toward their charges, but the friar teachers often tried to use pedagogical methods that went beyond verbal instruction. They stressed the use of pictures, plays, drama, processions, fiestas, music, dancing, singing, prizes, and awards. The major goal, however, was always to convert and to make conversion stick.

In some of the most successful variations on primary education the Christianizing effort was combined with attempts to change the economic basis of life as well as the religious. Peter of Ghent's school for Amerindians in Mexico City was such a school, producing artisans, carpenters, and masons as well as artists. *San Juan de Letran,* also in Mexico City, was originally a clinic and orphanage that became a primary school for mestizo boys and girls, stressing the trades and vocations as well as a prime function of training teachers for primary schools. In many places special classes for Indian girls were set up to stress the European domestic arts as well as religion. And very widespread was the less formal but effective practice of teaching the catechism and some of the basics of literacy to the children of the village or town in the *atrio,* or courtyard, of the church. Some of these patio schools reached thousands of children, and many adults, in more or less well organized classes taught by friars, assisted by Amerindians who had attended primary school, and supervised by adults in the community, who also often attended the classes.

Still more effective in promoting the transformation of Amerindian folk societies in the direction of the specialized, differentiated, and urban ways of life characteristic of traditional civilization was the mission effort on the borderlands of New Spain to the north where Christianizing and civilizing efforts went hand in hand in developing new forms of settled community life:

> Indians accordingly were taught agriculture and stock raising and a variety of crafts. . . . Franciscans in California developed elaborate economic complexes, the native inhabitants of which built aqueducts, dams, and reservoirs and cultivated gardens, grain fields, orchards, and vineyards. Indians constructed buildings, learned carpentry and masonry, operated gristmills, raised cattle and sheep, tanned hides, wove textiles, and made wine, shoes, soap, and candles, all under Franciscan supervision. . . . everywhere in the borderlands they introduced plows, European plants and seeds, and new agricultural techniques in addition to Christianity.[14]

The missionaries even developed a form of cooperative "technical assistance" whereby the more advanced Amerindians of Mexico helped to civilize the less advanced Indians of the future United States—and they made some of the same mistakes their modern successors have made:

> Indians from the south were introduced on the frontiers as aides in these processes of civilization. They came as colonists, teachers, and models, the purpose being to instruct by example in orderly social living, agriculture, and

---

[14] Gibson, op. cit., pp. 196-197.

political officeholding. . . . The full native community had judges and police, a *cabildo,* a jail, and other institutions for the maintenance of internal order, all under the supervision of the Spaniards. But it should be added that these programs often lapsed, most missionaries had little understanding of the social organization of the peoples among whom they worked, and appointments to native office were sometimes made arbitrarily and thoughtlessly.[15]

Of course, the story was not simply one of mistakes or miscalculations in the civilizing process; it was also one of deliberate "uncivilizing," whereby Amerindian students in the mission schools of Mexico were used as major agents in destroying the Aztec temples, idols, and even manuscripts of great religious and cultural value. They sometimes did this with overly fanatical zeal. Students also furthered the uncivilizing process by spying on their parents. Some missionaries justified the destruction of the religious traditions of the Amerindian civilization as necessary for the building of Christianity. Others condemned it as an affront to humanity itself.

No matter how benevolent and Christian, conversion was a program designed to impose European standards upon non-European peoples. The common attitude of the clergy was one of authoritarian paternalism, and in various degrees the regime that they imposed was maintained by force, with whipping posts, stocks, and prison cells. . . . it is obvious that no program could be too tolerant, for this would defeat the purpose and weaken the effort to substitute Christianity for paganism.[16]

At the secondary level of education there was promise of designing a new kind of college appropriate to a social transformation which would honor the culture of the indigenous civilization as well as adopt some of the values of the alien civilization. The most famous of such attempts was the *Colegio de Santa Cruz* which the Franciscans established in Mexico City, to which came Amerindian students from all over New Spain. It was a boarding school with strict and severe regulations and it gave a high quality Latin education in the humanistic liberal arts with some of the sharpest Franciscan intellectuals of the sixteenth century as teachers, including Bernardino de Sahagun. It soon proved, for those willing to look and listen, that Amerindians were fully capable of mastering a Western education. The students and graduates assisted Sahagun in writing his monumental history of Aztec civilization and engaged in the construction of Nahuatl vocabularies, grammars, textbooks, and translations. The graduates not only became translators and interpreters but also teachers in primary schools for whites as well as Indians and clerks in government administrative offices. One graduate, Antonio Valerino, became the only Indian governor in Mexico during the sixteenth century.

But critics arose to argue that such an intellectual education for Indians would only lead to heresy and possibly to rebellion, and in 1555 the Council of Trent forbade the creation of an Indian priesthood. As a result, *Santa Cruz* began to decline

[15] Ibid., p. 198.
[16] Ibid., pp. 199-200.

late in the sixteenth century, and secondary education turned more and more to the creole population with the standard humanist curriculum of the Jesuits' *ratio studiorum* dominating. The opponents of the *Colegio de Santa Cruz* were probably cruelly correct in their judgment that a large scale development of secondary education for Amerindians would have led to the rise of an indigenous intellectual elite—and rebellion.

In the short run, secondary education would have provided increasingly competent members for the bureaucracy, the civil service, and the teaching profession (had these functions also been opened to Amerindians). And in the long run it would have produced an intellectual elite that might have taken the leadership in achieving self-government and independence, as happened so widely in the twentieth century in many of the new nations of Asia and Africa. But this did not happen in Spanish America. Instead, the Spaniards did not educate Amerindians, still less Africans, for self-rule. They imposed a white traditional Western society on top of subject populations, and they concentrated their educational attention upon the intellectual elite of the ruling white classes. Eventually, it was the upper class creoles who threw off Spanish peninsular rule in the early nineteenth century, but this did not change the society very much. Social transformation and genuine modernization in Latin America had to wait until the twentieth century.

One of the reasons for the continuity and stability, some would say stagnation, of Hispanic society in America for some three to four hundred years was the traditional character of higher as well as secondary education. Predominantly religious and thoroughly aristocratic, the twenty-six universities that were founded to the end of the eighteenth century carried on a heavily medieval university tradition, responding to the new currents of the Enlightenment almost a century later than in Northern Europe or in Northern America. The first move to establish a university in the New World had been made by the Dominicans when Pope Paul III authorized the founding of the University of St. Thomas Aquinas in 1538 in Santo Domingo with all the privileges and rights pertaining to the Universities of Alcalá, Salamanca, or other Spanish universities. We have already mentioned the Universities of Mexico and San Marcos which began operation in 1553 long before Santo Domingo was functioning.

Other major universities were founded in Bogota, Guatemala City, Cordoba, Quito, Havana, and Caracas.[17] At first the Dominicans, and then later the Jesuits, were the most enterprising in promoting the establishment of universitites, often engaging in bitter disputes over jurisdiction and privileges. Typically, a major university boasted the four medieval faculties of arts, theology, law, and medicine. The faculty of arts was usually held in fairly inferior position, often scarcely distinguishable from the *colegio* and usually considered to be preparatory to the highest prestige faculty of theology, which meant that the universities were basically training grounds for the clergy. Law also became popular for the growing administrative classes in the course of the seventeenth century, but medicine was often in low repute because of the absence of competent physicians as teachers. The popularity of university study as a sign of upper-class status is attested to by the estimate that some 150,000 university

---

[17] See Germán Arciniegas, *Latin America: A Cultural History*, Knopf New York, 1967, pp. 150 ff.

degrees (including 30,000 doctorates) were granted in Spanish America during the colonial period.

Too often, however, the acquisition of a university degree was looked upon by the American creoles as a badge of equality or even superiority to the peninsular Spaniards with whom they had to compete for public and clerical office. So a university education became not so much a professional preparation for superior accomplishment or public service to the general welfare as a credential of upper-class status. Consequently the impetus to change the medieval university curriculum or adapt it to the conditions of America was fairly slight:

> In Spanish America the universities' systematized, authoritarian pedagogy made them the custodians of a pre-established knowledge. The parading of knowledge became the scholar's goal. Scholarship depended upon intellectual intensification and memorization and verbal manipulation rather than investigation or innovation of any kind.[18]

In sum, to the middle or end of the eighteenth century the secondary and higher educational patterns transferred from Spain to Spanish America turned out to be predominantly classical, humanistic, literary, and Christian with the aim focused upon training an educated clergy and with pedagogy confined largely to a pedantic formalism. The scientific realism that was becoming so important in Europe and North America in the seventeenth and eighteen centuries scarcely affected Spanish America. It was almost all Renaissance and Counter-Reformation in style and purpose.

The early Franciscans who argued that the Amerindians could be Christianized through their own languages without induction into the full panoply of Spanish culture and language may have been humanitarian and anthropologically wise, but as it turned out Hispanization won the day in Latin American education. The crown wanted the Spanish language as a common tongue for ruling a vast empire beset by large numbers of indigenous oral languages. Charles V had set out in a *cedula* of 1550 to order the establishment of schools to teach Spanish to the Amerindians, but this was not carried out, and Philip II in 1596 simply said Spanish teachers should be available in the villages to teach any Indians who wished to learn Spanish. As a result of the policy of Hispanization of education and the virtual exclusion of Amerindians and Africans from formal education, the speaking of an Amerindian language became one of the major signs of subjection and lower-class status even more important in some respects than biological race. This has led to a classification of members of Latin American society on the basis of "social race," including such sociocultural factors as education, language, custom, or wealth as well as ancestry or appearance.[19]

In the Philippines

The Spanish conquest of the Philippines had far different results for the education of Filipinos from that of Amerindian America. Augustinian friars accompanied Legaspi in 1565 when he renewed Spanish claims to the Philippines, nearly 50 years after the

---

[18] Gibson, op. cit., p. 131.

[19] See Wagley, op. cit. chap. 5, for a fascinating discussion of "social race."

islands had been touched by Magellan. Within fifteen years the Franciscans, Domini-cans, and Jesuits had all arrived, and by 1600 it is estimated that some 400 mission-aries were at work. Even though the Philippines were officially ruled from Mexico City as an outpost of New Spain and such institutions as *audiencia* and *encomienda* were imported from New Spain, the secular clergy never gained predominance over the missionary orders in the same way they did in Spanish America. For their part the four orders maintained an aggressive, almost conquistadorial zeal for Christianization not only of the Philippines but also of China and Japan. Only Spanish or Spanish-Neapolitan clerics were allowed in the Philippines, so the effort possessed a homo-geneity not achieved in the rest of Asia.

As a result of this massive mission effort and the absence of a matured literate civilization among the Filipinos the Spanish efforts at Christianization were more successful in the Philippines than those of any Western nation in Asia. The missionaries learned the local languages, established primary schools widely through the islands, introduced the Roman alphabet for the vernacular languages, and spread literacy to large numbers of Filipinos through both religious and secular subjects.

Unhampered in their devotion to educating as well as Christianizing the Filipinos by a large immigration of colonial Spaniards, the missionaries did not divert education from the indigenous population. Indeed, secondary schools and colleges as well as primary schools were established to train an indigenous priesthood and teaching cadre. By the mid-seventeenth century some of the Hispanic and humanistic studies, stressing Latin, Greek, philosophy, theology and even law and medicine attained university status. Because there was only a thin layer of Spanish officials to administer the islands on behalf of the Spanish crown, the educated Filipinos began to serve the bureaucracy as clerks and lower officials as early as the seventeenth century. Eventually, the secondary and higher schools produced a Western-educated Spanish speaking elite who formed the nucleus of anti-Spanish movements in the nineteenth century. In this respect Spanish education in the Philippines served a purpose closer to that of English education in India, or French education in Vietnam than Spanish education did in New Spain.

In the classic cases of Western imperialism three discernible patterns of educa-tion emerged. Where a relatively small but rotating class of Western administrators ruled Asian or African peoples on behalf of the sovereign at home, one pattern of education was to raise up a small indigenous elite trained in Western education as the British did in India, and the British and French did in Africa. A second pattern was the one we have described for Spanish America: a Western education primarily for the Western colonists who established their society on top of an indigenous civilization. Despite being a minority in the population, the white colonists nevertheless dominated the political and economic as well as the cultural and educational scene.

In French Canada

A third pattern was that of the British and the French who went to North America to establish their particular fragments of European civilization, paying relatively little or no attention to the indigenous societies they found in their way, striving mainly to ignore them or to drive them away. As it turned out, the version of education transplanted to the British colonies of the Atlantic seaboard of North America relatively soon took on a character of its own which was eventually to influence not only the very roots of the Western European education from which it sprang but also the development of education in some of the traditional societies of Asia and Africa. Meanwhile, the version of Western education transferred to the New France of Canada was to become one of the most conservative elements of a highly traditional and relatively unchanging society.

Although the St. Lawrence was explored by Cartier as early as 1535, the first permanent settlements were not made in Quebec until 1608 under the leadership of Champlain. Soon thereafter the teaching orders of the Catholic Church began to establish schools: the Gray Friars as early as 1616, followed by the Jesuits, the Sulpicians, the Ursulines, and the Sisters of the Congregation of Notre Dame founded in Montreal in 1657. Most of these schools concentrated on the rudiments of reading, writing, arithmetic, religion, and a bit of geography and history. The Jesuits provided what secondary or higher education there was, a *collège* in Quebec that offered the standard classical, humanist course. For a population that amounted to around 10,000 persons by 1700 the church orders had established some two dozen schools, a notable achievement in comparison with the availability of primary schools in France itself.

The founding of new schools tapered off toward the end of the seventeenth century, reflecting no doubt the drastic decline in new immigration from France after 1681. In fact the 1660s and 1670s marked a significant turning point in French Canadian history. Prior to that time the colony had been fostered by a series of trading companies that had stressed the commercial importance of the fur trade and had attracted a fairly liberal variety of bourgeois Frenchmen, including Huguenots. In 1663, however, the colony was transferred out of the hands of the Company of New France into the hands of a royal governor and an *intendant* (administrator) directly responsible to Louis XIV and his ministers in Paris. From this point forward the absolutism and the economic mercantilism that were reaching a high point in France were increasingly reflected in French Canada. From 1665 to 1672 under an especially vigorous *intendant,* Jean Talon, population increased and the colony reflected the dynamism of the highly centralized regime of France at the height of its European power. Under the stimulus of Bishop Francois Xavier de Leval in the 1660s, Jesuit and Sulpician seminaries were founded in Quebec and Montreal for the advanced training of Catholic priests and, reflecting the economic momentum in France itself, technical schools for promoting the trades and agriculture were also established.

Absolutism, however, began to take its toll. A seigneurial system of land tenure injected a kind of feudalism into New France that lasted much longer than in old France. While it was less severe in its demands for dues and obligations required of the *habitant* who worked the land, it nevertheless contributed a traditionalizing factor to Quebec society that saw three-hundred-year-old remnants surviving to the 1960s. Absolutism also mandated carefully restricted immigration in order to keep the outflow from France under strict control. While 10,000 people left France for Canada in a matter of 150 years to the mid-eighteenth century, the English sent out as many as 45,000 to 50,000 to their American colonies in a matter of two or three decades in the mid-seventeenth century. By 1750 French Canada had grown to approximately 50,000 population, while English America had grown to 1 million, even though France was probably twice as large as England.

Even more important than the numbers, perhaps, was the character of the immigration. Protestants had never been particularly welcome in New France, but after the revocation of the Edict of Nantes in 1688 as many as 200,000 Huguenots fled from France to the profit of Holland, Germany, and English America but not of French Canada. The loss of their urban skills and the quieting of the ferment of their intellectual and religious dissent further served to strengthen the traditional character of New France, already homogenized by the absence of lawyers and judges and Jansenists who had struggled against the growth of Louis' absolutism in metropolitan France.

To be sure, the absolutism did not become the despotism that brought on the French Revolution, but it did serve to build a social and cultural tradition far different from that which began to develop in the English colonies to the south by the end of the seventeenth century. The seeds of modernism much more rapidly grew to a healthy growth in the more liberal and heterodox soil that developed in Anglo-Protestant America in the eighteenth and nineteenth centuries. Indeed the plants that produced those seeds in sixteenth- and seventeenth-century England were considerably different from those of the France of the same period.

CHAPTER VIII

THE DISPERSION
OF ANGLO-PROTESTANT
EDUCATION
(1400 A.D.-1700 A.D.)

A. LUTHERAN AND CALVINIST VARIATIONS ON THE REFORMATION THEME

One of the far-reaching trends that the Protestant Reformation accelerated in northern Europe was the spread of civil control of education and the accompanying idea that education from top to bottom ought to be sponsored by the state for sectarian religious puposes. Lutheran and Calvinist reformers promoted this movement across the face of Western Europe. For example, when the Lutheran church in German lands became closely allied with the state, the church and its schools virtually became a branch of civil administration in which the clergy and teachers were appointed by the head of state. Thus, under the stimulus of Luther and his followers, Bugenhagen and Melanchthon, the Protestant rulers were urged to reform their schools by civil action. As a result, several of the German states and free cities issued civil codes for the conduct of schools.

The school code of Württemberg in 1559 was one of the most far-reaching, providing for the establishment of vernacular elementary schools to teach boys and girls reading, writing, arithmetic, music, and religion. These schools were to be established in every village and to be taught by the church sexton. Latin secondary schools were also to be set up to train boys for leadership in the church and state and for the university at Tübingen. Other states followed the Württemberg code, notably Saxony in 1580.

Another important code was issued by the state of Saxe-Gotha in 1642, providing for compulsory attendance, higher salaries for teachers, free textbooks, supervision of instruction, a graded class system, and more realistic studies. Other important cities that reorganized their schools by action of the civil authorities were Brunswick, Weimar, Nuremberg, Hamburg, Wittenberg, and Strasbourg. In the seventeenth century several states enacted compulsory attendance laws, including Württemberg and Saxony. This effort to spread vernacular education in Lutheran lands met with considerable success. Older Catholic parish schools and town schools were reorganized wherever possible or legislated out of existence, and new schools were established. Denmark and Sweden also took steps to reform their schools along Lutheran lines.

The vernacular curriculum included reading Luther's translations of the Bible and Aesop's *Fables* and learning his catechism, singing the Lutheran hymns, possibly studying some history and arithmetic (although the earlier reckoning schools maintained their superiority in arithmetic), and performing some physical activity. The basic four R's (reading, writing, arithmetic, and religion), along with music and some history and physical education, became the staple curriculum of the common vernacular schools in Lutheran lands.

Despite his interest in vernacular education for the common people, Luther always felt that the Latin school was the prime educational agency for promoting the Reformation in Germany. This confluence of humanism and evangelical religion proved to be particularly efficacious in Germany. Even though early gains for humanism had been made in the mid-fifteenth century by Agricola and by Reuchlin,[1] it was not until Luther came under the influence of Erasmus between 1500 and 1520 that the real reformation of German schools began. In those days of intense religious controversy, Luther became convinced that it was the classical school which would best prepare Lutheran leaders to defend and propagate the Lutheran faith in competition with Catholic leaders. Luther wanted even the elementary schools to teach Latin; but when he despaired of the abilities of the common people, he put more emphasis than ever upon the secondary schools and upon rhetoric as the chief instrument of persuasion.

Luther's faithful lieutenant, Melanchthon, who had charge of reorganizing secondary education in Lutheran Germany, was a thoroughgoing classical humanist as well as a dedicated religionist, loving Greek as well as Latin and contemptuous of the vernacular. Melanchthon was extraordinarily active in establishing classical schools. He also wrote numerous textbooks on the seven liberal arts, being careful to select only those authors who were duly pious. Also influential was Johann Sturm, whose organization of secondary schools into regular classes on the basis of proficiency laid the foundations of the German *gymnasium.* In his school at Strasbourg Sturm divided the curriculum into ten graded classes, each to be taught by a different teacher and each to follow a prescribed curriculum. Learning Latin was the exclusive task of the first three years, then Greek was added from the fourth class on. In the senior section of six years the course branched out to the seven liberal arts and the lectures were open to the public. Throughout, Sturm sought to combine Christian teachings with detailed study of the literary classics. He was one of the most successful practitioners of the *pietas litterata.* He helped to prove the generalization that there was a stronger alliance between religion and humanism in northern Europe than in Italy.

In Germany, the courts and the schools accepted the humanist learning before the universities did. Lectures on classical antiquity were attempted as early as the

---

[1] Reuchlin had been outstanding in his promotion of Hebrew as a scholarly classical language. In his defense of Hebrew writings against those who would burn the books of Jews as heretical, he was able to strike an early blow against the book burners and in favor of tolerance and intellectual freedom in the field of scholarship.

latter part of the fifteenth century, but they met with little response by the universities until after 1500. Then, as the religious reformers adopted the new learning, it gradually was accepted by the universities under the leadership of a reform group at Erfurt and Tübingen and especially at Wittenberg and Nuremberg under the impetus of Melanchthon. However, the Reformation wars, dogmatic religion, and oppressive state control virtually turned the German universities into centers of theological-mindedness. Lutheran rulers molded their universities to serve Lutheran purposes, and Catholic rulers did likewise for Catholic purposes. The universities at Wittenberg, Leipzig, Frankfurt, Tübingen, and Rostock became Lutheran, while new Lutheran universities were founded at Marburg, Jena, Strasbourg, and Konigsberg. Although the union of theology with humanism had preserved some of the vitality of the humanistic interests, most German universities had sunk to a low level under the weight of theological interests by the end of the seventeenth century. The revival during the eighteenth-century Enlightenment was to see the German universities emerge into the first rank in the world, a position they maintained until the Hitler regime of the twentieth century.

Calvin's theocratic theory, according to which the state was essentially an arm of the church, stimulated the growth of civil control of education in Calvinist countries even more than in Lutheran lands. In Geneva, the state set up religious schools and enforced attendance for the benefit of the church. In the Netherlands, when the Dutch Reformed Church came into power, it proceeded to adapt the town schools already in existence to its religious purposes. The Synod of the Hague in 1586 provided for the establishment of schools in the cities, and the Synod of Dort in 1618 provided for the establishment of schools to give free instruction to poor children in all villages under the control of civil magistrates. In Scotland where King James I had decreed in the fifteenth century that public schools should be maintained as one means of reforming the clergy and promoting literacy, the General Assembly of the Presbyterian Church, following John Knox's proposals in the *First Book of Discipline,* recommended to the Scottish Parliament as early as 1560 that primary schools should be set up in every parish and secondary schools in every major town. After the Presbyterian Church was made the state church in 1592, Parliament passed laws in 1616, 1633, and 1646 providing for schools in every parish.

Like Luther, Calvin strongly advocated vernacular schools in which children could be taught his catechism, the three R's in the vernacular, and the singing of hymns. The Huguenots carried this type of school into France, and the German Reformed Church (teaching in German, of course) attempted to do the same in the territories of western Germany. In the Netherlands the Dutch Reformed Church set up what may have been the best vernacular schools of any country in Europe. Here again, stimulated by the practical needs of the commercial cities of the Netherlands, the Dutch schools taught the three R's and religion for boys and girls. This system doubtless had an influence upon the Puritans of England and America, as well as on the Dutch settlers in America.

There was a long tradition of devotion to classical studies in the Low Countries. One example of this tendency is furnished by the clerical and lay society known as the Brethren of the Common Life, founded in the Low Countries in the fourteenth century by Gerhard Groot. The members of this society spent much of their time earning their livelihood by copying manuscripts. Gradually they began to give instruction in the town schools and eventually established their own schools in such cities as Deventer, Brussels, and Antwerp. Their orientation remained heavily medieval, but the classics were introduced into their curriculum in the late fifteenth century. Out of this tradition came the greatest of the humanists, Erasmus, who was also the chief exponent of the *pietas litterata.*

In Geneva, Calvin also put great emphasis upon the study of the classics in order that "true" religious scholars might read the Scriptures in the original languages of Greek, Hebrew, and Latin and not be obliged to depend upon Catholic interpretations. He once said that only those boys who could not study the classics profitably should, as second best, study the vernacular. Calvin had taught at Strasbourg and modeled his schools upon Sturm's. He shortened the curriculum to seven years and introduced some vernacular French, but the prime object was still to train leaders in classical scholarship and rhetoric in order to defend and propagate the Calvinist faith.

Calvin's higher institution of learning, the academy at Geneva, was the capstone of his educational system. The academy was apparently very successful at the outset, enrolling several hundred students the first year. Emphasizing constant religious devotions, the curriculum included the classics, the usual liberal arts, ethics, poetry, physics, and theology. Obviously designed to prepare preachers, theologians, and teachers for the Calvinist world, Geneva was used as the model for the University of Leiden in the Netherlands, University of Edinburgh in Scotland, and Emmanuel College of Cambridge University in England. Of the several universities established in the Netherlands in the sixteenth and seventeenth centuries, those at Leiden, Amsterdam, and Utrecht became outstanding centers of scholarship and Calvinist religion. The Scottish universities founded in this period under Presbyterian auspices achieved special preeminence during the eighteenth century, notably Edinburgh and Aberdeen.

B. THE EDUCATIONAL REVOLUTION IN ENGLAND

In the two and a half centuries between 1400 and 1650 England proved to be the scene of the most spectacular developments in Western education. This radical turn of events was the result of a peculiar interplay of the social and educational forces that were operating in other parts of Europe and the world. These included the political drive to national authority, in which the crown and Parliament vied for power, the struggle among social classes in which the rural gentry and urban commercial classes were strengthened, the relatively amicable religious settlement among Protestants and Catholics, and a fairly reasonable kind of settlement of the tension between humanist and medieval learning. We shall first sketch briefly the interweaving of the forces that produced the "new" education in England and then describe the overall characteristics of the expansion and structure of English education as they took form toward the end of the seventeenth century.

Forming the New Tradition:
Humanist, Protestant, Civil, and Gentle
While the Renaissance ferment was bubbling over into educational programs and practices in Italy and in the Low Countries during the fifteenth century, relatively little humanist activity was touching English education. But this does not mean that

significant movement was lacking in England. Very important expansionist trends were under way that were to mix in with humanist influences when they did flood into England in the sixteenth century. The development of town life led to demands that schools be set up by the municipal borough governments. Even though the English towns were smaller than the bustling cities of Italy and northern Europe, they nevertheless took steps to establish their own schools as well as undertake greater control over such other civic affairs as trade, markets, and hospitals. This was one sign that the urban middle classes were seeking more educational training for advancement in civil as well as commercial careers. Private teachers, borough schools, and foundations for chantry schools all gained considerable support.

The monopoly which the church had exerted over education for a thousand years was being challenged in England as it was in the cities of northern Europe. The right of the church foundations to license new teachers was being questioned, and the right of parents to send their children to any school they pleased was asserted by a statute of labourers as early as 1406.[2] Outside the towns, as the gentry steadily gained a larger place in the administrative as well as the economic life of the country, they began to promote the spread of village and parish schools as well as joining with the upper aristocracy in contributing to foundations which would support a priest or two to pray for their souls and to teach school on the side.

During the fifteenth century the endowment principle in England went beyond the medieval chantries to include foundations designed specifically for the establishment of grammar schools. When wealthy individuals or groups contributed money for the founding of schools, secular control was being exerted where church control had been dominant before. The first of these foundations, which was the origin of the English public schools, was instituted by William of Wykeham in 1382 at Winchester in connection with New College, Oxford; the second was founded at Eton in 1440 under Henry VI in association with King's College, Cambridge. The teachers were thus not directly responsible to church authorities, for the schools had a corporate existence independent of church control. Boards of trustees were set up for the general supervision of the schools, and, in some cases at least, these included representatives of merchant or craft guilds as well as the gentry and aristocracy.

As control of grammar schools became laicized, so did the teachers themselves. This trend reflected in part a change in the character of university education itself, which began to shift away from the tradition that clerical training was the only professional discipline that led to teaching. Undergraduate teaching in the colleges of liberal arts became a career goal in and of itself. In fact, when God's House was founded at Cambridge about 1439 William Byngham specifically intended that it should prepare undergraduates to be teachers in the grammar schools. Such a radical proposal, that a teaching college should in truth be also a teachers college, was, however, nearly 500 years ahead of its time.

The usual historical judgment is that with the opening of the sixteenth century the golden age of English humanism dawned with a remarkable succession of scholars

---

[2] Joan Simon, *Education and Society in Tudor England,* Cambridge University Press, London, 1966, p. 24.

preaching the glories of classical learning as they had discovered it in Italy.[3] There had been a long background of scholarly contact between England and Italy, but the upsurge of interest was stimulated by Erasmus, John Colet, Thomas Elyot, Thomas More, and Juan Luis Vives, to name only the most familiar, during the first three decades of the sixteenth century. This was the period when the humanists were campaigning vigorously for the new learning (as described in Chapter 6). It was not until the 1530s, however, that enough teachers had been trained to enable the programmatic ideals to be put into practice in the schools.

The prime model was created in 1510 when John Colet was able to refound the medieval cathedral school at St. Paul's into a publicly endowed grammar school under the control of one of the leading guilds, the Company of Mercers. Its doors were open to the public; it represented the new urban culture of London. It promoted a Christian way of life, but its medium was the classical tradition of *pietas litterata*. Although it was not the first humanistic school, its historic prominence and the influence of Colet helped to introduce classical humanism into the dozens of other grammar schools that were soon to follow. The stress was usually upon learning the rules of Latin and Greek grammar, declensions of nouns and conjugations of verbs, and the reading of such authors as Cicero, Horace, Vergil, Cato, Aesop, and Erasmus. Colet was even able to enlist the help of Erasmus and Lily in writing texts to be used in the schools.

By the 1530s the humanist appeals began to take effect. The gentry pressed for a classical education for their children, and the Protestant reform movement had grown strong enough to attack the Catholic Church on its own grounds and to reorganize the educational enterprise according to its own lights. The propertied classes, however, did not listen to appeals that they establish courtly schools for their own children as had become common in the courts of Germany and France.[4] Rather, they turned to the grammar schools and the university colleges to give the education they now felt was suitable for a governing class. The Protestant reformers, alternately led and egged on by Henry VIII and Edward VI, provided the organizing thrust that actually changed the schools and universities and produced what became an extraordinary educational revolution.

The religious reformation of the middle decades of the sixteenth century is now looked upon not as a period of destruction or retardation as formerly pictured by some historians of education, but as a period of educational advance, reform, and progress.[5] After the Church of England had been established by the Act of Supremacy in 1534, the Protestant rulers of England issued edicts of one kind or another about schools and universities in accordance with their assertion that the king was the supreme head of the church. The Chantry Acts under Henry VIII and Edward VI

---

[3] See Kenneth Charlton, *Education in Renaissance England,* Routledge, London, 1965, chap. 3. For a view that the usual tribute to the early Oxford Reformers is misplaced and that the real florescence of English humanism did not occur until Elizabethan times, see R. R. Bolgar, *The Classical Heritage and Its Beneficiaries,* Harper Torchbooks, New York, 1964, pp. 310-315.

[4] See the proposals by Thomas Starkey, Richard Maryson, Sir Thomas Elyot, Sir Humphrey Gilbert, and Lawrence Humphrey in Charlton, loc. cit.

[5] This is the burden of the revisionism of Joan Simon, Kenneth Charlton, Mark Curtis, and Lawrence Stone, albeit they differ amongst themselves on major points.

dispossessed the Catholic foundations for chantry schools, and Henry VIII took over the monastic schools. Universities were inspected and supervised by agents of Henry VIII and Elizabeth I. Henry VIII made the church primers required reading in schools. Thus the beginning church book became the beginning schoolbook. The Oath of Supremacy under Elizabeth in 1562, which required all teachers to swear loyalty to the monarchy and to subscribe to the Thirty-nine Articles of Anglican faith, gave supervision of grammar schools to bishops. In general, civil control of education in England during the Reformation tended to match that of Lutheran and Calvinistic countries, whereas the Latin countries adhered primarily to the traditional conception that education was a function of the Church and that schools should be established by religious and private sources.

When the Catholic Church was largely eliminated from the religious scene in England, the foundations of the monastic and chantry schools were confiscated and much effort went into the refounding of the schools under public or private auspices. For a time elementary education was provided in a rather haphazard and unsystematic way. Parents taught their children whatever they could, hired a tutor if they could afford one, or sent their children to the parish priest if he could and would teach them their letters. In time, however, more or less formal instruction was given in *petty schools* or in the preparatory department of a grammar school, called the *petty classes*. By and large, education was available principally to those whose parents could afford to provide it. Of course, as the merchant class grew in wealth and numbers, more parents could afford education, and proposals were made for charity schools for the poor. Formal education came to be available to approximately half the population of England—the upper half.

Much more systematic interest was expressed in a classical secondary education. Many new grammar schools were established—perhaps as many as 500 such schools were newly founded or refounded during the Reformation. The financial stimulus for this interest came substantially from the gentry and the new middle classes, whose desire to improve their social status kept pace with their improving economic status. As funds were poured into the endowments for Latin grammar schools, the bases were being laid for the English public schools. The desire to give free instruction to poor children was doubtless a motive in this movement, as witness the plea of Archbishop Cranmer that poor boys be admitted to Canterbury School. On the whole, however, the clientele for these schools came from a fairly wide range in the population above the working classes. Some grammar schools were "public" in the sense that the funds and income were used for the benefit of the schools rather than for the private profit of those who conducted them. They were also "public" in the sense that all children were free to attend them if they could pay the tuition or gain a free scholarship. They were not "public" in what came to be the American sense, that they were open to all free of charge because they were supported by public funds or taxation. The most notable of the public schools were Winchester, Eton, Westminster, St. Paul's, Shrewsbury, Rugby, Harrow, Charterhouse, and Merchant Taylors'.

Partly as a result of humanist consensus on pedagogical ideology and partly as a result of royal edicts, the curriculum of the Latin grammar schools achieved a remarkable standardization of content. Beginning as early as 1529 a canon of the

Canterbury Convocation prescribed not only that teachers be orthodox and of upright character and that they teach morals and Christian doctrine to the boys but also that they teach only the grammar authorized by designated church officials. Soon after the Church of England was established, Henry VIII decreed in 1542 that William Lily's grammar should be taught throughout the realm and none other. Edward VI, Elizabeth, and the constitutions of 1604 reconfirmed this regulation. Such prescriptions and the models set by the leading public schools achieved an essential uniformity by mid-sixteenth century.[6]

At the university level the Oxford Reformers, a group of scholars aiming at the general reform of church and society as well as of education and aided by Henry VIII, had earlier been able to make substantial gains for the new learning. Lectures on Greek were read at Oxford in the late fifteenth century; but neither Oxford nor Cambridge made official provision for humanistic studies until the early sixteenth century, when Erasmus began to present the new learning at Jesus College at Cambridge.

Soon the first avowedly humanistic colleges recognizing Greek and Hebrew were founded. Erasmus taught at Cambridge for four years from 1511 on, and Vives taught at Oxford in 1522. Even greater advances toward humanistic studies were made at Cambridge when Aristotle began to be studied from the commentaries of the humanists, Agricola and Ramus, rather than from the glosses of the medieval scholastics. Thus humanism steadily gained ground in the subjects of both the trivium and the quadrivium. The founding of Trinity College, Cambridge, in 1546, with its several fellows in Greek along with the regius professorships in Greek, Hebrew, and civil law, appointed earlier by Henry VIII, finally set the seal upon the transition from the medieval to the humanistic tradition.

This meant a decline in the importance of logic and a reemphasis upon grammar and rhetoric. In the hands of the humanists, grammar lost its purely medieval aspect, expanded to include the grammar and literature of classical Latin, Greek, Hebrew, and other Oriental languages. Rhetoric also began to receive the greater attention characteristic of the humanists' interest in the style and form of written and oral speech. Under the influence of Ramus, logic was simplified and freed of the complexities of scholastic treatment. As the classics became "polite letters" particularly suitable for the education of a gentleman, the Renaissance tended to reaffirm the literary conception of a liberal education, which the Hellenistic Greeks and Romans had praised so highly.

This humanistic interest was associated with religious sectarianism as the various colleges at Oxford and Cambridge took sides in the Reformation conflict of religious ideologies. Humanistic and classical studies were used as new weapons with which to fight old theological battles. Some colleges became Anglican, and others remained Catholic. When Catholics were excluded by Queen Elizabeth in 1575, the contests were then fought between Anglican Protestants and Puritan Protestants. The Puritans

---

[6]For a useful brief summary see Mark H. Curtis, "Education and Apprenticeship," in Allardyce Nicoll (ed.), *Shakespeare in His Own Age,* Cambridge University Press, London, 1964, pp. 57-66; for a detailed survey, see T. W. Baldwin, *William Shakspere's Small Latine and Lesse Greeke,* University of Illinois Press, Urbana, 1944.

went mainly to Cambridge, where endowments had been made favorable to them, especially at St. John's College, Emmanuel College, and Sidney Sussex College. These colleges became the avowed centers of a militant Puritanism, eventually training many of the people who went to America in the seventeenth century. Theology remained the predominant study at the highest levels aimed at training clergymen who would be well versed in Latin, Greek, Hebrew, and the art of disputation so that they could go forth and defend their religious doctrines against all assailants.

The system of college instruction as opposed to university lectures was more firmly embedded than ever by the Reformation emphasis upon mental, moral, and religious discipline. The college retained its communal aspects, marked by the hall and quadrangle, in which masters and students lived and studied together. The continued enforcement of celibacy upon masters and tutors also helped to preserve the communal life of the English college long after the Reformation had seen its disappearance in German universities. The English college with its discipline and prescribed curriculum provided the model for development of higher education in America, Harvard being a virtual copy of one of the colleges at Cambridge.

The principal ingredients of the liberal-arts course consisted of (1) the medieval liberal arts (grammar, rhetoric, logic, arithmetic, geometry, astronomy, but no music); (2) the philosophy of Aristotle (ethics, politics, physics, and metaphysics); and (3) the Renaissance studies of classical humanism (Latin, Greek, Hebrew, and rhetoric). The Reformation made all these studies more or less subservient to religious and sectarian interests, as well as to the demands of a political state closely allied with the church. Since each of these historic traditions was based upon a belief that liberal education should consist essentially of linguistic and literary studies, the Reformation educators assumed that the best way to develop a man of action was through the study of books. (The courtly academies were a denial of this principle, but they did not receive much acceptance in England.)

There is general agreement that royal and secular direction of the universities increased during the middle decades of the sixteenth century at the expense of clerical and religious influence. There is also general agreement that enrollments began to increase markedly in the 1560s, reaching a peak around 1583, and that the students came increasingly from the upper classes. But there is considerable disagreement concerning how fundamentally the universities were changed and what role they played in society during the century from 1560 to 1650.

In 1533 the Act for Restraint of Appeals gave full authority over the universities to the crown, removing the papacy from any jurisdiction. In 1571 the universities were designated as legal corporations by authority of the royal charters granted to them by the crown and Parliament. These acts, one under Henry VIII and the other under Elizabeth, symbolized the transfer of ultimate authority from the Roman church to the English crown. Politically, this meant that the vice-chancellors were to be responsible to chancellors who were lay statesmen (rather than clerical) and that public boards of visitors would be inspecting the loyalty of teachers to the crown and to the Church of England. Academically, it meant that the humanistic and Anglican slant to the curriculum would be speeded in the effort to oust or play down the Aristotelian and the medieval curriculum. For example, Thomas Cromwell's visitors in 1535 required that daily public lectures be offered in Latin and Greek, that lectures on the Bible replace scholastic lectures, that degrees in canon law be discontinued, that all students be taught the liberal arts, and that the philosophy of Aristotle and Duns Scotus be balanced by the humanist teachings of Agricola and Melanchthon.[7] When Henry VIII endowed regius professorships at Cambridge in Greek, Hebrew, civil law, divinity, and medicine in 1540 and when the statutes of Trinity College, Cambridge, were authorized by the visitors in 1549, the imprint of the humanist tradition was sealed by royal authority. The signal had been given that university education henceforth was to be regarded as the prime road for advancement of the upper classes as well as the lower classes, a road to be travelled to the secular professions and public services, as well as to a clerical career. The upper classes had finally got the humanists' message. Now that the *studia humanitatis cum pietas litterata* had been widely accepted in the grammar schools and universities, they would become in effect a prerequisite for achievement in church and state, in profession and trade, in city and country during the coming hundred years.

By 1550 the humanist influence had established the classics as the heart of English secondary and higher education. It helped to establish Latin grammar schools as preparatory institutions for further study in the universities. Above all, humanism established the tradition that no person might be counted as truly educated who had not had training in the classics. This was, to the humanist, the mark of the scholar and the gentleman. The aim of education had been broadened to include preparation for service in the secular life of the times, in the state as well as in the church, in the social life of the nobleman and gentry, and in the work of the merchant. But, for any of these purposes, the humanist insisted that the common background of the truly educated and cultured person must be knowledge and training in the classics. The great tradition in English education had been established by the joint effort of humanist, crown, gentry, and religious reformer.

The Educational Explosion

In the hundred years from the mid-sixteenth to the mid-seventeenth centuries the basic structure of a national system of education took recognizable form in England, a structure that was to be generally maintained until the nineteenth century. At the same time, a revolution of major proportions produced the highest rate of literacy in the general population and the greatest proportion of young men attending university-level education in any society in history up to that point. These structural and functional developments together helped to produce the social and cultural conditions which propelled England into the age of modernity ahead of other nations.

Two key generalizations concerning the period 1550-1660 have been made by Lawrence Stone. One is the factual expansion of schooling:

> . . . educational facilities at all levels increased at a tremendous pace during
> this period. It has been estimated that by 1660 up to 30% of all adult males
> were literate; that there was a school for every 4,400 persons (which may be

---

[7]For details see Simon, op. cit., chap. 7.

compared to the 1870 figure of one for every 23,700); and that the proportion of the male population undergoing higher education was larger than at any time before the Second World War.[8]

The other generalization attributes much of English florescence to organized schooling:

> ... the extraordinary increase in quantity at every level ... [wrought] a change of such dimensions as to create an entirely new intellectual environment. ... the cultural achievements of the age of Bacon, Raleigh, Ben Jonson and Donne are extraordinary by any standards, and cannot be entirely unrelated to the formal educational background from which they emerged.
> ... it must be assumed that the formal educational system, whatever its admitted deficiencies, was to no small degree responsible for this remarkable cultural efflorescence.[9]

The outline on page 266 of the hierarchy of classes as they existed in sixteenth and seventeenth century England, illustrates the evident point that the florescence of which Stone speaks applies largely to the upper classes of nobility and gentry, and somewhat less to the urban middle classes and the growing class of free men in both city and country. So that while we may say that organized education was becoming increasingly available to the upper 50 percent of the population in England during the early modern period, it is clear that it does not include the lower half of the population comprising the working classes. But still, the gains were remarkable. They undoubtedly helped prepare England to become the first nation to lead the West toward modern civilization. The gentry and the urban middle classes with their educational advantages supplied much of the modernizing leadership which spearheaded England's seventeenth-century revolution and briefly gained power in 1649.[10]

It will be seen at once from an inspection of Figure 8.2 that England's seventeenth-century educational structure was not particularly democratic in the modern sense of that term. Probably half of all boys and a vast majority of girls did not attend a formal school at any time during their lives. The organized institutions varied widely in their arrangements for admission, selection, or "graduation" of their students. In comparison with a modern, centralized, national school system, England's seventeenth-century system was loosely organized indeed. But it had much more coherence and was bound together by more common expectations than has often been assumed.

Petty schools. In this period English elementary schools, commonly called petty schools, spread widely through the rural sections of England, in the parishes and villages, as well as in the towns and cities. The growing economic prospects of the

[8] Marius B. Jansen and Lawrence Stone, "Education and Modernization in Japan and England," *Comparative Studies in Society and History,* vol 9, p. 216, January 1967.

[9] Ibid., p. 218.

[10] See C. E. Black, *The Dynamics of Modernization, a Study in Comparative History,* Harper & Row, New York, 1966, chaps. 3 and 4.

yeoman farmer helped this process along. They joined with gentry and urban classes in contributing funds for endowed schools to give free instruction to village and town children. Typically, the petty school took children (often girls as well as boys) from about the ages of four years to eight years and gave them two or three years of basic instruction in English literacy. They were vernacular schools concentrating on reading, spelling, and writing of the alphabet and single sentences in English. The instruments were a hornbook, containing the alphabet, syllables, and a prayer, the catechism, a religious primer, and selections from the Bible. The teacher was the local curate, a clerk, a poorly paid schoolmaster, or even a housewife in her home. The petty schools were the seventeenth-century Protestant versions of the medieval chantry schools, now stressing English learning and now much more available than ever before. The evidence for their availability stems from the conclusion that by 1640 half of the adult males in favored towns and cities and a third in villages were literate.[11] Most petty schools were separate institutions, albeit small and poor, but many grammar schools began to institute classes for the *petties* to give the English rudiments to boys who had not already acquired them.

Social reform, as well as religious reform, was a prime motivation for the spread of schools. The incidence of poverty, vagrancy, thievery, begging, prostitution, and rioting in English towns and villages was alarming indeed. Then, as now, many humanitarians turned to education and the schools for aid. They argued that national backwardness and social unrest were intimately connected with ignorance, and therefore education could aid in the cure. Curtis quotes an Elizabethan schoolmaster on the "benefits of learning:"

> Knowest thou not what profit and commodity learning bringeth to the children of Adam? Look upon the barbarous nations, which are without it; compare their estate with ours; and thou shalt see what it is to be learned, and what to be unlearned. They for want of learning can have no laws, no civil policy, no honest means to live by, no knowledge of God's mercy and favour, and consequently no salvation nor hope of comfort. We by the means of learning have and may have all these things. Therefore in that thou dost enjoy thy lands and livings, in that thou mayst procure such things as thou wantest, it is the benefit of learning. In that thou sleepest quietly in thy bed, in that thou travelest safely on the way, in that thieves and enemies do not spoil thine house and household, kill thy children, take away thy life, it is the benefit of learning. Nay, go further. In that thou thyself runnest not to the like excess of iniquity— art no thief, no murderer, no adulterer, it is the benefit of learning. Dost thou not here see what a plentiful harvest of all good fruits learning bringest forth?[12]

After a boy had learned his English letters he was then ready for more schooling. At that point came a kind of parting of the ways which can perhaps be described as follows. He could go on to a further education which was academically oriented to the

---

[11] See Lawrence Stone, "The Educational Revolution in England, 1560-1640," *Past and Present*, no. 28, pp. 42-44, July 1964.

[12] Curtis, op. cit., p. 55.

Exhibit 8.1   Class Structure in Seventeenth-Century England

I. *Upper Classes* (the aristocracy; the "Gentle"—about 2% of the population)
   A. *Nobility* (titular peerage; great landowners—60 to 100 members)
      1. Duke
      2. Marquis
      3. Earl
      4. Viscount
      5. Baron
   B. *Upper Gentry* (large landowners and proprietors)
      6. Baronet
      7. Knight
   C. *Lower Gentry*
      8. Squire—landed proprietors; justices of the peace
      9. Gentleman (armigeral gentry)—Small landed proprietors—Highly trained professionals (clergy, lawyers, physicians, public officials, university dons)

II. *Lower Classes* (the "Ungentle"—about 98% of the population)
   D. *Urban Middle Class*
      10. Merchants
      11. Bankers
      12. Large employers
      13. Urban wealthy
      14. *Bourgeoisie*
   E. *Free Classes*
      15. Yeomen, small landowners, freeholders
      16. Self-employed shopkeepers or tradesmen
      17. Clerks
      18. Skilled artisans and craftsmen
   F. *Working Classes* (about 50% of the population)
      19. Unskilled wage earners or hired laborers on farm, in mine, factory, or shop
      20. Propertyless cottagers, renters, or tenant farmers
      21. Household servants
      22. Vagrants

classical humanities and which made possible a higher education, or he could go on to a practice-oriented education which would prepare him more directly for a job. The main agencies of academic education were the Latin grammar schools and the two universities. The main instruments of the practice-oriented education were the English schools, the system of apprenticeship, and the so-called "Third University."

Latin Grammar Schools. We said earlier that England developed the structure of a national system of education and that an educational revolution was in the making in

Figure 8.2　England's National System of Education (1550-1650)

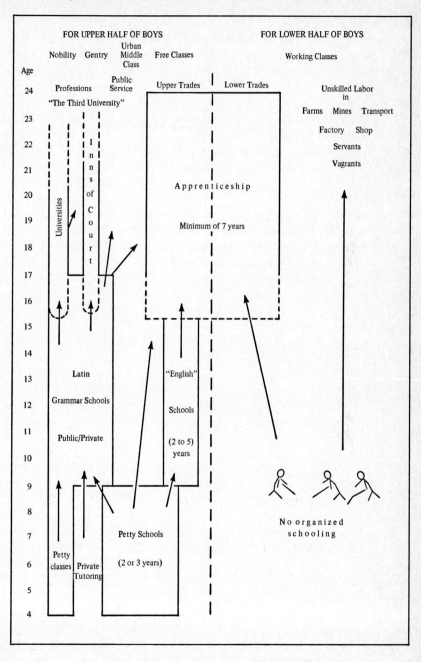

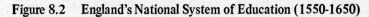

the late sixteenth and early seventeenth centuries. Such a statement can be misleading if the term *national* is viewed as implying a centrally planned or administered system, or if *revolution* is taken to imply a populist or mass uprising. Remember that *national* meant that ultimate authority was shifted from religious and clerical control to civil authority, both national and local or municipal, and that the revolution meant that access to education was greater than ever before in history, not that universal education was achieved or even attempted. Indeed, at the time that literacy was increasing, and larger numbers of boys were attending grammar schools and universities, the main impact of the educational system during Elizabethan times was conservative; that is, it tended to maintain the established order and distinctions among the classes. If the upper classes had *not* sent their sons to the schools and if the working classes *had* flooded into the schools, then a true revolution would have been in the making.

As it was, literacy may have reached from a third to a half of English boys in this period, but it can be assumed that fewer than one-third of the age group, nine to sixteen, actually went on to a grammar school education. What that figure actually was can probably not be determined with very much accuracy. It may have been one boy in eight or ten. In any case, it has been estimated that by 1660 there was one grammar school for every 4,400 persons in the total population.[13] This is fairly revolutionary when it is realized that the comparable figure in the mid-nineteenth century was one to every 23,750 person. To achieve such a state of affairs in mid-seventeenth century meant a vast investment of money and resources in endowed grammar schools, as well as a great outpouring of entrepreneurial effort by private teachers who made a business out of teaching school for a fee.

A word about the distinction between the two. By and large a "public school" was one which had been chartered or authorized by a public authority. It was constituted as a corporate body with a board of trustees or managers who held the property in trust and to which endowments could be given. The corporate body employed the teachers and gave general supervision in school affairs, using the income for the benefit of the school and not as income or profit for themselves. Such a public school was also theoretically open to all who could meet its standards and pay its fees, although some became known as socially exclusive and others as catering particularly to the "free" students who came on scholarships.

In contrast, a private school was one which had no such public authorization or corporate existence. It simply consisted of the teacher who sought or accepted students on a tuition or fee-paying basis. It therefore had no scholarships or free places, or provisions for continuity beyond the life and activity of the teacher or the proprietor. Small, unendowed, private grammar schools were scattered all over the country, even in small villages. They added their bit to meet the desire for advancement in the respectable trades as well as for university preparation leading to the professions and public service. They were responsive to the growth of a professional middle class. For a time they may have provided as many as half the entrants to the universities, although by the end of the seventeenth century the majority were coming from the free or public grammar schools.

[13] W. K. Jordan, *Philanthropy in England, 1480-1660,* Allen and Unwin, London, 1959, pp. 278-291.

Oxford and Cambridge. Perhaps the most extraordinary aspect of the educational explosion of the century we are considering was the "invasion" of the two universities, which of course meant Oxford and Cambridge.[14] There was an initial boom in the 1560s and 1570s, then a lull of twenty years, and another upsurge in the first forty years of the seventeenth century. In the mid-seventeenth century the number of students was higher than it was to be for another 200 years. It is estimated that about 2.5 percent of all seventeen-year-old males entered the universities in the 1630s. This proportion was not equalled again until the 1930s and was not surpassed until after World War II.

Historians have differed about the significance of this boom in higher education. Kenneth Charlton and Joan Simon find it to be interesting but by and large of only moderate and temporary importance. Charlton admits that large numbers of upper-class young men poured into the universities, but he finds that they did not stay very long, did not ordinarily take degrees, were not very serious about their studies, and did not mix with their inferiors. In general the universities continued in their basically medieval paths, more or less indifferent to the modern study of science or technology.[15]

A quite different and much more optimistic view of the role of Oxford and Cambridge in this period is given by Mark H. Curtis.[16] He finds that they changed markedly in content, in method, and in social role. From having been training grounds for the clergy they became training schools for the lay professions and public bureaucracies. Instead of appealing largely to those young men who needed scholarship support in their journey to the church, the universities began to attract significant numbers of upper-class youth. The social composition at Oxford showed an average of about 50 percent gentlemen, 41 percent plebian, and 9 percent clergy in the years from 1515 to 1639. Perhaps the proportion of gentlemen is a bit high, but figures for St. John's College, Cambridge, show nearly 40 percent gentry, nearly 40 percent artisans, shopkeepers, and plebian, and more than 20 percent professional and clerical.[17] The point is that a wider spectrum of social classes was represented than at any prior period in history.

Curtis argues also that the liberal arts curriculum of the universities was broadened to include a fair proportion of the developing mathematics and science of the day, modern history and geography, modern foreign languages, and modern authors. The group of scientists who formed the Royal Society met at Wadham College, Oxford, in 1662. The college's warden, John Wilkins, had written "The Discovery of a World in the Moone" in 1637, just 332 years before man made his first direct contact with the moon. To be sure, scientific subjects were not prescribed in the statutes which continued to be highly humanistic, but Curtis argues that the growing emphasis upon tutorial instruction in the colleges rather than upon university lectures enabled the tutors to respond to their students' interests in public affairs and modern

[14] For excellent short analyses, see Stone, op. cit.; and Lawrence Stone, *The Crisis of the Aristocracy, 1558-1641,* Oxford University Press, London, 1965, chap. 12.

[15] See Charlton, op. cit., chap. 5.

[16] See Mark H. Curtis, *Oxford and Cambridge in Transition, 1558-1642,* Clarendon Press, Oxford, 1959.

[17] See Stone, *The Educational Revolution in England,* loc. cit.

studies by extrastatutory reading and tutoring. In their ever-growing reliance upon the teaching of undergraduates and decline in professional studies in law, medicine, and theology the English universities turned more and more to the humanistic liberal arts as the corpus of knowledge needed by the educated young man for a career in public affairs and the civil service. The ideal of the generalist rather than the professional specialist was indeliby embedded in English society and English university education from this period forward.

Even though Curtis may be too optimistic concerning the extent to which the universities promoted social mobility, commonality among social classes, and the practical studies of relevance to the social problems of the day, I believe that Lawrence Stone correctly assesses the consequences of university expansion to be of fundamental importance in the intellectual and cultural revolutions that marked seventeenth-century England:

> It was precisely between 1590 and 1690 that England boiled and bubbled with new ideas as no other country in Europe. What is so striking about this period is . . . the widespread public participation in significant intellectual debate on every front. . . . This was the great age of theological disputation conducted at a high level of sophistication and followed by a large and passionate audience; of wide-ranging political theorizing, democratic, authoritarian, even proto-Marxist, but all involving a rethinking of conventional assumptions about the nature of the State; of a reexamination of a host of social problems from the role of women to the merits of enclosures, from censorship to the duel; of a major conceptual breakthrough in scientific thought; of the invention of the modern theatre; of the development of new techniques and standards for historical research; of the foundation of England's great tradition of antiquarian and topographical scholarship; and of the application of statisfical method to create the new discipline of Political Arithmetic. If one allows a lag of about twenty years, both the beginning and the end of this age of unprecedented intellectual vitality coincided fairly closely with the rise and fall of the graph of higher education. It is tempting to think that the relationship was something more than a coincidence.[18]

Practice-oriented Education

Our knowledge of the practice-oriented means of education whereby Englishmen in the hundred-year period from 1550 to 1650 sought and obtained knowledge they deemed directly relevant to their careers or to their aspirations for economic improvement is considerably more sketchy than that relating to the grammar schools and universities. In part this is due to the less well organized character of such education and the consequent scarcity of records; in part it is due to the long tradition of educators and historians who felt that such knowledge and such activity was somehow not really education, at least it was not formal schooling. But it now seems evident that England developed in this period a remarkable network of private English schools that were directly oriented to teaching practical subjects, a formal system of apprenticeship operating under public authorities and involving some emphasis upon literacy

---

[18] Ibid., p. 80.

education as well as technical skill, and an opportunity for acquiring professional training as well as technical knowledge in organized institutions in the city of London, a development sometimes referred to as England's "Third University."

"English Schools." Giving a name to the practice-oriented schools of early modern England is historically gratuitous, for they had little in common with the grammar schools. The most distinctive thing is that they were regularly taught in the English language, whereas the grammar schools existed for the purpose of teaching students to read, write, and speak Latin. If it did not sound a bit pretentious, these might well be called prototechnical schools. They were the direct ancestors of modern technical schools, but they were less systematic because the fields of technical knowledge were themselves just being systematized and regularized. This was an age of extremely rapid technical improvisation, and the thirst for knowledge about it was enormous. A great outpouring of manuals and self-help books written in English tried to meet the demand. One of the best discussions of this phenomenon is that by Kenneth Charlton.[19]

Charlton makes much of the fact that this practice-oriented education was informal in character. By that he means that it was not carried on in the regularly constituted public educational system, but rather by the publication of books and manuals that were read by persons who wanted to use the information. I grant that the reading of self-help manuals is informal education, but Charlton also indicates that many of the authors he cites were also teachers and conducted private schools. I would argue that regular instruction in private schools by a teacher who advertises for and accepts students on a fee-paying basis should qualify as a part of organized or formal education. Therefore I have used the term *English schools* or prototechnical schools to sum up a widely ranging and diffuse, but nevertheless very significant, development.

One of the most common types of school had to do with teaching the subjects most pertinent to rapidly expanding commerce and trade. These included arithmetic, Italian double entry bookkeeping, accounts, letter writing, and useful knowledge about currency, exchange, weights and measures, credit, and the like. Such subjects had long been taught in the municipal schools of Italy, Holland, Flanders, and northern Germany. England did not follow their example by setting up municipal schools, but it was widely recognized that Dutch prowess in international commerce was related to their mercantile schools. So private schools appeared in substantial numbers in London and other commercial centers. Merchants, aspiring merchants, and upward-bound craftsmen found such knowledge very practical indeed.

Another fertile ground for technical instruction was the art of navigation and the mathematical sciences that were required for pilots and seamen. Here the examples of Italian, Spanish, and Portuguese schools, as well as Dutch, proved to be useful. Not only were schools set up in London and in other port cities specifically to train pilots, but special mathematical lectureships were established in London for systematic instruction on a high level and aimed at the technical and practical applications of astronomy and geometry to navigation. Somewhat less common but also involving the application of mathematics to practical affairs was instruction in surveying. Texts and

[19] Charlton, op. cit., chaps. 8, 9.

manuals were written for agriculture, but even though the proposals for agricultural schools and colleges grew more insistent in the middle of the seventeenth century, no such institutions seem to have been established.

Perhaps the best known institution that had a practical orientation was Christ's Hospital founded in 1552 under Edward VI to try to deal with the problems of children bereft of homes, family, and educational opportunity. It took in orphans and poor children of free men and gave them a home. It also maintained a petty school and a grammar school to enable them to find a useful and productive place in society. Above all, it provided instruction in practical writing, arithmetic, commercial accounts, and other subjects that would enable the boys to enter the world of trade and commerce with some educational skills. Christ's Hospital provided a supply of merchant's apprentices to the East India Company when it began operations in India in the early sixteenth century.[20] This is an early example of the interlocking relationships of social change at home, the problems of urbanization, the humanitarian spirit, the commercial enterprises overseas, and education. These forces were to continue to interact upon one another as the Western nations reached out to the rest of the world in the succeeding four centuries.

Apprenticeship.   While the English schools approached the problem of training for practical life through a kind of formal school that taught subjects that would be of direct use in later employment, the English also faced the problem of education and employment from the other side. They instituted a national policy with regard to apprenticeship, formalizing induction into the trades, with literate learning to be involved, when necessary, with the primary goal of direct training for effective functioning as a skilled member of the trade.

The Elizabethan Statute of Artificers in 1563 was a ground-breaking move to set up national standards of skill in the trades, taking much control over apprentices away from the guilds and putting it into the hands of civil magistrates. It stemmed in part from mercantilist efforts to maintain a healthy agrarian sector of the economy as the shift began to take place from agriculture to commerce and urban life; in part to keep laborers down on the farm and to maintain standards in the city trades; and in part to stave off the social anarchy that could arise from peasant revolts and unrest as small landholders or tenants were thrown out of work. The statute provided that any person between the ages of sixteen and sixty not otherwise employed could be compelled to work on the land for a year at a time, except for apprentices and students in school or university. Exemption from the "farm draft" for students was a long-standing arrangement.

Apprenticeship was thus expected to be the common method of entrance upon a job for nearly half of the population, excepting professional careers requiring a substantial academic type of education or for unskilled jobs requiring no education. (See Figure 8.2) The Statute of Artificers set uniform standards for apprenticeship for some thirty trades, requiring a minimum of seven years, and requiring that the period

[20] Ralph Braibanti (ed.), *Asian Bureaucratic Systems Emergent from the British Imperial Tradition,* Duke University Press, Durham, N.C., 1966, p. 89.

of apprenticeship extend to age twenty-four. Most apprentices began their service around the age of sixteen. Property qualifications were required of the apprentices' families for entrance to some of the higher prestige trades (merchants, goldsmiths, clothiers, and the like), but not for more manual workmen like carpenters, bricklayers, and smiths. The obligation between apprentice and master was a mutual one sealed in a contract or indenture in which the master agreed to teach the skills and secrets of the trade while the apprentice agreed to serve faithfully the master, usually living in his house and benefitting from his home life as well as the close supervision by individual contact, especially helpful in the midst of the sprawling and brawling city of London. The trades, of course, varied, as did the competence of the master in the amount of literate learning that was required or could be taught. But that such teaching must have been taken seriously is indicated by the fact that Edmund Coote wrote a book entitled *The English Scholemaister* aimed to assist those masters who were faced with the teaching task.[21]

Even though the apprenticeship system did much to enable England's economy to move from an agricultural base to commercial capitalism, the conditions of subsistence for those in the towns, as well as in the rural regions, proved to verge on the desperate for vast numbers of Englishmen. Reacting to this situation, the government enacted a series of poor laws, particularly those of 1598 and 1601, which tried to bring order to earlier legislation. In general, the welfare state principles of modern times were enunciated with respect to the poor who had not been able to survive the ravages of depression, war, enclosure, epidemic, or hard-core poverty. The local parishes were charged with the obligation to care for the poor and to levy taxes for such purposes. The Poor Law of 1601 authorized the churchwardens and overseers of the poor to enforce compulsory apprenticeship for poor boys and girls between the ages of five and fourteen and continuing to age twenty-four for men and age twenty-one for women. While the poor laws undoubtedly produced benefits in comparison to the desperation of vagabondage, they also had their darker side. Employers exploited them as a means of obtaining cheap labor from those who could not help themselves.

The "Third University."   At the peak of the practice-oriented structure of education is what has been called "The Third University of England," defined by Sir George Burk in his treatise of 1615 as "the Foundations of all the Colledges, Auncient Schools of Priviledge, and of Houses of Learning and Liberall Arts, within and about the most Famous Cittie of London." In thus calling the City of London England's third university, Sir George was not using the term university precisely, but he was making a telling point about the wide opportunities for formal teaching and learning that existed outside the degree-granting structures of Oxford and Cambridge. And much of the opportunity if not most of it was indeed related to the newer and more practical fields of knowledge for which there was a great thirst and which the proper universities could not regard as legitimate subjects of university study. Curtis lists these as "surgery, hydrography, navigation, cosmography, various foreign languages, calli-

[21] For an especially useful short description, see Curtis, "Education and Apprenticeship," p. 66-70.

graphy, brachygraphy (shorthand), stenography, military arts, dancing, printing, heraldry, art of revels, art of memory, and alchemy."[22] He adds such modern foreign languages as Italian, Spanish, French, Dutch, Polish, Persian, Turkish, Russian, and Arabic. The exact locale of the teaching of such subjects is not wholly clear, but the presumption is that private-venture schools of the type we have mentioned provided the most ready source.

What is more clear is that an increasing number of formal public lectureships were established by endowments and benefactions and often administered by corporate bodies established for the purpose. Among these were the Lumleian lectureship in surgery and the Goulstonian lectureship in pathology under auspices of the Royal College of Physicians; the Smith lectureship in mathematics; and the very widely known professorships of Gresham College, which almost paralleled the liberal arts and the professional faculties of the orthodox universities—rhetoric, geometry, astronomy, music, law, medicine, and divinity. The competence of the scholars who held these lectureships easily rivalled in quality much of the work conducted at Oxford and Cambridge. Thus they were often far above the standard of learning often associated with the terms *adult education* or *self-help education.* They did much more. By linking the practical with the academic they helped to prepare the English mind for the modern world, indeed to propel it into it.

Perhaps the best known and probably the most influential components of England's "Third University" were the Inns of Court, the principal centers for the professional study of secular law in England. They had grown out of the custom of informal living together adopted by the practitioners of the common law when they came together to attend the fairly brief sessions of the king's court held in London four times a year. Gradually, they established four major inns where they could room and work together near the courts. These were Gray's Inn, Lincoln's Inn, the Inner Temple, and the Middle Temple. By the end of the fourteenth century they began to take on the task of initiating younger members into the profession in a professional system of training which borrowed the concept of personal instruction from the apprentice pattern and lectures and discussions from the collegiate academic ideal.[23] Charlton argues that by the end of the sixteenth century the quality of the training declined as the senior lawyers became too busy to attend to their teaching duties and the Inns became so popular that many young men attended rather more for the benefit of the free social life in London than for the serious business of professional preparation. Many attended the universities before they came to the Inns.

In any case, the Inns attracted a far larger proportion of young members of the nobility and gentry than of the urban commercial or professional classes. Stone estimates that four-fifths of all entrants to the Inns of Court between 1570 and 1630 were from the upper classes.[24] This was one more educational means by which the upper classes in the sixteenth and seventeenth centuries changed radically their

[22] Ibid., p. 71.

[23] For an excellent brief description of the Inns of Court, see Charlton, op. cit., chap. 6.

[24] Stone, "Educational Revolution," pp. 58-59.

intellectual and professional function in society and thus enabled themselves to maintain their role as a governing class in the centuries ahead.

Lawrence Stone makes the persuasive argument that the educational revolution in which the English upper classes engaged, from the petty school at the bottom to the universities and Inns of Court at the top, had two major political effects. In the short run, it enabled the gentry classes to compete more effectively with the nobility, and thus weakened the nobility in the decades before the civil war. But in the long run, as the peerage itself took part in the educational revolution, it in turn was enabled to survive as a ruling elite.[25] Thus, by not developing the kind of courtly academy which had been popular among the Italian, German, and French nobility and by not following the proposals of Sir Humphrey Gilbert, Thomas Starkey, or Nicholas Bacon that separate academies should be set up for the nobility, the English nobility strengthened rather than weakened itself between 1560 and 1660. That education, by being spread more extensively among the free classes from the artisans to the peerage, could serve to strengthen those groups that had access to it was a lesson that eventually was learned in the nineteenth century when education was finally extended to the working classes too.

C. THE DISPERSION OF ANGLO-PROTESTANT EDUCATION TO AMERICA

In an especially evocative phrase Carl Bridenbaugh speaks of "The First Swarming of the English" to describe the outpouring of thousands of people from their homeland in England in the early seventeenth century to places as near as Ireland, Holland, and France, and as distant as India to the East, the island Indies to the West, and the shores of the North American continent.[26] The vast majority went to Virginia and to New England in the New World during the great migrations of the 1620s and 1630s. Bridenbaugh estimates that approximately 80,000 people (perhaps 2 percent of the total population of England, which was growing from 4,000,000 to 5,500,000) packed up and left England between 1620 and 1642, as many as 58,000 sailing across the Atlantic to find homes on such islands as Bermuda and Barbados, as well as on the mainland. Other West European nations were sending colonists to North America too, but up to 1650 the vast majority came from England.

The U.S. Census Bureau estimates that the total population of the mainland American colonies in 1650 was a little over 50,000.[27] They were distributed as follows:

[25] Stone, *Crisis of the Aristocracy*, p. 722.

[26] Carl Bridenbaugh, *Vexed and Troubled Englishmen, 1590-1642*, Oxford University Press, New York, 1968, chap. 11.

[27] U.S. Bureau of the Census, *Historical Statistics of the United States, Colonial Times to 1957*, Government Printing Office, Washington, D.C., 1960, p. 756.

NEW ENGLAND		SOUTHERN		MIDDLE	
Massachusetts	14,037	Virginia	18,731	New York	4,116
Plymouth	1,566	Maryland	4,504	Delaware	185
Connecticut	4,139				
New Hampshire	1,305				
Maine	1,000				
Rhode Island	785				
Totals	22,832		23,235		4,301

Of this total 1,600 are estimated to be Negroes, distributed with approximately 400 in New England, 500 in New York, 400 in Virginia, and 300 in Maryland. Inasmuch as the vast majority of the 4,300 people in the Middle colonies were not English (Dutch, Swedish, French), this means that approximately 44,000 out of a total 50,000 were English, divided almost evenly between the colonies of New England and the Chesapeake region.

The outward trek from England began slowly in the first decade of the seventeenth century with the forming of the London Company to stimulate colonization of Virginia, but the going was very slow until the accumulating social ferment began to boil over in the late 1620s. Everything seemed to be wrong at home—depression, epidemics, crop failures, royal attacks upon Parliament, and Archbishop Laud's religious persecution of the Puritans. In contrast, the glowing reports of new lands and new hopes began to sound better and better. Coupled with these, a notable company of Puritan leaders began to add a deeply felt religious drive to all the others; here was man's best hope to establish the Lord's society upon earth.

The chief motive for the Puritans was far less focused upon lucrative trade than it was for those who were attracted to the Caribbean islands or to the Chesapeake plantations. They were apparently devoid of the desire for military conquest that prompted the Spanish in Central and South America. This fact produced a remarkable difference that eventually had fundamental significance for education. Bridenbaugh puts it this way:

> The exodus of the English Puritans to New England, 1629-42, was, and still is, unique in the annals of migration. . . .
> The most striking fact about this remarkable movement is that, once it got under way, by dint of able leadership, it quickly generated a dynamic momentum of its own. Here was no artificially stimulated, haphazard outpouring of individual Englishmen to serve mercantile ends. The massive religious concern of the English people, and of the Puritans in particular, impelled these emigrants to abandon England to save their souls; only secondarily did economic or social considerations figure in their decisions. A majority of the rank and file, as well as the leaders, believed firmly that they had discovered the Northwest Passage to Utopia where they could be "merry in the Lord" and eventually attain everlasting salvation.[28]

[28] Bridenbaugh, op. cit., pp. 434-435.

Of particular note is that the Puritans went to New England in groups—family groups and church congregation groups. Colonists that prayed together tended to stay together, to work together, to rule together, and to educate together. In contrast, the Caribbean and Chesapeake plantations sought to persuade and did persuade a high proportion of single men to go to work in the fields, and to earn their passage by indenturing themselves as servants or bonded farm hands. Bridenbaugh estimates that in 1625 one-third of the population of Virginia consisted of indentured servants; by 1692 more than three-fourths in Virgina and Maryland were indentured. New England had its share, but far fewer in comparison with the family groups who came from a wide cross section of the English classes. Almost all were free men and free women, few from the nobility or upper gentry, and few from the lowest classes of farm hands, rural vagabonds, city rogues, or day laborers. They paid their own way. They came from the most populous sections of southeastern England, and they carried with them the educational traditions of the most advanced regions of town and city life in the England of the day.

All the evidence seems to point to the fact that the rate of literacy was even higher than in England and the proportion of university graduates was probably higher than in any other society in the world up to that time. It is estimated that there were 130 university graduates in New England in the 1640s. Of these, the vast majority (possibly ninety) were ministers. This could mean a ratio of something like 1 university graduate for every 100 to 200 people, perhaps 1 to every 40 or 50 families. When the much larger number who had attended grammar schools or English schools is added, the educational complexion of transplanted English society gave New England a basic head start over its sister colonies. Samuel Eliot Morison finds the high educational level of New England to be a significant factor in the earlier development of an active intellectual and cultural life as compared with the slower development in Virginia, Maryland, Bermuda, and Barbados.[29]

The American colonies as a whole may not have have been exactly "born free," but the New England colonies were certainly born well educated, and the other colonies lagged not far behind. Each segment of English society proceeded promptly to recreate on American shores much of the structure and form of the English strain of Western civilization which they represented. When these qualities were planted and nurtured in different settings they eventually produced the American variation of Western civilization. But the relatively high level of education among English colonists gave them the initial advantage in Anglicizing the other European colonies that dotted the American coastline.

In the process of civilizational transplanting, the motives that sent the English, Scottish, Dutch, Swedish, French, Germans, and other north Europeans to America were a result of the course of events in their homelands. Some came because of political or religious persecutions; others came in the hope of greater economic security than was possible at home; and still others came in a spirit of adventure, desperation, or compulsion. Some were sent out to serve the political and mercantile

[29] Samuel Eliot Morison, *The Intellectual Life of Colonial New England,* New York University Press, N.Y., 1936 (reprinted by Cornell University Press, Ithaca, N.Y., 1960, pp. 14-15).

purposes of the ruling classes at home, but, comparatively, the economic patterns of feudalism with their rigid class stratification never gained the firm foothold in the Anglo-Protestant colonies that characterized Latin-Catholic America. The soldier of fortune and the military adventurer were so rare that the North American colonies were spared much of the economic exploitation and military oppression that flourished in Central and South America.

Yet, curiously, the Latin-Catholics not only sent to America more military conquerors and economic exploiters but they also sent out more missionaries than did the Protestants. The Spanish missionaries, as we have seen in the prior chapter, constituted a vast educational instrument of the civilizing and Christianizing spirit that flowed out from Latin Europe in the sixteenth and seventeenth centuries. By comparison, the effort of the Protestants in America during the seventeenth century was feeble indeed. They, of course, did not have at hand anything like the well-organized associations of mendicant friars or Jesuits who had fanned out virtually around the entire world. Besides, they were not confronted with the enormous populations of settled Amerindians who had developed well-organized traditional civilizations of their own. And the Puritans, at least, came to America primarily to establish their own forms of civilization for themselves, not particularly or primarily to civilize the indigenous populations they found.

To be sure, the English crown proclaimed, as the Spanish and Portuguese had done, that the high purpose of colonization was to bring civility to the savages and barbarians of the New World. They urged their proprietors and colonists to Christianize the natives by conversion and by education. As early as 1617 James I encouraged the founding of schools for Indians in Virginia, and plans were even made for an Indian college to be established at Henrico, but the massacre of 1622 discouraged the idea in Virginia for decades to come.

In the middle of the century much greater success was achieved in New England, especially by Reverend John Eliot who preached to the Indians in their own language, established "praying towns" to bring European methods of agriculture and urban ways of life to the Indians, and of course brought literacy and education to them. But herein lay a basic handicap for the Protestants, and especially the Puritans. Whereas the Catholic missionaries would convert thousands of Indians by baptism and oral participation in the liturgy, the Puritans required enough literacy so that each individual could read the Bible for himself, either in English or in his own language. The Anglo-Protestant task of conversion thus had to be longer and more complicated than the Latin-Catholic task.

Even so, strenuous efforts were made by Eliot, Reverend Jonathan Mayhew, and a few others. The Puritan Parliament even went to the length of establishing in 1649 the Society for the Propagation of the Gospel in New England to assist Mayhew and Eliot in their good work with the Indians. By 1675 it is estimated that some 20 percent of the Indian population of New England had been Christianized (around 2,500 persons). An Indian school building had been built at Harvard, and a few Indian children attended the public schools of Massachusetts, as well as the schools in Eliot's praying towns. But again King Philip's war slowed down interest in 1675 in educating what had become a fearful enemy.

As with the blacks who were brought as slaves from Africa or the West Indies in the course of the seventeenth century, the major efforts at educating the Indians did not develop until the onset of the civilizing mission that swept through the Western societies, including America, from the beginning of the eighteenth century onward. (See Chapter 14.) The judgment of a report to the Virginia Company in 1622 was probably agreed to by all but the most zealous, tenacious, and persistent of the seventeenth-century advocates of bringing civility to the Indians:

> The way of conquering them is much more easie then of ciuilizing them by faire meanes, for they are a rude, barbarous, and naked people, scattered in small companies, which are helps to Victorie, but hinderances to Ciuilitie: Besides that, a conquest may be of many, and at once; but ciuility is in particular, and slow, the effect of long time, and great industry.[30]

It was all well and good for the gentle humanists like Erasmus, More, and Elyot, or their successors like Henry Peacham or Richard Braithwaite a hundred years later, to sit in their comfortable studies and write in elegant Latin or English about the way that a classical education could combine with gentle birth to form the characters of European aristocrats so that they would become wise and kind rulers. But the harsh realities of bringing such an education to the uncivil folk peoples on the frontier of the New World in an unfriendly, even brutal, environment were quite another matter. Even the connotation of the word *civility* used by the English to sum up the idea of establishing a political order based upon justice, reason, and compassion, was too gentle for the arduous process required in America, Africa, or Asia.

Once the wilderness was pushed back a little and the clear and present dangers surmounted for a while, then the regrouped forces of religious revival and humanitarian zeal could infuse a new and more vigorous spirit toward educating the "natives" around the world. In the eighteenth century even the words were to change; gentle "civility" became triumphant "civilization," the goal of the aggressive civilizing mission of the West.

Establishing a Religious Civil Society

The actual political institutions set up in New England in the early seventeenth century were a mixture of Calvin's theocratic conception of the state and the constitutional liberties being won by Englishmen in Parliament at home. The result was a covenant or compact theory of polity: the state was viewed as a gift of God by which men obeyed his command to establish a government on earth. Thus the state must be the protector and supporter of the church, to do its bidding and enforce its pronouncements. This theory, however, had to be reconciled with the fact that political authority flowed from the Crown.

The charter granted by the king to the Massachusetts Bay Company in 1629

---

[30] Edward Waterhouse, "A Declaration of the State of the Colony and. . . . A Relation of the Barbarous Massacre . . . ," (1622), Document no. 210, in Susan Myra Kingsbury (ed.), *The Records of the Virginia Company of London,* Government Printing Office, Washington, D.C., 1933, vol. 3, p. 557.

vested the government in a governor, a deputy governor, and the free men (stock-holders) of the company who elected the General Court, which exercised legislative functions of government. The Puritans quickly established a religious basis for this arrangement by passing laws that gave voting privileges only to those male persons who were church members as well as landowners. The estimate has been made that even in 1674 only about one-fifth of the men in the colony fulfilled these requirements for the suffrage. While there was no popular government in the modern democratic sense, the basis for representative government was present from the beginning. When Massachusetts was transformed into a royal province in 1691 and government vested in a governor appointed by the Crown, the religious qualification for voting was abolished, and only the property qualification remained.

In the course of the seventeenth century the English established hegemony over the Atlantic seaboard colonies. The Dutch West India Company, which sent over its first permanent settlement in 1630, directed the affairs of New Netherland from Holland. A Swedish trading company formed in 1624 sent settlers up and down the Delaware River from 1638 on. After mid-century, however, a second wave of colonization began to take place which, in the course of twenty to thirty years, began to change siginificantly the course of colonial development. In 1655 the Dutch governor of New Netherland wrested control of the Delaware from the Swedes, but in 1664 the English took over all of New Netherland and made it an English royal colony, with its mixture of Quakers, New England Puritans, French Huguenots, Swedes, Finns, Germans, Scots-Irish, and English.

When William Penn received a large grant of land from Charles II, his advertisements extolling the advantages of free government, economic opportunity, and religious freedom induced many to flock to Pennsylvania, beginning in 1681. Attracting 7,000 to 8,000 settlers by 1685, Pennsylvania rapidly became one of the most populous colonies, made up as it was of many different nationalities and religious sects. By 1700 not only Quakers but English, Welsh, German, French, and Dutch, each with their own distinctive religious beliefs, had poured into eastern Pennsylvania.

The London Company took the lead in settling Virginia for commercial purposes at a time when England very much needed raw materials. A governor and a council of wealthy families were set up soon after the London Company was formed in 1606-1607, and by 1619 a representative assembly called the House of Burgesses was established as well, consisting of two representatives from each county elected by the free (property-owning) citizens. Late in the century the Carolinas were established on a similar pattern. Maryland was founded by a grant of land to Lord Baltimore in 1634 as a haven for Catholics, but other colonists poured in so rapidly that by 1700 the Catholics were outnumbered by Puritan and Anglican settlers.

The political-religious events in England had much to do with stimulating emigration to the Anglican colonies of the South. Just as the Puritan exodus to New England had been accelerated by the persecution of Puritans by Archbishop Laud in the 1630s, so the establishment of the Puritan Commonwealth in 1649 tended to drive Anglicans and royalists to the southern and middle colonies during the 1650s. Likewise, the revocation of the Edict of Nantes in 1685 by Louis XIV in France enriched America by sending many French Huguenots to the middle colonies, and the Thirty Years' War in Germany (1618-1648) eventually sent many Germans to America hoping for a greater measure of religious tolerance.

In New England the land originally granted by the king to the Massachusetts Bay Company was in turn granted to groups of people who held much of it in common for joint use as pasturage and for other purposes. The farmers typically lived together near the meetinghouse, church, and school and went out to work their farms, which radiated from the population center. This provided a degree of community association not found in the same degree in the southern colonies. Similarly, such a compact social community became much more self-sufficient in providing its own food, clothing,and shelter. A variety of skilled workmen became an integral part of the town life, providing useful articles for other members of the community and giving a diversified character to New England economic life. It could thus support merchants, farmers, sailors, fishermen, shipbuilders, and a host of specialized workers. This reliance upon skilled labor rather than unskilled labor meant that slaves never became the economic asset in New England that they did in the South.

Two things should be noted concerning the population of seventeenth-century New England. One is that the whole spectrum of the class structure of society in England below the nobility and above the working classes (see Figure 8.1, p. 266) was transferred to New England. The other is that the beginnings of a more democratic society were evident in the policy of town making and land granting. The policy of granting free land to small holders so bolstered the free classes that a large share of economic democracy eventually provided a firm basis upon which later political and social democracy could be built.

These democratic tendencies, however, had to struggle hard against the privileges imported from England by the gentry and merchant classes, who had preferential status in the matters of voting, less severe punishments for minor and major offenses, and favored distinctions in matters of title, dress, and seating in church. These distinctions eventually led to a conflict between the agricultural interests of the backwoods farmers and the commercial interests of the towns, and between the skilled artisans and the merchants within the towns. In Virginia, the original population was similar in class structure to that of New England, except for the larger proportion of indentured servants. It was not until after 1680 that the introduction of tobacco led to the growth of the importation of Negro slaves from Africa, a fateful development for the future of the New as well as the Old World.

Following the patterns of church-state relations developed in Reformation Europe, most of the colonial legislatures instituted establishments of religion in America. This meant two things. First, it meant that the state gave financial support to a single, preferred church. This was done by levying taxes upon everyone and granting public lands to be used by the church to pay salaries of the established ministers, to erect church buildings, and to maintain church services.

An establishment of religion meant, secondly, that the state enforced by law the doctrines of the perferred church, requiring people to attend its public worship and prohibiting public worship according to any other religion. Those who persisted in holding or expressing dissenting views were subject to trial in civil courts and punishment by fine, jail, or torture. Dissenters were denied the right to vote or hold public office.

In New England, the Congregational Puritan form of church organization was established by law by the Massachusetts and Connecticut legislatures, and in fact if not by specific law in New Hampshire, but no church was established in Rhode Island. There, religious freedom was sturdily maintained by Roger Williams and his followers in line with the principles of separation of church and state expressed by the Anabaptist sects of Europe. Rhode Island thus became the principal haven for religious dissenters in New England, as Pennsylvania was in the Middle Colonies.

In the South the Church of England was from the first established in Virginia by the terms of the charter of 1607 to the London Company and by many subsequent laws promulgated under the company and by the legislature. Even so, it was difficult for the church to flourish in the early seventeenth century because the lack of towns, the sparse and dispersed population, the poor salaries paid to the clergy, and the primitive conditions of life made it hard to persuade able priests to leave their parishes in England. Although Maryland was first settled largely by Catholics, a law of toleration was passed in 1649 permitting trinitarian Christians to worship as they pleased, until the Church of England was established by law some half century later.

The general religious profile in the seventeenth-century colonies was thus mixed: established churches in New England and the South; considerable toleration in Rhode Island, Pennsylvania, and Delaware; and considerable uncertainty and change in New York, New Jersey, and Maryland. By 1700 nearly 300 churches had been established in the English colonies. Most of them were Calvinist (Congregational, Presbyterian, Dutch Reformed, and French Reformed).

Despite the sectarian and political quarrels that divided one group from another, the dominating world outlook among the colonists was, of course, basically Christian. Whether Catholic or Protestant, Calvinist or Lutheran, English or Dutch, church member or not, the prevailing atmosphere of belief and attitude was that of Christianity. Puritan and Quaker, separatist and Anglican could quarrel about the proper way to reach salvation, but they all agreed that salvation was important. They could disagree concerning the role of the clergyman in bringing the individual into proper relationship with God, but they all agreed that making one's peace with God was the prime purpose of life. The Calvinist may have emphasized total depravity a little more, and the Quaker may have stressed the "inner light" of conscience, but they both operated from a point of view that was generally at odds with the new philosophy of science that was developing in Western Europe.

The basic structure of the Christian tradition was reenforced in the New World with every shipload of colonists. They assumed, and were constantly reminded by their preachers and by easy-to-read devotional books that human nature was divided into a material and a spiritual element, the body partaking of nature and the soul linking man's spirit to the highest spirit of all. Calvinism was perhaps more gloomy and pessimistic than any other sect about the inherent depravity of human nature, but all Christian faiths put some stock in the fall of Adam and hence the need for men to seek forgiveness and grace by expressing faith in Christ's sacrifice. By exercising this godliness in their daily lives, they would be saved. Finally, it was assumed that all knowledge emanated from God and was implanted in man for his purposes. This meant that the highest type of knowledge was revealed to man through the Scriptures. Knowledge of lower nature was deemed important only as it revealed the superior nature of God and his handiwork. This traditional outlook on the world, on human nature, and on knowledge and learning dominated the education of seventeenth-century America.[31]

Some of the Puritan spokesmen who wrote for and about children took pains to emphasize that children, born in sin, must be taught to fear God, obey his command-ments, and submit to their parents' authority. One of the earliest catechisms designed especially for children was written by the Puritan divine, John Cotton, and entitled *Spiritual Milk for American Babes Drawn out of the Breasts of Both Testaments for their Souls Nourishment.* Cotton emphasized that, since children were infected with original sin and naturally inclined toward evil, they must be especially obedient to parents, teachers, ministers, magistrates, and all others in authority. They should pray constantly, repent their sins, attend church, learn their catechisms, and observe strict discipline in all that they did. Cotton even proposed that rebellious children, if sufficiently incorrigible, should be put to death.

One of the most elaborate Puritan statements of attitude toward children in the seventeenth century was a booklet written by Cotton Mather in 1699, entitled *A Family Well-Ordered.* The first part of the book told parents how they should bring up their children to be pious, to fear God, to pray, and to obey their elders. Parents must constantly be on the alert to keep their children under control, to rule them with an iron hand of authority, justice, and fear. If "charging them" to be good did not work, the rod should be vigorously applied. The second part was addressed to the children themselves, painting a vivid picture of the torments and punishments in store for the undutiful child in the endless darkness of eternal Hell. The dutiful child, on the other hand, could expect reasonable well-being if he behaved himself, gave proper reverence to God, and gave obedience and recompense to his parents.

It is no wonder that educational method should have relied so heavily upon instilling fear in children, demanding obedience, and resorting to strict discipline, physical as well as mental. An authoritarian age produced authoritarian education.

The Standing Order in Education

The pattern of institutions just described, often known collectively as the "standing order," was a complex arrangement serving the interests of the ruling groups who held political, economic, and religious power. Clearly, organized education in seventeenth-century America was shaped by the institutions and outlooks of the standing order. The main support for a state system of education was to be found in the authoritarian collectivism of Calvinist or Anglican America, rather than in the libertarian individu-alism of Rhode Island, where few steps were taken toward state promotion of education.

[31] For a particularly illuminating discussion of the devotional manuals and the role of family and clergy in colonial education, see Lawrence A. Cremin, *American Education: The Colonial Experience, 1607-1783,* Harper & Row, New York, 1970, especially chaps. 1, 4, and 5.

The principal impetus for organized education on the part of civil authorities arose in New England, where Calvinist ideals of religion and education prevailed. At first the initiative in establishing schools was taken by the various towns before the colonial legislatures added their authority to the process. As early as 1635 the town of Boston voted to establish a grammar school to be supported by private subscription and by income from a parcel of land set aside for this purpose by the town. Before the end of the century some thirty New England towns had made similar provisions for the establishment of schools; notable among those were Charlestown, Ipswich, Salem, Dorchester, New Haven, Hartford, Cambridge, and Roxbury. The principle was soon fairly well established in New England that the towns should not only take the initiative in seeing that schools were established but also take at least partial responsibility for supporting them. Financial support came from several sources: tuition from those parents who could afford it; rate bills levied on families in proportion to the number of children they sent to school and the amount of time spent there; income from town lands, fisheries, or tolls; fines and licenses; and property taxes.

The next step in civil control of schools came when the colonial legislatures stepped in to prod those towns which had failed to establish schools on their own initiative. The Massachusetts Bay Colony took the lead in this process in two school laws that had considerable influence upon other colonies. In the law of 1642, the state assumed the authority to tell town officials that they had the power to require parents to educate their children. The law did not establish schools, nor did it require the towns to establish schools. It did call for compulsory instruction of children by parents or masters. It set up the minimum essentials to be taught (reading of English, knowledge of the capital laws, the catechism, and apprenticeship in a trade). It gave the selectmen authority to see that the parents obeyed the law and to enforce the ruling by fines and compulsory apprenticeship.

Apparently, however, neither the parents nor the towns responded with enough alacrity to suit the General Court, for five years later another law was passed that went still further in establishing the authority of the state over education. In the law of 1647, the legislature required each town of 50 families to provide an elementary school teacher, and each town of 100 families to establish a Latin grammar school. The law made it legally permissible for towns to levy taxes for the support of such teachers and tried to give teeth to enforcement by levying fines upon towns that failed to live up to the provisions of the law. If parents would not attend to the instruction of their children, then teachers and schools must do so.

The state now asserted its right to require towns to establish schools and to delegate to civil authorities the right to manage, supervise, and control schools. As yet the principle of compulsory attendance at schools was not enunciated. Parents were still free to teach their own children, to hire tutors to teach them, or to send them to school, as they wished. The state was trying to make it more likely that children would actually receive instruction by making public instruction more easily available. In 1650 the colonial legislature of Connecticut passed a law like that of the Massachusetts law of 1647; New Haven followed suit in 1655. Similar developments took place in Dutch New Netherland where at least twelve towns had established their Calvinist schools by 1650.

What the New England colonies did was to combine (1) their Calvinist Puritan belief that education was required for the achievement of the true Christian commonwealth, and (2) the Anglican tradition that state control over the apprenticeship of poor children, as expressed in the Statute of Artificers of 1563 and the Poor Law of 1601, was necessary to protect the standing order from crime and disorder. The state in New England was establishing its right to require vocational education through compulsory apprenticeship at the same time that it required education in language and reading as the basic ingredients of civility.

In a more general sense, the New England colonies were reflecting the general expansion of education that marked England from the mid-sixteenth to the mid-seventeenth centuries. They were a part of the English educational revolution described in the prior chapter. They reflected, too, the concern by local and central government for education, which had been developing for a century in England. Instead of waiting for the home government to promote education in America, they took upon themselves the governmental jurisdiction over education which the highest political authority in England had already exerted in the national laws on apprenticeship and poverty.

The New England version of civil authority in education boiled down to this: the colonial government could require parents to have their children educated (either by themselves or by teachers); the central government of the colony could require local towns to appoint teachers or establish schools; public funds could be raised by taxation to pay the teachers; and public teachers were subject to direct supervision and control by such governmental authorities as the General Court, the town meeting as a whole, the selectmen, or a special education committee.

Teachers of town schools were usually appointed at town meetings or by the selectmen with the approval of the ministers. Teachers of church schools were usually appointed by church officials or clergymen. This meant that the qualifications of teachers were passed upon by towns, by churches, by royal companies, by royal governors, and often by the bishop of London in the case of Anglican teachers. It meant, too, that the most important qualification for teaching was religious orthodoxy.

Licenses for teachers were regularly issued by civil authorities in all the colonies—another evidence of civil control of education. Teachers were supervised and inspected by clergymen, selectmen, and committees that visited the schools to see if students were actually learning correctly the grounds of religion and the rudiments of reading, writing, and arithmetic. Tenure thus depended mainly upon religious orthodoxy, civic loyalty, and good moral character. In general, teachers possessed about as good moral character as the rest of the population as far as drunkenness, profanity, legal and financial troubles, or crimes of violence or sex were concerned. Most teachers were men, but women also found a place—as keepers of dame schools in New England and as substitutes in the summer when the men were in the fields; similarly, the wives of planters in the South sometimes carried on instruction for their children.

The colonial legislatures in Virginia and elsewhere in the South possessed the same legal authority to legislate on educational matters, had they wished to do so. They could have established, supported, and directly administered their own schools, as in New England, if they had wished. However, they chose not to pass laws requiring all children to be educated but rather assumed, as in Anglican England, that any parent who could afford to educate his own children should do so, that the church, through its parishes and vestrymen, rather than the state was the proper custodian of schools, and that the state should concern itself primarily with poor and orphan children of the underprivileged and lower classes.

In this respect Virginia reflected the fact that the Church of England dominated educational policies there. Instruction was provided by private tutors when parents could afford to pay them, by any parish priests who had the ability or inclination to do so, and by endowed schools. Several such endowed schools were established by interested persons in order to provide free education for those who could not afford it. The first of these was made by Benjamin Syms in the 1630s. Usually the endowment took the form of gifts, bequests of land, produce, or livestock to be used for the sustenance of the teachers. In general, however, free education in the South meant charity education for the poor, and upper-class parents naturally did not want that kind of free education for their children.

Here was a considerable difference, even in the seventeenth century, between New England and the South that was to have lasting importance. New England soon built up a tradition of free education being perfectly proper for self-respecting members of the community, whereas a stigma was long connected with free education in the South because of its connection with charity. The principal educational concern of the state in the South was for orphans or children of poor and indigent parents who could not take the responsibility of educating their children. In Virginia, for example, an act of the legislature in 1642 required guardians and masters to give their apprentices proper training. A law in 1636 stated that an orphan child should be educated at the social level of his parents. If his parents had not been free, the child was to be apprenticed to a trade and given proper moral and religious training. Several acts made apprenticeship and religious instruction compulsory for poor children in order to protect the rest of society from a possible vagabond and "dangerous" class. In these respects the South followed the tradition of the English poor laws but did not show the zeal for popular education through public schools that is reflected in the Puritan New England laws of the same period.

It was this zeal for popular education that eventually came to distinguish the American modernization process of the late eighteenth and nineteenth centuries. Despite the differences between the New England and the Southern approaches, they were both English and both Protestant. By the end of the seventeenth century the major cast of American education was definitely Anglo-Protestant. Non-English schools were to survive into the nineteenth century, but they definitely became a minority phenomenon. The non-Protestant schools had even less chance of surviving unchanged.

In Maryland, for example, some Jesuit schools were established on an endowed basis; but by the end of the seventeenth century the Catholics were such a small minority that their schools had virtually disappeared. A similar fate overtook the Latin school conducted by two Jesuit priests in New York. In Spanish Florida the Franciscans established as early as 1606 a classical school in connection with a seminary at St. Augustine. By 1634 several mission schools were flourishing, but they soon declined as a result of the wars with the Indians and the English colonies. In New Mexico, Franciscans had established some fifty missions that carried on active educational work among the Indians until the uprising of 1680 virtually wiped them out. Although Latin-Catholics were not able to withstand English competition in eastern America in the seventeenth century, they dominated education in the Spanish southwest and California until once again overwhelmed by waves of Anglo-Protestants in the nineteenth century. By that time new Catholic immigration from central and southern Europe began to challenge the prevailing Anglo-Protestant patterns that had been transplanted throughout most of the United States.

The Types of Schooling Transplanted

Schools in seventeenth-century America, from the lowest to the highest, were expected to promote piety in conformity with the religious mission of the European Reformation. Whether the schools were Puritan, Dutch Reformed, Anglican, Lutheran, Huguenot, or Quaker, their primary purpose was to teach the respective grounds of Christian faith. Furthermore, the aim to teach children to read was grounded in the Protestant belief that civil society, as well as the religious community, would be better served by a literate citizenry than by an illiterate one. But that was not all. Education should not only serve piety and civility but the economy as well; children should be taught a useful trade by their parents but should be apprenticed to others if parents failed to give them the vocational training that would enable them to support themselves through the practice of a trade. As early as 1685 a Quaker writer, Thomas Budd, proposed that American children should learn a useful trade in public schools along with their academic studies, but like those of the realistic proposals in England, his ideas did not catch on. The humanistic tradition was too strong for that. Schooling was considered to be a literary matter.

Humanism, entrenched in the grammar schools of America from the beginning, explains why the colonists relied upon apprenticeship, as in England, for the vocational training they so badly needed in a frontier society. The education of those who would rule in church and state, the humanists had taught them, was, properly conceived, the study of classical language and literature, shaped to serve the purposes of piety, the *pietas litterata*. So it was that, in the midst of a wilderness, Latin schools were set up as the proper form of school for privileged boys to attend, leaving to apprenticeship the job of training the majority of young people for the skilled vocations.

Vernacular Elementary Schools. All the American colonies in the seventeenth century made some provision for teaching children to read in a vernacular tongue. If parents could not do it themselves, they were expected to see that others taught their children. In New England the town schoolmaster or the women in charge of private dame schools taught reading, and sometimes writing, in English, along with the Puritan catechism. The Massachusetts law of 1642 said nothing about writing as a general requirement, but by the end of the seventeenth century it was not uncommon for writing schools (including arithmetic) to exist alongside reading schools.

If a child was exposed to more than reading and the catechism, he was lucky.

The basic reading materials were a hornbook, a primer, the Bible, the catechism, and the psalmbook. With minor variations, the same story applied to the Dutch schoolmasters in New Amsterdam who taught in Dutch, the Anglican schoolmasters and tutors of the South who taught in English, the Huguenots who taught in French, and the Lutherans who taught in German or Swedish.

There was little uniformity in the number of hours a day during which schools were open or the number of days a year for which they operated. Much depended upon the sense of responsibility of the teacher and his community. In general, the Calvinist communities were likely to be most zealous in keeping schools open the year round. In the hands of a conscientious teacher, hours were likely to be long and arduous, marked with prayers, hymn singing, memorizing, severe discipline, and corporal punishment. "Spare the rod and spoil the child" was the universal maxim. The newer theories of sense realism as the basis of educational method being formulated in Europe had not yet touched these shores. Pupils of all ages went to the same teacher, who may have taught two, three, or several dozen in the same room. The room was at the teacher's home, the church, the town meetinghouse, or in some specially constructed shelter, likely to be rough and inhospitable in winter or summer.

By and large, poor as the colonial petty schools may look to twentieth-century eyes, they produced a remarkably high level of literacy in comparison to the world of their day. It is estimated that in the middle of the seventeenth century some 90 percent of men and 40 percent of women in New England and perhaps half those proportions in Virginia could write their names (a minimum test of literacy).[32] While many adults of this period could have picked up their literacy in their homelands, the literacy rate of the late seventeenth century rose rather than fell.

Classical Grammar Schools.   The humanist respect for the classical languages as basic to scholarship and religion was carried intact from Europe to the New World. American secondary schools, following the English model, were called "grammar schools" or, more correctly, "Latin grammar schools." Their major and almost only task was the teaching of Latin grammar. Sometimes such schools instituted preparatory departments for teaching the younger boys the four R's in English. In general, when they appeared in America the grammar schools had lost the vital spirit of humanism that had characterized the better European classical schools of the Renaissance. Their main job was preparation for college work, although the ideal was also to prepare boys for public service and for any occupation into which they might go, especially the ministry, the magistracy, and teaching.

These schools, therefore, were not particularly adapted to the immediate social demands of time and place. It is no wonder that they were not too popular among the great majority of people. As a result, the fines for failure to set up such schools were several times raised by the colonial legislatures of New England in an effort to compel reluctant towns to establish them. Even where they were maintained as town schools, they tended to be class schools frequented by the more wealthy families.

---

[32] For a brief summary of several studies of illiteracy, see Morison, op. cit., pp. 82-85; and Cremin, op. cit., chap. 17.

Perhaps the most famous grammar school teacher of seventeenth-century America was Ezekiel Cheever. What went on in his schools at Ipswich and Boston has had to be reconstructed from the books he wrote and from the testimony of some of his famous students, among whom was Cotton Mather. From these sources it is clear that students studied a combination of religious books and secular classical authors— Cheever's own grammar, Lily's *Grammar,* the Bible, Aesop's *Fables,* Vergil's *Aeneid,* Cicero's *Orations,* Ovid's *Metamorphoses,* St. Paul's Epistles, and selections from Corderius, Erasmus, Ovid, Horace,and Cato (the fourth-century Latin author of the *Distichs*). Hours were long, discipline was strict, and punishment severe and frequent. Other grammar schools probably approached this curriculum in essentials if not in breadth. Some grammar schools also taught the rudiments of Greek if they sought to prepare students to meet the entrance requirements of Harvard College.

Humanistic Sectarian Colleges.   One of the most remarkable educational feats of the New England Puritans was the creation of a college within a half dozen years of the founding of the Massachusetts Bay Colony. When Harvard College was established by order of the General Court in 1636, it turned out to be virtually a copy of one of the many colleges that constituted the English universities. It happened to follow Cambridge more closely, inasmuch as so many of the early Puritans who came to America had attended Cambridge University. Morison lists approximately 100 Cambridge and 30 Oxford men who had come to America by 1646;[33] of these university graduates 90 were clergymen. John Harvard, who gave his name to the young college, was a graduate of Cambridge, and Henry Dunster, the president who formulated the first well-defined curriculum, was a graduate of Magdalene College, Cambridge.

The Harvard curriculum of 1642 reveals a striking similarity in content to that of the English colleges.[34] Here were six of the seven medieval liberal arts: grammar, rhetoric, logic, arithmetic, geometry, and astronomy; music had disappeared. Here were some of the studies of Aristotle's moral philosophy (ethics and politics) and his natural philosophy (physics). Here was a strong infusion of Renaissance humanist learning in the emphasis upon Greek, Hebrew, and "Eastern tongues" (Aramaic and Syrian). The Reformation concern with religion was reflected in the study of "Divinity Catechetical" on Saturday mornings and the worship services on weekdays and on Sundays. Ancient history was offered during an hour on Saturday afternoons for freshmen in the winter months, and the "nature of plants" was a similar hour for freshmen in the summer (neither of these appeared in later statements of the curriculum). This first curriculum was entirely prescribed, with the basic language of instruction being Latin. The course of instruction consisted of three years of study continuing around the calendar, winter and summer alike. By 1655 it had become a four-year course, still completely prescribed.

If the amount of time devoted to the several studies of the 1642 three-year

[33] Samuel Eliot Morison, *The Founding of Harvard College,* Harvard University Press, Cambridge, Mass., 1935, p. 40 and Appendix B.

[34] Samuel Eliot Morison, *Harvard College in the Seventeenth Century,* Harvard University Press, Cambridge, Mass., 1936, vol. 1, chaps. 7-13.

course is translated into modern terminology, the relative amount of class time would look something like this:

HUMANITIES		
Greek	18%	
Hebrew and Eastern Tongues	18%	
Rhetoric	18%	72%
Logic	9%	
Divinity	9%	
SCIENCE AND MATHEMATICS		
Arithmetic, geometry, and astronomy	12%	
Physics	3%	15.5%
Botany	0.5%	
SOCIAL STUDIES		
Ethics and politics	12%	12.5%
History	0.5%	
Totals	100%	100%

The preponderance of emphasis upon the humanities is obvious. Foreign languages alone occupied one-third of the time, to say nothing of the fact that most textbooks and lectures in all subjects were in Latin. If to these are added rhetoric and logic, the study of language in its various forms amounted to nearly two-thirds of the curriculum. Language and mathematics combined came to three-fourths of the program. The subsidiary role of the social and scientific studies is thus patent. Erasmus and Calvin might have been pleased with this curriculum, but neither Aristotle nor Cicero would have been pleased with the relatively little attention to philosophy, science, and social studies.

In the course of the seventeenth century some modification in this first curriculum began to be made. The logic of Aristotle was being tempered with that of Petrus Ramus, Johann Heinrich Alsted, and Bartholomaüs Keckermann. The astronomy of Aristotle, Ptolemy, and Dante was being modified by Copernicus. With the use of a telescope acquired in 1672, one of the tutors, Thomas Brattle, made observations of the Great Comet of 1680 which proved useful to Newton in his calculations. In general, however, Harvard reflected relatively little of the great scientific discoveries and speculation that were so much a part of the intellectual ferment of realism in seventeenth-century Europe. But then Harvard was not so very much different from most European universities in this respect.

At first Harvard had only three classes, but a fourth was added by 1655, following the European model of four years of undergraduate work leading to the B.A. degree. After a three-year interval, the M.A. degree was granted upon payment of a fee, defense of a thesis, and evidence of good moral character. Often the first item was the most important requirement.

The undergraduate curriculum was completely prescribed, all students in a class studying the same subjects at the same time, and all taught, in Dunster's day, by the president himself. The college was small, students varying from twenty to fifty in number. The students were considerably younger than now, probably ranging from thirteen or fourteen to seventeen or eighteen years of age. Discipline was severe, and riots were frequent; much of the restlessness doubtless resulted from the fact that the methods of teaching were almost entirely bookish, and the food was poor. The students listened to the instructor read the assigned books, read the books themselves, recited from the books, drew up outlines from the books, disputed on questions drawn from the books, and gave declamations.

Harvard set the pattern for American colleges and universities for more than a century. When the College of William and Mary was established in 1693 in Virginia and Yale in 1701 in Connecticut, they did not differ markedly from the Harvard model of Renaissance-Reformation higher education.

This pattern helped to transplant to America the fundamentals of traditional Western education. In fact, it was accepted so wholeheartedly and defended so vigorously against criticism that American colleges were slow to respond to the modernizing influences that appeared in the eighteenth and nineteenth centuries. The close connection between religion and humanism kept the colleges from adapting themselves readily to the "realistic" economic, scientific, and philosophical currents. Prospective lawyers and physicians found no specific training in college, but had to rely upon apprenticeship to practicing lawyers and physicians. Prospective surveyors, navigators, shipbuilders, farmers, and businessmen, to say nothing of skilled workers, found little direct help in preparing for work that was very important to American development. Their needs were not to be met by higher education until the modernizing movements of the late eighteenth and nineteenth centuries.

In the first American colleges we find a confluence of three strains of thought which flowed from 500 years of European higher education.

1. From the late Middle Ages came the seven liberal arts and Aristotelian philosophy that had long constituted the round of arts studies deemed necessary for an educated person and for entrance to later professional study in European universities.
2. From Renaissance humanism came the classical languages and literature of Graeco-Roman civilization, widely accepted throughout the West as the best means of preparing leaders for church and for state, the civilizing studies par excellence.
3. From the Reformation came the conviction that higher education should be an instrument for Christianizing friend and foe alike and for preparation of Christian ministers who would defend and propagate their doctrinal orthodoxies.

The medieval idea that an education in the liberal arts should be preparatory to professional studies was narrowed somewhat by the Reformation insistence upon the primacy of sectarian theology, but it was at the same time enlarged by the Renaissance vision that education should prepare for service in the secular as well as the religious world. The basic ambiguity and latent conflict among these three ideals were thus present from the beginnings of American higher education. Ideally, they would support each other in the liberalizing, civilizing, and Christianizing work of higher education. They all agreed that a liberal education should primarily be based upon linguistic and literary studies. Each held to the notion that an education through books was the best way to develop a man of action. But each had its own notion concerning what books of the past and what great men of antiquity were best suited to serve as examples in developing the great men of the present. Aristotle and Ramus, Cicero and Calvin, Erasmus and Bacon, Copernicus and the Scriptures—each found their place in the curriculum under different auspices, but they eventually became uneasy bedfellows.

All three ideals agreed on one other thing. They sought to educate the leaders rather than the followers in church and state. The liberal education common to England and America in the seventeenth century, despite its relative accessibility, turned out to be too limited in scope to meet the demands of a society that insisted upon an ever expanding educational opportunity. The first American higher education was basically intellectualist rather than practicalist. Its stress upon the books, languages, and literatures of the classical humanities revealed this bias. There was little deliberate effort to shape the received traditional education so as to give a direct preparation for an active life of work or public service in a new world.

The fact remains, however, that the original classical education brought to America had a strong professional leaning. It was highly useful for certain occupations, namely, the "higher" professions of leadership in the community—the ministry, the magistracy, and teaching. These were the occupations in which language training was most useful. It was not so useful for the "lower" occupations of farming, trading, or artisanship. It eventually became useful for medicine and law in the course of the eighteenth century.

The eighteenth century, however, began the process of broadening the range of occupations deemed worthy of a free man and thus began to broaden the idea of a liberal education. This modernizing process eventually gave a distinctive American flavor to the liberal education transplanted from Europe. The colonial American colleges of the late eighteenth and early nineteenth centuries began to toy with the idea that they might produce educated Americans rather than educated Europeans. But no matter what was to come, the first century of transplanting insured that North America's education would be indelibly Western. It was a fateful development for human civilization that the education of half the new world traced its original roots to the west of Europe, sometimes following respectfully and dutifully the lead of Europe, sometimes rejecting it scornfully and impatiently. In both stances, American education performed as progeny are wont to do toward their parents in a modern civilization.

PART III

THE FLORESCENCE
OF MODERN
EDUCATION
IN THE WEST
(1700 A.D.-THE PRESENT)

CHAPTER IX

THE TRANSMUTATION
TO MODERNITY
(1700 A.D.-THE PRESENT)

The social and cultural changes that gathered speed in the heartland of Western civilization from the beginning of the eighteenth century to the middle of the twentieth century were so portentous for the future of mankind that they can justly be compared with the other major transformations in the human career: the evolutionary process through which prehuman men became human; and the original civilizational process through which certain folk societies were transformed into the first agrarianate civilizations of Asia and Africa. The third great transformation of man, the transmutation of traditional civilization into modern civilization, was to bring even more radical changes in the human configurations of the entire world.

We have already pointed to the intimations of modernity that began to appear as early as the fifteenth and sixteenth centuries. From that time forward, the process of modernization originating in Western Europe gained strength with unprecedented historical speed, soon embracing a large part of Western civilization and eventually influencing fundamentally the rest of the world's civilizations as well as the remaining precivilized folk societies. By the middle of the nineteenth century the transmutation in the heartland of Western civilization had proceeded to the point that an enormous gap yawned between the West and the rest of the world, yielding a decisive difference in what Marshall Hodgson aptly called "social power."[1] The difference rapidly upset the cultural balance among the civilizations of the Afro-Eurasian ecumene, a balance that had roughly obtained for some 2,000 years:

> Individual Europeans might still be less intelligent, less courageous, less loyal than individuals elsewhere; but when *educated* and *organized in society* the Europeans were able to think and to act far more effectively, as members of a group, than could members of any other societies. European enterprises, such as firms or churches or, of course, governments, could muster a degree of power, intellectual, economic, and social, which was of a different order from what could be mustered among even the most wealthy or vigorous peoples in the rest of the world.[2]

[1] See Marshall G. S. Hodgson, "The Great Western Transmutation," *Chicago Today*, University of Chicago Press, vol. 4, no. 3, Autumn 1967.

[2] Ibid., pp. 40-41. Italics added.

This social power of Western civilization was a product of several factors to be identified shortly, but it should be noted that it appeared earlier in some parts of the West than in others. So, first, a word about the term *the West* and its ambiguities. In its most general sense, Western civilization is largely to be identified with the civilization that arose in Southern and Western Europe around 1,000 A.D. It grew out of the survivals of the Graeco-Roman world in Europe, and, from the sixteenth century onward, it began to impinge upon all the older civilizations of Africa, Asia, and the Americas and upon folk societies in all the major continents and islands of the world. Not only did the transplantation of European institutions to South and North America bring the major Amerindian civilizations of the New World generally within its sphere of influence, but, in the eighteenth and nineteenth centuries, significant parts of eastern Europe and Russia were brought into the Western orbit, and colonial outposts of the West were planted in outlying reaches that stretched around the world, from the tip of Southern Africa to Australia, New Zealand, and the islands of the Pacific.

Not only did the massive onset of modernity in the late eighteenth and nineteenth centuries distinguish the West in general from the non-West, but its prototype forms of polity, economy, and education appeared first in only a few societies of the West, serving to set them apart for a time from the larger conglomeration of societies that constituted traditional Western civilization as a whole. The earliest modernizing societies, led by Britain and France, constituted the vanguard nations that paved the way for the rest of Europe to follow; they set the general pattern which the more traditional sectors of eastern Europe and Russia eventually emulated. And, of course, it was the earliest modernizing nations of Western Europe that developed their social power to the extent that they not only vied among themselves for supremacy in Europe and America, but they eventually competed with each other in their intrusions upon the traditional societies of Asia and Africa.

The line of demarcation between Western Europe and Eastern Europe was indefinite and shifting, but, by and large, in 1700, it extended southward from the mouth of the Elbe River along the Bohemian mountains to the head of the Adriatic Sea. To the west of this line the modernization process proceeded much more rapidly and pervasively than to the east. As the rise of strong and modernizing rulers in Hohenzollern Prussia, Hapsburg Austria, and Romanov Russia replaced the declining powers of the Holy Roman Empire, Poland, and the Ottoman Empire in central Europe, the line between East and West moved eastward in the course of the eighteenth century. By 1850 the modernizing heartland of Western civilization had come to embrace roughly the societies of Europe from the Atlantic to Berlin and Vienna as well as the transplanted European societies in North America from the Atlantic to the Mississippi. (See Figure 14.1, p. 487)

With respect to economic development, Britain is usually acknowledged to have been the first society to industrialize, followed by France, the Low Countries, the United States, and Germany. Just as Britain is taken as the prototype society of the industrial revolution so are France and the United States taken as the prototypes of the democratic revolution, which erupted in much of Western Europe in the late eighteenth century. In the view of R. R. Palmer, the democratic revolution of 1760 to 1800, although marked by a series of outbreaks in different countries, was actually a single revolutionary movement of Western civilization.[3] These two modern revolutions, one economic and one political, originated in the heartland of Western civilization.

Another way to put the point is that of C. E. Black who defines several patterns of political modernization. The nations that were able to complete the transfer of political power from traditional to modernizing leaders by the end of the nineteenth century were the United Kingdom, France, and the United States, followed by Canada, the Low Countries, Germany, Italy, and Denmark.[4] Others began the process before the middle of the nineteenth century but did not complete it until the twentieth century: Australia, New Zealand, Norway, Sweden, Spain, Portugal, Austria, Czechoslovakia, and Hungary. The first two of these were offshoots of Britain in the New World; the rest were European societies struggling to achieve the democratizing movements initiated during the French revolution. All other nations of the world (with the exception of Uruguay) either did not begin the consolidation of their modernizing leadership until the second half of the nineteenth century, or they have not yet completed the transfer from a traditional to a modernizing leadership.

The difference in timing between the first nations to achieve political or economic modernization and those that followed have had enormous ramifications for the history of the world since the eighteenth century. Whether the difference is that between primary and secondary modernizers,[5] or between "advanced nations" and "follower societies,"[6] or simply the dichotomy between the developed and underdeveloped nations, the rich and the poor, or the modern and the traditional, the differences have plagued the entire world to this day. Indeed, many social science scholars believe that the international problems posed by the nations of the Thrid World (the newly independent states of Africa and Asia) are more likely to demand attention than the confrontations between the "West" (United States and its allies) versus the "East" (the Soviet Union, China, and their allies).[7]

It is time to make more explicit the meaning of modernization. Social scientists in recent years have been at some pains to define its essence. Marion J. Levy, Jr., sociologist at Princeton, finds the key to modernization in the degree to which a society's social structure reflects the use of inanimate sources of power rather than human or animal energy.[8]

Joseph Elder, sociologist at the University of Wisconsin, defines the essence of

---

[3] R. R. Palmer, *The Age of the Democratic Revolution, a Political History of Europe and America, 1760-1800,* 2 vols., Princeton University Press, Princeton, N. J., 1959, 1964.

[4] C. E. Black, *The Dynamics of Modernization; a Study in Comparative History,* Harper & Row, New York, 1966, pp. 90-91.

[5] Dankwart A. Rustow, *A World of Nations; Problems of Political Modernization,* The Brookings Institution, Washington, D. C., 1967, p. 10.

[6] Reinhard Bendix, "Tradition and Modernity Reconsidered," *Comparative Studies in Society and History,* vol. 9, pp. 330 ff, April 1967.

[7] "Protagonists, Power, and the Third World: Essays on the Changing International System," *The Annals of the American Academy of Political and Social Science,* vol. 386, November 1969.

[8] Marion J. Levy, Jr., *Modernization and the Structure of Societies; a Setting for International Affairs,* Princeton University Press, Princeton, N.J., 1966, vol. 1, p. 11.

modernity "as corresponding to 'secular education,' that type of education endorsing the establishment of objectifiable evidence for proof of phenomena in opposition to the type of education that endorses tradition or faith as the basis for proof of phenomena."[9] C. E. Black, historian, stresses the particular historical setting which produced modern societies:

> "Modernization" may be defined as the process by which historically evolved institutions are adapted to the rapidly changing functions that reflect the unprecedented increase in man's knowledge, permitting control over his environment, that accompanied the scientific revolution. This process of adaptation had its origins and initial influence in the societies of Western Europe, but in the nineteenth and twentieth centuries these changes have been extended to all other societies and have resulted in a worldwide transformation affecting all human relationships.[10]

Three interrelated points that these definitions imply deserve special underlining. The first is that organized scientific knowledge and the technological tools that flowed therefrom played a fundamental role in the social changes that characterize the modern as distinguished from traditional civilization. The second is that those societies which first achieved modernization not only organized themselves socially, politically, and economically, but they gave to organized education a strategic role to play in the production of knowledge and its dissemination. Black stresses a third point, the spread outward from the West to the rest of the world. Here again the role of education became a key factor along with the political, the economic, the technological, and the religious.

Reinhard Bendix emphasizes the fact that tradition and modernity are not simply mutually exclusive social systems or typologies, as some sociologists are inclined to make of them. Rather, the original modernization breakthroughs were culminations of long historical processes in which tradition does not disappear [especially as in education] but is modified and carried along in the process. Particularly useful is the point made by Bendix that external stimuli have been potent factors in inducing modernizing change in one country after another. The first modernizing societies became models or reference societies for others to emulate. "The economic and political 'breakthrough' which occurred in England and France at the end of the eighteenth century, put every other country in the world into a position of backwardness. . . . Ever since the world has been divided into advanced and follower societies."[11] Bendix rightly argues that this gap puts a premium upon the diffusion of ideas and techniques and social institutions as the means by which the follower societies try to catch up or close the gap. Modernization is thus not a simple matter of nationalizing or industrializing or democratizing a society. It is a most complicated matter that relies heavily upon the role of intellectuals, of educated government

---

[9] Joseph Elder, "Brahmans in an Industrial Setting: a Case Study" in William B. Hamilton (ed.), *The Transfer of Institutions,* Duke University Press, Durham, N. C., 1964, p. 141, n. 14.

[10] Black, op. cit., p. 7.

[11] Bendix, op. cit., p. 330.

officials, of the deliberate advancement of knowledge (especially that knowledge which leads to the solving of practical problems), and the dissemination of education among the populace.

The effort to deal with nearly 300 years of Western educational history in a few chapters is, of course, bound to fail in any sense of coverage or completeness. There is one compensating factor, however. The educational models of the most influential Western nations were relatively few. Despite their many real differences, the educational institutions and ideas emanating from British, French, German, and American sources became the most common reference systems of the modern period since 1700. This was so either because they were most widely transplanted throughout the world or because they were thought to be especially effective in promoting the modernization of their own societies and thus most worthy of emulation by similarly aspiring states. This is not to say that Dutch, Belgian, Italian, Spanish, or Portuguese educational influences were not widespread or not important in this period, nor that Scandinavian, Russian, Japanese, Indian, or Chinese education did not become so later. It is simply to say that the peculiar combination of modernizing forces reached special peaks of social power in four societies of the West.

The combination of modernizing ingredients, albeit in different proportions, consisted of centralized national authority, intellectual and scientific creativeness, democratic aspiration, industrial and technological advancement, urbanization, religious expansionism, and faith in education. These ingredients gave a relatively sudden and peculiarly decisive advantage to four of the societies of the West. They were not by any means all beneficent, but they gave a head start toward erecting the political, commercial, military, religious, educational, intellectual, and scientific networks that established large-scale Western hegemony in the modern world.

This hegemony was viewed by some as symbolizing the worst evils of colonial and imperial exploitation, and by others as embodying the highest values of the "civilizing mission" of the West. Whatever the angle of vision, Western hegemony exerted a powerful influence upon the entire world. Indeed, the power of modernizing Westerners was a mixture of dynamic and aggressive confidence in themselves, combined either with a humane or humanitarian desire to bring the advantage of their advancement to others, or with an arrogant or cruel ethnocentrism based upon feelings of racial or national superiority. Their power sometimes rested upon the rewards of their own efficient organization, hard work, and ingenuity; sometimes upon their indolent exploitation of others. Their attitudes ranged from expansive, imaginative, and future-oriented visions for themselves and for others to the reactionary and small-minded myopism of tradition-bound and insufferable insularity.

In any case, the combination of ingredients gave the modernizing Westerners the advantages of speed and power, of impact and leverage for disruptive change that far exceeded, even though for a much shorter period of time, those of the other vast proselytizing civilizations of the past: the Mesopotamians in the Middle East, the Greeks in the Middle East and the Mediterranean, the Romans and Christians in the Mediterranean and Europe, the Moslems in Europe, Africa, and Asia, the Hindus in South Asia, and the Buddhists in South and East Asia. In contrast to these the Westerners spanned the world.

I have selected seven major ways in which modernizing leaders in the heartland of the West achieved their social power in the eighteenth and nineteenth centuries:

They mobilized the political power of the nation-state.
They railed against religious establishment and rallied round religious freedom.
They lit the secular lamp of enlightenment.
They ignited the torch of democratic revolution.
They energized massive industrial urbanization.
They preached redeeming faith in popular education.
They launched their "civilizing mission" to embrace the world.

The first six will be discussed in this and succeeding chapters of Part III; the seventh will be discussed in Part IV.

A. THE MOBILIZING POWER OF THE NATION-STATE

The process of nation building which had been underway for a long time in Western Europe came to fruition by the end of the nineteenth century. Political authority at the national levels of government gained the upper hand over the conflicting localisms and the competing particularities inherited from medieval times. This centralizing movement signaled a widespread decline of local autonomy and the transfer of the center of political gravity from the locality to the nation. Where the feudal institutions had been strongest, as in France, the centralizing reaction was strongest; where feudal institutions were virtually absent as in British North America extreme centralization was less necessary. But the essence of modernity in government was not simply greater political institutionalization as described in Chapter 6, but rather the growing capacity of the political system to cope with an increasing range and complexity of public and private affairs and to cope with them rationally, effectively, and adaptably.

Especially important in this regard was the development of efficient bureaucracies for the conduct of the public business. A succinct summary of Max Weber's views which are basic to many definitions of a modern system of public administration is given by Joseph LaPalombara:

> The crucial characteristics of bureaucracy, in the classical sense, are: (1) specialized, highly differentiated administrative roles, (2) recruitment on the basis of achievement (measured by examination) rather than by ascription, (3) placement, transfer, and promotion on the basis of universalistic rather than particularistic criteria, (4) administrators who are salaried professionals who view their work as a career, and (5) administrative decision making within a rational and readily understood context of hierarchy, responsibility, and discipline.[12]

The necessity of building a well-developed system of organized education to give

---

[12] Joseph LaPalombara (ed.), *Bureaucracy and Political Development,* Princeton University Press, Princeton, N.J., 1963, pp. 49-50.

the professional training required for bureaucratization was apparent to the modernizing leaders of the West. They may have differed as to the content and character of that education and as to the classes of society who should have access to it, but they all agreed that an education beyond the rudiments was important in a modernizing society as a means of professional preparation and as a means of recruitment into the governmental service.

Organized education was seen as important in the political process in another major way, as a primary agent in developing the attitudes, knowledge, and behavior patterns appropriate to a national political system; a process that political scientists like to call political socialization.[13] In layman's language, this is education for citizenship, and it was in this period of mobilization of the nation-state by the modernizing leaders of the West that education was fully enlisted into the service of building or strengthening nationality. Since that time education and nationalism have been close allies, and the schools have been expected to assist in welding disparate groups into an identification with the nation-state, whether it be a monarchy or a republic, whether it be autocratic, democratic, socialist, fascist, or something in between. This may serve to remind that modernization may take place in nation-states of different political ideologies, but modernization has not been particularly effective in those societies that have not attempted or have failed to achieve authoritative government, command over the peoples' loyalties, and the capacity to tax and conscript manpower, all of which have customarily been associated with the modern nation-state. So far, modernization has been closely associated with nationalism.

As the national state became the acknowledged unit of political authority of the modern world, as contrasted with the medieval and feudal world, the sovereign state was assumed to be entirely independent of any legal or moral authority beyond its own borders. No matter whether the state was an absolute monarchy, a constitutional monarchy, or a republic, it was recognized to be the supreme political power possessing the right to determine its own boundaries, its own form of government, and its own internal arrangements.

In the process of building political nationalism, most states appealed to the idea of cultural nationality. People began to think of themselves primarily as Frenchmen, Englishmen, Germans, Italians, Poles, or Americans. Each nationality laid claim to a common historic background, a common language, common customs, and perhaps a common religious, artistic, and institutional life. More than ever before, the people of one nationality clamored to be joined together in one political unit. Great efforts were exerted to make the boundaries of the state identical with the lines of cultural nationality. To this end it became supremely important to foster in the people a strong feeling of loyalty to their state and pride in their nationality. It was only natural, then, that education should be used as a prime means to develop the spirit of nationalism.

Between 1700 and 1850 Great Britain and France were the principal large nation-states in Europe. Most of the rest of the people of the world lived in relatively

---

[13] See, e.g., Gabriel A. Almond and G. Bingham Powell, Jr., *Comparative Politics; a Developmental Approach,* Little, Brown, Boston, 1966; and James S. Coleman (ed.), *Education and Political Development,* Princeton University Press, Princeton, N.J., 1965.

small states which were more or less autonomous, or they lived under huge sprawling empires more or less loosely ruled by hereditary dynasties. Within two decades after 1850 several other powerful nation-states appeared on the world scene. Politically, they had unified and centralized the political functions for the peoples who now lived within their national boundaries: unified empires for Germans, Japanese, and Russians; unified kingdoms for Italians and Austro-Hungarians; and unified representative governments for Americans and Canadians. In the following century nearly all the peoples of the world would aspire to live in nation-states patterned on one or the other of these forms and with educational systems to suit.[14]

Firmly in control of Parliament, the landed classes in England were able to modernize themselves and the state without reliance upon a strongly paternalistic monarch and without the opposition of a repressive military regime, or a reactionary feudal aristocracy. The upshot was that England was able to modernize without the worst excesses of a bloody revolution and without repressive centralization. The educated gentry and middle classes provided the local and national bureaucratic framework within which the British nation-state could function so effectively that it could challenge France for colonial supremacy in the world and be the first to industrialize at home.

As a result of the vast colonial possessions acquired in the eighteenth century, British influence ranged from America and Canada in the West through Africa in the South and to India and Australia in the East. The Treaty of Paris in 1763 made Britain the world's leading commercial and colonial power, a position that was maintained even after the loss of the thirteen American colonies a few years later. By mid-nineteenth century the British under Queen Victoria were confident that all was well with the world—so long as Britannia ruled in it.

At the opening of the eighteenth century, France under Louis XIV was the great nation of Europe and of the world. However, the series of wars with England and other countries during the long reign of Louis XV (1715 to 1774) lost for France not only her colonial supremacy but her commanding place in Europe—until the day of Napoleon.

When Napoleon emerged as a military strong-man, acquired virtually dictatorial powers under the Constitution of 1799, and ended the revolutionary life of the First Republic by making himself emperor in 1804, he enormously strengthened the central power of the state in France by establishing a powerful bureaucracy and system of justice based upon his famed legal code. Embracing such revolutionary principles as equality before the law, freedom of contract, and civil rather than religious authority to be administered in the centralized geographic units, known as *departments*, the French civil service enabled France to become politically more modern than Britain. Even though its bureaucratic structure was designed to appoint and promote on the basis of merit and to relate its educational system directly to the governmental structure, France failed, however, to orient its educational system sufficiently to the business, industrial, and economic needs of the modern world. In this respect France eventually fell behind Britain, the United States, and Germany.

[14] For a brief but perceptive analysis, see Hans Kohn, *The Age of Nationalism; the First Era of Global History*, Harper Torchbooks, New York, 1962, 1968.

Situated strategically in central Europe and at the same time a crossroads for the warring armies of eastern and western powers, Prussia emerged from the eighteenth-century wars not only intact but strengthened and expanded under the Hohenzollern line which had ruled Brandenburg from the fifteenth century. Under Frederick William I (1713 to 1740), the Prussian kingdom became a highly centralized modern state, a civil-service bureaucracy was established, and a strong army was developed. Then, under Frederick II (the Great) (1740 to 1786), Prussia became a first-rate political and military power to be reckoned with thereafter in the destinies of Europe.

In addition to expanding Prussian territory and attempting to bring other German and non-German states under his control, Frederick tried to make Prussia self-sufficient by making internal improvements, levying protective tariffs, distributing free grain, and lowering taxes. His strong paternalistic monarchy in Prussia not only strengthened his own power but served to mollify the discontented merchants and lower classes to such an extent that no revolutionary movement was able to achieve the strength it had in France. Frederick the Great thus became known as one of the "enlightened despots" of eighteenth-century Europe.

However, the liberal promise of late eighteenth-century Prussia extended only a decade or so into the nineteenth century. After the defeat of Napoleon and the onset of conservative reaction flowing from the Congress of Vienna in 1815, the Prussian kings more than regained the territory they had lost to Napoleon. Frederick William III and Frederick William IV far outdid the French monarchy in making the school system into an engine for maintaining the authority and instilling loyalty to the ruling House of Hohenzollern. Despite the short flurry of liberalism in the "Revolution of 1848," the way was well-paved for the German Empire of William I and Bismarck, uniting north and south Germany in 1871. Prior to 1815 Prussia had been largely an eastern state (i.e., east of the Elbe). As it shifted toward the heartland of the west in the nineteenth century it rapidly took on the trappings of a modern nation-state but did so under the auspices of increasingly repressive, despotic monarchy. Meanwhile, the other Western nations were becoming less repressive, less authoritarian, and more democratic in their political systems. By late in the nineteenth century their educational systems reflected these differences.

In the United States the trend was unmistakably in the direction of expanding the role of the federal government in the affairs of the new nation following the War of Independence. Born in an international war of revolution, the new nation's efforts to keep out of foreign wars and entangling alliances lasted only a short time. Although Adams and Jefferson stayed out of the actual fighting of the Napoleonic wars, Madison finally plunged in. As a result of the War of 1812, a new spirit of nationalism set out to win a continent by treaty, purchase, and war with Mexico and with the various Indian tribes. Although the Jeffersonian Democrats adhered to a narrow conception of the functions of the federal government in comparison with that of state governments, their presidents often actually helped to enlarge the federal government's powers. Jefferson concluded the Louisiana Purchase in 1803 which added vast territories to the nation; Monroe annexed Florida and formulated the doctrine that warned European nations away from the shores of the Americas; under Polk, Texas, California, New Mexico, and Arizona were added to the western territories, until the boundaries of the nation spanned a continent. In all these ways Democratic administrations laid the groundwork for a vast nation in which the power of the federal government was bound to expand. Decentralized political authorities could no longer be sufficient.

As the Civil War approached, however, the Democratic party began to stress the rights of states to govern themselves, and the Republican party took up the cudgels for a strong federal government. Inheriting the arguments for a permanent union as set forth by Daniel Webster and other Whigs, the Republicans gave to Lincoln the task of preventing the federal government from falling apart in civil war. The power of the federal government emerged from the Civil War immeasurably strengthened, and in general continued to expand in the succeeding century.

B. RELIGIOUS FERVOR AND RELIGIOUS FREEDOM

One of the thorniest aspects of the first modernization process was the confrontation between establishments of religion and those seeking separation of church and state. The establishments of religion were looked upon as citadels of the traditional standing orders that had to be stormed if the forces of modernity were to be victorious. The political struggles over disestablishment were constant, severe, and often debilitating. Only in the United States was a reasonably clear-cut victory won for the separation of church and state. This was undoubtedly one of the reasons why the United States was able to forge ahead so rapidly in its modernization. There were no enormously powerful land-owning churches to hold off political reform or economic development as they did in Eastern and Southern Europe, and for a time in France, England, and Germany.

But it also turned out that political action based upon a secular theory of natural rights was not the only, perhaps not even the most important, aspect of the disestablishment process. The political role of nonconformist, dissenting churches, or radical Protestant sects who believed in the free exercise of religion without interference by government in religious creed or practice proved to be indispensable. "Separatists" like the Quakers, Baptists, Methodists, and Mennonites were opposed to establishments of religion on principle, but even those who *were* believers in a close alliance between church and state (Presbyterian, Congregationalist, Lutheran, Catholic) began to see the values of separation in societies where *they* were not the dominant church. Thus, the religious heterogeneity of the American colonies helped to undermine the religious establishments which had benefitted from laws that imposed the doctrines of the preferred church and taxes that were levied upon everyone for the support of the established clergy.

The power of the established churches in Europe, however, generally remained strong in the nineteenth century, gaining adherents as a reaction set in against the rationalism of the Enlightenment. The state churches did have their troubles with liberal governments, for they were likely to be conservative and to side with the absolutist parties against the new liberalism. The Catholic Church in France, subject to bitter attack throughout the Enlightenment, was disestablished by the French Revolution. Thereafter, its fortunes fluctuated with the political pendulum. Regaining some of the privileges of an established church as a result of Napoleon's Concordat of 1801, it gained strength under the Bourbon restoration, lost ground under the Second Republic, came back under the Second Empire, and finally lost its favored position under the Third Republic. In England the Church of England retained its preferred and central place. It was generally allied with the Tories, the aristocracy, and the wealthy, but the growing liberalism in England permitted greater toleration for the nonconformist churches than on the continent. Even Roman Catholics gained some liberties following the Catholic Emancipation Act of 1829.

This was in marked contrast to the lack of toleration that persisted in those countries, like Spain, Italy, and Austria, where the Catholic Church continued to be the established church. In most Catholic countries the Church remained in virtual control of education despite growing interest by the state. Charles III in Spain, affected by the Enlightenment, drove out the Jesuits and hoped to set up secular schools and require state examinations of prospective teachers, but his plans never were realized. In Austria, Maria Theresa tried to adopt Frederick the Great's plans for state education and reform of schools; and Joseph II planned to set up a centralized system of all educational institutions in the Empire. Though the hopes of these enlightened despots may have been in the modern vein, the difficulties of issuing edicts from the top down were too great to achieve much success in a short time with peoples not accustomed to the privileges of education.

In most Protestant countries the educational systems continued to function in the hands of the state churches. The Scandinavian countries continued their Lutheran schools, and the Netherlands and Scotland their Calvinist schools. In Switzerland the Helvetic Society in 1762 began to work for union of the several loosely federated cantons into a stronger national state, with a national system of education as an integral part of the plan.

A noteworthy development for education in the eighteenth century was the emergence of aggressive new religious organizations and churches, some of them beginning as reform movements within the established churches. In German Lutheran lands the Pietistic movement under the leadership of such men as Spener, Francke, and Zinzendorf sought to revitalize and reform Lutheranism. In England, the Wesleyan movement launched a similar revivalistic effort to replace the formalism and ritualism of the Anglican church by more good works and evangelical spirit. The Baptists and Quakers represented still more radical protests against the authoritative practices of the established churches.

Many other religious groups, large and small, began to gain strength and confidence as a result of the more liberal attitudes of the eighteenth-century Enlightenment. These sectaries contributed their share to the revivalistic feeling that welled up in great areas of Europe and America. The movement became so widespread that historians have named it the Great Awakening. Hundreds of thousands of people were swept up on a wave of a religious emotionalism sometimes reaching the proportions of hysteria. This movement had special effects on education in England, Germany, and

America. A lively missionary spirit stimulated education and philanthropic efforts in informal as well as in organized ways.

The Great Awakening was a popular movement often at odds with the rationalism of the Enlightenment. Whereas the Enlightenment promoted a secularization of society, i.e., removing religious sanctions for the conduct of public affairs, the evangelical movement tended to regard the religious spirit as the all-embracing force in human affairs. In this respect they came into conflict, especially over the value of religious creed versus secular knowledge in schools. But evangelism and secularism often joined hands. They cooperated in attacking the established churches, working for the separation of church and state, and achieving freedom of religious worship; and they cooperated in philanthropic and humanitarian movements of social reform, including the effort to relieve the suffering of the underprivileged in the newly industrializing cities and to extend the opportunities for free or charity education to the children of the poor.

In the course of the eighteenth century the American states moved toward religious freedom as a basic part of their liberal revolution, but the transition from a single establishment of religion to full separation of church and state was a tortuous and painful process. The essence of a single establishment of religion was that every person had to pay taxes to support the established church whether or not he belonged to that church or believed in its doctrines. In several colonies an intermediate step was taken. This permitted more than one religious group to use the power of the state to help support their own ministers and church services. I have called this a "multiple establishment of religion."[15] For example, in Massachusetts, Connecticut, and New Hampshire where the Congregational churches were established, the Anglicans were given the special privilege of applying their religious taxes to the purpose of supporting their own Church of England ministers. Later, *all* Protestant societies were given this privilege in the organic laws that governed these states after the Revolution.

A similar proposal aroused a bitter controversy in Virginia during the Revolutionary period, but it was defeated under the leadership of Jefferson and James Madison. Instead, the Virginia statute for religious freedom drawn up by Jefferson and adopted in 1786 became a model for other states throughout the nineteenth century. Fresh from this battle, Madison saw the necessity of guaranteeing religious freedom and separation of church and state in the federal constitution. As a result, he led the fight for a bill of rights in which the First Amendment proclaimed, "Congress shall make no law respecting an establishment of religion, or prohibiting the free exercise thereof."

Reflecting the unmistakable trend toward religious freedom, eight states had already disestablished their state churches before the First Amendment determined national policy. This toppling of the standing order of the colonial period was one of the most important triumphs of the Enlightenment over the Reformation in American life, heralding radical changes in the control and program of education in the nineteenth century. Without it, a common public education would have been impossible.

---

[15] For a full history of this process, see R. Freeman Butts, *The American Tradition in Religion and Education,* Beacon Press, Boston, 1950.

The influx of an increasing diversity of religious groups during the eighteenth century helped to create the political conditions wherein religious freedom could become a reality. Large numbers of German Lutherans, Moravians, Mennonites, and Scots-Irish Presbyterians settled in Pennsylvania, and Methodists and Baptists settled in virtually all colonies. The established churches could not survive the rising political power of these growing sectarian groups.

The strength and vitality of the churches in America were in no small measure the result of the principles of religious freedom and the separation of church and state embodied in the First Amendment and in the bill of rights of the several state constitutions. Virtually every state as it came into the Union in the nineteenth century adopted the principles that the state guaranteed freedom of religious conscience and that the state would not use public funds to aid or support any churches or their schools.

In sum, the secularization of public affairs was one of the basic elements in the modernization process. This did not mean that religious values had to be separated from political decisions, but it did mean that no longer would the official clerical institutions be supported by public funds and no longer would the clergy *by virtue of their office* be empowered to make political decisions on behalf of the citizens. Although there were countless twistings and turnings in the road from Cotton Mather's rule of the sectarian clergy over education in 1700 to the establishment of laicized state boards of public education in the 1850s, it was a perfectly visible road.

C. THE SECULAR LAMP OF ENLIGHTENMENT

The eighteenth-century Enlightenment was a reaction against the traditional civilization of the old regime in Europe—against absolute monarchy, closed economic systems, rigid social stratification, religious authoritarianism, an unscientific world view, the doctrine of original sin in human nature, and the domination of intellectual life by medieval conceptions of knowledge. Underlying this protest was a growing faith in the powers of man, in science, and in human reason. This age of reason preached the humanitarian faith in progress that man, by taking thought, could reform his institutions as a means of promoting the general welfare. These currents of thought helped to shape the pervasive liberal and democratic ideals that came to mark the heartland of the West. They formed the intellectual pillars upon which the social structures of modernity rest. As the reformers sought a justification of their revolt against traditionalism and absolutism, they formulated the conception of natural law and natural rights as instruments with which to attack all forms of entrenched interests. The conception of natural law, borrowed from the new science, was applied to human nature, to society, to economics, to politics, to learning, and to education.

Peter Gay begins his masterly study of the Enlightenment with a perceptive overview and ends it, appropriately, with a discourse on education:

> The men of the Enlightenment united on a vastly ambitious program, a program of secularism, humanity, cosmopolitanism, and freedom, above all,

freedom in its many forms—freedom from arbitrary power, freedom of speech, freedom of trade, freedom to realize one's talents, freedom of aesthetic response, freedom in a word, of moral man to make his own way in the world.[16]

At the end of his two volumes, Gay rightly refers to education as "the logic of enlightenment," the very basis of programmatic reform:

> But education was more than a theory or a hope for the philosophes; it was also an experience—in fact, it lies at the heart of their experience *as* philosophes. I have defined that experience as a dialectical struggle in which the philosophes first pitted classical thought against their Christian heritage that they might discard the burdens of religion, and then escaped their beloved ancients by appealing to the science of nature and of man; *this pursuit of modernity was the essential purpose of their education.* Indeed, their experience was an education in the most specific possible sense. Each philosophe recapitulated in his private development the course that the Enlightenment was prescribing for mankind in general; each first sensed his opportunity for engaging in this liberating and exhilarating struggle, and equipped himself for it, in his school.[17]

Peter Gay's thesis is pregnant with suggestions for viewing the formative role of education in promoting social reform during the Enlightenment and after. It makes suspect the easy dichotomy sometimes assumed by latter-day developmental economists that the humanities are wholly tradition-bound and the sciences entirely forward-looking. That the philosophes could use the classical studies as powerful weapons in attacking the religious traditions of their day and then pave the way for modern reforms in society and in education finds a certain parallel in the twentieth-century independence movements led by Asians and Africans who were brought up on a classical Westernized education.

But the fact remains, too, that the Enlightenment philosophes were not content to remain with the world views or the social views of their beloved ancients. They believed the modern world could only be unlocked by the secular sciences and their application to man, to society, and to education. They found their patron saints in Bacon, Fontenelle, Newton, and Locke, not in Aristotle, Cicero, or Vergil. For all their attraction to and competence in the classical style the philosophes from Montesquieu and Voltaire to Condorcet, Turgo, and Kant would have to side with the Moderns in their struggle with the Ancients. Just as the Renaissance humanists proclaimed their own superiority over the medievalists by appealing to the classics, so the philosophes proclaimed *their* superiority over the humanists by appealing to science. The idea of progress as a historical process of social improvement was no longer simply a description of the historical record of the past. It became a faith for the future, that

---

[16] Peter Gay, *The Enlightenment: an Interpretation,* vol. 1, *The Rise of Modern Paganism,* Knopf, New York, 1966, p. 3.

[17] Ibid., vol. 2, *The Science of Freedom,* Knopf, New York, 1969, p. 502. Italics added.

indefinite improvement could be achieved if men purposely applied themselves, their reason, and their knowledge to the task of reforming their institutions.

Above all, the progressive development of knowledge was at the root of all other progress. It was not only normal and natural, nay inevitable.[18] It was no accident that Condorcet's great essay was entitled the *Progress of the Human Mind*. Condorcet not only viewed progress as a process of social development through ten stages from folk societies to his present, but he viewed these stages as anchored in the development of the human mind as it progressed from irrationality to rationality. And, significantly, the tenth stage, the last and greatest, was to be marked not only by liberty, equality, and democracy but by universal education, the fountainhead of the development of knowledge and of intellect.

Never have scholars and intellectuals been so confident that knowledge could improve society. Taking their cue from the physical sciences, they carried on investigations that led to major advances in nearly all organized bodies of knowledge. Preeminent in expanding the horizons of knowledge were the scientists and mathematicians. In the fields of astronomy and physics Newton's formulation of the law of gravitation began a new era of science that rapidly found expression in the newly developing biological sciences, social sciences, and humanities. For a Newton in physics there was a Leibnitz in mathematics, a Pasteur or Darwin in biology, a Voltaire or a Ranke in history, a Malthus or a Ricardo in economics, a de Tocqueville or a Bryce in political science, a Saint-Simon or a Comte in sociology, a Locke or Hume, Kant or Hegel in philosophy, a Bentham or a Mill in social theory, and a Rousseau or a Condorcet in education.

As a result, science gained tremendous prestige and authority in the intellectual life of the modern western world. The term *science* came to have at least three meanings. (1) It referred to all bodies of *organized knowledge* that developed systematic and consistent statements of tested beliefs. (2) It came to mean more specifically the *experimental method* for the discovery and refinement of knowledge, relying upon careful observation, the formulation of hypotheses, the elaboration of consequences, and the testing and verifying of the hypotheses under controlled and measurable conditions. (3) It came to mean a general *philosophy,* or *world view,* according to which both natural phenomena and human events follow orderly regularities that can be observed by the senses, measured accurately, and expressed in quantitative terms.

On the American side of the Atlantic the Enlightenment began to glow with increasing brightness from 1715 onward. By the end of the eighteenth century Unitarian religious beliefs began to temper the stern Calvinist outlook on sin and depravity, preaching the inherent goodness of human nature and the infinite perfectibility of man. A deistic outlook began to view the world in Newton's terms as a great machine operating according to natural laws rather than the capricious will of a personal God. The Franklins, Winthrops, and Jeffersons were relatively few before 1800, but they began to multiply thereafter.

---

[18] For an important analysis of the idea of progress varying from the standard view of J. B. Bury, see Robert A. Nisbet, *Social Change and History, Aspects of the Western Theory of Development,* Oxford University Press, New York, 1969. chap. 3.

One of the most impressive facts concerning the intellectual life of the United States during the nineteenth century was the enormous and rapid expansion that took place in nearly all fields of organized knowledge. Few developments had so great or so direct an effect upon the character of American education. The investigative methods of science played a key part in this process.

As masses of material were added to the traditional bodies of knowledge, many new and relatively independent subjects came onto the educational scene. The older bodies of knowledge were divided and subdivided into ever more specialized elements. A college professor of natural philosophy like Benjamin Silliman at the beginning of the century could take for his field the whole range of organic life, but by the end of the century he was more likely to be a botanist, zoologist, physiologist, geologist, or chemist. What had simply been called natural philosophy came to be subdivided into such specialized physical sciences as astronomy, physics, chemistry, mineralogy, geology, meteorology, and physical geography. In the same manner moral philosophy was transformed and differentiated into the social sciences of history and political economy. Indeed, by the end of the century a scholar could no longer take even the whole of one of these newer fields for his special interest but had to specialize in ever more narrow aspects of zoology, or physics, or history.

This process of expansion and specialization of knowledge was hastened not only by the attempt to apply scientific methods to nearly all fields of knowledge but also by the organization of professional associations of scholars and specialists in the various fields. The success of the scientific method was soon apparent as scientists were impelled by colleges and universities, by business and industry, and by the government to investigate the whole range of natural and physical phenomena. Practical and profit motives were strong, as well as the theoretical impetus. The desire to create better machines for the production of goods, to improve agricultural products, to find better sea lanes, and to develop ocean and overland transportation all played their parts.

With the growing importance of knowledge of so many kinds, it was only natural that there should be differences of opinion concerning the uses to which knowledge should be put—indeed, concerning its whole purpose. One outlook, strongly akin to the humanistic tradition, held to the ideal that knowledge is valuable primarily for its own sake. Literature, language, science, history, art, and music are the hallmarks of culture and scholarship that express the most refined and purest sentiments of human nature. According to this genteel tradition, the quiet, reserved, and undisturbed pursuit of truth or expression of beauty should not be jarred by the harsh realities of the outside world. Romanticism, escape literature, the remote, the sentimental, and the adventurous were marks of the genteel tradition, exemplified by such writers as Longfellow, Lowell, and Holmes.

In opposition to this exaltation of scholarship, whether in the humanities or the sciences, as an adornment of the cultivated mind, was the belief that knowledge has a social function to perform and should not merely hide away in its ivory tower. This view, linked to the modernism of the Enlightenment, took several forms. One was a nationalistic emphasis, which began to glorify the new American republic, its ideals, its people, and its setting in a new continent. Literature, history, and science were stimulated by this nationalistic zeal to turn knowledge to the improvement and development of the new nation.

Another form drew its inspiration from business enterprise and industrialism, which idealized the practicality of life and insisted that knowledge should promote the practical business of living. This stimulus included not only the desire to use technology to improve the productive capacity of the nation but also the optimism that practical knowledge is the open-sesame by which the individual may advance himself on the social and economic scale.

A third form was the belief that knowledge should be devoted to the welfare of the great majority of the people in a democracy. The test of literature, science, social science, and art should be their functioning in the public interest. Knowledge must not be locked up in its intellectual hideaways; it must not be neutral to injustice and corruption; it must not be confined to an aristocratic elite; it must not defend the privilege and entrenched interests of the status quo. Rather, investigation should be undertaken with a view to the improvement of democracy, and its fruits should be spread as widely among the population as possible by means of popular education.

As a matter of fact, the scientific movement proved to be one of the most important factors in breaking down barriers between intellectuals and the common people. The interest in scientific facts amounted to a popular rage. Societies for the dissemination of scientific knowledge sprang up in all parts of the country, and thousands of people were brought into closer touch with the marvels of science through mechanics' institutes, libraries, popular books, and lyceum lectures.

Whatever else the Enlightenment may have bequeathed to modern civilization it affirmed the value of knowledge in the improvement of social institutions. From Montesquieu, Voltaire, and Franklin to Jefferson, Bentham, and Mill, the faith in rationality assumed that the world of man as well as the world of nature was basically comprehensible and, if not orderly on the surface, could be made orderly by the uses of reason and especially of scientific reason. More than that. The world of man and of nature could not only be understood by acquiring knowledge, it could be controlled, managed, and improved by taking thought and applying the resources of reason and knowledge to the task. This faith in knowledge—and thus in education—was of the essence of modernity. Of all the sources of social power upon which Western civilization drew as it moved from tradition to modernity this was the fountain that nourished, or the lamp that illumined, the others.

But illumination was not all either. Fundamental efforts to understand the world and man are characteristic of traditional civilized societies as well as modern. All traditional civilizations had great respect for knowledge as the reservoir of wisdom, or sacred writ, or spiritual nourishment, or intellectual satisfaction. The Greeks spread the gospel of rationality as the spearhead of a civilized way of life. The distinctively modern is, however, the energizing power that knowledge endows upon those who use it, applying it to practical affairs.

Aristotle had separated theoretical knowledge from practical knowledge, and the West followed his lead for nearly a thousand years. It was the Enlightenment that gave enormous momentum to consummating an alliance between the two which produced the technological revolutions of the nineteenth and twentieth centuries. The Greeks had the word for it, τέχνη, an art or regular method of making a thing, which has come into the English language as *technology*. A latter-day Greek philosopher, Emmanuel G. Mesthene, defines technology as "the organization of knowledge for practical purposes."[19] This is the essence of the matter. Such organization includes not only physical tools and machines, but linguistic, mathematical, and intellectual tools in general. Along with harnessing physical energy, these are the sources of the social power which has marked modern Western civilization for some 300 years. Organizing linguistic, mathematical, and intellectual tools for practical purposes became a special province of modern Western education.

Of course, this power has not been viewed with as much unalloyed enthusiasm by everyone as by the philosophes of the eighteenth century and the utilitarians of the nineteenth century. The old regimes and the standing orders being attacked by the philosophes scarcely welcomed their admiration for knowledge as a means of changing institutions. Nor did a growing crescendo of voices that began to be heard throughout the West in conservative reaction against the modernity, the freedom, the individualism, the progress, the practicality, and the rationality of the Enlightenment. The lamp was dimmed or at least it flickered fitfully in the face of the growing winds of disenchantment with the success of the Enlightenment. These took various forms: a reassertion of the traditional values of spiritual, moral, and religious authority, a claim for the needs of the social bonds of community as over against rampant individualism, the importance of the nonrational springs of behavior as against the rational, the complaints about alienation in the face of secular, profane, progressive trends that degrade and cheapen the quality of life.[20]

The conservative reaction against the enthusiasms, the confidence, and the optimism of the Enlightenment belief in the efficacy of knowledge has had its effects upon Western education on both sides of the Atlantic. These will be treated later, but the immediate result was to raise the religious tone of much of the education offered to the populace and slow down the liberalizing reforms that were seeking to modernize educational institutions in the afterglow of the Enlightenment. The overall result, however, was only to delay the intellectual momentum of the Enlightenment ideals in education, not to reverse them.

D. THE TORCH OF DEMOCRATIC REVOLUTION

Few of the Enlightenment philosophes contemplated that their programs for social reform would lead to the violent overthrow of the established order. To be sure, they attacked the evils of church, monarchy, and ignorance, but they did not visualize the lamp of enlightenment becoming the torch of revolution. Their faith in men of reason did not extend easily to faith in the great masses of poor, downtrodden, uneducated

---

[19] Harvard University Program on Technology and Society, *Fourth Annual Report, 1967-1968*, Harvard University, Cambridge, Mass., p. 44.

[20] See, for example, Robert A. Nisbet, *The Sociological Tradition*, Basic Books, New York, 1966.

men, the rabble, the *canaille,* the *sans culottes.* But their preachments against special privilege and in favor of wider participation by the populace in the political process led inexorably to the egalitarianism and popular extension of citizenship that formed the basis of the democratic revolution, described so persuasively and penetratingly by R. R. Palmer.[21] This movement, linked intricately with the growing power of the nation-state, the reformism of the Enlightenment, and religious freedom is the fourth major element of the modernization process that characterized the societies of Western civilization in the period from 1700 to the present.

One of the most illuminating aspects of Palmer's interpretation is that the democratic revolution was a single revolutionary movement that broke out in different parts of the heartland of the West in the latter decades of the eighteenth century.[22] The manifestations that appeared in America and in France were the prototypes for all the others. The American revolution was first to take place and the only one to succeed without major reaction. The French Revolution, more extreme and more violent than the others, was associated with the most powerful nation-state in Europe until Napoleon was defeated and the Congress of Vienna in 1815 heralded a major reaction in Europe.

Palmer makes the point that the revolutions did not spread from America or from France to the rest of the West. Rather, each country had its own agitations, its own protests, and its own assaults upon the established orders, which from the mid-seventeenth to the mid-eighteenth centuries had become ever more aristocratic, more closed, more elite, more self-perpetuating and hereditary, and more privileged. Even the parliaments, assemblies, councils, and diets were less responsive to the needs of the common people. Each country had its revolutionary upheavals aimed at achieving greater equality, more participation in government by a greater share of the populace, and greater protection for the civil liberties and civil rights of citizens in a free political community. Reform movements appeared in England and Ireland, and short-lived republics were set up in Holland, Belgium, Switzerland, Italy, Hungary, and Poland in the 1780s and 1790s. But by 1800 the established orders had regained their powers, and the republics had reverted to aristocracies or monarchies, except for France which maintained its republican facade until Napoleon declared the empire in 1804.

In general, Palmer's analysis of the adversaries has interesting educational ramifications.[23] Those who were likely to be anti-French and anti-revolution were likely to include those who had only a moderate amount of education (the highest social, economic, and governing classes) as well as those who had little or no education (the lowest wage-earning or dependent classes). (France and the United States were major exceptions to this generalization.) Those who were likely to be pro-French and prorevolutionary were those who were the best-educated: the intermediate classes or

[21] R. R. Palmer, *The Age of the Democratic Revolution; a Political History of Europe and America, 1760-1800,* 2 vols. Princeton University Press, Princeton, N.J., 1959, 1964.

[22] Palmer, op. cit., vol. 1, *The Challenge,* chap. 1.

[23] See Palmer, op. cit., vol. 2, *The Struggle,* chap. 1.

those whose status was changing. These were the professionals in medicine, law, and teaching, students, literate craftsmen or shop keepers, and small businessmen or merchants who saw advantages in modernization. Palmer puts it this way:

> In any case, sympathy for the new order everywhere varied in direct proportion to communications, to the contact between town and country, the state of the roads, the reading of newspapers, the frequency of inns and of travelers, the habit of small farmers selling their own produce in a market. Rural communities that had the least contact with the outside world were least interested in a new legal and political order.[24]

It is not too much to say, therefore, that the more widespread literacy was among the populace and the more influential were the educated professional classes the more likely was the outlook to be in favor of the ideals of the democratic revolution. Intentionally or not, the incidence of education seemed to have a bearing upon the attitudes toward democracy as a phase of modernization. Exceptions of course were evident. In England the educated gentry class of the seventeenth-century revolution had taken a more conservative turn and had even restricted educational opportunity during the eighteenth century, so that literacy in 1780 was probably no more widespread than 200 years earlier. In Germany the educated classes were largely in the service of the "enlightened" rulers who were trying to modernize from the top down without extending democratic rule to the populace.

By and large, however, an even more fateful relationship between the democratic revolution and education began to take form: the more conservative or reactionary the outlook, the less disposition to extend educational opportunity; the more radical and revolutionary, the greater the demand for widespread education. The educational outlook of Palmer's five categories of opinion toward the revolution might be said to follow this pattern:

> Reactionary conservative monarchists who wanted to return to the privileges of monarchy, to maintain an established church, and to permit little or no social change would limit education to the few.
>
> Conservative constitutional monarchists who believed the old regimes needed some modernization and liberalization of citizens' civil and property rights would extend education modestly to more people.
>
> Constitutionalist revolutionaries who believed in substantial changes within an ordered system of property rights and representative government would extend primary education rather widely under state control.
>
> Jacobins, largely of middle class origin, who accepted universal suffrage and political democracy as their goal in the overthrow of established monarchy, aristocracy, and church proposed universal education.
>
> Popular revolutionary democrats, made up of the *sans culottes*, the lower classes, the underprivileged, the downtrodden workers, and the dependent people of the streets of Paris were the most militant activists and the least educated. Most of all they wanted respect and recognition as well as bread and

[24] Ibid., p. 21.

direct democracy. They also wanted more public education for all, including vocational training.

Extreme popular revolutionism boiled up to power, even for a short time, only in France. It was the extremity of this phase of the French revolution that provoked conservative reactions in many parts of Europe. Especially in England did the counter-revolution take hold and result in strengthening the established order. As a result of the reaction, the pressure for democratic public education in England was slowed in favor of voluntary, philanthropic, and religious sponsorship of education. The counter-revolution in France started a social pendulum that swung between reaction and liberalism throughout most of the nineteenth century, now favoring liberal, secular, democratic education, then swinging back to conservative, religious, and aristocratic education. Only in the United States was the success of the democratic revolution itself matched by the widening access to education. The democratic revolution in education helped the United States by mid-nineteenth century to begin to overtake England and France in the modernization process. Popular education helped to broaden the base of political and economic participation.

Having had its political revolution a century earlier than in France, England was in a position to modernize economically and industrially at the end of the eighteenth century even though it remained highly conservative socially. Thus, England was the first modernizing society, but then France had the opportunity to become more modern than England as a result of its revolution in the late eighteenth century. France modernized its bureaucracy, separated church from state (under the First Republic), and established under state control higher educational institutions of science and technology that began to devote themselves to public service and the application of science to modern life. But the conservative reactions that periodically slowed the democratic gains created a political instability that weakened the French drive to modernity.

Samuel P. Huntington points out that political modernization involves three elements: the participation of the mass of the people, the rationalization of legitimate authority in the transition from feudalism to centralized nation-states, and the differentiation of political structures according to legislative, executive, and judicial functions.[25] He points out that European and British political systems achieved the latter two characteristics before America did, whereas the United States went further and faster toward extension of political participation among the populace. It also moved rapidly to develop another of the characteristics of political modernity, the political party as a means of aggregating the demands of various interest groups into specific and alternative courses of political action. In these respects the modernization process in the United States forged ahead of that in England and France.

Because of the lack of entrenched constituted bodies or a privileged upper class of a feudalistic nature, democratic revolutionaries in America did not lean, as they did on the European continent, toward a strong, unitary, centralized government capable

[25] Samuel P. Huntington, *Political Order in Changing Societies,* Yale University Press, New Haven, Conn., 1968, chaps. 1 and 2.

of dealing with a deeply entrenched landed aristocracy. American democratic republicans like Jefferson rather favored local self-sufficiency and feared centralized homogeneous governments. In contrast, modernization by centralized government or by business aided by government was favored by anti-democratic Federalists like Hamilton.[26] The American party system was thus first formulated around the varying responses to the democratic revolution as it manifested itself in France, in the European wars of the French Revolution, and in radical Whig thought in eighteenth-century England. What was remarkable was that in large part both of the major American political parties that emerged by the mid-nineteenth century were agreeing that widespread public education was not only desirable but necessary to the well-being of the new Republic.

In his landmark study Bernard Bailyn has identified five major sources of the origins of revolutionary thought among the American colonists.[27] One was the classical literature of politics made familiar by the prevailing humanist education in Latin grammar schools and colleges. Allusions to Aristotle, Plato, and other Greeks were common, but special emphasis went to Republican Rome, to Cicero, Sallust, and Tacitus. A second source was the literature of Enlightenment rationalism and reform, ranging from Montesquieu and Locke, to Voltaire and Rousseau, Grotius and Pufendorf. A third and fourth stream consisted of the English tradition of common law with its emphasis upon equity, justice, and rights, and the American Puritan covenant theology that envisioned a special destiny for America in God's contract with man.

The fifth source, and in Bailyn's view the most important, was the radical ideology that stemmed from the seventeenth-century English Revolution and Civil War. Embracing such men as John Milton, James Harrington, Henry Neville, and Algernon Sidney, this tradition was carried on in early eighteenth-century England by opposition politicians independents in Parliament, and coffee-house radicals. Their writings directly shaped the ideas of Americans as early as the beginning of the eighteenth century, increasingly from 1730 on, and above all from 1760 to the Declaration of Independence.

Bailyn makes special point of his belief that the reforms which the American revolutionaries sought most vigorously were *political* reforms, not the reconstruction of the social order as a whole. Much social reform had already been achieved, in 150 years of history, in the direction of greater social equality and the absence of a privileged and hereditary aristocracy. What *was* oppressive was the power of Parliament and of royal officials to compel obedience of colonists from afar. Americans were thus especially concerned to do away with the repressive compulsion and the unwarranted power of standing armies and repressive officials. They came to agree that a check on such tyranny and the achievement of a self-sustaining liberty were the main goals of their revolution.

In the course of working out how this could be accomplished, the English idea that the major constituted orders—crown, nobility, commons—should each have its

---

[26] See Palmer, op. cit., vol. 2, chaps. 1 and 16.

[27] Bernard Bailyn, *The Ideological Origins of the American Revolution,* Harvard University Press, Cambridge, Mass., 1967, chap. 2.

own organ of government to balance and check the others was transformed into the idea that the different interests in society should be organized into parties for political action to work out their differences and arrive at agreements *within* the legislative branches of government itself. This development of the political party as an agency of interest aggregation marked a significant step in the modernization of the political process. When it was further determined that political office should be held only on the basis of merit or election and not upon the basis of birth, heredity, family, rank, or wealth, the democratic revolution moved the political systems of the West still further along the road of transmutation to modernity.

Enormously important for the future of American political life was the extension of the ballot to wider and wider elements in the population. At the beginning of the nineteenth century the privilege of voting was limited by property, religious, and racial qualifications, but by the middle of the century white manhood suffrage was virtually won. In the 1820s and 1830s especially, the new states of the West came into the Union with constitutions guaranteeing universal manhood suffrage (at least for white men), and many of the eastern states liberalized their voting requirements under the impact of the Republican-Democrats. The election of Andrew Jackson in 1828 is usually taken as the signal that the process of extending the vote to small farmers and laborers was well on its way.

While the possibility of social as well as political advancement for white workers increased, the social status of those who remained in the South declined as wave after wave of Negro slaves were brought in from Africa and the West Indies. In 1700 Negroes already represented about 10 percent of the total population, about 27,000 out of 250,000. By 1780 there were 575,000 Negroes in the United States out of a total population of 2,780,000. This represented something like an increase of 100,000 in each of the prior decades. By 1860 the Negro population reached nearly 15 percent of the total (4,400,000 out of 31,400,000). It was much higher in the South, reaching something over one-third of the total. With the invention of the cotton gin, the South turned more than ever to cotton, further entrenching Negro slavery until the time of the Civil War. The denial of rights to black Americans was, of course, the greatest failure of the democratic revolution.

By the middle of the nineteenth century, the United States was no longer merely a hothouse in which European institutions and ideas flourished as replicas of the Old World. A new environment, new soil, and new atmosphere produced a way of life that began to make its own distinctive contributions to Western civilization. Not the least important of these was the public school idea, an idea which in its own way was just as symbolic of the success of the democratic revolution as black slavery was symbolic of its failure. Eventually, these two had to come to grips with one another—a schoolhouse divided against itself could not stand.

E. THE MAGNET OF INDUSTRIAL URBANIZATION

In describing the transmutation to modernity it has been customary for social scientists to speak of the industrial revolution as the heart of the matter. And the essence of the industrial revolution has usually been located in the application of machine technology to the mass production of goods. The development of the steam engine in the 1770s was a key element in the process, dwarfing all previous power-driven techniques of harnessing wind and water. But the industrial revolution was not a simplistic matter of increasingly complex technology, tools, and power-driven machines. While the technological advances were historically vastly important, the transformation to modernity resulted from the interaction of several strands of social power. We have already mentioned four of these: the development of the power of the nation-state, the power of Enlightenment knowledge (especially scientific and practical), the power of religious freedom, and the power of the democratic populace.

In addition to these, another factor was involved: the fundamental character of urban life changed as the preindustrial city became the industrial city. The importance of the role of the urban way of life as a basic element in the rise of traditional civilization itself has been traced earlier in this book. Now, it should come as no surprise that the rise of modern civilization should be associated with the rise of the modern city. Whether industrialization can take place without urbanization is a nice theoretical question for the modernizing nations of the later twentieth century to ponder, but the historical fact is that in the first modernization experience the two went along indelibly together. I have therefore chosen to treat the two together under the term, *industrial urbanization.* The matter is put succinctly by Melvin Kranzberg:

> From the very beginnings of civilization the hearth and home had been the center of production and of life. The Industrial Revolution had transformed all of society by taking men away from the traditional agricultural pursuits which had formed their main occupation throughout history and introducing them to novel ways of working and living in factory and city.[28]

Under the stimulus of trade, commerce, and agricultural reform, urban growth had begun to accelerate during the eighteenth century, well before the onset of massive technological industrialization. The way had long been prepared by the world-wide trade that Westerners had pursued in their seaborne search for markets from the sixteenth century onward.[29] The industrial revolution came to a head in the period 1750 to 1830,[30] dates that are as useful as any in identifying what I have called the onset of industrial urbanization. It is the period in which the textile industry led the way to industrialization in Britain, and it is the period in which the industrial city appeared in the modernizing nations of the West, especially in Britain, France, the United States, and the Low Countries. In these countries the industrial cities began to dominate the rest of their societies in ways that preindustrial cities had never before been able to do, except perhaps in some of the ancient city-state systems and in a few

---

[28] Melvin Kranzberg and Carroll W. Pursell, Jr., *Technology in Western Civilization; the Emergence of Modern Industrial Society, Earliest Times to 1900,* Oxford University Press, New York, 1967, vol. 1, p. 217.

[29] For details of the background of the industrial revolution, 1600-1750, see Ibid., Part II.

[30] See Ibid., Part III. For a particularly valuable short survey, see Gideon Sjoberg, "The Origin and Evolution of Cities," *Scientific American,* vol. 213, no. 3, pp. 55-62, September 1965.

of the traditional centralized bureaucratic empires.[31] In the typical traditional society, it was the other way round, the countryside dominated the cities.

What modernization did was to establish the hegemony of the cities and enable the urban populace (middle classes and lower classes) to overthrow the traditional political system, as in France, or to forge alliances between the urban middle classes and the rural landed classes, as in England and in Germany. In all three cases, the rural populations were relatively passive politically, until urbanization and industrialization were well-advanced through the efforts of the urban classes and their allies in the countryside. The one exception was the United States. "In eighteenth century America, the war of independence, the norms of equality and democracy, the relatively high levels of literacy and education, and the relatively widespread distribution of land ownership (outside the south) combined to produce extensive agrarian political participation *before* the rise of the city."[32]

The point is that the pivotal power to change a society and to influence all aspects of a society was beginning to move to the city: ... "the transformation of Western nations into city-dominated societies is an inescapable fact."[33] "The industrial city ... formed the wave of the most thoroughgoing social revolution we have ever known."[34]

Each scholar may be pardoned for seeing in his subject the important catalysts of social change deserving the term *revolutionary.* So now we must reckon not only with the democratic revolution, the industrial revolution, and the scientific revolution but also with the urban revolution, encapsulated in the industrial city. Central in the rise of the industrial city was the emergence of the urban middle classes to positions of political as well as economic power.

Not only did the industrial and urban revolutions embrace the change from hand labor to machine production, making production increasingly specialized, differentiated, mechanized, and interdependent, but two other factors were crucially important. One was what might be called *technicalization,* the increasingly deliberate rationalizing of the whole process. In the early stages of the Industrial Revolution much was achieved by skillful artisans tinkering with machines and tools to produce the inventions that enabled the textile industry to mechanize. But by 1850 much more deliberate steps were being taken to apply science and scientific experimentation to the processes of production. An increasing number of specialists, highly trained in science and the application of science to technology, became necessary. Advanced schools of technology made their appearance in France, Britain, the United States, Germany, and elsewhere as signs that invention would be done less by tinkering mechanics and more by the deliberate experimentation of scientists, engineers, and technologists. The other major factor was the development of social organizations that

---

[31] See Samuel P. Huntington, *Political Order in Changing Societies,* Yale University Press, New Haven, Conn., 1968, pp. 72-77.

[32] Ibid., p. 74. Italics added.

[33] Leonard Reissman, *The Urban Process; Cities in Industrial Society,* Free Press, New York, 1964, p. 15.

[34] Ibid., p. 18

enabled capital to be accumulated and invested in large-scale productive as well as commercial enterprises. Stock companies, banks, and corporations became the typical social inventions that enabled the industrial revolution to take place.

Accompanying the political and economic growth of the industrial city went an increase in social mobility and class fluidity unknown in the more rigidly stratified agrarian and urban societies of traditional civilizations. Other social manifestations included a nuclear family arrangement more loosely knit than the traditional family units, a heightened emphasis upon assignment to positions on the basis of earned achievement rather than social ascription, and a greater stress upon an intellectual and managerial elite oriented to scientific and practical knowledge rather than solely to a literary, humanistic, or wisdom literature. Above all, a broadened base of literacy and the institutions of mass education accompanied the industrial urban phenomenon. Significantly, widespread education was considered to be as essential to the existence of a modern industrial urban society as it was to a nationalized, enlightened, and democratic society.

In defining the essence of the industrial city as contrasted to the preindustrial city Gideon Sjoberg has this to say:

> Mass education, where selection tends to be according to ability, is interlinked with the fluid class and family systems; *it is a must if the industrial city is to prosper.* At the same time only a highly industrialized system can educate all of its members. . . . Not only has the availability of formal education reached monumental proportions, but knowledge is becoming ever more widely diffused through mass communication media.[35]

Whether literacy and mass education come first, and industrial urbanization follows, or whether it is the other way round is a matter of considerable dispute among scholars. Daniel Lerner's famous formula for the modernization process has it that urbanization leads to literacy, literacy to mass media (as soon as industrialization makes them possible), and the mass media lead to greater participation in political and economic affairs. Lerner argues:

> Only after a country reaches 10% of urbanization [the proportion of persons living in cities over 50,000] does its literacy rate begin to rise significantly. Thereafter urbanization and literacy increase together in a direct (monotonic) relationship, until they reach 25%, which appears to be the "critical optimum" of urbanization. Beyond this literacy continues to rise independently of the growth of cities.[36]

Lerner's model was built upon contemporary twentieth-century data, so the question remains as to the historical sequence of development where the data are very

---

[35] Gideon Sjoberg, *The Preindustrial City; Past and Present,* Free Press, New York, 1960, p. 341. Italics added.

[36] Daniel Lerner, *The Passing of Traditional Society: Modernizing the Middle East,* Free Press, Glencoe, Ill., 1958, p. 59.

difficult to come by and much research remains to be done. Nevertheless, the interrelationship of education and industrial urbanization seems to be extremely significant. C. Arnold Anderson generalizes from a number of historical studies that "about 40% of adult literacy or of primary enrollment [in school] is a threshold for economic development."[37]

In any case, the historical advantage of the West in the modernization process seems to have stemmed largely from the educational factor as well as from the governmental, the scientific, the democratic, the secular, and the technological. It can be no accident that the most advanced countries economically are also the ones with the highest incidence of school attendance and literacy.

In America as in Western Europe urban growth in the eighteenth and nineteenth centuries was preparing the way for industrialization. This sometimes comes as a surprise, for the United States is often pictured as a society facing an early wilderness in the seventeenth century, expanding to vast frontier spaces in the West during the eighteenth and nineteenth centuries, and only becoming citified in the late nineteenth and twentieth centuries. Historical scholarship in the past 30 years, however, has done much to counteract this image of a rural agrarian America only lately urbanized.[38] The importance of town life in colonial New England and on the sea coast of the middle colonies has long been recognized, but the transformation of towns into cities and the generative role in social change they have played in the prerevolutionary as well as the antebellum period in American history has only recently become clear.

The proportion of urban dwellers in the American colonies may have been around 10 percent in 1690. While this seems small today, nevertheless, it was a decisive factor in colonial life compared with a wholly rural or plantationlike colony, and the crucial role of the urban centers in American society began to accelerate from the 1740s to the end of the eighteenth century. Then the proportion of people living in urban centers rose dramatically during the second quarter of the nineteenth century. In 1820 7 percent lived in urban centers (700,000 out of 9 million); by 1860 one-fifth of all Americans (6 million out of 31 million) lived in centers of 2,500 or more. While the total population was increasing something over three times from 1820 to 1860, the urban population was increasing something over nine times. This was the most rapid growth rate in American history. Noteworthy, too, was the rapid rise in the size of cities. In 1820 the United States boasted twelve cities of 10,000 or more; by 1860 there were 101, with more than 12 percent of the entire population living in them. Eight cities contained over 100,000, and more than 6 percent of all Americans lived in them. New York, over the million mark, was the third largest city in the world. All this *before* 1860.

Important too was the cultural and educational leadership of the cities on the western frontier as well as of those on the eastern coast. The usual image is that the western migrations of the early nineteenth century were led by covered wagons loaded with people aiming to settle on farms in the rural regions of the west, but it is now clear

[37] C. Arnold Anderson and Mary Jean Bowman (eds.), *Education and Economic Development,* Aldine, Chicago, 1963, p. 347.

[38] See Bibliographical notes, p. 585.

that town dwellers went west just as farmers did. In fact, the towns and cities of the pre-Civil War period in the west are described by Richard C. Wade as "the spearheads of the frontier." The inland cities, founded on rivers and lakes and at convenient transportation junctions, developed common as well as unique urban characteristics that carried the urban way of life from the Atlantic through the vast American continent to the Mississippi and beyond. They not only set up printing presses, libraries, theaters, museums, and lecture circuits, but, above all, they established elementary schools, academies, normal schools, colleges, and universities. The proliferation of American institutions of higher education cannot be understood without understanding the proliferation of towns and cities throughout rural America.

In counteracting the famous frontier thesis of Frederick Jackson Turner that the expanding frontier gave America its distinctive characteristics, Charles N. Glaab argues that "American expansion was largely a function of urban expansion, and ... the civilization which pushed the edge of wilderness always toward the Pacific drew most of its impulses and took most of its direction from cities."[39]

As people flocked to the manufacturing centers, first in the New England and Middle states and then in the Middle West, the crowded cities belched forth desperate conditions of congestion, filth, squalor, and disease. The slum areas became a startling threat to health, sanitation, morals, and human dignity, the effects of which are still plain in the decaying core areas of all large cities today. People came to the cities not only from the rural areas of America but from many countries of Europe and Asia. Meanwhile, the labor movement in America arose, as elsewhere, as a protest and reaction against the excesses of industrial capitalism. The skilled workers began to organize into trade unions or craft unions in order to improve their bargaining power and keep wages up. In 1827 in Philadelphia fifteen trade unions joined together to form the Mechanics' Union of Trade Associations. Meeting with preliminary success, the movement soon explanded, and a political party was organized in 1828 called the Workingmen's Party, designed to agitate for legislation that would extend the rights of labor, including free public education as one of the means of improving the condition of working people.

To improve the social conditions of the masses caught in the clangor, grime, and crunch of industrial urbanization, innumerable voluntary societies dedicated themselves to alleviate poverty, abolish Negro slavery, soften criminal codes, improve prison conditions, extend women's rights, prevent intemperance, and help the insane, the blind, the deaf, and other handicapped. Approaching reform in a variety of ways, some groups took to the city streets to achieve a more humane community life for the downtrodden and disadvantaged masses. Others, religious and socialist communities alike, went off by themselves to the country to seek the perfect life apart from the destructive influences of an industrial and capitalistic society. In all, there were dozens of different experiments like those at Oneida, New York, New Harmony, Indiana, or Brook Farm in Massachusetts, reflecting the ferment of reform ideas that emerged in reaction to the sordidness and stifling quality of industrial urban conditions.

But the achievement of social reform in the face of massive industrial urbanism

---

[39] Charles N. Glaab and A. Theodore Brown, *A History of Urban America,* Macmillan, New York, 1967, p. 51.

required a vastly greater organized enterprise than could be put forth by such small and isolated community projects. The major role in voluntary efforts for social reform was to be played by large-scale religious denominations and voluntary secular societies which launched nationwide and worldwide campaigns usually combining social welfare and education. Even these, however, could not do the job alone. Every modern nation had to turn to government and to large-scale, organized, state-sponsored education even to begin to cope with the problems loosed upon mankind by his determination to live an ever more industrialized and urbanized way of life.

F. THE FAITH IN POPULAR EDUCATION

We come now to a sixth major ingredient of modernity—a redeeming faith in the power of massive educational endeavor. One might even go so far as to say that this is the single most distinctive characteristic of a modern civilization in contrast to a traditional civilization or a folk society. It might be argued that universal schooling was even more distinctive of the modernization process than the other ingredients just discussed: After all, the nation-state had parallels in the great bureaucratic empires of the past; the Enlightenment really grew out of the Hellenic belief in rationality as a way of life; democracy had its roots back in the Greek city-states and the Roman Republic; industrial urbanization was simply a more intensified growth of the urban way of life that began with the Sumerians, the Egyptians, the Indians, and the Chinese. By contrast, it might be argued, elaborate large-scale systems of organized education embracing a large part of the total population were something genuinely new under the sun, something that no premodern societies had even visualized, let alone tried to establish. But I shall not try to argue the case here.

Characteristics of Modernity in Education
It is enough to argue that organized education was one of the essential elements in the process that characterized the appearance of modernity in the heartland of Western civilization. It was finely interwoven with the other strands we have just considered, and it was an indispensable part of the modernizing means by which the West exerted its impact upon the rest of the world, a matter we shall turn to in Chapters 14 and 15. Meanwhile, we need to examine as closely as possible how education was involved in the development of the early modernizing Western societies, how it was affected by the other major factors in modernity, and how it in turn made them possible or gave them added impetus. As a preview and a kind of checklist for the reader, I shall point briefly to five major characteristics that have distinguished modern education from traditional education since the beginning of the eighteenth century. I make no claim that the list defines a model or typology by which to measure the extent of modernity or of traditionality in an educational system, but it may serve as a beginning guide for those who may be inclined to do so.

Large-scale Participation.
Large-scale Participation.   The first and most obvious characteristic of modern education is that there is a great deal of it. The modernizing trend for 300 years has been to

provide more education for more people. To achieve this, large-scale educational systems have been organized, especially on a national basis and especially by governments rather than solely by voluntary or private effort. Some governmental efforts have been highly centralized, others a combination of local and central effort. But the trend has been unmistakeable: from education for the relatively few to education for the relatively many—and at all levels of the organized educational system. The most modern systems have come close to universal education for nearly every child at the primary school level, to widespread education at the secondary level (as high as 70 to 90 percent of the age group), and to expanding availability at postsecondary levels (as high as 30 to 50 percent).

The trend toward popular education has involved making it increasingly free of charge by means of public support and compulsory in attendance through the primary grades and even through secondary school. Whether the society has been democratic or monarchical or socialist, equalitarian or authoritarian, the trend to modern education has involved greater participation by larger numbers and for a longer period of time than in traditional societies. The latter have usually held the opportunity for formal or organized education fairly close to the ruling classes or intellectual elite. Modern education makes *some* provision for education of all classes and strata in a society, whether the levels are defined by wealth, status, race, occupation, or whatever.

A basic counterpart to the popularization of education on a massive scale has been the emergence of highly organized, large-scale, and coordinated *systems* of education. As education has become modernized it has necessarily been bureaucratized. By and large, the trend has been toward greater centralization of the educational organization, as it has been in most other types of modern organization, and this has meant an increasing tendency for government to become the major source of control and support in place of family, or church, or class, or voluntary agency. And, furthermore, the nation-state has tended to become the ever more powerful agency of government in its relationship to local or regional units of government.

Modern educational systems have varied in two major ways. One axis of difference is the degree to which the system is disjointed or integrated; the other is the degree to which it is authoritarian or libertarian. A disjunctive system is likely to divide into two or three disconnected tracks, designed for different groups in the population. There may be separate schools for different racial, religious, ethnic, or linguistic groups, or for different social or occupational classes, or for different levels of intelligence and academic ability. A disjunctive system typically makes it difficult for a person to cross from one track to another. An integrative system tries to weld together into an organized whole the disparate groups in the society by maintaining common schools open widely to all, or at least making it relatively easy to move from one track to another, providing in effect a ladder which all may climb on the basis of their achievement rather than on the basis of personal, family, or social preferment.

Some modern systems have differed on another basis. Some have maintained an authoritarian system which has assigned students to schools on the basis of decisions taken by central governmental or academic authorities; others have permitted considerably more subsystem autonomy for local governmental groups or local educational institutions to make decisions; or for individual students, families, and voluntary groups to follow their own choices regarding their educational preferences and careers. Although generalizations are precarious, the modern ideal has often looked to an educational system that is basically integrative as well as libertarian; while the traditional system has leaned toward the disjunctive and the authoritarian.

Secular and Scientific. Another characteristic marking the transition from traditional to modern education has been the trend from the sacral to the secular, from the humanistic and classical to the scientific. This secularizing tendency has taken two major forms. One has been the gradual laicizing of control, as the principal bodies that authorize and support modern education have shifted from the hands of church, voluntary, and private bodies to governmental authorities. To be sure, while church and state were allies, the education they sponsored was both governmentally controlled and religiously permeated. But the overall trend has been toward separation of the churches from the states with the balance of educational power moving to the states, even where religious bodies remained in local charge of schools.

The other major secularizing trend pertains to the content of subjects and methods of teaching in organized educational institutions: the curriculum has increasingly made way for scientific materials based upon rational, logical, and experimental methods of inquiry rather than upon the fideistic authority of revealed religious faith or classical wisdom literature.[40] The term *scientific*, of course, refers not only to the subject matter of the physical and biological sciences but also to the social and psychological sciences; it has modified the literary, linguistic, artistic, and humanistic studies as well.

Practical and Professional. As education has become more available and more secular it has become increasingly technical and practical, i.e., the effort has been made to concentrate on the application of knowledge to the physical, economic, and social conditions of life. This has most often taken the form of subjects and institutions that stress direct preparation for occupational work. It has ranged from the most intensive and highly intellectual academic training for a career in the learned professions to very specialized and narrow training for specific crafts and trades that depend largely on mechanical skills. A modern system of education in contrast to a traditional education has embraced preparation for a wider and wider range of occupational tasks, until the formal educational system offers vocational training for virtually all skills required in the society, whether this is done in complex, comprehensive educational institutions or in narrowly specialized ones.

Much argument has been spilled over the steady encroachment of crass practical and vocational motives upon the sanctum of academic learning. This has been a steady drumbeat of debate ever since the quarrels between the Ancients and the Moderns of the seventeenth century. But the fact is that modern education has come to embrace much of the technical and vocational training that in a traditional system was relegated to apprenticeship systems. Part of this development is due to the social demands arising from the increasingly complex character of modern, large-scale industrial

---

[40] Recall that Elder defines modernity as corresponding to secular education. (See p. 298)

society; part is due to the recognition of the usefulness to society of knowledge that is organized for practical purposes. When the Enlightenment faith in the power of knowledge was added to the dynamism of industrial urbanism, the practical and professional momentum of modern education could not be resisted.

When educational institutions, especially universities, deliberately set out to produce knowledge through research enterprises a new dynamism was added to modernity. The research-minded characteristic became so strong after mid-nineteenth century that it could well be counted a sixth aspect of modern education. The expectation was that sooner or later the knowledge would be of practical value. If sooner, it was thought of as "applied" research, or policy research, growing out of specific problems to be solved; if later, it was "pure" research stemming from the intellectual interests of the researcher. The conflict between pure and applied research has touched nearly all aspects of modern higher education. In both cases the stress upon the value of research in producing new knowledge has been a modernizing force in contrast to the traditional priority upon the transmission of received knowledge. The "new" knowledge may be required by political modernization, by economic modernization, or by religious modernization as well as by the requirements of national or personal development. Whatever the rationale, the argument of usefulness for society and for the individual has been a potent force in modern education.

Differentiated and Diversified. As with almost all other institutions in a modern society, educational institutions have become increasingly organized along specialized and differentiated lines. Education has become a department or a ministry in national governments; large bureaucracies to administer national, state, and local systems of education have been created; specialized administrators, inspectors, supervisors, and innumerable specialist officials as well as specialist teachers have appeared on the scene to manage and conduct an enormously complex institution to which many nations assign a major part of their annual budgets. In some developing countries, education has become the largest industry; in some advanced countries, as many as one fourth to one third of all the individuals are involved directly as educators or as students.

The educational profession has thus become one of the largest occupational groups in a modern society which, characteristically, begins to stress the service occupations along with the productive. Training for the educational profession has thus become increasingly specialized and differentiated, specifically focusing upon training for education as a career rather than simply assuming that teaching will be an incidental by-product of a generalized humanistic education. A modern system of education thus tends to increase the length and raise the academic level of training required of teachers and qualified professionals, just as modern societies have in general increased the educational qualifications for a vast number of specialized occupations.

As modern educational institutions took on more and more of the specific functions that were performed by family, church, or occupational guild in a traditional society, they reflected the general trend toward functional specificity and structural differentiation that characterizes all modern institutions. Some modern educational systems reflected this trend by establishing specialized selective institutions to serve the society's differentiated functions: academic institutions for university preparation of the socially or intellectually elite; vocational and technical institutions for the skilled trades; teacher-training institutions for preparing primary school teachers; and specialized faculties for different technical and professional careers.

Other educational systems began to provide comprehensive, multipurpose institutions designed to embrace many social functions within a single framework: a primary school for all children, a comprehensive secondary school that includes academic as well as technical studies, multiuniversities that range across nearly all the occupational categories of a complex modern society. Educators and politicians and public alike have continued to debate which type of institution provides the better occupational training, equality of opportunity, range of individual choice, and contribution to national development.

Ambivalence Between Achievement-oriented and Learner-oriented Pedagogy. Underlying modern systems of education is the faith that massive educational endeavor involving the vast majority of people is the best insurance that both society and the individual will be able to achieve their respective purpose. Obviously, different societies have different goals; a particular society may have conflicting goals within itself; and those who run the educational system may have different purposes from those who support the system and those who are expected to learn from it. But, by and large, modern systems of education typically have an achievement orientation different from that of a traditional system, which only had to deal with an elite few. Advocates of a modern system believe that mass education can have a formative influence upon the kind of society they want to achieve as well as enable the learner to become the kind of person he wants to be. How to arrive at a balance between achievement-oriented pedagogy and learner-oriented pedagogy in a mass system creates continuing tensions for modern education.

On the side of society, the modern educational system is expected to mobilize the populace to promote the national welfare, or assist economic development, or contribute to political socialization and recruitment, or strengthen the power of the nation to resist its enemies and support its friends, or generally to contribute to the stability and security of the society as well as to the health, welfare, and development of individuals in the society. Thus, all sectors of the society are expected to put forth the effort to learn, to acquire the competences that will enable them to contribute in expected ways.

Indeed, achievement is to be evaluated or examined on the basis of what has been learned, and public recognition is to be made by the assigning of appropriate credentials in the form of marks or grades or diplomas or degrees. Classification within the lower institutions and admission to higher institutions are made on the basis of some kind of assessment of achievement. Thus, a major function of a modern educational system is that of certification, i.e., public acknowledgment that certain individuals have acquired the standards of competence required for particular tasks in the society. Certification may range all the way from an assessment of minimal literacy in the first years of schooling to professional assessment of medical, legal, or scientific competence at the doctoral and professional level.

On the side of the student, his perception of what is important to achieve is often quite different from that which is expected of him. The task of a modern education has been made infinitely more difficult because of the factor of mass compulsory education in which the achievement aspirations of students and teachers cannot automatically be expected to coincide. Many students or their parents see the educational enterprise as its managers do, a means for their social integration, upward social mobility and personal improvement, or financial gain. Assessment on the basis of competence rather than social class or inherited ascribed status becomes a means of opening up for them formerly closed occupations that had been reserved for a particular privileged elite.

The problem still remains of creating an educational experience deemed valid and valuable by all those who are required to attend universal schools or who are able to attend advanced institutions in increasing numbers. The modern educational profession has been pushed to the limit of its ingenuity to adapt educational methods and curriculum to the wide range of interests and capabilities of all students so that they can best fulfill themselves as individuals and as participants in their society.

No traditional society has ever had to grapple with this ambivalence between achievement-oriented and learner-oriented pedagogy on the scale and intensity that modern societies have had to do. The educators of traditional societies were able to select a clientele best fitted to the kind of education they offered, or weed out those not interested in or incapable of mastering the required education, or simply to ignore the extent to which the student learned anything. In the latter case it was enough if the "right" student was exposed, even though he did not catch on. To be sure, modern educators do all these things too, but it is much harder to surmount educational dissatisfaction when virtually everyone in a society has become involved in education in one way or another. Each of the Western nations has found this out in its own way, some sooner, some later; and the new nations are beginning to experience the problem. In every modernizing society there has been an ambivalence, a powerful drive on both fronts, a drive to make the educational system serve the goals of achievement as set by its managers and a drive to enable education to serve the goals of the learners as seen by them.

G.   THE EDUCATIONAL GAP BETWEEN THE WEST AND THE REST

The period from 1700 to 1850 not only marked the rise of modern education along these six lines in the West, it marked the period when the leadership of education in the modernization process gradually broadened from the European nations to include the United States in the heartland of the West. (See Figure 14.1 p. 478) Through the eighteenth century, major creative movements in educational theory and practice were arising in Britain, France, Germany, and Switzerland; but by the middle of the nineteenth century, some of the distinctive characteristics of modern education were originating with more and more power in the United States. From the mid-nineteenth to the mid-twentieth century the United States not only overtook Europe in economic development but began to set the pace in some aspects of educational modernization as well, notably in the spread of popular education and the turn to the secular and the practical.

However this may be, by the middle of the nineteenth century the overall framework of modern education in the West makes a striking contrast to traditional educational patterns that changed little in some parts of Europe and outside the West. The general tendency was for the Western nations to borrow heavily from each other as each saw ways in which its own modernization might be hastened and strengthened. In turn, each began to export its own brand of education to major sectors of Africa and Asia.

In general, the fifty-year period from around 1870 to World War I is widely agreed to be the climax of the modern period in the civilization of Europe, a time when its influence was greatest upon the rest of the world and when its confidence in itself was highest. It had achieved extraordinary industrial development through the use of science and rational forms of social organization, high standards of living and material progress, lowered death rates and infant mortality, and increasing literacy, life expectancy, and productivity. On most of the basic characteristics of modernity defined earlier in this chapter the European countries were making high marks: the mobilizing power of the nation-state was exceeding anything hitherto seen as a result of centralizing political authority into a single polity and differentiating political structure according to political functions;[41] the faith in the power of knowledge generated by the lamp of the Enlightenment continued apace, still burning despite the gloom of World War I and its waves of pessimism; the torch of the democratic revolution had been dimmed by successive setbacks or resistance, but on the whole, representative governments were on the increase; participation by greater numbers of individuals and social groups was increasing in most societies; and the magnet of industrial urbanization had taken on new electronic powers. While religious brotherhood had not finally won the day, the reaches of religious freedom and safeguards for religious pluralism were greater than in 1850. And solid gains were being made in extending education to more and more people, even if not everywhere on an egalitarian basis.

Measured in both political and economic terms the nations of the West acquired an enormous advantage over the traditional societies of the world by the end of World War I. In C. E. Black's terms they were moving to economic and social transformation following 1850 while many other peoples were still trying to consolidate their modernizing leaderships for effective political action.[42] Political modernity may be defined as more effective political mobilization, wider participation, cultural secularization, or political institutionalization, i.e., the use of rational and secular procedures

---

[41] Samuel P. Huntington, "Political Modernization: America vs. Europe," *World Politics,* vol. 18, p. 378 ff, April 1966.

[42] C. E. Black, *The Dynamics of Modernization; a Study in Comparative History,* Harper & Row, New York, 1966, p. 76.

for making political decisions and administering society through efficient managerial organizations.[43] In whatever technical terms the political scientists may use, the Western governments were mobilizing their organizations and their technological competence to enhance manyfold the social power they had begun to develop in the seventeenth, eighteenth, and early nineteenth centuries.

In economic terms the industrialization that had originated with Britain in the late eighteenth century took on momentous changes after 1870. Britain had acquired enormous initial advantages from the harnessing of coal and iron to the production of steam power by means of an extraordinary flowering of technological inventiveness and capitalist entrepreneurship. But Britain began to rest on its laurels after the first half of the nineteenth century, and the Germans, followed by the Americans, moved deliberately to apply scientific research and theoretical investigations to the field of technology and to the management of such social organizations as banks, corporations, and specialized bureaucracies. Thus industrialization was promoted both by efficient management and by research in electricity, chemistry, and other fields of scientific knowledge.

A linkage between education, technology, and industry proved to be the keys which enabled Germany and the United States to move more rapidly to overtake the original lead that Britain and France had taken in the industrial revolution. Specialized education ranging from lower trade schools through secondary level technical schools on to the universities and higher technological schools proved to be important catalysts in the process. Thus the nations of the West were the first to move into a stage of technological maturity early in the twentieth century and into a stage of high mass-consumption by mid-century, closely followed by Russia and Japan, while most of the rest of the world was still in the traditional stages of a subsistence economy or preparing for a stage of economic takeoff.[44]

By 1950 some 60 percent of the world's population was still engaged in agriculture, but in the early-industrializing societies of the West it had dropped to 20 or 10 percent (as low as 5 percent in England). Even the character of urban life changed drastically when a distinctively new kind of urban settlement appeared, the modern metropolis which Hans Blumenfeld defines as a "concentration of at least 500,000 people living within an area in which the traveling time from the outskirts to the center is no more than 40 minutes."[45] The two types of settlement that had marked civilization for 5,000 years, the village and the city (preindustrial and industrial), were now joined for the first time by a third form of settlement. It was a huge composite built upon an extreme form of specialized division of labor, cooperation of workers, and interconnections between central city, business and manufactur-

---

[43] See, for example, Gabriel A. Almond and James S. Coleman (eds.), *The Politics of the Developing Areas,* Princeton University Press, Princeton, N.J., 1960; Gabriel A. Almond and G. Bingham Power, Jr., *Comparative Politics; a Developmental Approach,* Little, Brown, Boston, 1966; and Samuel P. Huntington, *Political Order in Changing Societies,* Yale University Press, New Haven, Conn., 1968.

[44] W. W. Rostow, *The Stages of Economic Growth,* Cambridge University Press, London, 1960, chap. 2.

[45] Hans Blumenfeld, "The Modern Metropolis," *Scientific American,* vol. 213, p. 64, September 1965.

ing areas, urban and suburban residence areas, and open districts. The metropolis now encompassed as much as 10 times the population and 100 times the area of the largest industrial cities. This basically new form of human settlement was made possible toward the end of the nineteenth century and increasingly in the early twentieth century by the invention of the telephone, elevator, street cars, subways, and automobile. The modern metropolis made its first appearance in the West but in the course of the twentieth century began to appear in all parts of the world as the modernization process took hold in the economic and social realm as well as in the political.

In all this advance toward modernization, however, there were not only vast disparities between the West and the rest of the world, plainly evident by the end of the nineteenth century, there were also great differences in development among different zones of civilization within Europe itself.[46] After 1870 the inner zone of Western Europe was generally more developed industrially, scientifically, technologically, and educationally than the outer zone. In sum, it was more modern than the societies of the Iberian peninsula, southern Italy, Ireland, and Eastern Europe in general. These regions were less industrial, more exclusively agricultural, less literate, and by and large looked to Western Europe for educational and cultural leadership. These were the regions whose modernization depended in large part upon adopting the technology, ideas, and educational patterns of the more rapidly developing parts of the West. As far as modernization is concerned, most of Latin America, the South of the United States, and the eastern regions of Russia were similar in their "backwardness" to the outer zone of Europe.

As Russia borrowed from the primary modernizers and then exerted the enormous driving power of the revolutionary movements of 1905 to 1906 and of 1917, the Soviet Union began to modernize itself with unprecedented speed eventually exerting tremendous modernizing influence over much of Eastern Europe and the mainland of Asia in the fifty years after 1917. Thus Russia overtook much of the West in the twentieth century as the United States had in the late nineteenth. These two were joined by a third modernizer, Japan, which beginning in the late ninteteenth century borrowed with great speed and effectiveness the panoply of modernization from the generative modernizers. Within a half century Japan had so mobilized its technological and social energy that it moved ahead to join the most modern nations of the West by the 1950s.

The disparities referred to here could be substantiated by any number of economic or social indices, but none is more important than education itself, revealing a telling relationship between the extent of education and stage of political, economic, and social development. A useful list was provided in the early 1960s by the economists Frederick Harbison and Charles A. Myers when they developed a composite index by which to rank seventy-five countries according to the level of their human resource development.[47]

The composite index which Harbison and Myers decided to use to measure

---

[46] For discussion of this concept see R. R. Palmer and Joel Colton, *A History of the Modern World*, 3d ed., Knopf, New York, 1969, pp. 557-559.

[47] Frederick Harbson and Charles A. Myers, *Education, Manpower, and Economic Growth; Strategies of Human Resource Development*, McGraw-Hill, New York, 1964.

modernization and which correlates highly with economic development is basically an educational index. It consists of the arithmetic total of (a) enrollment at the level of secondary education taken as a percentage of the age group, 15 to 19, and (b) enrollment at the level of higher education as a percentage of the age group, 20 to 24 (multiplied by a weight of 5 because of the greater importance of higher education in modernization.[48] The seventy-five nations were then divided into four levels and labelled as shown in Exhibit 9.1: underdeveloped, partially developed, semiadvanced, and advanced. For our purposes, the rankings provide a rough measure of the level of modernization in the educational systems of the seventy-five countries, ranging from least modern to most modern.

It can readily be seen that the most advanced level (IV) is made up in large part of the countries of the West that were earliest or most active in their modernizing efforts. Here are the primary modernizers, located largely in the inner zone of Western Europe, and the European offshoots of that zone, the United States, New Zealand, Australia, Canada, and Russia. The outer zone countries of Europe are all in the semiadvanced level (III). The Latin American countries are divided between semi-advanced and partially developed (level II); most Asian countries are classified as partially developed (level II); and most of the new African states are classified as underdeveloped (level I).

Thus our disparities have a fundamentally educational base: Europe's education by and large is more extensive than that of the rest of the world as of mid-twentieth century; and Western Europe's education is more extensive than that of Eastern and Southern Europe. Much of this advantage arose from the historical fact that the Western European countries and their offshoots began their economic and political modernization before most of the rest of the world did. It is significant that all sixteen nations classified as advanced are either Western societies that began their economic modernization in the late eighteenth or early nineteenth centuries, or have been markedly influenced by the West in the nineteenth and twentieth centuries. And, in terms of C. E. Black's category of modernizing leadership, twelve of the sixteen began their political modernization before 1810, while Japan, Russia, and Finland began such consolidation in the mid-nineteenth century.[49] (Israel is a special case of twentieth-century origin.)

There is not only a rough correspondence between the level of educational development and economic, and political modernization, there is a rough historical correspondence: the earlier the modernization began, the more modernized the countries are. This, of course, does not apply in an exact one-to-one correspondence. Britain was first to launch a political revolution and first to industrialize, but it is not first in the composite index of the late 1950s. Japan and Soviet Russia were relatively late to industrialize, but are very high on the index. The reason the United States, Japan, and Russia are so high is certainly related to the speed and thoroughness with which they modernized their educational systems. Japan and Russia borrowed heavily

[48] Ibid., chap. 3. Most of the data are from the late 1950s.
[49] C. E. Black, *The Dynamics of Modernization,* pp. 90-94.

Exhibit 9.1 Four Levels of Educational Development in the 1950s

Seventy-five countries ranked according to the educational index of Harbison and Myers*

Level I Underdeveloped		Level II Partially Developed		Level III Semiadvanced		Level IV Advanced	
Sudan	7.5	Iraq	31.2	Norway	73.8	U.S.A.	261.3
Uganda	5.5	Peru	30.2	Uruguay	69.8	New Zealand	147.3
Senegal	5.5	Turkey	27.2	Czecho-slovakia	68.9	Australia	137.7
Haiti	5.3	Jamaica	26.8	Poland	66.5	Netherlands	133.7
Nigeria	5.0	Pakistan	25.2	Yugoslavia	60.3	Belgium	123.6
Kenya	4.7	Ecuador	24.4	Italy	56.8	U.K.	121.6
Liberia	4.1	Lebanon	24.3	South Korea	55.0	Japan	111.4
Congo	3.6	Malaya	23.6	Hungary	53.9	France	107.8
N. Rhodesia	2.9	Ghana	23.2	Chile	51.2	Canada	101.6
Ivory Coast	2.6	Paraguay	22.7	Greece	48.5	U.S.S.R.	92.9
Tanganyika	2.2	Colombia	22.6	Taiwan	48.4	Finland	88.7
Saudi Arabia	1.9	Brazil	20.9	Venezuela	47.7	West Germany	85.8
Afghanistan	1.9	China (Mainland)	19.5	Costa Rica	47.3	Israel	84.9
Somalia	1.6	Iran	17.3	Portugal	40.8	Argentina	82.0
Nyasaland	1.2	Tunisia	15.2	Egypt	40.1	Sweden	79.2
Ethiopia	.7	Bolivia	14.8	South Africa	40.0	Denmark	77.1
Niger	.3	Dominican Republic	14.5	Spain	39.6		
		Burma	14.2	Cuba	35.5		
		Libya	10.8	India	35.2		
		Indonesia	10.7	Thailand	35.1		
		Guatemala	10.7	Mexico	33.0		

*Adapted from Frederick Harbison and Charles A. Myers, *Education, Manpower, and Economic Growth; Strategies of Human Resource Development,* McGraw-Hill, New York, 1964, pp. 45-48.

from the West in their periods of defensive modernization.[50] Israel began its career as an independent state in 1948 with a basic stock of Western-educated cadres of high-level manpower that gave it a head start toward modern education over most of the other nations of the Middle East, Africa, and Asia. Argentina had been more energetic than most Latin American states in developing its educational system along the lines of nineteenth-century models in Western Europe and the United States.

Much more research is required, but it does look as though the nations of Western Europe may have been overtaken in their modernization not only because of the special political and economic zeal displayed by the United States, Russia, and Japan but also by the imbalance in their educational developments and the continuing power of traditional education which slowed down their modernization, particularly in secondary and higher education. It was not until after World War II that the swell of educational reforms began to gain major proportions in Western Europe, several decades after it touched the other three countries.

Even more important, however, than the differences in educational development among the various nations of the West is the educational gap between the advanced Western nations and the nations of the Third World in Asia, Latin America, and Africa. Not only did the Western societies gain a large head start before World War II, they also continued to forge ahead in the 1950s and 1960s. UNESCO's International Commission on the Development of Education found that the industrialized nations increased their spending on education from $50 billion to $120 billion between 1960 and 1968, while the developing nations (with two-thirds of the world's population and three-fourths of its young people) increased their spending on education from less than $5 billion to less than $12 billion. Meanwhile the gross national products of the advanced nations were increasing by 78 percent while those of the developing nations increased by only 62 percent. The linkage between education and national productivity was inescapably clear—and the disparities were profoundly disturbing: "The ever-growing gap between industrialized and developing countries had produced the fundamental drama of the contemporary world."[51]

In the following four chapters we turn to those major nations of the West (Britain, France, Germany, and the United States) whose educational systems enabled them to modernize most rapidly and become models for much of the rest of the world. In the final two chapters we return to the impact of Western education upon the non-Western world, how it promoted modernization among traditional societies and yet failed to overcome the disparities it had helped to create.

---

[50] Ibid., pp. 71 and 121.

[51] Edgar Faure, et al., *Learning to Be; The World of Education Today and Tomorrow*, UNESCO, Paris, and Harrap, London, 1972, p. 49.

CHAPTER X

EDUCATION IN THE MODERNIZING STATES OF EUROPE
(1700 A.D.-1860s A.D.)

A. THE VOLUNTARY APPROACH IN BRITAIN

At the opening of the eighteenth century Britain's educational institutions reflected the impact of the traditionalizing forces set afoot by the Stuart Restoration of the 1660s and at the same time began to reverberate to the calls for reform expressed in the educational thought associated with the Glorious Revolution of the 1690s. The Baconian and Puritan reformers of the seventeenth century had been damped down by the Clarendon Code of laws passed by the Cavalier Parliament in the 1660s in the effort to root out Puritans and other dissenters from public office, from pulpits, and from schools and colleges, all in favor of extending the role of the Church of England in religion and education as well as in law and public order. The response of many Puritan clergymen and schoolmasters had been to refuse to take the oaths of loyalty or to subscribe to the Anglican articles. Thus, as nonconformists, they were obliged to move into the remoter places of England and Scotland where they continued to preach and where they set up Dissenters' Academies to train a supply of ministers and to provide private schools for the education of their children.

For over a hundred years the Dissenters' Academies and private mathematical schools in England along with their secondary school counterparts in Scotland were the major modernizing forces in British education; they were distinguished by their devotion to the sciences and their more modern and practical studies alongside their classical and religious studies. Although they kept alive and nourished a clientele of persons who eventually sparked the industrial techniques of the middle and later eighteenth century, they nevertheless were relatively small islands of modernization in a great sea of traditional education.

Meanwhile, major voices of educational reform began to lay a theoretical groundwork in empirical philosophy and psychology upon which subsequent reformers relied very heavily in France and in America as well as in Britain. Trying to conceive of human nature in a way that would be appropriate to the kind of physical universe that Newton had described and yet not to give away the basic tenets of Christianity, John Locke set out to elaborate the laws of human nature in a scientific manner. His basic assumption was that human nature is not innate but is a result of the impact of environment upon the unformed and pliable raw material of the human organism. At the same time, Locke did not become a materialist; he believed in a human nature consisting of a soul and a mind, each having certain independent qualities.

Applying Baconian and Newtonian conceptions of science to the study of the mind, Locke tried to formulate the natural laws of learning. He maintained that the child is not born with a preexistent mind or with innate ideas concerning God, justice, or morality. Rather, the newborn child merely possesses a blank tablet (*tabula rasa*) upon which perceptions from the outside world are imprinted. Ideas, values, and knowledge have their origin in sense experience received from the external environment of things and people. In his essays, *Of the Conduct of the Understanding* and *Essay Concerning Human Understanding,* justifying in theory the practices of sense realism in education, Locke opened the way to a pedagogy that would develop all the senses of the child, not merely through reading, but through the active senses of sight, taste, smell, touch, and hearing.

In his *Some Thoughts Concerning Education* Locke argued that children learn best when they are interested in what they are learning, and the best way to gain their interest is through play, which provides pleasurable incentives and prevents the building up of aversions to education. Much of modern learner-oriented education was anticipated by Locke as he described the education appropriate for a gentleman's son who will find useful in his adult life such practical and interesting subjects as English, drawing, arithmetic, writing, shorthand, geography, history, science, mathematics, and even the values that can be achieved through manual activity in carpentry, gardening, and active sports of all kinds.

Besides the political, religious, and humanistic aims, the Enlightenment also emphasized education for social status. Perhaps the most famous suggestions for the education of a gentleman's son were made by Locke in his *Thoughts*. The aims of education as stated there were, in order of importance: virtue, wisdom, breeding, and learning. Virtue is acquired through practice in sound moral habits; wisdom is acting with foresight and prudence in the management of one's personal and social affairs; breeding is correct behavior, bearing, and manners; and learning is the achievement of intellectual power through mental training, rather than through the acquisition of mere facts or knowledge. These ideals not only reflected the attitude of the English upper classes but played a major role in rationalizing the gentlemanly ideal of liberal education in American as well as British colleges.

More radical in their empirical views, David Hume and David Hartley put almost exclusive emphasis upon the five outer senses as the sources of ideas and ruled out Locke's mental faculty of reflection as they developed their theory of associationism which became the forerunner of much of the experimental and scientific psychology of the nineteenth and twentieth centuries. To Hartley the basic natural law of learning was the fact that sensations coming from the external world, repeated often enough, leave traces in the nervous system. When different sensations are thus associated, the occurrence of one sensation will call up a memory of the others. Simple ideas are thus built up into complex ideas largely by association. The principles of associationism sound a good deal like twentieth-century doctrines of synaptic connections, conditioning, and the laws of frequency and recency. The empirical theory of knowledge and learning was carried still further in the nineteenth century by John Stuart Mill who argued that universal and necessary truths can be built up by experience through the inductive methods of science. Mill thus provided the theoretical basis upon which empirical philosophy and behavioral psychology later attempted to reduce all mental processes to that of physical association.

Traditional pedagogical method in England did not respond very rapidly to the secular or the rational post-Enlightenment theories of a Locke or a Hartley or a Mill, but the tempo of proposals for institutional reform did begin to pick up in the later eighteenth century, reaching a crescendo of activity in the middle of the nineteenth century. As a result of the spread of ideas which can justly be called modernizing and as a result of organized efforts by middle class and working class groups, the English educational system began to take on more and more modern characteristics. The universities were the first to be reformed, by the concerted efforts made by royal commissions to break the stranglehold of the Church of England upon university governance and to modernize the curriculum. New types of more practically-oriented secondary schools were founded by the middle classes; the traditional great public schools were effectively opened to the upper middle classes; and the beginnings of state responsibility gave a new impetus to providing elementary schools for the working classes which voluntary and religious societies had begun. The path to modernity was tortuous but in the long view of a century and a half, it was clear.

Voices began to be raised on behalf of a more secular, practical, and state-supported education that would be spread more widely, indeed universally, among all the people. Such voices came with more frequency and insistence from the midlands and north of England and from Scotland, the more active generative centers of industrialization and urbanization in Britain. The English dissenters with their scientifically-oriented academies and the Scottish Presbyterians with their state system of public schools and practically-oriented interests fed these currents of educational reform which bubbled up out of Edinburgh and Glasgow and out of the urbanizing centers in and around Birmingham and Manchester.

A significant element in promoting educational modernization along with the industrial revolution itself was the rash of literary and philosophical societies that became active in the 1760s and 1770s. The Lunar Society (a prophetic name) in Birmingham may have been the most successful in bringing together scientists, technologists, and industrialists and igniting the sparks of the technological revolution. Such men as Matthew Boulton, James Watt, Joseph Priestley, Erasmus Darwin, R. L. Edgeworth, Thomas Day, and Josiah Wedgwood combined knowledge of science, inventiveness in technology, and industrial pragmatism to an unusual degree.

Some also made the implications of the transformation they were seeking in education quite explicit.[1] Outstanding was Joseph Priestley whose *Essay on a Course*

---

[1] For an excellent analysis of the " Forerunners of Educational Reform, 1760-1800" see Brian Simon, *Studies in the History of Education 1780-1870,* Lawrence and Wishart, London, 1960, chap. 1.

of Liberal Education for Civil and Active Life (1768) aptly summed up in its title the key concepts of modernity in education: *civil* and *active*. Though he did not advocate state-controlled education, he did stress the need for modern studies in history, policy, science, manufacture, and business in place of traditional classical studies. This was a theme spelled out in detail by R. L. and Maria Edgeworth in their book curtly titled *Practical Education.* They insisted that poor teachers were more to blame for pupils' failures than the absence of ability. Their methodology had all the earmarks of a twentieth-century discovery method of learning.

"Lit and Phil" societies which sprang up in Manchester and in other northern cities revealed interests similar to those of the Lunar Society. In a sense they provided an intellectual climate which nourished the establishment of scientific and practically-oriented academies to take the place of the Dissenters' Academies. Notable among these were Warrington Academy (1757), its successor, Manchester Academy (1786), Hackney, and the Manchester College of Arts and Sciences (1783).

Although these "Lit and Phil" societies and new academies were aimed primarily at a more practical education for the middle classes, a few British voices were raised late in the eighteenth century in favor of state support of education for all. Adam Smith argued for state education, but not for the reasons advanced by the French reformers. Smith was interested in the protection of the "better" classes in society from the delinquencies and dangers to property that might rise from an uneducated and illiterate mass of people who might derive wrong ideas from the French Revolution. The specialization of work in the factory, which is a key to industrialization, leads to the suffocation of intellectual activity, so a school should be placed in every community to counteract the tedium of specialization. Therefore, he urged public education for the poor as a means of aiding the lower classes to obtain a useful occupation and a realization of their "proper" place (of inferiority) in society. Much the same notion was expressed by Malthus. These early expressions for state-supported education in Britain had uppermost in them a desire to protect the economic interests of the propertied classes, a far cry from what the lower classes themselves were interested in.

By and large, the reaction against the democratic revolutions in France and America and the upsurge of conservative thought and action in church and state in Britain stifled for two or three decades the efforts for modernization in British education. Symbolically, Joseph Priestley and Thomas Cooper fled to the United States while a new evangelical fervor fastened even more firmly a class-inspired religious hold upon elementary schools. The agencies of this process were voluntary, religious, and charitable associations, which raised funds by subscription and then established free charity schools for the poor who could not otherwise pay for the education of their children. It had long been accepted that self-respecting parents would pay tuition for their children's education, while the children of the poor would be served by free charity schools such as those provided by the Society for Promoting Christian Knowledge (1699) under Church of England auspices.

The philanthropic measures begun in the eighteenth century were extended and redoubled in the early nineteenth century, largely as a result of the deplorable industrial conditions facing the working classes in the factory towns of England and Wales. Added to the sympathetic humanitarianism aroused by the industrial revolution were the religious sentiments stimulated by religious revivalism. There was also a desire to protect the vested interests of the upper classes against the unruly, ignorant, and undisciplined mob of workers now crowding into the unhealthy and congested cities.

Whereas the French Revolution stimulated the liberals of France and Germany to propose national state school systems for the benefit of the people, it stimulated the liberals of England to form charity organizations to help the underprivileged. Whereas the reaction against the French Revolution led the conservatives of France and Germany to use their state school systems to keep the people in their place, it prompted the conservatives of England to form still more voluntary societies in order to provide a little education to make the people satisfied at small cost. Any number of charitable agencies set out to furnish "ragged" schools for the poor and under-privileged, soup kitchens, orphan schools, reformatories, industrial schools, thrift brigades, and the like. Virtually all the religious denominations organized school societies to provide charity education for the poor.

The most innovative agencies concentrated on three types of schools—Sunday schools, infant schools, and monitorial schools. The Sunday school movement was initiated in 1780 in Gloucester by Robert Raikes, a newspaperman who sought to provide education for lower-class children who worked in factories from sunrise to sunset for six or seven days a week. Such schools taught the three R's and the catechism to working children during their free time on Sundays. Another specific educational response to the industrial revolution was the infant school, sponsored by Robert Owen, Scottish manufacturer, philanthropist, and socialist. In addition to agitating for reducing the hours of child labor, Owen was instrumental in establishing schools for three-, four-, and five-year-olds whose parents worked all day in the factories. These schools likewise taught religion and some elements of the three R's, although much attention was directed at simple play, singing, dancing, and nursery care.

A third means of making education available to larger numbers of children was the monitorial system developed almost simultaneously by Joseph Lancaster, a Quaker, and by Andrew Bell, an Anglican chaplain with the English army in India. Monitorial instruction meant that the older children were used as monitors, or helpers, for the teacher. The teacher taught the monitors a lesson, and then each monitor taught the lesson to ten or twelve smaller children by repeating what he had learned. The small children recited aloud in unison whatever was being taught. Wall placards and charts, forecasting in a modest way the mass audio-visual techniques of a later educational technology, were used to aid in group instruction and to save money on books. The subject matter was still principally the catechism, reading, writing, spelling, and arithmetic. Corporal punishment was abolished, and a system of merits and rewards was substituted to enlist the interest of children. Children began to enjoy the marching, the activity, and the rewards; mass education could be fun, or at least noisy.

Lancaster's idea, first put into school practice in 1798, took organized form in 1808 in the Institute for Promoting the British System for the Education of the

Labouring and Manufacturing Classes of Society of Every Religious Persuasion. Its name was changed and its international outreach reflected when in 1814 it became the British and Foreign School Society. Not to be outdone by the nonconformists the Anglicans organized a competing society to support Andrew Bell's version of monitorial education. Tories who really did not believe in popular education nevertheless came to support the Anglican effort so precisely summed up in the 1811 name, The National Society for Promoting the Education of the Poor in the Principles of the Established Church throughout England and Wales. Between them, the British and Foreign Society and the National Society dominated elementary education in England for most of the early nineteenth century.

Despite pedagogical reform in theory and institutional reform in practice, the elementary schools of England remained essentially reading schools. When all else is said and all the major exceptions are noted, the fundamental task of the schools was literacy. This was very greatly needed, for the estimate is made that literacy in England in 1780 was probably no greater than it had been 200 years earlier. However, attention to writing and arithmetic was growing in response to the middle class interest in such studies for their usefulness in the trades and commerce. Singing and music also gained a larger place as religious revivalism stimulated hymn-singing and as a nationalistic spirit began to stress patriotic songs.

The most common means of teaching reading were the catechisms, hornbooks, psalters, and especially the primers, usually containing the Creed, Lord's Prayer, Ten Commandments, and Psalms. In the middle of the eighteenth century new aids to reading took the form of spelling books. One of the most famous of these was Dilworth's *New Guide to the English Tongue,* which included lists of words, with their proper pronunciation, rules of grammar, prayers, and some fables and moral precepts. Arithmetic books also appeared at this time, giving further recognition and stimulus to this increasingly popular subject of the elementary school curriculum.

As would be expected from the English voluntary system, the preparation of elementary school teachers in the nineteenth century was largely carried on by the voluntary religious societies. Proposals for the public training colleges for teachers met much the same fate as proposals for state schools. The result was that the government granted financial aid to the voluntary societies to help them support their training institutions, of which there were thirty-two in 1860 and forty in 1870. All but two of these were receiving government aid and were being inspected by the government, but the teaching staffs regularly represented the denominational faith that controlled the schools. An early training college for thirteen-year-olds at Battersea, offering a three-year course to a teaching certificate, became a model for many others.

In 1846, England set up an apprenticeship system of teacher training in which a pupil-teacher, age thirteen, was assigned to a regular teacher in the school and received a government grant for support. The regular teacher also received payment; and the regulations for their working and teaching together were laid down by the government. Practice schools were often maintained in connection with the teacher-training institutions. Much of the stimulus to teacher training came from the monitorial system of the day, for the large numbers of pupils required new techniques of teaching to replace the time-worn individualized instruction.

With the defeat of Napoleon and the return to peace following 1815, the campaign for educational reform got underway once again in Britain. This time it was part of the general reform movement closely linked with the effort of the middle classes to gain more power in the established agencies of government which were still largely in the control of the landed gentry. The Radicals in Parliament, led by Lord Henry Brougham and David Ricardo, and the Utilitarians, whose chief theoreticians were James Mill and Jeremy Bentham, became the spearhead for the age of reform.

It was during this period that the goals for modern education in Britain received major definition. The refrains heard more and more from now on were: universal education, free education, compulsory education, secular education, useful education, and scientific education. The variations on the theme cannot be played out in detail here.[2] The point is that the middle-class spokesmen, like Brougham, Mill, Bentham, and Place, and working-class spokesmen, like Robert Owen, Richard Carlile, William Thompson, Thomas Hodgskin, and William Lovett all developed similar conclusions from quite different assumptions and intentions.

Up to 1832 the working and middle classes cooperated to achieve some of the reforms of the Radicals and Utilitarians. Lord Broughan introduced the first bill to be brought into Parliament advocating universal, compulsory elementary education to be provided by the state (1820). But it had no chance of success while children worked all day long in the factories. The Radicals also set up Mechanics Institutes for the adult education of workers in the industrial centers, and organized the Society for the Diffusion of Useful Knowledge (1826). Meanwhile, the workers themselves organized scores of Corresponding Societies and Hampden Clubs which conducted systematic classes of lectures, readings, and discussions on political, scientific, and public affairs. Some of these societies conducted their own schools on the Sunday school or infant school model.

Eventually, the Reform Act of 1832 was passed, gaining greater representation in Parliament for the middle classes in the towns and cities, but not extending the suffrage to the propertyless working classes. Also the Education Act of 1833 was passed, but the ringing cries for universal, free, compulsory, secular education were far from embodied in it. Lord Brougham had retreated from his secular stance; a very mild measure was passed that approved not more than £20,000 to aid the two voluntary Protestant religious societies to build schoolhouses "for the education of the Poorer Classes in Great Britain." A Factory Act at the same time prohibited labor of children under nine years of age, restricted the labor of those between nine and thirteen to forty-eight hours a week or nine hours in a single day, and of those from thirteen to eighteen to sixty-nine hours a week or twelve hours in a day. These achievements, difficult as they were to come by, strike the present-day observer as something less than revolutionary. A token step toward compulsory education was made by requiring children under thirteen to have two hours of schooling a day, but with no funds allotted for enforcing the regulation and with children working eight hours a day in the factories, the two hours a day in school could not amount to much even where it was tried.

Because the workers got neither the suffrage nor the ten-hour day they had been

[2] Ibid., chaps. 3-5.

agitating for and precious little advantage from the education acts, they split off from the middle-class Radicals in 1838 and formed their own independent political movement, the People's Charter. Some Chartists were still interested in universal, practical education, perhaps best exemplified by William Lovett's *Chartism* written while he was in jail from 1839 to 1840. His proposals for free, compulsory, nonsectarian common schools controlled by elected committees with the power to raise taxes and pay teachers sounded very much like the kind of system that was actually being achieved in the United States at the time. But other Chartists, more cynical about the value of education in improving the lot of the working man, dubbed Lovett's proposals "Knowledge Chartism." Instead, they would concentrate on first gaining the suffrage so they could abolish child labor and reduce adult labor to ten hours a day; only then could a useful system of national education result. Unfortunately for the working classes, neither of these goals came about. Chartism was suppressed, it disintegrated from 1848 on, and workers turned from political action to economic action with emphasis upon bargaining for better wages and hours.

Meanwhile, government support for religious schools was to be the typical form of national interest in English education for the next thirty-five or forty years. Several times in the 1840s and 1850s the amounts of state aid were increased and extended to other school societies as well as to the National Society and the British and Foreign School Society. In time, the national money could be used by the societies for maintenance and current expenditures as well as for the building of schoolhouses. In 1839 a Committtee of the Privy Council on Education was appointed to administer the funds and provide inspectors to visit the schools to which money had been granted. For ten years James Kay-Shuttleworth was secretary of the Committee. In 1856 this committee was transformed into a Department of Education.

Stimulated by the arguments of Kay-Shuttleworth and others that the industrialization of the country made it necessary for factory foremen and skilled workers to be able to read and write, and that social revolution could only be avoided if education was improved, many liberals were not satisfied with the halfhearted measures of support to voluntary societies. In 1850 a National Public School Association was formed to agitate for free, compulsory education supported entirely by the government through taxation. In the 1850s many working men's organizations and trade unions also supported public education, such as the Working Men's Association for Promoting National Secular Education.

This move, of course, met great opposition from conservative and religious groups. The Anglicans wanted to maintain religious education; the dissenters wanted religious schools, but did not want the Church of England to have a monopoly in the field; and both opposed the liberals, who advocated secular schools. In the midst of the agitation Parliament appointed in 1858 a committee known as the Newcastle Commission, whose investigations led it to recommend in 1861 that no change in the existing voluntary system was desirable and that free, compulsory education was undesirable, for the evils of a compulsion that invaded the individual's rights outweighed its advantages. The individuals whose welfare would be most damaged were, of course, the employers whose rights to employ the children of the workers as they required them would be restricted if the children were attending school.

At the time of the Newcastle Commission it is estimated that about one-third of elementary school children were in private schools (860,000) while two-thirds were in the voluntary schools of religious and nonprofit societies (1,675,000). Of the voluntary schools, only about one-third received any state aid (which had grown to £663,000 by 1858) and 80 percent of these were Church of England schools. The result was that the children of the working classes who went to school at all attended for about four years, and 80 percent had dropped out by age eleven. This is what the Newcastle Commission found to be on the whole satisfactory and to compare favorably with other countries.

Within a decade, however, the Newcastle Commission was in principle partly repudiated. Craft unions, cooperative societies, school leagues, reform associations, and a great outpouring of group political agitation joined in a clamor for tax-supported, nonsectarian, free, compulsory elementary education, all bywords of a modern education.

Finally, while Gladstone and the Liberal party were in power, an elementary-education act known as the Forster Act was passed in 1870. The country was divided into school districts under the jurisdiction of local school boards. The voluntary school societies were given a year to establish schools in any districts where they were needed. If this was not done, the school boards were authorized to establish public board schools and to provide teachers to be supported partly by taxation and partly by fees from those parents who could afford to pay. They were to be free only for those who could not pay tuition. The local boards were also authorized to make attendance compulsory from the ages of six to thirteen if they wished. The religious question was solved by requiring the instruction in the board schools to be nonsectarian if the local board wished to allow any religious instruction at all, while the voluntary schools could give religious instruction, provided that children were not compelled to receive such instruction if their parents did not wish it.

All in all, elementary education was now established in Britain as a social right of all children rather than a gift of charity, but the goal of universal, free, secular education as visualized by the modernist reformers for more than a hundred years was still far from realization. Britain now had in effect a dual system of schools. This disjointed national system consisted of elementary schools for the working classes and secondary schools for the middle and upper classes. This disjunctive system of education reinforced the class fabric of English society for another century, very possibly slowing down the modernization process itself. While it was modern in its extension of formal education to the working classes, it did not deliberately seek the social mobility characteristic of an integrative type of modern education. While it was generally libertarian rather than authoritarian, the admission to secondary and higher education was rigidly selective rather than comprehensive. Tradition continued to wield a heavy hand on the educational institutions beyond the primary school.

During the eighteenth century English secondary education was ruled by the endowed grammar schools in which the Latin grammarians held the fort against mounting criticism by the middle class. The traditionalists insisted that Latin grammar was the only means of achieving the truly disciplined mind of the liberally educated person. The Church of England often sided with the grammarians, invoking the intention of the founders of the endowed grammar schools in the sixteenth and seventeenth centuries who had stipulated that Latin and Greek should be taught free to worthy students. The grammarians insisted that these terms meant that nothing *besides* Latin and Greek could be taught; even the boards of control could not dislodge a determined master who knew his common law.

Gradually, however, the grammar schools became so pedantic in their teaching, so brutal in their discipline, and so marked by unrest and rioting among their students that their clientele fell off markedly. It was then that these schools began to be reformed in the nineteenth century. They kept their classical emphasis but began to yield to Locke's conception of the education proper for a gentleman. The point of view of the pedantic scholar or grammarian had never appealed very much to the middle classes; so, when the schools began to play up the importance of virtue, wisdom, and breeding as defined by Locke in his *Thoughts* and play down scholarly learning, the middle classes became more interested as Thomas Arnold at Rugby showed the way to reform.

Long before that time, however, the modern response to new educational trends had taken place in the Dissenters' Academies conducted by nonconformist clergymen for their congregations. Starting as Latin schools in the late seventeenth century they soon paid considerable attention to the realistic studies that would appeal to the middle classes. By the beginning of the eighteenth century the academies were teaching, in addition to the classics, English language and literature, modern foreign languages, mathematics (geometry, astronomy, trigonometry), natural science and anatomy, history, geography, politics, and philosophy (ethics, logic, and metaphysics).

By the middle of the eighteenth century science and mathematics played a larger role than ever, and commercial subjects became more important. Toward the end of the century the Dissenters' Academies began to decline as the conservative trends in society and the Church of England grew stronger. Thereupon, the nonconformist groups and the industrial middle classes turned to two new types of schools. In 1779 when the ban on nonconformists as teachers was lifted, a spate of private schools appeared in the industrial cities and towns to give a directly practical education for the commercial occupations, emphasizing such studies as surveying, bookkeeping, accounting, and the like. Many were private-venture day schools; others were boarding schools. Some helped to train the people who were pushing forward the industrial revolution; others were small, poorly staffed and equipped, fly-by-night money-makers, conducted primarily for profit.

A still more important type of school was the proprietary school conducted in a more businesslike and efficient way by joint stock companies organized by businessmen and tradesmen. In these, the income was fed back into the corporation controlling the school. The Liverpool Institute, a day school in 1825, may have been the first of many that mushroomed in the industrial cities. In London the University College School (1828) and the City of London School (1836) set the pattern for such schools that catered particularly to the middle classes. In the 1840s and 1850s the proprietary schools began to appear in boarding school form, thus reaching for the social advantages of the upper class public schools but at the same time consciously preparing boys for modern business and professional careers in the armed services, the civil service bureaucracy, engineering, colonial administration, and the managerial posts of church, industry, and state. The roster of such schools included Cheltenham, Marlborough, Haileybury, Malvern, Rosall, and Wellington.

In these ways English secondary education began to take on differentiated forms of specialization that roughly corresponded in ascending order of prestige to the major social and economic strata of the middle and upper classes: private-venture day schools, proprietary day schools, proprietary boarding schools, day grammar schools, boarding grammar schools, and the great "public" schools. But there was still no formalized organization or national system to secondary education as a whole, and the middle classes were growing restless at their virtual exclusion from the highest prestige schools. So the next step beyond setting up new schools outside the establishment was to attack the citadels themselves and seek to make them over into a mold more consonant with the life style to which the upper middle classes would like to become accustomed.

The great "public" schools had long set the standards and ideals for all other types of secondary school in England. The nine great "public" schools were usually considered to be Eton, Winchester, Charterhouse, Westminster, Rugby, Harrow, Shrewsbury, St. Paul's, and Merchant Taylors'. In these, the classical humanities continued to play the central pedagogical role. The English gentry set great store not only by the classics as the special symbol of intellectual superiority but by the corporate life of the boarding school as a molder of the religious, moral, and intellectual life and of the manners and behavior appropriate to a gentleman's son. The community life of the English secondary schools was one principal way in which they differed from their counterparts in France and Germany. Despite the hold of the "public" schools upon English life as exemplified by such famous schoolmasters as Thomas Arnold of Rugby, criticisms and attacks upon them increased during the early nineteenth century. Demands for a more democratic and more practical type of education continued to be made, including recognition for science as an essential ingredient in a liberal education.

After the middle of the century Parliament responded to the dissatisfaction being expressed by appointing two major commissions to study the conduct of the secondary schools. The Clarendon Commission (1861) ended its study of the nine "public" schools by justifying the classical curriculum as the principal determinant in the molding of the English gentleman and rejecting the establishment of a course for modern studies as demeaning. Class bias supported the traditional academic bias in the proposition that half the curriculum be given to the classics, one-eighth to science, and three-eights to all else, including modern language, history, and the arts. In general, the public schools were given a clean bill of health; the lower orders would find it even harder to gain the free places formerly reserved for them.

The Schools Inquiry Commission under Lord Taunton then studied all other endowed secondary schools and found a great diversity of quality and teaching standards, in a large part bad. This commission which studied 800 endowed schools made several far-reaching suggestions concerning reform of the curriculum, closer state supervision of the achievements of students and certification of teachers, and a more systematic organization. The Taunton Commission recommended making some sort of order out of the secondary school maze by establishing three grades of schools in descending order along class lines: first grade schools of the boarding type in which boys of the professional and upper middle classes could be prepared for the universities; second grade schools in which boys of the shopkeeper, mercantile, and trading classes, and well-to-do tenant farmers could prepare up to age sixteen for middle-level occupations; and third grade schools in which boys of small tradesmen, artisans, and tenant farmers could obtain an education up to age fourteen.

Even these suggestions apparently were too radical, however. Parliament largely ignored the report and passed instead the Endowed Schools Act of 1869, which appointed a commission to help the endowed schools to make more satisfactory plans for managing their own endowments. Public administration of "public" schools was too radical a step along the road to modern education for England to take in the middle of the nineteenth century.

With all the intellectual activity and scientific progress in Britain during the Enlightenment, it might have been expected that the English universities would have been leading the way. However, academic tradition and the tenacious hold of the Church of England and the aristocracy kept the English universities behind the times throughout most of the eighteenth century. Despite a few brilliant names, such as Newton, Gray, and Blackstone, the favored studies at Oxford and Cambridge continued to be the classics, logic, and scholastic philosophy. Some gains were made in introducing Newtonian science and mathematics, especially at Cambridge. Chairs in chemistry were established at both Oxford and Cambridge as early as 1685; modern history was established at Oxford in 1724; and a tripos, or honors examination, in mathematics was established at Cambridge in 1747. But these were relatively small ripples in the great sea of classicism. There was no effort to train professionals for government service by direct study of the political or economic sciences as in Germany.

However, the Scottish universities were able to make major reforms by the middle of the eighteenth century. At Edinburgh, the professors of Latin, Greek, logic, and natural philosophy were joined by professors of mathematics and moral philosophy, who gave lectures open to voluntary attendance. By 1750, the courses of study in the arts at Edinburgh and Glasgow were far more modern than those in the English universities. The utilitarian spirit of reform at Aberdeen involved recognition of such activities as writing, bookkeeping, and French. Here, then, are early evidences of modern trends: the impact of the new science upon the arts curriculum; the valuing of useful, or practical, subjects as equivalent to the older studies of a liberal education; and the actual practice of the voluntary, or elective, principle.

The English universities began to recover a measure of their old vitality with the beginning of the nineteenth century. Oxford reformed its examination system from within so that a student needed more adequate preparation for passing his examinations. Honors courses in mathematics and classics were designed to permit greater specialization than the regular "pass courses" and to provide added inducements for the student to attain a high degree of scholarship. At Cambridge, mathematics continued to gain in importance during the early nineteenth century; it had been the first subject in which a tripos (honors-course examination) was held (1747). Then triposes were added in civil law (1815), classics (1824), moral sciences (1851), and natural sciences (1850).

But in the view of such acerbic critics as Sidney Smith, James Mill, Jeremy Bentham, and Sir William Hamilton the Oxford and Cambridge colleges were the epitome of uselessness. The critics were all pretty well agreed that until the hand of the Anglican Church was lifted the colleges would not be able to expand to include the modern languages and history, experimental philosophy, and the whole range of social study embraced by political economy.

In exasperation at the unresponsiveness of the Oxford and Cambridge colleges, radicals and utilitarians like Mill and Brougham and liberal Whigs turned to the establishment of a new institution that would consciously seek to prepare for the modern professions. In 1828 University College, London, was formed by a joint stock company, taking cues from the University of Edinburgh, from German universities like Berlin, Bonn, and Munich, and from Thomas Jefferson's new University of Virginia in the United States.[3] The intention was that the new college should be secular in curriculum and control, and that it should depart from the residential, tutorial, and class systems of the traditional colleges by stressing a professoriate whose lectures would cover all the major fields of modern knowledge, as well as the classics. It was even contemplated that a chair in education be established, but this proved to be far too radical. Of the original two dozen professors, half came from Scotland, a fourth from overseas, and a fourth from Cambridge.

In an effort to counteract the secular intent of University College, the Tories and the established church created a competition in King's College (1828). Not surprisingly, it quickly received a charter, whereas it was eight years before University College got its charter. Both colleges then became constituent colleges of the new University of London, intended to be primarily an examining and degree-granting body. But as happened at the secondary level, the middle classes were not satisfied with having a separate institution of their own. Influential as it was to become in setting a pattern for the modern universities of England later in the nineteenth and in the twentieth century, it could not match the prestige and preferment in public office that went to graduates of Oxford and Cambridge. So those walls had to be stormed. The assault was primarily in the hands of two royal commissions appointed in 1850.

Even before that time, rumblings of discontent were bubbling up within the universities, especially from the ranks of the university professors who had relatively little voice in the governance of the universities compared with the fellows of the endowed residential colleges who constituted the corporate and financial authorities. Thomas Arnold represented the moderate modernists who would try to make the upper classes more socially useful and the middle classes more civilized. John Henry (later Cardinal) Newman typified the traditionalist who was ready on behalf of faith and reason to resist all encroachment by the modernists. By mid-century restless professors like Benjamin Jowett were convinced that genuine reform could be achieved only when the Church of England monopoly was broken. Only Parliament, by

[3]Ibid., p. 21.

removing religious tests on these matters, could open matriculation and degrees, as well as the seats on the governing corporations, to nonconformists.

When the Royal Commissions began their work the colleges set up the cry of autonomy, arguing that the Commissions had no authority over them. The long-standing issue of the right of government in the name of national welfare to reform a university that was not doing its part in national development, a confrontation so familiar in the developing nations of the second half of the twentieth century, was having a dress rehearsal in the mid-nineteenth. As far as modernization is concerned, the government's intervention speeded the process.

The Oxford Commission found students lazy and idle, underachieving and dissolute, the curriculum irrelevant to the social needs of England, and the whole institution geared to training clergymen for the Church of England rather than for the public affairs of a modernizing Britain. The recommendations included greater attention to specialization of professors and students, to mathematics, science, and technology, and to the responsibilities of careers in the public service; all these familiar themes of modernity. The university bills when passed (for Oxford in 1854 and for Cambridge in 1856) abolished the Church of England religious test for degrees, but the test for faculty members on the governing boards remained until 1871.

So Britain took a major step toward modernization when it opened the traditional universities to the nonconformists of the middle classes, but this was by no means the broad participation in higher education that came to mark a fully modern educatonal system, especially as developed in the United States. The English universities were still far behind the technical faculties of France and the professional research institutes of German universities. England achieved its modern education by the explosive and intermittent efforts of innumerable voluntary groups, some stable and large in scope, others ad hoc and fleeting. When England finally got around to sustained governmental action in the field of education, as in the period from 1850 to 1870, more happened in higher education than at any time since the educational revolution of the later sixteenth and early seventeenth centuries. But one could argue that because France, Germany, and the United States turned earlier to large-scale governmental action, they approached modernity in their educational systems more rapidly than did Britain.

B. THE SWING OF THE PENDULUM IN FRANCE

Prior to the French Revolution the control and support of schools in France were largely in the hands of the various teaching orders of the Catholic Church. At the elementary level, for example, the Institute of the Brothers of the Christian Schools by 1790 provided charity education in over 125 schools for the poor and unfortunate; and several orders of sisters, principally the Ursulines and the Congregation of Notre Dame, gave elementary instruction to girls. In addition, there were scores of *petites écoles* taught by private teachers for boys and girls whose parents could pay the fees; and in the larger towns there were writing schools preparing clerks and accountants for commercial jobs. The estimate is made that near the end of the eighteenth century something less than half the males and about one-fourth of the females of France were literate.[4]

When the Jesuit schools were closed in France by royal edict in 1764, and the order was suppressed by the Pope from 1773 to 1814, this left an enormous gap in French secondary education. Their schools were transferred to the Oratorians and other teaching orders or simply stood vacant. Secondary education was, however, available in the colleges of those universities which had Faculties of Arts. All told, there were more than 70,000 students in some 500 *collèges* in France in the 1780s, most of which were heavily classical, humanistic, and religious.

The philosophes proposed greater attention to practical and technical education to prepare boys for a trade or a career in business and commerce, but the response by the regular elementary and secondary schools was limited. A few trade schools and schools for drawing and design did appear for the lower classes as well as military and naval schools for the nobility. Some charity schools began to give some attention to manual arts, but by and large the elementary and secondary schools were slow to take up *practical studies,* a term usually intended to refer not only to the mechanical and industrial arts but to such nonclassical studies as French history, language, and literature, mathematics, science, geography, political economy, art, music, and physical education

The classical and humanistic bias also applied to the twenty-one universities which boasted twenty-one faculties of law, eighteen faculties of medicine, eighteen faculties of theology, and eighteen faculties of arts. They continued to be heavily traditional in content and teaching. The *Collège de France* did embrace a wider range of sciences, but the universities continued to be the preserves of conservative religious groups backed by the Bourbon monarchy, which kept a watchful eye on their political and social doctrines as well as their religious teachings.

Nevertheless, the modernizing needs of the nation for new professional and technical training were being met by establishing separate institutions outside the universities. All told there were more than seventy of these specialized schools prior to the Revolution, ranging from engineering, mining, military and naval science, and veterinary medicine to art and music. Chief among these was the School of Bridges and Highways formalized by Turgot in 1775 and the School of Mines in 1778. These advanced technical schools were major factors in building a competent corps of trained manpower contributing to the nationalizing power of France. Much of the expertise thus developed went into the revolutionary wars that kept France occupied—and victorious—on the continent of Europe for some 25 years until the final defeat of Napoleon in 1815.

This then was the educational situation under the *ancien régime:* charity schools for the lower classes conducted by the teaching orders of the Catholic church and private "little schools" available for a fee; classical secondary schools conducted by the teaching orders of the church; technical schools for practical occupations supported by

[4]H. C. Barnard, *Education and the French Revolution,* Cambridge University Press, London, 1969, p. 8; and C. Arnold Anderson and Mary Jean Bowman (eds.), *Education and Economic Development,* Aldine, Chicago, 1965, pp. 332-340.

the state; and universities dominated by the church offering a traditional education in the arts and in the learned professions of medicine, law, and theology. There was little or no system or national design for education of the populace; and relatively little attention to the new science and philosophy of the Enlightenment.

Naturally, the philosophes began to turn their literary and intellectual guns upon the need for educational reform. From the middle of the eighteenth century to the onset of the Revolution the theoretical outlines of modern education were being drawn up by such philosophes as Rousseau, Helvétius, Condillac, and Diderot, while specific programs for institutional change were presented by such statesmen and men of affairs as Chalotais, Rolland, Turgot, Mirabeau, Talleyrand, and Condorcet. All told the plans spelled out almost all possible variations on the major themes of modern education: Remove the church from its dominant place in education and substitute the civil authorities who will appoint and pay lay teachers. Extend education to the people, and, if need be, make it universal, free, and compulsory. Remove the slavish memorizing of books, reduce the classics, and substitute the practical studies of science and the ethical studies appropriate to a democratic society. In sum, educate the natural man for a life of freedom and patriotic citizenship in a just state and modern society.[5]

The most elaborate educational plan was drawn up by Condorcet at the request of the Legislative Assembly (1791-1792). Condorcet proposed a complete national system of secular schools to provide equal opportunity for all children, free, compulsory, and universal. The aim was to develop citizens devoted to the civic, national, and democratic purposes of the state. He proposed that primary schools for ages six to ten should be established throughout the country within walking distance for all pupils, one school for approximately every village of 400 people. Next, intermediate or higher primary schools should be located in all medium-sized towns to provide two or three more years of education, and especially a technical or vocational education, for the common people. Third, there should be 100 secondary schools, or institutes, located in the largest towns to provide not only classical education but a wide variety of subjects adapted to the occupational needs of the people. Of special interest here are agriculture, mechanical arts, and training for teachers of the primary schools. Finally, there should be nine *lycées* to provide higher and professional education, to take the place of the traditional universities and to teach all the major branches of knowledge. Capping all would be a National Society of Arts and Sciences through which scholars could exert influence over the whole educational system. Condorcet's plan was not put into practice, but it provided germinal ideas for generations of later plans and laws.

After the Republic was established in 1792 by the National Convention (1792-1795), several attempts were made to set up a state system of schools and to repress the church schools by confiscating their properties and by suppressing the teaching orders. The Lakanal law of 1794 provided for a primary school for every 1,000 people, to teach the three R's in French, along with geography and nature study. They were also to instill republican ideals by teaching patriotic songs and stories and inculcating the doctrines of the Declaration of the Rights of Man. The Daunou law

---

[5] For a very useful summary of the many proposals for educational reform, see Barnard, loc. cit.

of 1795 provided that each of the several thousand communes should establish a primary school for the three R's, and a secondary, or central, school should be established for every 300,000 people to give a scientific, secular, and practical education, emphasizing drawing, mathematics, natural history, physics and chemistry, history, political economy and legislation, and belles lettres as well as the classical languages and grammar. In these respects the central schools for pupils thirteen to sixteen years of age resembled technical schools with an academic bias rather than the classical *collège*. In addition courses were to be taught by specialist teachers and were to be elective rather than organized into a single prescribed curriculum.

The central schools were a most interesting modernizing experiment. Within four or five years 100 such schools had been established, but it must be remembered they replaced more than 500 *collèges*, and they only lasted six years before they were abolished by Napoleon in 1802. They had, however, opened the way for middle-class children to gain direct preparation for careers in business, industry, the government, and the armed services.[6]

Far more influential perhaps than any other concrete institution-building undertaken by the revolutionary governments was the establishment of a series of advanced specialized technical schools. The church schools had been abolished, repressed, or intimidated. The universities had been suspended. A constant series of reports, proposals, projects, laws, and decrees went undiscussed or unenforced in the midst of the rapidly changing fortunes of revolution and continental wars. All this meant that educational opportunity in general had been greatly retarded in the twenty-five years from 1790 to 1815; despite the grandiose plans for universal education fewer students attended primary and secondary schools in 1815 than forty or fifty years earlier. And what gains toward modern education *were* made in the form of secular and scientific education were largely nullified by the return of the Church to education under Napoleon and the restored monarchy. But in the field of technical and professional education the revolutionary government under the Convention broke new ground.

Many of the technical schools that had been established before the Revolution were either left undisturbed or strengthened and multiplied; for example, the schools of arts and crafts provided shopwork in several trades, and the Conservatory of Arts and Crafts became an outstanding museum of the industrial arts. Other schools provided instruction in the fields of military ammunition and arms, military science, military health, oriental languages, mining, and fine arts. The crowning achievement was the *École Polytechnique* to serve as a school of technology giving a common course for engineers of both military and civil types. Advanced courses in all the basic sciences and mathematics and their applications were offered to students who were very highly selected. The rigorous standards made it one of the most sought-after institutions in France. From this fundamental theoretical training a student could go on to greater specialization in applied schools of mines, bridges, and highways, and the various specialties of civil and military engineering. As Artz points out, these schools helped to make France a pioneer in technological education, for it was the only

---

[6]See Frederick B. Artz, *The Development of Technical Education in France 1500-1850*, Massachusetts Institute of Technology Press, Cambridge, Mass., 1966, pp. 125 ff.

country in the world where engineering was a respected learned profession in the early nineteenth century.[7]

Beginning with the Directory (1795-1799) the Republican political forms were maintained, but the extreme equalitarianism and democratic Republicanism were tempered by a return to middle class interests. With the take-over by the Consulate (1799-1804) Napoleon began to give his own personal stamp to the Republic's political forms. This meant for education a reinforcement of modernity with respect to efficient organization, central authority, differentiation of institutions, and professional training; it meant a return to tradition as far as religious control was concerned.

The most significant modernizing trend in France in the first half of the nineteenth century was the building of a strongly centralized and highly organized state system of education. When Napoleon came to power, he moved to reinforce the national character of schools, but at the same time his Concordat of 1801 with the Roman Catholic Church, quickly followed by the law of 1802, returned primary schools to church control. Napoleon was favorably impressed with the work of the Institute of the Brothers of the Christian Schools; furthermore, he was really more interested in secondary education than in primary education. It was through the secondary schools that he expected to train a loyal and efficient corps of officials to help carry on his government. It was therefore important for him to do away with the practically-oriented and republican-minded enthusiasm of the central schools.

The law of 1802 provided the framework for a national system of secondary schools under state control. Although private secondary schools were permitted to continue, the way was paved for two major types of secondary schools that dominated French education for a century and a half, namely, the *lycée* for the larger towns and the *collège* for the smaller communes. The *lycée* provided the preferred road to university study in a seven-year course for ages eleven or twelve to eighteen. It was typically a residential boarding school, received national funds for the construction of buildings and payment for teacher's salaries, catered to the aristocratic classes of society by charging fees, and maintained a strongly classical and humanistic course of study, topped off by philosophy, logic, and mathematics. The *collège* also gave preferment on the road to the higher faculties, but it received a greater share of support from the local community and therefore was usually not so well-endowed, physically or intellectually, as the *lycée*. In the educational prestige hierarchy it ranked below the *lycée*.

Soon after Napoleon established the Empire (1804-1814) his decrees of 1806 and 1808 brought all French education under his direct and personal control. The University of France was established as the supreme administrative organization to supervise all the educational institutions of France. It was not a university in the usual Western sense, but more nearly a centralized national department of education embracing as a corporate body all the public teachers of the nation. A supreme master to be appointed by the emperor was the highest educational official. He received advice from a superior council of education made up of twenty-six or thirty members, also appointed by the emperor.

---

[7]Ibid., p. 161.

The whole country was divided into twenty-seven administrative subdivisions, known as academies, each academy to be headed by a rector, advised by a council, and aided by inspectors, all appointed by the supreme master. The purpose of this hierarchy of public officials was to bring all public and private schools closely under national surveillance, provide inspection of the schools, supervise the teachers, and examine the students. Despite changes and modifications, the framework of French educational organization remained essentially as defined here for 150 years. It consisted of four types of institutions: primary schools, secondary schools, university faculties, and other "establishments of higher education."

Napoleon's contribution to educational modernization was in the organizational efficiency at the secondary and higher levels rather than at the primarly level. His general view of primary education was summed up in 1808 when he stated that the schools should teach the Roman Catholic religion, inculcate fidelity to the Emperor, and produce obedient citizens devoted to the church, state, and family. We have noted that when Napoleon was overthrown in 1815 there were fewer students in primary schools than forty to fifty years earlier, and more than half were still in private rather than state schools.

But at the higher levels Napoleon was strongly in favor of full state control. The imperial university gathered in its embrace a total of seventy-eight separate university faculties. Some were remnants from the medieval university corporations that had been abolished by the Revolutionary government, and some were newly constituted. But they were no longer university institutions comparable to those in Britain or Germany. Instead, there were twenty-seven faculties of arts, fifteen faculties of science, thirteen each of law and medicine, and ten of theology. University instruction carried on in these separate faculties operated under strict regulations laid down by the Ministry of Education. Attendance at lectures and exercises was compulsory; the courses of instruction were prescribed for each year; and state examinations had to be passed before the student could be promoted from one year to the next.

Much of the active scientific and applied research went on outside the faculties, in establishments of higher education. These were the technical and professional schools we have already described. But a significant new one was added in 1808. This was the *École Normale Supérieure* located in Paris and designed to prepare teachers for the *lycées* and *collèges*. Its standards for selection and completion of the two-year course were very high. The Superior Normal School eventually came to be looked upon as a *grande école,* emphasizing university-grade instruction in classics, mathematics, and other subjects appropriate to the secondary schools. By the middle of the century the most important degrees were awarded at the Superior Normal School in classical literature and grammar, philosophy, history, science, and mathematics, but students could also take courses at the Polytechnic School and Museum. The acquisition of subject matter and of systematic knowledge was considered to be the chief instrument in the teacher's preparation for teaching. Graduation from a secondary school was requisite to entrance to the Superior Normal School.

The specialization and differentiation of professional training for secondary school teachers was a most significant modernizing step on two counts. In the seventeenth and eighteenth centuries the training of teachers had been conducted largely by religious orders, and it had been aimed at primary school teachers. Now France made it a state matter and a secondary-school matter.

It was nearly a quarter of a century before primary education began to receive the kind of attention that Napoleon had given to secondary and higher education. During the constitutional monarchy of Louis Philippe who ruled from the July revolution of 1830 until 1848 and under the leadership of Guizot as minister of public instruction, a law of 1833 provided the framework for a French primary system that would become more popular and widespread even if not more equalitarian. This law required each commune to establish a state primary school, pay the teachers, and provide the school building (usually as a dwelling for the teacher as well). Fees were to be charged those parents who could pay, but poor children could attend free of charge. If the commune could not afford to provide a school, the state was authorized to give help. Private schools (most of which were religious schools) were permitted to continue in operation, but the teachers of these schools had to be certified by the mayor of the commune as well as by the church. Likewise, the religious emphasis was somewhat lessened in the state primary schools by requiring that a child could not be forced to receive any religious instruction which his parents did not wish him to have.

In addition, a new type of advanced education was to be provided by higher primary schools in the principal towns and cities of the departments, the ninety-odd legal and political subdivisions of France. The higher primary schools were designed to offer to those who completed the primary schools a vocational preparation in commercial, agricultural, or industrial subjects appropriate to the region. Furthermore, a primary normal school was to be established in each department for the training of teachers who were to teach in the primary schools. The Guizot law was naturally opposed by the church as a threat to its schools and the freedom of parents to choose religious schools. Nevertheless, primary schools increased by 50 percent in fifteen years, from 42,000 in 1832 to 63,000 in 1847; pupils increased from 2 million to 3,500,000, and normal schools from fourteen to seventy-six. More than that, there is some evidence that literacy rose from less than 50 percent to more than 65 percent.[8]

The advance in literacy was potentially more important for the modernization process than any particular reform in the primary schools curriculum. The law of 1833 virtually fixed the primary school curriculum at the three R's and moral and religious instruction. This curriculum was somewhat broadened in 1850, when primary schools were allowed to include, if they wished, such studies as history, nature study, geography, drawing, and music.

The practical and secular aspects of modernization were, however, more fully embodied in the higher primary schools which were designed to improve vocational competence on the farms and in the factories and cities. But the higher primary schools had a difficult time achieving social acceptance because of the opposition of the secondary schools. The upper classes would not send their children to schools of inferior status, and the working classes often could not afford education beyond the rudiments because they needed the older children at home to contribute to the family income.

[8] Ibid., p. 190.

In the long run one of the most powerful moves in the direction of modernization may have been the establishment under the law of 1833 of a widespread state-supported system of secular normal schools, an institution widely copied in the Western world. Courses in pedagogy and methods of teaching modeled somewhat on Pestalozzian lines were introduced into the normal schools in the 1830s and 1840s. Apparently these newfangled ideas were considered dangerous, for the normal schools were the targets of particular reproach by the reactionary elements of the Second Republic and Second Empire.

During the struggles to establish the Second Republic of 1848, it was apparent that an ardent democratic spirit motivated many of the primary teachers. They issued strongly worded proposals to make primary education free, compulsory to age fourteen, and a democratic agency for the achievement of greater opportunity by the common people. But as soon as the conservatives and monarchists gained the upper hand in the short-lived Second Republic, they set about to quash the liberal movement in education, especially through a law of 1850 which made it easier for the clergy to sit on the educational councils and to teach in the public primary and secondary schools than had been the case under the July monarchy. The hierarchical system of state and local inspectors was reinforced, so that the means were provided of hunting down the liberal teachers, who were charged with instigating the Revolution of 1848. As soon as Louis Napoleon became emperor in 1852, the process of liberal-hunting was intensified; teachers were discharged and even exiled; private and religious schools were urged to compete with the public schools; and the normal schools were put under close surveillance to ensure that they did not become soil for the growth of liberal social or educational ideas.

The curriculum of the primary normal schools was thereupon narrowed, shorn of its courses in theory and methods, and reduced to the acquisition of the subject matter of the primary school subjects. Even the Superior Normal School received its share of rebuke. Its degrees in philosophy were suspended, or withheld from students who were suspected of liberal views, and instructors were forced to leave. After the establishment of the Third Republic the curriculum of the primary normal schools was expanded again, but all the details of entrance, subjects taught, textbooks used, and qualifications of the instructors in the normal schools were determined by the Ministry of Public Instruction. The system, completely closed and under state control, aimed at training efficient, competent teachers loyal to the Republic.

Although the provisions for teacher training in France, Germany, and England differed, they all held to the principle that elementary school teachers should receive a preparation different from that for secondary school teachers. This disjunctive principle followed from the social and educational distinctions that were maintained in the two-track system of schools. Inasmuch as secondary schools were preparatory to and closely allied with universities, it was expected that universities or "superior" institutions should prepare teachers for the secondary schools. Inasmuch as elementary education did *not* lead to the universities, it was necessary to establish separate and "inferior" training institutions to prepare teachers for teaching in the lower schools. Social and educational inbreeding of teachers was accepted as normal and proper so long as a disjunctive system of education was maintained.

It is something of an anomaly that the land of the most extreme equalitarian democracy should have developed a system of education whose major purpose was the training of an educated elite to serve in the highest offices of government, army, civil service, teaching, and the liberal professions. And two of the major avenues for preparing the elite were a rigorous selection of teachers and a rigorous selection of students. The French approached modern education through the gates of a highly centralized and hierarchical national system, through enormous stress upon scholarly achievement based upon a standardized, prescribed national curriculum and a recurring system of public examinations of increasing difficulty, as the means of admission to higher institutions and many civil positions. Like England, France adhered to a dual set of differentiated institutions, the primary for the working classes and the secondary and higher for the middle and upper classes, with relatively little chance for transfer from one to the other. Comprehensiveness was achieved by a maze of differentiated institutions each with its specialized purpose and each having little in common with the others.

Because of its enormous emphasis upon achievement, the last aspect of educational modernity that France came to accept was learner-oriented pedagogy. The anomaly of this is heightened by the fact that the most extreme exponent of child-centered education was Swiss-born, French-adopted Jean Jacques Rousseau. In reacting violently against the traditional belief that men are born in original sin, Rousseau went to the opposite extreme to insist that human nature is essentially good. The child is born with inherent impulses that are right; it is social institutions that distort the individual into ugly and vicious behavior. Stemming from the doctrine of the inherent goodness of human nature, Rousseau argued in *Émile* (1762) that learning takes place best when the child is free to develop and grow according to his natural impulses. Restrictions upon his growth should be removed, and a pedagogical setting provided in which the child can engage in those activities which genuinely interest him. Echoing the realism of the day, the best learning comes when the learner is dealing with physical objects, with the manual arts, and with persons in a natural way. Learning is hampered by too great insistence upon the intellectual discipline of the tools of rationalism, namely, mathematics and language.

However one assesses his views, they reflected a modern tendency in the education of the West that steadily gained ground in 200 years, despite recurring setbacks. Yet, Rousseau's chief service to modernity was a delayed one. It lay in directing attention to the desirability of studying the child, so that education can be adapted to the characteristics and needs of the learner as he progresses through the natural stages of development from infancy to adulthood. His conceptions of freedom, growth, interest, and activity eventually proved to be powerful leverages against an overweening authority and absolutism in education outside of France. Whether French education would have embraced Rousseau's theories sooner if the Revolution had not been diverted by Napoleon and the recurring reactionary regimes of the nineteenth century is, of course, impossible to say. More than 100 years passed in France before the time seemed propitious. It was not until the mid-twentieth century that the French educational establishment seemed ready to give more than passing attention to learner-oriented education.

C. MODERNIZATION FROM ABOVE IN GERMANY

At the beginning of the eighteenth century the German-speaking peoples of Central Europe were still divided into hundreds of medieval, particularist political units. Germany then consisted of some 300 kingdoms or princely states pockmarked with another 300 free cities and a thousand imperial knights. No wonder that the task of creating a national state out of such a plethora of local authorities was greater and later than in France or Britain. However, some of the more energetic German states, notably Prussia, began to push hard toward consolidating neighboring territories into larger and more centralized state systems. In this process, the middle classes found a major outlet for careers as bureaucrats and civil servants in the service of the various rulers. This function of preparing official personnel for the governmental bureaucracies gave a characteristic professional role to higher education in many German states. Along with their proclivities toward embracing science and technology, it gave the German universities a head start toward modernity. The modernizing rulers also quickly turned to organizing centralized systems of education clearly differentiated as to class structure, with particular concern for practical studies, but still predominantly religious in tone and only occasionally learner-oriented.

Early in the eighteenth century a stimulus to modernization came from the religious enthusiasms of August Hermann Francke who had caught the humanitarian desire to aid the unfortunate as well as the religious desire of Pietism to spread the gospel. At Halle, Francke established a series of institutions that virtually ran the gamut of a complete educational system: a free school for poor and orphan children; a vernacular German school at the elementary level; a Latin *gymnasium* for fee-paying students at the secondary level; a higher school (*pädagogium*) originally intended for noble students but eventually something of a scientific academy; and, finally, a teacher-training institution that prepared university students to teach in the elementary and Latin schools. In Francke's Latin school the curriculum was much broader than in the usual classical school, including not only religion and the ancient languages but also mathematics, physics, botany, anatomy, history, geography, painting, and music. In his *pädagogium* the realistic studies found an even larger place; considerable provision being made for the study of mechanics and work with glass, copper, and wood, along with laboratory work in natural history and the physical sciences.

Francke gained the support and interest of King Frederick William I, who established several hundred schools in Prussia on the model of his institutions and issued school laws in 1713 and 1717 making it compulsory for all parents to send their children to school. Tuition fees were to be paid for poor children by the communities. In 1737 a general school code authorized government aid to build schoolhouses and pay schoolmasters, almost a century before equivalent action in England.

National control in Prussia was pushed another step forward when Johann Hecker, a Pietist clergyman and educator, joined forces with Frederick II, who had a philanthropic concern for the poor and downtrodden but no democratic urge to give them a voice in their own affairs. Saving their souls, making them better workers, and shaping them into loyal subjects were the prime motives of Frederick, as indeed it was of the other "enlightened" rulers of the eighteenth century. Hecker applied an empirical outlook in the new schools he established, whose very name *realschule* gives a clue to his interest in sense realism. Actual objects (*realien*) were used to illustrate the lessons from books: small-scale models of ships, buildings, and machines, life-size examples of everyday articles, and collections of plants, rocks, and small animals. The overall emphasis upon practical work in mathematics and science was clear.

Frederick asked Hecker to draw up his famous school code of 1763 which laid the basis for a national system of elementary education in Prussia, some seventy years before France did so. In these regulations achievement-oriented education was the rule, religion and literacy playing the predominant roles and the state setting standards for the church teachers to meet. Attendance was made compulsory from five to thirteen years of age, and specific school hours were prescribed. Children were required to pass state examinations prepared by the clergy. New state inspectors were entrusted with the regular supervision of schools. Teachers had to obtain a license and be approved by the state inspectors as well as by the church consistory before they could be employed. Curriculums, textbooks, and the qualifications of teachers were prescribed in detail. In 1765 Frederick issued a similar school code for the Catholic county of Silesia, which he had conquered and won from Austria. These were important transition steps toward a modern national system of education.

The final step in establishing full state authority over Prussian schools came in 1787 under Frederick William II, when a school code took the supervision of schools out of the hands of the clergy and put it in the hands of a state ministry of education, a central agency of education to control all elementary and secondary schools. It also instituted the leaving examination, which all graduates of a secondary school had to pass for admittance to the university. The principles of state education under state control for authoritarian purposes were thus established in Prussia just before the Revolution broke out in France.

Although the scientific and practical goals of a modern education were being forecast in a few German schools like those of Hecker's *realschule* and Johann Bernhard Basedow's *philanthropinum,* they could not invade the classical secondary schools. The *realschulen* had to be set up as separate institutions. Nevertheless, the traditional secondary schools were not standing still; they began to reflect a new and enlivening interest in the classics as promoted by such humanists as Lessing and Herder who argued that the Greek classics even more than Latin were the fountainheads of good taste and reason. As the French influence was cast off in the middle of the eighteenth century and a new crop of German literary men turned to Greece for their inspiration, the old Latin schools became *gymnasiums,* the very name harking back to the ancient Greek schools of that name and the curriculum giving larger place to Greek language and literature. That was not exactly a move toward the modern, but an important change *was* taking place in the German universities, destined to influence educational modernization throughout the West.

A vital intellectual life was allowed to develop in Germany in the eighteenth century by the rulers who professed an enlightened care for the interests of their people. Under Frederick II, for example, Enlightenment science, philosophy, and literature gained favor not only at court but also at the universities, which began to lose their narrowly ecclesiastical character and to take on the air of public institutions intended to train the loyal citizen and the competent civil servant. At the University of Halle, founded in 1694, Christian Thomasius, the rationalist, and Francke, the Pietist, led a revolt against Lutheran orthodoxy. After 1706 Christian Wolff infused the new science and rationalism into Halle, insisting upon the liberal right and duty of free investigation. Philosophy, separated from traditional theology, began to adopt the garb of modern mathematics and physics. Another step forward occurred when a university was founded at Göttingen in 1734. Here the ideas were even more liberal than at Halle; almost complete freedom was given to a professor once he had been appointed. Other universities, both Protestant and Catholic, following the lead of Halle and Göttingen, gradually adopted the new learning.

In sum, the modernizing changes of the Enlightenment influenced the German universities more quickly and more fundamentally than they did the English or French. Scholastic Aristotelian philosophy was superseded by a rational philosophy founded upon the principles of the physical sciences and mathematics. The hard-and-fast curriculum was loosened up by the principle of freedom of teaching and learning. Sheer exposition of a canonical text gave way to the scholarly systematic lecture. The formal disputation was replaced by the research seminar. Finally, the German language ousted Latin as the medium of instruction.

As the eighteenth century ended, however, with its cataclysmic upheavals, the German states were neither ready to join in with active revolution by overthrowing their traditional governments as in France and America, nor ready to repress the revolution with overpowering counterforce as in Europe farther east. R. R. Palmer calls the German response the "revolution of the mind," an ambiguous development which seemed to approve of the liberal movements in theory but not to put them into practice.[9] Whereas the revolution peaked in France in the last decade of the eighteenth century its climax in Germany arrived in the first decade or two of the nineteenth century, while it was receding in France and the United States.

This was the period when the German drive for national identity took on a tremendous momentum, along with a cultural efflorescence matched only a few times in Western civilization. This was the period of Goethe and Schiller, Herder and Schleiermacher, Mozart and Beethoven, Fichte, Kant, and Hegel. It was the time when the princely rulers were motivated to modernize their realms from the top down with the aid of their bureaucratic civil servants, the middle classes, and university intellectuals and against the opposition of the privileged aristocracy of the Holy Roman Empire and established church. The universities became centers of radical thought, combining German nationalism with liberal pleas for freedom of the spirit and intellectual inquiry—so long as thought did not become too activist in revolt against the established order. Freedom of teaching and freedom of learning rallied the university communities—so long as they did not spill over too much into the realm of political action.

During the reign of Frederick William III (1797 to 1840) the struggles between conservatism and liberalism in German education were touch and go. For ten to fifteen

[9] R. R. Palmer, *The Age of the Democratic Revolution*, vol. 2, *The Struggle*, Princeton University Press, Princeton, N.J., 1964, chap. 14.

years after the defeat of Prussia by Napoleon in 1807, it looked as though liberalism might win. Prompted by such men as Fichte and von Humboldt, the king allowed liberal ideas to be expressed as a means of regenerating Prussia and nationalizing Prussian education. These men felt that Prussia could be rejuvenated by an integrative system of education of the ladder type in which every child would have an equal opportunity of climbing as far as his talents would enable him to go. In this way the class distinctions that divided Prussia socially might be lessened.

For a while it looked as though educational reform might parallel the social reforms of 1807 to 1811, when serfdom was abolished, towns were made independent of feudal control, and peasants gained a large share in the ownership of land. Fichte was made head of the University of Berlin, founded on liberal principles in 1809, and von Humboldt was put in charge of Prussian education. Teachers sent to study learner-oriented Pestalozzian methods in Switzerland came back to become heads of the public teacher-training schools and provincial departments of education. Elementary education in Prussia was on the way to becoming the most enlightened and modern in the world, especially attracting the attention of French and American educators in the 1820s and 1830s. The basic curriculum was broadened to include nature study, geography, drawing, and music, in addition to reading, writing, and arithmetic as Johann Friedrich Pestalozzi recommended.

Pestalozzi was not the radical secularist that Rousseau was. He always put traditional religous and moral instruction of children at the top of his list of important aims of education. To be sure, he talked of social reform, and he had allied himself with liberal groups; but he looked upon reform of society as a thing to be achieved by helping the individual to help himself. Apparently even this approach went too far for the conservatives of Prussia and France, but his humanitarian sympathy for the downtrodden and underprivileged touched a responsive chord among philanthropically minded middle classes. Likewise, Pestalozzi's emphasis upon the practical activities of children, starting with motor skills and leading to vocational competence in farming, trade, and industry, attracted those who were dissatisfied with the exclusively literary and linguistic emphasis of most schools of the day.

Above all, however, it was Pestalozzi's conception of learning that appealed to educators who were looking for new ways to teach the children of the common people. In this respect, too, Pestalozzi did not offend by his radicalism but attracted favorable attention by his application of Locke's empiricism and Rousseau's naturalism without giving up a regard for religious sensitivity. His theory of individual development of the learner thus became his most effective contribution to modernity in educational theory and method. He looked upon the child as a unity made up of separate faculties of moral, physical, and intellectual powers, all of which were to be harmoniously developed by the teacher.

The natural instincts of the child should provide the motives for learning, rather than prodding and compulsion from without. Cooperation and sympathy are the means to achieve discipline, rather than physical punishment. In this way the natural powers of the child can develop and can be freely expressed. It is the job of the teacher to adapt instruction to the individual child according to the various stages of his natural development. Since sense perceptions provide the most important elements in the development of the mind of the young child, it is necessary for the child to rely at the earliest stages upon observation of actual things and natural objects rather than upon books and reading. Pestalozzi devised a whole series of object lessons in order to give full play to the child's senses of sight, touch, and sound and as the means of acquainting him with the fundamentals of language, number, and form. Plants, animals, special models, tools, drawing, modeling, music, and geography were important items in Pestalozzi's program for developing the perceptive faculties. Such methods made a startling impression upon educators accustomed only to the reading of books, memorizing, and reciting. Pestalozzi's emphasis upon proceeding from the particular to the general, from the concrete to the abstract, was particularly impressive at a time when children were learning Latin with little understanding of its meaning.

Most important of all, Pestalozzi's methods were so systematically developed that it was soon recognized that a new kind of teacher training was necessary. Henceforth, teachers would need to study the nature of the child more closely in order to guide his development properly and to adjust instruction to his requirements and interests. Once this need had been recognized, an enormous step forward had been taken. At last primary schoolteaching could be looked upon as a profession that required special and professional preparation and not merely as a task for someone who could do little more than make quill pens or whittle strong birch rods—and use them. Pestalozzi made a lasting contribution to the rise of the modern professional educator who needed to know pedagogy and understand the learner as well as know the rudiments of the subject he was trying to teach.

Conducting his schools at Burgdorf and Yverdon with sympathy and gentleness, Pestalozzi tried to recapture the ideals of a sound family life with its emphasis upon mild discipline, loving care for children, and religious and moral inspiration. He broadened the conception of what the primary school curriculum should contain and perhaps more than any other single person, helped to introduce into it instruction in geography and nature study, drawing, and music, along with the more commonly accepted studies of reading, writing, and arithmetic. After Pestalozzi the truly modern primary school education could no longer be routine parroting limited to the three R's. His were perhaps the first schools of joy and love to gain wide attention. But this was not the mood of nineteenth century Germany.

Reliance upon piety and moral instruction as a means to the development of loyalty to the nation became important in German elementary schools. History and literature extolling Germany were put into the curriculum as a means of instilling national loyalties, and physical education as a foundation for military training. In these ways social and educational traditionalism began to regain the upper hand as the short-lived liberal trends came under attack soon after the Congress of Vienna in 1815. Pestalozzian ideas of the regeneration of society through education began to give way to religious, disciplinary, and military obedience. Frederick William III valued education, not as a modernizing agency for the reform of society, but as a means of making the common people satisfied with their lot, happy in their appointed place, and loyal to the king. By 1830 the hopes of the liberals for an integrative system were dashed, and a disjunctive two-track system of education was firmly established—elementary schools for the common people (*volkschulen*) serving over 90 percent of the population, and secondary schools for the upper classes serving less than 10 percent. The repressive Carlsbad decrees of 1819 were designed to stamp out liberalism among the faculties and students of the universities.

His hand strengthened by conservative reaction in Austria and Prussia, Frederick William III retreated from the libertarian movement and reestablished religious and authoritarian control of education under his personal supervision. The department of public instruction was shifted from the Department of Interior to the Ministry of Religion, Education, and Public Health. The country was divided into provinces and subdivided into counties and local committees, each with a school board representing the various religious groups in the community. School inspection was put into the hands of local ministers or priests.

The basic elementary school curriculum throughout the latter part of the nineteenth century was shaped by religion and nationalism designed to produce obedient, loyal, and humble subjects of the monarchy. The methods of instruction were likewise shaped to emphasize discipline, obedience to the authority of the teacher, and reliance upon the authorized textbooks, rather than the development of initiative or resourcefulness among the students.

In the first half of the nineteenth century the classical *gymnasium* won its way as the standard secondary school of Germany. A nine-year school for boys from the ages of nine to eighteen years, it was the preferred road to the universities, public office, and the army. It emphasized, above all, the study of Latin and, to a lesser degree, Greek, mathematics, science, history, and geography. Religion continued to hold a high place. When the leaving examination (*abitur*) taken at completion of the *gymnasium* was recognized for admission to the universities, the hold of the *gymnasium* upon German education was ensured.

Repeated attempts by modernizing liberals to increase the amount of science and introduce the modern foreign languages were turned back; even the efforts to make classical study a creative and liberalizing experience in the spirit of a new humanism in the 1820s were defeated. The supremacy of a narrower study of Latin grammar was supported by the repressive Carlsbad decrees, which reinforced strict supervision of the curriculum and weeded out any teachers or students who dared to deviate from the straight and narrow path of obedience and loyalty to the king.

On the whole, however, the German universities were able to make substantial strides toward freedom for the individual professor and for the individual student. Despite the reactionary attempts in the early decades to stamp out liberalism in the universities, von Humboldt made of Berlin a university of independence and freedom. Instruction was carried on not in the form of a prescribed curriculum, but in an academic atmosphere in which the professor had freedom to teach what he thought best and the student freedom to study what he desired.

As the interest in speculative philosophy and classical humanities was overshadowed by the rise of research in mathematics and the physical sciences, an ever-increasing specialization took place, a sure sign of the onset of modernity. Consequently, the number of departments increased; the number of professors in each department multiplied many times; and the greater need of specializing in order to reach a competent degree of scholarship led to the free use of the elective principle.

The student was not required to follow a round of prescribed studies but was free to select the field of study in which he wished to specialize and to attend the lectures he needed in order to pass the examinations and obtain his degree. The faculties of the German universities became models for graduate and professional schools everywhere. The English and American types of undergraduate college were not a part of German higher education; their functions were to be served by the *gymnasium*. The highest ideal of the German university was the training of the research specialist.

The concern for professional specialism had long spilled over into the preparation of teachers. At Francke's institute in Halle special attention had been given to the problems of prospective teachers, and Hecker established regular seminars for training teachers at his *realschule* in Berlin. Frederick the Great was so impressed by Hecker's work that he urged teachers to attend his *realschule*. Other teacher-training institutions were established in Austria, Saxony, and Silesia. The new humanists of the eighteenth century also influenced teacher education, not so much through special pedagogical training as through a thorough grounding in classical scholarship for the teachers who would man the *gymnasiums*. This scholarly conception of teacher education assumed that all a good teacher needed was mastery of subject matter.

As a result of the modernizing thrust of the liberal movement in the early nineteenth century, the teacher-training institutions of Prussia became models for the world to follow. Before 1840, standards were raised in the preparation of elementary school teachers by borrowing much from Pestalozzian practices. New teachers' seminaries were set up under state control, the curriculum was broadened, and courses were introduced in methods of teaching, theory, pedagogy, and didactics. In 1848, liberal teachers linked their proposals for a more democratic school system with the idea that elementary teachers should be trained in the universities along with secondary teachers, but that proved to be a far too radical and presumptuous idea.

The threatened revolution of 1848 brought a stern reaction from Frederick William IV (1840-1861) who, far from looking upon education as a means of social improvement, viewed the schools as a means of counteracting unauthorized religious and political ideas. He rebuked the elementary school teachers of Prussia for their part in the revolutions of 1848, charging that they had been instrumental in stirring up the people to the outrageous act of requesting a constitution. His regulations of 1854 were designed to reemphasize obedient habits and proper respect for religion and the king. He especially concentrated on the teacher-training institutions as a means of carrying out these aims. Once again the attempt to liberalize German education had failed; the potentiality of education had been recognized by the ruling classes, and they were more than ever determined that the schools should be used for their purposes, not those of the lower classes.

The repressive regulations of 1854 struck down dangerous instruction in pedagogy dealing with the methods and theory of education, a move designed to limit instruction in the teachers' seminaries to those safe subjects that were taught in the elementary schools. Some of the professional content, however, was restored by regulations of 1872, which gave more freedom to such secular subjects as history of education, theory, psychology, and logic. But the hierarchical, disjunctive German system did not permit university instruction for elementary teachers.

However, the early liberal movement did effect certain changes in the preparation of secondary school teachers. Some of the universities began to give special instruction in pedagogical seminaries for prospective teachers who were required to pass state examinations before they could acquire certificates to teach. These examinations included major subjects offered in the secondary schools—classics, mathematics, science, history, and geography. A year of practice teaching was also required for all new teachers. Such developments soon attracted the attention of educators in various other nations, both libertarian and authoritarian, who sought to borrow ideas for the improvement of teacher-training institutions along German models.

Indeed the quest for emulation was radiating in all directions from the primary modernizing centers of western Europe. Not only did Britain, France, and Prussia influence each other, there were other centers of creativity in Switzerland, in Austria, in Poland, in the Low Countries, and in Scandinavia. But up to the middle of the nineteenth century the major Western powers were the most influential generators of educational modernization, as they were in political, economic, and scientific development. The lines of their influence were in the main directed outward from the west European heartland. In the long run of history it was a momentous fact that the two most powerful outliers of Western civilization began to tune in on the modernization wave lengths. The people of the British colonies in North America were able to do so much more rapidly, for reasons described in a later chapter, while the people of the vast Russian empire were slower to respond in their own terms.

D. FLIRTATION WITH MODERNITY IN RUSSIA

In the century and a half from 1700 to 1850 the enormous weight of the traditional society of Russia began to respond but slowly to the challenge of the modernizing states of the West. The leadership in this effort to modernize came largely from the defensive interests of some of the tsars who saw that Russia's traditional strengths built upon enormous land areas and massive manpower were being overtaken by the much smaller but more technologically advanced nation-states of the West.[10] In this period several of the tsars attempted to modernize Russia from above, borrowing some of the agencies of Western education as a basic part of the task. The process was slow and partial, because the policies of the tsars were inconsistent and piecemeal at best, always beset by the mountainous inertia and resistance of the Russian Orthodox Church and the conservative landed aristocracy who proved to be even more obdurate to change than their counterparts in Germany, France, or England. Besides, only a few of the tsars themselves and their advisers saw the need or the possibility of modernization. And when they did, they were often divided as to the role that education should play: whether Russia should follow the expansive, secular,and large-scale models being developed as the patterns for modern education in the nations of Western Europe, or whether it should simply borrow a few technical and scientific practices from their

---

[10] For a reminder concerning the concept of defensive modernization, see C. E. Black, *The Dynamics of Modernization; a Study in Comparative History,* Harper & Row, New York, 1966.

educational institutions designed to give modern training to a very limited elite that would man the chief offices of the upper bureaucracy and army. There was little sustained commitment even among the most avid modernizers beyond the effort to preserve and strengthen the traditional elites; little or no desire to broaden the basis of social participation or to include wider segments in the governance of Russia.

Peter the Great (1689-1725) is usually acknowledged as the first of the Russian tsars to take major steps to bring secular, and especially scientific and technological, education from the West to strengthen the army, the bureaucracy, and the landed aristocracy which he was determined to bring firmly under his control. Up to his time nearly all education from top to bottom was in the hands of the Orthodox Church whose prime concern was to train its own clergy. The debut of organized Western education in Russia is usually reckoned to be the establishment in 1701 of a school of mathematics and navigation in Moscow, modelled on schools in Britain and taught in English. Other military, engineering, and medical schools followed, with preparation to be supplied by elementary cyphering schools so that the sons of the nobility could learn the three R's, a service the church soon absorbed. Peter made a preliminary stab at establishing a broader type of higher education following advice from such German scholars as Christian Wolff and Leibnitz. This resulted in the founding of the Academy of Sciences at St. Petersburg in 1725, but the first genuine university did not appear until the University of Moscow was established in 1755, some 500 years after universities were first organized in Western Europe. Peter found the nobility reluctant to follow his lead.

Catherine the Great (1769-1796) went much beyond Peter in her early efforts to develop a large-scale Russian system of secular education. She had the advantage of a full-fledged Western education imbued with the Enlightenment doctrines of Locke, Rousseau, Montaigne, and Diderot. She established schools for girls taught in French and she kept doggedly asking for advice not only from French educators but also from English, German, and Austrian. Indeed, she promulgated a law in 1786 that visualized a large scale system of national education from primary schools (for the towns) through secondary schools and advanced institutions, including teacher-training schools.

Some of the modern ideas were there, but the will and the way to achieve them turned out to be absent, as Catherine recoiled from the French Revolution into a more reactionary stance toward the end of her reign. While some gains had been made, it is estimated that by the end of the eighteenth century there were some 550 educational institutions in all of Russia, enrolling something over 60,000 students, with perhaps 10,000 of these having gone beyond elementary schooling. Government had extended education to perhaps 0.33 percent of the male population of the Empire.[11] Such reforms as Catherine *was* interested in scarcely scratched the surface of Russian society.

The third Russian tsar to promote modernization was Alexander I (1800-1825) who began his reign by establishing a central ministry of education for the first time in

[11] Arcadius Kahan, "Social Structure, Public Policy, and the Development of Education and the Economy in Czarist Russia," in Anderson and Bowman, op. cit., chap. 19, pp. 364-365.

Russia, somewhat along the model of Poland, and then promulgating laws during the first decade of the nineteenth century, that smacked of Condorcet's plans for a complete state system of schools. Although these laws did not open up education to the serfs or to the lower classes, they did have the effect of more closely integrating the educational institutions with the state bureaucracy. Teachers were given bureaucratic rank, and officials were required to have an advanced education. To this end, several new universities were founded. In these ways, especially under the influence of German models of alliance between the bureaucracy and the culture of the academics, modernization proceeded for a time under Alexander I. He, too, reverted to reaction, joining with Austria and Prussia in the Holy Alliance against the liberalism that was developing in Western Europe attendant upon the fall of Napoleon.

Nicholas I (1825-1855) went still further in slowing down the already faltering modernization process. Religious subject matter was reemphasized in the schools, Western content in the social studies was excised from the *gymnasium* courses, foreign travel was reduced, and secular studies in the universities were censored. As so often with repression, these moves toward reaction served to alienate the growing groups of intellectuals who had already received some glimpses of modernity in the secondary schools and universities. Nicholas I thus solidified against his policies this new class of intelligentsia who were the educated members of the nobility, the upper middle classes, and the clergy who had learned lessons of liberalism from the West. Some were for going further and faster to embrace the West; others were predominantly slavophile in their approach to the West. But in any case, the universities and technical institutes proved to be continuing centers of criticism, dissent, and eventually of revolution.

Thus, despite conservative and even reactionary political, economic, and religious policies, modernization was gradually taking place in Russia at the upper levels of society. As Germany had earlier shown and as Japan and Russia itself were later to show, modernization could come authoritatively from above as well as democratically from below. As the imperial bureaucracy was improved by increasing educational standards and as industrialization took place, even before 1860, the groundwork of modernization was being laid. Perhaps the growth of the technical schools and the advance of science were more important in this regard than any other aspect of the challenge of modernity posed to Russia by the rapid encroachments of the West not only upon its frontiers in Europe but in Central Asia and East Asia. By mid-nineteenth century it could be argued that the expansion of schools embracing science and technology was crucial for Russian industrialization, which had actually progressed fairly far in establishing the preconditions for economic takeoff.[12]

[12] William J. Blackwell, *The Beginnings of Russian Industrialization, 1800-1860,* Princeton University Press, Princeton, N.J., 1968.

CHAPTER XI

PERSISTENT ISSUES IN MODERN EUROPEAN EDUCATION
(1860s A.D.-THE PRESENT)

A. GRADUAL CURES FOR DISJUNCTIVITIS

Between the mid-nineteenth and mid-twentieth centuries the countries of Western Europe moved with varying speed to provide universal, compulsory, free elementary education. If some 40 to 50 percent of primary school age children were actually attending school in 1800, more than 90 to 95 percent of children age ten to eleven were attending by the beginning of the twentieth century. This increase with its attendant spread of literacy, which contributed substantially to the economic development and the political nationalization of the major West European countries, followed by several decades a similar development in the United States. But there were two major differences in the expansion of education between the two major branches of Western civilization. In the first place, primary schools in Europe were distinctly separate from secondary schools, different in kind and quality of education offered, taught in separate institutions, by teachers trained separately, to children of recognizably separate social classes. In the second place, the West European nations did not move in the nineteenth century, nor indeed until virtually mid-twentieth century, to open up their secondary and higher education in ready response to the increase in primary education.

I have dubbed this separation between primary and secondary education with all its attendant dualisms and distinctions a kind of academic disjunctivitis that robbed the modernization movements in West European education of much of their energy, dynamism, and effectiveness, qualities which American, Russian, and Japanese education exhibited earlier and in higher degree. The more usual description of this difference is that the American and Russian systems were basically single-track systems, extending end-on from primary schools through general secondary schools, a track over which all children were normally expected to travel, at least until the end of the compulsory schooling period, whether that be fifteen or sixteen or even seventeen or eighteen years of age.

In contrast, the Western European states, when they did expand primary education in the late nineteenth century, maintained dual systems in which primary schools were designed to parallel the secondary schools and not normally to intersect. Primary schools were free for the lower classes (lower middle classes, artisans, industrial working classes, and peasants), whereas secondary schools were attended by the urban middle, upper, and professional classes who could afford to pay tuition. Primary education was designed for basic literacy leading directly to the working force or to vocational schools designed to train for the technician levels of employment in agricultural or industrial occupations; secondary education was basically intended as preparation for the university and for the higher professional, technical, and managerial positions in society.

The West European countries, faced with the pressures to provide some kind of education beyond the rudiments of primary school education, typically introduced into their systems sharp transfer points for most children at about the ages of ten, eleven, or twelve. At this point, children could go in one of three directions. Most would continue on to the end of the compulsory attendance period in short or upper primary schools for two, three, or four years or a terminal general education. This was the function of the secondary modern school in Britain, the higher primary school and the *collège d'enseignement générale* (CEG) in France, the *realschule* in Germany, the *école voyenne* in Belgium, and the higher primary school in the Netherlands. Normal schools for training primary school teachers stressed this form of short secondary education along with pedagogical training.[1]

A second possibility for pupils from the lower middle and working classes who finished the primary school was attendance for one, two, or three years at some form of specialized vocational or technical school. Such schools provided a specialized, job-oriented training for the trades, mechanics, agriculture, or commerce with little or no general education. Usually they did not lead to higher education, although the tendency as the twentieth century wore on was to upgrade some of the secondary schools even to the extent that they would lead to higher technical schools.[2] Nevertheless, technical schools attracted relatively few youths of ages fifteen to seventeen.

The third possibility, the most sought-after and the most difficult to enter, was the long, general secondary school designed primarily as preparation for entrance into institutions of higher education. These were the grammar schools in Britain, the *lycées* in France, and the *gymnasiums* in Germany and pre-Soviet Russia. The other countries have a variety of names for their schools, but all give an equivalent general cultural education emphasizing the academic subjects of language, science, mathematics, and

---

[1] For full discussion of the short (or upper primary) forms of secondary education and the long (or preuniversity secondary schools), see Raymond Poignant, *Education and Development in Western Europe, the United States, and the U.S.S.R., a Comparative Study,* Teachers College Press, New York, 1969, chap. 1.

[2] Ibid., pp. 92-138 for extended comparative discussion of the varieties of vocational and technical schools.

social studies. Common to all, the method of selection traditionally favored special examinations measuring achievement in the primary school subjects or scholastic aptitude, or both. Sometimes these examinations were framed by examining bodies external to the individual schools, as in the case of the famous examinations at the age of "eleven plus" in Britain. The effect of limited access to the schools of general secondary education was to nourish an intellectual elite which combined academic superiority with social class exclusivity. Such an educational structure served to maintain predominance for the middle and professional classes in the managerial, administrative, and ruling functions of their respective societies.

The democratizing pressure that built up in the twentieth century in all Western European countries called for some means whereby a broader range of social classes could gain access to the long preuniversity secondary schools and thus to the universities. Despite the gains being made, however, the statistics seemed to show that by 1962 to 1963 only 27 percent of British pupils aged twelve to thirteen, 21 percent of French, and 14 percent of West German, were being admitted to preuniversity secondary schools, in comparison with 99 percent of American and Russian children attending general secondary schools.[3]

These figures dealing with *entrance* to secondary schools, however, may not give a fair picture, because the types of secondary schools are not comparable. Yet there is a similar disparity in the percentages of students in the age group who *complete* a long or preuniversity secondary school program and acquire a certificate. In 1950 the percentages in Western Europe and in Russia hovered around 5 percent, while in the United States it was 50 percent. Some ten years or so later the percentages had increased sharply, but the disparity was still great; 7 percent in Italy, 8 percent in West Germany, 10 percent in the United Kingdom, 12 percent in France, and 15 percent in the Netherlands compared with 30 percent in the Soviet Union and 70 percent in the United States.[4] The march to secondary and higher institutions which began in earnest in the 1950s and gained momentum in the 1960s paralleled the expansions that had taken place in the United States some three to four decades earlier.

By the beginning of the 1960s the disparities at the higher education level were as marked as at the secondary. While the Western European countries were admitting around 5 to 10 percent of the relevant age groups to higher educational institutions, the Soviet Union was admitting around 16 percent and the United States 35 percent. Similar disparities obtained with regard to the proportions of the age group that completed an institution of higher education with a first degree: the average for France, Germany, Italy, and the Benelux nations was 4 percent; for Great Britain 5.6 percent; the U.S.S.R. 8.2 percent; and the United States 19.6 percent.[5] The disjunc-

---

[3]Ibid., p. 56.

[4]Ibid., p. 59.

[5]Ibid., p. 264. Other estimates vary somewhat, e.g., the *Report of the Committee on Higher Education* (Lord Robbins, chairman), Her Majesty's Stationery Office, London, 1963, p. 44, gives the U.S.S.R. 7 percent, Great Britain 9.8 percent, and the United States 17 percent in 1961 to 1962.

tions in the educational systems of the Western European nations resulted in a slow rate at which senior cadres of manpower were trained and limited access to higher education for the lower classes. Both results served to put brakes upon modernization.

As the second half of the twentieth century opened, most European universities were faced with momentous decisions concerning their future.[6] For nearly 800 years the universities of the West had served two major social functions. From their origins in the later Middle Ages to the early modern period they provided an advanced literate education for the managerial elites required to man the offices of church and state: the clergymen, the jurists, the magistrates, the civil service administrators, and the teachers and scholars. In a second period, from the industrial urbanization of the late eighteenth century and early nineteenth century to World War II, the universities widened their efforts, albeit sometimes slowly and reluctantly, to serve the expanding professional needs of modernizing societies, the growing cadres of the military, the national bureaucracies, and the corporate bodies engaged in commerce and industry as well as in scholarly, scientific, and technological affairs. Still, the training was basically for an academic elite.

Following World War II the vista of mass higher education was opened up by the United States, Russia, Japan, and the Philippines, a mass education that began to encompass a large proportion of the age group and promised even to approach a majority. Such a prospect entailed enormous diversification to cover the wide range of tasks and occupations required in highly industrialized and urbanized technological societies. The European universities were beginning to open their doors, but they were not sure they wanted to enter fully into this third stage of development which they saw materializing in the three nations with the highest gross national products. George Bereday and Frank Bowles agreed that in the 1950s the European universities were as yet showing relatively little signs of internal reforms designed to shape their roles in response to the needs of economic, political, or technological modernization.[7] By the late 1960s, however, the stirrings of reform went in two directions: the opening of the university doors to increased enrollments, and their recurring closing down by student unrest and dissent.[8]

France

With the establishment of the Third Republic in 1871, the educational pendulum in France began to swing once more toward democratic and egalitarian ideals. This was not achieved without bitter struggles between forces which can be generally subsumed under the heading "republican, anti-clerical left" on one side and "anti-republican

[6]For an interpretation based upon a large-scale study conducted by OECD, see George Z.F. Bereday, *Towards Mass University: U.S.A., U.S.S.R., and Japan,* Organization for Economic Cooperation and Development, Paris, 1972.

[7]Ibid.; Frank Bowles, "Education in the New Europe," *Daedalus,* vol. 93, pp. 373-395, Winter 1964.

[8]See OECD studies; Brian Holmes and David G. Scanlon (eds.), *Higher Education in a Changing World,* Evans Brothers, London, and Harcourt, Brace, New York, 1972; and Roy Niblett and R. Freeman Butts (eds.), *Universities Facing the Future: an International Perspective,* Evans Brothers, London, and Jossey-Bass, San Francisco, 1972.

Catholic right" on the other. The primary schools were the principal battleground. As they became free, compulsory, and secular, they became the shield of the Third Republic itself; and the primary school teachers, the *instituteurs,* became the secular missionaries carrying the republican message of light to combat the forces of darkness throughout the land.[9] The master designer of the primary school as an instrument of national renewal following the defeat in the Franco-Prussian War was Jules Ferry, minister of public instruction, ably supported by F. Buisson, a Radical-Socialist deputy in the National Assembly whose educational proposals became official Radical Party doctrine.[10]

Through a series of laws in the 1880s Ferry shaped the modern form of French primary education. In 1881 fees were abolished in the primary schools; in 1882 compulsory attendance was required between ages six and thirteen; in 1886 the Ministry of Public Instruction was given complete control over the details of curriculum, selection of textbooks, examinations and appointment of teachers, and payment of all primary teachers' salaries. Frenchmen came to believe that a strongly centralized system of state education was the road to national unity, no matter whether the controlling polity was monarchy, empire, or republic.

Meanwhile, the French educational system remained disjunctively class conscious. Primary education remained almost the sole preserve of the lower classes, secondary education being reserved for the upper classes. There were sporadic attempts to open the secondary schools to lower-class children through scholarships, but not much progress was achieved. In 1911 some 80 percent of scholarships went to children of the middle classes, 14 percent to artisan, worker, and small employers, and 6 percent to peasant children.[11] More attention was gradually given to a practical education in the higher primary schools and to technical and trade schools beyond the higher primary schools, but the secondary schools remained virtually aloof from the lower classes. "The *baccalauréat* was a badge of membership in the bourgeoisie."[12]

Following World War I, considerable agitation for educational reform was aroused by a band of secondary and primary school teachers on General Pétain's staff at Compiegne late in 1917. According to the manifesto of *Les Compagnons de l'université nouvelle,* the road to the rise of a new France lay in the erection of a unitary school system open freely and equally to all children, the *école unique.* There should be a common primary school, then selection on the basis of merit for all to attend a full secondary school appropriate to talents. Special attention should be given to the reform of teacher education, better trade and technical education at the secondary level, more modern scientific research in the universities, and greater opportunity for girls at all levels. For several decades the *école unique* was a consum-

---

[9] For an excellent brief background, see John E. Talbott, *The Politics of Educational Reform in France, 1918-1940,* Princeton University Press, Princeton, N.J., 1969, chap. 1.

[10] David Watson, "The Politics of Educational Reform in France during the Third Republic 1900-1940," *Past and Present,* no. 34, pp. 126-137, July 1966.

[11] Talbott, op. cit., p. 19.

[12] Ibid., p. 18.

ing political issue between the Radical, Socialist, and Republican parties on one side and the Monarchist, Clerical, and Conservative parties on the right.

With the establishment of the provisional government for the Fourth Republic in 1944, a committee for the reform of French education was appointed under the leadership of Paul Langevin; in 1947 this committee published its report. As planned, compulsory education would be raised from thirteen to fifteen years of age, the number of secondary schools would be greatly increased, especially in the scientific, technical, and vocational fields. All in all, the reform looked toward greater equality of educational opportunity, more secular control, less centralized authoritarianism in French education, and more attention to individual aptitudes and the learning processes of children. To these ends it was proposed that education be organized on the unitary basis of a ladder system of schools. The sharp division between primary and secondary education was to be eliminated. All education between the ages of seven and eighteen was to be a unified system known as the *premier degré* (first level), leading from a common education between ages seven and eleven to a period of educational and vocational orientation between ages eleven and fifteen, and finally to a choice of practical, professional, or theoretical education between ages fifteen and eighteen. All higher education was to be looked upon as the *deuxieme degré* (second level), consisting of advanced professional and technical preparation in the universities, institutes, and higher schools.

While the reform of French education in these directions made some headway, great difficulties arose from the unstable political character of the Fourth Republic, the severe economic problems, and the constant pressure of the Catholic Church upon the state schools. The financial situation kept the public school system from expanding, whereas the Catholic schools increased rapidly despite the legal restrictions against them.

With respect to the structure of French education as a whole, however, major reforms finally began to take place in France in 1959, soon after the inauguration of the Fifth Republic with Charles DeGaulle as president. The main thrust was to move up the common education available to all children alike from the primary school to include the first cycle of the secondary school. Not only were all children to attend a common primary school to age eleven, some 80 percent of them would continue for four more years in a common program designated the first cycle of secondary education. After that, around age fifteen, they will be separated to attend one of three types of upper secondary school: the *lycée* which continues to be the model of academic secondary school leading to higher education; the college of general education (C.E.G.) which provides a more modern and less classical specialization than the *lycée*; and the college of secondary education (C.E.S.) which is intended to be a kind of comprehensive institution providing a wide range of diversified offerings.

England
Viewing the hundred years from 1870 to 1970 as a whole, it was clearly not a century of steady progress from traditional toward modernizing forms of education in England. There was much backing and filling, halting and hesitation, conflict and com-

promise. By and large, it can be said that the political forces which generally supported the modernization of British education over this period were the Liberal Party, the Labour Party and movement, and nonconformist religious groups; while traditionalism in education was generally supported by the Tories and Conservatives, the Church of England, and the Roman Catholic Church.

The Forster Act of 1870 had been a victory for the modernizing forces to the degree that it had made it possible for local elected school boards to use taxes to support elementary schools. By the Free Education Act of 1891 the local boards could provide education free for children without a test for poverty. Thus, in the course of the 1880s and 1890s an elementary education was fairly quickly made available to large numbers of British children. In 1872 there were some 8,700 pupils in board schools, by 1883 there were a million and by 1896 two million. Meanwhile, the voluntary schools run by the churches, mainly by the Church of England, grew from a million in 1870 to two and a half million in 1896.

But mere expansion by no means satisfied the working class leaders who began to form new organizations from the 1880s onward in order to link political action with trade union organization. These increasingly adopted a socialist orientation and platform.[13] Preeminent in the writings of such leaders as William Morris, H. W. Hobart, Annie Besant, and Margaret McMillan was the doctrine that not only was education a right of all children, but it must be provided free in common secular schools. Only in such schools could children learn the lessons of reason and science free from the trammels set by orthodox religion and upper-class biases. Through the efforts of the Social Democratic Federation, the Independent Labour Party, the Fabian Society, the Trades Union Congress, and other groups, men and women of working-class orientation were elected to local school boards to try to achieve such educational goals for their children. Considerable gains were made in the course of thirty years to the turn of the century, including the establishment of higher elementary schools to extend the period of schooling for lower class children.

Meanwhile, however, many leaders of the Church of England and Roman Catholic Church became increasingly alarmed at the spread of state secular schools and the threat they posed, both economically and socially, to the grammar schools which sorely needed funds. When the Tories were in power from 1895 to 1905, political pressure was stepped up to stem or to reverse the trend. The culmination of their effort was the Balfour Act of 1902 which was bitterly opposed by Labour and socialist groups, by Liberals, and by nonconformist religious groups, but nevertheless was passed by a majority of 123 in Parliament after fifty-seven days of debate.[14]

This Conservative act set the basic character of public control until near the end of the Second World War. It abolished the old school boards and handed over public educational responsibility to the newly organized agencies of local government, namely, county councils and county borough councils. These were less likely to be

---

[13] For this story see Brian Simon, *Education and the Labour Movement, 1870-1920,* Lawrence and Wishart, London, 1965.

[14] Ibid., chap. 7.

oriented to working class interests than the school boards. They could levy taxes for the support of other than elementary schools (i.e., secondary schools if the council chose to do so) as well as elementary schools. The old board schools came to be known as council schools, that is, schools provided at public expense and under public control of an education committee of the local councils. Privately and religiously sponsored schools continued to be known as voluntary schools. Conservative and ecclesiastical groups were able to insert provisions into the act that gave public tax funds to these voluntary schools in return for a minority voice on the boards of management of the schools. Liberals and reform church groups fought this aspect of the law—but to no avail—because it meant public support of religious instruction, especially favoring the Church of England.

Under Robert Morant as a permanent secretary, the National Board of Education insisted upon clear distinctions being made between an elementary education for the vast majority of children and a secondary education that was wider in scope and more advanced for the few. While the labor and liberal groups stepped up their clamor for an educational institution that would be open commonly to all children, the class system was solidified by a scholarship system to enable a few selected children to attend secondary schools in free places.

Britain went into World War II with a doubly disjunctive system; not only did it have the disjunction between primary and secondary education largely based upon social class, it also had a dual system within primary education itself, the board or council schools on one side run by public authorities and the voluntary schools on the other run by church authorities, both with public funds in support.

The movement for thorough reform, however, gained strength in the late 1930s and during the years of the Second World War. Finally R. A. Butler, president of the National Board of Education, presented to Parliament in 1943 a white paper on educational reconstruction, the major proposals of which became the Education Act of 1944. These proposals were promoted by the Trades Union Congress, Cooperative Union, National Union of Teachers and the Workers' Educational Association, along with the Labor party and liberals in the Conservative party. The provisions of the act called for gradually extending the principle of free public education for all.

The National Board of Education was transformed into a Ministry of Education, which was to have greater centralized powers of leadership, control, and direction. Each local educational authority was to make provision or secure appropriate facilities for three stages of education, somewhat analogous in principle to the ladder system, in which every child would have a chance to progress as far as his needs and abilities would carry him.

The three stages were as follows. *Primary education* included ages two through eleven; nursery schools or nursery classes were to be provided for children from two to five and separate primary schools for children from five through eleven. *Secondary education* was to include ages twelve through eighteen; attendance was to be compulsory through age fifteen and through age sixteen as soon as practicable. *Further education* was defined as being all education beyond the school-leaving age of fifteen or sixteen. It included compulsory attendance at county colleges for one day a week or two half-days a week through age eighteen for those who were not in full time attendance at some other educational institution. It included adult education as well as technical, commercial, and art education.

General provisions of the act included such welfare principles as the following: education to be provided according to the parents' wishes insofar as possible, including boarding-school provisions; special provisions made in separate schools or classes for any disability of mind or body; free medical inspection and treatment; free milk, meals, and clothing for those who needed them; enhanced facilities for recreation, social, and physical training in camps, playing fields, day centers, playgrounds, and swimming pools; and prohibition of child labor or any employment that the local educational authorities deemed harmful to the pupils' health or educational opportunities.

As the Second World War ended, it was clear that England had made major gains in formulating plans for a more modern form of national education by the characteristic methods of gradualism and compromise. It was to be another twenty years, however, before the rigid distinctions between primary and secondary education would begin to give way to a more genuinely integrative system of education based upon common schools at the elementary level and comprehensive schools at the secondary level.

An Education Act of 1945 for Scotland incorporated most of the principles just mentioned, and an Education Act in 1947 did the same for Northern Ireland. In 1872 Scotland had established the basis for a single-track system of schools almost seventy-five years before England and Wales had done so. Consequently, the vast majority of Scottish children had attended local public schools for a long time and had attended comprehensive secondary schools somewhat analogous to American high schools.

Germany

Modernization took place in the United States, Britain, and France generally under the impetus and auspices of liberal and democratic forces in which the middle classes and working classes had varying but interactive roles to play from the 1850s onward. In general, they operated in and through the forms of representative government and by and large reflected the leadership of urban educated classes. Borrowing terms from the typology of Barrington Moore, Jr., without necessarily accepting the underpinnings of his theory, this road to modernization could be called the liberal revolution from below.[15] Organized groups in society contested for the political power of government and shaped educational policies when they were successful. Generally speaking, educational reforms consonant with modernization largely favored expansion of education of the middle classes, a process which was more or less rapidly shared with the lower classes, more rapidly in the United States and less rapidly in Britain and France.

In contrast, the road to modernization in nineteenth-century Germany could be

---

[15] Barrington Moore, Jr., *Social Origins of Dictatorship and Democracy; Lord and Peasant in the Making of the Modern World,* Beacon Press, Boston, 1966, p. 413 et passim.

characterized as a conservative revolution from above, largely engineered by an authoritarian monarchy which mobilized the landed aristocracy (Junkers) and a growing middle class to impose a coordinated political organism upon the scores of large and small political units.

Up to the First World War, German education remained strongly dualistic in structure as well as centralized in administration. The two-track system was maintained: children at six years of age went to their respective schools, lower-class children to the *volksschule* and upper-class children to the *vorschule,* a preparatory course of three years before entering one of the secondary schools at nine years of age. Education was compulsory from six to fourteen, and separate schools were maintained for boys and girls wherever possible. The religious control of education continued to be vexatious.

After the First World War the liberal and socialist forces of the Weimar Republic tried to reverse the aristocratic character of German education, much as was being proposed by labor and popular groups in Britain and France. In the attempt to democratize the schools a unified four-year fundamental course for all children from ages six to nine was established, called the *grundschule.* The idea was to provide a common educational background for all children and to postpone their allocation into separate elementary and secondary schools until the age of ten. It was also designed to give more opportunity for the children of the lower classes to pass over into the several secondary schools by means of scholarships and free tuition. The second four years of the elementary school, known as the *oberstufe,* was strengthened as a means of preparation for the trade, technical, and continuation schools; and more attention was given to the *mittelschule,* which led to minor business, clerical, and official positions.

In these ways the Weimar Republic attempted to make the opportunities more flexible for the masses of German children and to increase their opportunities for social and economic advancement. More authority for educational direction was given to the federal states of which the Republic was composed in order that the systems could be somewhat decentralized and adapted to local needs. The churches in the various states also maintained a strong position in the public schools. The Roman Catholic Church, for example, supported the Republic because Prussia and the empire had favored Protestantism, whereas under the Republic it could promote its cause even in the Protestant strongholds.

As a result of the public denominational system there was little pressure for large numbers of private schools; only a very small proportion of German children went to private schools (some 3 or 4 percent in the middle 1930s). There was some agitation for a unified school system (*einheitschule*) along the lines of the proposed French *école unique,* but tradition was too strong and the life of the Republic was too short.

When the Nazis came to power in 1933, their first aim, of course, was to gain complete control of the educational system of Germany for their own purposes. This meant destroying the power of the federal states in education as well as in all other political matters and establishing a more completely centralized system of education than the empire had ever dreamed of. It meant, too, that the Nazis set about in all the ways they could think of to break the hold of the churches upon the schools. They would brook no opposition and no loyalties other than to the party.[16]

On the surface, the Nazis also attacked the two-class, aristocratic system of education by turning their attention to building up the elementary schools at the expense of the secondary schools, with a corresponding drop in enrollment in the secondary schools. But in reality the aim was to use the mass schools to instill the Nazi ideology of followership in all young children and then create a new elite, based not upon economic class or intellectual achievement, but upon loyalty to the party. The Nazis perhaps went further in complete control of schools for political purposes than any other nation up to that time. They showed the world what a power education could be in achieving political and social ends. They showed, too, how destructive of humane values a partially modern education could be when it is used to promote some aspects of modernity (the nation-state, knowledge as power, and industrial urbanism) and at the same time is used as a weapon to stifle other aspects of modernity (democracy and religious freedom).

When Allied occupation authorities began their work in Germany in 1945, they immediately turned their attention to ways and means of creating a truly free and democratic education, a task of enormous proportions because the Nazis had done their work so well and because there was relatively so little democracy in German education to build upon. The Potsdam agreement of 1945, which divided Germany into four occupied zones, stipulated that Nazi and militaristic doctrines should be eliminated from German schools. By 1947 the four occupying powers agreed upon several points of school reform that sounded very democratic: equal educational opportunity for all; free texts and school materials and scholarship grants; compulsory attendance for ages six to fifteen and part-time attendance to eighteen years; a ladder system, rather than a two-track system, of elementary and secondary schools; democratic citizenship education; international understanding; health and physical education; educational and vocational guidance; education of teachers in universities; and participation by the German people in the reform of their educational system. The United States and the Soviet Union would have abolished the denominational schools, but England and France would not agree.

By 1950 to 1951, however, it was clear that earlier agreements had resulted in little of common meaning between the Russian zone of the East and the British, French, and American zones of the West. The Russians proceeded to abolish the private and denominational schools and to infuse the entire system of East Germany with Communist doctrine. Rule by fiat became the order of the day. Textbooks incorporated the dialectical materialism of Marxist-Leninist ideology; teachers were selected on the basis of their political reliability and loyalty to Communism; Russian language and literature were emphasized; and instructions issued to teachers ordered Russian pedagogical methods to be used, Russian heroes to be glorified, the ideals of

[16] See, for example, I. L. Kandel, *The Making of Nazis*, Teachers College, Columbia University, New York, 1935.

freedom to be denied, and teachers to become active in the Communist party. Such great emphasis was put on scholarship grants that some 60 percent of university students in the social science fields were being subsidized by the state. Plans were made to increase the number of university students in the East zone. The entire objective was to create a younger generation molded by Communist philosophy in the shortest possible time.

In the Western zones much more attention was paid to the wishes of the German people. Reform was conducted by discussion rather than by fiat. This meant that educational traditions could be reasserted. As a result, much of the old two-track system was retained, with upper classes divided from lower classes. Furthermore, the denominational school system wherein religious instruction was supported by public funds was reestablished, especially upon the insistence of Catholic groups and aided by the power of the dominant Christian Democratic party. Religious influences grew steadily stronger.

Russia

Taking the period from 1850 to 1950 as a whole, one of the most momentous social facts for the entire world was the emergence of Russia from the wings of the European political stage to the front and center. By the end of the period the most powerful actors were no longer the nations of Western Europe but the outliers of Western civilization, the Soviet Union and the United States. Not least of the factors involved in the new role for Russia, along with its industrial development, the Communist Revolution, and the military outcomes of the twentieth-century wars, was the modernization of Russian education. This process was building up, albeit in fits and starts, well before the massive commitment to modernization given by the Communist regime following the Revolution of 1917.[17]

However, the disastrous defeat at the hands of the Turks and British and French in the Crimean War led to a reassessment of the Empire's social and economic hierarchy as well as to its educational provisions. Alexander II (1856-1881) began his reign, as several of his predecessors had, on a wave of liberal reforms. The serfs were emancipated in 1851, education was assigned to newly created local administrative units (zemstvos) which were elected in the districts and provinces. From 1864, primary and secondary schools were to be administered by the school boards of the zemstvos. Within twenty years there were some 18,000 secular schools so established, including three types of secondary schools similar to the German *gymnasium, realgymnasium,* and *realschule.* Universities were permitted a reasonable amount of self-government and encouraged to develop new programs of scientific research and secular philosophy. For a decade or two under such liberals as A. V. Golovnin, N. I. Pirogov, and Constantin D. Ushinski, it appeared that Russia was on the highway to a modern educational system to rival those of the West. Certainly, in the fields of

[17] See Bibliographical Notes, pp. 586, 588.

science, literature, and music Russian intellectuals more than held their own, Lo-bachevsky, Mendeleev, Pavlov, Tolstoy, Chekhov, Dostoievsky, Tchaikovsky, and Rimsky-Korsakov, to name only a few popularly known in the West.

But then Alexander II turned away from liberalism following an attempted assassination on his life in 1866. While considerable repression followed, this was not wholly a brake on modernization as such. Dmitry Tolstoy (not related to Leo Tolstoy) as minister of education (1866-1880) pushed forward the standardization of the school curriculum, upgraded teacher training, instituted a system of inspection, tried to centralize the administration of education in the hands of the state, and otherwise nationalized Russian education at the same time that he was cutting down opportunities for the lower classes and for women for higher education. His autocratic methods alienated liberal educators, many of whom continued to unite and agitate for more freedom. In any case, the zemstvos were able to keep at work and to continue to expand secular education throughout the century. Even under the still more repressive measures of Alexander III (1886-1894) enrollments in primary and secondary schools continued to expand, and a new system of technical schools at the middle level was instituted, while higher technical institutes expanded into new specialized fields to respond to the great numbers of students who flocked to the technical and scientific studies in the 1860s and 1870s.

As the universities and technical schools grew in numbers and importance, their liberal and radical ideas became more and more a threat to the established regime which in turn took increasingly sharper steps of repression. In the 1880s the ministry of education rescinded the liberality of autonomy for universities, discriminated against Jews in the universities, repressed minority languages in favor of Russian, aided church schools, restricted lower-class children in the *gymnasiums,* and generally took an antimodern stance.

In response, the unrest grew sporadically throughout the higher institutions of education, and various temporizing moves were made in response during the reign of the last tsar, Nicholas II (1894-1917). At almost the last moment, so to speak, early in the second decade of the century, a number of fairly comprehensive proposals for establishing a full fledged modern system of education were made. These followed the defeat at the hands of the Japanese in Asia in 1904 to 1905, the great general strike of October 1905, and the creation of the imperial Duma in 1906. If the several bills for establishing universal, compulsory, free, secular, elementary education could have been passed and put into effect, at least one of the pressure points of frustration against the regime might have been eased somewhat.

As it was, enrollment continued to increase up to World War I, by which time there were some seven to eight million students of all ages in schools and universities. It is estimated that literacy in Russia in 1897 was approximately 21 percent (29 percent of men and 13 percent of women; 45 percent in urban areas and 12 percent in rural). By 1920 the overall percentage of literacy had increased to 33 percent (42 percent among males and 25 percent among females). The literacy rates were much higher than this in urban centers; for example, among cotton mill workers in the

Russian Socialist Federated Soviet Republic in 1918 it was 77 percent for males and 37 percent for females.[18]

So there was a fairly well established infrastructure of educational institutions in imperial Russia at the time of the Revolution of 1917. The tsarist regimes had not been utterly negligent in trying to modernize the educational system, but they certainly provided too little too late. While there was a substantial cadre of trained manpower in the technological fields, the opportunities for the great masses of people were far behind those of Western Europe and the United States.

When the Communists came to power they set out to modernize Russian education by centralizing, secularizing, and socializing it. They confiscated the school properties of the Orthodox church, abolished private schools, and moved to establish a universal, compulsory, and free educational system completely under state and party control. The early years of the regime established the goal of a unitary nine-year school, of which the first seven were to be compulsory. These consisted of a four-year elementary cycle, ages seven to eleven, a first cycle of secondary education of three years, ages twelve to fifteen, and a second cycle of secondary education of two years, ages fifteen to seventeen. At various times the nine-year school became a ten-year school; then for a while it was expanded to an eleven-year school under the Khrushchev reforms, and then returned to a ten-year school in 1964.

The first part of the ten-year school which all children attend in common is called in literal English translation of the Russian "the compulsory, incomplete secondary, eight year, labour, general, polytechnical school" for ages seven to fourteen. After completing this program the student may fulfill the compulsory attendance requirements to age seventeen by going to the complete secondary, labour, polytechnical school for both general and vocational education; or he may go to specialized technical schools or vocational schools (technicums) aimed at particular occupational skills.[19]

Obviously, at the outset of the Communist regime not all children could be accommodated at once or spared by families to attend the full eight or nine or ten years of schooling, so many had to be satisfied with the four-year elementary cycle, or the incomplete secondary education, or with part-time or evening or correspondence classes. Nevertheless, the ideal of a common school which all children would attend alike to the compulsory age of seventeen years was one of the Russian revolution's major accomplishments on behalf of modernization. The age-old dualistic system which had created so much disjunctivitis for so long in Western Europe was done away with in spirit and very largely in practice. The unitary complete secondary school was one of the principal agencies of modernizing nation-building.

---

[18] See Arcadius Kahan, "Social Structure, Public Policy, and the Development of Education and the Economy in Czarist Russia," in C. Arnold Anderson and Mary Jean Bowman (eds.), *Education and Economic Development,* Aldine, Chicago, 1964, chap. 19, pp. 367-369.

[19] *World Survey of Education, IV, Higher Education,* UNESCO, Paris and New York, 1966, pp. 1134-1135.

B. THE GRUDGING TREND TO THE SECULAR

The road to modernization in Europe since 1850 has been pockmarked by constant guerilla skirmishing and occasional pitched battles over the secularization of education. Road blocks and detours have slowed the process, and political compromises have sometimes been the only means by which educational institutions were able to survive the conflicts which swirled around the relations between church and state.

These were particularly apparent in the politics of education in France. With the establishment of the Third Republic in 1871 the idea that state education should be exclusively under lay control and imbued with secular knowledge freed from the teaching of religion and the influence of the church was one of the pillars of the republican doctrine of *Laicité*. And one of the most vigorous exponents of the view was the reformist minister of education, Jules Ferry. The general lineup of combatants ranged Republicans and secularists against Monarchists and Roman Catholics. For a century no overwhelmingly decisive battles settled the matter once and for all. In fact it was still very much alive in the Fifth Republic as the 1960s began.

In 1901 the secularists of the Third Republic passed the Association Act which provided that no religious order could exist without the approval of the government and no unauthorized order could teach in the schools. The next step was the Separation Act of 1905, which ended Napoleon's Concordat, disestablished Roman Catholicism as the state church, and required that within ten years all teachers in state schools must be laymen. But the Catholic Church, which continued to be the preferred church of most Frenchmen who adhered to any religious faith, held tenaciously to its position. Under the Vichy regime of Marshall Pétain following the defeat of France in World War II the church won back some of its privileges when a decree of 1942 cancelled the Association Act of 1901, restoring to the religious orders full legal status as public bodies. Under the Fourth Republic, Catholic clericalism continued to play a strong political role through the Popular Republican Party. The composition of the National Assembly was often so evenly divided that proposals to reestablish religious instruction in state schools or to give financial benefits to Catholic parents rocked the Republic as much as did the unpopular war in Indochina or the high cost of living.

In 1951 a shaky coalition of conservative and center parties finally agreed to compromise with the church. In September 1951, the National Assembly revised the secular policies of the Fourth Republic by passing two school-aid bills: one gave indirect aid to Catholic schools by granting scholarships at public expense to students in Catholic schools; the other gave direct aid to families of Catholic students by granting allotments to the Catholic parents' association. Despite such aid the proportion of children in Catholic schools was gradually decreasing; from about one-third in 1950 to one-fifth in 1959. In that year, the first of the Fifth Republic, the Gaullist government forces voted overwhelmingly in the National Assembly (427-71) to grant substantial state aid to Roman Catholic schools. Only the prewar Popular Front of Radicals, Socialists, and Communists opposed the move, plus virtually the entire professional teaching corps. Nevertheless, by the mid-1960s large amounts of public money continued to flow into Catholic private schools despite their decline in numbers.

On the persistent question of public support for voluntary private and religious schools in England, an elaborate compromise was worked out in the Education Act of 1944. The act provided that all schools receiving state support should begin each day with collective worship of a nondenominational kind for all pupils and also that religious instruction should be given in all schools, the pupils to be excused if parents so requested. In county schools run by local education authorities the religious instruction was to be nondenominational in accordance with an agreed upon syllabus drawn up by a conference of four committees representing the Church of England, other denominations in the local community, teachers' associations, and the local educational authority. In various types of voluntary schools denominational religious instruction could be offered by special teachers under complicated arrangements designed to satisfy a wide range of parental preferences. This all meant that the religious element remained strong in English schools.

As soon as William I became emperor of the Second Reich in 1871 and set out to use education as an instrument to unify the diverse elements of his new empire, he immediately ran up against religious opposition in the several German states. In pursuit of his *kulturkampf* against outside alien forces in the affairs of the new Germany, Bismarck tried to remove the control of school inspection from the clergy; but he soon abandoned this effort and left inspection largely in church hands. The General School Regulations of 1872 recognized that the different religious groups in the German states should have a voice in the educational system. State schools should be constituted as Protestant, Roman Catholic, or Jewish, according to the dominant elements in the community. Where the community was divided, each kind of school should be maintained, or special instruction should be given by each of the different faiths. This arrangement resulted in a public denominational school system in which the state maintained public schools for the benefit of the various religious groups. No concerted lay movement developed in Germany to demand secular state schools as in France. Religion continued to play a substantial role in German elementary schools.

In Germany under the Nazis the churches received their most severe setbacks. Hitler took every means at his disposal to attack the clergy, destroy their power, and wean the younger generation away from religious teachings. The Nazis tried to set up a Nazi state church devoid of Christianity; they persecuted Roman Catholic, Protestant, and especially Jewish leaders. By court order and otherwise, children were taken from parents who tried to teach Christianity, pacifism, or resistance to Nazi ideas. Hitler tried to rewrite Christian history, claiming that divine guidance was on his side; in his anti-Jewish outbursts he even claimed that Christ was not a Jew but a good German Aryan. The churches, however, held out as best they could and throughout the Nazi regime constituted one of the few opposition forces to the Nazis. With the victory of the Allies the German churches once more became free to undertake activities and reassert their influence in the schools.

In Russia before the Communist revolution the Greek Orthodox Church held a dominant position in the political life of the country, the clergy ranking with the nobility among the privileged classes. When the Communists came into power, they immediately set about to liquidate the church as a bulwark of the old capitalistic and czarist regime. Karl Marx' dictum that religion is the "opium of the people" was echoed by Lenin, and Stalin asserted that the party stood for science, whereas religion was diametrically opposed to science. Church properties were confiscated, and the clergy forbidden to preach, teach, or undertake charitable activities. In educational and cultural activities, the youth were taught that communism had no place for the old religion.

In the new Soviet constitution of 1936, however, the principle of religious freedom was stated, but few gains were made until the Second World War, when more official permissiveness was expressed by the government. The church was no longer considered to be a threat to the security of the state, for it had supported the war against Germany. Although the church by no means recovered its lost ground, it was estimated in 1945 that there were more than 16,000 Greek Orthodox churches functioning in the Soviet Union, compared with 54,000 before the Revolution. The church remained definitely in a subordinate position, maintaining itself as long as it did not oppose the communist regime. Constant charges of anti-Semitism and of persecution of Jewish schools in Soviet Russia emanated from the United States and Israel.

C. THE RISING FORTUNES OF TECHNICAL SPECIALISM

Despite all the momentous developments in the biological and physical sciences and in the social sciences, which generally secularized the intellectual world of the West between the 1850s and 1950s, the curriculum in the schools tended to change more slowly in Britain and France than in Germany, Russia, or the United States. While this is too complicated a problem for easy answers, one of the reasons must surely be found in the strength of the classical humanistic tradition among the educated elites of Western Europe, who took the role of the Ancients in giving highest priority to the literary classics in the preuniversity secondary school programs against those Moderns who would broaden them to include the sciences, the social studies, and the technological studies.

By and large, viewing the century since 1850 as a whole, the modernists were gaining against the stubborn resistance of the traditionalists. Generally, however, the modern studies gained their early successes by being offered in institutions *outside* those strongholds of the classical tradition, the French *lycée,* the English grammar school, and the German *gymnasium.* When the modern studies finally did gain a larger place in these preferred institutions, they often remained in a subordinate position. Raymond Poignant's comparison of the study of the sciences and mathematics in Russia and in the Common Market countries showed that *all* students in Soviet secondary schools receive longer training in those subjects than do the students in Western Europe who have chosen to *specialize* in the scientific programs. And only a third to two-fifths of secondary school students chose the scientific sections.[20] Later comparative studies reveal that innovations that sprang up in the late 1950s and early 1960s had more to do with new methodologies than with new and more modern subject matter in the courses offered in general secondary schools.[21]

Still, making all allowances for the strength of tradition, the momentum for modernizing reform was obviously gathering speed from mid-nineteenth century onward. This applies to what we have identified earlier as three ingredients of modern education: the secular and scientific, the practical and the professional, and the differentiated and diversified. The interrelationships among these factors are so complicated that they cannot possibly be unravelled here. They are simply lumped together here under the heading technical specialism, the increasing tendency to organize knowledge in specialized and calculated ways to achieve concrete goals for practical purposes.

In the main, the provisions for education to develop technical specialism in Western Europe were more scattered and diffuse, and suffered more from lower prestige in comparison with university forms of higher education than has been the case in the United States or in Soviet Russia.[22] Frank Bowles points out that Europe could recover relatively quickly and go on to expand economically after World War II without making major changes in education related to economic development, because it already had a large reservoir of trained manpower from its partly modernized prewar educational system. But he argues that continued social and economic development cannot be maintained unless the European educational systems radically change their approaches to technological education in the future. They must do this as the American and the Russian systems did in the 1930s when they expanded the training of personnel for the technical, administrative, and service professions through the state universities in the United States and the polytechnical programs in the Soviet Union. If the universities do not respond, new kinds of higher education will need to be developed to break the blockages.

The Robbins report on higher education in England made much the same point when it compared British higher education with the European continent, Russia, and the United States. The hierarchical system of Europe not only assigns lower prestige but attracts fewer numbers to technological and professional studies compared with university studies. The crux of the matter is that the universities dominate the higher education scene, but they are the least diversified in their offerings of a practical and professional nature, and thus they do not produce the variety and range of trained

[20] Raymond Poignant, *Education and Development in Western Europe, the United States, and the U.S.S.R.; a Comparative Study,* Teachers College Press, New York, 1969, pp. 43-47.

[21] See, for example, Ursula K. Springer, *Recent Curriculum Developments in France, West Germany, and Italy,* Teachers College Press, New York, 1969; "Ten Years of European Educational Reform, 1956-1966," a special issue of *Comparative Education Review,* October 1967; and Edmund J. King, *Education and Development in Western Europe,* Addison-Wesley, Reading, Mass., 1969.

[22] See, for example, Poignant, op. cit., chap. 2; Bowles, op. cit., pp. 373-393; and the *Report of the Committee on Higher Education,* (Lord Robbins, chairman), Her Majesty's Stationery Office, London, 1963, chap. 5.

personnel with the competences required for the advanced stages of modernization. In contrast, the systems in Russia and America display much more variegated patterns of professional training, both within and outside of the universities, and no such rigid caste system of institutional types.

Germany

The educational instruments that promoted the modernization process in nineteenth century Germany were the secondary schools, technical institutions, and universities that prepared the classes that marched in the vanguard to modernization. Chief designer of the German experience was the Hohenzollern monarchy which was able to enlist extraordinarily capable administrative leaders, of whom Bismarck was only the most outstanding in his loyalty and zeal to create a unified German nation. To this end, a powerful bureaucracy was built up, based not only upon loyalty to the monarchy but upon devotion to the performance of duties of office. A high standard of achievement and competence was set as the test of fitness for appointment and promotion. And, of course, the military was a major factor, for it could keep the powerful landed Junkers in line by providing them with an outlet for their inherited feelings of class superiority, and it could provide the middle classes with the law and order necessary for expanded industrialization, commerce, and profits.

It was recognized that a new kind of education would be needed if the upper classes were to produce the scientific and technological expertise required for industrialization; and if the lower classes were to achieve a more effective and widespread literacy and loyalty as well as the technical skills required to build a unified national state out of scores of particularistic polities. While the outward forms of parliamentary government were gradually developed, they were generally less effective than the bureaucracy and the military in promoting industrialization. They could not become the chief instruments whereby the social structures could be modified to achieve democratization as an ingredient of modernization. Germany tried to modernize without applying the torch of the democratic revolution; neither the bourgeoisie, the working class, nor the peasants could effect fundamental reform from below. Militarism and autocracy to which the upper classes rallied stood resolutely in the way, with the exception of the short-lived Weimar Republic, until after World War II.

What was lacking in democratic reform as a touchstone of modernization in education, Germany made up in promotion of an education that stressed the scientific and technological, the practical and the professional, the differentiated and the diversified, an exaggerated achievement orientation, and an extraordinary emphasis on research. This was a brilliant galaxy in the cosmos of modernity, attracting attention and emulation throughout much of the world in the nineteenth century. The linking of science and research to technology, the specialization of technical training for particular jobs, the managerial and administrative skills, by which to rationalize the economy and society all commanded admiration—as well as trepidation.

The fatal flaws turned out to be the authoritarianism, the arrogant militarism, the absence of a humane concern for the welfare of the common people, and indifference, even contempt, for individual difference and cultural diversity. Worse still, the educational system, for all its glory in the pursuit of pure knowledge and its application of science to technology, did not counteract the undemocratic forces that marked German modernization. The academic doctrines of freedom of teaching masked a political alliance between the state and the professorate that demanded loyalty to the established imperial order in return for the privileges and perquisites of high bureaucratic status. Professors were coopted into the bureaucracy, paid good salaries, given security of tenure, granted the right to select their colleagues, and awarded high rank in society as part of the ruling elite. Fritz Ringer refers to them as members of the "German mandarin caste."[23] While the higher technical institutes trained specialists for the new industrial society, the orthodox mandarins of neo-Kantian or neohumanist persuasion bemoaned the onset of modernity, the erosion of *kultur*, and the efforts to democratize or modernize the schools.

Meanwhile, vocational and continuation schools became very popular in most German cities as a means of training skilled workers for the industrialization of Germany. More than any other nation, the Germans sponsored this type of education through local institutions. The regulations of 1872, recognizing the need for an education beyond the elementary level, looked to the establishment of intermediate, or middle, schools for the children of artisans, small merchants, and tradesmen who could go beyond the rudiments of education but were not expected to have the advantages of the secondary school.

By the middle of the nineteenth century the classical *gymnasium* had become the highest prestige secondary school in Germany, the preferred route to the bureaucracy, the army, public office, church, and university. The *abitur* awarded as the certificate of achievement of a secondary education on the basis of leaving examinations became, like the *baccalauréat* in France, an automatic key of admission to the universities. While the *gymnasium* thus stood at the peak of upper class secondary education with its major stress upon Latin and Greek as the epitome of humanistic culture, Germany moved faster than either Britain or France to build up studies in science, mathematics, and technology, at both the secondary and higher levels. The modernizing revolution from above had this advantage, that it could effect changes in education more quickly and efficiently than in the more libertarian societies.

If the universities were reluctant to accept or to promote the applications of science to technology, the government could and did establish new institutions to do so. Thus appeared the famous German *Technische Hochschulen* in the nineteenth century to specialize in the most advanced study of the sciences and mathematics and their application to such professional and technological fields as medicine, veterinary science, agriculture, and engineering as well as economics, commerce, and public administration. These technical or polytechnical institutions relatively soon acquired university level status; indeed the trend in the twentieth century was to affiliate with university institutions. They helped to develop the high-level manpower that speeded Germany's modernization. They added diversification to higher education by multiplying differentiated institutions. They had a similar effect upon secondary education.

---

[23] Fritz Ringer, *The Decline of the German Mandarins: the German Academic Community, 1890-1933,* Harvard University Press, Cambridge, Mass., 1969.

The achievements in science and the gains of the industrial revolution after the middle of the nineteenth century meant that newer types of secondary schools were recognized, if not on a par with the *gymnasium,* at least far above elementary schools. One of these was the *realgymnasium,* which represented a compromise with the humanists according to which Latin was retained but Greek was omitted in order to give more time to science and modern languages. Although these schools were attacked by educational traditionalists on the basis that they failed to give real mental discipline, they were finally accorded the right to give leaving examinations in science, mathematics, and modern languages entitling the successful to the *abitur* and entrance to the universities.

A third type of school also gained some recognition on the fringes of secondary education against the objections of the conservatives. This was the *oberrealschule,* which was so radical that it omitted Latin as well as Greek and shaped its curriculum entirely around the sciences, mathematics, modern languages, and social studies. It was, of course, attacked as utterly lacking in culture and discipline because it omitted the classics. All these schools were nine-year institutions, but each had its six-year counterparts principally in rural areas, from which students could go on to the nine-year schools.

The multiplication of secondary schools went much further in Germany than it did in France or England, especially under the impetus of the democratic educational reforms of the Weimar Republic. Whereas France really had only two versions of the same type of academic secondary school (*lycée* and *collège*) as roads to the universities, Germany provided at least six types of schools that led to higher education in technical or academic subjects. Until the Nazi regime, however, the *gymnasium* continued to be the preferred route, much like the *lycée* in France and the public grammar school in England. Under the Nazis the German secondary school system was greatly reduced in intellectual and scholarly standing in comparison with the school systems of most other nations of the Western world. The secondary schools in Western Germany after the Second World War maintained their specialized character, but the number of different kinds of institutions was cut down.

The whole system of differentiated and specialized schools is quite rational so long as people are willing to have their children's social and economic niche in life decided at age ten. As the twentieth century wore on, modern German educators became increasingly concerned that so few young people were completing the long secondary education and qualifying for the *abitur* and entrance to higher education.

Up to the 1930s the German universities were widely regarded as providing the highest levels of teaching and research and thus as the best universities in the world. The renown of Berlin, Munich, Heidelberg, Göttingen, Halle, Jena, Freiburg, Hamburg, Bonn, Cologne, Frankfurt, Breslau, and Königsberg along with a dozen others was celebrated throughout the West. The freedom of teaching and learning for professors and students; the autonomy of the faculties of philosophy, medicine, law, and theology; the quality of specialized and empirical research; and the disinterested pursuit of science and knowledge were held up as models for the rest of the world to emulate.

Although all was not as roseate as the admirers from outside painted the German universities to be, often in order to gain reforms they desired at home, there is little doubt that the ideal of research was firmly embedded as a basic ingredient in the meaning of modern education by the example of the German universities as they developed in the nineteenth and early twentieth centuries. Specialization became the touchstone of competence; *Wissenschaft* the goal of the professor. Walter Metzer's cogent analysis puts it this way in his essay on the influence of the German university:

> The very notion of *Wissenschaft* had overtones of meaning utterly missing in its English counterpart, *science.* The German term signified a dedicated, sanctified pursuit. It signified not merely the goal of rational understanding, but the goal of self-fulfillment; not merely the study of the "exact sciences," but of everything taught by the university; not the study of things for their immediate utilities, but the morally imperative study of things for themselves and for their ultimate meanings.[24]

When the Nazis came to power, however, they made a shambles of the vaunted freedom of the German universities. They instituted a concerted drive to turn the universities to their own uses, to make party loyalty the principal requirement for students and professors, and to wipe out the "decadent" liberal notions that science and knowledge should be objective. Knowledge and science could no longer be nonnational or international in outlook but had to be subordinated to Nazi ideology, the ultimate in the politicization of the university. Professors who did not suit the Nazi ideas of race, religion, or politics were ruthlessly attacked. Many who could not or would not adjust their positions were weeded out or liquidated. New courses were announced on such subjects as folk and race, Nazi philosophy and race theory, foundations of National Socialist philosophy, and the nature of ancient German religions.

Even after the Second World War the agony of the German universities was not to end. They reestablished many of their fine traditions of specialized scholarship, but they also reestablished some of their aristocratic traditions of independence for the full professorship which came to be criticized by students and younger colleagues not so much as autonomy as autocracy. The unrest of the 1960s focused in Germany, as almost everywhere in Western Europe, upon the hierarchical powers of the privileged professor to dictate academic affairs from the sanctity of his chair or his feudalistic institute, the isolation of disciplinary specialisms from each other, the impersonalism and indifference to the welfare of the students, and a lack of relevance of the mainstream of academic interests to the flood tide of human concerns outside the universities. Each of the Western societies had made contributions to some aspects of educational modernization; none had as yet put all the pieces together to produce a fully developed modernity.

---

[24] Richard Hofstadter and Walter P. Metzger, *The Development of Academic Freedom in the United States,* Columbia University Press, New York, 1955, p. 373.

Soviet Russia

Stimulated by the desire to achieve rapid and massive industrialization Soviet Russia turned quickly to develop scientific, practical, and technical education. Within a few decades the curriculum of the complete ten-year secondary school gave first priority to the study of mathematics and the physical and natural sciences. Parallel to the general secondary schools were established special workers' faculties for the underprivileged urban classes in the factories and for the peasants on the collective farms as well as many vocational institutions and extension classes for adults in industrial, agricultural, commercial, and professional fields. Special attention was given at all levels to wiping out illiteracy and extending technical, cultural, and political education. Part-time education through evening classes and correspondence courses became a major feature of promoting achievement-oriented education throughout Russia.

In the formal educational system polytechnism was the leading idea. Students in a rapidly modernizing society should be immersed in studying the meaning of science and technology for the radical social transformation through which they were passing.[25] Therefore, an understanding of the various ramifications of science for industrial, political, social, and intellectual development of the people should be at the very heart of the general *and* polytechnical education. In Russia, polytechnical does not mean simply what it does in France, the offering of several specialized technical fields of study in a single institution. It does not mean only that students should be trained in a variety of specialized techniques for undertaking productive work. It is both a general education based upon the study of the sciences rather than the study of the humanities and a learning to play a technical role in achieving a modern society. In this respect polytechnism is thoroughly consistent with the idea of modern education. It is inherently secular and scientific as well as practical and professional.

In the 1920s the Soviet government instituted a thoroughgoing reorganization of higher education. The universities were made a part of the state system of education, and numerous specialized higher institutions were established, intended both to prepare specialists and scientific workers in such various fields as technology, agriculture, economics, law, medicine, teacher training, and the arts. Preference was given to students of proletarian origin and background, who received maintenance at state expense, and their curriculums played up social and political studies in order to spread the Marxist gospel. Physical education and military training were also made compulsory.

After 1929 the character of Soviet higher institutions changed once more, much as the lower schools had changed with the beginning of the first Five Year Plan and the onset of the Stalin regime: The stress was now upon the mastery of knowledge as a means of preparing professional and specialized scientific personnel. The doctrine that science must serve communism became the overall aim, much as the Nazis stated that science must serve national socialism. Higher institutions were set up in connection with many factories; thus, centers of production also became centers of education.

---

[25] For a clarifying short analysis, see Kenneth Charlton, "Polytechnical Education: an Idea in Motion," *The International Review of Education*, vol. 14, no. 1, pp. 43-60, 1968.

By 1946 the number of higher institutions which had expanded enormously had been brought under all-union control, except for the pedagogical institutes which were left to the ministries of education in the several republics. Very rapid increases in enrollments brought additional thousands of students into Soviet higher institutions in the postwar years. By 1955 the Soviet Union was producing more scientists annually than the United States was. The success of Sputnik in 1957 seemed to be a mark of success for the Soviet emphasis on science in education. By 1962 there were 731 Russian institutions of higher education enrolling nearly 3,000,000 students, over half of whom were enrolled part-time while continuing to work. The plan was to increase enrollments to 8,000,000 by 1980.[26]

The Soviet Union has become inordinately proud of its rapid modernization in the fifty years since the Revolution, and some leaders in underdeveloped nations have been inclined to accept on face value that it was the communist element that was the prime causative factor. Much more hard analysis and rigorous study will be necessary before such claims can be substantiated with confidence; it may just be that Russia's stress on education for technical specialism was an even more important factor.

France

Despite the great controversies that raged between the classicists and the modernists during the 1880s and 1890s, secondary education in the Third Republic did not depart radically from the humanistic tradition as the recognized road to preferment in public affairs and university study. To be sure the Moderns won a round or two in their bouts with the Ancients as they tried to gain a larger place for science and the modern languages in the *lycée* and *collège*. At one point Victor Duruy established two different courses in the last three years of the secondary school, when students were to have a choice between the classics and science, but the scientific course was always considered to be second rate. Teachers were not as well trained in science as in the classics; the humanists could therefore look down pityingly upon the scientific courses as undisciplined and feeble.

In 1902 a major victory was won for the Moderns when Louis Liard was able to introduce into the upper years of the secondary schools parallel courses, which emphasized various combinations of modern languages and science, alongside the classical course, which emphasized Greek and Latin. All courses were to include a certain amount of history, geography, mathematics, and science and to lead to the *baccalauréat*, but the newer courses were never fully recognized as equal in standards to the older classical subjects.

In reaction against the intrusion of modern subjects and after hot debates in the parliament of France, Léon Bérard sought to undo the reforms of 1902 by decreeing under a rightist government in 1923 that four years of Latin and two years of Greek were compulsory for all students in *lycées* and *collèges*. In 1925, however, a coalition government of the left restored the choice between modern languages and Latin, and in the highest grade of the *lycée* a choice was permitted between philosophy and mathematics. State examinations at the end of the secondary school led to the *baccalauréat* and admission to the universities or technical facilities.

The leftists could never quite solidify their educational reforms against the traditionalists' charge that they were subverting French culture and civilization by primarization of the school system. In 1936, Léon Blum, the first socialist premier to be elected in France under the popular front, appointed Jean Zay as minister of education. Zay's proposals and decrees began a major shift to learner-oriented education and an integration between primary and secondary education, but the Second World War intervened.

To the horror of the humanists, the Vichy government announced its intention to deintellectualize French secondary education along the lines of the German youth movement. Following the philosophy of "kitchen, church, and children," the proposal was to introduce manual training, domestic science, physical training, and other practical and vocational courses into the staid halls of the *lycée*. Fully as revolutionary was the proposal to abolish the philosophy course as the last year of the *lycée*. These proposals, of course, met determined resistance and were never fully carried out.

Under the Fourth Republic the dominant intellectual character of the secondary schools was maintained, but significant new trends began to appear. Even before the Second World War, the closely knit character of French secondary education began to loosen. An increasing number of scholarships went to able students irrespective of social class. Transfer from elementary to secondary tracks was made easier, gradual abolition of tuition fees had been achieved in 1937, and the newer subjects gained some respectability. In postwar France students could at last major in the physical sciences in the final year as well as in mathematics or philosophy. The emphasis upon classics in the lower grades was declining but continued strong.

The tremendous need for technical education as a basis for French industrial progress and military security was given little attention by humanistically minded secondary school educators. Vocational and technical education was offered in local preparatory vocational schools (two or three years) and topped off by national technical schools (three to four years). Rapid increases in enrollments in these schools gave hope that this phase of French education would finally receive the attention it deserved. But, most likely, it would continue to be separated from the humanistic and theoretical training available only in the secondary schools, unless genuine democratization could be achieved. Methods in secondary education might change, but even in the early 1960s the basic content was not being radically revised.[27] Much depended on whether the voices of reform were to be heeded or ignored.[28]

What the reformers had to cure was a deeply ingrained disjunctivitis whose symptoms were two disparate educational worlds. Primary schools led to higher primary schools which led to normal schools which trained teachers for the primary schools; and about the highest one could go was to the higher normal school to be

---

[27] See, for example, Springer, op. cit., chap. 6.

[28] See, for example, Jean Capelle, *Tomorrow's Education; the French Experience*, Pergamon Press, Oxford, 1967.

trained to teach in turn in the primary normal schools. From this route, traditionally, there was no access to the universities; it was a professional dead end, for only the *baccalauréat* could lead to the university, and the *baccalauréat* was the special preserve of secondary schools. As Talbott puts it:

> Under the Third Republic the *sans-latin* was the social counterpart of the *sans-culotte* of the Revolution. The educational system was a sort of self-propelled engine of social control, acting as a brake upon social mobility and as a counterweight to civic and political equality. It was one more means by which the working class could be held at arm's length from the chief beneficiaries of the Third Republic.[29]

It seemed possible, however, that the formative role of the educational system which had perpetuated class distinctions for so long and thus had acted as a positive shaper of French society might now be reversing itself and revving up its engines to break through the walls of social class. The march to the secondary schools would, as in the United States, in Russia, in Japan, and in Britain, soon beat demandingly upon the cloistered walls of higher education.

In general, French higher education by mid-twentieth century had not kept pace with advances in other countries. It has been wedded to traditional subject matters and to traditional methods of teaching and research. Its facilities and laboratories have been outmoded. Its lecture halls have been massively overcrowded; control centralized in the ministry; professors remote from students. The reform movement, as far back as the Langevin commission, urged a revitalizing to overcome the strict separation of the technical from the theoretical that has long marked French higher education. An example of this was the establishment of the National School of Administration to give better preparation for public officials. If this and similar movements were to be expanded to bring together the basic cultural and intellectual foundations and practical training experience, a new day might dawn in French professional education. Another suggestion has been to bring the specialized *grandes écoles* for technical training into closer association with the university faculties and research institutes.

But reform in France had to await, as it did elsewhere, the vast disruptions of student disorders of the late 1960s. A radical reorganization of French higher education under the Education Minister, Edgar Faure, was ordered by the DeGaulle government after it was almost toppled by the student riots of 1967-1968. It remained to be seen, however, whether overnight a century and a half of highly structured, formalized, achievement-oriented, examination-ridden, highly intellectualized education for a small elite could be democratized, decentralized, individualized, practicalized, and oriented to masses of learners as well as to the larger world of nations. If it could, French higher education might be reenergized and redirected on the road to modernity.

[29] Talbott, op. cit., p. 32.

England

Throughout most of the past century the pace and tone of secondary education in England has continued to be set by the public schools. Their classical, religious, and aristocratic patterns were generally imitated as far as possible by grammar schools. In the social estimation of England the public schools held high place as agencies for training leaders in government, business, and church, while at the same time they were increasingly criticized for their exclusive and selective character. Their hold remained strong on the preferred civil, political, and managerial positions in England.

Despite the larger number of free places and scholarships that were being granted in the secondary schools, class distinctions and the economic level of parents played a large role in the selection of clientele. Pupils from the elementary schools were constantly outclassed in the examinations for scholarships because of the largely classical and academic character of the examinations. Character training and gentleman-liness played a larger role in the public schools than severe intellectual training.

The Second World War brought new criticisms upon the public schools; proposals were even made that they be taken over by the government. Their future role remained uncertain for a time as genuine public secondary education expanded under the Education Act of 1944, but they continued to play a large role, in influence if not in numbers, so long as local autonomy and control over curriculum were left in the hands of headmasters and private school managers. The chances were, however, that they would never again play the exclusive and dominating role in a dualistic school system that was their privilege for so many generations.

During the postwar period four types of secondary schools marked the educational scene in England: grammar schools, secondary modern schools, technical schools, and comprehensive schools. The grammar schools sought to follow in large part the lead of the public schools in stressing a liberal arts education designed to prepare for the universities and the professions. The curriculum, highly academic in character, emphasized foreign languages, especially Latin or Greek, along with standard subject-matter instruction in English language and literature, mathematics, science, history, and geography. Some attention was given to manual arts, domestic science, and physical training.

The secondary modern schools took the place of the upper levels of the old elementary schools. They stressed the general academic subjects in the lower forms and then offered a more practical education appropriate to the vocational future of students, the occupational demands of the community, and the social life of the locality. Community or regional studies were often developed, and the later years of the school often permitted the students to acquire direct vocational or prevocational studies in shop and laboratory. These schools became the most popular secondary schools in England. Technical schools have also gained somewhat since their first appearance in 1905. They often claimed not to be vocational, industrial, or trade schools, but rather to stress those sciences and technologies upon which the dominant industries or businesses of the community rested.

Finally, in a few urban centers comprehensive schools have been established to bring together under one roof courses representing the grammar, the modern, and the technical emphases, giving students who specialize in one or the other type of study a chance to have a common social and community life. It was not until the 1960s that a major trend toward the comprehensive schools developed. In 1962 there were some 6,000 secondary schools in England. Of these 3,872 were secondary modern schools, 1,462 grammar schools, 325 of mixed type, 233 technical, and 138 comprehensive. About 75 percent of the students were in modern schools, 20 percent in grammar schools, and 5 percent in technical schools.

Because of the strength of the bias toward the humanities, bulwarked by the religious orientation of the main colleges of Oxford and Cambridge, the English universities lagged far behind the German and American universities in scientific research. In this regard their contributions to the modernization of Britain was far less than that of the German or American universities. Their emphasis was not so much upon research as upon instruction that would lead to the type of social, moral, and political character appropriate to the ruling classes of England. The close relationship between an Oxford or Cambridge degree and a high government position has long been widely recognized.

Over the years, however, opportunities for higher education more akin to that of American state universities have been steadily expanding. In addition to the great complex known as the University of London and the much older Scottish universities (St. Andrews, Glasgow, Aberdeen, and Edinburgh), several provincial universities were founded in the later nineteenth century (Birmingham, Bristol, Durham, Leeds, Liverpool, Manchester, and Sheffield). The number of British universities continued to gain after both world wars. The full-time enrollment jumped from around 50,000 in the period 1938-1939 to nearly 120,000 in thirty-one universities in the period 1962-1963.

Controversy over the place of the sciences and technology in relation to the humanities continues to be lively. It is especially related to the almost inevitable tendency of government grants to be made in a way that favors technological research, although the University Grants Committee has largely maintained the principle that government funds should be given with no strings attached and with the traditional autonomy of the universities preserved.

Further education now accounts for approximately one-fifth to one-fourth of all full time enrollment in higher educational institutions. Even more remarkable is the expansion of part-time study. In the early twentieth century the Workers' Education Association took the lead in expanding the arena of adult education, convincing the universities to cooperate in offering serious study opportunities outside the degree system. Fifty years later the institutions themselves were conducting with government support a wide variety of experiments ranging from new degree programs in old universities to the free swinging approach of the Open University.

D. THE TENDER SHOOTS OF LEARNER-ORIENTED PEDAGOGY

We have argued that a modern system of education not only recognizes that social roles should be assigned on the basis of personal achievement rather than membership in class, kinship, or racial categories, but also that the achievement motive be tempered by a concern for developing the interests and aptitudes of individual learners. The societies of Western Europe devised elaborate forms to honor achievement, but their demands for specialism in knowledge and their adherence to disjunctive systems of schooling prevented all but incidental attention to the needs of the mass of new learners that flooded their educational institutions. In this respect modernization was held back or slowed down.

The bias in favor of specialization is undoubtedly a sign of modernity in an educational system, insofar as it responds to the increasing requirements of specialization in knowledge. But the question then arises, specialization in what? And here the connection with modernization begins to falter, for the Western educational tradition strongly favored classical, academic, and literary specialization over scientific or technological specialization. This has been especially true in the high prestige universities as well as in the academic secondary schools that prepare for universities. So, while specialization may in a real sense be a sign of learner-oriented education if it reflects the genuine choices and interests of students, it may seem odd that relatively so few young people have chosen to specialize in the sciences in an age that depended so much upon them. It is not really so odd, though, when it is remembered that the formative power of high prestige education was combined with a humanistic tradition which, for all its high sounding cultural justification, was actually a highly practical as well as preferred road to the civil service bureaucracy.

Furthermore, the disjunctive structure of the West European educational systems was bulwarked by a whole set of academic motivations that were held in a sort of fieflike bondage to the prevailing examination systems. Somehow, the achievement-orientation characteristic of modernity got locked in with a certifying examination system that served traditional rather than modern purposes when it was applied to a mass participation society. This subject deserves much more investigation, but apparently written examinations began to be used on a fairly broad scale in the nineteenth century for two major purposes—to test the competence of students engaged in degree programs at the English universities, particularly at Cambridge, and to select persons for the civil service bureaucracies in France, Germany, and England. Both kinds of examinations had the motive to apply publicly acknowledged standards of evaluation as the basis for awarding credentials or certificates of competence. Both were intended to replace personal or family favoritism with objective and impersonal standards of achievement.

It has been argued that the long established system of written examinations in open competition for the civil service positions in imperial China influenced the introduction of civil service examinations in Britain.[30] However that may be, written civil service examinations were set up in both India and England in the 1850s. And in both places they seemed to parallel the ancient Chinese practice of stressing literary knowledge in the humanities as the prime bases of the written examinations. It even seems likely that the practice of written examinations for university certification

[30] See Ssu-Yü Têng, "Chinese Influence on the Western Examination System," *Harvard Journal of Asiatic Studies,* vol. 7, pp. 267-312, 1942-1943; and Y. Z. Chang, "China and English Civil Service Reform," *American Historical Review,* vol. 47, pp. 539-544, April 1942.

preceded written examinations for civil service credentials. Whether there was a direct influence from university upon governmental practice is hard to tell, but there was a clear affinity in the kinds of knowledge and intellectual skills tested in each case. The competences of university study and the generalist knowledge for public administration served to reinforce one another.

A similar development took hold in other West European countries. Gradually the examination procedures were applied to admission standards for the universities and examinations upon leaving from secondary schools. Then, when the pressure to expand primary education came along, the written examination became a prime means of selection for admission to the secondary schools from primary school. So what began as a reform to insure fairness and objectivity in judging competence for university graduation and for admittance to public office became a means of restricting admission to the very institutions that would best prepare for the higher examinations that led to preferment. This seemed to work with little complaint when the number of positions was fairly small and the potential pool was also fairly small and homogeneous.

But when the egalitarian demands for universal primary education began to take effect in the early twentieth century and when the demands for opening wider the doors to secondary education gained momentum at mid-twentieth century, the strongholds of selective written examinations also began to be assaulted. The examinations were criticized on the political grounds that they discriminated against the lower classes whose access to high standards of literary education was limited, and on the educational grounds that pervasive teaching to the examinations prevented the introduction of learner-oriented education that would better serve the wide range of interests and needs of a population that was compelled to attend school. On both grounds, the West European nations were relatively slow to respond, but the major signs of the postwar era in the 1950s and 1960s seemed to point to further diversification of the large-scale systems of education which the Western nations had been at such pains to establish during a century of political, economic, and educational travail.

Elsewhere the tender shoots of learner-oriented education bloomed every now and then for a short while, only to be stamped under the marching boots of aggressive nationalism or smothered by the heavy overgrowth of a lush traditionalism. Several examples come to mind.

The shift in mood and tone of English elementary education between 1870 and 1970 is far too complicated to be characterized briefly, but one thing can be said. The contrast between the idea of "payment by results" which dominated the lower schools in the last third of the nineteenth century and the informality and creativity of some of the infant schools in the second half of the twentieth century is startling indeed. However, the change to a learner-oriented education was so slow in coming that it could be argued the delay slowed down the modernization process itself in Britain.

As elementary education was extended to the working classes in the late nineteenth century its dominant tone was a rigid curriculum, taught to the book, "chalk and talk" endlessly repeated and memorized, ground into the heads of the docile children by severe discipline, in crowded, grimy, gloomy surroundings that reinforced the attitudes of passivity and dullness. The six years of the elementary school were minutely defined into six standards, or grades of achievement, that pupils were expected to master in sequence. And each year they were examined by external inspectors who then recommended allocation of national grants on the basis of the number of passes achieved in a school. Thus the teachers' task was basically to teach to the syllabus of the three R's in order to keep the money flowing to the school, so his salary could be paid. "Payment by results" anticipated the accountability movement and performance contracting in the United States by a hundred years. As the twentieth century opened, this ideal of achievement dominated the education of Britain's "second nation," the working poor.[31]

By any reckoning it was also a poorer education than was obtainable for a fee in the preparatory classes of the secondary schools. Learner-oriented education may have been slow in coming, but come it did, gradually and painfully, through the efforts of aggressive educational reformers as different as Margaret McMillan and A. S. Neill. By the 1960s the British pride in their infant school was attracting attention throughout the world. Just how this transformation in elementary education took place in infant schools (ages five to seven) and how it began to affect the junior schools (ages seven to eleven) is one of the success stories for learner-oriented education that could well be compared with the story of progressive education in the United States, a process that had gained widespread public notice some twenty to thirty years earlier. An excellent summation of the modern British view of informal education with stress on the freedom of children's activity and choice in a flexible setting under the guidance rather than the task-mastering of the teacher is contained in an official publication commonly known as the Plowden Report.[32]

In the last third of the nineteenth century, the opportunity for children of the middle classes to enter secondary schools and thus be prepared for higher positions in society expanded considerably. From being a fairly limited preserve for the landed classes, who continued to dominate English society until World War I, secondary schools began to admit a larger proportion of the business and industrial middle classes. When the Clarendon Commission studied the public schools in 1861, it reported on nine such schools; by 1900 there were some 100 grammar schools that claimed to serve the same purposes as the "great" nine, and by 1950 some 150.[33]

An intriguing social analysis of this process of broadening the clientele of secondary education—but only under severe limitations—is given by Lawrence Stone in a comparative study of the role of education in the modernization of England and Japan. Stone argues persuasively that the Victorian public schools deliberately maintained the Greek and Latin classics in their prime curricular position in the public

---

[31] See Simon, op. cit., for descriptions of the "payment by results" system and the growing labor criticism of the plight of the elementary schools.

[32] Central Advisory Council on Education, *Children and Their Primary Schools*, 2 vols., Her Majesty's Stationery Office, London, 1967.

[33] See Simon, op. cit., chap. 3, for a description of the process of consolidating the public schools into a system whereby they operated independently of elected governmental bodies and sought to serve a national and not just a local clientele.

schools as a means of inculcating the children of the new middle classes with the values and the badges of culture long held by the landed aristocracy. By this emphasis on a classical, formalistic, moralistic, curriculum, by the whole pattern of life imposed by the boarding school ethos, and by instituting a competitive examination system based upon the literary curriculum, the elite could maintain their power despite the modernization required to build an efficient bureaucracy for government at home and to conduct the expanded business of a vast new empire abroad. The clue was a "sponsored mobility" parallel to that of imperial China.[34]

Thus, the ideal of secondary education could be preserved in its purest form in the public schools as a bulwark for the upper class social structure while at the same time a larger number of children from the middle classes and a trickle of children from the lower classes could be socialized into the elite culture of "gentlemanly power."[35] The selective examination system for the primary schools culminating in the eleven-plus examination and a system of scholarships for free places were the instruments used to restrict competition, preserve the hierarchy and yet provide a limited upward mobility for the lower classes.

Labor saw the selective examination system as calculated to keep workers' children out of secondary schools while admitting the middle classes to them. The Trades Union Congress kept up a steady drum-fire of protest against the practice, arguing that the only solution was a publicly supported system of general secondary education for all children, offered in common schools open to all. But meanwhile a very strong bias toward selectivity on the basis of examinations was reenforced by the psychological testing movements of the 1920s and 1930s which affirmed that inherited differences in intellectual ability required different forms of education and that such differences could be accurately determined by aptitude tests as early as eleven years of age. The testimony along these lines of such educationists as John Adams, Percy Nunn, and Cyril Burt seemed to justify separate kinds of schools after age eleven and made it more and more difficult to rationalize secondary education for all children in a common school.[36]

As a matter of fact, the principle of selectivity maintained a strong hold upon British public and professional opinion throughout the first two-thirds of the twentieth century. Even where it was opposed on social and political grounds it was likely to be accepted on educational grounds. The eleven-plus examination survived all sorts of onslaughts, and the general examinations at ages fifteen or sixteen leading to the General Certificate of Education (Ordinary level) and at eighteen or so (Advanced level) all helped to sort out students for advanced study.

---

[34] Marius B. Jansen and Lawrence Stone, "Education and Modernization in Japan and England," *Comparative Studies in Society and History,* vol. 9, pp. 225-232, January 1967.

[35] For a long essay on the values of the elite culture as promoted by the English public schools and brief comparisons with the Chinese Empire, the Meiji regime in Japan, and the Jesuit order, see Rupert Wilkinson, *Gentlemanly Power; British Leadership and the Public School Tradition; a Comparative Study in the Making of Rulers,* Oxford University Press, London, 1964.

[36] See Brian Simon, "Classification and Streaming; a Study of Grouping in English Schools, 1860-1960," in Paul Nash (ed.), *History and Education, The Educational Uses of the Past,* Random House, New York, 1970, pp. 115-159.

By the late 1950s, however, there were signs that the assumptions about innate intellectual ability were to be resolutely challenged as psychologists and sociologists began to stress the environmental influences on the development of intelligence, including the role of social class.[37] Nevertheless, the pressure to gain admittance to the grammar schools rather than to secondary modern schools did not seem to let up. In fact, the secondary modern schools even tended to model themselves upon the grammar schools in the effort to prepare larger numbers for the external examinations leading to the universities.

Streaming–classifying students by ability–continued to mark all types of schools far more than in the United States. Such devices, fitted to the external examination system which dominated the university admission process, continued to place achievement well above learner orientation in British secondary schools. What may happen in the future, of course, is unpredictable, but international influences are likely to play a larger role than they did in the interwar years. There may be some significance beyond mere irony in the fact that in the opening years of the 1970s, Americans were being urged to emulate British infant schools[38] while the new headmaster of Eton was saying that the curriculum of his ancient school would be "tending more toward the American pattern with less specialization in the senior years."[39]

Whether Michael McCrum's speculation that Eton might turn away from specialization would be borne out remains to be seen, for the Crowther Report of the Central Advisory Council for Education (England) came out strongly for specialization in the later years of the secondary school (i.e., after age sixteen). The reasons were that specialization provided a means whereby the student could attach the acquiring of knowledge to a main intellectual interest, and it also was the best means of awakening interest, teaching clear thinking, and developing self-discipline in study. True, specialization may lead to narrowness, but that is probably better than shallowness. Thus the English boy or girl who continues education beyond the age of fifteen or sixteen is to be a specialist. Whatever justification in learning theory it may have, specialization helps him or her to pass the examinations in subject matters which are required for university entrance.

The Russian Bolsheviks, in their early zeal to be rid of tsarist institutions and practices, looked around the world for ideas they could borrow to help them build a new system. They looked to Britain, France, Germany, Scandinavia, Switzerland, and yes, to the United States which in the 1920s was exporting the progressive education of Dewey, Thorndike, and Kilpatrick to the far reaches of the world. For the decade of the 1920s, the Soviet educationalists were fascinated with a learner-oriented approach to the schools which they called pedology. With it they hoped to release the learner's energies and reorient the traditional views of the bourgeois teacher. They

---

[37] See, for example, P. E. Vernon (ed.), *Secondary School Selection; a British Psychological Society Inquiry,* Methuen, London, 1957.

[38] Charles E. Silberman, *Crisis in the Classroom; the Remaking of American Education,* Random House, New York, 1970, chap. 6.

[39] As quoted in *The New York Times,* "Eton Gently Sheds Aristocratic Ways," January 4, 1971.

used activities, project methods, student trips, and political ideology to instill the new political ideals in the younger generation and convert the teachers. Individual marks and competition were abolished as a holdover from capitalistic ideology, and ability to perform in group cooperative work was extolled as the ideal.

But after a decade pedology was declared a failure by the Central Committee of the Communist Party in 1931. The Communists felt secure enough to return to the more traditional methods in which the complete authority of the teacher was reestablished, organized and systematic knowledge was prized, and diligent study, passing of examinations, and hard work and good conduct by students were to be the educational means of building a highly modern industrialized nation in a short time.

After World War I the cultural florescence of the Weimar Republic, so enthusiastically described by Peter Gay,[40] prompted many elementary teachers in Germany to become enthusiastic over progressive methods of teaching. They emphasized individual freedom from restraint and integrated subject matter as a reaction against the excessively controlled, authoritarian, and intellectualized subject matter of the imperial schools. Stress was put upon the study of the local environment, trips, plays, music, and art as mediums of free expression. Printed courses of study were replaced by "suggestions." Much attention was given to child psychology, the interests of pupils, and pleasanter relations between teachers and pupils in the effort to replace the formal discipline of bowing and heel clicking characteristic of the Prussian military tradition. Such freedom and individualism were, of course, resented by many Germans, and the disappearance of such learner-oriented activity methods was little lamented in the reactionary swing of the pendulum under the Nazis back to strict control, obedience, discipline, and authority of the teachers.

In 1945 a remarkable experimental program in some French secondary schools was instituted for 5,000 eleven-year-olds to emphasize an activity program roughly analogous to some of the methods of American progressive education. These "new classes" were to be added successively each year to the next higher grade. The content of the program in the mornings was to be focused upon French language and literature, history, geography, foreign language, natural science, and mathematics. In the afternoons attention was to be devoted to choices among the fine arts, music, and the applied arts. Recreational, health, and physical education activities along with community studies were made compulsory. The underlying principles of attention to the growth and development of children, tests, and measurements, guidance, and better teacher-student relationships all trumpeted the coming of modern education to France. Attention to the creative talents of students and regard for their ideas and personality were supposed to break down the authoritarian methods of discipline by the teacher.

However, French education was not to be swept away by modern, learner-oriented education. The hold of tradition was too great, criticism of the newfangled "soft pedagogy" of these new classes was bitter and loyalty to the values of disciplined intellect was deep and strong. Lectures by the teacher and notetaking by the students

[40]Peter Gay, *Weimar Culture: The Outsider as Insider,* Harper & Row, New York, 1968.

remained the basic methods of instruction. Library facilities in the schools were virtually nonexistent and other kinds of instructional and audio-visual materials were scarce. The bleakness of a regimented boarding-school life somehow cast its shadow over the tender shoots, and they withered. Was the learner really all that important compared with the traditional values of French civilization?

CHAPTER XII

THE MODERNIZING MOMENTUM OF AMERICAN EDUCATION
(1700 A.D.-1860s A.D.)

Perhaps the most striking thing about American education in the years from 1700 to 1860 is that it started out in a more traditional pattern than that of England, France, or Germany, but it ended up more modern than its European counterparts. This is not to say that it was more modern in every respect by the mid-nineteenth century, but rather that the modernizing momentum was building up with such force that American education did overtake the other nations of the West in the course of the century following the 1860s.

The two characteristics of modern education in which the American sector of the West did seem clearly to forge ahead of the European had to do with the emerging consensus that popular education and practical education must be provided on a large scale through organized and public effort, both for the benefit of the development of the society as a whole and for the development of the individual. These generalizations are of course subject to the usual difficulties of comparative proof and to the exception that they did not apply to American blacks or Indians to any significant degree.

The growing consensus in America that universal, free, and compulsory elementary education should be established in schools controlled and supported under public auspices was a remarkable and distinctive achievement. This achievement was all the more remarkable because the American colonists had started out their colonial experience by relying for the education of their children far more upon family, church, and informal means than upon schools and universities, simply because the organized educational institutions were not as widely available in seventeenth-century America as they were in England, France, or Germany.[1] But in the course of the century and a half from 1700 to 1850 they not only caught up with the Europeans,

[1] This point is persuasively documented by Lawrence A. Cremin, *American Education: The Colonial Experience, 1607-1783,* Harper & Row, New York, 1970.

402

they established schools, colleges and universities in such numbers and with such enthusiasm that they overtook their former mentors, often to their remark and sometimes to their scandal.

One major reason for this development has to do with the character of political and economic democracy in America, nicely described by R. R. Palmer as the paradox of American attitudes toward the French Revolution.[2] In the mid-eighteenth century ordinary Americans already had more equality and liberty than their counterpart Frenchmen or Englishmen, less subordination to a strong central government, no all-embracing feudal obligations, and a less well-developed commercial, urban economy. So whereas the radical "democrats" of the revolutions in France, Switzerland, and Holland sought to build a strong centralized government that could serve their middle-class, professional, or working-class interests by removing the aristocratic landowners from the seats of power, the "democrats" or "republicans" in America were themselves the landowners and farmers of the west and south and the working-men of the eastern cities. They were traditionalists in their belief in agrarian self-sufficiency and in local government as guarantors of liberty; they were suspicious of unitary central governments and closed corporations as instruments of special privilege. Republicans, with Jefferson as the prototype, were, however, modernizers in their adherence to democratic participation in the political process, to equalitarianism in the social process, and to faith in the efficacy of secular, scientific, professional, and practical knowledge in the educational process.

By contrast, the Federalists in America, who were mostly anti-French and antidemocratic, were likely to be in favor of economic and national development as a benefit to the business and commercial interests of the cities. They were ready for the social change that could be achieved by a strong central government as it promoted banking credit, urbanization, trade, and sound money. In other words, with Hamilton as the prototype, they were ready to speed modernization under stimulus from a powerful central government, as were the democrats of France, but they were likely to be conservative with respect to maintaining established religion and aristocratic rule by the favored classes. They were also likely to favor scientific and professional knowledge as the means of training those best fit to rule.

The significant thing is that in America both the Republicans (and the Democrats who succeeded them) and the Federalists (and the Whigs who succeeded *them*) in large part came to agree that popular, practical education was a good thing for them and for American society.[3] There were, of course, exceptions on both sides and there were regional differences, but the net result of the century between 1750 and 1850 was an accumulating belief in the value of widespread public education, a belief that stemmed from the most radical theorists among the Democrats on the left to the conservative spokesmen among the Whigs on the right. The redeeming faith in the social power of massive educational endeavor was nowhere more strikingly evident,

[2] R. R. Palmer, *The Age of the Democratic Revolution; a Political History of Europe and America, 1760-1800,* vol. 2, *The Struggle*, Princeton University Press, Princeton, N.J., 1964, pp. 26-27, and chap. 16.

[3] For an illuminating discussion of this process, see Rush Welter, *Popular Education and Democratic Thought in America,* Columbia University Press, New York, 1962, Parts I and II.

and no nation came to it in more overwhelming and articulate numbers than in mid-nineteenth-century America. This was a chief source of the overtaking modernizing momentum that was to propel the United States first into the florescent stage of modern education. It was so basic that the faith in education actually shaped American political policies in distinctive ways. As Welter puts it, American democrats could afford extreme laissez faire political policies and thus did not need to revert to the class struggle, because they believed universal education would be the major solvent for an integrative society. Democratic public policy was simply "anarchy with a schoolmaster."[4]

A. MODERNIZATION FROM BELOW

Two factors that gave a distinctive character to eighteenth-century development in America were the influx of a variety of national groups with their diverse languages and religions and the dispersion of population from the settled towns of the seacoast into the back country. Both of these developments tended to weaken unitary state control over education by colonial legislatures and to strengthen on one hand the smallest unit of local government known as the district or precinct and on the other the autonomous religious community or private corporation. In either case the predominance of the town schools so popular in New England in the seventeenth century came to an end as educational authority was delegated by colonial legislatures to denominations, to corporate bodies, to individuals, and to local districts of government. Diversity gained the educational saddle in the management of schools by the end of the eighteenth century.

Outside of New England one of the most important means of providing education was the Church of England's Society for the Propagation of the Gospel in Foreign Parts (1701), which established many "free" schools for the charity education of poor and underprivileged children. Accelerated by the religious enthusiasms of the Great Awakening, thousands of people flooded into the various denominational churches. With rising emotions of altruism, philanthropy, and religious zeal, people were more than ever ready to pour money into sectarian religious schools and colleges—Presbyterian, Dutch Reformed, Anglican, Congregational, Lutheran, Moravian, Mennonite, Quaker, Baptist, and Methodist. Each denomination wanted its own religious doctrine taught in its own schools. Gradually, the several colonial governments began to permit the different religious groups to conduct their own schools in their own languages. In this sense denominational control of education was a gain for religous tolerance and recognition of the rights and values of religious pluralism, a step toward modernity in place of the uniformity required by an established church.

In New England, where the established churches stubbornly held their ground, the town schools became less convenient for the children of the backwoodsmen who pushed back from the seacoast towns to settle in the rural frontier regions of

[4] Ibid., pp. 3, 50.

Massachusetts, Connecticut, New Hampshire, and Vermont. To be sure, the country farmers wanted elementary education for their children, but they did not want to pay taxes for the town Latin schools that their children would probably not attend. The outlying districts therefore proceeded to agitate for release from town control of their local or district schools. Eventually, the districts achieved legal authority. The Massachusetts law of 1789, for example, authorized them to build their own schoolhouses, appoint their own teachers, set the length of school terms, and control the curriculum. By 1800 the local districts were empowered to levy their own taxes to support their schools

Just as community control of schools and decentralization of management were becoming basic tenets of the American practice in education, along came the new democratic ideology of the Revolution proclaiming that the state rather than the local community should provide primary schools for the common people and advanced education for the uncommon people. One of the earliest to argue this way was William Livingston, a leading Presbyterian in New York, who fought to dislodge the Church of England from its power center in the legislature and in New York City during the 1750s.

The most formidable spokesman, however, for a state system of education before independence was won was Thomas Jefferson. When he introduced into the Virginia assembly in 1779 a comprehensive document for the reform of the state's institutions, his bills called for the repeal of the laws of primogeniture and entail, abolishing taxation on behalf of the established Church of England, and setting up a state system of free universal education as a corollary to these political, economic, and religious reforms. His education bill proposed that free elementary schools be established throughout the state to provide secular education for all children, and that secondary schools should be available for the more intelligent youth. The most promising candidates should then be sent free to a reorganized and enlarged College of William and Mary, which would become in effect a public universisty to cap the state system. Jefferson's plan for education was not adopted by the Virginia legislature, largely through the opposition of religious groups and the College of William and Mary, but the ideal of free universal education had been stated, very much as it was later to be adopted in most American states in the nineteenth century. When the colonies were drawing up their constitutions as independent states during the Revolution, approximately half declared that schools should be established, or in some cases simply that schools should be cheap.

Scarcely had independence been assured when a flood of pamphleteers began to argue that a new education was needed for the new republic. Stimulated by the American Philosophical Society's prize contest for the best description of a liberal education suitable to a republican society, the chief spokesmen applied the main doctrines of the Enlightenment to the United States: education is the key to the perfectibility of man and the possibility of social progress.[5] Samuel Knox, Samuel

---

[5]For summaries of these proposals, see Allen O. Hansen, *Liberalism and American Education in the Eighteenth Century*, Macmillan, New York, 1926; and Frederick Rudolph (ed.), *Essays on Education in the Early Republic*, Harvard University Press, Cambridge, Mass., 1965.

Harrison Smith, Benjamin Rush, and Robert Coram among others stated the case for modernizing American education. Education should be practical, flexible, and adaptable to new conditions. It should be universally free in order to provide equal opportunity for all individuals as well as to prepare citizens for their responsibilities in a democracy. It should embrace a comprehensive system of elementary, secondary, and higher institutions under national control in order to contribute to secular rather than religous outcomes and to ensure the greatest progress toward social welfare.

Although these proposals for a national system of education were not put into practice because the tradition of sectarian and decentralized control of education proved to be too strong, some steps were taken by the central government that were to have lasting influence upon American education. While the American states were operating under the Articles of Confederation, two ordinances were passed under pressure from the northern states. They concerned the disposition of the vast public lands of the western frontier, the claims to which the various states had given over to the federal government. The Ordinance of 1785 established a policy for the sale of this public land, providing that the income from the sale of a section of land in the center of each township was to be used for common schools.

Two years later the Ordinance of 1787 confirmed this land policy and set forth the governmental principles to be followed when the Northwest Territory was settled (an area comprising the present states of Ohio, Indiana, Illinois, Michigan, Wisconsin, and part of Minnesota). The states carved out of this territory must assure free religious conscience, trial by jury, prohibition of slavery or involuntary servitude, good faith with the Indians, and common schools. This meant that the income from the school lands would be public funds dispensed by civil authorities and not by religious or private bodies. A pattern of public education was forecast for the whole region, not simply a continuation of charity or sectarian education.

When the Constitution was drawn up and ratified in 1789, no mention of education was made in it. Many members of the Constitutional Convention considered education properly to be a function of the churches or of local or state government rather than of the national government. The Federalists were interested in a strong federal government but not in education for the common people; therefore they did not desire a national system of education. The Anti-Federalists were interested in education for the common people but opposed a strong national government; therefore they did not want national control of education.

Nor did the Bill of Rights mention education. The Tenth Amendment, however, reserved to the states or to the people all powers not delegated by the Constitution to the federal government or prohibited by it. In the republican era to follow this was to be interpreted to mean that the states could assert their rights to establish and maintain public schools. But, all in all, the constitutional resolution meant that education in America would essentially be modernized "from below," by the lower branches of government and by voluntary effort rather than by the central government "from above" as in Germany or France.

What is sometimes forgotten, however, is that even before independence organized education, for all its lack of system, had become widely available throughout the colonies and had undoubtedly made it possible for diverse colonists to work together to achieve the revolution and form the new republic. Whether promoted by town or district, by established church or dissenting sect, by corporate body or individual entrepreneur, by the desire for personal advancement or political prestige, the predominant cultural pressure of the eighteenth century was toward getting more education rather than less. Lawrence A. Cremin concludes that by the late eighteenth century literacy in the American colonies was at least equivalent to that of England and possibly higher, even before the republican campaigns for common public schools began to move into high gear. Still more important is his judgment that by and large the schools encouraged what he calls a "liberating literacy" which led the individual to greater participation in ideas and affairs as contrasted with an "inert literacy" so often conveyed with a minimal amount of motivation by families or by informal means.[6] If organized education could be a principal instrument in bringing the new republic into being, no wonder that republicans turned with such faith to a massive public schooling endeavor as the indispensible ingredient for its preservation, prosperity, and progress. No longer would the make-do education, imposed upon families and churches and communities by the exigencies of the colonial experience, suffice for the modern nation-building process that lay immediately ahead.

B. A CENTURY OF REPUBLICAN EDUCATION

In the first century of the republic from the 1770s to the 1860s Americans planned, argued, built, criticized, and changed the institutions they had inherited from colonial rule. In many different ways they said that if a republican government and society were to endure and to prosper, then the people who elected the government, held office, made laws, and consented to be ruled must be educated as republicans.

The voice of the founding fathers was clear:

> If a nation expects to be ignorant and free, in a state of civilization, it expects what never was and never will be.
>
> Thomas Jefferson

> A people who mean to be their own Governors must arm themselves with the power which knowledge gives.
>
> James Madison

> The whole people must take upon themselves the education of the whole people and must be willing to bear the expense of it.
>
> John Adams

But this was not so easy to do. The people who had won the Revolutionary War—these so-called Americans—were not really Americans, at least not yet. They were "European ethnics." They were English, Scottish, French, German, Dutch, Swedish, and a good many more. And there were soon to be Irish, Italian, Hungarian, Polish,

[6]Cremin, op. cit., chap. 18.

and Russian as well. They spoke different languages and they had different customs. Some had no tradition of self-government; others were fiercely proud or jealous of rule by others.

When it was finally decided that they should all learn the same language and the same principles of republican government, a question arose as to how this was to be done. The republican answer was that it could best be done by a common school, taught in English, which all the children of all the people could attend together. Thus, they would learn how to live together, even though some people were poor and some rich, some had good manners while others were coarse and rude. It was decided that they must all be educated in this way if free government was to endure. The entire community had to give financial support, because if there are weak spots anywhere, the whole community of freedom would be weakened. So it was decided that the common schools must be supported by taxes paid by all.

A second question was who would control these schools. The only institution of a free society which serves everyone equally and is responsible to everyone is the government. Therefore the government should control the common schools. In order to keep the schools close to the people, the local governments, or if need be the state governments rather than the national government, should control the schools. In order to prevent the schools from being subject to political and partisan prejudice, a series of local boards of education separate from the usual executive, legislative, and judicial branches of government were established. These school boards, elected directly by the people, constituted a "fourth branch of government." They exerted direct control over local education under the general authority of the state governments, subject to the guarantees of equality and freedom laid down in the United States Constitution.

Under the First Amendment to the Constitution all Americans, each different religious group, had the freedom to establish their own schools. The choice for each American was whether the education that supports a free society should be conducted in separate schools in which religion provides the fundamental framework for all studies, or in common schools devoted primarily to the whole range of free institutions in America. If the citizens had decided the first way, the children would have been divided into separate schools for their entire education, with the division being along religious lines. The second choice provided that children would attend the same public school together for their common education, being separated only for their religious education, which would be conducted by the home, the church, or the synagogue. This was the classic decision between a disjunctive system and an integrative system.

In the century of republican education, most Americans eventually chose the common school, controlled and supported in common, and embracing a supposedly nonsectarian religious outlook. Their primary concern was to design a universal, free, comprehensive system of public schools that would promote modern republican institutions. For the first 100 years of the republic, the need for creating the common bonds and loyalties of nation building was paramount. Less attention was given to the claims of diversity, pluralism, or difference. This came later when the Union had been established, made secure against internal opposition, defended against outside invaders, and preserved despite a war between the states themselves.

The republican ideal of the first century of nationhood gave the following answers regarding the control of education: a modern society required public elementary schools to provide the basic information, literacy, and moral teachings required by every free man. For most Americans the term *free man* was limited to white men, until the Civil War legally admitted Negroes to citizenship. Even therafter, black freedmen were scarcely treated as free men, and Indians had by then become wards of the state.

Under the effective and determined leadership of an extraordinary galaxy of "public-school men," the idea of universal common schooling for white children was widely accepted in the new United States during the first half of the nineteenth century. Outstanding among these men were Horace Mann and James G. Carter in Massachusetts, Henry Barnard in Connecticut, Calvin Stowe in Ohio, Caleb Mills in Indiana, John D. Pierce in Michigan, Ninian Edwards in Illinois, Calvin Wiley in North Carolina, and Charles F. Mercer in Virginia. These men and their counterparts made countless speeches before thousands of people; wrote hundreds of pamphlets, articles, and reports; organized scores of groups and societies to agitate for common schools; and held dozens of positions in state governments or school systems.

They argued that the payment of tuition for schooling was unfair to children of poor parents who could not pay for an education. They argued that the older forms of public support, like the land grants from the federal Land Ordinances of 1785 and 1787, would not support schools on the vast scale now necessary. They argued that the term *free school* should no longer mean a school in which only poor children were given free education and all others paid tuition. They argued that class distinctions could be lessened only when a *free school* meant that *all* children were given a free education in common, and when the entire school system was supported by taxes levied upon everyone. Aiding their efforts were the newly formed labor unions, which demanded that the public schools provide universal education.

The states gradually accepted the responsibility of establishing free public school systems. The state legislatures first passed laws permitting local school districts to tax themselves for such schools; later they sometimes gave state funds to encourage local districts to tax themselves; and they finally required all local districts to tax themselves in order to establish public schools.

By these means the local freedom of districts to ignore the need for schooling for their children gave way to the larger freedom to be gained by a total population enlightened by education for all. Local community control was gradually limited by requirements set by state constitutions, legislatures, boards of education, and superintendents of schools. It was decided that a modern society would be better served if education were planned by the central authority of the states rather than left wholly to the completely decentralized control of local school boards. This was not done without bitter conflict, for many believed that state as opposed to local control would be so undemocratic as to destroy freedom.

But in the 1820s, 1830s, and 1840s, it was decided that a state government, responsive to public control, could serve freedom as well as, if not better than, the hundreds of local school districts could do. If a local district were left free to provide a poor education or no education at all for its children, those children would be deprived of their birthright to an education that would prepare them for free citizenship. Thereby, the state's own freedom would be endangered. A smaller freedom must be limited in the interests of a greater freedom. To guarantee the larger freedom, the state must exert its authority to see to it not only that schools were available to all but that all children actually attended school. Massachusetts led the way by passing a compulsory attendance law in 1852.

The solution was a genuinely creative one. By the 1850s authority for providing public education was spelled out in state constitutions and laws. State authority for education was carried out by state superintendents of schools responsible to a state board of education, elected by the people or appointed by the governor. New York State created the office of state superintendent of schools in 1812. Massachusetts established a state board of education in 1837 with Horace Mann as secretary, and Connecticut did likewise in 1839 with Henry Barnard as secretary. Other states followed. These state agencies could then set minimum standards for all the schools of the state. Meanwhile, the direct management of schools would be left in the hands of locally elected school boards, local superintendents, and locally appointed teachers. Local management served the cause of flexibility, diversity, and freedom—what political scientists were later to call "sub-system autonomy."

This arrangement was designed to assure that schools would serve the whole public and would be controlled by the public through special boards of education, not through the regular agencies of the state or local governments. This is why in the United States the usual term is *public schools,* not *state schools* or *government schools,* as they are often called in those countries that have centralized systems of education.

But what about religious instruction in these common public schools? It was soon evident that if common schools taught the doctrines of a particular church they would violate the freedom of conscience of all those who did not agree. Many Protestants felt that the common schools could find a common religious outlook and teach it. They found the common religious doctrines of Christianity in the Bible (the Protestant Bible, that is). If the schools would teach only the nonsectarian principles of Christianity as contained in the Bible, they argued, all sects would be satisfied.

This solution might have been successful if America had remained exclusively Protestant. But immigration had brought increased numbers of Roman Catholics and Jews. Besides, many Americans had never officially belonged to any church. Catholics charged that the so-called nonsectarian schools were really Protestant in character and that they were therefore sectarian. Catholics therefore established their own schools and demanded a share in the public tax funds to support them. Protestants and Jews opposed the giving of money to parochial schools. Most states finally decided to prohibit sectarian control over common schools and to prohibit the use of public money for private schools under sectarian control. Especially bitter struggles between Protestants and Catholics were settled, at least for the time being, by legislation in New York in 1842 and by constitutional amendment in Massachusetts in 1855. Nearly every state had a similar struggle and enacted similar laws.

By the end of the first century of republican education, the general decision was that a free society was better served if the majority of children went to common, nonsectarian schools than if they went to separate, sectarian, religious schools. The argument for common schools was that nonsectarianism would provide a greater measure of national unity and social integration than could be achieved when each sectarian group shepherded its own children into its own schools. The range of communication among children would be restricted if each group continued to run its own schools, different in religion and language from others. Separate schools would create a disjointed society and perpetuate divisions among the people—thus narrowing their outlooks and reducing free interchange of ideas. Free common schools would more certainly serve the cause of free institutions. They would help to form an integrative society rather than perpetuate a disjunctive society. This belief made it possible for the United States to build a modern system of nearly universal free elementary schools sooner than any other country in the world.

At the end of the first century of the republic, secondary schools, however, were still largely in private and religious hands. This fact did not seem undesirable to most Americans of that particular period. The private academies provided considerable opportunity to those who could afford some education beyond the essentials. Likewise, most of the 200 colleges were under private and religous control. This, too, seemed reasonable to the majority of Americans at that time. Elementary education for all at public expense would be sufficient to guarantee the basic security of a republican government; advanced education for leadership in the state and in the professions could safely be obtained privately by those who could afford it.

A few spokesmen, however, began to argue that a free society needed *free* secondary and higher institutions as well as free elementary schools. The public high school, for example, appeared as early as 1821 in Boston, but public high schools did not come to dominate the secondary school field for another half century or more. Indeed, some working-class people were suspicious that free public high schools were really upper-class institutions in disguise and would thus serve only the advantaged classes while being supported by taxes on everyone. Thus the era of republican education tried to get along with common schools at the elementary level, but with secondary and higher institutions divided along denominational lines. In general, while the elementary schools served most everyone, the academies, colleges, and universities catered to the wealthier, upper classes rather than to the ordinary people.

The major failure to achieve the reformers' goal of a common universal school was the system of segregated schools for Negroes, which appeared occasionally in the North, as well as generally in the South. In fact, it was the Roberts case in the Massachusetts Supreme Court in 1849 which set forth the principle that separate schools for Negroes were permissible so long as their facilities were equal to those of the white schools. Charles Sumner's argument that separate schools violated the equal rights of Negroes was rejected by the court. Nevertheless, Massachusetts and other Northern states moved soon thereafter to abolish their segregated schools by law. But it would be another century before substantial gains were made in achieving common schools by law in the South and in fact in the North. That was one of the things with which the black revolution of the 1950s and 1960s was concerned. Disregarding this condition, the general shift from predominantly private and voluntary to predominantly state controlled and supported elementary schools was a spectacular achievement in a rapidly expanding society characterized by hundreds of overlapping political jurisdictions and with no centralized educational authority.

In higher education, however, the result was quite different. Between the mid-eighteenth and mid-nineteenth centuries a series of decisions was made in favor of the private institutions that helped them maintain their predominance in American higher education until well into the twentieth century. During the middle of the eighteenth century the Great Awakening prompted the several Protestant denominations to set up colleges that would be supportive of their faiths and would aid the training of ministers in their particular beliefs. Princeton was founded by the Presbyterians of New Jersey in 1746, Kings College (Columbia) by the Anglicans of New York in 1754, Brown by the Baptists of Rhode Island in 1764, Rutgers by the Dutch Reformed of New Jersey in 1766, and Dartmouth by the Congregationalists of New Hampshire in 1769. The College of Philadelphia, built upon Franklin's Academy, was given a nondenominational charter in 1755. Together with Harvard, William and Mary, and Yale, these colleges comprised the institutions of higher education founded in the colonies before the Revolution.

With the surge of democratic ideals embodied in the Revolution, republican arguments for a complete system of education under state control began to apply not only to the lower schools but to a university at the top. Long suspicious of the closed corporation as an engine of privilege, the democratic forces took what seemed to them a logical step—namely, to transform the private and religous colleges into state and secular institutions. On the whole, however, they successfully resisted several attempts by the colonial legislatures to increase their control. An especially bitter struggle took place in Connecticut as an outgrowth of the religious revivals and the antagonisms between the "Old Lights" and the "New Lights." Yale College had remained staunchly Calvinistic and conservative, whereas the New Light forces felt that Yale should be more responsive to the religious needs of the revivalistic groups, inasmuch as it received public moneys paid by all groups alike. But President Thomas Clap won the battle for the Old Lights, insisting that Yale was a private autonomous college and not a public institution and therefore had the right to require strict religious discipline of its students, no matter what religious views their parents might hold or from what sources, public or private, the funds came.

If Virginia had followed Jefferson's lead in 1779, the College of William and Mary might have become one of the earliest state universities, but the Church of England successfully resisted the change. Indeed, the very first state university might have been achieved in New York in the 1750s had the battle over the founding of King's College turned out differently. Two factions were in conflict. One, representing the Church of England and the Tory classes loyal to the crown, wanted the new college to be Anglican and founded by royal charter. The other, representing dissenting Presbyterian and democratic forces under the leadership of William Livingston, wanted the college to be public, nonsectarian, and founded by enactment of the colonial legislature. But the "church party" won the fight and the college became King's College, the original name to be changed to Columbia only after the War of Independence.

When the college in Philadelphia, which had originally been nonsectarian, came under Anglican and Tory control, the democratic forces in Pennsylvania in 1779 set out to convert it into the University of the State of Pennsylvania. The old college, however, refused to give up its charter, continuing to exist for ten years alongside the state university. In 1789, when the religious and political interests in the state were realigned, the original college was given back its charter, and the University of Pennsylvania became a private and independent institution, which it has since remained.

Finding it difficult to transform the private colleges into public colleges, the democratic forces began to establish new institutions created from the beginning as state universities. Four were established before 1800, in Georgia, North Carolina, Vermont, and Tennessee, significantly, in states where no colonial religious college had been established. The real impetus for state universities, however, arose in the nineteenth century, when a remarkable democratic experiment began in higher education no less than in elementary and secondary education. No other country had ever tried to establish so many institutions of higher education.

In response to a new religious awakening almost every denomination was active in founding colleges as a means of spreading their religious faith, as well as of providing a general education for the youth of the land. The most active denominations were the Presbyterians, Methodists, Baptists, Congregationalists, Roman Catholics, and Episcopalians. They worked individually as well as jointly in such organizations as the Society for the Promotion of Collegiate and Theological Education at the West. According to Donald G. Tewksbury, 182 permanent colleges were established before the Civil War, along with dozens more that died after a time.[7]

Despite the prevailing belief that higher education should be under religous control, the movement for state universities gained increasing momentum in the nineteenth century. This precipitated a series of legal battles which culminated in the famous Dartmouth College case of 1819, when the Supreme Court decided that Dartmouth College was a corporation whose charter from the king of England had the force of a contract which the state could not impair under the protection of the United States Constitution. The decision had far-reaching economic and political ramifications, but it meant specifically for American colleges that the philanthropic endowments of private colleges would be safe from encroachment by the states. This encouraged private donors to give money to private colleges, and, conversely, it stimulated the states to establish their own universities under state control.

Twenty state universities were founded before the Civil War, even though they met vigorous opposition from the private and religious colleges in many ways. The religious groups often tried to prevent the passage of enabling laws in the legislatures, and they tried to transfer state moneys and land grants to religious institutions. Even after the establishment of some state universities, the religious groups often continued their efforts to insert religious interests in the new universities or to reduce their funds

---

[7]Donald G. Tewksbury, *The Founding of American Colleges and Universities Before the Civil War*, Teachers College, Columbia University, New York, 1932.

to insignificance. The score in the contest between state and church for control of higher education was more than even. For the few cases in which states tried to take over private institutions, there were many cases where religious groups tried to control the state universities.

Until the Civil War the state universities lagged far behind the private colleges in their influence upon American higher education. However, with the passage of the Morrill Act by Congress in 1862, a new era began. It granted to every state 30,000 acres of public land for each of its members in Congress, the money to be used for the establishment of agricultural and mechanical colleges that would teach the liberal arts as well as the sciences appropriate to agriculture, engineering, mining, and forestry. Some of the states set up separate "A and M" colleges; others gave the money to their already established universities. With this impulse the state universities were propelled on their way to becoming a major force in the modernization of education and American society. Characteristically, they made more widely available a popular education that was increasingly secular and scientific, practical and professional, diversified and comprehensive.

C. GROWING POPULARITY OF THE PRACTICAL AND THE PROFESSIONAL

Much as Englishmen had done, Americans sought to meet the rising demands for a modern, "useful" education by trying to reform their established educational institutions, and then, failing that, they set about establishing new institutions. In the course of 150 years the trend was perfectly plain. The town supported Latin grammar schools in New England and the religiously sponsored grammar schools elsewhere were not particularly interested in the new commercial life of the seacoast towns in the eighteenth century. The Latin grammar schools were primarily college-preparatory institutions attracting the relatively few students destined for the major learned professions in church and state. Well before the American Revolution a growing demand for more practical and modern education was passing the grammar schools by.[8]

Therefore, two new types of secondary schools appeared, comparable to those in England—private-venture schools run by enterprising schoolmasters and academies run by corporate bodies of interested men. As a result, the Latin grammar schools began to disappear in the eighteenth century, as did the private-venture schools after a period of great popularity. This left the field of secondary education largely to the academy as the new republic got under way. But during the nineteenth century the academy became more academic, more elite, and less attuned to the needs of a growing, industrial, urban population, so still another new institution was invented, the public high school. By mid-century it had challenged the academy in popularity and was ready to move on to become the standard vehicle of American secondary education in

---

[8]See, for example, Jon Teaford, "The Transformation of Massachusetts Education, 1670-1780," *History of Education Quarterly,* vol. 10, pp. 287-307, Fall 1970.

the century to follow. The Latin grammar school in New England had been public, but not particularly popular or practical. The private-venture schools and the academies were more popular and practical, but not public. Finally, the high school epitomized the modernization process by striving to become popular, practical, and public.

Responding to the interests of the rising commercial and trading classes early in the eighteenth century, private-venture schoolmasters began to teach practical subjects that had more direct vocational value and thus more relevance than the classics. The basic language of their private schools was English; thus, for the first time in America there was a conscious attempt to adapt educational institutions to a changing social situation. Inasmuch as their aim was not primarily preparation for college, the curriculum of these schools was not prescribed or circumscribed by college entrance requirements. Rather, they were free to offer any courses for which there was a demand, or for which a demand could be created. Their clientele was made up of children of merchants, clerks, bookkeepers, accountants, mechanics, engineers, and seamen.

As the first major "alternatives" to public education in America, the private schools were more flexible and responsive than the town Latin grammar schools; they admitted anyone who wished to study and could pay the fees, adults as well as youth, girls as well as boys. Students took whatever courses they felt would be valuable to them; there was no diploma, degree, or prescribed curriculum. Classes were held at whatever hours students could come, early in the morning before working hours, at the noon hour, late in the afternoon, or in the evening after working hours. As a result, a broadened clientele of middle-class youth could go to school while they worked.

High on the list of studies taught by the private venture schools were those practical modern subjects so long disparaged by humanists: commercial subjects (bookkeeping, accounting, penmanship, and commercial arithmetic) designed to prepare clerks, accountants, bookkeepers, merchants, and bankers for jobs in business and trade; and mathematical subjects (algebra, geometry, astronomy, trigonometry, calculus, navigation, surveying, optics, fortifications, and gunnery) were taught for their vocational usefulness in such increasingly important occupations as navigation and civil and military engineering. In many cases the mathematical teaching in the private schools was fully as rigorous as that found in some of the colleges. The modern languages, which found little acceptance in colleges or Latin grammar schools, were also quite common in the private schools—French as the polite language of high society, and Italian, Spanish, and Portuguese as the commercial languages of importance. Geography and history were widely advertised as of general value for everyone and of special value to traders and navigators. In addition, the private schools offered the classics for any who wished to prepare for college.

The private schools did another thing that most Latin grammar schools did not do: they opened their doors for advanced education to girls. Some private schools allowed girls to attend with boys, some held special classes for girls, and others catered particularly to girls. The most common subjects for girls were reading, writing, arithmetic, geography, and French, but many other subjects were also offered in different schools—the general subjects of English grammar, history, and Latin; the vocational subjects of bookkeeping, accounting, and the modern languages; and the polite accomplishments of drawing, painting, singing, instrumental music, sewing, and penmanship. Hence the groundwork for advanced education for girls was being laid, upon which were later built the academies for girls, the "female seminaries," and eventually the colleges for women.

Because the private-venture schoolmaster was an individual enterpriser seeking students where he could and adapting himself to varying interests of people, there was no continuity or formal organization to carry on his work when he passed from the scene. Therefore, in the middle of the eighteenth century, a corporate type of private school took form. Typically, a group of men organized themselves into a board of trustees along the model of the English corporate schools. The state would then grant a charter to this board of trustees, constituting it a corporation and authorizing it to own property, receive money, endowments, and bequests, and conduct the affairs and control the policy of a school. Many such corporate boards were granted the right by the state to be self-perpetuating.

Such schools were thus able to maintain continuity, achieve permanence, and build distinctive traditions. Early examples were the William Penn Charter School and Franklin's Academy in Pennsylvania, the Newark Academy in Delaware, the Washington Academy in New Jersey, the Dummer Academy and Phillips Academy in Massachusetts, and the Union School at New London, Conn. Henceforth, the private corporate school was to become an important aspect of American education. The state had formally delegated part of its authority over education to private institutions. How much control the state would exercise over these private schools proved a matter of much controversy.

In his outline for an academy Benjamin Franklin embodied the prevailing tendency of the private schools to offer utilitarian subjects for vocational preparation as well as classical languages for college preparation, but he shaped these into a clearly differentiated and organized structure. He proposed that the new academy should have three departments, English, Latin, and mathematics; students should be allowed to choose their course according to the several occupations or professions for which they were preparing.

Franklin's proposals included a diversifying modernity that was in sharp contrast to the heavily classical curriculum of the Latin grammar schools. Franklin not only proposed writing and drawing; arithmetic and accounts; geometry and astronomy; rhetoric and oratory; and logic; but also English grammar, composition, and literature; history (universal and national history, ancient customs, moral, religious, and political); ancient and modern languages (Greek, Latin, German, French, Spanish); sciences (observation, experimentation, and natural history); history of invention, commerce, and manufacturing; and agriculture, gardening, and mechanics. Franklin thus reflected the Enlightenment streams of influence—empiricism, sense realism, and the new science—as well as his own experimental, commercial, and utilitarian interests. Significantly, also, he made no mention of religious or sectarian instruction, except for the history of religion, which was well within the deistic outlook. His was a major step in the promotion of practical, modern, and scientific studies. Although the private venture schools had met a modernizing need, they did not carry the prestige of the classical and religious traditions of the Latin grammar schools. The theory behind

Franklin's academy had been to combine the practical and modern with the classical, but he too went too far for eighteenth-century America, for he had left out the religious ingredient.

The institutions that definitively replaced the Latin grammar schools absorbed into themselves not only the principal influences of the Enlightenment but also those of the Great Awakening; not only the classical, the practical, and the scientific, but the religious as well. The academies that were to have real influence for more than a century were founded in the later part of the eighteenth century by the churches or by individuals with strong religious interests. The Dissenters' Academies in England had shown that religious schools could have a broad and diversified curriculum, and the Great Awakening gave the American impetus to establishing such schools for religious as well as practical purposes. The classics were of course included, for the supporters of the academies were primarily middle-class parents who wanted their children to be able to go on to college. In general, the academies combined the aims of college preparation with religious piety and vocational efficiency.

The academies differed in other respects from the Latin grammar schools and the private schools. They were usually boarding schools in which the students lived together away from home. Academies for girls were not uncommon. Often acting as local substitutes for colleges, many academies were sooner or later transformed into colleges. Commonly, too, they were nonpublic institutions, supported by tuition from parents or by endowment from churches and wealthy individuals. Support also came from several of the states, as the academies caught the public fancy and became centers of the deliberate efforts to train teachers. Despite their private and usually religious character, the academies were more modern than the Latin grammar schools because of their wider appeal, their broader and more elastic curriculum, and their more comprehensive aims. They helped to introduce into the secondary school curriculum English grammar, composition, and literature, English rhetoric, history, mathematics, the modern languages, some commercial subjects, and, especially for girls, the social arts of dancing, music, drawing, and needlework.

As the newer subjects became popular, there was greater demand for useful textbooks in these fields. The first text in English grammar used in America was Thomas Dilworth's *New Guide to the English Tongue*. Soon American authors tried their hands at writing English grammar, notably Noah Webster and Lindley Murray. The most noteworthy textbook in arithmetic was written by Isaac Greenwood, private schoolmaster and professor of mathematics at Harvard College, the title of whose book, published in 1729, revealed his practical outlook—*Arithmetic Vulgar and Decimal with the Application thereof to a Variety of Cases in Trade and Commerce*. Other texts began to appear in history, geography, the commercial subjects, practical mathematics, and modern languages. As the academies began to emphasize subjects requiring a command of English, they also began to institute preparatory departments to give the younger children a grounding in the fundamentals before they entered the academy proper. If this process had continued uninterruptedly, the United States might have produced a disjunctive or dual system of schools quite similar to that of the West European countries.

However, in the 1820s and thereafter, the modernizing forces in the United

States began to demand a type of secondary school that would give, at public expense, a more useful education for children who had completed the primary and grammar grades of the elementary schools. The public high school was designed to meet this demand and to overcome the growing undemocratic, class character of the academies. The laboring groups had no access to an advanced education of a more practical and non-college preparatory sort so long as the Latin grammar schools and the tuition-charging academies continued to be the only secondary school institutions.

Therefore, in Boston in 1821 an "English classical school" was established, (it later became the English high school) designed for boys of twelve years of age or older who were not planning to go on to college. It was originally a three-year high school emphasizing English, mathematics, science, and social studies. In 1827 Massachusetts passed a law requiring that such high schools be established in every town of 500 or more families. By 1860 there were over 300 such high schools in the country, most of them located in Massachusetts, New York, and Ohio.

At the outset the high school was more practical than the grammar school in the sense that it stressed an "English education," i.e., a curriculum taught in English and stressing the modern subjects of science and social studies. It was not, however, a trade or technical school preparing students for specific jobs. In general, the so-called vocational studies received attention, in the middle of the century, in private institutions outside of the public high schools; they were gradually admitted to the expanded high schools or to special vocational high schools later in the century.

Not only were more boys going on to secondary school, but opportunities for girls expanded as a part of the new experiment in democratic secondary education. In the early nineteenth century this took the form of "female academies" and "female seminaries." They had to ïight the traditional social attitudes, which insisted that woman's place was in the home to rear children and care for a family and that women were inherently inferior intellectually to males. The female academies, therefore, offered home economics or domestic science as well as the literary subjects when they were established by the early leaders—by Emma Willard at Troy, N.Y., in 1821; by Catherine Beecher at Hartford, Conn., in 1828; and by Mary Lyon at Mount Holyoke, Mass., in 1838. With this much gained, the advancing political and social democracy of the time began to make it possible for the sphere of women's activities to be expanded to include business, industry, and the professions, especially teaching. When this happened, and as a corollary to it, girls were admitted to high schools on a coeducational basis.

During the later colonial and early republican periods, the interest in modern science and practical utility gradually began to affect the curriculum of some of the American colleges, but most held to the religious and humanistic traditions of earlier days. The exceptions, however, were noteworthy, for they pointed to the tide of modernity that began to run more and more swiftly from the mid-eighteenth century onward.

By the beginning of the eighteenth century, the new Enlightenment science had begun to creep into the traditional studies of Harvard. The logic of Descartes, the geometry of Ramus, and the physics of Newton gradually gained a hearing. The astronomy of Copernicus, Galileo, Kepler, and Gassendi began to replace that of

Aristotle, Ptolemy, and Dante. In 1728, Thomas Hollis established a professorship of mathematics and natural philosophy to which he contributed books and "philosophical apparatus." By 1769 these included skeletons, globes, microscopes, and mechanical instruments, as well as the transactions of the English Royal Society and the French Academy of Sciences.

As the first Hollis professor of mathematics and natural philosophy, Isaac Greenwood wrote books on arithmetic, meteorology, mine damp, and the aurora borealis. He did much to bring the college into closer touch with the practical spirit of the age and to attract to Harvard practical-minded young men who might otherwise have gone to private venture schools or into business. His successor, John Winthrop, who held the post from 1738 to 1779, proved to be the most accomplished scientific investigator in America next to Benjamin Franklin. By 1743 the Harvard curriculum included Enlightenment science and philosophy in the form of Isaac Watts's *Astronomy* and Locke's *Essay Concerning Human Understanding*. In these ways Harvard had begun to show a definite interest in the new science and philosophy, though the paramount emphasis remained upon the classical languages and mathematics. By the end of the eighteenth century the change had been made from the old Aristotelian science and philosophy to that of the Enlightenment.

When the College of William and Mary received its royal charter in 1693 under Anglican auspices, it proclaimed the current religious purposes—namely, to train ministers, to educate youth piously in good letters and manners, and to extend Christianity to the Indians. Its curriculum, similar to that of the Oxford colleges, did not change much during its first eighty-five years of existence. When Thomas Jefferson tried unsuccessfully to modernize its course of study in 1779, there were only six instructors, two in divinity and Hebrew, one in logic, rhetoric, and ethics; one in physics, metaphysics, and mathematics; one in Latin and Greek; and one for teaching Indian boys the elements of religion.

Jefferson's proposals for the reform of William and Mary as submitted to the Virginia legislature in 1779 incorporated the modernizing ideals of the Enlightenment. He would have broadened and secularized the curriculum in the following ways: theology and Bible study would have been replaced by study of the ancient languages and ecclesiastical history; modern foreign languages would have gained preeminence over the classics; great attention would have been given to the pure and applied sciences and to the social sciences in place of Aristotelian philosophy; and law and medicine would have had a prominent place. In general, the whole tone and purpose of the College would have been designed to prepare young men for leadership in public affairs, practical pursuits, and professional service, rather than for narrow scholarship, aristocratic intellectualism, or religious sectarianism. But Jefferson's proposals came fifty years too soon.

Developments at Yale were more characteristic of the times. The traditional religious temper at Yale became even more marked under the spell of the Great Awakening. In 1735 the Connecticut General Court declared anew that the "one principal end proposed in erecting this college was to supply the churches in this Colony with a learned, pious, and orthodox Ministry." Even so, during most of the eighteenth century its curricular development largely paralleled that of Harvard—the original course was changed gradually in the direction of the new science and philosophy of Newton and Locke.

The most significant difference, however, between Yale and Harvard up to the time of the American Revolution seems to have been that Yale gave greater emphasis to the religious nature of college education and the desirability of continuing the prescribed curriculum for religious ends. Whereas the religious position of Harvard had been considerably liberalized, the following statement of President Clap in 1754 illustrates the more traditional position of Yale:

> Colleges, are *Religious Societies,* of a Superior Nature to all others. For whereas *Parishes,* are Societies, for training up the *Common People;* Colleges, are *Societies of Ministers,* for training up Persons for the Work of the *Ministry....* *Some indeed, have supposed, that, the only Design of Colleges, was to teach the Arts, and Sciences.... But, it is probable, that there is not a College, to be found upon Earth, upon such a Constitution.* [9]

Most of the colonial colleges were generally similar in their loyalty to this tradition and to an emphasis upon the study of divinity, the classics, mathematics, and philosophy. Their histories up to the Revolution showed little that was radically different, with a few notable exceptions. With the founding of King's College (Columbia) in New York City in 1754, President Samuel Johnson leavened the strictly sectarian character and aim by the formal toleration of religious beliefs and a broadening of the scope of liberal studies. With the establishment of the College of Philadelphia in 1755 (University of Pennsylvania), the traditional literary and aristocratic conception of liberal education was frontally challenged by the first provost, Reverend William Smith. It is likely that Smith's curriculum for the Philadelphia college was framed in the image of his own Scottish training and the course that had shortly before (1753) been revised at King's College, Aberdeen. His "Scheme of Liberal Education" embraced the greatest diversity of subjects of any college in America at the time; three "Schools of Philosophy" included instrumental philosophy (technology), moral philosophy (social science), and natural philosophy (physical science).

Because the colonists followed the pattern of the English colleges, they did not institute the formal professional studies in law, medicine, or theology that characterized the medieval university. Education for these professions during most of the eighteenth century was gained by apprenticeship to a practicing lawyer, physician, or clergyman. No specialized instruction in law was given until 1793, when a Kent professor of law was established at Columbia.

Similarly, professional training in medicine was acquired when boys in their teens were apprenticed to physicians, to do the menial work and pick up what information they could. As a result, American medicine lagged considerably behind European medicine during the eighteenth century. However, as the study of science

[9] Thomas Clap, *The Religious Constitution of Colleges, Especially of Yale-College in New Haven,* T. Green, New London, Conn., 1754, pp. 4, 12.

began to gain ground, as more physicians came to America from England and France, and as such men as John Morgan brought back ideas from Edinburgh and London, special instruction in medicine began to appear in a few colleges, notably at those colleges where science had received particular emphasis—the College of Philadelphia, King's College, and Harvard.

Training in theology fared somewhat better because of the religious bias in most colleges. Students with a bent for theology could do special work with the professor of theology, who was often the president, or the young graduate might stay on after receiving his B.A. degree and receive individual theological instruction. He could then be apprenticed to a clergyman or teach school while awaiting the call to a pastorate.

The most thoroughgoing formulation of the ideal of a modern university was made by Thomas Jefferson. In his plans for the University of Virginia in 1818, Jefferson struck the major notes of modernity time and again: its secular public service purpose, its professional function, and its scientific and practical orientation:

> To form the statesmen, legislators and judges, on whom public prosperity and individual happiness are so much to depend; [These are the men of public affairs who will lead the new republican society.]
>
> To expound the principles and structure of government, the laws which regulate the intercourse of nations, those formed municipally for our own government, and a sound spirit of legislation, which, banishing all arbitrary and unnecessary restraint on individual action, shall leave us free to do whatever does not violate the equal rights of another. [Here is the stress upon the study of politics and society in the service of republicanism and freedom.]
>
> To harmonize and promote the interests of agriculture, manufacture and commerce, and by all well informed views of political economy to give a free scope to the public industry; [A statement that proclaims the university's responsibility to promote the economic development of a modernizing society.]
>
> To develop the reasoning faculties of our youth, enlarge their minds, cultivate their morals and instill into them the precepts of virtue and order; [A goal that echoes the usual traditional academic statement of the purposes of a college education.]
>
> To enlighten them with mathematical and physical sciences, which advance the arts, and administer to the health, the subsistence, and comforts of human life; [The stress is upon the modern studies and their practical application to social service.]
>
> And, generally, to form them to habits of reflection and correct action, rendering them examples of virtue to others, and of happiness within themselves. [All leading to the formation of exemplary republican conduct.] [10]

Jefferson proposed that ten schools be established to carry out these aims. He still found room for the classics in one of the schools, but he found no room for religion. The other nine schools were to consist of: modern languages; pure mathematics; physico-mathematics; physics (natural philosophy); botany and zoology; anat-

---

[10] Saul K. Padover, *The Complete Jefferson,* Tudor Publishing Company, New York, 1943, pp. 1098, 1100-1101.

omy and medicine; political economy (government, law, and history); municipal law; and ideology (grammar, rhetoric, ethics, belles lettres, and fine arts). The heavy professional and social service orientation is patent. Also clear was Jefferson's belief that a modern university should be conceived on a large scale, attractive to scholars who had specialized in the various fields of modern knowledge, supported by the state, free from sectarian religious control, and encouraging the student to prepare himself for a secular career by making available a broad range of fields from which he could choose.

The whole tone of Jefferson's proposals was much like that of William Livingston's and Benjamin Franklin's a half century earlier. All three were prominent men of public affairs who had turned their attention to the role that education could play in the modernizing of a republican America. Each of these public men was exhorting the academic brethren to reform higher education as a means of transforming their traditional society into a modern society.

Some of the academic brethren were indeed trying to reform their institutions from within. One of these was George Ticknor, who brought to Harvard in 1819 German ideals of advanced scholarship and of freedom for teacher and learner. Interested in promoting the modern languages, Ticknor set out to break up the prescribed classical curriculum, substitute election of studies, and institute methods of thorough scholarship. His justification for these reforms was that Harvard must meet the demands of students and the community for a useful education in scientific, technical, and mechanical studies; incidentally, such reforms would meet the competition of rising technical schools.

In response to such currents of unrest, a number of colleges took steps toward reform. The most common approach was to set up separate courses, parallel to the prescribed classical regimen. Thus the integrity of the classical curriculum leading to the B.A. degree would remain unimpaired, but there would still be a chance for students to get an education in the "scientific," "literary," or "English" studies. In these new, parallel courses, the classical studies were either diminished, or they entirely disappeared to make way for the physical and biological sciences, English and modern languages, and the social sciences.

A radical plan by Jacob Abbott was adopted by the board of trustees of Amherst College in the 1820s to train boys for occupations that would be useful for the social improvement of a rapidly modernizing society—namely, commerce, business, international trade, farming, and teaching—but it faded rapidly. The reformers did not reckon sufficiently with the difficulty of attracting able boys to the "lower" occupations. The new courses did not usually set such high standards for admission as did the classical course; that is, they did not require as much Latin or Greek. They were allowed to grant, not the bachelor of arts degree, which was jealously reserved for the classical course, but only a diploma or such new degrees as the bachelor of science, bachelor of philosophy, or bachelor of letters.

Another approach was the establishment of independent technical schools, as represented by Rensselaer Polytechnic Institute, Worcester Polytechnic Institute, and Massachusetts Institute of Technology. Stephen Van Rensselaer, for example, established his school in 1824 with the purpose of ". . . affording an opportunity to the farmer, the mechanic, the clergyman, the lawyer, the physician, the merchant, and in short, to the man of business or of leisure, of any calling whatever, to become practically scientific."[11] It was emphasized that students would not only receive literary exercises but also would be given proper development of manual abilities by appropriate muscular exercises. In this way the student was to become familiar with the most important scientific manipulations and "particularly with those which will be most useful in the common concerns of life." Here was a direct challenge to and eventually a source of keen competition for the literary colleges.

A third response was made by a few of the older colleges which attempted to meet the competition by establishing affiliated schools of science separate from their regular colleges but on the same campus. In this way the college could retain its classical emphasis and give a traditional training to those students who wished to become clergymen, teachers, scholars, or merely "cultured" persons, whereas the scientific school could give a training to those who were intended for careers in business or industry. Such were Sheffield Scientific School at Yale, Lawrence Scientific School at Harvard, Chandler School of Science at Dartmouth, and others at Princeton, Pennsylvania, Columbia, and elsewhere.

The practical and technical studies offered in the private academies and colleges, in West Point Military Academy (1802), and in the technological and scientific schools made a direct contribution during the economic takeoff period of industrial production which marked the two decades of the 1840s and 1850s. But despite the calls for modernization, despite the efforts to transform the traditional arts colleges, neither Jefferson's vision of a grand university, Ticknor's efforts to reform Harvard's academic curriculum, nor Abbott's efforts to set up a parallel course won the day in the early decades of the century. They remained undercurrents of modernizing dissent in a massive sea of academic resistance.

The hand of the academic conservatives was strengthened by three unlikely allies. The first was a resurgence of fundamentalist, sectarian religious revivals that swept through the land and the colleges. Especially pronounced at Princeton and at Yale, they became the pacesetters for those 182 permanent colleges founded before the Civil War. Reenforcing the disciplinary and classical tone of the colleges, the religious momentum set the seal on the college as a residential guardian standing *in loco parentis* for the morals of students, as well as for their minds.

A second obstruction to change came from the extreme egalitarian and anti-intellectual wing of Jacksonian democrats who did not believe that higher education could benefit the working classes but was simply another bastion of privilege serving only the establishment rulers of the day. The very idea of a university giving special training for an intellectual career was seen to be an undemocratic symbol of inequality. At the opposite pole politically was a third opponent to modernization in the universities, the proslavery Southern landowners who listened nervously to the calls for greater access to higher education for mechanics, farmers, and tradesmen, seeing them as somehow a threat to their position. As the Civil War approached, a stifling atmosphere settled over

---

[11] From a circular purporting to be the first prospectus of a school of science in the English language, quoted in *U.S. Bureau of Education Circular of Information*, no. 3, 1900, p. 484.

those colleges that might harbor the voices of reform. The curious mixture of religious conservatives, anti-intellectual egalitarians, and proslavery racists each in their own way slowed down the tempo of modernization in higher education.

Probably much more directly influential within the academic community itself, however, was the voice of the classical humanist who had long been chafing under the onslaughts of Enlightenment empiricism, practicality, and antireligious rationality. Paramount among these voices was the famous Yale Faculty Report of 1828, written by President Jeremiah Day and the noted classicist James L. Kingsley. Together they framed an eloquent and persuasive document proclaiming that the purpose of the college was a general liberal education, *not* the preparation of the specialist for a vocation, a profession, or a practical career. Therefore the curriculum must remain prescribed, so that all students would be assured of a balanced education. And, above all, the preeminent core of the prescribed college curriculum must continue to be the Greek and Latin classical studies without knowledge of which no man could be called liberally educated. Not only did this appeal to the gentlemanly instincts of academic prestige but also to the collegiate opinion molders who viewed the classics as the proper handmaidens of Protestant theology.

At mid-century, however, the clamor of the modernizers became more insistent, claiming that economic development, industrialization, and urbanization required more and more highly trained manpower. In the 1840s Captain Alden Partridge, erstwhile superintendent of West Point and founder of Norwich University, urged Congress to grant land for establishing state schools of agriculture, science, engineering, and business. In the 1850s Professor Jonathan Turner of Illinois College urged Congress to give public land to the states so they could set up "Industrial Universities for the People" (1853) in which the working classes would have the same opportunity to prepare for their livelihoods as did the higher professional classes. To this end the industrial universities should train teachers of agriculture and mechanical arts for the secondary schools. By 1860 at least three states (Michigan, Maryland, and Pennsylvania) had established state agricultural schools.

Meanwhile, reform efforts were continuing within some of the well-established institutions. President Francis Wayland, after visiting many universities in Europe, advocated that Brown University be transformed into a genuine university by offering work in all the major branches of knowledge and by devising new courses to meet the mechanical, agricultural, and industrial needs of the people. He argued that the older colleges must adapt themselves to meet the needs of all classes of society or lose essential patronage to the newer technical schools. Another mid-century proponent of university building on the European model was Henry Tappan at the University of Michigan. Taking inspiration from the German universities, Tappan argued that a genuine university must be secular, supported by the state, offer courses in all the subjects of human knowledge, ensure freedom of research and of study, adapt itself to the needs of the state, and become the capstone of a complete state system of education.

The time was not quite ripe, however, for such ideas. Wayland retired in dismay and disgust at the small gains he was able to make in opening up Brown to the lower classes in society, Tappan was driven from Michigan for trying to import alien, elite, Prussian ideas into rural, egalitarian Michigan. But the tide was just about to turn in their favor. The war measure to aid the states in developing agricultural and mechanical colleges, as proposed by Senator Justin Morrill of Vermont as early as 1859 and signed by President Lincoln in 1862, was to become a watershed date in the history of Western higher education. A decade earlier the English royal commissions had cautiously opened the doors of Oxford and Cambridge to the middle classes. The Morrill Act opened the doors of scores of state institutions to an ever-growing flood of students who stamped the seal of popularity upon the practical and the professional ingredients of modern higher education in America.

D. AMBIVALENCE BETWEEN ACHIEVEMENT AND LEARNER-ORIENTED GOALS

We have said that one of the characteristics of modern education is that it seeks a balance between the achievement that society expects from the products of its educational systems and the system's efforts to adapt education to the learning capabilities and talents of the students it teaches. In the period from 1700 to 1850 the balance in American education, as elsewhere in the West, was tipped heavily in favor of the achievement of society's goals.

The achievement expected in elementary schools was literacy wrapped in piety and moral behavior. From the days when Cotton Mather laid his charges upon the dutiful child of *A Family Well-Ordered* (1699) to be obedient and prayerful, when Jonathan Edwards' *Faithful Narrative of the Surprising Work of God* (1736) revelled in four-year-old Phoebe Bartletts' religious anguish and sense of sin, the Protestant ethic enjoined the child to work hard to achieve salvation. From the mid-eighteenth to the mid-nineteenth centuries two additional motivations permeated the educational system's efforts to socialize its students. They must work hard to become loyal patriots in order to help the nation achieve its destiny as conceived by a Noah Webster or a George Bancroft. They were enjoined to work hard to make a decent and honest living as embodied in Benjamin Franklin's *Advice to a Young Tradesman* (1748). The intertwining of these three achievement motivations prescribed the dominant social task and tone of American education—to hew a self-reliant, individualistic, middle-class morality into the pillars of a white, Anglo-Saxon, Protestant society.

The most influential of the early reading books was the *New England Primer,* first published in America just before the beginning of the eighteenth century. It illustrates above all how learning to read was thoroughly imbued with religious sentiments. It commonly began with the alphabet in capital and small letters, followed by lists of syllables and words emphasizing moral concepts. Little children learned their letters by spelling and memorizing such words as: abusing, bewitching, confounded, drunkenness, faculty, godliness, impudent, everlasting, fidelity, glorifying, and humility. Then came the edifying woodcuts illustrating the letters of the alphabet accompanied by religious, moralistic rhymes, many of them reflecting the gloomy outlook of Puritanism. Reading material followed under such headings as "The Dutiful Child's Promises" and "An Alphabet of Lessons for Youth," culminating in the Lord's Prayer, the Apostles' Creed, the Ten Commandments, the names of the books of the Old and New Testaments, religious verses and stories, and finally the Westminster catechism. The Roman and Arabic numerals were learned as a means "for the ready finding of any Chapter, Psalm, and Verse in the Bible."

Later in the eighteenth century newer editions of the *New England Primer* began to reflect patriotic sentiments commensurate with the outlook of the new nation. For example, the early rhyme describing the letter K expressed loyalty to the king of England: "Our King the Good, No man of blood." After the Revolution, patriotism became the motif: "Kings should be good, Not men of blood;" "The British King, Lost states thirteen;" or "Queens and Kings, Are gaudy things." Other changes made the patriotic point as plain as could be: "Whales in the sea, God's voice obey" became "Great Washington brave, His country did save."

Not only did the patriotic motif begin to appear after Revolution but also a good deal of other secular material was inserted. Stories about punishments for bad boys and girls no longer involved eternal suffering in hell but stressed the withholding of oranges, apples, cakes, and nuts. Furthermore, the practical value of learning to read began to seem more enticing to youthful ambitions than its use in reading the Bible. For example, the *New England Primer* exhorted pupils in the following manner:

> He who ne'er learns his A.B.C.
> Forever will a blockhead be.
> But he who learns his letters fair
> Shall have a coach to take the air.

The *Primer* began to lose ground after the Revolution as more sprightly reading books appeared, one of the most famous being Noah Webster's "blue-backed speller," *Elementary Spelling Book,* probably the most widely used schoolbook for a century. Emphasizing moralistic and patriotic sentiments, it symbolized the ideals of a newly Americanized civility, one of whose goals was universal literacy.

William Holmes McGuffey's graded readers, published in the 1830s and 1840s, carried the achievement motive into nearly every part of the land. It is estimated that 12 million copies were sold between 1836 and 1920. The readers were not so much interested in adapting literature to the learner as in putting generations of young and immature readers in touch with the common stock of modern English literature. And, above all, the selections set before the youth of America the ideals of achievement that served the cause of modernization on a large scale. Henry Steele Commager sums up their underlying ideology this way:

> It was a middle-class, conventional, and equalitarian morality, one that derived from Benjamin Franklin and his careful rules of good conduct, rather than from the Puritan austerity of a John Adams, or the Enlightenment of a Jefferson. Industry, sobriety, thrift, propriety, modesty, punctuality, conformity—these were the essential virtues, and those who practiced them were sure of

success . . . a job, a farm, money in hand or in the bank. Failure was, just as clearly, the consequence of laziness or self-indulgence, and deserved, therefore, little sympathy.[12]

Less well known but distinctively American, an elementary textbook, *First Lessons in Political Economy,* written in 1835 by the Reverend John McVickar, professor at Columbia College, deftly wove together the texture of individual effort with a laissez faire economic system operating according to natural laws as the best guarantee for national development. In a last chapter on "How to Make Money," McVickar dotted the i's and crossed the t's of the achievement motif in the American dream:

> If he has good health and is industrious, even the poorest boy in our country has something to trade upon; and if he be besides well-educated and have skill in any kind of work, and add to this, moral habits and religious principles, so that his employers may trust him and place confidence in him, he may then be said to set out in life with a handsome capital, and certainly has as good a chance of becoming independent and respectable, and perhaps *rich,* as any man in the country. "Every man is the maker of his own fortune." All depends upon setting out on the right principles, and they are these:
> 1. Be Industrious—time and skill are your capital.
> 2. Be Saving—whatever it be, live within your income.
> 3. Be Prudent—buy not what you can do without.
> 4. Be Resolute—let your economy be always of today, not tomorrow.
> 5. Be Contented and Thankful—a cheerful spirit makes labor light, and sleep sweet, and all around *happy,* all of which is much better than being *only rich.*[13]

There is no doubt that the ideology of hard work instilled by the schools contributed to the rapid modernization of the United States. It is probably significant that a similar achievement orientation in the century to come pervaded the approach to modernization in capitalist Japan and in Communist Russia and China. Stripped of the goal of getting rich, McVickar's gospel spelled out a basic formula useful to the modernizing leadership of all shades of political ideology: industriousness, prudence, resoluteness, and contentment.

In comparison with the stress on achievement, American schools gave relatively minor attention to learner-oriented pedagogy up to mid-nineteenth century. Yet there was a growing undercurrent of effort to adapt teaching materials to the learner's interests or abilities. As early as 1706 the instruction of the Society for the Propagation of the Gospel in Foreign Parts to its Anglican teachers not only enjoined them to develop in their charges good manners and the virtues of honesty and truth, but also to be kind and gentle to the children and to be sparing with corporal punishment.

---

[12] *McGuffey's Fifth Eclectic Reader,* 1879 ed., New American Library, New York, 1962, p. viii.

[13] John McVickar, *First Lessons in Political Economy; for the Use of Primary and Common Schools,* Hilliard, Gray, and Co., Boston, 1835, pp. 86-88.

Similarly, the Quaker teacher, Anthony Benezet, advocated patient understanding of innocent child nature, special attention to different aptitudes, and emphasis upon the pleasant and interesting rather than upon laborious drudgery.

The most elaborate and perhaps the first entire book written in America on schoolteaching was that of Christopher Dock, a Mennonite schoolmaster in Pennsylvania during the mid-eighteenth century. He described at length how he taught his children at different age and ability levels, appealed to their desire for praise and avoidance of blame rather than fear of the rod, and in general tried to instill a common understanding, sympathy, and mutual love between pupil and teacher. "Soft pedagogy" is at least 200 years old and deep in the American religious and educational tradition—but not as old nor as deep as the harsher puritanical emphasis upon the need for unflagging achievement.

With the great influx of children into the common schools in the nineteenth century, it soon became clear that the little one-room district school with its individual teaching methods for a wide range of ages could no longer suffice. Two major changes in elementary school organization were made—the development of the class method of teaching and the graded system of grouping children by age levels.

By the end of the Civil War children aged six to ten were grouped into a primary school for grades one through four, and children aged ten to fourteen in a grammar school for grades five through eight. The development of the graded and class system was doubtless influenced not only by the increased number of children but also by the example of the European systems, especially the German and French, as reported by such Americans as Horace Mann, Henry Barnard, Calvin E. Stowe, and John Griscom. A teacher could specialize somewhat by teaching only one grade and age level by the class method, rather than teaching the whole range of children individually. The graded system, first receiving attention in Boston in the middle of the century through Superintendent John D. Philbrick, soon spread throughout the country. Its impact was heavily on the side of standardizing education rather than individualizing it.

Throughout the first part of the century a series of imports from Europe attempted to loosen up the increasingly unwieldy system. From England came the Sunday schools and the infant schools, which helped to spread the idea that formal educational systems had a responsibility to very young children and to the underprivileged. The monitorial schools, also from England, helped to show that class instruction could not only be reasonably efficient in handling large numbers of children but that discipline through rewards and social punishment could replace corporal punishment.

From Germany came the ideas of Pestalozzi and Froebel. More attention was given to the study of nature and concrete objects; the practical usefulness of geography, drawing, music, home economics, and industrial arts was recognized; and a psychological rather than a strictly logical organization of subject matter like that of Warren Colburn's mental arithmetic in 1821 was supposed to meet the learning needs of individuals. Friedrich Froebel's kindergarten tried to combine moral and religious socialization with directive play and group activities for preschool children. Elizabeth Peabody established a kindergarten taught in English in Boston in the 1860s, and William T. Harris added kindergartens to the public school system in St. Louis.

Among the other foreign influences which were increasingly learner-oriented was the increasing attention to education for the deaf, blind, crippled, and feeble-minded. After a visit to France in 1816, Thomas H. Gallaudet helped to establish a school for the deaf in Hartford, Conn. in 1817, and state schools for the deaf appeared as early as the 1820s. and 1830s. Also from France came the stimulus to education for the blind, through the efforts of Dr. Samuel Gridley Howe, who helped to establish the Perkins Institute for the Blind in Boston in 1832. The study of feeble-minded children was a part of Édouard Séguin's work in France and Gallaudet's work in the United States. The first state institution was the Massachusetts School for Idiotic and Feeble-minded Youth in 1851. Private schools for crippled children were established in New York in the 1860s.

In the regular common schools the introduction of drawing, music, and physical education was intended to enliven the curriculum beyond pure literacy, piety, and patriotism. By the 1860s some schools in Boston, New York, Philadelphia, and cities of the West were beginning to include drawing. The teaching of drawing was influenced on one hand by the practical interest in mechanical drawing for its uses in commerce and industry and on the other hand by the psychological desire to develop children's manual and physical skills along Pestalozzian lines as a means of developing their individual capacities. In the 1830s and 1840s Lowell Mason wrote instruction manuals for music teachers and persuaded the Boston public schools to introduce music into the system, whence the idea spread to other cities. Physical education in the form of calisthenics, exercises, and playground activities began to appear in schools in the 1850s and 1860s, and some educators became interested in the study of hygiene and physiology under pressure from antialcohol and antitobacco reformers.

By and large the long-range interest in a learner-oriented education depended upon the rise of specialized institutions of teacher education. So long as children were viewed as miniature adults who simply had to be poured—or hammered—into the adult mold there was little reason to study the child, his distinctive characteristics, his stages of development, or his learning processes. When discipline—mental, moral, or intellectual—was the chief end of education, there was little reason beyond efficiency to be concerned with classroom management or pedagogical methods. When religious orthodoxy was the chief qualification for a teacher, teaching competence could easily be measured by the clergy and required little pedagogical training.

But when childhood came to be viewed as a valued period in the total lifespan of human development, when differing individuals began to be viewed as warranting individual study, and when unprecedented numbers of children began to pour into the public schools, then teacher education began to be considered a worthwhile field of professional study, important and desirable in its own right. To be sure, the predominant hold of the ideal of discipline and the preoccupation of the several disciplines of knowledge with their own substances virtually left teacher education to those concerned with elementary education and younger children. Such persons were generally on the low end of the academic totem pole. So teacher training was widely ignored or neglected in the regular colleges and universities, because it was viewed as fit largely for the teachers of small children, and such teachers in a disjunctive system did not need higher education themselves.

But with the tremendous expansion in publicly supported education during the nineteenth century, increased provision for the preparation of teachers was clearly necessary. In the early years of the century such training of teachers as was done in the liberal arts colleges and the academies gave little in the way of specific attention to the task of teaching; rather, it was felt that knowledge of the subject matter to be taught was enough. For elementary school teaching, the qualifications beyond religious orthodoxy and good moral character were vague and informal.

As early as the 1820s, however, a definite movement to institute specific preparation for teaching gained headway. Borrowing somewhat from French and Prussian examples, a few normal schools were established to prepare teachers for work in the elementary schools. The word *normal* came from the French word meaning a model or a rule, connoting that the object of the institution was to provide a model for the way teaching should be conducted. The first normal schools in America, such as those promoted by Samuel R. Hall at Concord, Vt., in 1823 and by James G. Carter at Lancaster, Mass., in 1827, were private institutions. The first state normal school was established in 1839 at Lexington, Mass., at the instigation of Horace Mann and Charles Brooks, with Cyrus Peirce as principal. By 1860 there were eleven state normal schools in eight states.

Since most of the early normal schools admitted students directly from the elementary grades, they were really secondary level institutions with the courses of study varying in length, two years being the most common. In general, the curriculum was devoted to study and mastery of the elementary school subjects, with some additional work in the philosophy, psychology, and history of education. Nearly all normal schools eventually included some sort of observation and practice teaching either in a model school conducted by the normal school or in the public schools. In 1851 Cyrus Peirce stated the learner-oriented goals of the early normal schools as well as anyone could:

> . . . make better teachers; teachers who would understand, and do their business better; teachers, who should know more of the nature of children, of youthful developments, more of the subjects to be taught, and more of the true methods of teaching; who would teach more philosophically, more in harmony with the natural development of the young mind, with a truer regard to the order and connection in which the different branches of knowledge should be presented to it, and, of course more successfully.[14]

The success of Prussian and French state systems of teacher training helped to spur the American states to develop public normal schools. The report of Victor Cousin on the Prussian system was given wide currency in America, along with the reports of such Americans as Horace Mann, Henry Barnard, Calvin Stowe, Charles Brooks, John Griscom, William C. Woodbridge, and Edward Sheldon. In Oswego, N.Y., Edward Sheldon, waxing enthusiastic about the educational methods of Pestalozzi,

---

[14] Merle L. Borrowman (ed.), *Teacher Education in America, a Documentary History,* Teachers College Press, New York, 1964, p. 65.

brought some Pestalozzian trained teachers to Oswego in the 1860s to help his staff improve their teaching. When Oswego became a state normal school, these ideas were taken up by other normal schools, and the influence began to spread rapidly in the United States. Other influential normal schools were the Illinois State Normal University at Normal, Ill., and the New York State Normal College at Albany. A few liberal arts colleges began to give lectures on the art of teaching and pedagogy, notably New York University in 1832, Brown in 1850, and Michigan in 1860.

In addition to the notable extension of preservice training for teachers in educational institutions, some steps were taken to improve the quality of teaching through in-service training for teachers already on the job. Teachers' institutes of one or two to five or six weeks' duration were started by Henry Barnard in Connecticut in 1839. The idea spread rapidly to other states. Several universities began to give extension courses on and off the campus, home-study courses, and library lectures.

Periodicals for teachers appeared as far back as the *Academician* (1818), William Russell's *American Journal of Education* (1826-1831), and, above all, Henry Barnard's *American Journal of Education* (1855-1881). Textbooks for teachers began with Samuel R. Hall's *Lectures on Schoolkeeping* (1829), but their influence was rather slight until the professors of education at the end of the century began to publish books on a wide variety of topics. Another important means of improving the status and quality of the teaching profession was the relatively large number of teachers' organizations that sprang up in the nineteenth century. Among the more important ones were the American Institute of Instruction (1830), consisting mostly of New England scholars and college educators, and the National Teachers Association (1857), which became the National Education Association in 1870.

Organized education of youth and adults outside of the regularly constituted school and university systems took tremendous strides in the nineteenth-century United States. The spread of knowledge was promoted by philanthropic and humanitarian agencies, as well as by some commercial ventures. These organized movements spread through all social classes in the population, including the laboring classes of the cities as well as the white-collar and professional classes. Mechanics' institutes, workingmen's and merchants' libraries, and lectures for industrial and commercial workers imbued thousands of ordinary people with the idea that knowledge gave power. The Boston Apprentices' Library was formed in 1820, and the Boston Mechanics' Institute was founded in 1826. In 1829 the New York Apprentices' Library had 10,000 volumes, and by the middle of the century it was serving three-quarters of a million working-class people. Mercantile libraries for young workers in business offices also became very popular after the 1820s. Many of these organizations sponsored lectures, discussions, debates, and public events of various kinds. Employers and philanthropically minded members of the wealthier classes also promoted adult education in such widely popular forms as the Lowell Institute in Boston (1836), Cooper Union in New York City (1859), and Peabody Institute in Baltimore.

On a larger scale, and serving the rural regions as well as the urban communities, the lyceum movement served as one of the most important agencies for adult education in the mid-nineteenth century. First organized by Josiah Holbrook in

Millbury, Mass., in 1826, the lyceum sponsored lectures, forums, public discussion, and reading material on all kinds of scientific and social subjects, including support for the public schools. Beginning as local discussion groups, the lyceum circuit eventually commanded the services of some of the best speakers and orators of the day. By 1834 some 3,000 communities boasted lyceums.

In sum, the widespread availability of formal educational services outside as well as inside the schools enormously speeded the process of modernization of the United States in the middle decades of the nineteenth century. The thirst for knowledge was as evident in rural communities as in urban. The proliferation of small colleges and of normal schools in innumerable small towns gave a kind of access to advanced education for rural classes that up to that time was unparalleled. They contributed significantly to the rural transformation of America that preceded and then accompanied industrial urbanization. The normal schools provided an occupational upward mobility for thousands of rural young people and helped to make rural life a more satisfying mode of existence for an educated person than was commonly the case in countries where the magnet of the major cities was irresistible to anyone with a literate education. Many of the developing nations of the world were struggling with just this problem in the second half of the twentieth century.

CHAPTER XIII

THE AMERICAN FAITH
IN MASSIVE
EDUCATIONAL
ENDEAVOR
(1860s A.D.-THE PRESENT)

In the prior chapters we have viewed the hundred years since 1860 or 1870 as a period in which education in the heartland nations of the West became more popular, more secular and scientific, more practical and professional, more differentiated and specialized, and more achievement-oriented as well as more learner-oriented. These characteristics also became a model for educational development, in greater or lesser degree, for the less modern Western societies and for many traditional non-Western societies, either through their own efforts or perforce through external pressure or control. Of course, the modernizing tendencies were opposed, obstructed, or delayed in various degrees, but the tendency to emulate them was so widespread and so rapid that the century may very well be called the dispersive as well as the florescent period of modern Western education.

Because of the speed with which educational modernization in the United States overtook the momentum of France, Britain and Germany in the course of the century, the United States also began to set the pace for the West in the social power of organized knowledge and research, mass participation in the political process, industrial urbanization and technology, and the vitality of pluralistic religious association. But not without great travail and dislocation.

In its efforts to achieve a large-scale system of popular education that was effectively universal, comprehensive, free, and compulsory the United States was beset by four interrelated, persistent, and inflammatory issues: the tension between federal and state powers in education, the conflict between the public and the private interest in education, the role of religion in education, and the gap between the practices of segregation and the ideals of equal educational opportunity for minority racial, and ethnic groups, especially of blacks. Each of these conflicts tore at the fabric of

433

national unity and delayed the process of achieving modernity in education. None stayed completely resolved; what seemed to be fairly well settled at one time could burst into angry conflict at another time.

As the century wore on it became clear, too, how interrelated were the four problems.[1] What was being fought out in one arena had serious repercussions in another, sometimes threatening the very existence of the political and social order. But the general trends of a hundred years were clear. Enough of a settlement was reached in each arena to mark the century as one of overall educational modernization.

A. THE ACCELERATION OF LARGE-SCALE POPULAR EDUCATION

Whereas the ideal of the first century of the American republic had been to provide *some* education for all white children and much education for a few, the democratic goal for the second century of the republic was, quite simply, more education for more people. The march to the schools came faster, the lines stretched longer, and the students grew older. In general quantitative terms, modern education in the United States came to mean elementary education for all, secondary education for the vast majority, and higher education for a rapidly expanding number (reaching toward a small majority).

The American statistics for elementary education are relatively easy. Well over half the children age six to thirteen were attending elementary schools in 1870, three-fourths in 1900, and 99 percent in 1970. Virtual universal elementary school attendance was achieved. The literacy figures correspond. In 1870 the literacy of all persons over age ten was 80 percent; by 1900 it was 90 percent; by 1940 it was 97 percent where it has hovered ever since. What the functional literacy may be is, of course, another question, for it is clear that simply writing one's name and reading a few sentences from a graded reader does not qualify a person for effective functioning in a highly modernized society. As recently as 1945, 30 percent of the jobs in the labor force were classified as unskilled, presumably requiring only minimal literacy. But by 1970 the proportion of unskilled workers had dropped to 15 percent and the estimate was that by 1975 it would be as low as 5 percent.

More than simple or inert literacy is required of those in skilled jobs, to say nothing of all the other social, political, and cultural necessities of modern society. Special handicaps accrue to those whose access to education has been limited by racial segregation or ethnic discrimination. For example, white literacy in the United States is over 98 percent whereas nonwhite literacy is less than 90 percent. A large proportion of nonwhites are thus still handicapped in achieving skilled jobs, even if racial prejudice were not a factor in employment. And when unskilled jobs virtually disappear, literacy becomes the sheerest minimum essential for employment in a modern society.

The march to the secondary schools has been even more remarkable. The numbers virtually doubled during each decade in the early twentieth century from

[1]See R. Freeman Butts, "States' Rights and Education," *Teachers College Record,* vol. 58, no. 4, pp. 189-197, January 1957.

about 500,000 in 1900 to 1,000,000 in 1910, 2,500,000 in 1920, nearly 5,000,000 in 1930, and about 7,000,000 in 1940. After a decline in the 1940s, the numbers increased spectacularly from the 1950s until they reached around 14,000,000 in 1970. In 1890 less than 7 percent of children age fourteen to seventeen attended a secondary school (grades nine to twelve). By 1930 this percentage had jumped to more than 50 percent; by 1940 to nearly 75 percent; and (after a decline in the 1940s) had climbed to some 94 percent by 1970. This comes close to universal secondary education, something not dreamed of by the republican leaders of the first century of American nationhood, nor by modernizing leaders of most nations of the world until very recently.

Another way to put the point is that by the late 1960s the median number of years of schooling completed by all Americans over age twenty-five was twelve. This means, of course, that half of American adults had more than a secondary school education. Again, the educational disadvantage of nonwhites is revealed by the fact that their median years of schooling is nearly three years less than that of the total population. But the march *through* secondary school and on to college may be even more remarkable in the long run. In 1870 it was estimated that 2 percent of the seventeen-year-old population graduated from high school. This percentage would not be enormously different from that of other modern countries, and it rose only gradually for several decades. But nearly 30 percent of seventeen-year-olds were *completing* secondary school by 1930; 50 percent by 1940; 60 percent by 1950; and 75 percent by 1970.

With 94 percent of high-school-age youth actually in high school and with 75 percent graduating, it is not surprising that the numbers going on to postsecondary education would also increase. By 1950 about 30 percent of high school graduates were going on to college; by the 1970s it was 50 percent, and the projections were that it would continue to increase. Frank H. Bowles has pointed out that in 1900 when 11 percent of the high school age group was in high school about 4 percent of the college age group was in college.[2] Twenty-five years later, in only one generation, the percentage of college age youth actually in college had risen to 11 percent and the high school percentage to 50 percent. Then another generation later 90 percent of the high school age group was in high school, and 50 percent of the college age group in college. So he projects that another generation will see a very high percentage (if not 90 percent) of college age youth actually in college. Whether the drastic unrest that affected higher education during the 1960s will modify the projection or not, the generalization as it applies to long-range modernization is extremely suggestive: In 1900 the educational requirement for general admission to adult life in modernizing America was completion of an elementary-school education; in 1930 it was completion of a secondary-school education; around 1985 it will be completion of four years of higher education.

Such a development of more education for more people has not struck many observers of the American scene as particularly desirable, but it is an essential characteristic of modernity, a trend that is taking place and will take place no matter

---

[2] Frank H. Bowles and Charles M. Holloway, "The Coming Age of College," *American Association of University Professors Bulletin*, vol. 46, no. 3, pp. 271-276, September 1960.

how reluctantly it is agreed to, if the modernization process itself takes place. Of course it may be delayed. There may be talk in some countries about *gradually* extending education anywhere from age fifteen to eighteen. In 1958 only 25 percent of French youth stayed in school until age seventeen and 15 percent to age eighteen; projections seemed to show that this would increase by 1975 to 50 percent of seventeen-year-olds and 35 percent of eighteen-year-olds.[3] This puts France roughly twenty-five years behind the United States on this one factor of age in school (not considering how much or what is learned in those years). Perhaps no conclusions can be drawn from such facts as to the speed or timing of modernization in the two countries, but the point is that the general direction is the same wherever modernization is taking place.[4] The upward pressure from universal elementary education will be extremely difficult to stop or to reverse, once the process has begun. It may be delayed by all sorts of political and economic and social measures, but the pressure for educational expansion as an integral condition of modernization has been all but universal.

How the United States came to achieve large-scale popular education without the prodding of a centralized government or a centralized educational authority is a difficult matter for modernization theory to answer. A clue perhaps is found in Samuel P. Huntington's analysis of political modernization in which he compares the continental European, British, and American experiences.[5] In two aspects of political modernization the United States lagged behind Europe: (1) the nationalizing of authority into a single, centralized, national polity and (2) the differentiation of political structures to correspond to new specialized functions in such way as to give supremacy to the legislative functions of the law-making body without serious challenge from judicial review of the courts or an independent executive.

But in a third characteristic of political modernization, the United States led Europe, that is, the rapid broadening of political participation to most of the populace. Because of the relative absence of violent social conflict, pervasive international war, and a feudal legacy of rigid social and property classification, the United States did not need to create a strong centralized government to institute social reform as in Europe. Thus, the Americans were able to modernize their society through diffuse and local governmental agencies while maintaining for a longer period of time the traditional forms of government they had transported to the New World, with the invention of federalism as the chief political innovation.

In sum, federal participation in educational control and support was slow and late in coming, but large-scale *public* control and support were achieved principally through widespread state and local efforts. The mass participation of citizens in

[3]Edmund J. King, *Other Schools and Ours; a Comparative Study for Today,* Holt, New York, 1967, p. 75.

[4]See, for example, the comparative figures for the countries of the European Common Market in the chapter by Philip J. Idenburg, "Europe—In Search of New Forms of Education," in George Z. F. Bereday (ed.), *Essays on World Education: the Crisis of Supply and Demand,* Oxford University Press, New York, 1969, pp. 277-296.

[5]Samuel P. Huntington, "Political Modernization: America vs. Europe," *World Politics,* vol. 18, no. 3, pp. 378-414, April 1966; and *Political Order in Changing Societies,* Yale University Press, New Haven, Conn., 1968, chap. 2.

American public educational affairs has always bewildered Europeans accustomed to centralized authority in education. The United States was able to modernize its education from below, because the incentive to produce education on a large scale was widely dispersed throughout the population who saw its value for economic, social, political, and cultural advancement. No matter how widely this incentive was spread, the major motivating force, in education as well as in society in general, came from the middle classes.[6]

Despite the enormous expansion in educational attendance throughout the system, drastic inequalities continued to exist in the quality and amount of education available to various groups in the population. The more highly industrialized and richer states spent more on education and thus provided better opportunities for their citizens. By 1970 several states were spending only one-half to one-third as much per pupil as other states were spending. The poorer states, mostly in the South, had to exert greater effort than the richer states even to maintain this relationship.

It was clear, too, that, within the states, the urban and industrial areas were more advantageously situated than the rural and farming regions. So long as local units provided the bulk of school support, those units with greater population and greater wealth could spend more money on their schools. Likewise, great inequalities existed in the provision of educational opportunities for black and other minority children as compared with white children; in the southern states the average expenditure per black child was about one-fourth to one-half what it was for each white child. Thus, in general, the inequality was enormous, either because some communities simply did not have enough money to provide decent education, or because they did not wish to spend equal amounts for all groups in the population, or both.

Attempts to equalize these discrepancies took several forms. Within the states, equalization funds were set up to distribute state aid to the local communities on a basis that would help the poorer districts. Forward-looking states adopted the general principle that the entire wealth of the state should be tapped to serve the entire population of the state. Various kinds of formulas were developed to give state aid to communities on the basis of their need and ability to raise funds for schools, the number of children to be educated, and their willingness to tax themselves as fully as possible for the support of schools.

Likewise, many states set out to consolidate local rural school districts into larger units in order to provide more efficient schools at less cost. By pooling their resources on a county basis, local districts could provide fewer but better schools, served by school buses and manned by better-paid and better-trained teachers. The consolidation movement met vigorous opposition from many enthusiasts for local and decentralized control, who feared that the county or state would usurp their rights, but the trend toward consolidation made steady headway despite continuing opposition. By the middle decades of the twentieth century 100,000 school districts had been consolidated into less than 18,000.

In general the states were willing, even eager, to receive financial aid from the

[6]See, for example, Henry J. Perkinson, *The Imperfect Panacea: American Faith in Education, 1865-1965,* Random House, New York, 1968.

federal government, but they were not willing to have the federal government extend its control over the state systems of education.ᐟ Several bills were introduced into Congress in the 1870s and 1880s proposing direct federal support for general education, but they were never enacted into law. It was recognized, however, that the federal government should have a share in the field of national education in some measure. Consequently, a federal Department of Education was established in 1867. Fearing that such a department might get out of hand, several states raised such strong objections that the separate department was transformed into an Office of Education within the Department of Interior. In 1870 it became the Bureau of Education. Despite its change in name, its function remained primarily that of collecting information and statistical data, conducting research, and disseminating information concerning the status and progress of American education. At a time when France and Germany were building strong national systems of education, the United States was unwilling to take steps that would put very much control in the hands of the national government. For 100 years the Office of Education was a poor stepchild in the federal bureaucracy. The forces of decentralization prevented educational modernization in the national government until well into the twentieth century.

It became clear, however, especially during the depression of the early 1930s, that genuine equality could not be achieved for all American children unless the federal government entered the field of school support in a substantial way. The real stumbling block was the determination of the Roman Catholic Church to oppose federal aid unless it included their parochial schools. Curiously enough, the role of the two major political parties has reversed since the nineteenth century. Whereas it was the antislavery Republicans who had sponsored federal-aid bills in the 1870s and the 1880s, it was the pro-welfare Democrats who favored federal aid to education in the 1940s and 1950s.

More and more groups were coming to realize the need for federal funds, but many continued to fear federal control. Southern whites opposed any bill that would provide for equal distribution of funds to Negro schools. Most Protestant and Jews opposed any bill that would give federal aid to Catholic parochial schools as well as to public schools. Roman Catholics opposed any federal-aid bill that ruled out support for private and parochial schools. Taxpayers' alliances and economy groups opposed all federal aid of any kind. With these groups pulling and hauling in different directions, the problem became ever more acute.

Despite the fact that no bill for general federal aid to education had been passed by mid-century, the federal government was spending some 3.5 billion dollars a year by 1950. This reflected the accumulations over six or seven decades of piecemeal response by Congress to special demands rather than to carefully planned and integrated programs. Only a few of the outstanding developments can be mentioned here.

In general, the key was specialized support for particular categories of practical, vocational, and professional education. A few examples are the Hatch Act (1887) for agricultural research, the Smith-Lever Act (1914) for agricultural extension services, and the Smith-Hughes Act (1917) for training secondary school teachers of vocational subjects. The New Deal added the category of relief for depression-affected persons and aid for vocational training under such programs as the Civilian Conservation Corps (1933), the National Youth Administration (1935), the Works Project Administration, and the Public Works Administration. Then the emergency of World War II and postwar national defense became key categories including war training programs in technical skills, G. I. Bill educational benefits for returning servicemen, national defense research in the sciences and technology, aid to local school districts affected by war industries, and the National Defense Education Act of 1958 to aid studies critical for national welfare.

Though the cold war motivation was foremost in the minds of congressmen when they passed the National Defense Education Act to provide scholarships, loans, and grants for mathematics, science, and foreign languages, audio-visual aids, and guidance and testing services to identify talented youth, the academic community accepted the program because it gave further indication that education was becoming a high priority in federal policy. Later on, assistance was rendered to humanistic and social science fields of study as well as to the sciences and mathematics. The promotion of scholarly study of the languages, history, and cultures of major areas of the world little known to Americans was of great significance in correcting the pervasive provincial emphasis on Europe and the United States that dominated most curriculums of colleges and universities. Non-Western studies were given an indispensable boost. But NDEA only paved the way for further support that did not need to come wholly under the umbrella of national defense. Increasing appropriations for other special purposes in higher education, especially through research, traineeships, and fellowships, and the construction of new buildings were solidified in the Higher Education Act of 1965. Within a year the annual grants were amounting to 2.5 billion dollars.

Finally came the most important new piece of federal legislation in the field of education since the Morrill Act of 1862. The Elementary and Secondary Education Act of 1965 was a brilliant piece of political legislation that was able to overcome the long-standing road blocks that had stood in the way of federal aid for general educational support for nearly 100 years. Key personalities in the achievement were Francis Keppel, who had been brought from the deanship of Harvard University's School of Education to be Commissioner of Education, and President Lyndon B. Johnson whose strong support for the bill did indeed justify his oft-stated desire to become known as America's "education president."

The bill turned out to have something for most interested parties. It recognized the growing need to give special attention to the poor of the urban ghettos and the rural slums; this meant special attention to blacks, Puerto Ricans, Mexican-Americans, and other minority ethnic groups. So Title I provided funds to states and localities to improve schooling for educationally deprived children (five-sixths of the total) using a quantitative formula based upon child population, family poverty, and need of the local district for funds. In this way most of the 18,000 school districts in the United States were entitled to some aid.

The bill also recognized the need to provide something for parochial schools, so Title II made it possible for school library resources, textbooks, and other instructional materials to go to private as well as to public schools, with the caveat that no such aids should be used for religious instruction and all aids continue to be owned by public authorities. The child benefit theory had won the day over heated opposition. By this time most people were ready to gloss over the question of separation of church and state which had agitated Americans for some 300 years in order to get the benefits of massive federal support for education. This issue was not finally decided by any means, but a major breakthrough was made from which there would be greater and greater difficulty in turning back.

Innovation had become a byword among critics of educational practices in the public schools, so Title III enabled the federal government to establish "supplementary educational centers and services" that would enable ambitious school systems that wanted to try new practices to bypass the established state and university systems. Title IV provided federal funds to support educational research, demonstration, and training by universities, by private profit-making research organizations, and by individuals. Again these research and development centers and demonstration laboratories were viewed as ways to go around the established state organizations and educational institutions. To mollify the states somewhat, Title V gave them funds to strengthen their departments of education.

All through the bill were provisions that no federal official could exercise control over the educational program. What this meant when federal officials could decide what grants to make and what not to make in Titles III, IV, and V, and when religious schools could receive federal funds directly from the Office of Education even if state policy prohibited the use of such state funds for such purposes, was a fine distinction that could make a great difference. As so often happened, the process of modernization was promoted at the cost of compromise with traditional forces. Centralization and science were promoted at the risk of slowing down secularization.

Despite the objections to the passage of the bill and the ambiguities raised by its administration, the decade of the 1960s can be viewed as a significant watershed in the history of American education. In a word, the United States was modernizing its federal role in national education. A century after the federal government enunciated the principle in the Morrill Act that the government should promote national development through aid to higher education, and a century after it established a fairly forlorn shadow of what other governments had built into their national ministries of education, the United States finally enunciated the practice, if not the principle, that the national welfare depended upon massive support from the federal government. Within a decade the federal support to education jumped to 10 billion dollars a year, not much when compared with other agencies of the federal government, but massive when compared with the relatively few millions spent prior to the 1960s. So a bill that started out to provide some thing for all interested groups may be looked back upon as a symbol that the United States government was not only belatedly modernizing its education by centralizing support, but perhpas as a sign of the opening of the postmodern era when basic research and applied knowledge in the educational field would become one of the most powerful formative elements in the creation and very survival of a worldwide civilization.

B. THE UNEASY COEXISTENCE OF PUBLIC
AND PRIVATE EDUCATION

The American system of education has included both public and private schools, but, as in other nations, the paths of the public and the private interest in education have often crossed and tangled. The going is especially rough in a society that decides to welcome religious and cultural diversity and yet is determined to build a unified nation. Thus, in the decades of the late nineteenth and early twentieth centuries the United States went through what so many of the new nations of Asia and Africa are now going through on their roads to modernization—the crises of identity and of legitimacy. The new Americans, made up of many different ethnic, linguistic, religious, and cultural stocks, had to achieve a common sense of identity, to come to feel that they belonged to their new homeland, and somehow to reconcile the tugs of their traditional roots against the pull of the new. In this process the building of a public school system was deeply involved.

In the century of heavy immigration prior to the 1920s some 35 million people came to America. During the first half of that century the vast majority of immigrants had come from northern Europe; in the second half of the century, especially after the 1880s, two-thirds of the immigrants were from southern and eastern Europe, from Italy, Austria-Hungary, Russia, Poland, a very large proportion being Roman Catholic or Jewish in faith and most crowding into the urban centers. The foreign-born population of large cities came to be 30 to 40 or even 50 percent of the total. Some of these groups established their own private schools in the effort to preserve their traditional religious and ethnic ways of life in the face of the modernizing secularism of the new land. Others turned avidly to the public schools in the hope that free education would open doors of opportunity that had been so firmly closed against them in the old country.

In general the public schools set out to acculturate the immigrant, often lower-class and rural in background, to the standards of middle-class America. This is what masses of younger immigrants sought, and what many older immigrants feared or resented. The generation gap between first, second, and third generations of immigrants was traumatic indeed. And relations with the "natives" were not easy, sometimes bitterly hostile. As "native" Protestants felt their way of life challenged by Roman Catholics and Jews, they often turned upon them as undemocratic and un-American.

In the early part of the twentieth century the flood of immigration from Europe reached its peak. In 1930 the proportion of first- or second-generation citizens of foreign birth was very high; some 12 percent of the total population was foreign-born, and another 20 percent had foreign-born or mixed parents. In addition, some 10 percent of Americans were black. Therefore, substantially less than 60 percent of Americans were native white persons with native-born parents. The United States was truly a mixture of nearly all the nationalities of the world; but, despite the ideal of welcome to all peoples, Americans still consciously or unconsciously fostered group prejudices against the more recent immigrant groups.

It was in this setting of pulling and hauling between the values of a common national identity, crudely called Americanization, and the values of a cultural pluralism based upon religious and ethnic diversity that the relations between public and private education were hammered out. In the chauvinistic and nativist outbursts preceding and following World War I, many efforts were made to restrict and even abolish the schools being run by religious, ethnic, and private groups. This was often undertaken by indirection. For example, between 1917 and 1921 more than thirty states required that the medium of instruction in the public schools should be the English language. This was clearly aimed at parochial and immigrant schools being conducted in foreign languages.

Thereupon began a process by which the constitutional provisions in the Bill of Rights were interpreted to mean that *national* policies should take precedence over the powers of the states in the field of education. This was a fundamental transformation looking to the modernizing of American education: the strengthening of centralization in the federal government, and a limitation upon the particularist powers of the states in the field of education. The first controversies in the transforming process arose over the relative rights of public and private schools in the 1920s; then they arose over the religious question in the 1940s; and finally in the 1950s they centered around segregated education for blacks. In all three issues the Fourteenth Amendment of the Constitution was involved—no state shall "deprive any person of life, liberty, or property, without due process of law; nor deny to any person within its jurisdiction the equal protection of the laws."

In 1925, the Supreme Court struck down a law passed by the state of Oregon in 1922 requiring that all children between the age of eight and sixteen must not only attend school, but they must attend a *public* school. The proponents of this law echoed the arguments made for the common schools a century earlier: all children needed a common education for citizenship, and immigrant children could best be given this instruction when all classes and creeds attended school together; religious prejudice and juvenile delinquency could most easily be prevented in public schools, and loyalty to America most effectively promoted.

The court reaffirmed the right of the state to compel all children to attend some school and reasonably to regulate all schools, but it declared that the state could not unreasonably interfere with the liberty of parents, protected by the Fourteenth Amendment, to educate their children by sending them to a private rather than a public school if they saw fit. Thus the principle was established that private schools, so long as they met the reasonable standards set by the state, could exist alongside the public schools:

> The fundamental theory of liberty upon which all governments in this Union repose excludes any general power of the States to standardize its children by enforcing them to accept instruction from public teachers only. The child is not the mere creature of the State; those who nurture him and direct his destiny have the right, coupled with the high duty, to recognize and prepare him for additional obligations.[7]

[7]*Pierce v. Society of Sisters*, 268 U.S. 510 (1924), p. 535.

The Oregon case, of course, did not prevent continuing debate and controversy about the meaning and value of public education as compared with private education. But the test was what the people did. Most Americans continued to believe that the public schools should be the principal agency whereby the youth of America was to be educated, but a persistent and growing minority believed that private schools were better and that they should receive aid from public sources.

Up to the 1930s less than 10 percent of elementary and secondary children were in nonpublic schools, but then the percentage began to rise. By 1949 to 1950 it was 11.8 percent, during the early 1960s it hovered around 13 to 14 percent, but then began to decline after 1965 until it dropped back to around 10 percent by 1971. Approximately 90 percent of nonpublic school enrollments were in Roman Catholic schools as a result of steady and strong campaigns undertaken by Catholic leaders to get all Catholic children into Catholic schools. Some Protestants, too, were redoubling their efforts to expand the number of their denominational schools. These were potential threats to the idea of a common school system established with such cost and effort in the nineteenth century.

By and large, however, a considerable consensus was achieved concerning the meaning of public education in the United States. It is significant that Americans speak of public schools rather than state schools or government schools as in many other countries. The term signifies an institution that is or should be directly responsible to the people rather than one of many arms of the regular branches of government. Indeed, a distinctive form of government (the elected, lay board of education) was designed to keep the schools responsive to local community interests and somewhat free of the regular bureaucratic regimes of the other branches of government.

The consensus ran something like this. To be public rather than private a school should have certain characteristics. To the degree it had them it is public; to the degree that it does not, it is private.

1. A public school primarily serves a public purpose rather than a private purpose. It is not simply for the personal or private gain of the teacher, the proprietor, or the board of managers. It is not simply for the personal enjoyment or individual enhancement of the student or his family. It may indeed enhance the vocational competences and personal development of individuals, but if this was *all* it did, it could well be a private school. Instead, a public school will serve the common values necessary for the general welfare of the society, the dissemination of useful knowledge, and the responsibilities of citizenship.

2. A public school is under the exclusive control, ownership, and management of public authorities responsible to the people directly or to publicly designated officers of the civil government. Public bodies, whether legislatures, courts, or boards of education supervise, inspect, and approve policies, budgets, expenditures, and operation of the public schools.

3. A public school is supported by public funds, largely raised by taxation at the local, state, and federal levels. It does not rely heavily upon direct financial charges upon the student or his family in the form of fees or tuition. It thus is effectively free, especially at the elementary and secondary levels where compulsory education predominates. There is, however, much fuzziness about this

characteristic, as private schools demand public funds for their assistance but insist upon continuing to be private in control.

4. A public school is open freely and equally to all persons irrespective of social class, religion, race, sex, or national origin. A public school ideally is thus a school common to all in the society and does not select, divide, separate, or segregate pupils on grounds other than achievement. In sociological terms, it is based upon achieved status not upon ascribed status. Parents have a right to send their children to public schools as well as to private schools. This ideal has been violated more than any of the others; witness segregated schools for blacks, American Indians, and Spanish-speaking groups.

5. A public school is likely to be less religious or less sectarian and more secular in character than private schools. This is true either on the principle of religious freedom and separation of church and state or simply because diverse religious groups that share the school cannot agree on the specifics of religious instruction in doctrines, creeds, or devotional exercises to be held. This characteristic has also been violated or in dispute through much of the past century. To this issue we turn now. It has been a peculiarly volatile aspect of the public-private problem.

C. CONTINUING TENSION BETWEEN THE SECULAR AND THE RELIGIOUS

Perhaps more than any other people, Americans have proliferated and segmented their religious groups. By the end of the nineteenth century some 150 denominations claimed their religious loyalties. If the Protestant churches were generally grouped together, they represented some 18 million members, of which the Methodists, Baptists, Presbyterians, Lutherans, and Congregationalists were the largest. The Roman Catholic Church, larger by far than any one Protestant church, represented some 10 million members. Jews accounted for perhaps 1 million. Throughout the nineteenth century the number of church members had increased more rapidly, in proportion, than did the total population (76 million in 1900). Organized religious groups continued to increase, until in 1960 more than 100 million people representing 250 denominations were counted as church members, well over half of the total population of the country. The largest single denomination was the Roman Catholic Church, with some 35 million members; the principal Protestant denominations totaled some 60 million; Jewish congregations, 5 million; and Eastern Orthodox, 2.5 million.

The strength and diversity of the churches in America were in no small measure related to the religious freedom and the separation of church and state embodied in the First Amendment and in the bills of rights of the several state constitutions. Virtually every new state as it came into the Union in the nineteenth century adopted the principles that the state would guarantee freedom of religious conscience and that the state would not use public funds in support of churches. Up to 1876 the states voluntarily followed these basic principles of separation of church and state. After 1876 the Congress stipulated that new states must adopt irrevocable ordinances to the same effect. At the end of the nineteenth century the American people came closer to agreeing to these principles than at any time in their history. As applied to education, it was widely, though by no means universally, accepted that no public funds would be given to aid religious schools and no sectarian religious instruction would be given in the public schools. Though the public schools were professedly nonsectarian, they were generally Protestant in orientation and often in explicit practice, as so clearly described by David B. Tyack.[8] The other side of the coin, the effort to reserve public funds exclusively for public schools, was more nearly won by the end of the nineteenth century than at any time before or since. The whole set of issues, however, was to be reopened again in the middle of the twentieth century on the national as well as on the state and local levels.

While the ideal of religious freedom was often tarnished by outpourings of religious prejudice, it was also put under severe strain by the genuine differences of belief among men of good will concerning what role religion should play in the educational life of the nation. These differences came to explosive conflict in countless debates, resolutions, campaigns, laws, and court cases during the middle decades of the twentieth century. Beginning around 1930, four decades of religious and public controversy seemed to be leading to a fundamental redirection of the 150-year secularization trend. On one hand, secularization has meant the withdrawal of public funds from support of religious institutions. This was clearly involved in the First Amendment's mandate that "Congress shall make no law respecting an establishment of religion." In this sense, the trend toward modernization of American education slowed down in the 1950s and 1960s, as public funds increasingly poured into private and religious educational institutions.

On the other hand, the secularization involved in reducing the amount of religious instruction or observance (even of a nonsectarian sort) that could be required in the public school program has tended to be strengthened under the impact of a series of major Supreme Court cases. At mid-century, America seemed to be going in two different directions on two interrelated issues involving religion and education. The lineup was something like this:

In answer to the question "should public funds be used for religious schools?" there were three types of answers.

1. In the main, the Roman Catholic Church answered "yes." Since the parochial schools provided a public service by helping children to meet the compulsory attendance laws, it was only just that parochial schools be aided in this task in order to relieve Catholic parents from the burden of "double taxation," that is, of paying public school taxes and also supporting their own schools. No harm would come to the principle of separation of church and state so long as the state aided all churches equally and fairly and did not show preference for one church above others.

2. The second answer given by many Catholics and many Protestants was a qualified "yes." Here it was argued that the state should not give *direct* support

[8] David B. Tyack, "Onward Christian Soldiers: Religion in the American Common School," in Paul Nash (ed.), *History and Education: The Educational Uses of the Past,* Random House, New York, 1970, chap. 8.

to religious schools because that would violate the separation of church and state, but it was perfectly proper for the state to use public funds for such *indirect* aid as paying for bus transportation of children to parochial schools or providing them with free textbooks, free lunches, and free health and medical services. Since such auxiliary services were welfare benefits to the child and not aids to the school, they should be given to all children, no matter what school they attended. The majority decision of the United States Supreme Court in the Everson case in 1948 seemed to support this practical adjustment, although the constitutional principle was there clearly stated to be that "no tax in any amount, large or small, can be levied to support any religious activities or institutions, whatever they may be called, or whatever form they may adopt to teach or practice religion."[9]

3. The third answer to the question about public funds for religious schools was "no." This answer was given by many Protestants, most Jews, and most public school educators, including the National Education Association. This position argued that indirect aid, as well as direct aid, to religious schools should be prohibited if the values of the long struggle for separation of church and state were to be maintained. Either kind of aid would violate the First Amendment of the Constitution and in effect reintroduce "an establishment of religion" in the United States. Not only was genuine separation required on principle, but there seemed to be no place logically to stop once aid was begun even on a small scale.

By 1970 it began to look as though those who held the third position had lost their case and were being proved to be correct that there was no place to stop. *Indirect aid* approved under the child benefit theory of the Cochran case as early as 1930 permitted free textbooks to parochial school children at public expense. Only seven states permitted the use of textbooks until New York State's 1965 law was upheld by the Supreme Court in 1968. The Everson case applied the principle to bus transportation in 1947. The School Lunch Act passed by Congress in 1948 authorized the use of federal funds for school lunches in parochial schools even if state regulations prohibited the use of state funds for the purpose. The main breakthrough came with the Elementary and Secondary Education Act of 1965. By the late 1960s, thirty-six of the fifty states had enacted some variation of indirect aid to church-related and private schools.

Direct aid to private and religious institutions of higher education was gaining even more momentum. The National Defense Education Act of 1958 followed the pattern of the GI Bill of 1944 permitting students to use their scholarships at private institutions as well as public. In addition, the National Science Foundation began to make unrestricted grants directly to private colleges and universities, and the Higher Education Facilities Act of 1963 and the Higher Education Act of 1965 began to pour money into private church-related institutions for nonreligious purposes. The Higher Education Amendments of 1972 proposed to make direct federal grants for the first time to all types of colleges and universities, a precedent-setting measure.

While direct aid was expanding at the higher education level the private and parochial school proponents were campaigning for a number of "freedom-of-choice"

[9]*Everson v. Board of Education,* 330 U.S. 1 (1947).

plans, whereby parents would be given tax credits or vouchers out of public tax funds which they could use to defray the expenses of educating their children either at public or private schools of their choice. (Note that white parents in the South could benefit from such a plan by using public funds to send their children to free private schools for whites only.) The argument here was that parents were entitled to public support for the education of their children, and they should be free to decide what kind of school they would send their children to with such support.

Seeing the success of direct aid to private higher institutions from federal and state funds (New York State began to give all private colleges and universities a money grant for each degree granted), the private school forces turned openly to seek direct aid. Pennsylvania led the way in 1968 with a law that would use public funds to pay part of the salaries of private school teachers in certain nonreligious subjects: modern languages, mathematics, physical sciences, and physical education. In 1969 Connecticut and Rhode Island followed suit; seven other states turned down similar proposals; and twenty-two were still debating. These laws for "purchase of services" were immediately tested in the courts.

In June 1971 the Supreme Court declared in two 8 to 1 decisions that the Pennsylvania and Rhode Island laws were unconstitutional, because the state aid given to church-related schools violated the First Amendment's guarantee of the separation of church and state. In a succinct historical statement going back to the Everson case, Chief Justice Warren E. Burger summed up the cumulative criteria developed by the court over many years to test the constitutionality of laws on this subject. "First, the statute must have a secular legislative purpose; second, its principal or primary effect must be one that neither advances nor inhibits religion; finally, the statute must not foster an excessive Government entanglement with religion."[10]

Of particular importance is the warning that inserting direct public support for the teaching process produced a divisive political potential far exceeding that from support of indirect nonideological services like bus transportation or lunches. It looked as though another watershed had been reached which would halt a three- to four-decade trend toward aid for church-related elementary and secondary schools. Whether the court's decision would diminish or increase the political divisiveness remained to be seen. The New York State legislature went right ahead to pass a 1971 law that would provide 33 million dollars a year for "secular educational services for pupils in nonpublic schools." As expected, a federal court promptly declared the law unconstitutional in January 1972, and even more promptly the governor and legislators swore they would find some way to aid the parochial schools with state funds.

Significantly, at the higher education level the trend toward public aid seemed to be gaining. Although in a Maryland case in 1966 the granting of state funds to three sectarian colleges to construct new buildings was declared unconstitutional, a definitive case was undertaken in Connecticut with the intention of testing the constitutionality of the Higher Education Facilities Act of 1963 which granted federal money to private institutions, sectarian as well as nonsectarian, for the construction of

[10] *Lemon v. Kurtzman*, 403 U.S., 602 (June 28, 1971). See also *Early v. DiCenso* 403 U.S., 602 (June 28, 1971).

academic facilities. In a June 1971 concurrent decision the Supreme Court upheld by the narrowest of margins, 5 to 4, the use of federal funds for buildings at four Connecticut colleges. The majority found that so long as the buildings were used for nonreligious purposes (library, science, language, laboratories, and music and fine arts) the grants did not violate the three tests of constitutionality enumerated by Chief Justice Burger. The majority decision hinged on the differences between religious permeation of primary and secondary school teaching in contrast to the freer and more secular intellectual environments of colleges and universities. The minority found no such determining differences. In any case the Court had once again affirmed that the state's interest in aid to education must be to promote a secular purpose, not religious.

Meanwhile, the secularization of the public school program proceeded its tortuous way through the courts of the land. The response to the question, "should religious instruction be given in the public schools?" also elicited three types of response. The first and possibly that of the "silent majority" was simply "no." While it was seldom argued that the public schools should be actively irreligious, a dominant view was that religion was a matter for home, church, and private belief, not for the public schools.

A second response to this question, given principally by many Protestant and Roman Catholic leaders, was "yes, religious instruction should be given in the public schools." Such adherents of this position would like to see their own sectarian religion become the basis of public school instruction, but they knew that this was a practical impossibility so long as several strong churches continued to compete in the United States. In the 1940s the most promising way to insert sectarian religious instruction in the public school program seemed to be the weekday released-time plan. This gave parents the opportunity to have their children receive instruction in their preferred faith by approved instructors for certain hours set aside each week on condition that children leave their regular classes and attend religious classes.

The United States Supreme Court stirred up a great controversy when it decided in the McCollum case in 1948 that such religious classes used the tax-supported public school system to aid religious groups to spread their faiths and thus could not be conducted within the public school buildings of Champaign, Ill.[11] Religious groups were mollified somewhat, however, when the Supreme Court decided, in the Zorach and Gluck case in 1952, that the New York City plan of released-time instruction was permissable because the religious classes were held off the school property.[12]

The campaign for released-time, however, faded in the 1950s in the face of the difficulties of administering the programs and their general inadequacy. Instead, the campaign to inject required religious prayers and Bible reading grew in momentum. This was a third general answer to the question, saying in effect, "yes, there should be more religious instruction in the public schools, but it should be nonsectarian instruction." This position was taken almost entirely by Protestants who argued that the

[11] *McCollum v. Board of Education,* 330 U.S., 203 (1948).
[12] *Zorach and Gluck v. Board of Education,* 343 U.S., 306 (1952).

common basis of so much of American culture was Christian in its origin that these common religious teachings could form the basis of nonsectarian instruction. Most often this took the form of reading the Bible in the schools each day. Under Protestant stimulus, some twelve states passed laws requiring Bible reading and some twenty-five other states permitted the practice in one way or another.

A decade later, however, two decisions pretty well decided the matter. As early as 1951, in the heat of the afterglow of the McCollum case, the New York Board of Regents had urged local boards of education to institute nonsectarian prayers in the public schools. Some time later the Board itself approved such a prayer, but in the Engel case the U.S. Supreme Court found in 1962 that such a prayer was "a religious activity" promulgated by public authorities and wholly inconsistent with the establishment clause of the First Amendment.[13] A year later in a Pennsylvania and Maryland case the Supreme Court similarly found that the compulsory recitation of the Lord's Prayer and reading from the Bible was an unconstitutional invasion of religious liberty by an agency of government.[14] Although these cases seemed to settle the legal question, the hue and cry did not die down. In fact a strong movement got underway to amend the Constitution specifically to permit Bible reading and religious prayers in the public schools. The Becker amendment in 1964 was finally sidetracked, but not before a major public controversy.

From the mid-1960s onward the organized effort to link religion and education more closely turned away from the effort to inject more religious instruction in the public schools and toward public support for sectarian schools. The height of the religious rancor of the 1950s had passed, the ecumenical movement of better feeling among Christians was symbolized by the second Vatican Council called by Pope John XXIII in 1962, the fiscal crises hit parochial schools harder and harder, and the public school establishment was being belabored year after year for its failures in urban and ghetto education.

All in all, the century and a half of faith in public education was being challenged from many sides. It therefore was harder for the educational profession to continue to persuade the public that public schools should be the sole recipients of public funds. The flight of the middle classes from the Northern cities to the suburbs or to private schools paralleled the flight of white segregationists in the South to private schools. Many in both groups were willing if not eager for public funds to follow their children; and the hard-pressed Catholics pressed relentlessly for public relief in their efforts to provide a religious education for their children.

So, in a sense, it was not surprising that the fortunes of secularization declined as public support for parochial education rose, and they rose as religious instruction in the public schools declined. In fact, the two were related. If the public schools were to become increasingly secular, the religious-minded majority could see little harm in providing some public support for parochial education, even if it meant some Protestant taxes going to some Catholic schools. Besides, white Protestants in the South

---

[13] *Engel v. Vitale*, 370 U.S., 421 (1962).

[14] *Abington Township District School v. Schempp*, 374 U.S., 203 (1963).

could see value in white taxes following white students to all-white private schools. For the first time in 150 years it was seriously broached that a series of alternative *free private* school systems might replace the free public school systems that had been so laboriously built up. Some states actually began to flirt with the idea of abolishing their public school systems. And some critics began to suggest that *all* schools ought to be abolished and society "deschooled." But few took such proposals seriously, least of all those who had been denied equal access to schooling.

What *could* prove to be a more serious threat than abolishing schools was a frontal attack upon the idea of compulsory education itself. This was a principle that few modernizing societies had questioned in their efforts to build national unity and achieve equality of educational opportunity. But there had always been an undercurrent of opposition to the idea of compulsory education from those who did not *want* to modernize. Sometimes this stemmed from political or economic conservatism, sometimes from religious. A particularly important case arose in *Wisconsin v. Yoder* in 1971 in which the state of Wisconsin disputed the right of Amish parents to keep their children out of school after they had completed the eighth grade. The Amish defied the compulsory attendance laws on the ground that secondary and higher education are inimical to their traditional religious beliefs and agrarian way of life.

The state of Wisconsin appealed to the Supreme Court on the grounds that such defiance would weaken the right and obligation of states to maintain a stable and democratic social order by ensuring an educated populace. Now the argument took on a new flavor, not simply the right of religious minorities to follow their religious beliefs, but also a radical note that compulsory education is at root a means of repressing the majority as well as the minority and of making them conform to the established order of things as represented in the public schools of the state. The wavering boundaries of freedom and control, of equality and justice were to have yet another test in the precincts of education.

By the 1970s it seemed easier to achieve liberty for private schools to exist and for religious freedom to be protected in the public schools than to achieve equality of educational opportunity for blacks, Indians, Mexican-Americans, Puerto Ricans, and other minorities. In the 1950s the hottest educational problem was freedom; in the 1960s it was equality. Until both could be reasonably solved, the American ideal of modern education could not be fully achieved.

D. ETHNIC DISJUNCTIVITIS IN EDUCATION: A NEAR-FATAL SOCIAL DISEASE

In comparing their educational systems with those of Europe, Americans have commonly pointed with some justifiable pride to their unitary, single-track or ladder character as more democratic than a two-track or dual system. There is, of course, considerable truth to the generalization. European school systems grew up as social class systems: primary schools for the working classes leading to the skilled and unskilled occupations and secondary schools for the middle and upper classes leading to the universities or higher technical schools and the professional and managerial occupations. The two systems were parallel to each other with relatively little chance for crossing over from one to the other. The inbred separation was perpetuated by training teachers for primary schools in institutions separate from those training secondary school teachers. I have called this disjointedness or separatism the disease of disjunctivitis which afflicted all major European systems in the eighteenth and nineteenth centuries and was carried around the world by the Western empires in the nineteenth and twentieth centuries.[15]

In contrast, the American system much more easily leads students from the elementary school to the secondary school and on to the postsecondary and higher educational institutions. No selective examinations are required for a child to pass from the primary school to the secondary school. Primary schools are not reserved for the working classes. Everyone is expected, even required, to go on to a secondary school. Teachers are trained for both types of institutions in many colleges and universities.

There are, of course, financial, regional, and social barriers that produce differentiated drop-out patterns in rural-urban, poor-rich sectors of American society. But, by and large, the system has not been based upon academic barriers that produce occupational or professional dead ends which bar a primary school product from ever attending a university because he was in turn barred from attending a secondary school because his examination at age eleven or twelve did not entitle him to cross over.

While this general analysis has large elements of truth in it, the fact remains that the American system has harbored a far more deadly strain of the disjunctivitis virus than the European systems themselves. American disjunctivitis has been based upon racial or ethnic discrimination rather than upon social class or academic attainment. It has too often been overlooked as simply a minor fault in the American ideal of universal, free education. It must now be recognized as a disease which can have fatal consequences for the very existence of American society if not alleviated and cured. Its consequences extend far beyond the one-tenth of the population that is black, or the smaller racial groups made up of American Indians, or peoples that come from East Asia and the Pacific islands.[16] It infects as well the larger minority groups of Spanish-speakers from Puerto Rico to Mexico. And in the end it is a virus that affects equally the white majority in whose outlooks and attitudes the depredation of the disease of racial segregation continues to fester as denials of the very ideals of equality, freedom, and justice which America has claimed as its contribution to Western and world civilization.

The Black/White Virus

Americans, black and white alike, have made three major efforts in their history to cure racial disjunctivitis and its symptoms of segregation and inequality in education.

[15] R. Freeman Butts, "Teacher Education and Modernization," in George Z. F. Bereday (ed.), *Essays in World Education,* Oxford University Press, New York, 1969, pp. 111-123.

[16] The 1970 Census, in round figures, lists 178,000,000 Americans as white, 22,600,000 as black, 800,000 American Indian, 600,000 Japanese, 435,000 Chinese, 340,000 Filipino and 720,000 "other" (including Korean, Hawaiian, Aleut, Eskimo, Malayan, and Polynesian).

The first, as we have seen, was in the three Revolutionary decades following 1776, but the hopes for universal republican education implied in the new state bills of rights were shortlived. The second major effort to wipe out disjunctive racial education and institute integrative education was in the Reconstruction decade immediately following the Civil War, but this effort was more than cancelled in the periods of "redemption" and repression that followed during the next fifty years. The third effort, beginning slowly in the 1930s, began to pick up speed and impact in the civil rights campaigns and the resistance movements of the 1950s and 1960s.

Reconstruction (1860s and 1870s)   In the Civil War years preceding Appomattox the revolutionary ideal of equality for all men was restated with ever-greater conviction by the President and the Congress of the United States. In his commemorative address at Gettysburgh (1862) and in his official declaration in the Emancipation Proclamation (1863) Abraham Lincoln took his stand. In passing the Thirteenth Amendment abolishing slavery (ratified in 1865) and in establishing the Freedman's Bureau Congress began to make reparation to American Negroes for 250 years of enslavement. Before the end of the Civil War, too, northern humanitarian and religious associations began to send relief teams and teachers to aid the freed slaves in those parts of the South that were being liberated by Union armies. But under the relatively mild and tolerant policies of Andrew Johnson and the presidential reconstruction of 1865 to 1867, the white ruling classes of the southern states moved rapidly to institute new social control over the freed blacks by means that had not been necessary in order to control them under slavery.

Prime means of such social control was the adoption of legal Black Codes imposing unequal restrictions upon freedmen in the form of segregated transportation facilities, hotels, public accommodation, and schools. This policy prompted an angry reaction from Radical Republicans who instituted a decade of congressional reconstruction with the passage of the act of reconstruction in 1867. Under military rule the southern states were required to adopt new constitutions protecting the equal civil rights and voting rights for Negroes. These principles were then embodied in the Fourteenth Amendment (1868) and the Fifteenth Amendment (1870) and spelled out in more detail in the Civil Rights Act of 1875.

It is clear from the history of the passage of the Fourteenth Amendment that it was intended to be a sweeping legislative measure to abolish the racial codes and practices of the states by means of federal jurisdiction over state actions in the civil rights field. In its centralizing intent the Fourteenth Amendment was a modernizing step of the first magnitude—if it had been carried out as intended. It was not until the mid-twentieth century that the Supreme Court made the Fourteenth Amendment into an instrument by which the Bill of Rights of the U.S. Constitution was applied to the states.

Although universal, free, compulsory education in *mixed* public schools (the term then used for integrated schools open to white and black alike) was the goal of most black leaders during Reconstruction, it was achieved in law in only two states of the South—in the 1868 constitutions of Louisiana and South Carolina. Most of the new biracial state governments proclaimed the values of the free public school systems as a sine qua non of equal civil rights for blacks, but remained vague about mixed schools in order to avoid entanglement with the Fourteenth Amendment.

In practice, integrated schools were few and far between. The leap from no education for slaves to full and equal education for freedmen would have been enormous under the best of circumstances and good will. Mixed schools had neither. The hostility of southern whites to any schools for Negroes was widespread and intense, to say nothing of mixed schools. The attitude of northern whites was ambivalent, many believing that separate schools for Negroes were the only possible alternative, some believing they were indeed for the best. And many blacks themselves were just as glad to get *any* education. If the choice had to be between *some* education with inequality or theoretical equality but *no* education, they opted for some education.

In the 1860s, education for freedmen in the South was still largely a phase of the civilizing mission that had poured out of the Western nations on the waves of religious, humanitarian, and philanthropic motives. (See Chapter 14.) Nearly fourscore philanthropic societies, mostly in the North, were organized to send teachers to the South. The American Missionary Society was foremost with over 500 teachers at work by 1864. There were secular associations, too, with headquarters in all the major cities of the North and Midwest. The societies worked in tandem with the Freedmen's Bureau of the federal government, the latter providing buildings and the former providing the teachers for Negro schools, 1,000 in 1867, 3,000 in 1868, and 10,000 in 1869.

Joining with the civilizing mission of the freedmen's movement from the North, a public school movement, largely initiated by black members of state legislatures in the South, began to enroll increasing numbers of children in school in the 1870s and 1880s. The proportion of black children in southern schools moved from 5 percent in 1850 to 10 percent in 1870 to 35 percent in 1890. It then dropped until 1910, when it started up again. Some southern states did much better than others; for example, in 1868 Arkansas had 28 percent of its black children in school, by 1870 it had jumped to 50 percent.

Despite the fact that several hundred thousand freedmen were taught in the freedmen's schools, private and public alike, and though dozens of colleges were founded (some eighty by 1895), the hostility of white southerners toward the civilizing mission never eased. And soon the crusading spirit and subscription funds from the North began to die down. The sustaining funds then began to come from the philanthropic foundations that found an outlet in the education of the freed Negroes of the South.

While segregated schools in practice were being extended to a wider and wider circle of Negroes at the grass roots level, the policy for the next fifty years was being fought out at the federal level. Charles Sumner, the abolitionist Radical Republican who had gained his legal baptism in arguing the Roberts case in Massachusetts, which he lost, went on to the victory of the Fourteenth Amendment. But for a decade thereafter he led a continuing but losing fight to put into federal law a prohibition against segregated schools in the states of the South. His backers in the Sumner phalanx in Congress also tried to incorporate mixed schools in the several federal-aid bills they introduced in the early 1870s, especially those sponsored by the black representative, Legrand Pierce, but a powerful coalition of conservative Republicans and Southern Democrats prevented all such efforts—just as they did for a decade in the 1950s and 1960s. The Sumner phalanx almost succeeded in the long debates over the Civil Rights Act, but it was finally passed in 1875, only after the provisions outlawing disjunctive, segregated schools were dropped. Once again, the political decision was that it would be better to have *some* education for blacks in segregated schools rather than no education at all.

The upshot of a decade of acrimonious debate over the matter of segregated schools was that Congress decided *it* would not intervene in the problem, but would leave the matter to the courts. The courts in turn decided that *they* would not construe the federal judiciary power broadly enough to intervene in the civil rights affairs of the states. And the presidency looked the other way throughout.

"Redemption" (1870s and 1880s)   The failure to achieve a uniform national policy of integrative schools through action of the federal government meant that the Reconstruction promise of modernization of education in the South went unfulfilled for nearly 100 years. White southerners began to regain political control in their states in the early 1870s, a process they liked to refer to as a "redemption" which saved the South from the alien rule of the North. When President Rutherford B. Hayes signalized the end of Reconstruction by removing the last of the federal troops from the South in 1877, it may have seemed like redemption to white southerners, but it seemed like the same old repression to blacks, for it meant a renewed and still harsher inequality for them.

All seventeen of the southern states and Washington, D.C. reinstituted new and more severe Black Codes, regulating association among the races in public places, conveyances, theaters, and hotels and relegating Negroes to an inferior status in all cases, including, of course, segregated schools. So by 1880 the southern states had achieved in practice segregated schools for Negroes (though the constitutions in some states were not changed until the 1890s), while most northern states were deciding in favor of legally integrated schools, either by legislative action or judicial decision. A nation half integrated and half segregated led to an insidious disjunctivitis on a national scale, a disease that was to continue to undermine the social health of both halves.

The Supreme Court had forecast its eventual support for redemption when it declared the Civil Rights Act of 1875 to be unconstitutional on the grounds that the federal government could not protect citizens from discrimination against each other on the basis of race or color and that states could be held in check only with respect to *civil* rights (like voting) and not *social* rights (like frequenting restaurants and hotels). When it came to matters of legal separation, the test was to be equality, not integration.

Efforts to break down the Jim Crow laws in transportation and education were met by decisions of state and federal courts upholding the principle that segregation was legal so long as *equal* facilities for both races were maintained. This doctrine went back at least as far as the Roberts school case in Boston in 1849 when the supreme court of Massachusetts decided that Boston could maintain a segregated school system. The separate but equal doctrine was firmly incorporated in *Plessy v. Ferguson* in 1896 when the United States Supreme Court upheld the right of railroads to segregate passengers according to race so long as equal facilities were provided. The Plessy case, setting a seal of approval upon the power of states to deal with civil rights free from federal intervention, provided the legal precedent for segregated public schools until the middle of the twentieth century. In 1899 the case of *Cumming v. Board of Education* applied the separate but equal doctrine to public schools.

Repression (1890s to 1920s)   As the nineteenth century turned into the twentieth century the American dream of equality turned into the nightmare of repression. The three R's of sixty years of postbellum education for blacks in the South could be summed up as follows:

Reconstruction	integrated and equal schools
Redemption	separate but equal schools
Repression	separate but unequal schools

The disjunctive disease was running its course with ever more devastating effects. Generations of black children were being taught what it meant to be inferior and were learning the lessons perforce. Generations of white children were being taught what it meant to be a superior race and were learning the lessons only too well. In the South as a whole expenditures that had been approximately in the proportion of $3 for whites and $2 for blacks in the 1870s became by 1930, $7 for white and $2 for blacks. No matter what the laws said or what the courts said the practice was clearly not only separate but also unequal.

Despite the efforts of some forward-looking southerners and humanitarian northerners, the Negro schools continued to be a disgrace in a democratic nation, a massive roadblock in the way of modernity. White teachers received little enough in salaries; black teachers received a pittance, averaging $1500 a year in some states. In 1910 no rural Negro school included an eighth grade; no Negro school provided as much as two years of high school. Elementary schools operated about four months a year, taught by teachers with an eighth-grade education. By 1900 compulsory-attendance laws were not to be found in any southern state. Less than half of all the children in the South actually attended schools, and only one out of every seventy who started the first grade ever reached the eighth grade. The modern trends toward universal, free, and compulsory education were being thwarted by the forces of social, political, and educational tradition.

Once it was clear that the Reconstruction ideal of integrated and equal education was unattainable under the political conditions of redemption, and once it was equally clear that even the redemptive ideal of separate but equal education was not going to be honored by the white majorities in the southern states, those concerned with Negro education, both northern and southern, white and black, had to decide what to do under the repressive practices of separate and unequal education. During the fifty years of repression, the predominant response of the promoters of Negro education was to accept the conditions under which Southern white majorities would permit Negro education at all and then to persuade them to support it. This attitude of accommodation or compromise has been termed the "great detour" by Henry Allen Bullock of Texas Southern University in his prize-winning historical study of Negro education.[17]

The chief Negro spokesman for the moderate response was Booker T. Washington who founded Tuskegee Institute on the model of his mentor, General Samuel Chapman Armstrong, the founder of Hampton Institute. Armstrong's humanitarianism, strongly tinged with paternalistic attitudes of racial superiority, led him to argue that the differences between the races meant that there should be a different and special kind of education for Negroes. This special education should be an industrial education to fit Negroes for the kinds of jobs they were to fill in a segregated society—practical courses leading to the skilled trades, and moral education leading to the virtues of hard work, frugality, thrift, and honesty characteristic of the Puritan ethic.

Booker T. Washington echoed these sentiments publicly for many years, becoming the symbol of the moderate and reasonable Negro leader who was willing to eschew the radical Reconstruction doctrine of equality and integration and ready to work to expand educational opportunities for Negroes under the segregated system. This meant a strong emphasis upon useful industrial education as the prime means to economic sufficiency for Negro workers and a stress upon the value of the dignity of labor as the means to proving merit and achievement as the principal road to economic efficiency in a segregated social, economic, and political system.

The merits of this educational response to repression have been vigorously debated in recent years, much to the discredit of Booker T. Washington and his supporters for acceding so wholeheartedly to the castelike system of legal and customary segregation. Whatever else may be said, it is a fact that enormous amounts of northern money poured into the South from a number of new philanthropic foundations. School attendance increased rapidly from around 30 percent of Negro children (age five to nineteen) in 1910 to 60 percent by 1930; literacy (age ten and over) moved up from around 19 percent in 1870 to 84 percent in 1930; and an educated black leadership was being trained in the segregated Negro colleges.

The spearhead of the separate Negro education movement was the Conference for Education in the South, first convened in 1898 at Capon Springs, West Virginia, which led to the policy activities of the Southern Education Conference and the financial activities of the General Education Board.[18] In a matter of two decades the Conference persuaded the South to support universal public education for whites and to provide widespread special education in rural, manual, and industrial trades for

---

[17] Henry Allen Bullock, *A History of Negro Education in the South from 1619 to the Present*, Harvard University Press, Cambridge, Mass., 1967.

[18] Ibid., chap. 4.

Negroes. Not only did Rockefeller money pour into the General Education Board for Negro education in the South, but several other foundations turned special attention to the problem. Prominent among these were the funds built by George Peabody, John F. Slater, Anna T. Jeannes, and Julius Rosenwald.

But some whites and some blacks were never happy about all this emphasis upon vocational education for Negroes. It smacked too much of intellectual superiority toward an inferior race. Two of the most distinguished representatives of both races spoke out instead for an academically rigorous education for blacks. William T. Harris, U.S. Commissioner of Education and noted philosopher, argued strongly for the same kind of intellectual education for the black elite as for the white elite. This meant a college education in the classics, the only really practical education that would give bright Negroes the kind of preparation for leading their fellows out of the precivilized state of slavery into an advancing Western civilization.

Although not necessarily devoted to classical education literally in Greek and Latin, W.E.B. DuBois spoke eloquently for his fellow blacks on the side of an intellectually rigorous higher education which would produce the black leadership capable of breaking the chains of inequality and segregation. Undoubtedly the most distinguished black intellectual of the early twentieth century and himself educated at Fisk, Harvard, and Berlin, DuBois bitterly attacked the accomodating views of Booker T. Washington as a sell-out to the repressive caste system of segregation. To be sure, many blacks needed a technical education for earning a living, but even more important is the need for higher education of the most able blacks, "the talented tenth," to become the professional leaders of their people. "Was there ever a nation on God's fair earth civilized from the bottom upward? Never. It is, ever was, and ever will be from the top downward that culture filters."[19] Above all, the highest priority for higher education is to produce the competent teachers to man the schools for Negroes from top to botton. This is the most important task that American higher education could undertake in achieving justice and equality for black Americans:

> If Hampton, Tuskegee and the hundred other industrial schools prove in the future to be as successful as they deserve to be, then their success in training black artisans for the South, will be due primarily to the white colleges of the North and the black colleges of the South, which trained the teachers who today conduct these institutions.[20]

In the early decades of the twentieth century the dominant tone of compromising moderation reflected by Washington and the philanthropic foundation executives like Barnas Sears of the Peabody Fund began to be challenged by a rising note of protest against the failures of the "great detour" that was supposed to lead from the paths of inequality to the highway of equality by going through the swamps and byways of segregated education. To be sure, more Negro children were in schools,

[19] W. E. Burghardt DuBois, "The Talented Tenth," in *The Negro Problem*, James Pott and Co., New York, 1903, p. 45.

[20] Ibid., p. 60.

literacy was rising, but inequality was not giving way: Negro school terms were shorter than white, school attendance was smaller (largely because of a tenant farm system), less money was spent on Negro schools, teachers salaries were lower, buildings, equipment, and facilities were inferior, industrial education was really artisan training for a decaying traditional agricultural way of life, not the technical training needed for a modern industrial and urban way of life, and almost everywhere Negro institutions were qualitatively second- and third-rate compared with white. The Negro schools were performing much the same function as that of the disjunctive primary schools of Europe, perpetuating a lower class, not to say a caste system for the maintenance of a traditional society.

Restitution (1930s to 1960s)   After a decade of reconstruction, two decades of redemption, and five decades of repression, leaders of the black community and their white allies began in the 1930s the drive for restitution, a return to the original ideals of equality and freedom envisioned by the American revolution and a restoring of the practices of equal and integrative education that had been promised by Reconstruction. Patience, compromise, and accommodation were no longer enough. The promise of equality had been held out for nearly 200 years only to be withdrawn when it came to practice in education. Now, increasing numbers of black Americans and white Americans began to feel that the time for restitution of the promise of equality had come—in voting, in jobs, in housing, in welfare, in public facilities, and in education.

Stirred by hopes for a genuinely new deal for blacks by President and Mrs. Franklin D. Roosevelt the overwhelming majority of black Americans shifted their political loyalties during the 1930s from the party of Lincoln, Sumner, and Reconstruction to the party of Roosevelt and Truman. President Harry S. Truman's Committee on Civil Rights issued in 1947 its sweeping indictment of segregation and discrimination based upon race, color, creed, or national origin. The report entitled *To Secure These Rights* proposed a broad legislative and educational program to eliminate segregation and discrimination from American life. Although Congress did not act on Truman's full legislative program, considerable gains were made in the fields of housing, equal travel facilites, and voting rights. When President Truman ordered the armed forces to be integrated in 1948 a Democratic president had finally placed the office of the President on the side of civil rights and put the segregationists on the defensive for the first time in seventy-five years.

The next agencies of government to act were the state and federal courts, prompted to do so by the legal attack upon the inequalities in segregated education that began in the 1930s under the aegis of the National Association for the Advancement of Colored People. Under pressure from the NAACP, some southern states began to equalize facilities and the salaries of Negro and white teachers in their separate school systems.

Then the NAACP turned to higher education, where it was felt the walls of segregation could more easily be crumbled. The details of this campaign for legal restitution of constitutional civil rights in education cannot be told here, but it began in the mid-1930s and climaxed in the mid-1950s. In successive cases the Supreme

Court ruled that universities in several states had to provide equal facilities for Negroes as for whites under the equal protection guarantees of the Fourteenth Amendment: the case of Gaines at the University of Missouri law school (1938); Sipuel at the University of Oklahoma law school (1947); Sweatt at the University of Texas law school (1950); and McLaurin at the University of Oklahoma graduate school of education (1950). As a result, a small but recognizable stream of black students began to flow into the white universities of the South; perhaps as many as 2,000 by 1954. But these early cases did not settle the constitutionality of the doctrine that public education for blacks could be separate and still be equal.

To this task the NAACP turned its efforts in the early 1950s, launching concerted legal actions to wipe out segregation itself in the public schools of the seventeen southern states and the District of Columbia where segregated school systems were still authorized by law. In December 1952 the Supreme Court was specifically asked to overthrow the separate but equal doctrine of *Plessy v. Ferguson.* On May 17, 1954, the Supreme Court issued its momentous unanimous decision in which the Plessy doctrine was indeed reversed and segregated schools were declared unconstitutional under the Fourteenth Amendment because they denied equal educational opportunity to Negro children. The court held that segregation in separate schools in and of itself produced inequality, even though the physical facilities and tangible factors like salaries might be equal.[21]

Ready compliance was achieved in orderly desegregation in some of the border states and in Washington, D.C., but the problem was by no means fully settled, for even though the Court's decision was a great and historic policy statement, reaffirming the best of the American tradition of devotion to equality of educational opportunity, it met with open defiance in many parts of the South. The attitudes inculcated for 200 years would not be easily or quickly changed.

From the mid-1950s the confrontation over civil rights spilled from the courts to the campuses, the schools, the restaurants, the buses, the streets, and the countryside of the South. Both sides announced "massive resistance." The blacks undertook nonviolent resistance to the repression of segregation. The whites undertook legal resistance and on occasion violent opposition to what they claimed to be the invasion of the rights of the states by the federal government. Hundreds of White Citizens Councils were formed, 101 Southern Congressmen signed a manifesto pledging to reverse the school desegregation decision, and the Ku Klux Klan made yet another appearance.

Martin Luther King emerged as the leader of the nonviolent mass civil rights movement which rose to national consciousness with the Montgomery bus boycott in 1955 and swelled in power and effect until the march on Selma in 1965. Violence broke over the campuses and schools as crowds of white resisters as well as state officials opposed the entrance of black students to the educational institutions. Authurine Lucy was driven away from the University of Alabama in 1956; and black children were turned back from schools in Baltimore, Maryland, Sturgis, Kentucky,

---

[21] *Brown v. Board of Education*, 347 U.S., 486 (May 17, 1954).

Mansfield, Texas, Clinton, Tennessee, and Little Rock, Arkansas, to name only a few that hit the national headlines. Finally, President Eisenhower sent federal troops to Little Rock in 1957 to enforce the Supreme Court's orders in a genuine showdown of federal and state power.

In the early 1960s the tempo of desegregation picked up and so did the violent resistance. In 1961 it was Charlayne Hunter and Hamilton Holmes at the University of Georgia; in 1962 it was James Meredith at the University of Mississippi, with two dead. In 1963 it was rioting and bombing of a Negro church in Birmingham and Medgar Evers assassinated in Jackson, Mississippi. In 1968 it was the assassination of Martin Luther King. From 1963 on, demonstrations erupted in the northern ghettoes, and the riots of the cities in the summers of 1966 and 1967 surpassed all previous violence in the South. The impatience, the frustration, the anger were welling up over the whole country. It looked for a while as if decisions would be made in the streets and the jails rather than in the courts or in Congress.

But the legal confrontation on matters of education continued into the 1960s with slow but general success. In fact by the end of the decade the educative effect of the law in persuading white public opinion to accept desegregation in the South turned out to be remarkably significant. A decade that began with the governors of Alabama, Mississippi, and Georgia "standing in the school house door" to bar the entrance of Negro children ended with the governor of Virginia escorting his own thirteen-year-old daughter to the John F. Kennedy high school in Richmond, opening in September 1970 with 70 percent black children and 30 percent white.

The year 1964 was a turning point in the progress of desegregation, a full ten years after the Supreme Court's major decision. Now the Congress finally got into the act. The progress in Congress seemed to be excruciatingly slow for those civil rights reformers who thought the Supreme Court had settled the matter in 1954, but the Senate filibuster seemed invincible. The first halting step in seventy-five years led eventually to the Civil Rights Act of 1957 which, reminiscent of the Civil Rights Act of 1875, could be passed only after the school desegregation provisions were deleted. But the momentum continued to build up, under pressure from President Lyndon Johnson and from the emergence of new and more aggressive civil rights organizations, the Southern Christian Leadership Conference, the Student Nonviolent Coordinating Committee, and the Congress for Racial Equality as well as a more activist stance by the NAACP and the National Urban League. The momentous March on Washington led by Martin Luther King in 1963 provided an urgent setting for the historic breakthrough which came when the filibuster was finally broken and the Civil Rights Act of 1964 was passed.

This Civil Rights Act now put all three branches of the federal government behind the drive for black equality in education. Title IV authorized the Justice Department to initiate law suits on behalf of individuals to compel compliance with desegregation in the schools and to give assistance to school districts in desegregation; and Title VI put financial teeth into the operation by authorizing the withholding of federal funds from state or local agencies, including school districts, that continued to discriminate. This last provision turned out to be especially significant in the light of the passage of the Elementary and Secondary School Act of 1965 which poured new federal funds into the nation's schools for disadvantaged children, most of whom belong to black or ethnic minorities. And the consensus was building up overwhelmingly on the side of the federal authority against state's rights. The 450 resolutions, legislative acts, and other actions of the southern states to slow down or erode desegregation were slowly but surely nullified by federal courts. Of especial significance was the decision of the Supreme Court in 1964 that the closing of public schools in Prince Edward County, Virginia to avoid integration was unconstitutional as was the payment of tuition grants to white private schools that were set up after the public schools were closed.[22]

In the course of the next half dozen years the pace of desegregation in the South picked up remarkabley despite the foot dragging and guerrilla warfare of delay and opposition. Ten years after the Supreme Court's decision the eleven states of the deep South in 1965 had enrolled only 6 percent of Negro pupils in desegregated classes; in 1971 it was 39 percent and virtually all of the slow-moving school districts in the old South had submitted plans to desegregate. The Supreme Court had become increasingly impatient with the delay. In October 1969, it changed its 1954 command to desegregate schools "with all deliberate speed" to "end segregation at once."[23]

As the decade of the 1960s ended, it became clear that the fact of separation was outlasting the outlawing of legal segregation. The most active scene of the problem shifted from the legal segregation of the South to the de facto segregation of the northern urban centers. As might be expected some courts said the schools themselves cannot do anything about de facto segregation when it results from residential patterns that produce all white or black neighborhoods, but other courts said that if neighborhood schools result in segregation then they must be modified or abandoned. The most common method of modifying was to transport children by bus from one school to another to achieve proportions in all schools that approximated the racial proportion in the school district or community as a whole. In April 1971 the Supreme Court decided that Southern school districts could constitutionally assign pupils to schools in such a way as to achieve racial balance to correct a previously segregated system. This can be done by altering attendance zones and by transporting pupils from one zone to another. The Court summed up its history of a decade and a half by saying that "the constant theme and thrust of every holding from Brown 1 to date is that state-enforced separation of races in public schools is discrimination that violates the equal protection clause [of the Fourteenth Amendment]. The remedy commanded was to dismantle the dual school system."[24] This decision nailed down the lid on the constitutional question: the South had to replace its legal dual system with a legal unitary or integrative system. It did not touch the de facto question in the northern and western states where the percentage of blacks in majority white schools remained at around 27 percent whereas in the South it approached 40 percent.

[22] Griffin v. Prince Edward County School Board, 377 U.S., 218 (1964).

[23] Alexander, et al., v. Holmes County (Mississippi) School Board, (1969).

[24] Swann v. Charlotte-Mecklenburg (North Carolina) Board of Education, 402 U.S. 1, 91 S. Ct., 1267 (1971).

Meanwhile an explosive political issue was in the making as the percentage of blacks in large northern cities who attended majority white schools was actually declining. Thus neighborhood segregation in northern city schools was increasing at the same time that the South was making substantial headway toward desegregation. A curious ambivalance surrounded the problem of school busing. In a nation which every day in 1971 transported nearly 20 million public school children by bus (42 percent of the total), millions of parents wanted state aid to enable their children to be transported by bus so they could acquire religious instruction in Catholic parochial schools, while millions more did not want their children to be transported to public schools outside their neighborhood in order to achieve an integrated schooling that would alleviate the disease of disjunctivitis. Not all minority groups favored busing. Chinese-American parents in San Francisco brought suit to prevent their children from being bused to integrated public schools.

As the 1960s drew to a close a major debate arose not only concerning the constitutionality of using bus transportation to achieve integrative schools, but questions began to be raised about the wisdom of integration itself, this time by blacks. Just as restitution of the right to an equal and integrated education was being won in practice as well as principle, the black power adherents within the civil rights movement not only repudiated nonviolence as the prime social technique of confrontation but began to put integration in a lower order of priority than an insistence upon black independence, black separatism, and black control of black institutions. From 1965 on the black nationalism of Malcolm X, the Black Panthers of Eldridge Cleaver, the black power of Stokely Carmichael and H. Rap Brown echoed and reechoed these demands.

Militant activists thus justified the running of schools in black neighborhoods by the black community itself rather than by the white establishment of the larger school district; the appointment of sympathetic black teachers; the firing of unsympathetic white teachers despite the tenure qualifications stressed by the organized profession; and the special emphasis upon the black experience through black studies which could only be properly taught by black teachers. In September 1970 the Congress of Racial Equality rejected the goal of integration and officially adopted a position of black separatism, approving a public school plan in Mobile, Alabama that would provide for "desegregation without integration."

This separatist movement, termed "withdrawal to resegregation" by Bullock, was criticized and opposed on educational as well as racial grounds. James S. Coleman, the sociologist-author of a massive study that showed that black students did better academically in integrated than in segregated schools, argued that integration was of more assistance to ghetto children than compensatory education.[25] And Kenneth B. Clark, the noted black psychologist whose findings so influenced the Brown decision of the Supreme Court in 1954, made the added argument that segregated schooling was even more harmful to white children than to black. It instills hypocrisy, prejudice, and psychological instability. The goal of America for its bicentennial year in 1976 should be full-scale integration in the North as well as in the South. "By then we could

[25] James S. Coleman, *Equality of Educational Opportunity*, U.S. Government Printing Office, Washington, D.C., 1966.

be well on our way to a more civilized way of living. We could, after 200 years, free sensitive young Americans from the feeling of need to rebel randomly, irrationally and self-destructively."[26]

Dr. Clark's views added a sobering thought too seldom considered by white segregationists who thought they were protecting white children by imposing racial disjunction or by black separatists who thought they were aiding black children by seeking racial disjunction. Both failed to see that the welfare of both blacks and whites hinged upon achieving a genuinely equal and a truly integrative education. The diagnosis of the near-fatal social disease of disjunctivitis was persuasively stated by the National Advisory Commission on Civil Disorders as it sought to discover the causes of the riots that wracked the cities and the very foundations of the United States in the mid-1960s. "Race prejudice has shaped our history decisively; it now threatens to affect our future. White racism is essentially responsible for the explosive mixture which has been accumulating in our cities since the end of World War II."[27] Segregated education has been at the root of these attitudes as much as discrimination in housing and employment. How can racial disjunctivitis be cured? By equal and integrated education as the first priority, and by compensatory education where needed. If America could make restitution quickly enough, its bicentennial might become genuinely a celebration for freedom and equality as well as civilized modernity.

The Red/White Strain

While the graph of black and white disjunctivitis in American education was rising and falling in the century following the Civil War, a variant of the same disease, a red and white strain, was infecting another whole sector of American life. Less immediately and directly in the forefront of the consciousness of most Americans, the educational plight of the American Indian was no less poignant in its impact upon the spirit and outlook of a whole people. Because the Indians were far less numerous than the blacks, were farther removed from the major centers of population, and had blocked so painfully the trails to the open lands of western America, concern for the welfare of the Indian was less prevalent and less pronounced than for the freed blacks. And because their dealings were largely with the federal government itself and their sense of common identity so weakly developed, the Indians' efforts at self-help were either less efficacious or longer-delayed than those of black Americans.

In the years following the end of the Civil War the Plains Indians continued to resist the encroachment of settlers upon the lands west of the Mississippi which they believed were rightfully theirs and which had been assigned to them by treaty after treaty with the federal government. However, by 1890 when effective military resistance closed, most Indians had been pushed back within reservations defined by the federal government and for which the government took formal responsibility.

[26] Testimony before the Senate Select Committee on Equal Educational Opportunity, *The New York Times,* April 21, 1970, p. 31.

[27] *Report of the National Advisory Commission on Civil Disorders,* U.S. Government Printing Office, Washington, D.C., 1968, p. 5.

As the Indians began to make do on the reservations, their plight attracted the attention of religious humanitarians who preached the need for Christianizing and civilizing the Indians, as they had done for black Americans and for Africans and Asians in their own homelands. They even convinced President Ulysses S. Grant to assign the reservations to the several denominations which ran them virtually as their own private religious domains.

In 1887 a new policy was enunciated in the General Allotment Act, or Dawes Act. Viewing the reservations as unwarranted prisons for the Indians, the act's sponsors sought to free the Indians from their constrictions so that they could more quickly drop their tribal ways and become civilized. They argued that the best way to assimilate Indians into American life was to make them into citizen farmers by breaking up the common tribal lands of the reservations and allotting separate plots to individual Indians who could gain full title after twenty-five years. The trouble was that many Indians did not want to become farmers or did not know how to farm. In any case white promoters managed to deprive the Indians of most of their lands. A total of 138 million acres of Indian lands in 1887 had dwindled under the Dawes Act to 48 million in 1932.

Reprehensible as the economic treatment of Indians was, the massive deprivation of the Indians' sense of dignity and self-respect was even worse. Prey, on one side, to the sordid and mercenary dealings of private entrepreneurs as well as by bureaucratic hirelings in the Indian Service, and, enveloped, on the other hand, by the self-righteous and self-serving piety of zealous missionaries, the Indians could take little hope from the education they had been promised. By and large, they were subjected to an education whose main purpose was to assimilate them into American life by inducing them to give up their Indianness and accept the teachers' values of white Christian middle-class Americanism. For some fifty-eight years following the Civil War this was the prime goal of educational effort.

Three principal types of special schools undertook the task. Mission schools run by Catholic and Protestant denominations under contract with the government dominated the 1870s and 1880s. They concentrated on the three R's, some vocational and agricultural education, and of course, religion. They often were taught in the Indians' languages as the best way to lead them to conversion. This subsidy of sectarian education by government was one of the outstanding violations of the doctrine of separation of church and state which was gaining ground in the rest of the country. In 1917 these arrangements for operating Indian mission schools at government expense were ended.

In the 1880s and 1890s government day schools run by the Bureau of Indian Affairs on the reservations began to outdistance the mission schools in number and influence. They were universally taught in English in order to speed up assimilation through the learning of non-Indian knowledge, skills, and values. In addition to the government reservation day schools, a number of boarding schools were established off the reservations with support from the Bureau of Indian Affairs (some eight of them by 1887). Many educators felt that the quickest and most efficient way to transform the Indian child into an American was to remove him from his tribal setting, give him strict, even military, discipline, combine work with study, and saturate him with English language and civilized customs. The most influential of these schools was at Carlisle, Pennsylvania, founded in 1879 by General Richard Henry Pratt who was an aggressive and unrelenting assimilationist, devoted in his way to the transformation of his wards. "Kill the Indian, and save the Man" was the epitome of his educational goal, helping the child to vanish as an Indian and reappear as an American.

In the early decades of the twentieth century the spirit of progressive reform that began to appear in so many aspects of American life found expression in the rise of Pan-Indianism, an effort to find a common identity that transcended tribes and led to a future in which the Indian could find pride in his Indianness and still come to terms with the modernizing Western civilization of America.[28] However wanting in other respects they may have been, the boarding schools, especially at Carlisle and Hampton, had made it possible for a cadre of young Indians to receive an education in English that enabled them to communicate with one another and to exert leadership in the kind of intellectual association and national organization that eventually could promote fundamental change in the Indian condition. An important spearhead in reform ideology was the Society of American Indians, founded in 1911, whose middle-class and professional leadership, pride of race, and commitment to democratic political methods paralleled those of the National Association for the Advancement of Colored People.

In the 1920s the climate of the Indian environment began to change. In 1924 the Snyder Act conferred citizenship upon all Indians, and attention was drawn to the shortcomings in the administration of Indian Affairs, including of course Indian education. Then reform became official policy in the New Deal, symbolized by the Indian Reorganization Act of 1934 (Wheeler-Howard Act) administered by John Collier as Commissioner of Indian Affairs. The allotment policy of the Dawes Act was ended, self-government by tribes was promoted, revival of Indian culture was encouraged, and educational facilities improved. Assimilation was still the ultimate goal, but it was now to be accomplished by the retaining of such elements of their traditional culture as the Indians themselves wished to retain.

Once again, however, a major setback occurred under the Eisenhower administration when a resolution of Congress in 1953 declared its intention to terminate federal relations with Indians as soon as possible in order to speed assimilation. This would mean that tribal lands would no longer be tax-exempt and the tribes themselves would be dismantled under allotment plans. Despite the reversal and dismay it caused, this policy was never carried through, and the 1960s saw a rapid upswing in attention to Indian affairs. The Kennedy administration reaffirmed the Collier policies under Phileo Nash in 1961, and the American Indian Chicago Conference of ninety tribal groups declared that education was the key to the salvation of the Indian people. In July 1970 President Nixon formally renounced the 1953 policy of forced termination and reaffirmed the integrity and right to existence of all Indian tribes and Alaskan

---

[28] For an original analysis, see Hazel W. Hertzberg, *The Search for an American Indian Identity; Modern Pan-Indian Movements,* Syracuse University Press, Syracuse, N. Y., 1971.

native governments. Not only must the relationship between the government and the Indian communities not be abridged without the consent of the Indians, but the communities must be given control over the federally funded programs of education, including membership on school boards.

The decade of the 1960s was a period of extraordinarily rapid growth in Indian education. The National Study of American Indian Education conducted by Robert J. Havighurst of the University of Chicago for the Office of Education detailed the growth as well as some of the problems. Indian children in 1970 were predominantly in public schools (63 percent) with 31 percent in government schools conducted by the Bureau of Indian Affairs (half in boarding schools and half in day schools), and 6 percent in mission schools. The report recommended that the boarding schools be eliminated for elementary school age children, but they probably would still be needed for such isolated communities as the Navaho and Alaskans. The most striking expansions in the decade of the 1960s were the growth of the Indian population in urban centers (30 percent in 1960; 38 percent in 1970) and the proportion of young people going through secondary school and on to college: 55 percent of the age group finished high school; 20 percent entered college and another 10 percent entered other types of post-high-school institutions; and 5 percent graduated from four-year colleges.[29] These are relatively high proportions of attendance in comparison with other American low income groups.

But the attendance numbers, of course, do not solve the problems of education of Indians. If anything, they simply bring them into the mainstream of American educational problems: rural-oriented youth transferred to an urban environment that is more alien and hostile than the reservation and more contemptuous of poor vocational skills; a curriculum that pays virtually no attention to the Indian heritage; teachers who have little training, understanding, or appreciation of the special need for respect and dignity of a people who must be able to move skillfully between the traditional culture of tribal folk society and a modern urban civilization and be able to find values in both.

The La Raza/Anglo Hypertension

A third minority group whose treatment by the dominant American majority produced a debilitating educational disjunctivitis was La Raza. Standing in numbers in 1970 between the 23 million black Americans and the 800,000 American Indians were the 10 million Americans with Spanish surnames. Only the Indians have been on the North American continent longer than the Spanish-speaking peoples, but the latter's plight in educational discrimination was the latest to come to national consciousness in the United States. Despite the presence of Spanish-speaking peoples for more than 400 years within what is now the continental United States, their confrontation with the dominant, English-speaking Americans is only a little more than 150 years old, and for most of that time it was largely a regional matter of the American Southwest

---

[29] The National Study of American Indian Education, Robert J. Havighurst, Director, *The Education of Indian Children and Youth, Summary Report and Recommendations,* Center for Urban and Regional Affairs, University of Minnesota, Minneapolis, December 1970, pp. 43-46.

(principally the present states of Texas, New Mexico, Arizona, Colorado, and California).

Although La Raza was in the process of formation from the time of arrival of the Spaniards in Mexico in the 1530s it was not until the early 1800s that they came face to face with the English-speaking Anglo-Americans. *La Raza* (literally, "the race", but meaning "my people") is a term that points to the mingling of traditions that arose from the encounter of Spanish and Amerindian peoples in the New World, a heritage in which the Spanish language and culture play a prominent role. It embraces the descendants of Spaniards who did not mix ethnically with Indians, of Indians who did not mix with Spaniards, and of those who did. It includes Mexican-Americans, Puerto Ricans, Cubans, and other Latin Americans who have settled in the United States. The term now carries not only an ethnic and cultural connotation, but also a sense of belonging and pride in a common tradition and destiny as distinguished from Anglos, native English speakers.

From the time when La Raza's civilization was carried above the Rio Grande in the late sixteenth century, New Mexico was the heartland of the interior provinces of Mexico under Spanish rule for over a century. Then La Raza pushed into Texas after 1700 and to California after 1769. In each case the educational enterprise was conducted by Spanish missionaries. Following the Louisiana Purchase of 1803, Anglos from the United States began to push into the Southwest, at first encouraged by the newly independent Mexican government in the early 1820s, but the welcome was short-lived. As a result of Texan independence from Mexico in 1836 and the war between Mexico and the United States that ended in 1848, the Spanish-speaking Mexicans above the Rio Grande became Mexican-Americans, a conquered people in their former homeland. The Treaty of Guadalupe Hidalgo of 1848 guaranteed the rights of American citizenship to those Mexicans who chose to remain north of the Rio Grande, but the promise of equal rights went unfulfilled over a century in which Mexican-Americans were deprived of equal access to political, economic, social, and educational opportunity.

Sorry as the educational performance was, it had less to do with legal discrimination and segregation in the schools than was the case with blacks in the South. More important was the discrimination, both intended and unconscious, against the Spanish language and the cultural traditions of La Raza as practiced by the Anglo-oriented educators who imposed their culture upon the Mexican-Americans of the Southwest from the mid-nineteenth century on. One of the principal agencies of the process was the public school system transferred from the East and Midwest to replace the Catholic mission schools which had been the principal educational arms of the region under Spanish and Mexican rule. Lacking the legal compulsion that enforced segregated schools for blacks in the South and lacking the legal "protection" that provided special separate schools for Indians, the educational discrimination against Mexican-Americans was largely one of custom and attitude. This ranges from blatant imposition of Anglo values to subtle denigration of the Spanish-Indian heritage.

After 1850, the Anglo-Americans who flooded into the Southwest came from a rapidly modernizing America to find a traditional civilization little changed from the sixteenth century. As with colonizers in other parts of the world, the Anglos brought a restless and exploitative temper, faith in the superiority of their own institutions, and contempt for the backward peoples they found. Some were eager to take advantage of the backwardness and proceeded to deprive the Mexican-Americans of enormous areas of land. Others, feeling more kindly, brought their own institutions to help reform and assimilate the culturally deprived. The Roman Catholic Church sent such reformers as Archbishop Jean Baptiste Lamy to Santa Fe to build missions and schools. Secular reformers established the public school systems in the territories and in the new states when they were admitted to the Union.

Between 1910 and 1940 La Raza was greatly enlarged as hundreds of thousands migrated from Mexico to search for jobs and to escape the unrest of the Mexican revolution. Most immigrants were uneducated, unskilled, and unwelcome to the already established Mexican-Americans. Many pushed on to work on the farms, factories, and railroads of the upper Midwest and to take the place of laborers from China and Japan whose migration to the Far West had been cut off by the Chinese Exclusion Act of 1882 and the Japanese agreements of 1907.

The general story of education for Mexican-Americans was all too familiar. The curriculum of the public schools was basically the same as that for the English-speaking peoples of Anglo United States. It was not only not adapted to the needs of the Spanish-speaking children, it deliberately sought to "kill the Spaniard and save the American." All children had to be taught in English and to speak only English in school with punishment meted out for those who used their mother tongue. Naturally, teachers thought Mexican-American children were inferior intellectually, and naturally they did not do well on I.Q. tests administered in English and reflecting the Anglo, middle-class, professional orientation of the test writers. Naturally, too, the children sensed and resented the disparagement of their culture and of them as individuals.

Despite the inadequacies and failures, however, the public school system did eventually open up opportunity for a leadership to emerge, determined to achieve for La Raza the full promise of American citizenship: the civil and political rights being demanded by blacks and Indians, greater educational opportunity, a better economic deal, and above all a greater respect, pride, and dignity to be accorded to their heritage, history, and culture as a people. From 1940 onward the reawakening accelerated, fed not only by a new aggressiveness in the Southwest, but by an influx from Puerto Rico and Cuba; 800,000 Puerto Ricans moved to the mainland in a matter of three decades. By the late 1960s more than 80 percent of all persons with Spanish surnames were living in cities, and 70 percent lived in three states, New York, Texas, and California. The problems of La Raza were no longer regional but national. The urbanization that characterized all of America and that was exacerbating the plight of all minority city dwellers now encompassed La Raza—inferior education, segregated housing patterns, a constricted ghetto life, low-paying jobs or no jobs, and cultural deprivation, all complicated, even more than for blacks, by the fact that their mother tongue was a foreign language.

While the legal battles over disjunctive education for La Raza have not been so spectacular as in the case of the Black Codes, nevertheless there has been a certain parallel. Beginning about the same time as the black desegregation campaigns, court cases were brought in the 1940s by Mexican-American parents who claimed that even if there was no legal segregation there was de facto segregation by school board regulation, usage, and custom.[30] The courts found for the parents, but, as was so often the case elsewhere, practice was harder to change than law. As late as 1970 a federal judge ruled that Corpus Christi, Texas was actually operating a dual school system for Mexican-Americans and ordered the board of education to submit a plan for desegregation as provided in the Brown case.[31]

Thus the educational rights of America's two largest identifiable minorities were linked in a common cause, the cause of stamping out a disjunctivitis that produced major imbalances in school attendance, school achievement, and school satisfaction. When the average years of schooling in California was twelve for Anglos, ten for blacks, and eight for La Raza, the disease was still rampant. The imbalances in attendance, teaching staffs, school board memberships, and administrative staffs were documented for La Raza by the U.S. Commission on Civil Rights as well as for blacks.[32] What is far more difficult to document in human terms in the history of education is the decivilization of La Raza and the attempts, sometimes successful and sometimes disastrous, to reeducate a people nourished in a traditional civilization but determined to live in a modern one. This is the history of education that awaits to be written. It is a story that has special particularities for the minorities of the United States but it is a basic part of the American phenomenon of educational modernization.

It is symbolic that just as the Brown case in 1954 which set off massive integration of Southern schools was brought on behalf of black children so was a major case in 1971 brought on behalf of Mexican-American children in the schools of east Los Angeles. Both appealed to the equal protection of the laws as guaranteed by the Fourteenth Amendment. Both were aimed at curing different forms of disjunctivitis. On August 30, 1971 the California State Supreme Court decided in *Serrano v. Priest* that the state's system of financing public schools through local property taxes invidiously discriminated against poor children because it made the equality of education provided in local schools dependent upon the wealth of the local school district in which they happened to live. The court said: "by our decision today we further the cherished idea of American education that in a democratic society free public schools shall make available to all children equally the abundant gifts of learning. This was the credo of Horace Mann which has been the heritage and the inspiration of this country."[33]

---

[30] See, for example, *Mendez v. Westminster School District of Orange County (California)* 64 F. Supp. 544, affirmed 161 F. 2nd 744 (9th Cir. 1947); *Delgado v. The Bastrop Independent School District,* Civ. No. 388 (D.C. W.D. Texas 1948).

[31] *Cisneros v. Corpus Christi Independent School District,* Civ. No. 68-C-95 (D.C. S.D. Tex. Corpus Christi Div. 1970.)

[32] U. S. Commission on Civil Rights, *Mexican American Education Survey,* report 1: "Ethnic Isolation of Mexican Americans in the Public Schools of the Southwest," Government Printing Office, Washington, D.C., April 1971.

[33] *John Serrano, Jr., et al. v. Ivy Baker Priest, 96 Cal., RPTR., 601.* (August 30, 1971).

This case quickly had widespread repercussions, first in Minnesota and Texas and other states on federal constitutional grounds, and then in New Jersey on grounds that the local property tax system violated the *state* constitution. If the principle is upheld in the Supreme Court, a national reassessment of the entire financing of American public education would be underway, a process that would have fundamental reverberations not only in racial and ethnic relations but in public financing, taxpaying, housing, welfare, and social patterns in general.

Fully as momentous for its consequences, socially and politically as well as educationally, was a ruling in January 1972 by the federal discrict court in Richmond, Virginia, that the urban Richmond school district (about 70 percent black) be merged with two surrounding suburban school districts (about 90 percent white) in order to form one metropolitan school district in which the schools would be roughly racially balanced according to the combined district's proportions of two-thirds white and one-third black.[34] If this approach to achieving integration and educational equality under the Fourteenth Amendment is upheld by the Supreme Court, it could mean that state authorities in the northern states could not draw school district lines according to residential patterns, thus protecting the white flight to the suburbs and producing racially imbalanced schools in both urban and suburban regions. In other words, the de facto segregation of schools that follow segregated residential patterns in the northern metropolitan areas is just as unconstitutional as the de jure segregation imposed by the dual systems of schools established by law in the southern states. Similar cases were being taken in many metropolitan centers of the North.

These two major developments, along with the volatile busing issue, promised to make 1972 a critical year on the road to equality of educational opportunity, possibly surpassing even that of the 1954 segregation decision. In less than twenty years the South's disjunctive school system was largely dismantled. But in the meantime the large-scale migrations of blacks from the South to the northern cities and of whites from the cities to the suburbs shifted the arena to the metropolitan regions of the entire country. The explosive mixture of racial tensions, financial pressures of taxation, and political and legal issues found expression in a case brought in Denver to determine whether the busing of children in cities of the North is a constitutional means of overcoming de facto segregation as well as de jure segregation.[35] Symbolically, the case was brought on behalf of both black and Mexican-American parents who asked the courts to remedy the overwhelming concentration of minority children in inner city schools.

No matter what the legal conclusion of all this ferment may turn out to be, the issues revealed not only a determined drive to realize the historic goals of American equality by curing the educational system of its disjunctive virus but also a deep malaise of fear, racial antipathy, and proneness to violence and strife that might stand in the way of such cure. On one hand, a French observer found great hope that Americans would consummate the social progress and cultural innovation through

[34] *Bradley v. School Board of the City of Richmond,* Civ. No. 3353 (E.D. Va., January 5, 1972).
[35] *Keyes v. School District No. 1, Denver,* No. 70-507, October 1971, Term Sup. Ct.

which they have set the pattern for the modern societies of the world.[36] On the other hand, an opinion poll in 1971 showed that almost half of Americans themselves were afraid that unrest and violence would lead to a real breakdown in the unity, political stability, and law and order in the country.[37] Which view would be realized in the 1970s would depend in no small degree upon the resolution of the educational tensions that were coming to a head in that decade.

E. THE IDEOLOGY OF MODERNITY IN AMERICAN EDUCATION

In view of the stormy issues surrounding the road to modernity in the control of education, it should go without saying that the modernization of pedagogy in the United States was not a smooth or continuous process. It would take volumes to chart the course through the arguments, the debates, the speeches, the books, the plans, the revisions, the experiments, and the untold effort that went into a century of program planning, proposing, resisting, or just plain drift. The principal modernist challengers of tradition sometimes appealed to the methods and assumptions of empirical science and sometimes to the methods and outlooks of the newer policy-oriented social sciences, but the major signposts on the road to modernity were clear. The direction of the century was unmistakably toward the secular and scientific, the practical and the professional, the differentiation and specialization of knowledge, and empirical research on human behavior.

That distinctively American contribution to the modernizing of intellectual outlooks in the later nineteenth century, the philosophy of pragmatism, marshaled the broad principles of evolutionary theory to attack the hold of the genteel tradition on American education. From the restless and expansive temper of American life and from the example of Darwinism and the new sciences, Charles Peirce, William James, and John Dewey formulated a pragmatic philosophy that required knowledge to be validated by the tested experience of human beings rather than by appeal to a remote authority of religion or traditional philosophy. As the nineteenth turned into the twentieth century the experimentalism of John Dewey and his followers made it even more difficult for advocates of a closed intellectual system and conventional body of truth to hold their own.

For more than fifty years Dewey was the chief apostle of modernity in American philosophy as well as in American education, heralding a revolt against the prevailing religious, disciplinary, and humanistic tradition which ruled elementary and secondary education throughout most of the Western world. He argued that schools should strive to emphasize moral goals based upon democratic civic and social experience, vocational and practical usefulness, and individual development in the light of the rapid modernizing changes that were taking place in Western civilization.

[36] Jean-Francois Revel, *The New American Revolution Has Begun*, Doubleday, New York, 1971.
[37] Albert H. Cantril and Charles W. Roll, Jr., *Hopes and Fears in the American People*, Universe Books, New York, 1971.

According to Dewey, education has two sides, the psychological and the social, neither of which should be subordinated or neglected. On the one hand, since the basis for learning is the psychological nature of the individual child, the teacher must utilize the activity springing from a child's nature and make it coincide with his own efforts. On the other hand, teachers must be familiar with the basic characteristics of modern civilization in order to interpret properly the child's activities and help transfer them into socially desirable channels. Education proceeds by the participation of the individual in interactive relationships with his fellow human beings. Dewey attacked both the older achievement orientation of formal indoctrination and the newer type of achievement education, which attempted to train the individual slavishly for a specific adult occupation. He proposed instead that the child be put in complete possession of all his powers, capacities, skills, and judgment. If there is any key to Dewey's pedagogical theory it is the need for a balanced tension between achievement-oriented education and learner-oriented education. Education is an active process whereby immediate experience is continously redirected toward more significant social behavior.

Dewey considered the school as primarily a social institution; it is that organized form of social life in which are concentrated all the factors that will most effectively and rapidly bring the child to share in the accumulated knowledge and skills of civilization. Modifications of method and curriculum should consist in efforts to meet the peculiar needs of modern society, marked by the application of science to the means of production and distribution, by industrial urbanization, and by rapid means of communication. Habits of discipline and responsibility that were earlier formed in an agrarian and closed family system of economy must now rely upon the school to help mold the habits and character of urban children.

Thus Dewey believed the school to be a fundamental formative agency in social progress toward the attainment of a democratic civilization. In order to achieve social as well as political democracy a new social education is needed. This social education should endeavor to make civic and vocational interests the means of promoting a more satisfying common life, but the subject matter and method of the school should also be adapted to child needs. Dewey argued that introducing the child too abruptly to special studies that have little relevance for his own experience is a pedagogical mistake.

As the twentieth century progressed, Dewey's general outlook not only drew upon the philosophy of pragmatism and science but attempted to devise a theory of education that would adequately assimilate evidence and findings from the new social science disciplines. Of prime significance here were the concepts of culture and society and their roles in the development of individuals. To understand individual behavior and to formulate desirable goals for education, one must study the vital connection between the school and the civilization in which it functions. Such study requires educators to turn to anthropology, sociology, political science, economics, and history as social science aids in building the foundations of American education. Dewey found the goals of the American form of Western civilization and of its schools to reside in the ideals of democracy and the intellectual ideals of free and disciplined intelligence.

Meanwhile, a second kind of modernizing influence pursued its persistent course in the name of empirical science. It, too, gave support to both sides of a dyad that combined achievement-oriented pedagogy with learner-oriented pedagogy. Experimental psychology, as it developed in the United States in the nineteenth century, gave close attention to the empirical bases of learning, recognizing that sensory, motor, and physiological processes greatly affect mental development. Influenced by the laboratory methods of European researchers, by the theory of evolution, and by the actual experimentation of such innovators as G. Stanley Hall, Joseph Jastrow, James McKeen Cattell, and Edward Lee Thorndike, learner-oriented pedagogy received substantial boosts from the empirical psychologist as well as from the pragmatic philosopher.

Believing fully in the scientific method, a growing company of behavioral psychologists assumed that human nature could be investigated and analyzed by empirical methods with as much precision as the physical universe and physical phenomena. Discarding dualistic conceptions of human nature, they described man as a complicated machine whose behavior could be predicted and even controlled with a high degree of accuracy and certainty. Man was therefore looked upon as an inherent part of nature, although somewhat more complex in his structure than the animals. Even so, it was assumed that much could be learned about man from the scientific study of animals. Most American psychologists in the first half of the twentieth century were brought up in the atmosphere of a scientific behavioralism.

The experimental methods that had been envisioned in the later nineteenth century developed with enormous rapidity in various fields of psychology, learning, instincts, individual differences, and emotions. E. L. Thorndike attacked the introspective and faculty psychology of an earlier day. At Teachers College, Columbia University, he virtually created educational psychology as he attempted to apply the methods of the exact sciences to educational problems. With the publication of his three monumental volumes, entitled *Educational Psychology,* in 1913, attention in the United States began to turn more and more to an objective psychology for the answers to problems of original nature, learning, and individual differences.

Under the impact of Thorndike's connectionist psychology, mental discipline received a major setback, especially in elementary and secondary school practices of the United States. Thorndike argued that transfer of training occurs only when the content or the method of a school subject is similar to the use to which it is to be put. In other words, if students are to be educated for specific ends, they should study those subjects which contribute directly to those ends. This theory gave great support to the new scientific and social studies for which there was a growing demand throughout the country. Hence, specialized studies and differentiated courses received psychological justification. One more bolt was firmly fastened in the accelerating engine of modernization.

An eminently practical way in which the scientific method was applied to the study of pedagogy was the measurement movement which boomed across the educational frontiers in the 1920s and 1930s. The modernist faith in science was simply stated: Whatever exists at all exists in some amount; anything that exists in amount can be measured; and measurement in education is, in general, the same as measurement in the physical sciences. Objective testing in the form of achievement tests in most school subjects was perhaps the most widespread feature of scientific measurement procedures in the 1920s and thereafter.

Much reliance was also put upon aptitude testing and the measurement of the intelligence quotient (I.Q.). Lewis Terman developed and refined the Binet tests, making them suitable for American use in the Stanford Revision; Thorndike and others helped to develop group tests of intelligence for the army in the First World War; and vast use was made of group tests of all kinds in the Second World War. There was much discussion concerning the permanence of the I.Q. and the extent to which it was determined by heredity or molded by environment. It was assumed by many psychologists that intelligence tests measured inherited capacity and not achievement, but others pointed out that most tests relied upon some kind of acquired knowledge as evidence of original ability and that favored cultural groups (like the middle and professional classes from which the testers themselves came) had a head start over less-favored groups. The battles between the advocates of heredity and of environment, between nature and nurture, became still more severe when applied to the question of comparative intelligence of the races, a subject that would not lie still.[38]

Whatever the technical merits of a particular controversy the general trend of psychological, sociological, and anthropological scholarship of a hundred years was to discount racial characteristics as determiners of intellect or educability and to emphasize the formative influence of social, cultural, and educational environments upon groups and upon individuals. Differences in ability ranged more widely *within* human groups than *between* groups. Modernity lay with equalitarianism of inherited ability among major racial and ethnic groups, with differences resulting from diversity of cultural development. An integrative society is reckoned to be more modern than a disjunctive society that seeks to perpetuate assumed innate inequalities and inferiorities.

The long-term evidence of behavioral psychologists and empirical testers was on the side of modernity rather than tradition. With one hand, they produced the achievement tests that fortified with massive support achievement-oriented pedagogical practices in the schools. With the other hand, they produced aptitude tests, intelligence tests, emotional adjustment tests, and clinical tests that enable educators to identify particular learners who needed the special attention of teachers, guidance counsellors, and clinicians. None but a modern system of education has adumbrated such a corps of scientific diagnosticians and therapists as part of the basic educational enterprise. Traditionalists often found these developments an unnecessary, if not an appalling, invasion of intellectual and emotional privacy.

The aggressive drive to modernity in American education represented by the progressives, the pragmatists, the experimentalists, and the behaviorists was met with

---

[38] See, for example, Arthur R. Jensen, "How Much Can We Boost IQ and Scholastic Achievement?" *Harvard Educational Review*, vol. 39, no. 1, pp. 1-123; Winter 1969; seven psychologists replied in the *Harvard Educational Review*, Spring 1969, and Jensen replied to them in the Summer 1969 issue.

vigorous resistance from many quarters. The most vociferous voices in favor of traditional educational values came from religious leaders of both Protestant and Catholic persuasion and from educators who reaffirmed humanistic and intellectualistic positions. In general they called for education to cultivate the central significance of spiritual values in human personality. New humanists of a variety of persuasions reflected a defensive reaction against the progress of modern civilization and reasserted the role of the great intellectual, literary, and religious heritage of the West as the prime essential in educational content and method. Science, technology, and the social sciences were viewed as diluters of the traditional formative values to be served by the humanities in the educational program.

Gaining wide public notice in the 1940s and 1950s, allies of literary humanism, sometimes known as intellectualists, agreed in many respects with the humanists but had a less exclusive interest in the literary humanities. Believing that religious doctrine could not be the synthesizing agency for American education, the intellectualists turned to the traditional academic disciplines for their standards of educational value. Identifying education with cultivation of the intellect they tended to disparage the physical or emotional aspects of human activity as proper objects of education. Knowledge in its highest intellectual forms (philosophy, religion, and the humanities) should serve to give order to the lower forms of empirical knowledge of practical affairs.

These fundamental assumptions led intellectualists to decry the preoccupation of American education with scientific, technical, vocational, and professional studies, with practical experience, and with the freedom and interests of students as means to effective learning. They outlined what they believed to be the permanent studies that all youth should achieve if they aspire to be educated human beings. Primary place in liberal education should be given to the reading of great books, the study of formal grammar, rhetoric, logic, and mathematics. When a student has acquired competence in such basic academic disciplines, they argued, he will be fully equipped to solve the problems of practical conduct and experience. The distinctive function of school and college is, however, intellectual in nature and not practical or moral. An educational institution should be a sanctuary of scholarship, not a public service station, nor a training ground for the professions, nor an assembly line for the governmental or industrial bureaucracies.[39] The modern world is too much with us.

But it proved to be inescapable.

F. THE MODERNIZATION OF EDUCATIONAL PROGRAMS

Of the several modernizing trends that have characterized American education since the 1860s the elementary schools reflected the learner-oriented approach more than did secondary or higher education. This does not mean that all elementary schools became child-centered nor that there was a unilinear movement in that direction, but

[39] See Robert Paul Wolff, *The Ideal of the University*, Beacon Press, Boston, 1969.

the overall trend in the course of the century was to give greater attention to the variety of talents and capacities of the children who trooped in increasing numbers to the elementary schools. In the object teaching of the Pestalozzian reformers and the Froebel kindergarten of the 1870s, the child study movement of Francis Parker and G. Stanley Hall of the 1880s, the humanitarian reformers and progressives of the 1890s, the project method of the 1910s, the child-centered progressives of the 1920s, the activity programs and the experience curriculum of the 1930s and 1940s, the "discovery method" of the 1950s, and the informal or "open" education of the new naturalists in the 1960s. the themes echoed and reechoed: The schools stress too much conformity, rote memory, false competition, irrelevant subject matter, and authoritarian expectations of rigid achievement, all of which kill the child's spontaneity, curiosity, creativity, and individuality. The cure is to start with the interests, concerns, needs, and experiences of the learner and make the school more joyful, exciting, alive, interesting, creative, relevant, practical, and individualized.

The predominant trends to modernity in American secondary schools came in the form of practical and scientific studies, differentiated courses within the comprehensive high school, and an achievement orientation related to social mobility, direct vocational training, and preparation for college. The basic fact in the secondary-school curriculum was the rapid proliferation in the number of studies. No European country experienced anything like it. At the beginning of the nineteenth century ten to twelve titles would have covered most of the subjects taught in the academies. By the end of the century a hundred titles would not have done the same for the public high schools.

All sorts of nonacademic studies entered the secondary-school curriculum, originally as noncollege preparatory subjects. Manual training, industrial arts, home economics, commercial studies, and agriculture received their prime impetus from vocational and practical motives, but the pressure rose to admit them to the charmed college-preparatory circle. Naturally, the college educators began to worry about this unrestrained expansion, or what they called dilution, of the secondary-school curriculum. They saw utter confusion developing in the public high schools, which apparently were bound to teach anything to anyone. When these ill-prepared high school graduates came knocking at the doors of the colleges for admission, what were they to do? It was one thing when the colleges could count upon most secondary-school graduates having studied the classics and mathematics; it was disturbing when they began to study such modern subjects as science, English, and the social studies; but when they began to offer manual training, home economics, or art and music, the colleges felt that the line had to be drawn.

The high schools for their part were interested in offering wide and flexible courses of study to their students who represented an ever higher proportion of youth of high school age. The colleges, on their side, were more interested in having students come to them with certifiable achievement in the subject matter that they authorized. The best way to remedy the situation from the point of view of the colleges was to bring order into the high schools by standardizing the high school curriculum for those who wished to go to college. This they set out to do in the way they knew best, by working through college entrance requirements. They tried accrediting systems through regional associations and through committees of the National Education Association dominated by college educators.

In so far as the standardization movement gave some order to the college entrance chaos that had been precipitated by the vast expansion of secondary education, it was a modernizing influence, but in its effort to limit college entrance studies to the accepted academic studies, it exerted a traditionalizing brake on curriculum development. However, the practical, differentiated, and learner-oriented trends were not to be denied. No other nation had ever tried to educate 80 to 90 percent of its secondary school age population, let along try to do it in a comprehensive secondary school. It was literally something new under the sun.

It meant that students with a much wider range of social and economic background as well as of scholastic aptitude were going to the public high schools than ever before. It meant that also the aim of college preparation was no longer the dominant purpose of the high school. Whereas about 75 percent of the high school graduates had gone on to college in 1900, only about 25 percent of high school graduates were going to college in 1950. With these changes, it became clear that the traditional elite and relatively exclusive character of secondary education must give way to a kind of secondary education that would meet the needs of the vast majority of students it dealt with. As early as 1917, 80 percent of the public high schools in the North Central Region offered courses in manual training and home economics; more than 70 percent had typing and music; and over 40 percent, art. And the Smith-Hughes Act granting federal funds for vocational education was just being passed in that year.

So, for the next fifty years subjects and courses expanded enormously. The high schools were flooded with specialized courses in English, social studies, science, mathematics, commercial and vocational studies, home economics, art, music, foreign languages, and physical education, to say nothing of driver education, auto mechanics, or radio electronics. This multiplication of subjects meant that the elective system became common practice, and the subject curriculum of separate, isolated, and discrete subjects carried the day. The University of Chicago recognized the trend as early as 1911 by accepting for entrance three units in English, seven units from the other academic fields (mathematics, science, foreign language, and history), and as many as five units in any other high school subject.

Meanwhile, modernity in American higher education was symbolized by the rise of the comprehensive university to overshadow the undergraduate liberal arts college. In the large university's professional, technical, and graduate schools was most clearly to be seen the growing predominance of the secular and scientific, the practical and professional, the differentiated and specialized, and research-mindedness.

In the middle of the nineteenth century the four-year college had been the prevailing institution of higher education in the United States. However, by the middle of the twentieth century it had lost its unique position, as the junior college nibbled away at its first two years and as professional and technical education started to bite into its second two years. The professionalization of the liberal arts colleges was another symbol of the modernization trends. The undergraduate colleges themselves reflected the enormous growth of the sciences in relation to the humanities, the proliferation of identifiable fields of study in which faculty and students could specialize, and the reflection of practical and public service-oriented motivations among the educational institutions, the students, and their parents.

The growth of differentiated and specialized fields of knowledge at the graduate level is illustrated by the fact that in 1900 some 250 earned doctor's degrees were granted by twenty-five institutions. By 1960 nearly 200 institutions granted some 10,000 doctorates. The separate fields in which the doctorate was awarded totaled 150 at World War I (about forty-five major branches of learning); they had grown to 550 in 1960 (about sixty to eighty "real" fields).[40] The central fields of graduate study leading to the doctorate were chemistry, history, botany, education, physics, mathematics, English, economics, philosophy, psychology, zoology, geology, and political science.

While the doctorate was not supposed to be a professional degree, but rather a scholarly and learned degree, the trend was definitely toward the use of the degree in preparing for positions in government, industry, business, and professional practice rather than primarily in university teaching and research. The doctorate was, of course, the prime certification and professional requirement for university and college positions. Still further evidence was the fact that professional doctorates amounted to more than a third of the total number in 1960, the physical and biological sciences more than a third, the social sciences a fifth, and the humanities about a tenth. The trend toward professionalization was even more marked at the master's degree level, nearly three-fourths being in the professional fields (nearly half in education alone). At the undergraduate level a similar picture emerged.

Technical and professional education in the universities not only gave greater attention to the long-established professions of law and medicine but also began to give much greater recognition to the newer occupational fields that were struggling to become full-fledged professions. Among these were agriculture, business, education, journalism, architecture, social work, nursing, and library science. The junior colleges and community colleges vastly increased the opportunity for postsecondary education in general as well as for technical education. As the college and universities expanded to meet these practical needs, however, many critics arose to attack the universities for what they were doing. In general, the critics seemed to range themselves into two opposing groups, the defenders of tradition and progressives who argued for modernization.

The traditionalists who formed an unbroken link with the scholarly traditions of the past, wished to preserve as far as possible the humanistic conception of a liberal education. They claimed that the universities had degenerated into mere service stations for all sorts of industrial, commercial, and agricultural enterprises. They insisted that the university must return to its proper function of scholarly achievement by improving the intellectual quality of university training. On the other hand, the

[40] Bernard Berelson, *Graduate Education in the United States,* McGraw-Hill, New York, 1960, pp. 24-42.

modernizers said that society was now so complex and changing so rapidly that higher education must give the student an integrating and unifying experience in order to prepare him more directly for living in an interdependent world wide civilization.

Whatever form such revisions took and whatever the specific details with which they were worked out, at least two aims predominated. One was to give more attention to the needs of the individual student and greater meaning to his college study than was possible in large, impersonal courses and lectures. The second was to relate college study more closely to the fundamental problems of modern civilization and to give students a more integrated approach to their study of and participation in modern life.

The modern-oriented educators realized that the emergency demands of World War II for vocational, technical, and scientific training reflected not only the needs of a nation at war but required a new look at the crises facing a modernizing nation in peace. In the face of an appallingly rapid and vast technological explosion they realized that they could not maintain the old snobbery concerning practical education but rather that both cultural and professional aims must be synthesized into a new outlook appropriate to the modern world. They realized also that no amount of training, whether intellectual or cultural or scientific or technological, would be worthwhile if it was not oriented to a responsibility for achieving and maintaining a just, a free, and an equal society in the United States and a just and peaceful order in the world. But they had to reckon with a world which was in the revolutionary process of reacting against 500 years of domination by the West.

PART IV

THE DISPERSION OF WESTERN EDUCATION AND THE MODERNIZATION OF TRADITIONAL SOCIETIES

(1700 A.D.-THE PRESENT)

CHAPTER XIV

EDUCATION
IN
THE "CIVILIZING MISSION"
OF THE WEST
(1700 A.D.-1860s A.D.)

A. THE GLOBAL SPREAD OF WESTERN EDUCATION

While the Western nations were struggling to modernize their societies and their educational systems at home they were also radiating outward their educational influence to every part of the earth. They were doing this in three ways. They were transplanting their societies to new ground, they were influencing other peoples who remained at least nominally independent of their control, and they were bringing vast areas of the world under the direct control of their governments.

Properly speaking, the story of the modernizing education developed by European civilization in the seventeenth to twentieth centuries should include the process whereby the several segments of European nations when transplanted to various parts of the world developed differing political, economic, social, and educational institutions. It would be extremely interesting, for example, to test the educational implications of the thesis posed by Louis Hartz that "when a part of a European nation is detached from the whole of it, and hurled outward onto new soil, it loses the stimulus toward change that the whole provides. It lapses into a kind of immobility."[1]

It would be interesting indeed to try to compare the strands of the British and French in their uses of education in Canada, or the British and the Dutch in South Africa where relations with the majority of black Africans produced such a drastically different configuration from that in Canada. And, similarly, how the British settlers in Australia and in New Zealand developed different styles of life, not least of their

---

[1] Louis Hartz (ed.), *The Founding of New Societies; Studies in the History of the United States, Latin America, South Africa, Canada, and Australia*, Harcourt, Brace & World, New York, 1964, p. 3.

differences being their treatment of the aboriginal peoples they found when they arrived in the Southern Seas. Fascinating, too, are the variations on the European themes that arose in the lands and islands of the Americas south of the United States where the Latin and North European cultures were fused with Amerindian, African, and East Indian societies.

But this book is not and cannot be a world history of education. Unfortunately, it cannot even be a history of the whole range of ways in which Western education was dispersed throughout the world and molded in turn by the peoples of the several continents to their own uses. Such a story has not even been attempted on the scale that is necessary. It must await another book and another time.

So too must we pass by the story, yet to be told coherently on a worldwide canvass, of the way Western education was used by those Asian societies that maintained their independence in the face of Western expansion from the eighteenth century onward. In a sense, Russia was one of the defensive modernizers, but Russia was also predominantly European in contrast to the Asian peoples of Japan, China, Thailand, Turkey, Iran, and Afghanistan. However else Russia differed from the west of Europe it had a long tradition of Greek Orthodox Christianity as well as frontier confrontations which linked it to the West in ways which the Moslem, Hindu, Buddist, Confucian, and Taoist educational traditions of the East did not. The ancient literate traditions of these societies, combined with the fact that they did not fully succumb to Western imperial rule, meant that they responded to the enticements of modern Western education in ways that differed from those societies that *were* subjected to colonial rule.

The history of education in the societies of defensive modernization during the nineteenth and twentieth centuries is thus not *primarily* the story of the impact of the West no matter how important a factor that may have been. In some cases, as in Japan, it "took"; in others the result was more ambivalent. But the point is that all the independent traditional societies sought to modernize themselves in one way or another by borrowing from or emulating some aspects of Western education. In all cases of defensive modernization certain rulers took the lead in promoting Western education from above; some were more successful than others. Most spectacular and speedy was the example of Japan; least successful was that of China. In between were Turkey, Thailand, and Afghanistan.

The appeal of Western science and technology was especially strong. Necessary for this purpose was the study of the Western languages whereby the sciences could be studied and absorbed, most commonly English, French, and German. Common too was the bringing of Western scholars to advise on establishing institutions and systems of education and teachers from the West to conduct schools for members of the royal families, the court, the aristocracy, the bureaucracy, the army, or prospective teachers. And inherent in most cases was the practice of sending young men abroad to the Western nations for advanced specialized training in the field of education.

Despite the importance of these topics this part will concentrate only upon two themes of particular significance in the global spread of Western education. This chapter deals with the "civilizing mission" of the eighteenth and early nineteenth centuries, and the next chapter deals with the imperialist mission of the later nineteenth and the twentieth centuries.

B. THE PRINCIPAL INGREDIENTS OF THE CIVILIZING MISSION

If the transformation from tradition to modernity had been confined to Western civilization, it would have been momentous enough, but it was also inextricably intertwined with another phenomenon which carried the impact of the West to the rest of the world in a peculiarly poignant form from 1700 onward and which Westerners summed up as their civilizing mission to the world, a mission that relied at root on education. It was not only a reaction against the evils and inhumanities wrought by the new industrial urbanization and by the revival of slavery but also a growing confidence by the West in the superiority of its own Christian civilization. The civilizing mission was compounded of nationalistic pride, commercial aggressiveness, religious evangelism, humanitarian and philanthropic fervor, belief in natural rights, devotion to equality and liberty, confidence in the power of knowledge, and a psychological search for ethnic identity.

Above all, the civilizing mission centered upon a growing feeling that the peculiar style of society, culture, and thought being achieved by Westerners was somehow superior to that of peoples of the Old World of Asia and Africa as well as to that of the indigenous peoples of the New World of the Americas. Thus, the Westerners felt impelled to carry their civilization to the rest of the world, and, if need be, to impose it upon others for *their* good as well as for the good of the West. They felt the mission to civilize those who were less fortunate or less informed or less intelligent was an obligation laid upon them either by God or by their national destiny, or by both.

All this was summed up by the French as their *mission civilisatrice* and by the British as their civilizing mission. In fact the very word *civilization* first came into use in the middle of the eighteenth century, probably coined by the French philosophes (perhaps by Mirabeau in 1756). At first the term was rejected by Samuel Johnson in his English Dictionary of 1772 in favor of *civility*, but it was soon picked up by English and Scottish writers as well as by French. The term *civility* had been current in English usage as a converse for barbarism. But what the eighteenth century proponents did was to inject two new notions of enormous significance. One was the idea of progress, which viewed civilization as a state of development radically superior to that of all other societies of the past; the other was a self-consciousness about that superiority which called forth a missionary zeal to spread it to all those who had not had the good fortune or the wit to achieve it for themselves. The call to spread the word included the mission to educate.

To be sure, all civilizations had displayed something of the same feeling of superiority toward their barbarians. Successive rulers of Mesopotamia had it, Egyptians had it, Chinese and Indians, Aztecs and Incas, Greeks and Romans, Arabs, Turks, and Russians all had it. We have already mentioned the versions of it that the Portuguese and Spanish carried to Asia and America in the sixteenth and seventeenth centuries. It may well be that a common characteristic of all prior civilizations was their proselytizing effort to civilize the nonurban barbarians who pushed against their walls or who were visited in their own lands by the civilizer when he went abroad.

But this time it was different. Now it was the rapidly modernizing societies that were caught up in an especially virulent version of the civilizing mission. Between 1700 and 1850 it was the modernizing British, French, and Americans (and, to a lesser degree, the Dutch, Danes, and Germans) who took the lead away from the traditionalizing Portuguese and Spanish and who fashioned their emerging modernity into an extraordinarily powerful engine of social control over vast numbers of people throughout the world. Their efforts dwarfed even those of the Greeks and Romans in the extent of territory affected, the varieties of peoples involved, and the revolutionary changes wrought in the traditional civilizations and in the folk societies they touched. (See Figure 14.1.)

That the civilizing mission of the West in its educational aspects was an integral part of the modernization process is a fact too seldom recognized as such by those who tend to identify or limit modernization to economic or technological development. It also elicited contradictory attitudes ranging from the most noble to the most cynical. In its responses to the ugly, evil, and abhorrent aspects of industrialism, urbanization, and chattel slavery, it produced extraordinary sentiments of benevolence and altruism. But it also shared the love of nationalistic power, the intolerance of religious dissent, the excesses of political revolution in the name of democracy, and the exploitation, rootlessness, and deprivations of industrial urbanization, all of which made the modernization process itself an unlovely thing. Above all, the rise, spread, and power of a particularly virulent form of racial slavery brought out the whole range of human feelings, from cynical apology and defense of the practice through moral indifference to outraged revulsion and determination to destroy it.

In sum, the period from 1700 to the 1860s ran the gamut from expressions of the highest and most elevated of religious, moral, and political ideals to actions that resulted in the worst degradation of millions of human beings that could be imagined up to that time. In this period some Westerners enslaved millions of Africans, imposed forced labor upon millions of Amerindians and Asians, and established racial systems of exclusion and discrimination against millions more whose products they paid for or traded upon. While slavery had been practiced in all prior civilizations without serious questioning, it was carried to particularly brutal extremes in the English colonies of the West Indies and the southern colonies of North America.

In the same period, other Westerners came to recognize the enormity and immorality of the slave system and eventually convinced their fellows to abolish the system. As they recoiled in increasing horror and outrage at the degrading and inhumane practices of the slave trade, Western reformers developed the ideology of the civilizing mission as a rationale for its mitigation through education. It is to the everlasting discredit of some Westerners that they revived a traditional institution and promoted it so ruthlessly. It is to the everlasting credit of other Westerners that they did what no other civilized societies had ever done before, devise an ideology *ha

Figure 14.1 Dispersion of Western Education via the Civilizing Mission (1500-1750)

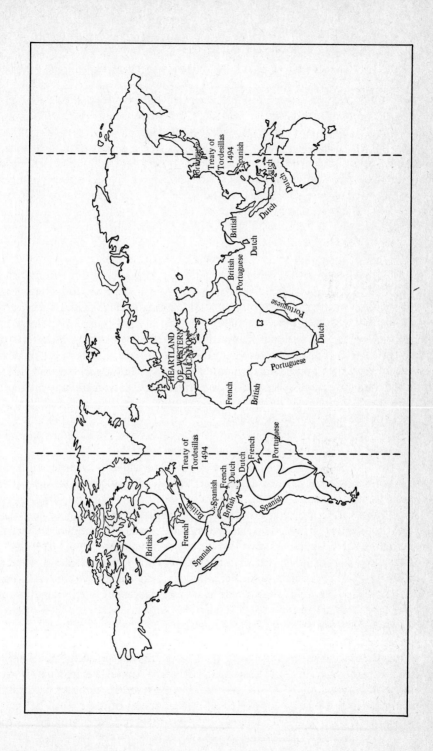

enabled them to denounce the institution in principle and then organize the political power to abolish it in practice.

The contradictions, tensions, and conflicts brought on by these confrontations have torn at the foundations of Western civilization for nearly 300 years and have left a legacy of hate, fear, prejudice, and mistrust whose evidences are all too clear in the modern world. The chasm between Western ideals of modern civilization and the reality of slavery, the contrast between Enlightenment and Christian professions of equality and the goals of democratic revolution on one hand and the actual practice of racial slavery on the other, have indelibly marked the transformation to modernity. While the extension of slavery may have stimulated the commercial and industrial aspects of modernization in the eighteenth century, the institution of slavery stood in the way of social, political, intellectual, and educational modernization in the nine-teenth century. In contrast, to the extent that the civilizing mission put its stress on educating the disadvantaged and the downtrodden, it was by and large a modernizing influence.

The ideology of the civilizing mission as it was developed by British and French protagonists in the eighteenth and early nineteenth centuries had three main ingre-dients: a religious evangelism based upon Christian equalitarianism; a secular philoso-phy of enlightenment based upon the natural rights of mankind; and a spirit of philanthropy and humanitarianism arising from a feeling of benevolence toward others and a desire to promote their welfare. To be sure, these ingredients may be difficult to separate, for they all sometimes appeared in the same individual or group, but they do mark distinctive approaches which cumulatively and in combination produced enor-mous social energy and impact upon the world. Something new had certainly been added to the contacts among peoples.

Christian Equalitarianism and Evangelism

At least three aspects of Christian thought gave support to the religious impetus behind the civilizing mission of the West. The age-old notion that all men by virtue of their spiritual nature are equal in the sight of God gradually came to be used as a weapon in the attack upon the justification for slavery which argued that some men are naturally unequal to others and thus can legitimately be enslaved. Of course, many Christians for hundreds of years had rationalized the existence of slavery by arguing that a rational social or natural order required the subordination of some men to others, even though in the spiritual order they were all equal. Slavery had long been justified in Greek and Roman and medieval times on such grounds. Gradually, however, Christians agreed not to enslave Christians; and slavery within Europe died out, to be replaced by the serfdom of feudalism.

Nevertheless, the concept of legitimate slavery imbedded in Roman law was revived in the sixteenth and seventeenth centuries and applied to the non-Christian heathens of Africa, Asia and America. For nearly 300 years (roughly 1450 to 1750) few Christians actively opposed the enslavement of non-Christians on the grounds that all men were equal in the sight of God. In fact, biblical sanction in the story of Noah's curse laid upon Ham was often trotted out by way of justifying slavery as a punishment to be levied upon Ham's black descendants for the sin he commited. But, as the slave trade grew, Christians became increasingly troubled and divided over whether slavery was permitted or justified by Christian doctrine.

A second aspect of Christian thought to become embroiled in the ideology of the civilizing mission was the question of the unity of mankind, brought to the fore by the spread of enslavement of black men by white men. Did all men originally spring from one race (monogenism) which would make all men basically equal, or were there plural sources of the races of mankind (polygenism) resulting in some men being inherently inferior to others? The Roman Catholic Church was clearly on the side of monogenism, taking the Spanish *conquistadores* to task for the enforced labor system they fastened upon Amerindians. The Protestants of northern Europe, far less acquainted with the black strangers of Africa or the colored Amerindians of America and reluctant to accept a Catholic doctrine without question, were slower to adopt monogenism. They seemed somewhat more inclined to accept the notion that there was a natural hierarchy of races. Perhaps the Protestant stress on a rigorous process of induction into church membership by means of study, public profession of the faith, and formal learning led them at the outset to a somewhat more exclusive position than did the Catholic Church. Calvinists particularly laid a good deal of emphasis upon the arduous educational and instructional process involved in the conversion to Christianity.[2] It seemed to be easier to believe that African blacks with no tradition of literacy were an inferior race when they found it difficult to learn the Christian catechism or to read the Bible in English or French.

With the emergence of religious revivalism and evangelism accompanying the Great Awakening in the early eighteenth century, however, many Protestant spokesmen effectively moved to the monogenist view by preaching that *all* men could undergo the emotional experience of conversion and establish a personal and individual relationship with God through acceptance of the faith rather than through the traditional rituals of the Catholic Church or the traditional instructional process of the established Protestant churches. Preaching salvation to black men, red men, brown men, and yellow men now became a Protestant Christian duty as well as a Catholic Christian duty.

The sudden outburst of religious revivalism that swept much of northern Europe and North America in the eighteenth century was thus the third element in the Christian outlook that sparked the surge of the civilizing mission. In view of the fact that the Catholic missionaries had been in the foreign field for two centuries, the Protestants now organized themselves with unprecedented speed and vigor to pursue their mission overseas, as if to make up for lost time.

The Church of England had begun even before the Great Awakening to seek to convert the heathens in America and Asia by establishing the Society for the Propagation of the Gospel in Foreign Parts (S.P.G.) in 1701. The Danes and the Moravians were also active early in the eighteenth century. But the Great Awakening swept more

---

[2] Winthrop D. Jordan is particularly adamant that Calvinist exclusivity was *not* based upon the doctrine of predestination of the elect. See his *White over Black; American Attitudes Toward the Negro, 1550-1812*, University of North Carolina Press, Chapel Hill, 1968, chap. 5.

people, especially blacks, into the Methodist and Baptist ranks in America than into any other churches. Although much of the foreign mission enterprise was stimulated by a reaction against the African slave trade, the S.P.G. held on to the defense of slavery as a justifiable social institution at the same time that it sought to save the souls of the slaves.

It was eventually the Quakers more than any other Protestant group who began to argue that the spiritual equality of men could not justify or tolerate the ultimate inequality in social arrangements represented by bonded slavery. Above all others, John Woolman and Anthony Benezet symbolized the Christian conscience that finally awakened to the basic contradiction between the beatific theory of spiritual equality and the evil practices of enslavement. It was no accident that both the S.P.G. with its defense of slavery and the Quakers with their attacks upon slavery believed in educating the black slave. In one case education could be viewed as a means of making better slaves; in the other as a means of preparing for freedom. The civilizing mission was flexible enough to embrace both.

Around the turn of the nineteenth century the missionary movements burgeoned in Britain, in Europe, and in the United States. For example, in little more than a decade, members of the major Protestant denominations of Britain redoubled their overseas mission efforts aiming particularly at West Africa, India, and South Asia. Among these were the Baptist Society for Propagating the Gospel among the Heathens (1792), the London Missionary Society (interdenominational) (1795), the Scottish Missionary Society (Presbyterian) (1794), the Society for Missions to Africa and the East (1799) which became the Church Missionary Society (Anglican) (1804), and the Wesleyan Missionary Society (1814). On the continent, the Netherlands Missionary Society (1797) was followed by German missions organized at Basel (1815), Leipzig, and Berlin, and by the French at Lyons and Paris.

In the United States after independence several societies were formed in the 1780s and 1790s to carry forward the civilizing mission to American Indians that had progressed only fitfully during the colonial period. These included the Society for Propagating the Gospel among Indians and Others in North America, the New York Missionary Society, the Northern Missionary Society, the Western Missionary Society, and the like. The Congregationalists, Presbyterians, Methodists, and Baptists were especially active. In 1810 the first nondenominational effort in the foreign mission field was launched; the American Board of Commissioners for Foreign Missions was an outgrowth of revivalistic movements that provided an enormous moral outlet for college students' idealism of the time. American missionaries were sent overseas as early as 1812, especially to India (including Ceylon and Burma), the Middle East, and to Hawaii.

The Christian missionary enterprise was by all odds the most influential aspect of the civilizing mission in the field of education. Missionaries almost universally paid attention to schooling; on occasion, they even had to defend their efforts against those who saw no need to "civilize the natives," only to exploit them. They often allied themselves with a second and more secular ingredient of the civilizing mission.

Natural Rights Philosophy of the Enlightenment

Just as Britain was the source of much of the Christian impetus to the civilizing mission of the West, France was the major source of the secular philosophy of natural rights which prompted the Enlightenment belief that the political and social rights of Europeans should be extended to all men everywhere. Montesquieu, Rousseau, Diderot and other authors of the *Encyclopédie* kept up a running assault on slavery as an affront to the doctrine of natural rights. Abbé Guillaume-Thomas Raynal epitomized the Enlightenment belief that while slavery was contrary to nature nevertheless the benefits of Western civilization should be carried to the less civilized societies of the French colonies. He even argued that certain youths should be selected for special instruction in the values of Western (French) civilization so that they could form an elite corps of political missionaries to proselytize on behalf of the metropolitan society, an idea that appealed recurringly to the Western nations during the next 200 years.

In conformity with the democratic doctrines of their Declaration of the Rights of Man, the French revolutionaries of the First Republic abolished slavery in the French colonies by decree in 1794. The doctrine of assimilation made explicit in the Constitution of 1795 stipulated that the overseas colonies of France were to be considered an indivisible part of the French Republic, to be governed by the same laws as the metropole and to be extended the same benefits of civilization that Frenchmen enjoyed at home. This came to mean that an elite group in the colonies should have the same education as those in metropolitan France.

Unfortunately for the colonies, and for the West in general, slavery did not stay abolished by France, for it was reinstated in 1802 under the consulate of Napoleon. Like secular education, the doctrine of assimilation was set back each time a conservative monarchial or imperialist government came to power in France and revived each time a liberal or reform government came to power. Finally, with the onset of the Third Republic in 1871 the doctrine of assimilation and of *mission civilisatrice* was to reach its apogee in French imperialism. It is clear that the French colonies might have been the subject of a much more intensive educational and civilizing mission if French democracy had not been pulled and hauled so badly between 1790 and 1870.

Similarly, the promise of the Revolutionary era in America was not to be fulfilled as soon as its leaders hoped. As early as 1700 slavery had gained a firm foothold in the law and in the practice of all of the American colonies, and there was scarcely any real opposition to it on principle until the mid-eighteenth century when Quakers and some Puritans like Judge Samuel Sewall of Boston began to protest not only against the brutality of slavery but against its inherent repugnance to religion and morality. Until then it had simply been argued that within the system of slavery the Christian had the obligation to convert, to instruct, and to educate the slaves. Puritans Cotton Mather and Samuel Willard early in the eighteenth century and Anglican George Whitefield and the S.P.G. in the second quarter of the century had supported this idea.

Such efforts to convince slave owners that conversion would make better and more docile slaves rather than restless and rebellious ones were not very convincing to the slaveholders who so feared rebellion that they simply opposed any measure that might narrow the social distance between whites and blacks. Besides, they argued, if they happened to bother to make the case, efforts to educate slaves would be wasted because they were basically uneducable and incapable of schooling. In this stance, they were able to find support in the incipient sciences of anthropology and psychology which gave comfort to white racial superiority.

As they studied and categorized what they believed to be the distinctive psychological and moral characteristics of different races, some scientists insisted upon arranging the races in hierarchical order from highest to lowest. Europeans found no trouble in asserting that the white race was at the top and the black race at the bottom of the hierarchy of racial intelligence. In the hands of extreme polygenists like Charles White and the publicist Edward Long the argument came perilously close to denying that black Africans were even human. The defenders of the religious and natural rights of the Africans stoutly maintained to the contrary that opportunity for education, Christianization, and civilization would prove the basic intellectual equality of the races.[3]

As the eighteenth century wore on, it became increasingly clear that the equalitarian promises of the Enlightenment and of the democratic revolution were being thwarted for millions in the world who were held in slavery. Not only did the Christian equalitarians begin to see this, but the American secular missionaries for natural rights began to see it; John Wise as early as 1717, then James Otis, Benjamin Franklin, Tom Paine, Benjamin Rush, Patrick Henry, James Madison, and Thomas Jefferson. The natural rights proponents differed among themselves on some basic issues. Benjamin Rush believed that human nature was the same everywhere and that racial differences arose from the degree of civilization to which men were exposed. Thomas Jefferson bitterly opposed slavery because he believed all men were by nature entitled to political and legal equality, but he could not bring himself to the belief that blacks were intellectually equal by nature to whites. In the balance, the weight of the American Revolution's ideology told against slavery.

Yet, in two major respects the natural rights philosophy fell short of realizing its ideals in the United States. In the political rough and tumble of creating the Constitution and the new nation once the war was over, the desire to create the union won out over the desire to abolish slavery. Although the Continental Congress had prohibited the importation of slaves in 1774, it soon became clear that the sectional interests of the North were diverging from those of the South. The Constitutional convention candidly agreed to compromise by counting only three-fifths of the slave population of the states toward apportionment of taxes and representatives in Congress. To have insisted upon abolition at that point would have broken up the Union before it was fully created. However, it *was* agreed that the slave trade would be abolished in twenty years. The point is that even though the revolutionary doctrines of equality began to

[3] For absorbing details of these arguments, see Charles H. Lyons, *"To Wash an Aethiop White,"* *British Ideas about Black African Educability, 1530-1960,* Teachers College Press, New York, 1973.

be imbedded in the consciences of Americans in some realms of life, they were not effective in abolishing legal slavery in the South for another seventy-five years. The civilizing mission to educate and to free slaves at home became largely a function of northern protagonists, while the southern states began to throw up barriers against such efforts by passing laws prohibiting the education of slaves and by restricting free Negroes by means of separating white from black in hospitals, jails, residences, cemeteries, churches, and schools.

The second failure of the natural rights philosophy in the decades following the Revolution was the curious failure to stress the role of education in the transformation of slaves into citizens. At a time when education was clearly seen to be a major key to the civilizing mission overseas, there were only a few who advocated education for Negroes at home. The Quakers did and some of the northern cities set up black schools for black pupils, but seldom was education stressed as the panacea for the social improvement of the black race. Thomas Jefferson notably failed to do this, despite his leadership in promoting public education in Virginia. Only New York and New Jersey among the states tried the experiment of requiring slaves to be taught to read. Few took seriously a Democratic lawyer and politician of Boston, James Sullivan, when he argued for an equal and integrated education of blacks and whites as a means of lessening racist attitudes:

> The children of the slaves must, at the public expence, be educated in the same manner as the children of their masters; being at the same schools, etc., with the rising generation, that prejudice, which has been so long and inveterate against them on account of their situation and colour, will be lessened within thirty or forty years.[4]

It may not be so curious after all that Americans did not turn to a common education as a possible cure for slavery immediately following the Revolution, for the major campaigns for public education were still three or four decades in the future. By the time the public school movement really got under way in the 1830s and 1840s, the proslavery cause had become so hardened and deepened in the South that any kind of education of slaves could not be countenanced, and the clamor for uncompromising abolition so shrill in the North that the rising tide of protest took the equally intransigent form that nothing short of immediate and complete abolition would do. Proposals for an educational program requiring thirty to forty years of sustained effort could not gain much of a hearing by either side in the heightened tension of the abolition controversy.

Philanthropy and Humanitarianism
The first half of the nineteenth century witnessed in the West a remarkable phenomenon very difficult for many non-Westerners to understand. The spirit of humanitarianism, philanthropy, benevolence, or altruism was a complex syndrome of feelings, motivations, and activism on behalf of others. It was, of course, related to the springs

---

[4]Quoted in Jordan, op. cit., pp. 355-356.

of Christian evangelism and of secular belief in man's natural rights to freedom and equality. But it was more than either of these. It was a welling up of a desire to help others, a devotion to human welfare, a determination to put into action a spirit of good will that would result in the improvement of the conditions of life for the poor, the unfortunate, the oppressed, or the unenlightened. It was a reaction against the depredations affecting the lower classes caught in the rapid changes of industrial urban life within the modernizing nations of the West particularly in Britain and the United States, and against the degradations of Negro slavery and the slave trade. It was still more than that. It was also a growing desire to do something about the massive poverty, deprivation, and lack of the material necessities of life prevalent among the millions of people of color in Africa, Asia, and the islands of the Pacific.

One could be cynical about the whole phenomenon and simply charge it off as a giant hypocrisy on the part of people who themselves had caused the depredations, the degradation, and the deprivation. One could argue that it was simply a psychological easing of conscience over a sense of guilt caused by the exploitation wrought by the aggressive capitalist nations. They could do no less in recompense for their conquests and their subjugation of innocent peoples. One could argue that helping others to improve their conditions of life was simply a matter of economic self-interest, for the more goods the Asians or Africans produced or bought the more wealth would flow into the Western pocketbooks.

One could say, and many have said, all these things, and there still remains the fact that thousands upon thousands of Westerners were prompted to work, to give money, to contribute time, to dedicate their energies, and to leave their homes and give up their health and even their lives in causes that were intended to benefit others. The mitigation and abolition of slavery were outstanding examples, but the reform movements of the late eighteenth and early nineteenth century embraced many causes: to improve prison conditions and mitigate punishments for criminals, reduce child labor, prevent the excesses of alcohol, drugs, and tobacco, stem disease and improve health, give aid to the poverty-stricken, raise the status of women, reform the electoral systems and judicial processes, and, of course, extend the benefits of education to the ignorant and illiterate. Especially was education emphasized as a means of bringing improvement to the strange people in distant and outlandish places of the world.

The humanitarian and philanthropic motivation was a remarkable aspect of the civilizing mission of the West to the rest of the world. Innumerable organizations, societies, and associations were formed to carry into practice the stated ideals. Sometimes the associations were heavily religious. Sometimes the evangelicals were undistinguishable from the humanitarians, but sometimes they were quite distinct. The British Utilitarians or Benthamites of the early nineteenth century were scarcely less secular than the philosophes of the Enlightenment in the mid-eighteenth century. They believed that the goal of the ideal society was the greatest good of the greatest number and that human institutions could be reformed as a means of raising the quality of life. They often joined with the evangelical religionists in support of the good causes. And these two were often joined in turn by men of wealth, of commerce, of industry, and of government. Such mutual support in voluntary associations was a characteristic feature of the life of the West and of its outreach to the world in the first half of the nineteenth century.

C. THE CIVILIZING MISSION IN AFRICA

In the period before 1850 all of the modernizing nations of the West were more or less active in carrying out their civilizing mission to the world, but none more than the British, and none had more educational impact. In the following century of full blown imperialism, their chief Western competitors were the French, the Germans, and the Americans, but up to mid-nineteenth century the British surged ahead. The principal fields of endeavor to which the British turned, after the American colonies had been lost, were West Africa and India. Only the barest outline can be hinted at here.

The Westerners' contact with Ghana (which they called the Gold Coast) was long confined to the sea coast where they built forts or castles as enclaves for their small contingents of traders, administrators, chaplains, artisans, and their families. The Portuguese were the first to arrive in the late fifteenth century followed by the Dutch whose West India Company was formed in 1621 and then by the British, the French, and Danes. Merchant companies were formed in each country, sending out agents or governors to administer the forts, deal with the African chiefs and traders as virtual equals, and to compete with each other for trade in goods and slaves.

Gradually the English merchant companies gained the upper hand and then the British government took over the commercial enterprise in 1821 when Parliament abolished the African Company of Merchants and turned over administration of the forts to the royal governor in Sierra Leone (which had gone through a similar process of shift from commercial company to crown). Although there was considerable backing and filling on this matter, the British government by mid-nineteenth century was beginning to exert more and more control over affairs of Africans outside the forts as well as within, much of this done at the request or with the consent of African chieftains and traders located in the coastal towns. The British government was generally reluctant to get more deeply involved in African political affairs prior to 1865.

The first Western education in Ghana went on in the coastal forts and their associated villages. The Portuguese had schools in the sixteenth century; the Dutch in the seventeenth century; and the Danes and British in the eighteenth century. The responsibility for sending out schoolmasters originally rested with the merchant companies. The first English schoolmaster (1751) was Thomas Thompson who happened to have been a missionary for the S.P.G. in America and who came to Cape Coast Castle from experience in New Jersey. As Philip Foster points out, these schools had a hard time. They taught a few mulatto offspring of the garrision and a few sons of the African merchants in the seacoast towns, but they were on the periphery of the traditional societies of Ghana and their impact on the traditional societies was slight.[5]

---

[5] Philip Foster, *Education and Social Change in Ghana,* University of Chicago Press, Chicago, 1965, pp. 43 ff.

In general, they simply taught the three R's and religion on the pattern of the charity schools then being conducted for the lower classes in Britain.

While the commercial companies of the eighteenth century did make a bow toward education they did it stiffly and without enthusiasm. Actually, they had little or no intention of doing more than profiting from trade with the Africans, including the slave trade. The economic motive which brought the Westerners to the Gold Coast did not particularly foster education. When, however, it was combined with the religious-humanitarian-political complex of motives that made up the civilizing mis sion, then education began to play a more significant role. This happened in the early nineteenth century.

When the crown took over the Gold Coast forts in 1821, several government schools supported by public funds were set up. Foster points to the fact that the British were spending government money on schools in the Gold Coast even before they began to do so at home in England in 1833. By 1850, however, the trend had been reversed. The missionary societies had begun to arrive and to establish their schools aimed at spreading the Christian gospel among the Africans. In fact they soon took over the government schools as well.

The Wesleyan Mission concentrated on the urban centers of the seacoast setting up day schools and teaching in English; while the Basel Mission took to the hill country bringing the children into boarding schools and teaching them in the vernacu- lar. Foster argues that the Wesleyan approach was more effective, because it responded to the demands of the urbanizing Africans who wanted to engage more extensively in the money economy associated with European trade and saw the English education as a means of advancement to that end. In contrast, the leaders of the upcountry traditional societies felt that literacy, in English or even in their own languages, provided no particular advantage for participating in a traditional and agricultural society; indeed it could be a disrupting factor which they feared. The Ashanti who dominated the country to the north of the seacoast bitterly resisted Western education until late in the nineteenth century.

Thus, while the missionaries might see literacy as a means for conversion to Protestant Christianity, the Africans saw it as either unnecessary or as a means to advancement in the modernizing exchange economy of trade and commerce that was being imported from the West. To the middle of the nineteenth century political power did not rest with the British, but economic power did. Thus, Foster argues, the African demand for Western education was limited to the urban centers where an African merchant trading class was developing. These Africans came to agree with the missionaries on the value of an English Western education; the missionaries got converts; and the Africans got the means of preferment that would enable them to deal with the British on terms as equal as possible under the circumstances.

One of the most puzzling aspects to many Westerners about the impact of British education is that on the surface its academic, literary, and humanistic character did not seem to be appropriate to the rural, agricultural, traditional societies of Africa. Indeed it was not, but it came to be greatly sought-after by many Africans who could see the benefits in it for them. The British have often been criticized for foisting an inappropriate academic education upon an unsuspecting people, rather than making available to them an appropriate education. What Africans needed, it was sometimes argued, was training in agriculture, manual arts, trade and technical education, domestic arts, health science, and other such practical studies.

As a matter of fact, many efforts *were* made by British and other humanitarians and missionaries to provide a practical education in agriculture, the industrial trades, and commercial subjects. An excellent example can be found in an offical report of the Education Committee of the Privy Council to the Colonial Office in 1847 as follows:

(i) To inculcate the principles and promote the influences of Christianity by such instruction as can be given in elementary schools.

(ii) To accustom the children of these races to habits of self-control and moral discipline.

(iii) To diffuse a grammatical knowledge of the English language as the most important agent of civilisation.

(iv) To make the school the means of improving the condition of the peasantry by teaching them how health may be preserved by a proper diet, cleanliness, ventilation and clothing, and by the structure of their dwellings.

(v) To give a practical training in household economy and in the cultivation of the cottage garden as well as in those common handicrafts by which a labourer may improve his domestic comfort.

(vi) To communicate such a knowledge of writing and arithmetic, and of their application to his wants and duties, as may enable a peasant to economise his means, and give the small farmer the power to enter into calculations and agreements.

(vii) Improved agriculture is required to replace the system of exhausting the virgin soils, and then leaving to natural influences alone the work of reparation. The education of the coloured races would, therefore, not be complete for the children of small farmers, unless it included this object.

(viii) Lesson-books should teach the mutual interests of the mother country and her dependencies, the rational basis of this connection and the domestic and social duties of the coloured races.

(ix) Lesson books should also set forth simply the relation of wages, capital and labour, and the influence of local and general government on personal security, independence and order.[6]

This all sounds extremely logical—to a Westerner. But if one notes carefully the repeated statement that this is the type of education appropriate "for the coloured races" and "for the peasant," one may get a clue as to why the Africans did not respond as enthusiastically to such practical education as Westerners thought they should. A pervasive racial attitude of white superiority over black peoples is all too evident in this governmental position paper.

[6]H. S. Scott, "Education by the European," *The Year Book of Education, 1938,* Evans P Ltd., London, 1938, p. 709.

The missionaries and humanitarians were thus faced with an excruciating prob, lem. They were arguing vehemently that Negro slavery was an affront to mankind, for all men are basically equal in their spiritual being and natural rights; they carried education to Africa in large part to prove the point to their racist critics that black Africans were as educable as all other men; and they argued that the backwardness of African cultural, social, and economic conditions in comparison to those of the West was due to environmental causes and to an isolation that could be changed by bringing Western civilization to Africa. Yet the period from 1800 to 1865 was witnessing a massive rise of antiblack racism from scientific as well as political and proslavery sources with which they had to contend.

The unfortunate conjunction of the growth of a scientific racism in virtually all of the Western countries and the hardening of the lines of defense for slavery in the American South gave impetus to the belief that black Africans were innately inferior to whites and that this fact, rather than environmental conditions, was the basic cause of their cultural backwardness. It was no accident that the Privy Council Education Committee used the term coloured races in 1847. The term was current in the British press of the late 1840s as critics and publicists like Anthony Trollope, Thomas Carlyle, and Charles Dickens were having a field day at the expense of the humanitarians and evangelicals for their hopeless efforts at uplift and their misplaced benevolence toward Africans. Political leaders like Disraeli and Bulwer-Lytton, both so influential in the foreign relations of Britain to come, were attributing the glories of Western civiliza- tion, its art, its science, and its literature to the racial characteristics of white men.

And the budding science of anthropology was turning to race and to inherent racial characteristics to explain the difference in the social and cultural developments of different societies. Robert Knox preached Anglo-Saxon supremacy in Britain; le Compte de Gobineau preached Nordic supremacy in France; and Max Müller preached Aryan supremacy in Germany. They were but three of scores of scientists who formed the new anthropological societies in London, Paris, Berlin, Moscow, and New York. The net result was a pervasive adherence to white supremacy over black. And then along came the phrenology of Franz Joseph Gall, Johann Caspar Spurzheim, and George Combe to spread the gospel of phrenology which they felt conclusively proved the hierarchy of the races. The capstone seemed to be put into place by Darwin's theory of evolution which somehow was taken as putting the seal of "fittest" upon the white race of the species which had won out in the contests of natural selection and had ascended furthest from the lower forms of the species, while the black race had departed least from the ape-men who also inhabited Africa.

All th   the humanitarians and evangelical religionists back on their heels as they   to maintain the doctrines of equality of man. But the racists seemed   their side; while the evangelicals had only their traditional   s; and the humanitarians had only their radical natural rights   ian creed. This is a curious reversal of the roles that are usually   of modernization who commonly see in the churches the de-   of tradition and in science the advocates of the forces of   however, the opposite was true. In general, the missionaries and humanitarians defended the blacks, while the publicists and government officials were only too glad to call scientific racism to witness what they wanted to believe as justification for extending political and economic control over an inferior race.

Charles H. Lyons documents the growth of racial attitudes among investigating commissions that were sent to assess education in West Africa as early as 1841. From then on, and especially in 1846 to 1847, commissioners began to urge more model farms, more agricultural study, more trade training, more mechanical skills, more domestic science, more moral education, and, of course, more religious training. While the racial bias in such proposals was seldom made explicit to the Africans and while few Africans had any idea about all these matters being bruited in Europe and America, nevertheless it is clear that the Africans resisted, deliberately or instinctively, the imposition of an agricultural or technical education that seemed designed to keep them at the low level of manual workers and in a subservient position economically and politically when they could sense in all kinds of subtle ways and eventually to see for themselves that this was not the kind of education that the British government officials, or administrators, or merchants, or even the missionaries themselves had had. *That* was the kind of education the Africans came to want. They did not want an education "appropriate for the coloured races." They wanted the kind of education that was obviously appropriate for their white rulers.

When the missionaries saw that their education was more popular with Africans than their gospel, they put schools high on their agenda and worked through them to conversion. When the government later extended its control over more and more aspects of African life in the colonies, the officials acceded to the value of the literary education. But by 1864 much of the humanitarian optimism based upon equalitarianism devoted to civilizing the Africans had begun to subside. In the latter part of the century the civilizing mission had a much more overt racist tone to it. The white man's burden was becoming more prominent for all to see.

But before that time came, the humanitarians were in the forefront of the attacks upon slavery and the slave trade. When Granville Sharp was successful in getting slavery declared illegal in England by court decision in 1772, it soon became clear to some of the humanitarians that the 15,000 domestic slaves who had been freed by the decision and the thousands more who had fled to England from the West Indies very much needed help. When in 1786 a Committee for the Black Poor was formed, it was decided that the best way to help was to enable the freedmen to return to Africa and to establish a repatriated colony of their own. Having chosen Sierra Leone as the place, this was done in 1787, but the planning was poor, many died, and the whole thing became a vast discouragement.

Nevertheless, a trading company was formed by some of the outstanding humanitarians of the day, Sharp, William Wilberforce, the great abolitionist, Henry Thornton, and others, in order to try to rescue the experiment. This became the Sierra Leone Company in 1791 which now tried to rely not solely upon benevolence and goodwill but to combine sound merchant trading policies with philanthropic motives. This time colonists were solicited from Nova Scotia where many blacks who had fought for the British during the American Revolution had gone. More than a thousand sailed for Sierra Leone in 1792. In less than a year a schoolmaster had been sent by the Company to start a school, probably at the request of the Nova Scotians. But again, an excess of philanthropic zeal and a shortage of experience in successful colonizing led to great difficulties, exacerbated by an oppressive administrator who put profit above philanthropy. All this led to a series of insurrections by the black settlers amidst attacks by the native blacks.

As things went from bad to worse, the evangelicals and the humanitarians back home in England got to work again to organize the Society for Missions to Africa and the East in 1799 which became the Church Missionary Society (C.M.S.) in 1804, Thornton and Wilberforce again being involved. This was a case in which the abolition movement and the rising missionary movement coalesced around the plight of the Sierra Leone experiment. In 1808 on the same day that the abolition of the slave trade took effect in British colonies the Sierra Leone Company handed over the administration of the colony to the British government. The humanitarian pride and outlook were well expressed in their report which stated their goal as having established a colony which "may become an emporium of commerce, a school of industry, and a source of knowledge, civilization, and religious improvement to the inhabitants of the continent."[7]

Now, liberated slaves rescued by the British navy from slave ships plying the west coast of Africa were enabled to settle in Sierra Leone. Meanwhile another philanthropic society began to aid education. This was the African Institution formed in 1807 and functioning for two decades. Eventually, however, the Church Missionary Society became the dominant educational agency in Sierra Leone, first at the request of the governor and with government support, eventually (after 1826) by setting up its own schools when government support for its efforts was terminated. One of its principal achievements was the establishment in 1827 of the Christian Institution, later to be known as Fourah Bay College, which became an important center of advanced education for all of West Africa and beyond. It did not include the trades and practical education which had been established in a prior institution in 1816 by the Church Missionary Society. Rather it stressed an academic curriculum including not only English, but Arabic and local languages. The opportunity for academic study was extended when the Church Missionary Society Grammar School was opened in 1845, and one for girls in 1848. By 1868 there were seventy-eight schools in Sierra Leone enrolling nearly 8,000 pupils, a proportion estimated to be one out of every six in the total population; at this time the proportion in England was one in seven.

These latter points support the view that the African demand for a Western type of education was growing. The C.M.S. grammar school curriculum included English grammar and composition, Latin, Greek, mathematics, geography, Bible history, astronomy, the thirty-nine articles of faith of the Church of England, English history, writing, and music. This curriculum might not be what the government officials thought illiterate Africans ought to study, but it was what the English were teaching in their own grammar schools at home. And it aided the liberated Africans to find a place

---

[7]Quoted in D. L. Sumner, *Education in Sierra Leone*, Government of Sierra Leone, Freetown, 1963, p. 17.

for themselves in the urbanizing, commercial life of Freetown. In this respect the experience paralleled that of Ghana. But it was even more important, for in the late 1830s and early 1840s when some of the liberated slaves who had been snatched out of the Yoruba-speaking region of Nigeria began to return to their homeland, they took with them the desire for a Western education. This was only one example in which the Sierra Leone emphasis upon education made it an important source of supply of the Western-educated elites who eventually took more and more of the leadership of Africa into their own hands.

Western education was introduced into Nigeria on the wave of missionary activity that began in the early 1840s and lasted until the 1860s, when considerable hostility to them arose as a result of the wars and the annexation of Lagos by the British government in 1861. During this period the most influential missionary groups were the Church Missionary Society, the Wesleyan Methodist Missionary Society, the Foreign Mission Committee of the United Presbyterian Church of Scotland, and at mid-century the Foreign Mission Board of the Southern Baptist Convention of the United States. The missionary and the humanitarian roles preceded that of the government in Nigeria. The slave traders were of course ahead of all others, but it was a unique combination of evangelicals and humanitarian laymen who saw that the slave trade, while legally abolished, was still actively oppressing thousands of Africans.

The religious motive, humanitarian benevolence, the abolitionist cause, and commercial enterprise were impressively rolled together into the civilizing mission. The ideology expressing these goals was nowhere better stated than by T. F. Buxton, originator of the ill-fated Niger expedition of 1841. In his "Prospectus of the Society for the Extinction of the Slave Trade and for the Civilization of Africa" (a title to stir the emotions of the righteous philanthropist in 1839), Buxton added to Christianity the following ingredients of the civilizing mission:

> adoption of effectual measures for reducing the principal languages of Western and Central Africa into writing . . . prevent or mitigate the prevalence of disease and suffering among the people of Africa . . . encouragement of practical science in all its various branches, the system of drainage best calculated to succeed in a climate so humid and so hot . . . afford essential assistance to the natives, by furnishing them with useful information as to the best mode of cultivation; as to the productions which command a steady market; and by introducing the most approved agricultural implements and seeds. The time may come when the knowledge and practice of the mighty powers of steam might contribute rapidly to promote the improvement and prosperity of that country . . . assist in promoting the formation of roads and canals . . . manufacture of paper, and the use of the printing press.[8]

This is an excellent summation of the humanitarian view of the civilizing mission and, despite the reference to "natives," carried less of the tone of racial superiority than

[8] T. F. Buxton, "Prospectus of the Society for the Extinction of the Slave Trade, and for the Civilization of Africa," in an abridgement of the *African Slave Trade and its Remedy*, John Murray, London, 1840, p. 60.

many of the offical statements of the period. In a well-noted passage in his widely read book entitled *The African Slave Trade and Its Remedy* (1840) Buxton summed up the ingredients which would enable the Africans themselves to prevent the slave trade through the development of their own social and cultural potential:

> Let missionaries and schoolmasters, the plow and the spade, go together, and agriculture will flourish; the avenues to legitimate commerce will be opened; confidence between man and man will be inspired; whilst civilization will advance as the natural effect, and Christianity operate as the proximate cause of this happy change.[9]

Thus Englishmen developed a "noble purpose" to compensate for the sins of the slave trade. Given the circumstances of the intrusions already made by the Westerners, could they simply go away? The resounding answer given by Buxton, Henry Venn, and other humanitarians is echoed in our own day. They must stay long enough to give economic aid, technical assistance, and specialized training to an educated middle class of Africans who would in turn civilize and modernize their fellows.

The modernizing dreams of Buxton and Venn were, however, damped down by a resurgent imperialism. True, the Select Committee on Africa (Western Coast) in 1865 advised the British government to withdraw from Africa, after preparing the Africans to run their own affairs (as if they had not done so for hundreds of years), but this, of course, did not happen. Not all Englishmen were as convinced as Buxton and Venn were that Africans should be or indeed could be educated in the civilization of the West. What humanitarian education did do, in Nigeria as in Ghana and Sierra Leone, was to prepare those who lived in the urban centers to enter into the commercial sector of the society. This happened to give the Yorubas who lived in the coastal and nearby regions a head start among all the other tribes of Nigeria.

Ajayi discerningly notes that Western missionaries insisted upon observance of particular forms of personal conduct and relationships as evidence of civilization: the social amenities (games and afternoon tea, of course); Victorian courtesy, manners, obedience, reserve, and dress; monogamous marriage; fidelity (in sexual conduct); and Western habits of eating, drinking, dancing, and sanitary facilities.[10] Only those who have lived for extended periods of time in the closed compound of a boarding school in Africa can genuinely know how important to the inmates such matters come to be. In that setting all the nuances of feelings of superiority and inferiority, of affection and aversion, of command and discipline become ever more acute. Obviously, the high-sounding phrases or the laments of despair reported by the headmasters to the directors back home were affected by the personal and intimate matters that surged through the Mission compound walls and boarding schools of Africa.

When all else was said, however, the essence of the problem of uplift, or of social improvement, or of religious conversion, or of civilization for the peoples of a

---

[9] T. F. Buxton, *The African Slave Trade, The Remedy,* Benedict, New York, 1840, vol. 2, p. 218.

[10] J. F. Ade Ajayi, *Christian Missions in Nigeria, 1841-1891; The Making of a New Elite,* Northwestern University Press, Evanston, Ill., 1965, pp. 13-16.

traditional folk society revolved around the matters of literacy in the schools. The marks of distinction between a folk society and a civilized society since 3500 B.C. have been literacy and formal education as well as a differentiated urban society. The successor societies of Mesopotamian civilization had to learn the written language of their predecessors. Hellenizing meant learning Greek. Learning Latin was the propaedeutic to the rise of Western civilization. Is it so surprising that acquisition of a written language should be even more important in the process of fundamental social change in modern times?[11]

So while there was debate over the importance of conversion to Christianity or adoption of Western manners, or the teaching of practical studies, the value of learning a written language (either the Western language itself or Western literature translated into the vernacular) was agreed to by virtually everyone who admitted that the Africans could learn any language. This point was well put by the American leader of the Baptist missionaries in Nigeria, Thomas Jefferson Bowen, in 1857:

> Our designs and hopes in regard to Africa, are not simply to bring as many individuals as possible to the knowledge of Christ. We desire to establish the Gospel in the hearts and minds and social life of the people, so that truth and righteousness may remain and flourish among them, without the instrumentality of foreign missionaries. This can not be done without civilization. To establish the Gospel among any people, they must have Bibles, and therefore must have the art to make them, or the money to buy them. They must read the Bible, and this implies instruction. . . . which can not exist without . . . civilization.[12]

This implies clearly that while the Gospel may have first spiritual priority, the first practical priority must be the development of written materials and their use in teaching. To Protestant missionaries this meant, of course, translation of the Bible into the hundreds of spoken languages in use by those they would convert. No wonder then that Christian missionaries have been prolific agents for the development of written languages among the preliterate peoples of the world.

D. THE BRITISH MISSION IN INDIA

When the English and other Westerners turned their civilizing mission efforts to India, however, they found a much different situation. They now had to deal with a literate civilization much older than their own, whose educated elite already possessed one or more highly sophisticated literary languages, Sanskrit, Arabic, or Persian. The question was now, who was civilizing whom? The language problem became acute in the mid-nineteenth century. It remained so for more than another century.

[11] For analysis of several societies in Asia and Africa, see Jack Goody (ed.), *Literacy in Traditional Societies,* Cambridge University Press, London, 1968.
[12] T. J. Bowen, *Adventures and Missionary Labours in Several Countries in the Interior of Africa from 1849 to 1856,* Frank Cass & Co., Ltd., London, 1857, pp. 321-322.

In India, Western merchants preceded missionaries, schoolmasters, and government officials by many decades. The Portuguese were the first Westerners on the scene, as early as the beginning of the sixteenth century, followed in the seventeenth century by the Dutch and the British, the Danes and the French. By the middle of the eighteenth century the British East India Company (founded in 1600) had established its superiority over the other Western trading companies, receiving assistance from the British military (both navy and army) in extending its power over larger and larger sections of India itself. Then in turn it began to be more closely regulated by Parliament during the early nineteenth century, until full authority was transferred from the company to the crown in 1858, a year after the widespread "mutiny" by Indian troops in Northern India.

Although a few missionaries began to go to India early in the eighteenth century under the auspices of the Society for Promoting Christian Knowledge, the East India Company was not particularly enthusiastic about promoting English education until late in the century when prodded from London by the company's court of directors and by Parliament. These in turn had been importuned by the same evangelical and humanitarian groups who were interested in the missionizing and civilizing of Africa. For example, Parliament passed the Pitt Act in 1784 taking upon itself the responsibility for the welfare and civilization of the Indian people rather than leaving these goals to the company. Thereupon, the missionaries became active in the major presidencies of the company (Calcutta, Madras, Bombay) by establishing their English schools.

The leading lights of the company in India were not indifferent to all education, for they had been influenced by a few scholarly gentlemen who felt it was much better politically to promote the ancient religious languages of India (Sanskrit for Hindus and Arabic for Moslems) as well as the official language of India (Persian) rather than to risk the antipathy that might be aroused by being too pushy about importing the English language and literature. For example, in 1781 Warren Hastings gave company support to the efforts of Moslems in Calcutta to establish a *madrassa,* or Islamic college, to foster the traditional learning of Islam in Arabic. In 1792 John Duncan did the same for a comparable Sanskrit college of Hindu learning at Benares; and colleges for Persian learning were later promoted at Poona and Delhi. In 1784 Sir William Jones had formed the Royal Asiatic Society to promote Sanskrit, Arabic, and Persian studies, not solely for political reasons but because he, as an outstanding oriental scholar, believed they were genuinely among the superior languages of the world.

It was in this setting that the humanitarians at home began to redouble their efforts to get Parliament and the company to send British teachers to India and to encourage the missionaries to spread English education by giving support to the mission schools from government funds. This proposal was forwarded by William Wilberforce at the prodding of Charles Grant, a former company employee, during consideration of the twenty-year renewal of the company's charter in 1793. Wilberforce did not achieve his purpose against the opposition of those who were fearful that the spread of English education would promote unrest among the Indians as it had among the Americans.

But Wilberforce, Grant, and others of the humanitarian and evangelical party known as the Clapham sect persisted and achieved more success in the next twenty-year review of the company's charter in 1813. This time Parliament authorized (but did not require) the company to give financial support (10,000 rupees a year) to schools and other institutions that would be used for "the revival and improvement of literature and the encouragement of the learned natives of India, and for the introduction of a knowledge of the sciences among the inhabitants of the British territories in India."[13]

While the Indians were referred to as "learned natives," at least this was a step up from the terminology of "coloured races" and "peasants" which was used to apply to Africans. The current of superior attitude reflected in such terms was strong and deep among generations of Englishmen, and just as strongly and deeply resented by generations of Indians. Nevertheless, the British government was again committed to the use of public funds for government schools abroad nearly fifty years before it did so in England itself; and the Christian missions were allowed to extend their work to all company territories. The most successful school established in these early years was that of Alexander Duff of the Free Church of Scotland established in Calcutta. His work became a model for those who would promote English education in India rather than an oriental education.

Despite the mandate of the East India Company Act of 1813, the company officials moved ever so slowly; in the manner of stodgy bureaucracies they spent many years in making surveys of indigenous education. They interpreted the act to mean that *oriental* literature should be "revived," not English introduced. They were also very reluctant to interpret the act to mean that they should establish colleges as in England but rather should extend their support to Hindu and Moslem scholars for private study. But by 1823 a Committee of Public Instruction was set up in Bengal to administer the company schools which consisted of one English college, six oriental colleges, and a number of vernacular primary schools. The point of view of the Committee of Public Instruction was almost solidly orientalist in 1824.

But while the officials in India were going their orientalist way, the pressures at home were building up for an Anglicized education. The Utilitarians had joined the evangelicals in their generally low estimate of Indian languages, literature, and culture, plumping hard, as might be expected, for *useful* studies. James Mill himself from 1817 took up the cudgel for the necessity of educational reform in India. Meanwhile, in India a new Hindu college was established in Calcutta by David Hare and by the energetic Indian campaigner for English studies, Rammohun Roy, the outstanding nineteenth century Indian modernist. This college was the first Hindu institution to promote Western learning.

When in 1823 the Company's Committee of Public Instruction, ignoring all the ferment, planned to establish in Calcutta a Sanskrit college to complement the Islamic college there, the pot really began to boil. Despatches from London, written by James

---

[13] H. Sharp, *Selections from Educational Records, Part I, 1781-1839,* Superintendent Government Printing, Calcutta, 1920, p. 22.

Mill, were severely critical of the plan, hammering away at the need for studies based upon the principle of utility, namely English studies. And Rammohun Roy himself took up the cudgels in a persuasive protest that outdid other Anglicists in its contempt for Sanskrit knowledge as utterly useless and in his praise for English scientific studies as just what Indians needed most. Covered by elaborate and respectful professions of humility, and couched in beautifully turned English phrases (note his twist on the term *natives*), Roy made his case:

> When this seminary of learning was proposed, we understood that the government of England had ordered a considerable sum of money to be annually devoted to the instruction of its Indian subjects. We were filled with sanguine hopes that this sum would be laid out in employing European gentlemen of talent and education to instruct the natives of India in Mathematics, Natural Philosophy, Chemistry, Anatomy, and other useful sciences, which the natives of Europe have carried to a degree of perfection that has raised them above the inhabitants of other parts of the world. . . .
>
> [Instead] the Government are establishing a Sanscrit school under Hindu Pandits to impart such knowledge as is already current in India. This seminary (similar in character to those which existed in Europe before the time of Lord Bacon) can only be expected to load the minds of youth with grammatical niceties and metaphysical distinctions of little or no practical use to the possessors or to society. The pupils will there acquire what was known two thousand years ago with the addition of vain and empty subtleties since then produced by speculative men, such as is already commonly taught in all parts of India.[14]

For a decade the controversy between the Orientalists and the Anglicists took place at long range between London and Calcutta and locally in both places. Meanwhile the Whigs came to power in 1830 on a wave of liberal reform, and soon thereafter the first subsidies from government funds were made on behalf of voluntary schools in England in 1833. So when the company charter once more came up for review in 1833, it called for a ten-fold increase in the annual support for education in India. The character of the Committee of Public Instruction in Calcutta had now radically changed. Its brash thirty-four-year-old chairman, right out of England, and innocent of classical Indian literature, was Thomas Babington Macaulay, a fervid Anglicist. His famous Minute of 1835 turned the tide in favor of the civilizing mission of English education. He was contemptuous of Arabic and Sanskrit, assuring the committee that "a single shelf of a good European library was worth the whole native literature of India and Arabia" and that

> all the historical information which has been collected from all the books written in the Sanscrit language is less valuable than what may be found in the most paltry abridgments used at preparatory schools in England. In every branch

[14] Rammohun Roy, *The English Works of Raja Rammohun Roy,* The Panini Office, Bahadurganj, Allahabad, 1906, p. 472.

of physical or moral philosophy, the relative position of the two nations is nearly the same.[15]

For sheer cultural arrogance Macaulay surpassed most of the other early nineteenth-century "civilizers." He played heavily on the theme that there was a useful analogy between what the great Latin and Greek classics did for the civilizing of Englishmen during the Renaissance and the same values that the great English and European literatures could now bestow upon Indians, as indeed they had already done in civilizing the Russians. He ended his Minute with the notorious peroration:

> To sum up what I have said, I think it clear . . . that English is better worth knowing than Sanscrit or Arabic, that the natives are desirous to be taught English, and are not desirous to be taught Sanscrit or Arabic; that neither as the languages of law, nor as the languages of religion, have the Sanscrit and Arabic any peculiar claim to our engagement; that it is possible to make natives of this country thoroughly good English scholars, and that to this end our efforts ought to be directed . . . that it is impossible for us, with our limited means, to attempt to educate the body of people. We must at present do our best to form a class who may be interpreters between us and the millions whom we govern; a class of persons, Indian in blood and color, but English in taste, in opinions, in morals, and in intellect. To that class we may leave it to refine the vernacular dialects of the country, to enrich those dialects with terms of science borrowed from the Western nomenclature, and to render them by degrees fit vehicles for conveying knowledge to the great mass of the population.[16]

The governor of the Company, Lord Bentinck, accepted Macaulay's arguments and opted for English education. Despite grave doubts in London, including those of John Stuart Mill, who thought Macaulay demeaned too much the Indian classical languages, the Macaulay position became the dominant view. English replaced Persian as the official language of the law courts in 1837, and public examinations for civil service positions were made available to Indians in 1844. Missionaries expanded greatly their primary schools taught in the vernacular while government schools on the secondary level concentrated on English. Neither could cope with the demand. Whatever else may be said of Macaulay's view he was proved right that Indians were interested in English education.

By the time the next and final renewal of the East India Company's charter was made in 1853, the victory for the Anglicists had been sealed. The 1854 Despatch by Sir Charles Wood set the guidelines for the future: Each province would have a department of education and a Director-General of Public Instruction to oversee a system of vernacular schools for primary education, and build middle schools, institutes for teacher training, secondary schools and colleges that would teach English to prepare students for three new universities to be established in the three presidencies,

[15] Thomas Babington Macâulay, *Minutes on Education*, Baptist Mission Press, Calcutta, 1862, p. 107-108.

[16] Ibid., p. 114-115.

Bombay, Madras, and Calcutta. In addition, there would be a system of grants-in-aid to private schools, regardless of religious affiliation, if they provided a secular education and allowed governmental inspection.

Although the Wood Despatch is sometimes regarded as the "Charter of Indian Education," its principal early achievements were the establishment of departments of public instruction and the establishment of three universities in 1857. The enthusiasm of the departments for wide expansion of primary and secondary education was as limited as the funds. They adhered to the filter-down theory and left primary and secondary education largely to the missionaries and to Indian private enterprise which responded with surprising alacrity, keeping an eye on admission to the universities. Students flocked to the new universities in unprecedented numbers; that is, they flocked to colleges affiliated to the universities which did the examining and degree-granting along the model of the University of London.

Such response is not really surprising when it is remembered that the British penetrated India through the major sea ports, long-established commercial centers dominated by urban, literate elites that were predominantly Hindu. The principal spheres of influence left to Moslem rulers of India were the inland regions of northern India. Therefore, the English trading culture and its developing economic and political power became focal points for the Hindu classes to strengthen themselves vis-à-vis the Moslems of India. No wonder they eagerly sought preferment through an English education which would enable them to improve their status.

This intense competition between Hindus and Moslems was further complicated by the bewildering variety of castes, classes, religions, sects, and groups that made up the vastly heterogeneous Indian civilization. English education was thus seen as a means of defending against competitors a status already achieved or improving a status too long hopelessly outclassed by others that enjoyed more educational opportunity. No wonder the lower castes took to the missionary education which came from outside the social system that repressed them and which preached the equality of all men in the sight of the Christian God. No wonder the literate elite of the Hindu caste took to the English language which was no more alien to them than the imported Arabic of Moslems or the Persian of the Mogul rulers had been. In fact, their literacy in at least one language and their urban background gave them a head start in cultural and in economic preferment over the rural and inland populace.

Thus the outsider's civilizing mission to India sometimes exacerbated already existing divisions along ethnic, religious, linguistic, and commercial lines, as it did in West Africa. It promoted an unevenness in social, economic, and political development among different groups and different regions of the country. Even more than in those parts of West Africa where the literate patterns of a traditional civilization were absent, the literate Indians responded positively to the Western literary education. While Rammohun Roy spoke warmly of the virtues of Western science, the fact was that it was the traditional English literary and humanistic education that prevailed more than did the modernizing, scientific, technical, or utilitarian studies. The result in both cases was a high priority for English academic literary education. Language more than science was seen to be the principal civilizing agent. The preoccupation in the nineteenth century with the process of *Westernization* rather than with the process of *modernization* perhaps postponed the national development of India longer than might otherwise have been the case.

All in all, the British humanitarian thrust toward spreading Western civilization by Christian missions, by commerce, by government, and by education was far more elaborate and widespread during the first half of the nineteenth century than that of any other Western nation.[17] Catholic France, heavily engaged in wars on the European continent and wracked by internal conflicts between conservative, liberal, and radical forces, did not erupt with the evangelical vigor or the commercial aggressiveness that marked the Protestant nations of the West. To be sure, the French were making inroads into Africa, especially in Senegal and the Ivory Coast, but their educational influence did not match that of the British until the age of later imperialism opened Africa to Belgian and German intrusion as well as to British and French.

E. THE AMERICANS JOIN THE CHRISTIAN ENDEAVOR

While the humanitarian and evangelical impulses within the United States came close to matching those in Britain, the American outreach to the rest of the world was far less extensive up to the middle of the nineteenth century. This was due partly to its later arrival as a competitor in world trade, partly to the necessity of building stable and effective institutions of government and religion after the war for independence, and partly due to the preoccupation of the humanitarian impulse with the all-absorbing abolition of slavery. Britain was favored, if that be the word, on all these counts.

Stanley Elkins points to the fact that the contestants on both sides of the abolition struggle in the United States came to display increasingly closed minds as to alternatives or modifications of the system.[18] Opponents of slavery moved more and more to positions that demanded immediate and unqualified abolition. No compromise could be made with the moral evil of slavery as preached by William Lloyd Garrison and his *Liberator* from 1831 onwards. Immediate and uncompromising repentance of the sin of slavery was preached by students at Lane Theological Seminary and Oberlin College. The moral impatience of college students has a long history; moderation in opposition to slavery was taken as a sign of weakness. On the opposite side, the proslavery apologists found values in the system even when it was actually becoming financially unprofitable and inefficient as an economic system in the light of technical and industrial developments.

So neither side could come to consider institutional ways in which slavery could be changed, reformed, or abolished gradually, and in which the owners as well as the

[17] For examples drawn from the Bahamas, Ceylon, India, Egypt, Cyprus, and Nigeria, see Brian Holmes (ed.), *Educational Policy and the Mission Schools; Case Studies from the British Empire,* Routledge, London, 1967.

[18] Stanley Elkins, *Slavery, a Problem in American Industrial and Intellectual Life,* University of Chicago Press, Chicago, 1959.

slaves could be educated to a radical transformation of the system. The reason that few persons turned to education as a transforming agent for slavery seemed to lie in the fact that the humanitarians had little influence in the institutional centers of power in government, business, church, law, or education. These institutions in the United States were so fragmented and decentralized into competing governmental jurisdictions, competing churches, and competing businesses that there was no Establishment in the United States through which to work as compared with that in Britain.

Beyond that, American humanitarians did not work so effectively in and through the institutional arrangements they did have in order to effect social change. Elkins points out that the transcendentalists of the Concord community were intellectuals without institutional connections in government, law, industry, church, or university.[19] The idealistic utopians established separate communities to work out their own isolated panaceas at Brook Farm or New Harmony. This point cannot be carried too far, for much humanitarian enthusiasm did flow into the large scale public school movement as a transforming agent of social reform. But the point, I believe, applies with special force to American participation in the international aspects of the civilizing mission.

We have seen how William Wilberforce and Thomas Fowell Buxton and a powerful coterie of allies in Britain not only worked ceaselessly to organize missionary societies to spread the gospel overseas, but they also worked in commercial companies to develop trade in Africa and Asia, and they worked on Parliament through influential lawyers, politicians, highly placed social leaders, merchants, and government officials to mobilize the power and authority of government behind their mission projects.

By comparison, the American missionary societies were weak (until after mid-century when they eventually surpassed those of all other nations). The Colonization Society formed in 1816 to repatriate freed slaves to Africa was a relatively disjointed and feeble operation. Thirty years later when Liberia declared its independence in 1847, American Liberians numbered only 3,000 to 4,000 settlers. To strengthen the early humanitarian forays into Sierra Leone and Nigeria the British moved to stronger ties with commercial companies and, when these ran into difficulties, the ties with government were strengthened. Neither kind of development materialized to the same extent in Liberia. Meanwhile the colony was scarcely able to maintain itself against the odds of climate, the hostility of the local Africans and Western neighbors, and, of course, the ambivalent motives of a home society in which the friends of repatriation could scarcely be called friends of the blacks. Henry Clay, Speaker of the House of Representatives, spoke thus of the Liberia project:

> Can there be a nobler cause than that which, whilst it proposes to rid our own country of a useless and pernicious, if not dangerous portion of its population, contemplates the spreading of the arts of civilized life, and the

---

[19] Ibid., chap. 4.

possible redemption from ignorance and barbarism of a benighted quarter of the globe![20]

Another factor that needs a good deal of investigation is the policy of the American societies in sending Negro missionaries to Liberia on the theory that blacks could stand up better under the rigors of the African climate than could white men. In the 1830s and 1840s, highly qualified white missionaries were sent to conduct schools in Liberia. Many of them had been especially trained for missionary work through study of the classics and theology at Princeton Theological Seminary and had been sent out by the Western Foreign Missionary Society or by the Presbyterian Board of Foreign Missions.

By 1850 the number of highly trained white missionaries began to decline as the number of qualified black missionaries became available to pick up the main burden of the work during the second half of the century. Perhaps more important than the color of the missionaries or their training was the fact that the effort of the American missionaries was less broadly humanitarian (intended to improve the quality of life for the general population) and more narrowly focused on training American-Liberian blacks to become Christian missionaries to spread the gospel in Liberia. The lack of rapport between the blacks imported from America and the blacks of the villages of Liberia made it clear that there was no automatic bond of color that could surmount the differences in culture.

Conceivably, the American blacks could have "civilized" the general population of native blacks more effectively if they had set out to do so, but apparently the effort to raise the general educational level of the entire African peoples of Liberia was minimal. The social distance between the Afro-Americans and the Africans in Liberia remained as great if not greater than that between the imported black settlers and the natives of Sierra Leone. In neither case did the Afro-Americans give indication of wishing to give up their Western acculturation in exchange for the traditional folk society culture they found in Africa. Most Afro-Americans in Liberia did not regard themselves as Africans and they did not give equal rights to the Africans when they set up their American-style constitution.

The local blacks in the various West African colonies did seem to have one thing in common when faced with the Western education from outside. They recognized it as a means of advancement or preferment in the modernizing sector of society. The plaint from Rev. Jonathan Alward from Liberia in 1840 sounds familiar:

> They are actuated in part, by curiosity, but the strongest motive is the love of gain. They are a very avaricious people. Some of them seem to think that the white man is in possession of some secrets, as, for instance, the knowledge of writing, which would greatly assist them in trade, and they also know that we cannot settle in their country for any purpose without bringing some trade. But,

[20] Report of the meeting on the Colonization of Free Blacks, *Daily National Intelligencer,* vol. 4, no. 1236, December 24, 1816.

whatever may be the cause of their willingness to receive us, we may make use of it for good, and by a *very prudent* course gradually exert a salutary influence.[21]

To Rev. Alward the Liberians may have seemed simply avaricious, but his students were sensing more than he realized when they believed that the white man's secret of the knowledge of writing was indeed a powerful secret and an instrument of modernization even if not so intended by the penetrating missionary. Whether the civilizing mission could have been undertaken with less disruption or devastation of the receiving culture, with less imposition of alien and upsetting ideas, and with greater respect for the welfare of those affected is, of course, one of the great questions of modern history.

It is just possible that if the American and British, and all the other Western devotees of the civilizing mission, had listened more closely to the kind of advice given to the young American college students at Princeton Theological Seminary in 1833 by a British missionary from overseas, the process could have been still more civilized. The Reverend John Philip of the London Missionary Society argued that the general education of the entire African community was the necessary condition of a successful mission:

> If I have enlarged more upon the importance of early education than upon the importance of preaching to the people, it is because too many good people, and too many missionaries regard the latter as everything, and the former as of little importance; and because the duties of the one are more agreeable to the fancy, to the indolence, and to the vanity of the human mind, than the other. . . . *The gospel never can have a permanent footing in a barbarous country, unless education and civilization go hand in hand with our religious instructions.* [22]

Ironically, the Reverend Mr. Philip was writing to the Americans from the Cape of Good Hope in South Africa. But the majority of Americans were not listening, either to the plea for widespread education of Africans in their homeland or to the need for widespread education of Afro-Americans in the land to which they had been transported as slaves. In fact, most of the little education that was provided for slaves in the American South up to 1860 could well be thought of as a phase of the more general civilizing mission of the West. It is true that many slaves on the plantations were trained as artisans to undertake the diversified trades needed for large-scale farming and support of a plantation settlement, but this was largely for the economic benefit of the slave owner.[23]

---

[21] The *Foreign Missionary Chronicle*, vol. 8, no. 7, July 1840. Italics added.

[22] *A Letter from the Rev. John Philip, D. D. Superintendent of the Missions of the London Society at the Cape of Good Hope, &c. to the Society of Inquiry on Missions in the Theological Seminary, Princeton, New Jersey,* Princeton, N.J., 1833, p. 22.

[23] Marcus Wilson Jernegan, *Laboring and Dependent Classes in Colonial America, 1607-1783,* Frederick Ungar, New York, 1931 and 1960, chaps. 1-2.

It is also true that as many as 15 to 20 percent of adult Negroes could read in the post-Revolutionary period of the 1780s and 1790s.[24] In the South this was achieved largely as a result of humanitarian efforts to help the oppressed and of missionary efforts to teach English so that the Negroes could read the Bible. In the North the democratic revolutionary spirit led to the opening of some schools for blacks and by blacks themselves. If the motivations of the civilizing mission directed at the education of Negro slaves had been allowed to take on the full-scale power which was soon to be applied to popular education for whites, a widespread education for blacks might have resulted, and possibly the course of history changed.

But with the onset of the second quarter of the nineteenth century a reaction began to set in. Bloody insurrections in Haiti, an influx of free Negroes from the West Indies, and the growing demand for cotton which increased the demand for slaves all led to repressive measures designed to prevent uprisings among the slaves. In the South, these included the prohibiting of slave owners from teaching slaves to read and write, even if the owners desired to do so. Even in the North measures were taken to prevent free Negroes from teaching. As a result of the general repression, literacy dropped to around 10 percent by 1860.[25]

It is true, of course, that some slave owners continued to allow their slaves to be taught, some slaves taught themselves or gained help secretly, and in the North some schools and colleges were established for blacks, notably an academy in Washington, D.C. by Mrs. Myrtella Miner and one by Wilberforce in Ohio. Some white colleges like Western Reserve, Lane Seminary, and Oberlin admitted a few blacks. Bullock documents the permissiveness of indulgent or sympathetic white owners that enabled many Negroes to obtain an education and a wide variety of technical skills and thus to prepare themselves to exert leadership among the free Negro population. As a result of the "Hidden Passage" that was never wholly closed, the free Negro population grew at a more rapid rate than the slave population between 1790 and 1860.

Many of the slaves who gained an education despite the repression of the closed system in the South escaped to the North to become literate leaders for revolt and eventually for abolition. It was no accident that almost all the black leaders had been able to achieve some measure of education: Denmark Vesey, David Walker, Nat Turner, Thomas H. Jones, Lunceford Lane, Frederick Douglass, Austin Seward.[26] This was no mean achievement to be made against the enormous odds of the brutal slave system. The unextinguishable spirit of the blacks themselves and the surreptitious aid of sympathetic white humanitarians made the exceptions to mass illiteracy possible. So long as a literate leadership of 10 percent was tolerated, the blacks could produce an effective elite.

[24] Carter G. Woodson, *The Education of the Negro Prior to 1861,* Associated Publishers, Washington, D.C., 1919, p. 85 (reissued by Arno Press, New York, 1968).

[25] Ibid., p. 228.

[26] Henry Allen Bullock, *A History of Negro Education in the South, from 1619 to the Present,* Harvard University Press, Cambridge, Mass., 1967, p. 14.

When the Union Armies began to control various parts of the South and appealed to philanthropic societies for aid to help feed, clothe, and educate the freed slaves, the humanitarian agencies loosed their enormous energies to the task. The American Missionary Association, the Home Mission Society of the Baptist Church (North), the Freedman's Aid Society, the General Conference of the Methodist Episcopal Church, and many others joined in a new task for the civilizing mission, to prepare the freed slaves to become self-supporting and self-respecting citizens. With the onset of Reconstruction the civilizing mission itself began to undergo a transformation. In a word, it had to become a "citizenizing" mission, a goal that was proclaimed by the Fourteenth Amendment in 1868, but still not to be fully achieved a hundred years later. It took white Americans a long time to realize that a genuinely modern society could not be realized until that goal was achieved.

It took white Americans still longer to apply even the ideal of a principle of citizenship to the original Americans. The civilizing mission was, if anything, more reluctantly transformed into a citizenizing mission with regard to American Indians than it was with regard to American Negroes. The linkage of the Christianizing and the civilizing mission had its roots deep in colonial ideology, though not particularly widespread in practice. True, Harvard had made gestures toward educating Indians, and the College of William and Mary proposed to do so in the original charter of 1693 as did Moon's Charity School founded by Eleazar Wheelock when it became Dartmouth College in 1769. After the Revolutionary War the Anglican efforts of the Society for the Propagation of the Gospel in Foreign Parts to educate Indians were taken up by the several Americanized Protestant denominations which founded scores of schools for Indians. Humanitarians also established manual labor schools in the Indian communities, and even the government provided very limited funds to aid the work.

Noteworthy is the fact, too, that some of the Indians themselves wanted schools and the means of Western education. As early as 1791 the Senecas asked President Washington to send them teachers to help their children learn farming and the three R's. By 1850 the Cherokees had provided their own school system of more than twenty schools and 1,000 students. The other members of the Five Civilized Tribes, the Choctaws, Creeks, Chickasaws, and Seminoles, took similar steps to civilize themselves by establishing towns, farms, and churches as well as schools after they moved from the Southeast to the Indian Territory of Oklahoma following the Removal Act of 1830. There they hoped to organize themselves politically, economically, and educationally into a confederation and eventually become a self-governing commonwealth or state in the Union.

But white Americans in general and the federal government in particular could not admit of such self-government. Rather, Indian Affairs were a matter for the War Department from 1824 to 1849 when they were assigned to the Department of Interior. Eastern Indians were given lands beyond the Mississippi in return for leaving their lands in the east by action of Congress in the Removal Act of 1830. Whereupon the Supreme Court in 1831 declared the Indians to be dependent peoples analogous to the relation of a ward to his guardian. They were not to be regarded as independent nations, despite all the treaties that had been signed, nor as slaves, nor as citizens. Up to the Civil War they were simply to be Christianized and civilized by their friends—or robbed and cheated and despoiled by their enemies.

After the Civil War a humanitarian concern for the assimilation of Indians into modernizing America did increase and the Federal government's role enlarged, but the record up to then was not very encouraging. Martha E. Layman sums up the century between 1780 and 1880 as follows:

> The net results of almost a hundred years of effort and the expenditure of hundreds of thousands of dollars for Indian education were a small number of poorly attended mission schools, a suspicious and disillusioned Indian population, and a few hundred products of missionary education, who, for the most part, had either returned to the blanket or were living as misfits among the Indian or white population.[27]

The educational problems raised by the confrontation of the American Indian folk culture and American Western civilization were if anything more baffling than those facing Euro-Americans and Afro-Americans. In both cases the hope and the faith of the civilizing mission was that formal education was the answer. Were the discouraging results due to the shortcomings of organized schooling itself, or to the inappropriate purposes of assimilation, the poorly trained teachers, or the unbridgeable gaps of culture, language, or racial capacity? To the mid-nineteenth century the answers were not forthcoming. To most white Americans the Indian problem was far off in the wild West—for the pioneers, the cowboys, and the army to worry about. But the modernizing process would not let the matter lie there, the whole American West had somehow to be Westernized—that is, modernized—during the coming century. The problem would not go away. It became ever more acute, as we saw in Chapter 13.

[27] Martha E. Layman, "A History of Indian Education in the United States," unpublished doctoral dissertation, University of Minnesota, Minneapolis, 1942, p. 15.

CHAPTER XV

EDUCATION
AND WESTERN
IMPERIALISM
(1860s A.D.-THE PRESENT)

A. CONDUIT FOR A WORLDWIDE MODERNIZATION PROCESS

In the century following the 1860s the most portentous agency through which the impact of Western education was exerted upon the traditional societies of the rest of the world was modern imperialism.[1] For better or worse, imperialism dispersed Western education around the globe, stimulated the modernization of the peoples it touched, and helped to shape an international and cosmopolitan social order that forecast the emergence of a worldwide civilization. This is not to say that imperialism was a *good* way to achieve such results, but it *is* to say that imperialism, moderniza-tion, and cosmopolitanism were inextricably entangled with each other, and that Western education was a major ingredient of all three.

It is well to remember that imperialism is not a new phenomenon, nor is it a stranger to education. In fact, it boasts one of the longest records of existence in human history, roughly 4,500 years. If imperialism can be defined in essence as the direct rule over the territory and lives of one people by the government of another,[2] the history of imperialism goes back almost as far as the history of civilization itself. (See Exhibit 15.1—Imperialism at a Glance). A few centuries after urban, literate ways

---

[1] Imperialism acquired exceedingly complex connotations in the nineteenth century, and generally received a "bad press" in the cold war atmosphere of the mid-twentieth century. No matter what its connotations, use of the term cannot be shirked in dealing with the spread of Western education since 1850. See, for example, Richard Koebner, with Helmut Dan Schmidt, *Imperialism: the Story and Significance of a Political Word, 1840-1960,* Cambridge University Press, London, 1964; A. P. Thornton, *Doctrines of Imperialism,* Wiley, New York, 1965; George Lichtheim, *Imperialism,* Praeger, New York, 1971; Philip D. Curtin (ed.), *Imperialism,* Harper & Row, New York, 1971; Ronald Robinson and John Gallagher with Alice Denny, *Africa and the Victorians: the Climax of Imperialism* (c. 1961), Doubleday, Garden City, N.Y., 1968.

[2] Thornton, op. cit., p. 5.

516

of life appeared in Mesopotamia, Egypt, India, and China, bureaucratic empires also appeared, attempting to centralize their policies and utilizing organized systems of education to train men for offices in the imperial bureaucracies.

In all these premodern, traditional empires the organized systems of education were also instrumental in acculturating "foreigners" to the dominant cultures of the empires. This was true when successive conquerors took over an established empire, absorbed its culture and education, and adapted themselves to its civilization; for example, the Akkadians, Babylonians, and Assyrians who successively ruled Mesopotamia; the Mongols and Manchurians who ruled China; and the Germans who conquered Rome. It was also true when the empires spread over the territories of the peoples they conquered, bringing their education as instruments of their civilization, as, for example, in the Hellenistic, Roman, Arab, Aztec, and Incan empires.

Around the sixteenth century, imperialism took on for the first time in history a worldwide character. The premodern empires (except for the Greek city-states) were principally land-based empires with the rule of the farthest reaches of territory subject to the limited technology of overland travel and communication. With the onset of early modern times the seafaring peoples of Western Europe became the spearhead of waterborne empires that eventually encircled the globe, embracing large parts of the Americas, Africa, Asia and Oceania, as well as of Europe. Meanwhile, imperial thrusts outward were also being made by the expansionst, land-based peoples to compete with the aggressive Western Europeans: the Russians pushed eastward across the entire continent of Asia to the Pacific and southeastward into Central Asia; the Ottoman Turks pushed across North Africa and deep into Europe from West Asia; and the Chinese expanded north, west, and south from the Chinese heartland. In the course of 300 to 400 years this combination of Eastern and Western empires spread their cultural and educational institutions with greater or lesser intensity to the remote reaches of the globe.

By the middle of the nineteenth century this movement produced a critical movement in world history. The age-old balance among the traditional land-based civilizations of the Afro-Eurasian ecumene began to wobble uncertainly. Astonishingly soon it collapsed in the face of the overpowering surge of a new imperialism from the West. I prefer the term *late imperialism,* because it was not wholly new nor unrelated to the early modern imperialism, but it did have a distinctive character. Its most aggressive representatives were the rapidly modernizing nations of the West, Britain, France, Germany, the United States, and to a lesser extent, Holland, Belgium, Denmark, and Italy. These were the primary or generative modernizers who first took the lead in modernizing themselves in the heartland or inner zone of the West. That it was the primary modernizers who took the imperialist lead from 1850 onward was a fact of momentous import. It meant that late modern Western imperialism was exceedingly rapidly established over virtually all of Africa, as well as over much of Asia. It thus has carried the brunt of the reaction against imperialism and imperialists in recent years.

What is sometimes overlooked, however, is that the traditional Eastern empires, Russian, Ottoman, Japanese, and Chinese, all with an enormous stake in Asia, began to

Exhibit 15.1   Imperialism at a Glance

I. *Premodern Imperialism**–2500 B.C. to 1500 A.D.
   A. *Nonbureaucratic Empires*
      1. Old Persian Empires
         a. Ahmenid–sixth to fourth centuries B.C.–patrimonial
         b. Parthian–second century B.C. to third century A.D.–patrimonial
      2. Greek City-States–fifth to fourth centuries B.C.
      3. Republican Rome–fourth to first centuries B.C.
      4. Carolingian–eighth to ninth centuries A.D.–patrimonial
      5. Holy Roman–tenth to sixteenth centuries A.D.
      6. Feudal Europe–tenth to thirteenth centuries A.D.
      7. Feudal Japan–twelfth to sixteenth centuries A.D.
      8. Mongols–thirteenth to sixteenth centuries A.D.–nomad or conquest empires
      9. Early Arab Caliphates–seventh to eighth centuries A.D.– conquest empires

   B. *Centralized Bureaucratic Empires*
      1. Egyptian–twenty-eighth to sixth centuries B.C.
      2. Mesopotamian
         a. Akkadian ⎫
         b. Babylonian ⎬ twenty-fourth to sixth centuries B.C.
         c. Assyrian ⎭
      3. Hellenistic
         a. Ptolomies ⎫
         b. Seleucids ⎭ fourth to first centuries B.C.
      4. Roman–first century B.C. to fifth century A.D.
      5. Byzantine–third to fifteenth centuries A.D.
      6. Persian
         a. Sassanid–third to seventh centuries A.D.
         b. Saffawid (Safavid)–sixteenth to eighteenth centuries A.D.
      7. Indian
         a. Maurya–fourth to second centuries B.C.
         b. Gupta–fourth to fifth centuries A.D.
         c. Mogul–sixteenth to eighteenth centuries A.D.
      8. Chinese
         a. Han–second century B.C. to third century A.D.
         b. T'ang–seventh to tenth centuries A.D.
         c. Sung–tenth to thirteenth centuries A.D.
         d. Yuan (Mongol)–thirteenth to fourteenth centuries A.D.
         e. Ming–fourteenth to seventeenth centuries A.D.
         f. Ch'ing (Manchu)–seventeenth to twentieth centuries A.D.
      9. Later Arab Caliphates
         a. Abbasids–eighth to thirteenth centuries A.D.
         b. Omayyad Caliphate of Cordoba–eighth to eleventh centuries A.D.
         c. Fatimid Caliphate of Egypt–tenth to twelfth centuries A.D.
         d. "Imperial cult" in
            black African kingdoms–thirteenth to sixteenth centuries A.D.
      10. Aztec–fourteenth to sixteenth centuries A.D.
      11. Inca–fourteenth to sixteenth centuries A.D.

*The list of premodern empires is adapted from S. N. Eisenstadt, *The Political Systems of Empires: the Rise and Fall of the Historical Bureaucratic Societies*, Free Press of Glencoe, New York, 1963.

Exhibit 15.1   Imperialism at a Glance (Continued)

II. *Modern Imperialism*—1500 A.D. to the Present
  A. *Early Modern Imperialism*—1500 A.D. to 1860s A.D.
    1. Originating in Europe
      a. Expanding overseas from Europe—seaborne empires to: America, Africa, Asia
        (1) Portuguese
        (2) Spanish
        (3) Dutch
        (4) British
        (5) French
        (6) Danish
      b. Land-borne empire to Asia
        (1) Russian
      c. Principally internal to Europe
        (1) Swedish
        (2) Holy Roman
        (3) Austrian
        (4) Prussian
    2. Originating in Asia
      a. Ottoman—expanding to Europe and North Africa
      b. Chinese—expanding north, south, and west
      c. Japanese

  B. *Late Modern Imperialism*—1860s to the Present
    1. The Empires of the Primary, Generative Modernizers—Western Imperialism
      a. British
      b. French
      c. German
      d. American
      e. Dutch
      f. Belgian
      g. Danish
      h. Italian
    2. The Empires of the Secondary, Derivative Modernizers—Eastern Imperialism
      a. Russian
      b. Ottoman
      c. Japanese
      d. Chinese
    3. Defensive Modernization outside the Empires
      a. Thailand
      b. Iran
      c. Afghanistan
      d. Ethiopia

  C. *Disimperialism*
    1. Following the Napoleonic Wars
      a. Latin America
    2. Following World War I
      a. Eastern Europe
    3. Following World War II
      a. Asia
      b. Africa

mobilize their own societies in order to fend off the threat posed by the Westerners. Each in its own way proceeded to strengthen itself with the Westerners' own most powerful instruments of technology, science, and education. In adopting a stance of "defensive modernization" the Eastern empires borrowed much from the West, and it is in this sense that they may be called secondary or derivative modernizers as they too swept millions of "other peoples" into their imperial orbits. While the Ottoman Empire was dismembered by World War I and the Japanese empire was similarly dismembered by World War II, and while the Western powers underwent a massive surge to disimperialism after World War II, the rule established by the traditional Russian and Chinese empires over the peoples of vast territories in Asia has not been relinquished by the modernizing Communist governments.

In the decade of the 1860s imperialism began to take on a new coloration. Whereas early modern imperialism had been largely maritime and commercial in character, with relatively little territorial aggrandizement (except in the Americas), in its late modern form imperial governments began to exert direct control over the lands of the less advanced peoples. The rapid rise in the populations of the modernizing European countries created a push toward emigration that led 60 million Europeans to move out of Europe between 1840 and 1940, particularly to Asian Russia (Siberia, Caucasus, and Central Asia), Argentina, Brazil, Canada, Australia, and the West Indies. Britain moved ever more aggressively into India and expanded onto the Malay peninsula. The Russians moved across the Asian continent to found Vladivostok (1860) and marched into Turkestan to take Tashkent (1864). France moved into Mexico, North Africa, and Southeast Asia. In fact, the use of the term imperialism in its late modern sense was particularly applied to Napoleon III of France in the 1860s, as he sought to extend French influence in Mexico by setting up Maximilian as emperor and in Indochina by taking over Cochin China (South Vietnam) and Cambodia.[3]

The Asian empires were so vulnerable and nonprogressive (especially the Ottoman, Chinese, and Persian) that the Western imperialists, including Russia, found it relatively easy to add political jurisdiction and financial investment in land, mines, and railroads to their commercial activities. This was sometimes done by extracting agreements to give special privileges to the Western powers (extraterritoriality in China, capitulations in Turkey, spheres of influence in Persia to Russia in the north and to Britain in the south). Elsewhere, control was exerted through protectorates in which the external power ruled indirectly through local chiefs, sultans, or kings, or through colonies directly governed by Western officials sent in by the imperial power. Control was sometimes achieved in the classic way by absorbing within the empire peoples who lived in contiguous territories and stood in the way of the imperial thrust. (Russia moved to their east, and China, Brazil, and the United States to their west). By and large, the imperialist impact on traditional societies in Asia preceded that in Africa, but from 1880 onwards the outward push of the modernizers (secondary as well as primary) accelerated so rapidly that the imperial powers of West and East alike carved up virtually the entire earth among themselves (See Figure 15.1). The prepon-

[3]Koebner, with Schmidt, op. cit., pp. 1-26.

Figure 15.1   Western Education Follows the Course of Empire (c. 1900)

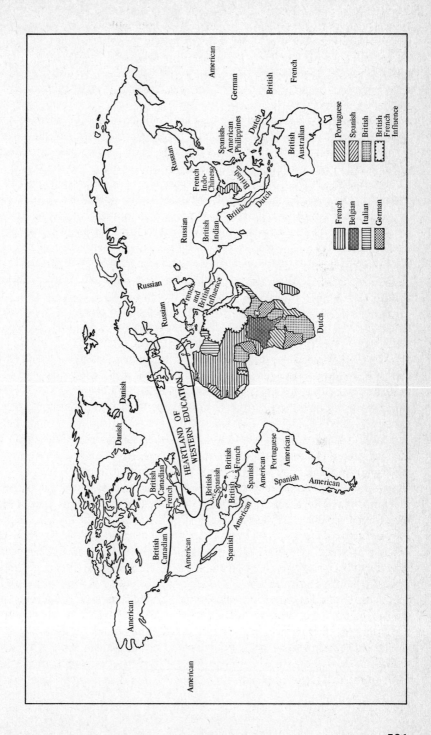

derance of power went clearly to the Europe-oriented societies; by the 1930s the colonies and ex-colonies of Europe covered almost 85 percent of the entire land surface of the world.

The most concerted and publicly announced actions of the Western nations took place between November 1884 and February 1885 when thirteen states of Europe and the United States attended the Berlin Conference and agreed upon the ground rules by which nearly all of Africa would be carved up. In the course of the scramble during the next fifteen to twenty years the lion's shares went to Britain and France with Germany, Belgium (or rather, King Leopold), and Italy gaining their lesser shares, and Portugal and Spain holding on to their earlier gains. Within two decades the rule of Africa was turned upside down. Whereas 90 percent of Africa was ruled by Africans in 1880, more than 90 percent was ruled by Europeans by 1900.

Although the United States did not participate in the carving up of Africa nor of the mainland of Asia, its imperialist thrust, headed southward and westward, paralleled in distance the far-flung engagements of Britain, France, Germany, Japan, and Russia. However, the United States empire in the Caribbean islands, Central America, and the Pacific from 1898 to 1920 was far smaller than that of the other major powers in size of territories (mostly islands) and magnitude of population.[4]

In seeking to illustrate the relatively sudden emergence of a global cosmopolitanism in the decade of the 1850s, William H. McNeill cites four events as symbolic of the beginning of the collapse of the traditional social orders in Asia: the Crimean War of 1853 to 1856, in which the Ottoman Turks defeated the Russians with British and French help, but during which the Ottoman political structure was severely weakened; the Mutiny of 1857 to 1858, which signalized the toppling of the Mogul empire in India and the substitution of direct British imperial rule; the "opening" of Japan to Western trade in 1854 by Commodore Perry's American fleet; and the Taiping Rebellion (1850-1864) in China which heralded assaults upon the Manchu rulers as alien supporters of an outworn Confucian society. In all cases the traditional orders were being attacked in a setting of ever-closer contact with the West. Within a decade or two of 1850, the major civilizations of the Middle East, India, China, and Japan, which had maintained a balance among themselves for some 2000 years and with the West for some 800 years, were beginning to be disrupted by the modernizing power of the Western nations.

In all these ways the West's modern imperial power not only generated an imbalance that put the older Moslem, Indian, Japanese, and Chinese empires on the defensive, but it began to create "a yeasty, half-formless but genuinely global cosmopolitanism . . . as the dominant reality of the human community."[5] McNeill points to the encircling of the globe by Western transport, communication, and technology, by the ideas embodied in knowledge of the sciences and practical arts, and by the secular vision of material progress and welfare. Palmer and Colton stress the fact that Western imperialism was the first phase in linking together the disparate civilizations, which had so long lived a separate existence, into what was to become an interconnected

[4]Robin W. Winks, "Imperialism," in C. Vann Woodward (ed.), *The Comparative Approach to American History*, Basic Books, New York, 1968, pp. 253-270.

[5]William H. McNeill, *The Rise of the West*, University of Chicago Press, Chicago, 1963, p. 727.

world society.[6] The second phase in the development of an interrelated worldwide civilization came with a speed unprecedented in the history of empires. As the late empires of the generative modernizers underwent a remarkable and speedy move to disimperialism in the mid-twentieth century after only a few decades of genuine power, their erstwhile dependent peoples demanded an even speedier modernization than ever before, this time with the assistance of their former rulers but on terms to be set by themselves. In both phases Western education played a significant role.

What Imperialism Meant to the Imperialists

The modern imperialist fervor of the late nineteenth century was a potent elixir. It was brewed with a base of religious and humanitarian zeal planted by the earlier civilizing mission now in full flower, reinforced with the acquisitive desire for economic gain to be realized from industrial as well as commercial development, backed up by the military might of powerful navies and armies, inspirited with the pride and prestige of a competitive nationalism, and topped off with the heady adventuresomeness to be gained from travel and daring-do in far away places. The more critical analysts of imperialism, from J. A. Hobson to Lenin, have made of it an image of unrelieved aggression by greedy capitalists, feeding on the profits to be obtained from the exploitation of native labor. That the economic motivation was present cannot be denied, but the Marxist-Leninist portrayal has been found to be entirely too simplistic. It underplays the sense of mission that motivated vast reaches of the Western peoples, without which the conniving of a few capitalists or political leaders would have been relatively fruitless.

Whether it was couched in terms of the "white man's burden" of the Englishman, the *kultur* of the German, the *mission civilisatrice* of the Frenchman, the "manifest destiny" of the American, or the "civilizing mission" of the Russian, the sense of crusade was pervasive throughout the populations of the West. It ranged from the religious missionism of evangelical Christians to the patriotic jingoism of the working classes of Britain, France, Russia, and the United States. The humanitarian protestations of the civilizing mission would not die. The Western powers continued to apply it to Africa:

> The Europeans thus developed a doctrine of imperial rule which, in the Livingstonian missionary tradition, justified white governance by linking pacification, economic development, technological innovation and moral uplift as a part of a coherent philosophy. At the Brussels Conference of 1890 the powers thus promised to fight the slave-trade, to build roads, railways and telegraphs, to prevent the unrestricted traffic in fire-arms and to "diminish inland wars between the tribes ... to initiate them into agricultural works and in the industrial arts so as to increase their welfare; to raise them to civilization and to bring about the extinction of barbarous customs such as cannibalism and human sacrifice."[7]

[6]R. R. Palmer and Joel Colton, *A History of the Modern World,* 4th ed., Knopf, New York, 1971, chaps. 15, 21.

[7]L. H. Gann and Peter Duignan (eds.), *Colonialism in Africa, 1870-1960,* vol. I, *The History and Politics of Colonialism, 1870-1914,* Cambridge University Press, London, 1969, p. 24.

The Russians also had spokesmen for their civilizing mission to Asians. As early as 1851 Friedrich Engels in a letter to Karl Marx said, "For all its baseness and Slavonic dirt, Russian domination is a civilizing element . . . in Central Asia."[8] A few decades later an aristocrat put Russia's mission more nobly when speaking of the need to liberate the oppressed peoples of the East: "All these people of various races feel themselves drawn to us, and are ours, by blood, by tradition, and by ideas."[9]

While the British, the French, the Germans, and the Americans could not have agreed to such sentiments about kinship by blood, they had the same supreme confidence in the superiority of their versions of Western civilization (as the Japanese and Chinese did in theirs). Therefore, they felt it was only right and just that they bring the benefits of their superior civilization to the inferior peoples. After all, it would be for their own good, even if a certain amount of force had to be used in order to achieve the law and order without which civilized advancement could not take place. A rational system of justice, of fair taxation, of health care, and of education was a necessary framework for an economic development that would benefit the dependent peoples, as well as the mother country. And even if no other benefits accrued to the colonial peoples, they would be able to drop their heathen and pagan ways and adopt the civilizing mantle of Christianity.

An imperturbable and righteous conviction of superiority permeated the assumptions of many imperialist spokesmen. Occasionally they made the conviction painfully explicit. F. D. Lugard gave the following advice to English missionaries respecting the way they should treat Africans:

> The essential point in dealing with Africans is to establish a respect for the European. Upon this—the prestige of the white man—depends his influence, often his very existence, in Africa. If he shows by his surroundings, and by his assumption of superiority, that he is far above the native, he will be respected, and his influence will be proportionate to the superiority he assumes and bears out by his higher accomplishments and mode of life. In my opinion—at any rate with reference to Africa—it is the greatest possible mistake to suppose that a European can acquire a greater influence by adopting the mode of life of the natives. In effect, it is to lower himself to their plane, instead of elevating them to his. The sacrifice involved is wholly unappreciated, and the motive would be held by the savage to be poverty and lack of social status in his own country. The whole influence of the European in Africa is gained by this assertion of a superiority which commands the respect and excites the emulation of the savage. To forego this vantage-ground is to lose influence for good. I may add, that the loss of prestige consequent on what I should term the humiliation of the European affects not merely the missionary himself, but is subversive of all efforts for secular administration, and may even invite insult, which may lead to

---

[8]Quoted in Edward Allworth (ed.), *Central Asia; a Century of Russian Rule*, Columbia University Press, New York, 1967, p. 37.

[9]John K. Fairbank, Edwin O. Reischauer, and Albert M. Craig, *East Asia, The Modern Transformation*, Houghton Mifflin Co., Boston, 1965, p. 469.

disaster and bloodshed. To maintain it a missionary must, above all things, be a gentleman; for no one is more quick to recognize a real gentleman than the African savage. He must at all times assert himself, and repel an insolent familiarity, which is a thing entirely apart from friendship born of respect and affection. His dwelling-house should be as superior to those of the natives as he is himself superior to them. And this, while adding to his prestige and influence, will simultaneously promote his own health and energy, and so save money spent on invalidings to England, and replacements due to sickness or death.[10]

Albert J. Beveridge made the rafters of the United States Senate ring with his declaration of dependence, announcing to the world that all men are created unequal and that some men (Americans) have the inalienable right to rule others (Orientals):

The Philippines are ours forever, "territory belonging to the United States," as the Constitution calls them. And just beyond the Philippines are China's illimitable markets. We will not retreat from either. We will not repudiate our duty in the archipelago. We will not abandon our opportunity in the Orient. We will not renounce our part in the mission of our race, trustee, under God, of the civilization of the world. And we will move forward to our work, not howling out regrets like slaves whipped to their burdens, but with gratitude for a task worthy of our strength, and thanksgiving to Almighty God that He has marked us as His chosen people, henceforth to lead in the regeneration of the world. . . .

It would be better to abandon this combined garden and Gibraltar of the Pacific, and count our blood and treasure already spent a profitable loss, than to apply any academic arrangement of self-government to these children. They are not capable of self-government. How could they be? They are not of a self-governing race. They are Orientals, Malays, instructed by Spaniards in the latter's worst estate. . . .

God has not been preparing the English-speaking and Teutonic peoples for a thousand years for nothing but vain and idle self-contemplation and self-admiration. No! He has made us the master organizers of the world to establish system where chaos reigns. He has given us the spirit of progress to overwhelm the forces of reaction throughout the earth. He has made us adepts in government that we may administer government among savage and senile peoples. Were it not for such a force as this the world would relapse into barbarism and night. And of all our race He has marked the American people as His chosen nation to finally lead in the regeneration of the world. This is the divine mission of America, and it holds for us all the profit, all the glory, all the happiness possible to man. We are trustees of the world's progress, guardians of its righteous peace. The judgment of the Master is upon us: "Ye have been faithful over a few things; I will make you ruler over many things."[11]

[10] F. D. Lugard, *The Rise of Our East African Empire*, Blackwood, Edinburgh, 1893 vol. 1, pp. 73-74.

[11] *Congressional Record*, Fifty-sixth Congress, First Session, pp. 704, 708, 711.

What Imperialism Meant to the Colonial Peoples

To the surprise of many imperial apologists, their colonial subjects did not always seem to take the same view of the benefits of imperialism that they claimed for it. Robin W. Winks gives a clue to the difference in his epigrammatic sentence: "Imperialism was a practice; colonialism was a state of mind."[12]

Dependent peoples could not particularly see the benefits to themselves when the alien agents of imperialism made all the important decisions, administered the laws and the courts, commanded the army and sometimes forced them to serve in it, lived in the best houses, had the most money, owned the most productive lands, managed the docks, factories, or shops, never worked in the fields, travelled in comfort, wore the finest clothes, and in general set themselves apart and above the inhabitants in their native land. As far as the subjects could see, most of the benefits went to the foreigners and few to themselves. The most obvious exception was the benefit that came to the few who were given an education. This was the best road to achieving the perquisites that surrounded the intruding "trade man," the "government man," the "army man," and the "religion man."

But even when material benefits were forthcoming to a clerk in an office, to a skilled worker in a shop or factory, to a teacher in a school, or to a minor government official, the benefit could easily be outweighted by a fear of the threat that the outsider brought to his traditional ways of life or by his resentment of the attitudes and behavior of the intruder. The threat ranged all the way from attempts to change his group habits (marriage customs, extended family, child raising, housing, magical beliefs, religious worship, and language) to condemnation of his habits of cleanliness, dress, and sexual conduct. While the less privileged might see the advantage in learning the written language of the rulers, the intellectual classes might see the Western languages as a threat to their own literary and religious traditions.

Above all, however, and perhaps least understood or appreciated by generations of Westerners who thought of themselves only as "doing good" for the unfortunate peoples of the world, was the sense of resentment that pervaded the dependent peoples' response to the imperialist enterprise. The economic exploitation could possibly be tempered by an improved standard of living as modern infrastructures of trade, commerce, industry, railroads, and shipping made more goods available and made them more diversified. The military life at least brought regular meals and clothes to the colonial soldier, along with discipline, hardship, and death. The establishment of law and order, even by outsiders, gave a certain sense of security and freedom from constant tribal or ethnic wars, raids, and reprisals. The preaching of the Christian gospel gave a hope for individual dignity and equality, at least in the next world. There were thus occasional ways to gain some sort of compensation from imperial rule. But from the humiliation of the race conscious attitudes of superiority there was no escape. All the other indignities could possibly be tempered by *some* advantage that modernization could eventually bring, but what possible advantage could come from psychological degradation?

[12] Winks, op. cit., p. 255.

In the long run it may be the airs of superiority surrounding the practice of discrimination, whether conscious or unconscious, whether deliberate or unknowing, that produced the greatest evil of late imperialism. The complex of attitudes that ranged from contempt and arrogance at one extreme to condescension and paternalism at the other indelibly shaped the colonial state of mind. This could take the form of smouldering resentment at the racial segregation, the class distinctions, the exclusive social and sports clubs, the ethnic slurs of everyday speech, the imperious call for "boy" to attend to all the wants of the master. Or it could be found in the self-immolation or self-humiliating obsequious compliance to all things that "master," "sahib," or "bwana" could possibly want. In between there was a vast mass of people with a confused loss of self-confidence and an uncertain sense of identity leading to profound psychic stress. A feeling of economic and political inferiority was one thing, and bad enough; a sense of psychological, racial, social, or cultural inferiority proved to be even more intolerable. The excesses of late imperialism in this regard may have helped to account for its fairly short span of existence. As historical imperialisms go, a life of less than 100 years was short indeed. Or perhaps it was the unintended result of a Western education that helped to speed the demise of the world's most all-embracing imperial thrust.

In any case, it is generally agreed that the rise of a Western-educated elite among the dependent peoples was one of the most significant elements in the attacks upon the worldwide imperial system and its exceedingly rapid decline in a decade or two after World War II. The German, Ottoman, American, and Danish holdings virtually disappeared in the aftermath of World War I. The Japanese empire was dismantled at the conclusion of World War II; and the British, French, Dutch, and Belgian empires were turned into several score of independent nations between 1947 and 1967. The territorial dimensions of only two of the pre-World War I empires did not shrink after World War II, those of Russia and China. In this process of revolt by the peoples of Asia and Africa against the imperialisms they had endured at the hands of both the primary and secondary modernizing nations, the role of the Western-educated elite has been of the greatest importance.

As the colonial critics of imperialism grew bolder and more eloquent, they struck out against political domination from the outside, demanding at first more participation and self-rule, and then the full independence due to a self-respecting modern nation. They attacked economic exploitation and demanded faster economic development; they deplored the military power of the empire as a menace; and they identified Christianity as a threat. This latter may have been one of the most difficult criticisms for those Westerners with genuine humanitarian and religious motivations to accept. After all, they did not think of themselves as exploiters or as oppressors; they thought of themselves as helpers, friends, and saviours.

But the Africans did not always see it that way. Abdou Moumouni describes how the well-intentioned schooling in French civilization appeared to young African students in West Africa in the 1920s:

> The curricula and texts of the period show that everything was directed at
> convincing the young African of the "congenital" inferiority of the Blacks, the

barbarity of his ancestors, and the goodness and generosity of the colonising nation which, putting an end to the tyranny of the black chiefs, brought with it peace, education, health measures, and so forth. The machinery of falsification is particularly evident in history courses (and with reason). Many Africans will remember all their lives the untruths they recited without understanding them: "Our ancestors the Gauls" . . . "Celebrate the brave chiefs who took the Samory! No more irons, no more slaves, to our conquerors, thanks" . . . "In her colonies France treats the natives like her sons," etc., etc., etc.[13]

Another recent study documents the feelings and attitudes of responsible African Christian leaders and laymen toward Western Christian missionaries in Ghana.[14] The things that most disturbed the Ghanaians included the following: the missionaries isolated themselves in segregated residential patterns and often lived in a big house on a hilltop (as Lugard had advised); they did not mix socially with Ghanaians nor share meals with them; they adopted a patronizing manner towards their "native" and "heathen" charges as that of master to servant; despite their supposed greater knowledge they were ignorant of Ghanaian religion, family, and social customs; they did not relate their Christian teachings to the local culture of ceremony and art; they deliberately tried to denigrate local craftwork and art forms and to substitute the imported Western forms of religious worship; they not only imported Western institutions in unmodified form, they also brought with them their Western religious rivalries and sectarian competition; in short, the Ghanaians looked upon the missionary as another instrument of imperialism.

Such an image would naturally be hard to take by missionaries who had dedicated their lives to "converting the heathen" in the service of God and the Christian gospel. The picture, of course, was not of unrelieved criticism, but the basic point seemed to be that the missionaries' theology was better than their anthropology. Of the positive contributions that the missionaries made to the Ghanaians, the stress on education was always deemed to be of the highest importance, despite the criticism for using the schools as recruiting agencies for the denominations.

Of all the elements of Western civilization diffused by the imperialistic system, the one that was most eagerly adopted by the nationalist leaders and their followers was Western education, especially insofar as it contributed to science, technology, and political and economic thought. If, indeed, "the future will look back upon the overseas imperialism of recent centuries, less in terms of its sins of oppression, exploitation, and discrimination, than as the instrument by which the spiritual, scientific, and material revolution which began in Western Europe with the Renaissance was spread to the rest of the world,"[15] it will be in large part due to a new realization that Western education played a key role in the imperial process that led to modernity for the greater part of the world.

[13] Abdou Moumouni, *Education in Africa*, Praeger, New York, 1968, p. 45.

[14] Harris W. Mobley, *The Ghanaian's Image of the Missionary; an Analysis of the Published Critiques of Christian Missionaries by Ghanaians, 1897-1965*, E. J.Brill, Leiden, Netherlands, 1970.

[15] Rupert Emerson, *From Empire to Nation, The Rise to Self-Assertion of Asian and African Peoples*, Harvard University Press, Cambridge, Mass., 1960, p. 6.

Without in the least attempting to justify imperialism as a social good, it seems clear that imperialism did speed up the process of modernization on a worldwide scale (although it should not be assumed that *that* had been an unmitigaged blessing), and that the attendant spread of Western education was one of the principal means of furthering that modernization. Whether the modernizing effects of Western education could have been spread around the world by some other means, without the disastrous evils of the imperialist system, is an unanswerable historical conjecture. However, if the independent nations of the late twentieth century are still determined to modernize, perhaps they can do a better job of it than the imperial nations of the late nineteenth century did. If they can, it may be because they learned something from their own history.

Much as it needs to be done, the concluding sections of this book cannot deal with the history of education in the process of modernization as it is taking place in sixty or seventy new nations. Nor can it bring together for comparative analysis the colonial educational policies and practices carried on by the globe-encircling empires of a century. What it tries to do is to generalize very briefly about some of the ways the major aspects of a modernizing Western education were applied to or were not applied to some of the colonial societies of the empires.

Some tentative generalizations may be drawn as to the ways the colonial education policies of the empires did or did not promote the modernization of the societies they affected. Such an effort is, of course, a hazardous intellectual and historical exercise, but I believe it must be undertaken even though the field is strewn with clashing points of view and ambiguous evidence. The peoples of the world will not delay the formulation of their educational policies until all the evidence is in. We must make judgments even as we pursue the evidence. In fact, by making judgments as explicitly and relevantly as possible in order that they may be tested with scholarly care, we may be hastening the gathering of the evidence itself.

My overall judgment of the role of education in the modernization process as conducted under imperial auspices encompasses two main points.

First, Western education enabled the modernization process in the traditional societies of the empires to be more rapid, and more disruptive, than it would otherwise have been if the empires had not diffused their education to the rest of the world in the late modern period at all. If, somehow, the vast regions of Asia and Africa had not been invaded by the education of the West, they would not have changed so rapidly nor would their traditional societies been as disrupted as they were. The less education was imported or made available, the less social change and less modernization took place.

The second point is that modernization in the colonial societies would have been still more rapid, much more humane,and possibly even less disruptive if the educational policies had been more deliberately designed to promote a more evenly balanced modernizing education in the interests of the people concerned and if more care had been taken to blend the traditional and the modern ingredients in a mix that would have led to an orderly and humane process of modern development. To be sure, the process of modernization could have seemed more beneficial if it had not been promoted under the auspices of an imperialism which inevitably had large elements of authoritarianism and exploitation in it, and which portrayed a racial superiority and social condescension that festered in the hearts and minds of the subject peoples. But even under these conditions of imperialism, Western education *might* have tempered the growth of the colonial mind, if it had remained truer to the egalitarian, integrative, and humanitarian ideals of the West's own Enlightenment and democratic revolution and had been primarily concerned to assist traditional peoples to create and manage their own modern societies. Instead, it too often reflected the disjunctive, selective, authoritarian, and proselytizing characteristics that continued to mark the more traditional sectors of Western education throughout the period.

B.   IMBALANCE AND DISJUNCTION IN COLONIAL EDUCATION

Even though the Western nations were developing large-scale educational systems at home and extending education to ever larger proportions of their own population as they moved to modernize their societies, they were far less energetic in doing the same for the peoples of their overseas empires. Their efforts just before the demise of imperialism became more significant, but they were too little and too late to enable the colonial peoples to achieve anything like a comparable state of modernization. One can only speculate that if the peoples of Asia and Africa had had some of the benefits of the large-scale educational efforts that went into the modernization process in the United States, Britain, France, Germany, or Russia after 1850, the present gap between the most modern nations and the least modern would not be so great.

This is not to say that education alone could have made the difference, but it surely would have made some difference. This can be seen in the differential development that did take place in various parts of the colonial world, for example, in India as compared with Burma, Philippines with Indonesia, and Senegal with Mali. It can be seen even more strikingly by the ironic fact that Japan, the non-Western nation which borrowed most heavily from what the Western nations were doing at home (rather than from what they were doing overseas), was able to match Western modernization most rapidly. It was obviously not education alone that made the difference, but virtually all observers agree that the Japanese government's aggressive efforts to establish a large-scale educational system, thus making education accessible to the vast majority of the Japanese people in the late nineteenth and early twentieth centuries, enabled Japan to become the first highly modernized nation outside the West and by the late 1960s the third most productive nation in the world.

In contrast, the Western powers were relatively slow and sluggish in applying their expertise in educational management to their colonial territories. Their governments were generally hesitant and vacillating in developing clear imperial policies in education. Not surprisingly, the governments did not give education a very high priority in their purposes or in claims upon their financial resources or investments. They put law and order highest on the list of priorities as being most essential for economic return. This can, of course, be attributed partially to the fact that the colonies during the late imperialism of the nineteenth century were looked upon primarily as sources of wealth and prestige for the benefit of the homeland and not primarily as societies needing economic, political, and social development for their own sakes.

Besides, the several religious groups were either already at work in the colonial territories or they were willing to pick up the educational tab and thus relieve the governments of that drain on their financial resources and obligations. This meant that at precisely the time when governments were expanding education at home under state auspices and thus speeding the long-term decline in the purely religious sponsorship of education (an almost universal sign of the modernization process in education) the governments were promoting, or at least permitting, the religious missions to take the major responsibility for providing education for their colonial subjects.

Thus the early educational policies of the Western powers (in Africa particularly) in the 1860s and 1870s left educational practice largely in the hands of Christian missionaries. Their practices varied among the denominations in different countries, as two recent volumes clearly show,[16] but in general the highest priority of the missionaries was not to adapt their educational efforts to the needs of the colonial peoples but to use Western education as a means of converting the people to Christianity, changing their customs and ways of life to conform with Western civilization, or indeed, to replace their traditional society with Western social, economic, and even political institutions. But they did not propose to substitute for the traditional education of the people the centralized, highly organized, and coordinated state systems of education which were being instituted back home. In many cases the missions opposed or resisted what they believed to be the state's intrusion into the educational sphere which they claimed as rightfully their own.

So, on the one hand, the missionary policies were genuinely disruptive of traditional society as they sought to transform the societies they were dealing with to conform to their own religious, moral, and "civilizing" outlooks. But, on the other hand, they were not particularly in favor of a coordinated and large-scale promotion of educational expansion by governmental authority. The former policy introduced social changes of vast importance which undoubtedly helped to create an educated leadership that eventually led to the national independence movements. The latter policy (or lack of policy) meant that a more carefully planned and balanced approach to providing education on a large scale for the majority of colonial peoples was delayed for many decades.

The imperial governments did begin to change their generally passive stance toward education after the mid-1880s. As they began more aggressively to extend their rule over larger and larger territories, they had to increase their whole apparatus of governmental administration, including education. This meant that the governments gradually began to drop their laissez faire policy toward the foreign missionary groups and to provide greater government support for education from state funds, greater

---

[16] David G. Scanlon (ed.), *Church, State, and Education in Africa*, Teachers College Press, New York, 1966; and Brian Holmes (ed.), *Educational Policy and the Mission Schools; Case Studies from the British Empire*, Routledge, London, 1967.

control over the mission schools, and finally greater energy in establishing government schools. This process took place earlier in some territories than in others and with greater zeal at some times and places than at others. Generally, imperial government interest in education for the colonies took on momentum from the 1920s onward; the real acceleration came after World War II, just before the independence movements heralded the rapid decline of Western imperialism.

British government promotion of education had begun earlier in India than in Africa, partly because governmental administration took over from the commercial companies earlier, but also partly because Britain was faced with an ancient civilization which, while heterogeneous in ethnic composition, exhibited widespread and massive traditions of Hindu and Moslem literary and religious cultures that required centralized attention. In contrast, the African territories consisted of much smaller ethnic and linguistic groups with no highly developed or common literate tradition outside the Arabic writing regions. Elsewhere, the oral tradition and the absence of formal educational institutions enabled the British rulers to move more cautiously and indeed to develop educational policies consonant with the administrative policy of indirect rule. In general, this meant that as far as possible the traditional rulers, chieftains or kings were maintained in nominal power while the British officials acted as advisers or resident authorities.

After 1885 the British policy in Africa began to soft pedal the missionaries' zeal for converting the whole way of life of Africans and to play up a policy of adapting Western education somewhat more to the needs of the Africans. As we shall see, this policy of adaptation had very rough going when it came to making education more practical and less academic. In the first place, even the energetic government officials were faced with what David G. Scanlon calls "the golden period of missionary effort in Africa" in the years from 1880 to 1920.[17] Still more patently the racialist attitudes of the government officials as well as of missionary teachers seemed to harden on the side of white superiority and black inferiority at about the time the policy of adaptation began to appear. For their part, black Africans saw in adaptation not a means to enable them to achieve equality with their rulers or to prepare them for self-rule; they saw it as a means of keeping them in their inferior place.

Theoretically, in contrast to the British policies of indirect rule, the French imperial policy was stated to be direct rule. All major officials, and indeed all minor officials, who administered French law and justice in the colonies were to be Frenchmen, and the law to be administered and the order to be maintained were to be French law and order. Educationally, the principle of direct rule was to be assimilation of Africans into French culture and civilization, not adaptation of French culture. In this respect the French policy of assimilation through education was similar to that of the missionaries who saw their task as conversion of Africans to Christianity and to Western civilization.

In theory, too, the organized system of centralized education which had developed at home in France could conveniently and systematically be transferred to the colonies overseas. The theory, however, was more easily stated than widely practiced.

---

[17] Scanlon, op. cit., p. 6.

It was not until 1896 that the first law to organize education in French West Africa was passed, not until 1903 that a general system was established by the Governor-General, Ernest-Nestor Roume, and not until 1924 that a fully organized system of education with differentiated levels and functions was envisioned. Even then the system was rudimentary: one year in a village school leading to rigid selection for admission to a regional primary school and then possibly on to an advanced primary school. In 1917 there were still only two full-fledged secondary schools in all of French West Africa. It was not until 1945 that certificates awarded in African institutions were granted equivalence to those in France and that active efforts were made to expand education in order to give Africans more general access to secondary and higher institutions.[18]

In principle, the French policy of educational assimilation was easier to manage than the British policy of adaptation. It meant that the French educational system, its various types of schools, curricula, and content could simply be transferred to Africa and conducted by French teachers. The purpose was to create an administrative and professional elite of Africans educated to be as nearly French in knowledge and outlook as possible. They in turn would aid in the process of shaping their African societies on the French model. In view of this purpose the French saw no need to transfer mass education to Africa, nor to make primary education free and compulsory as they were doing from the 1880s onward at home. Furthermore, they saw no need to offer instruction in the African vernacular languages.

All education for the educated African was to be in the French language from the very beginning of primary instruction, and the whole system should aim at achieving the standards of French teaching in France itself. High quality education for a few was obviously to be preferred to lower quality education for large numbers. This elitist concept grew even stronger after 1885 when so many Africans and Asians became a part of the French empire that to make all of them citizens under the egalitarian principles of the Third Republic would be to make Frenchmen at home a minority among the citizens of the French state. So assimilation came to mean citizenship only for those few who could meet the highest standards of education and occupation. Thus, by the 1920s, assimilation had given way to association, a kind of social contract between metropolitan France and the colonies. French policy had begun to look more and more like Britain's indirect rule and educational adaptation.

It was not until the Brazzaville Conference in 1944, near the end of World War II, that expansion of primary education was seen as a major goal of French education in Africa. To be sure, in the 1920s French colonial policy had begun to respond to the self-determination ideals that followed World War I, but these were embodied largely in plans to provide a larger ingredient of agricultural and vocational studies in rural primary schools, and the stress for those few students selected for secondary education would more than ever be focused upon achieving the standards expected in secondary schools in France itself. Meanwhile, the highly educated African elite had enthusiasti-

[18] See Michel Debeauvais, "Education in Former French Africa," chap. 2, in James S. Coleman (ed.), *Education and Political Development*, Princeton University Press, Princeton, N.J., 1965, pp. 75-91.

cally taken to and taken on French culture to a very high degree, thereby losing more than ordinary touch with the masses of people.[19] Combined with this, however, some of them reacted even more vigorously after World War II in the effort to reaffirm all that was African and non-Western in the concept of negritude.

By contrast, the British had embarked upon a much more difficult enterprise in their policy of indirect rule with its corresponding educational policy of adaptation. These policies produced a basic conflict of purpose which was never wholly resolved. The British, more than the French, intended to train up an educated elite that would fill a wide range of administrative posts in the imperial bureaucracy. The British had seen this possibility in India almost as soon as the empire was established there in the mid-nineteenth century, when English was made the official language and a civil service was instituted to which Indians were eventually admitted. They therefore transferred this idea to Africa. Implicit in it was the assumption that there would be a good deal more self-rule in their colonies than the French, Belgians, Dutch, or Germans contemplated. But this principle turned out to be at odds with the notion of indirect rule through the traditionally established local authorities. The trouble was that a new administrative elite would require a modern type of education for a modern type of political organization. Africans so educated were bound to come into conflict with the traditional African elites who were accustomed to rule on the basis of personal authority and appointment of family or kin to administrative posts.

So where the policy of indirect rule was most widely used, as in certain Moslem sections of Northern Nigeria, the Sudan, or princely states of India, the development of education for modernity fell far behind that where the British used a more direct rule through the crown colony scheme. Indeed, inasmuch as the Christian missionaries had had their least success in Moslem territories prior to British rule, the spread of a Western type of education was doubly handicapped when British dominion was established. Where the mission had been most welcomed or most successful and where the development of a commercial economy had been most rapid, the spread of Western education was most extensive, as for example in the coastal regions of Sierra Leone, Nigeria, and Ghana in West Africa, in the Buganda kingdom and in Nyasaland in the east of Africa, and in the urban and coastal regions of India.

The net result seemed to be that where government policy began to stress the importance of training an educated elite for administrative positions (even fairly low positions) the spread of education was more influential than in those colonies where education was limited almost entirely to the primary education that could be provided by the missionaries without much attention to the manning of a government bureaucracy. For example, in the Belgian Congo and in the German colonies where commercial or industrial exploitation overrode all other purposes, the main stress was upon primary education either for religious or vocational purposes, but in neither case did the effort contribute extensively to the process of modernization.

---

[19] For translations of several reports on French education in Africa, see David G. Scanlon (ed.), *Traditions of African Education,* Teachers College Press, New York, 1964, pp. 118-140. For condemnation of the African administrative elite on this count by a French-educated African scholar, see Moumouni, op. cit., pp. 48-62.

The overall result of both the policies of assimilation and of adaptation was that the imperial powers were relatively slow to provide coordinated systems of governmental education for their colonial subjects. The British did it earlier in India, Pakistan, and Ceylon than in Africa. They did it earlier in West Africa than in East Africa. The United States moved more rapidly than any of the others when it took over the Philippines, Cuba, and Puerto Rico in 1898 and, sooner than the others, announced self-government as the explicit goal of its imperial policies.

Table 15.1 illustrates how far the colonial possessions lagged behind the metropolitan countries in the provision of educational opportunity. In general, it may be seen that by 1950 when the postwar movements for independence were beginning in earnest, the gap was the smallest between the United States and its possessions, and largest in the Italian, Belgian, and Dutch cases. Britain's major Asian territories were ahead of their African territories, and with the exception of North Africa Britain's African territories were ahead of France's. Of the colonial powers the United States moved faster than the others to establish elementary schools on a large scale (in the Philippines and in Puerto Rico).

At the secondary level, an advanced education beyond the rudiments was made more available in Ceylon, India, and the Philippines than elsewhere. In general, virtually until World War II the British and French colonial governments promoted secondary education by providing financial support for private schools, principally of a boarding school type, rather than by setting up a system of government secondary schools. From the 1920s onward, they began to exert more energetic leadership, at least by establishing a few high prestige institutions in each major territory. At the end of World War II the most extensive systems of higher education in the colonial territories were in Singapore, Hong Kong, India, Pakistan, the Philippines, and Puerto Rico. Aside from these territories there were only a few thousand advanced teaching positions available in all of colonial Asia and Africa, and most of these were held by expatriates.

There has been much argument concerning which level of education makes the most important contribution to the modernization of traditional societies. This discussion has been especially active in recent years as the independent countries try to plan where they should invest their scarce resources. Although definitive generalizations from the history of colonial education are difficult to make, some tentative generalizations that need much greater testing with regard to the role of Western education in the onset of modernity are as follows:

1. Since 1850 only those societies that have embraced significant elements of Western education have shown significant movement toward economic or political modernization.
2. Those traditional societies in which literate primary education was most actively extended were those which were most likely to enter upon economic growth and development. Thus, insofar as the imperial powers failed to promote widespread primary education, they helped to delay economic modernization; and those societies or particular groups within a society that had greater access to primary education were most likely to be prepared for economic modernization.

Table 15.1 Some Comparative Enrollment Ratios in Former Colonial Territories of Western Empires: 1950 and 1965-1966*

	FIRST AND SECOND LEVELS ADJUSTED SCHOOL ENROLLMENT RATIOS		THIRD LEVEL NO. OF STUDENTS PER 100,000 INHABITANTS	
	1950	1965	1950	1966
BRITISH RELATED				
England and Wales	75	102	242 *a*	646
Scotland	81	81	454 *a*	958 (1965)
West Indies				
Jamaica	69	75	31	113
Trinidad and Tobago	70	76 (1963)	33	97
Barbados	59	79	32 (1951)	171
Asia and Oceania				
Singapore	50	85	192 (1951)	689
Hong Kong	30	80	150 (1955)	304
India	21	44 (1963)	113	235 b
Pakistan	20	27	93	258 c
Ceylon	68	81	56	126 d
Burma	12	50 (1964)	18 *e*	127
West Malaysia (Malaya)	40	59	5	179
Fiji Islands	65	76 (1963)	–	111 (1962)
Papua	44	49	–	88 (1965)

a Universities and degree-granting and teacher-training colleges only
b Not including intermediate and preuniversity courses
c Including arts and science colleges at the intermediate level
d Universities only
e University of Ragoon only
f Not including teacher-training colleges
g Including preschool education

*Data based upon UNESCO, *Statistical Yearbook,* UNESCO, Paris, 1968, pp. 69-91, 185-200.

School enrolment ratio is a percentage ratio obtained by relating the enrolment at a given level of education to the estimated population for the age group, i.e., five to fourteen years for the first level and fifteen to nineteen for the second level. The adjusted school enrollment ratios for the first and second levels combined as listed here are "an attempt to minimize the effect of the differences between the various national school systems and thus to improve the international data. . . . [They] should never be treated as a crude indicator of the situation and development of education in a given country and international comparisons should be made only in very general terms." (p. 69.)

Third level is defined as "degree-granting and non-degree-granting institutions of higher education of all types (such as universities, higher technical schools, teacher training colleges, theological schools, etc.), both public and private. As far as possible, the figures include part-time teachers and part-time students, but those for correspondence courses are generally excluded. Data on enrolment refer to students who are eligible to sit for examination and to receive degrees or diplomas; auditors are therefore excluded." (p. 185.)

Table 15.1   Comparative Enrollment Ratios (Continued)

	FIRST AND SECOND LEVELS ADJUSTED SCHOOL ENROLLMENT RATIOS		THIRD LEVEL NO. OF STUDENTS PER 100,000 INHABITANTS	
	1950	1965	1950	1966
Africa				
Sierra Leone	6	16 (1964)	13	38 *f* (1967)
Sudan	5	14	4	57
Ghana	15	72	4	56
Uganda	18	32	4 *d*	20 *d*
Lesotho	49	76 (1966)	4	41
Kenya	21	45	3 (1956)	40 *d*
Nigeria	14	25	0.8	18
Malawi	32	31 (1966)	–	11
Zambia	27	42	–	9
Tanzania	9	23	–	7
Egypt	25	53	165	194
FRENCH RELATED				
France	78	91	334	1,076
West Indies				
Martinique	83	98	–	194
North Africa				
Algeria	14	39	52	70
Tunisia	19	64	50 *d*	132 *d*
Morocco	12	38	15	56
Madagascar	19	41	6	51
West Africa				
Senegal	6	24	6	79 (1965)
Ivory Coast	5	32	–	56
Guinea	3	19	–	11
Mali	3	14	–	4
Dahomey	8	20	–	2
Upper Volta	2	8	–	0.6 (1965)
Mauretania	1	8 (1964)	–	–
Niger	1	6	–	–
Equatorial Africa				
Congo (Brazzaville)	21	76	–	121
Gabon	18	68	–	22
Central African Republic	6	35	–	–
Chad	1	20	–	–
Southeast Asia and Oceania				
South Vietnam	15	59	12	191

Table 15.1   Comparative Enrollment Ratios (Continued)

	FIRST AND SECOND LEVELS ADJUSTED SCHOOL ENROLLMENT RATIOS		THIRD LEVEL NO. OF STUDENTS PER 100,000 INHABITANTS	
	1950	1965	1950	1966
Cambodia	11	49	5	120 (1965)
New Caledonia	69	98	–	57 (1964)
Laos	9	32	–	9
BELGIAN RELATED				
Belgium	84	93	234	565
Democratic Republic of the Congo	29	52	1 (1954)	24
DUTCH RELATED				
Netherlands	82	91	603	1,310
Indonesia	27	47 (1964)	8	103 d (1967)
ITALIAN RELATED				
Italy	53	70	310	659
Libya	11	51	3 (1955)	132
Somalia	1	6	2 (1955)	2 (1965)
U.S.A. RELATED				
United States	100	93 g	1,508	3,245
Virgin Islands	103	129	–	2,446
Philippines	89	83	902	1,441 (1964)
Puerto Rico	72	97	548	1,669
Guam	71	94	–	1,868
Samoa	82	135	–	200 (1965)
Cuba	50 (1952)	77	364 (1952)	432

3. Those traditional societies in which Western types of secondary and higher education were given highest priority, even for a few, were most likely to move toward political modernization, as expressed in the manning of administrative and professional bureaucracies and in the achievement of national independence. Thus those imperial powers, whether they intended to do so or not, which promoted a Western type of higher education for their colonial subjects and the necessary preparation in secondary schools for entrance to college or university systems, were preparing the way for their political modernity more effectively than did those that concentrated on primary education or none at all.

4. Those traditional societies in which provision was made for a balanced access to all three levels of education had the greatest chance to achieve both economic and political modernization.[20]

[20] L. J. Lewis, *Education and Political Independence in Africa*, Thomas Nelson, Edinburgh, 1962, p. 2.

Whatever may turn out to be the validity of these generalizations after a great deal more comparative historical research, it seems clear that the European nations made the whole process toward modernization, both economic and political, more difficult for themselves and for the colonial peoples because their own educational systems possessed certain characteristics which they transferred to their colonies. I refer to the disjunctions, the dualism, and the separatisms that marked the European educational systems, a set of characteristics which I have summed up in the nonword *disjunctivitis.*

In some cases educational disjunctivitis was an active and virulent disease that tended to exacerbate ethnic, linguistic, economic, and political divisiveness in the societies the Westerners came to rule; in others it produced an enervating malaise which slowed down the preparation of colonial peoples for the economic and social transformation and the eventual integration of society which constitute the later stages of the modernization process.[21]

This fact was one of the great historical accidents of all time, namely that nation building had been proceeding in the major European states for a long enough time on so broad a front that they could build fairly united and integrated states, even with dualistic educational systems that had large elements of disjunction and segmentation within them. Britain, France, and Germany had relatively homogeneous cultures based upon a common language, literary tradition, and political and social institutions. The United States had rapidly absorbed vast numbers of the heterogeneous immigrants from Europe, partly at least as a result of developing a large-scale educational system built on an ideal of social integration (except for the minority blacks, American Indians, Mexican-Americans, and East Asians).

In contrast, the Africans presented to the Westerners literally hundreds of small-scale societies with little common cultural tradition, language, or comprehensive social institutions. Even the major African kingdoms were loosely built polities in which urban life was limited to a few towns based heavily on handicraft rather than industrial production. Literacy characterized only the tiny elite with knowledge of Arabic in the Moslem societies of the Sudan regions or of Western languages in the coastal regions where Christian missionaries had penetrated by 1850. Thus when the European powers transferred their educational institutions to the diverse, fragmented, particularistic societies of Africa, they compounded disjunctivitis. Educational systems were brought piecemeal and without an overall design for a comprehensive modern system of education (such as they were in the process of building for themselves). The institutions that were transferred, moreover, still had many of the earmarks of traditional disjointedness which Europe had not yet begun to give up to the degree that the United States had by 1900.

The characteristic and sharp distinction between elementary and secondary education was one of these earmarks. As we have seen, elementary education in Europe was designed to provide working-class people with a minimal literacy education, but it was not intended to lead on to higher education. This seemed to missionaries and government officials alike as naturally suited to most of those

---

[21] See C. E. Black, *The Dynamics of Modernization; a Study in Comparative History,* Harper & Row, New York, 1966, pp. 76-94.

Africans or Asians whom they judged to be able to achieve any Western education at all. If the prevailing notion at home was that most Englishmen, Frenchmen, or Germans did not really need more than a few years of fundamental education, how natural to believe that most Africans or Asians needed even less. Similarly, if rural and village schools in Europe or America were generally inferior to those in the cities, how natural to believe that elementary schools in the African villages or bush did not need the attention, equipment, facilities, or the quality of teachers needed in urban areas.

If education was to be left largely in the hands of missionaries, how natural to feel that those societies or regions which remained hostile to Christian efforts or did not respond with great alacrity could very well be left without the advantages of Western education. If there were a dozen different languages spoken by different groups in a given administrative unit, why try to teach in their languages when it would be so much better for them to learn the common Western language which would open up the doors to the literature of the Gospel and to modern knowledge. In fact, the missionaries before 1914 did an enormous amount of work in reducing nearly 200 African languages and major dialects to written form, many into school textbooks as well as into translations of the Bible. This effort was vastly important as one step in the transition from a preliterate folk society for many of the African peoples to a literate, modern way of life.

But then the traditional Western distinction between elementary and secondary education came into play again.[22] Recall that elementary education in Europe was based upon the vernacular and that secondary education rested upon the ancient Greek and Latin classics. The African or Asian oral languages were obviously vernaculars and thus not suitable as the means of instruction in secondary education. It appeared natural, therefore, to begin secondary education in Africa or Asia with heavy doses of the Western classics, and to make the medium of instruction in secondary schools English, French, or whatever Western language was being used by the imperial power. So it came about that in British domains elementary education was largely conducted in the vernaculars and secondary education in English. (The French, as we have seen, used French in elementary education as well.) Thus it was easy to transfer the habit, so common at home, of looking upon elementary education not only as lower than secondary education but also as inferior to secondary education. This assumption made it easy to think of English or French as the learned languages in relation to the African or Asian vernaculars, just as Latin and Greek had for so long been considered the learned languages in contrast to the common European tongues.

On top of all this, the West European nations had of course distinguished sharply between the training of teachers for elementary schools and the training of teachers for secondary schools. The former was conducted in normal schools or teacher training institutions that were no more than second level institutions. Because these institutions did not give the full academic courses characteristic of preuniversity secondary education, they were generally looked upon as inferior to the genuine secondary school (grammar school in England, *lycée* in France, or *Gymnasium* in Germany). With

---

[22] See, for example, R. Freeman Butts, "Teacher Education and Modernization," in George Z. F. Bereday (ed.), *Essays on World Education: The Crisis of Supply and Demand,* Oxford University Press, New York, 1969, pp. 111-132.

the secondary school course built upon the literary academic studies, the training of teachers for such studies should be provided in universities. Elementary school teaching, based upon the vernaculars, required no such higher instruction. Primary school teachers therefore, needed only a minimum of training beyond primary school itself. Indeed it was not usually possible to transfer to a secondary school after one had attended or even completed a primary teacher-training course. The presumption was widely held that the most able students would be selected for secondary schools, while the less able would go to teacher-training "colleges." This pattern was another sign of their inferiority.

So it was that elementary schools came to be considered of lower quality than secondary schools, not simply the first rungs of an integrated system that was expected to lead upward to secondary education. How natural therefore for the imperial governments, hard pressed for allocation of their colonial funds, to leave the training of primary school teachers to the missions, who were reasonably glad to accept the responsibility, for it enabled them to guide the training of their teachers for their schools. It was only after World War I that governments began to turn their attention to teacher training of Africans for the new government schools they began to establish. But advantageous as that was, a teacher-training college often led simply to a professional dead end, because it could not lead to a university or to a university degree, which was the recognized passport to secondary school teaching and other higher professions.

Thus it was that in English-speaking Africa the elementary education system came to be considered "African" while the secondary school system came to be "European" staffed largely by expatriates from Britain. The academic distinctions of superior and inferior, which were acknowledged at home to be a matter of class and intellectual differences, when transferred to Africa inevitably took on subtle connotations of racial superiority and inferiority, as well as intellectual. A system that severely limited secondary education to a relatively few at home naturally came to be looked upon as suitable only for a minute fraction of Africans. When it is recalled that the principal purpose of a secondary school was to act as a kind of selection process for admission to a university, the fraction became still tinier. Aside from Fourah Bay College in Freetown, Sierra Leone, the beginnings of higher institutions in British and French areas of Africa can largely be dated from the 1920s, when Achimota was established near Accra in Ghana, Makerere in Kampala, Uganda, and Ecole Normale William Ponty near Dakar.

A small stream of African students also began to go to the metropolitan countries for higher education in the 1920s. But the stream was thin indeed. Even as late as 1960 UNESCO figures estimated that the percentage of the twenty- to twenty-four-year-old population in the countries of Middle Africa enrolled in institutions of higher education in Africa *and* abroad averaged 0.2 percent. This ranged from .09 percent for Mali and Mauretania to 1.6 percent for Zanzibar and Mauritius. The average percentage enrolled in institutions in Africa alone represented only 0.1 percent of the relevant age group.[23] For comparison, the approximate figure for Britain and

---

[23] *The Development of Higher Education in Africa,* UNESCO, Paris, 1967, pp. 223-227.

France themselves was around 4 percent, the Soviet Union 8 percent, and the United States 12 percent.

It should be recognized that there was not only vast discrepancy in opportunity for education at all levels in different parts of Africa, but the imbalance also applied to different regions, to different religious groups, to different linguistic and ethnic groups, and to different occupational groups. The Moslem pastoral societies of northern Nigeria and Chad were not touched by Western education nearly so much as were the trading peoples of southern Nigeria, Ghana, or Nyasaland. The lower castes of India were not nearly so able to attain a Western education as were the Brahmin classes. The rural regions of nearly all areas were likely to receive less attention than the urban regions.

Above all, the most underprivileged group nearly everywhere was the female half of the total population. One of the most revolutionary aspects of Western imperialism as it touched the traditional societies around the world was the notion that girls should receive a formal education. But even here the late Victorians of Western Europe were not so sure that girls and women should have as much or as rigorous an education as boys and men. So the common practice was to provide separate secondary schools for girls, another form of disjunction which not only seemed more suitable to the traditional societies but which meant that access to higher education for girls inevitably was slower and more limited even than that for boys. Literacy figures for Asia and Africa into the 1960s continue to show that illiteracy is much higher for women than for men. This discrepancy has been and continues to be one of the most severe brakes on modernization throughout the world.

Insofar, then, as large-scale popular participation in education is a sign of modernity in society and in education, the forces of imperialism can be said to have started the process among the colonial peoples they ruled, but they by no means finished it. They gave to a few the opportunity to glimpse what might be, but their wholesale spread of disjunctivitis tended to consolidate, for a time at least, the already established distinctions between ruler and follower and served to keep alive the traditional practices of an elite type of education. Equality may have been an ideal at home, but the colonial practice overseas largely belied the ideal until the Asians and Africans were gradually able to force the issue. Ironically, their prime weapon was the very education that had been so carefully and sometimes grudgingly extended to them as an embodiment of the elite education of the West, not its democratic best.

C. THE MAKING OF ELITES: SECULAR AND SCIENTIFIC STUDIES

The secular and the scientific ingredients that played a large role in shaping modern education in the West helped in turn to form the Western-educated elites of Asia and Africa and helped to set them apart from the traditional ruling classes of the premodern societies of the empires. Even though the promotion of secondary and higher education was largely in the hands of religious missions until such time as government schools, colleges, and universities began to compete, the curriculum that was typically transferred from the West to the imperial territories included a good deal of secular content in both the humanities and the scientific studies. Indeed, such mixture was typical of secondary and college education in the West itself. Much more comparative study is required in this field as elsewhere, but my general impression is that the curriculum of secondary and higher education transported to the colonies tended to duplicate the metropolitan models even more closely than the elementary curriculum did. Part of this derived from the desire to maintain in the overseas institutions standards that would be comparable with those at home and partly from the assumption that since such education reflected the highest and best in Western civilization it was the most effective instrument for bringing civilization to the peoples of the empires.

Even though the curriculums thus transplanted may not have been as thoroughly permeated with the secular and scientific streams of knowledge as prevailed at home, they were definitely more oriented to the secular and the modern than were the traditional schools conducted by Islamic, Hindu, Buddhist, or Confucian scholars. All these schools emphasized traditional religious, moral or "wisdom" literature consisting of sacred texts to be copied, memorized, and commented upon. In contrast, the Western institutions were likely to stress the history, politics, economics, and social institutions of Europe from the time of the Greeks to the Victorians, as well as the philosophy, literature, and religion appropriate thereto. This emphasis upon studying the West was therefore likely to portray the religious conflicts of the Reformation, the clash of ideologies of the seventeenth century, the growth of rationality and political revolutions of the eighteenth-century Enlightenment, and the rise of modern science in the nineteenth century. The secular character of the literary, humanistic, and social studies in the Western curriculum served presumably as radical eye-openers to young men whose peers attended the non-Western schools of tradition or whose total educational experience consisted of the oral traditions of everyday life, tribal initiation ceremonies, or the bush schools of the nonliterate societies.

Secularism appeared, too, in the specifically scientific aspects of the Western curriculum. Again, while the range and scope of scientific studies probably did not match those of the more realistic secondary schools of Germany, France, Britain, or the United States, they certainly introduced an almost completely novel element into the education of those Africans or Asians who were admitted to Western-type schools. The knowledge of physical phenomena obeying scientific laws of regularity, cause and effect, and predictability for the future gave a kind of empirical base for rational and critical thought largely unavailable elsewhere in the traditional societies. Even so, scientific teaching was generally oriented to the textbook and relied relatively little upon practical experiments, laboratories, or other expensive items. How much more an experimental, critical, problem solving, or experiential methodology closely related to indigenous African techniques could have achieved is open to speculation.

Combining scientific and empirical knowledge of the natural and physical world with the Western literary and humanistic tradition from Plato and Aristotle to Locke and Mill, or to Rousseau and Voltaire, the Western-oriented schools helped to open vast horizons of new knowledge and insights for African and Asian students, a mixture of rationalism and nationalism that proved to be a heady brew.

Western educators of the empires have been criticized for not adapting their own curricula to their students' needs or for having little regard for the literature or cultural traditions of the colonial peoples. The assimilation policies of the French especially led them to transplant their Western syllabi and curricula without substantial change. While this undoubtedly helped to create African and Asian elites who were equipped to lead their own peoples into modernity faster than otherwise would have happened, it also created doubts, confusions, alienation, and a "provincial mentality" which, Edward Shils argues, continues to mark most of the Western-educated elites whose only modern culture is the culture of the foreign metropolis which sent them their teachers or to which they came as students. They stand as intellectual provincials in relation to the Western metropoles much as Roman intellectuals did to Greece, northern Europeans to Renaissance Italy, eighteenth- and nineteenth-century Americans to England, France, and Germany, and nineteenth- and early twentieth-century Russians to Western Europe:

India was, and remains, an intellectual province of London, Oxford, and Cambridge. The areas of Africa, once or still ruled by British, have become intellectual provinces of these same centers (and to a lesser degree, of British provincial universities). Africans in the French-governed territories are provincial *vis-à-vis* Paris, just as Indonesia, against its own will, still remains a province of the Universities of Amsterdam, Leiden, and Utrecht, and, insofar as it refuses them, of other European and American universities. Even in the violently nationalistic Middle East and even among the new generation of less sophisticated intellectuals the cultural life of the foreign metropolis still exerts its great attraction.

In each of the provinces, the possession of a degree from a metropolitan university is a claim to respect and to preference for an appointment in government or in education. The universities in the provinces are modelled on those of the metropolis, down to the syllabi of study, the required textbooks and sometimes even the questions on examinations.

The textbooks from which the student studies in college are usually from the metropolis. His most respected teachers have been educated there. In many of the new states, the language in which he is educated is the language, not of his own people, but of the metropolis. He comes to appreciate the values of going to the metropolis for further studies—under the urging of kinsmen and teachers who perceive the advantage which it confers and who also feel that it is intrinsically valuable to be "foreign returned." The novels he reads, the science he studies and practices, the principles of administration which he applies, the economic policy which he recommends or seeks to carry out, all come from the foreign metropolis.

The culture of a foreign metropolis is the only modern culture he possesses. If he denies that culture, he denies himself and negates his own aspirations to transform his society into a modern society.[24]

[24] Edward Shils, *The Intellectual Between Tradition and Modernity: The Indian Situation*, Mouton, The Hague, 1960, pp. 85-86.

Whatever else may be said of the transfer of Western educational institutions to Asia and Africa, the qualities summed up under the headings of secular and scientific undoubtedly contributed to the creation of Western-educated elites whose role turned out to be of incalculable importance for the entire world.[25] Shils points out that the intellectuals of Asia and Africa played a larger role in the creation of their new nations in the twentieth century than intellectuals have ever played at any other time in history.[26] He defines an intellectual to include all persons who have had an advanced, modern education in a college or university. In the past, revolutions leading toward modernization have been engineered principally by middle classes overthrowing an alliance of the landed aristocracy and traditional government, by peasants rising against established commercial and landed classes, or by strong centralized governments, often military-oriented, imposing their views upon the masses of the people.

Only in the colonial territories of the Western empires was the movement to independence led by intellectual elites consisting largely of professional and administrative classes that had in common their Western education. It is clear as well that modernization outside the Western empires depended to an enormous extent upon the Western-educated intellectuals, notably in Japan, Turkey, and China.[27] But the greatest success, and one achieved with the least help from the middle classes, peasants, military, or governments, was achieved by the indigenous intellectual elites of the Western empires, first in India and other parts of Asia and then in Africa.

Many of these young men obtained their advanced education in the Western countries themselves. They began to go to Europe in large numbers from Asia and especially from India as early as the 1890s, and from Africa some thirty years later in the 1920s. When they returned home, they engaged in the professional occupations, principally as civil servants and administrators in the governmental bureaucracies, as lawyers, as journalists, a very few as physicians, but, above all, as teachers, especially in the colleges and universities but also in the secondary schools. They associated with each other, being able to communicate across local linguistic and ethnic lines because they had English in common, or French. In these ways, the Western-educated elites became the spearhead of the ideas of nationalism and subsequently the actions that led to independence, in Asia in the 1940s and 1950s and then in Africa in the 1950s and 1960s.

The ideals of representative government and public liberties that motivated the independence movements in their early stages have been undergoing heavy weather from the rise of one-party systems and military coups, but the role of the intellectual

[25] See, for example, a small sample of recent studies of elites: T. B. Bottomore, *Elites and Society,* Penguin Books, New York, 1964; Frederick W. Frey, *The Turkish Political Elite,* Massachusetts Institute of Technology Press, Cambridge, Mass., 1965; Edmund Leach and S. N. Mukherjee (eds.) *Elites in South Asia,* Cambridge University Press, London, 1970; and Y. C. Wang, *Chinese Intellectuals and the West, 1872-1949,* University of North Carolina Press, Chapel Hill, 1966.

[26] Edward Shils, "The Intellectuals in the Political Development of the New States," *World Politics,* pp. 329-368, April 1960.

[27] See, for example, Frey, op. cit., chap. 1; Wang, op. cit., passim; and Herbert Passin, "Modernization and the Japanese Intellectual," in Marius B. Jansen (ed.), *Changing Japanese Attitudes Toward Modernization,* Princeton University Press, Princeton, N.J., 1965, chap. 13.

will be no less important whatever the political complexion turns out to be. The practical and professional demands of a civil service bureaucracy and the specialization and differentiation of a large-scale educational system with fully developed higher institutions will demand much of the intellectual classes of modernizing nations. One of the key problems facing all newly independent nations is how to achieve cultural, intellectual, and educational independence as well as political independence in a world that is moving toward global modernization. This may prove to be an even greater test of the ingenuity and talents of the Asian and African intellectuals than was the achievement of political independence itself.

D. CREATING COMMUNITIES OF MODERNIZERS: THE PRACTICAL AND THE PROFESSIONAL

Each of the societies which came under the rule of the large-scale imperialisms had its own distinctive forms of occupational engagement, some much more specialized, stratified, and highly developed, as in India, others more functionally diffuse, as in Middle Africa or Central Asia, whose occupational base was more akin to that of pastoral or settled agricultural folk societies. But the overall characteristic which the colonial societies had in common was their reliance upon the land rather than upon commerce or industry as the principal means of subsistence for the overwhelming majority of people.

In view of the interest of the imperial powers in the products of the land, either as raw materials for their expanding industries or as a basis for trade and commerce to supply the needs of their growing urban and mercantile population, the predominantly rural and underdeveloped characteristics of the economies of the colonial peoples posed one of the most persistent and controversial problems related to the role of Western education in Asia and Africa. From the early missionaries of the early nineteenth century to the economic planners and technical advisers of the later twentieth century this question plagued their efforts: should education for Africans and Asians be primarily academic and general or primarily practical and professional?

A common and recurring answer that has been given from the very beginning has been substantially as follows: since the vast majority of peoples in Asia and Africa will be supported by their efforts on the land for a long time to come, their education ought to stress direct preparation for rural and agrarian life. This means a practical education to enable them to subsist or possibly to improve upon their rural existence. As early as 1847 the Education Committee of the British Privy Council had recommended such an education for Africans to include training in agriculture, household economy, and health. This theme was reiterated over and over again in official statements and in advisory reports from the mid-nineteenth to the mid-twentieth centuries.[28] Proposals were not only reiterated, numerous efforts were actually made

---

[28] For a sample of such statements see Philip J. Foster, "The Vocational School Fallacy in Development Planning," in C. Arnold Anderson and Mary Jean Bowman (eds.), *Education and Economic Development*, Aldine, Chicago, 1965. pp. 142-166.

to establish model schools for farming and mechanical arts, industrial schools, and school plantations or gardens, and to inject agricultural and industrial courses into the regular primary and secondary schools, even to making them compulsory. All this effort was generally to little avail.

The famous Phelps-Stokes report of 1922 reflected the view that just as American Negroes should be trained by a practical education for rural life in the American South so should the school curriculum in Africa be adapted to African rural conditions. It emphasized the needs of African boys and girls as individuals, their health, their home life, their recreation, their character development, and their religious life. On the surface, the argument emphasized an adaptive education that would be appropriate to the "overwhelming majority of Africans [who] must live on and by the soil." Underlying the argument was the belief that the "industrial education" proposed by Booker T. Washington and Jesse Jones as typified at Tuskegee and Hampton Institutes would be as appropriate for the colonial societies of Africa as it was for the segregated societies of the American South.[29]

The general stress upon the need of Africans and Asians for an education appropriate to their stage of economic development has led to recurring criticisms of the Western imperial educational policies for having neglected practical and vocational education and for transferring to both continents their heavily literary and academic traditions of bookish education.[30] This theme and this complaint, however, have been challenged more and more by a view that points to two facts with respect to Africa: the authorities did try to promote a much more practical type of education than was actually instituted, but the Africans who had the opportunity for education were themselves eager for the literary and academic form of education far more than they were for a practical type of education oriented to the rural life or the technical types of industrial or mechanical endeavor which they associated with lower forms of occupation. Two especially knowledgeable observers of Western education in Ghana stress two interrelated points. John Wilson reminds us that literary education was universally seen by Africans as a possible escape from the dreary rigors of a life of subsistence on the land:

> The blunt truth behind this state of affairs in African education is that anyone who gets a taste of education at all can do no other than desire to escape from low subsistence farming economy and all that goes with it of physical and social circumstances. These are hard circumstances and the wonder is that African resistance, adaptability, and resourcefulness have been of such a high order as to survive them.[31]

[29] For thorough documentation of this point, see Kenneth James King, *Pan-Africanism and Education; a Study of Race, Philanthropy and Education in the Southern States of America and East Africa,* Clarendon Press, Oxford, 1971.

[30] See, for example, Guy Hunter, *Modernizing Peasant Societies; a Comparative Study in Asia and Africa,* Oxford University Press, New York, 1969, chap. 10; and Don Adams and Robert M. Bjork, *Education in Developing Areas,* McKay, New York, 1969, chap. 6.

[31] John Wilson, *Education and Changing West African Culture,* Teachers College Press, New York, 1963, pp. 30-31.

Philip Foster argues perceptively that a literary education similar to that attained by their British rulers was sought by Africans because they could see realistically that such an education led directly to the best jobs in the colonial society:

> Those who criticize the "irrational" nature of African demand for "academic" as opposed to "vocational" education fail to recognize that the strength of academic education has lain precisely in the fact that it is preeminently a *vocational* education providing access to those occupations with the most prestige and, most important, the highest pay within the Ghanaian economy. The financial rewards and the employment opportunities for technically trained individuals [in agriculture or the trades] were never commensurate with opportunities in the clerical field.[32]

The testimony of these and other scholars, African and non-African alike, thus raises serious questions about the easy judgment that practical education was not sponsored actively enough by the colonial powers. We are reminded that the educational provisions resulted from the interaction of the rulers and the ruled far more than is usually recognized. So long as the literary education was a sign of superiority, and technical or practical education was a sign of political and social inferiority as well as economic inferiority under the colonial system, the Africans were reacting with understandable feelings. They were searching for the higher vocations and professions as the payoff from their education, not simply staying where they were. They were seeking a way to escape not only from the drudgery and dead ends of subsistence farming in the village but to escape from the badges of social and political inferiority which vocational skills and manual industrial arts clearly displayed when compared with the higher administrative and professional skills to be achieved by academic education. They saw that practical education " adapted to their conditions of life" could mean the permanent inferiority of black men.

The story in India, however, appears to be somewhat different from that in Africa. While in both cases there was relatively little technical or industrial education, Robert I. Crane argues that the industrial policies of the British officials seem to have had a large role in the results.[33] He points out that even when the British educators in India decided to expand the scientific components in secondary schools the content was so bookish and so oriented to the examination system that it had little or no relation to technical or economic development. More important, however, was the realization by educational officials that if they trained large numbers of people in technical fields for which there was no developing industry and thus no jobs they would be creating a dangerous economic situation. But they did not use the same caution with respect to literary education, and thus the "educated unemployed" became a rampant political problem for India, as well as for many other colonial countries where education expanded rapidly.

[32] Foster, op. cit., p. 145; see also Philip J. Foster, *Education and Social Change in Ghana,* University of Chicago Press, Chicago, 1965, chaps. 3-5.

[33] Robert I. Crane, "Technical Education and Economic Development in India before World War I," in Anderson and Bowman, op. cit., chap. 9, pp. 167-201.

Crane also points out that even where technical education was developed in India it often focused upon reviving ancient handicraft arts (like fine brass work or embroidery) which did not particularly promote industrialization, or it provided training for Europeans rather more than for Indians. So the Indians discovered early, as the Africans discovered later, that the best jobs they could obtain under colonial conditions were the administrative, clerical, and bureaucratic jobs for which an academic and literary education was better direct vocational preparation than was a scientific, technical, or industrially practical education.

The Indian side of this equation was, of course, important along with the British. It was not only that the British education officers themselves generally had an academic education weighted on the literary and humanistic side, but also that the Indian classes who could afford to flock to the secondary schools and colleges were largely from the Brahmin classes who traditionally were not likely to enter mercantile, technical, or industrial occupations in any case; and, of course, the lower classes most accustomed to engaging in the arts and crafts were not likely to go to the literary schools at all. All this led the British entrepreneurs to come to the conclusion that Indians, to put it mildly, did not have a bent for technical skills and could not be trusted to fill managerial positions in factories.

Crane concludes that British policy in India with regard to technical education was marked by "much vacillation, uncertainty, and aimless compromise, both in the making of policy and in its execution."[34] The education officers, themselves trained in the humanities, could always find reasons why technical and industrial education was too costly. Besides, they had so little contact with business or industrial leaders they were not disposed to experiment or go much beyond the usual book, examination, and paper qualification system which characterized the humanities and the entrance to the government service.

Thus the British government policies not only held back technical education, they undoubtedly held back the development of modern industry and economic development in India. Above all, the universities of India paid little or no attention to technical education until well into the 1920s. Of course, professional education for law and medicine stood high in prestige, but by and large the technical institutes were of a lower level in both quality and quantity in comparison with the general academic colleges and universities. In summary, Crane's judgment is that education in India had an enormously formative effect on economic modernization—negatively:

> The obvious result was, of course, that the Indian economy remained singularly undeveloped and that its modernization was severely retarded. Though a number of different factors played upon the economy to keep it backward, the absence of anything like an effective system of technical, scientific, and industrial education was surely a considerable element of the causal complex. Perhaps equally regrettable, technical training in India did little or nothing to create a set of values—diffused among the population—which could have been the basis for a rapid modernization of the economy when the system of technical education eventually underwent transformation and improvement.[35]

[34] Ibid., p. 190.
[35] Ibid., pp. 193-194.

The contrast with the enormous acceleration that the expansion of technical education gave to economic modernization in the United States, Germany, Russia, and Japan in the nineteenth century (and much more recently in China as well as in India) makes the point much more positively. For example, in an empirical study of some seventy nations located in all parts of the world (except Africa), William S. Bennett, Jr. found a high positive correlation between growth in technological education and economic development.[36]

Another, and much neglected, element in the contrast between rapidly modernizing societies and the less developed colonial societies was the attention paid to teacher training. Most teacher-training programs for the preparation of primary school teachers in Asia and Africa were little more than postprimary schools concentrating on the technical pedagogy of teaching the primary school subjects. They usually did not even include an academic training equivalent to the level of the subjects of the secondary schools. Even so, they involved at least the rudiments of literacy and as such provided the teachers with an education that set them apart from the masses of illiterates in the populations.

The great pity was that primary school teachers found themselves living and working in the rural sector for which their training had poorly prepared them, and at the same time their lack of a secondary-level education cut them off from close contact with the cohesive urban professional elites. They could not act as effective intermediaries between the rural and the urban styles of life. One of the great opportunities for economic and political development was thus lost, because the gap between rural and urban sectors was, if anything, widened and deepened by the importation of disjunctive European educational systems which drew a sharp line between the training of primary school teachers in a rural climate of opinion and the training of secondary school teachers in an urban-oriented atmosphere. No wonder a boy with a modicum of education wished to escape from the countryside to the city if he could.

The opportunity was thus lost to achieve what was one of the more fortunate but little appreciated aspects of American teacher education in the nineteenth century. The normal schools and the teacher-training colleges were dispersed so widely throughout the United States that they contributed to rural development even when they did not teach rural subjects. They acted as an extension of the urban literate society to the countryside, and they relatively soon built up the academic training they offered to the level of the secondary schools that prepared for the colleges and universities. Before too long they were even providing a postsecondary level of general education to which the ambitious boy or girl could aspire without flocking to the cities. In this sense erstwhile teachers colleges helped to bridge the gap between rural and urban life, eventually providing a training for a diversified range of occupations which continued to include teaching but were not confined to teaching.

Up to the 1920s teacher training was so neglected in most colonial societies that when independence arrived thirty or forty years later a vast shortage of trained

---

[36] William S. Bennett, Jr., "Educational Change and Economic Development," *Sociology of Education*, pp. 101-114, Spring, 1967.

teachers existed in virtually every country. In contrast, the United States had begun its expansion of teacher-training institutes by the mid-nineteenth century, Japan in the late nineteenth century, and Russia in the 1920s and 1930s. By 1917 in the western Russian cities as many as 40 percent of elementary school age children were actually enrolled, whereas it was nearer to 2 percent in Uzbekistan. In the following years the Soviet regime pushed energetically ahead to train the teachers to man elementary schools for the vast rural regions to the east. In all three cases massive programs of teacher training accompanied the rapid extension of elementary education so that it could become virtually universal.

In the 1920s in Africa, however, teacher-training institutions outside those of the missions were just beginning to appear under government auspices. As late as 1924 Governor-General Ernest-Nestor Roume wrote to his fellow governors of the eight colonies of French West Africa (a territory which consisted of a total of 19 million people in 1950):

> As far as secondary teachers are concerned, I estimate that the average yearly number of graduates [for all eight colonies] should be about thirty-five. . . . Taking defections and failures into account, around thirty secondary school teachers will be available to you each year, or *four or five per colony.* This number seems to me to be sufficient to provide under normal circumstances against retirements and to satisfy the needs of a gradual extension of education proportionate to our financial resources.[37]

It was remarkable how the imperial authorities tended to underestimate the potential modernizing power of professional education not only for those who went into teaching but also for those who were selected to enter the clerical, executive, and administrative positions of the government and the other major institutions of colonial society. They found to their chagrin that the general, academic, literary education which both British and French educators believed was the best kind of training for a generalist in a bureaucracy turned out to be just the kind of education that helped to transform the Africans into nationalists.

What few realized explicitly was that a greater attention to professional education might have become the very key to leading their colonial peoples not only into independence but into the modern world, a view that Lucian W. Pye expressed so persuasively in his study of Burma:

> National development would be furthered as ever-increasing numbers of competent people meet in their daily lives the exacting but also psychologically reassuring standards of professional performance basic to the modern world. The emergence and interaction of such people as they fulfill their professional activities would provide transitional societies with communities of modernizers who would constitute islands of stability in an otherwise erratically changing world.

[37] Quoted in Moumouni, op. cit., p. 48. Italics added.

The concepts and standards of the modern professions can uniquely serve the dual functions of assisting the individual in realizing his potentialities while also providing the community with the skills and abilities necessary for national development. In nation building it is not just the society that needs modern skills; the people must also feel skilled in modern terms. As individuals, the intelligent and ambitious peoples of transitional societies can acquire the skills and competences appropriate to membership in the modern world and readily become the equals of citizens of industrial societies as teachers, lawyers, scientists, soldiers, and, yes, as administrators and politicians. They can achieve essentially modern standards even though their countries may still have inadequate school systems, undermanned legal professions, and militarily weak armies.[38]

E. LITTLE DIFFERENTIATION AND LESS DIVERSIFICATION

Earlier chapters in this book have emphasized a theme that has permeated much of current social science thought—the role of social differentiation in the change from tradition to modernity. We have traced the ways in which organized education contributed to the differentiating process in the civilization of the West. Now we mention briefly the way the organized forms of Western education speeded the differentiating process in greater or lesser degree in the traditional societies which came under imperial rule.

In traditional societies all over the world in the nineteenth century, the mission schools and the government schools of the Western type were often the first or the most pervasive specialized institutions with which isolated social groups came into contact. Countless thousands of Asians and Africans had their initial contact with the specialized function of education when the first Western teacher arrived in their midst and set up a school whose specialized function was the teaching of literacy. Along with the introduction of cash crops, a money exchange, and formal legal institutions functioning through magistrates, courts, district officers, and police, the school was one of the means by which the orderly conduct of social affairs began to shift from kinship and family authorities to differentiated institutions. In these ways the local people learned to divide society's labor among different groups specializing in particular social functions. As the people adopted the Western style of organizing themselves into an increasing number of functional associations to do the many tasks that family and kinship groupings had formerly done, the modernizing process got under way.

So two kinds of things happened. The first Western schools helped to introduce some differentiation into traditional societies, even though they did not represent the whole range of specialized educational institutions which had been developed at home. Gradually an increasing differentiation of educational institutions themselves was introduced. In general, the more rapid and the more effective the process of educational differentiation took place, the more ready for modernization a society became.

---

[38] Lucian W. Pye, *Politics, Personality, and Nation Building,* Yale University Press, New Haven, Conn., 1962, pp. 289-290.

The overall function of Western-style primary schools was of course to teach literacy, whose achievement marked those who acquired it with a remarkable specialty that enabled them to expand enormously the range of activities and occupations in which they could engage. However, in a limited, traditional society the range of activities was also limited, and the literate person often found himself differentiated away from his former kinship associates and toward those others who had also acquired literacy. An unaccustomed pattern of communication could thus take place across kinship, linguistic, and ethnic lines. As Western-type primary schools tried to diversify their curricula and programs of teaching to include agriculture, mechanical or craft skills, home economy, and the like, they were trying to add variety to the usually single purpose institution. We have seen that this was scarcely a huge success for much of the colonial period.

Increasingly, as governments became more active, they began with greater or lesser eagerness to introduce a number of second-level differentiated educational institutions. In some cases these were postprimary but nonacademic institutions set up parallel to the general secondary schools, housed and operated quite separately. They were schools with a vocational or practical bias that were intended to provide a terminal education for those who were going immediately to a job. They were of two general types—technical schools (agricultural, industrial, or trade schools), and teacher-training institutions for training primary school teachers.

The vast majority of the imperial systems of education followed a structure of second-level education that could be described as a selective system organized around two or three types of differentiated institutions but offering very limited diversification within the separate institutions. The general academic secondary school had a fixed and largely compulsory prescribed curriculum, with considerable academic specialization available at the upper levels but all with the single goal of preparation for the university. Admission to the general secondary school was commonly by examination at the end of primary school; the number admitted was far less than those who finished primary school. Likewise, the separate technical schools and teacher-training schools had limited variety in their curricula for they had very specialized occupational goals. In virtually all cases, the technical and teacher-training institutions were regarded both by educators and by students as less desirable alternatives to the academic, university-preparatory institutions. Indeed, very often the students and even the teachers in the former institutions had failed to gain entrance to the latter.

A second model of differentiated secondary education systems began to appear in some of the Asian and African countries in the early twentieth century. In this model the technical schools adopted a larger component of general education, somewhat similar to that of the university-preparatory institutions, but it usually was confined to the first cycle in the institution before the student began to specialize in technical or teacher education. This raised somewhat the academic level of the parallel institutions, but they still were usually sharply distinguished from the general academic schools. They were designed to provide a terminal education somewhat more advanced than in the first model but still not considered equivalent to the general secondary school and thus not leading to the university.

In a study of ninety-three countries in 1950 Frank Bowles found that forty-eight countries still had a system much like that of the first selective model and that thirty-eight countries had the second, modified form of selective system.[39] Only seven (the most modern systems) could be said to represent a third model, a nonselective structure in which comprehensive institutions providing both academic and technical education gave students a much more diversified offering and much wider options for choice among the specialized programs. The United States typified most fully the third or nonselective model of differentiation and diversification. Bowles and his staff found that in the short space of a decade after 1950, the trend was markedly away from the first selective model (twenty-seven instead of forty-eight), somewhat away from the modified selective model (twenty-nine instead of thirty-eight), and startlingly toward the nonselective model (increased from seven to thirty-seven).

Corresponding to the models at the secondary level the structures of higher education in the vast majority of the colonial territories followed the single purpose pattern of many European universities rather than the comprehensive or multiple purpose model of American universities.[40] In the former, teacher training for primary school teachers and technical training are not considered suitable subjects for study in universities, nor indeed is the subprofessional training for such occupations as nursing, librarianship, social work, accountancy, journalism, and any number of fields that have been admitted to higher degree status in the United States. The principal task of higher education is to carry students through a first degree in the major academic fields; research and the advancement of knowledge are suitable for separate institutes but not a major function of the university or college teaching faculty. This pattern has had the effect of restricting the fields of study to a fairly limited scope in comparison with the immensely diversified offerings of an American "multiversity."

Despite the uncertain success of the differentiated and specialized efforts in some territories, it is clear that those underdeveloped countries which did adopt relatively soon a series of more highly differentiated educational institutions were the countries which modernized most rapidly. As in the early modernizing countries of the West, the higher the level of education the greater the differentiation: organized divisions or departments within institutions of higher education became more specialized, and an increasing number of specialized, separate institutions were set up outside the usual college or university.

Joseph P. Farrell has developed an interesting method of comparing nations according to the amount of structural differentiation in their educational systems.[41] He has designed a scalogram by which to rank a large number of underdeveloped countries according to whether or not their educational systems include such differentiated structures as: (1) a ministry of education within the government to which is delegated overall administrative responsibility and authority for education in the

[39] Frank Bowles, *Access to Higher Education*, vol. I, *International Study of University Admissions,* UNESCO and the International Association of Universities, Paris, 1963, pp. 105-112.

[40] Ibid., pp. 73-76.

[41] Joseph P. Farrell, "The Structural Differentiation of Developing Educational Systems: a Latin American Comparison," *Comparative Education Review,* pp. 294-311, October 1969.

country; (2) an inspectorate within the ministry consisting of indigenous personnel whose function is to observe conditions and seek to maintain the standards of teaching; (3) a curriculum agency charged with developing syllabi and material; (4) special teacher-training institutes for preparing elementary school teachers and similarly for secondary school teachers; (5) special schools at the secondary level for vocational, industrial, and agricultural training for the skilled trades, crafts, or for particular industries; (6) special classes or schools for preprimary children and for handicapped children; (7) a higher educational institution called a university; and (8) specialized research institutes or separate teaching faculties for the various physical, biological, or social sciences, and professional education. It is clear that the list could be extended almost indefinitely if the attempt were made to describe the specialized structures that now characterize the most modern educational systems of Western Europe, the United States, or Soviet Russia.

But it is also clear that the underdeveloped countries have far fewer such structures. For example, among the eighteen Asian nations that Don Adams cites, Nepal, Laos, Cambodia, and Burma have the fewest of the structures listed above; Japan, India, Taiwan, and mainland China have the most; and Indonesia, North Korea, Pakistan, Philippines, South Korea, Thailand, Ceylon, Malaya, Afghanistan,and Mongolia are in between.[42] While many questions remain to be ironed out it is apparent that there is a general relation between degree of structural differentiation and level of modernization in education. It is apparent, too, that by and large the structures themselves are similar to those which originated in the countries of the modernizing West when they were solving their own problems of educational development. These structures have been adopted or emulated with varying kinds of modification by the underdeveloped nations of the world, whether they were subjected to imperial rule or not.

One aspect of educational differentiation which has been remarked upon earlier remains to be mentioned—the extent of diversification that is available within a single comprehensive educational institution. Most commonly in recent years, this has been a trend with an American coloration. We have seen how the American comprehensive high school attempted to bring within its scope a larger range of studies aimed at a wider spectrum of occupational goals than was common in the second-level institutions of Europe. In general, the latter tendency to set up separate institutions to achieve specialized academic purposes and to make each type of postprimary school more homogeneous with respect to occupational goal also generally involved separation of students along social-class lines. The European model tended toward high differentiation among specialized institutions but low diversification or variety of educational programs within each type of institution. The American model tended toward more comprehensive institutions with greater diversification of offerings, greater variety of academic programs and occupational goals, and a more heterogeneous range of social classes.

For reasons discussed earlier the educational institutions that the British and French transferred to their empires overseas were by and large the ones that had

[42] Don Adams, *Education and Modernization in Asia,* Addison-Wesley, Reading, Mass., 1970, pp. 183-185.

relatively little diversification within them—the grammar schools and the *lycées,* and eventually the university colleges and universities. This meant that the colonial peoples acquired an educational taste for the highest prestige type of academic education, for they were the only types offered in the most sought after institutions. If colonial students wanted diversity or variety of offering, say in science or technology, they had to attend what were generally regarded as second-rate institutions at home or seek such studies overseas. Since the mixing of heterogeneous intellectual and academic interests was slower to develop in the European empires than in the United States, the quest for greater comprehensiveness and greater diversification which has arisen in many newly independent states confronts the tradition which they inherited from Europe. The comprehensive high school and the comprehensive university ideas have been debated and tried in India, in Nigeria, and in a dozen other new states since 1950. It remains to be seen how widespread the movement becomes.

It is likely that as the growing demand for expansion of educational opportunity proceeds upward from the primary schools, as it is bound to do, a dissatisfaction with the highly selective character of the inherited European institutions will continue to rise in many parts of the world in the 1970s. The experience in Europe since World War II has been that the single-purpose, specialized, highly selective institution comes increasingly under fire. As the range of student talents and interests acceptable for development in the schools is widened, the demand for greater diversification within institutions is likely to rise. Where the egalitarian outlook begins to criticize highly selective institutions as closed preserves for an aristocratic elite, it also begins to push toward a more comprehensive institution freer of the stigma of inferiority on one side and the stigma of academic snobbery on the other. The comprehensive institution thus has the advantage that selectivity applies not so much to admission to the institution itself but to the variety of programs and occupational goals within the institution. The greatest advantage of all is the flexibility available to students to change programs appropriate to their talents and interests without the trauma aroused by suspicions of failure. The danger that faces a comprehensive institution is that in its efforts to avoid the stigmas of failure for students it fails to maintain the standards that are required for success in the occupational fields for which it professes to prepare students. This problem grows ever more serious as educational institutions are given greater responsibility for the task of certifying that candidates have met minimal and objective standards of competence upon which the public can rely. Achievement of such competence is a major goal of students in a modern educational system.

F. NOT YET A DYAD: ACHIEVEMENT THE PREDOMINANT MOTIF; THE LEARNER A MINOR CHORD

Taking the century of late imperialism as a whole the influence of Western education in the Asian and African countries was surely on the side of allocating educational roles and awarding certification on the basis of achievement rather than on ascribed status. To be sure, some of the early schools in Africa were designed primarily for the sons of chieftains, schools in India were likely to cater to Brahmins rather more than to any other caste, and the prevalence of fees gave preferment to the more affluent families. But, by and large, students were selected on the basis of merit as displayed by their achievement rather than by kinship, lineage, family, or social class. The ascribed status that Westerners had the most difficulty in overcoming was that of sex. They met with massive resistance in the effort to open educational opportunity to girls. Nearly everywhere in all the underdeveloped countries educational participation by girls was less than that for boys, especially at the higher levels. Nevertheless, as educational opportunity and rewards were assigned on the basis of achieved status, modernity overtook tradition.

But *achievement* was quite narrowly defined in most colonial educational systems. By and large, it was identified with the passing of written examinations, and it was celebrated with the award of certificates, diplomas, and degrees. Most European-oriented educational systems followed a model that could be described as limited access systems. Not only was primary education available to fewer than half the relevant age group, admission to secondary schools was based upon the passing of written entrance examinations. Typically, this meant that well under 20 percent of the age group was likely to be selected for admission to general academic secondary schools. Indeed, in some cases a whole series of examinations during primary school years would tend to eliminate most students from even entering secondary school.

Once admitted to secondary school, the whole climate of teaching and learning was supercharged with the leaving examination as the principal end in view of the entire system. Typically, those admitted would be reduced to around 10 percent of the age group by the end of secondary school, and still further to less than 5 percent who would continue on to university-level study.[43] All depended upon the pervasive written examinations from primary school to a university degree. This was achievement with a vengeance. Personal favoritism played relatively little part where the external examinations led to the British General Certificate of Education (G.C.E.) or some equivalent certificate. Excessive idolatry of the certificate in some societies (notably in India and Pakistan) sometimes led to strong pressures upon the readers to hand out passing marks.

All this meant that achievement was narrowly limited to the ability to acquire academic knowledge and repeat it in fairly standardized form on the written pages of the examinations. It meant too that the curriculum did not change easily, because it was locked into the examination system, and vice versa. Abilities to achieve in other ways than grasping written materials in prescribed books were not easily honored when all depended upon the examination results, a period of dread and trauma in countless schools and families around the world. Yet students' attitudes tended to rigidify the examination system even beyond the habits of teachers and readers. Attaining passing marks or high marks became so important that students would not stand for a teacher who tried to go beyond the syllabus or around it in order to stress

---

[43] Bowles, op. cit., pp. 90-93.

what he believed to be more important or more relevant topics for study and discussion.

The stress on examination results along with the tendency of students to seek only the high prestige (and high paying) jobs to which the examinations led combined to produce a widespread neglect of what in the West was deemed to be a learner-oriented education. Before 1960 very little attention was exerted by imperial education authorities to adapt education to the developmental needs or interests of the students—unless passing the examinations could be said to be the epitome of the students' expressed interests and needs. Even if this be granted for the few who were successful in achieving secondary school or university status, the needs of 90 percent outside the secondary schools or the 95 percent outside the universities did not loom as a major concern of the formal educational system. Only when a broad access system was instituted, as in the United States or Japan, did a learner-oriented view begin to gain headway. After 1960 this aspiration began to spread through most of the countries of the world as a cogent model of modernity in education.

A broad access system, as defined by Bowles,[44] has the following characteristics:

1. Universal primary education: approximately 95 percent of the age group finishes primary school and goes on to secondary schools without having to pass selective examinations.
2. Mass secondary education: approximately 90 percent of the age groups enters and 50 or more percent completes it.
3. Most secondary school students follow a common curriculum of general education, at least to age fourteen or so, before they begin to specialize.
4. Guidance and counseling services are designed to help students select among parallel programs designed to stress (a) further academic preparation for higher education, (b) technical education aimed at a job, or (c) further general programs designed as terminal education.
5. Achievement is reckoned by a variety of measures of student performance— marks on recitation in the several classes, internal examinations, daily or weekly records of teachers, and the like. There is no generally required examination at the end of secondary school which automatically certifies for admission to higher education.
6. The diversified programs and flexible standards set for different programs attempt to provide for the varying abilities and interests of a heterogeneous student body. A learner-oriented goal distinguishes this model from the limited access model.
7. Entrance to higher education is in the hands of the institutions themselves, rather than in those of an external examining body. As many as 15 percent of the age group, or more, is likely to be admitted to institutions of higher education.
8. Higher education becomes more diversified, especially as technical education and teacher education are advanced from secondary to higher levels, and the learner-oriented ideal gains impetus as students have before them a wider range of choices among many programs.

[44] Ibid., p. 90.

There is no doubt that the broad access ideology was gaining in virtually all parts of the world at the mid-twentieth century. This did not mean, of course, that it had easy going. Traditional loyalties would confine education to certain ascribed groups, whether males, upper castes, aristocratic ruling families, or particular kinship groups. The belief that girls, the lower classes, outcaste groups, or "those backward" tribal peoples could not really profit from education did not die easily. The belief that secondary and higher education, even primary education, should be reserved for those few who could demonstrate superior intellectual ability in the language of instruction, especially as signified by examination marks, was another tenacious holdover. The lament that lowering the barriers to admission would also "lower the standards" of achievement could be heard from seasoned educators in nearly every colonial land. But diversification and broader access were on their way, especially after independence was achieved in the new states.

How much the diversification was to be consonant with an achievement-oriented goal and how much with a learner-oriented goal is difficult to determine without more research. By and large, however, the principal impetus seemed to be coming from two major sources—the outlook that the good of the country and the needs of national development in the new states required diversification, and the pressures arising from the aspirations and demands that education be spread more equitably to larger and larger proportions of the population. In a real sense the latter could be looked upon as responding to the needs of learners, but it is impressive testimony to the power of a narrow view of achievement that enormous numbers of pupils drop out of school in the early grades for causes that must be related to the fact that schooling is not made appealing to them.

The problem of wastage and stagnation (two most expressive terms) was rampant in most of the colonial countries as they strove to modernize by attempting to move toward universal primary education and expanded secondary education. Wastage meant that enormous numbers of children who began school in the first grade would drop out as early as the second or third grade. UNESCO estimates that in Asia as a whole as late as the mid-1960s as many as 60 percent of children who began primary school dropped out by the fifth grade.[45] In some countries 50 to 60 percent drop out after the first grade (Burma, Laos, Pakistan); in others as many as 40 to 50 percent drop out after the second grade (India, Thailand, and South Vietnam). Stagnation (the repeating of a class by children who have failed it) is also a widespread indicator that achievement of the required knowledge of each grade level was required before the child could advance to the next grade. What achievement can mean in circumstances of massive wastage and stagnation can only be imagined. It may mean that aspiration of parents to educate their children may be low, finances inadequate, or the hardships of overcrowding and poor physical facilities are great. It certainly means that the quality of teaching is exceedingly poor, being in the hands of enormous numbers of untrained and unqualified teachers who have all they can do to read the pages of the textbook to the children, let alone develop and manage a learner-oriented program of instruction. Achievement-orientation continued to mean in vast areas of the earth a "chalk and

---

[45] *An Asian Model of Educational Development,* UNESCO, Paris, 1966, p. 88.

talk" routine by the teacher followed by notebook copying, verbatim memorizing, and rote repeating of formula by the pupils. Trying to develop a program that would appeal to children, enlist their enthusiasms, and develop their varying talents as well as encouraging achievement had only just begun when the late imperial era was dying.

Even more scarce than a learner-oriented ideal of education during most of the imperial era was the research-mindedness that was becoming a trademark of educational modernization in some of the countries of the West. Perhaps further investigation will reverse or modify this judgment, but Edward Shils strikes a most significant, if harsh and disquieting, chord when he points out that the vast majority of college and university teachers in India were expected to be "cram masters" rather than inspiring teachers:

> Indian higher education was not established for the purpose of advancing the quest of new truths. It was intended primarily to facilitate the inculcation of what had already been created or discovered, largely in other countries; it was intended to raise young men, and latterly young women, to the level of knowledge required for teaching, administrative work, and legal and medical practice. The Englishmen who came out to teach in India were in the majority very fine men who were devoted to their subjects, to their pupils and colleges and to India, but they were seldom creative scholars or scientists. Sir E. Denison Ross, Charles H. Tawney, Percival Spear, Humphrey House and a few others were exceptions to the general rule. The rest were diligent and conscientious pedagogues who believed that students had to be prepared for examinations rather than to become discoverers in their own right.[46]

To a very large degree Shils' analysis of the fate of the achievement motif and the research ideal may apply to much of the dispersion of Western education to the rest of the world under imperial aegis. Insofar as this is true, Western education by no means put its best modern foot forward. It did help to transform the traditional societies it touched in the many ways we have tried to describe, and thus it did stimulate modernization. But it did not, until very late in the era, apply to the colonial peoples the vast inspiriting elixirs which it was administering to its homeland populations. It did not try to humanize and liberalize the educative process on the basis of refined research into the nature of learning and of the learner. Nor did it try to infuse the humanities and the social studies with a steady flow of generalizations and evidence from the rapidly developing social sciences. In these and countless other ways the modern education of the West had helped to modernize the civilization of the West, but these generally played little part in the colonial heritage.

Perhaps the most important steps the West could take to make amends for this gap in its legacy to the peoples of Africa and Asia would be to assist them in developing educators with high-level research competence and a research-mindedness that would lead to a learner-oriented as well as to a society-oriented modern education. No greater contribution could be made in the long run than to establish research teams that would bring together scholars from countries that are at different stages of

[46] Shils, *The Intellectual Between Tradition and Modernity*, p. 47.

modernity who could view the interactions among cultures and societies from both sides of the equation.

In such a collegial process perhaps the provincialisms, the ethnocentrisms, and the particularities that have plagued the study of international social relations could be overcome or at least mitigated. Perhaps together they could not only inquire into the conditions required for but also design the outlines of an education that would help to humanize the modernization process by paying greater attention to the development of the individual, and which would at the same time broaden the nation-building processes by viewing them in international perspectives. Nationalism and national education were major elements in the original creation of modern civilization. Western educators now have the opportunity to take the next step and join with colleagues from other parts of the world in helping to create a postmodern, globe-encircling civilization for the future. One of the keys to this effort is sustained, cooperative, international inquiry into the role that education might play in a new civilization-building process, one that replaces inherited patterns of colonial rule and imperial mission with the practices of genuine freedom and equality among the peoples of the world.

UNESCO's International Commission on Educational Development has not only documented the ever-widening gap between the industrialized and the developing countries of the world but has argued that "it is difficult to see how this division can ever be overcome—quite the contrary—without an organized, rational transfer, an equitable redistribution, of the scientific and technological stockpile which has accumulated at one pole of the community of mankind. Clearly, education, as the mediator of knowledge, has a major role to play here."[47]

Herein lies the major task for international education in the future. I would stress even more than the Commission does the necessity for an organized, rational transfer and an equitable redistribution of the *educational* as well as the scientific and technological stockpiles that have accumulated in the West. This does not mean a one-way transplant of Western education; it means the promotion of a genuinely *inter*national educational enterprise. In another connection I have described the goals as follows:

> What we must do, somehow, is to form new kinds of co-operative associations among the educational institutions of the world. . . .
>
> Today we must avoid the attitudes and the mistakes of the "civilizing mission" of the past. We must remove the alien church, the alien government, the alien property owner, and the alien army from the control of education in the modernization process. We must promote a genuinely co-operative international education as the best promise of building the surest foundations for freedom in the future. International education should rely upon the open and free processes of education for the promotion of its ideas, not upon secret manipulation, brute strength, or furtive seeking of power. It should be under the control of the people concerned and not directed from afar. International educa-

---

[47] Edgar Faure et al., *Learning to Be; the World of Education Today and Tomorrow,* UNESCO, Paris and Harrap, London, 1972, pp. 49-50.

tion in the late twentieth century should provide a two-way process by which the self-determining peoples of the world seek to modernize themselves through education, just as Westerners did for themselves when they borrowed from each other during their period of rapid modernization. . . .

At the heart of any long-term engagement in international education must be the strengthening of the resources of the world's educational systems and especially of the universities and their constituent professional schools of education. . . . These associated universities for international educational development represent the next step beyond "technical assistance." Their collaborative efforts to train personnel, exchange staff and students, develop educational materials for use in schools and universities, and conduct co-operative research in international education will mark the coming of the "educational civilization."

. . . The stress upon professional schools is particularly important because, in a genuine sense, the major professions and their professional schools lie at the very heart of modern forms of organization and modern ways of life. If there is a single characteristic that distinguishes a modern society from a traditional society, it is a universal system of education leading to university-level work in the arts and sciences, which are in turn applied to the practical improvement of life through professional training and service. The effort to "professionalize" a traditional society is the very essence of the educational task in the modernization process. To succeed in this endeavor, the support of private agencies and of the governments and educational institutions of both receiving and sending nations must be enlisted. And all nations should take part as both senders and receivers. The one-way emissary is an echo of the past. All nations now should contribute their share of two-way educationaries.[48]

---

[48] R. Freeman Butts, "America's Role in International Education: A Perspective on Thirty Years" in Harold G. Shane (ed.), *The United States and International Education,* The Sixty-eighth Yearbook of the National Society for the Study of Education, part I, University of Chicago Press, Chicago, 1969, pp. 39, 42, 43.

EPILOGUE:
THE PROMISE
OF THE EDUCATION
OF THE WEST

All signs point to the third quarter of the twentieth century as a major watershed in human history. It was not simply one of those transitional periods that have become the clichés of history writers. It was a turning point from which there was no turning back. It was possibly even the beginning of the fourth great transformation in the human career, comparable in significance to the much longer and slower transformations that successively marked the evolution of *Homo sapiens* himself and his folk societies and cultures, the emergence of traditional civilization, and the rise of modern civilization. The incredible thing is that the outlines of a next stage in the human career began to take shape in a relatively short period of time in the latter half of the twentieth century.

Lest this seem to sound like an apocalyptic intonation, one need only try to identify for himself the most important date and event in recent history. Is it 1944 or 1945 when the atom bomb was first exploded or used? Is it the decade and a half beginning either with India's freedom in 1947 or with the Chinese communist victory in 1949 and ending with the independence of more than half the nations of the world? Is it the late 1960s which saw the landing of men on the moon and communication satellites sending immediate sight as well as sound around the world? Or is it the fact that the 12 billion computations turned out by the 1,000 computers in the United States every hour in 1956 would become 400 trillion computations per hour by 100,000 computers in 1976?

Whether these or any number of other data are adduced to point to the almost incomprehensibly rapid changes of the last quarter century, the point here is that they are basically the result of the application of knowledge, of science, of technology, and of social organization to practical affairs by the highly trained products of Western-type educational systems. The changes are so momentous that thoughtful analysts and predictors are beginning to say that we are moving into a form of society which they variously call postindustrial (Daniel Bell and Bertram Gross), postmodern (Peter F. Drucker and Amitai Etzioni), technetronic (Zbigniew Brzezinski), or postcivilizational (Kenneth E. Boulding).

Whatever term may win out in common or technical usage in the future, the formative role of modern Western education will be recognized as having contributed significantly to the technical and specialized intellectual expertise that produced the epoch-making changes of the third quarter of the twentieth century.

The question remained, however, concerning what direction the new age would take. Would modern civilization, which drew so much from Western influence, disintegrate, dissipate, and disappear in the pollution, the population explosion, the destructive weaponry, the ethnic, racial, and religious confrontations, or the national rivalries that it had produced over the past four or five hundred years?

Or would modern civilization be able to regenerate itself and move toward a worldwide civilization that could manage to achieve a more just, humane, and equitable condition of life for the peoples of the world? Much depends upon the role that education plays in the future. Will Western education become formalistic, congealing, constricted, and isolated as education became in the dispersive periods of Mesopotamian and Egyptian education? Will it become classical, formalistic, and imitative as education did in the dispersive periods of Indian, Chinese, and Hellenistic times? Or will it play an innovative, adaptable, and socially relevant role as it did in the formative periods of the major civilizations of the past? The hopes of mankind ride in part on what part Western education is to play in the emergence of a new civilization and what form that new civilization takes. Simply to be postindustrial, posturban, postimperial, postcolonial, or postmodern will not be enough. The new civilization to be viable must become truly transnational and worldwide.

The signs of the times were there if the educators of the world could but see them. The trends toward an emerging world civilization have been a long time in the making. The first phase actually was the imperialism of the Western peoples who were modernizing themselves and in the process carrying their impact around the world. Few would like to see that process repeated or emulated.

The second phase came to a head in the disimperialism of the decades following the second World War when the new states of Asia and Africa threw off the imperial controls of the West but did so by aspiring to the very nationalistic and modernizing trends created by the Western societies themselves. In spite of the political fragmentation that has marked the dispersion of modern Western civilization and the worldwide independence movements, a nexus of relationships was produced that began to take on the form of a world society, a world culture, and a world education.

The signs of the emerging world society were plentiful at mid-twentieth century. Some called it simply the international system; others coined more exotic terms such as sociosphere to be studied by xenology, the study of foreign or international systems. But the essence was the growth of world-spanning systems of communication and transportation, worldwide economic organizations for trade, business, industry, and finance, and thousands of voluntary nongovernmental associations as well as the host of intergovernmental organizations under the sponsorship of the United Nations, or regional associations, or bilateral or multilateral intergovernmental agreements. While the rhetoric of the nations continued to sound the tocsin of independent sovereignty, the nations of the world, large and small, most modern and least modern, were more interdependent than ever.

Whatever the terms used, the traditional human social systems based upon the local, contiguous areas of common culture, language, and customs of relatively small groups of people were being overlaid with the interconnected networks or systems of international association that were touching down in all parts of the world, especially in the urban centers. The nexus of cities became the anchoring centers of dissemination for the international network. The role of urban centers as interlocking points of cultural contact has long been familiar in the ancient as well as the modern empires, but the extent of communication, the extent of mutual interchange, and the growth of common ways of acting and organizing were never so great. Curiously, the nation-building explosions that swept over Asia and Africa at mid-century simply accelerated the trend toward transnational interdependence.

No matter which came first, the emergence of a world culture has paralleled, perhaps even made possible, the systemness in which the elements are so inter-related that one can speak of a worldwide system as a whole. Especially important in the emergence of a world culture has been the growing nexus of cultied cultures in which world-oriented educated elites have been the key figures.

Needless to say, many of the basic elements of the education of the elites came from the modern education of the West with its growing stress upon secular and scientific knowledge, rational, calculative, and scientific methods of thought, the aggressive application of science and techology to practical affairs, the expanding role of professional expertise resting upon experimental and theoretical research, and the dedication of popular education to the achievement of a more humane, egalitarian, and welfare-oriented society.

Again, some have referred to this world culture as a superculture or the Noösphere, a term used by Pierre Teilhard de Chardin to refer to the whole body of knowledge and images of cognition and values existing in the combined minds of men. At the root of much of this world culture was not only the global diffusion of modern science and technology, but the "increasingly inclusive and interdependent nexus of technical specialism" that has enabled invention and new discoveries in knowledge to increase at a geometric rate of progression.[1] The prime channels of transnational intellectual institutions have been the urban centers with their universities, professional associations, research and development centers, communication media, and publishing houses, a complex that has been summed up in the unlovely term knowledge industry.[2]

Again, whatever the term used, a set of structures of world education has accompanied and helped to produce the international systems of society and culture. At the heart of both is the network of formal education without which the Noösphere or the sociosphere could not long exist. Kenneth E. Boulding puts it bluntly:

> It is a slightly terrifying thought that all human knowledge is lost approximately every generation by the processes of aging and death and has to be

[1] Marshall Hodgson, "The Great Western Transmutation" *Chicago Today*, vol. 4, no. 3, p. 50, Autumn 1967.

[2] Fritz Machlup, *The Production and Distribution of Knowledge in the United States*, Princeton University Press, Princeton, N.J., 1962.

replaced in new bodies. If this process of transmission were interruped even for thirty years, the human race would revert probably to its paleolithic condition, or might even become extinct. . . . the noösphere of the modern world is so large and so complex that it requires a large formal educational establishment to transmit it. This establishment, furthermore, grows larger all the time.[3]

And it spreads from the more advanced societies to the less developed societies through the intergovernmental agencies of UNESCO, regional organizations, foreign aid and technical assistance programs, and countless international educational and professional associations.

The axial question to be put to the growing educational establishments of the nations of the world is whether or not they will contribute to the already emerging world society and world culture, or whether they will be so obsessed with the nation-oriented and ecologically destructive aspects of modern technological education that the coming of a genuinely human world civilization will be delayed or obstructed. Herein lies the challenge to Western education, which has promoted both the humane values of enlightenment, welfare, equality, and popular participation, but also has provided the training, the technical knowledge, and the expertise that enabled the wielders of massive industrial technology to threaten to make wastelands of much of the earth's lands, rivers, seas, and cities in the name of economic growth or national productivity. And it has been done on such a vast scale that all the peoples of the whole globe are involved. There is indeed no place to hide.

As Western education continues in its dispersive phase will it now be able to redirect its energies to the dissemination of a world outlook and thus enable a viable world civilization to be born, or will its energies be dissipated among the fragmented, self-serving, and narrowly conceived systems of 150 nation-states—and thus disintegrate and disappear?

If one takes the long view of history, the answer of course does not lie in the past, but the alternatives become clearer. One would hope that the deciders of the world's educational fate would make the choices leading to the coming of a world civilization. The human potentialities are certainly there. A race that could achieve the evolutionary complexities of *Homo sapiens* and then create the vast spectrum of folk cultures and societies and nourish them by becoming *Homo educans* was also able to produce the traditional and modern civilizations which rely so heavily upon the school. Thus man became *Homo scholasticus,* finding his educational and intellectual home primarily in the urban centers of the world ever since the cities of Sumer were first organized.

In Western terms even the words used to describe the process go back to the Greeks. The center of the civilized life for them was the polis, which became a metropolis, a mother of new cities. Others took the form of cosmopolis, a city to which people came from all around the world. Modern civilization has gone beyond the Greeks and created the megalopolis, the vast agglomerations of concentrated populations embracing 30,000,000 people in a concentrated area.

[3]Kenneth E. Boulding, "Education for Spaceship Earth" *Social Education,* vol. 32, no. 7, p. 648, November 1968, a special issue on "International Education for the Twenty-First Century."

Now the question is whether modern man can take the next step and create a world in which the civilized urban way of life will release the creative energies of men rather than stifle them. And the Greeks even had the word for that. The οικουμενη (Latinized to *oecumene*) was the term they used to designate *their* portion of the inhabited world which they had civilized or citified as opposed to the lands of the barbarians. They spread their ecumene, as we have seen, by establishing colonies and by governing Greek cities throughout the Mediterranean and Middle East. Since their time the nexus of citified cultures has spread around the world, creating a kind of ecumenopolis, or world urban way of life. This latter-day process has been greatly aided by the worldwide diffusion of the agencies of Western education, but seldom with a view of the world as a whole or with the welfare of all the peoples of the world in mind.

Here is the challenge to the education of the West in the future. Can it enable the learners of the world—and their teachers—to study and understand the world as a whole and to take their part in it? *Homo sapiens* was able to transform himself into *Homo educans* and into *Homo scholasticus.* Can he transform himself into *Homo ecumenicus*? Is this the promise of the education of the West?

I believe it is, but only if Western education can divest itself of its own ethnocentric and narrowly nationalistic preoccupations and infuse itself with a world orientation that seeks to enhance the best, not the worst, of the modernity it has helped to produce. Only then can it be in position to play its role in helping cooperatively to shape educational systems with other nations that will enable both:

> to move toward playing a responsible role in the coming world civilization, a civilization marked by increased reliance upon a scientific-rational outlook, by the rational-legal ordering of public behavior, by increased participation of ever larger numbers of people in public affairs, by the secular validation of the knowledge upon which decisions in human affairs are based, and by commitment to the primacy of humane values.
>
> ... what comes after a modern civilization based upon urban ways of life cannot be a return to a preurban or a premodern way of life, nor indeed can it be simply an extension of a suburban or exurban way of life. If there is to be a future beyond modern civilization, it must rest intrinsically upon an educational civilization, one in which the institutions and the plans for social change are based upon valid knowledge, in which the vast majority of people are enabled to profit from full educational opportunity, in which leaders are selected with due regard for their achievement, including their achieved education, and in which the universal elements of a rational education reach across national boundaries and contribute to the humane characteristics of modernity.

So what should we be doing in international education in the future? We should be trying to "educationalize" the process of modernization. We should be trying to see to it that this great transformation in the human career becomes more humane, more orderly, more peaceful, and more educative than it has ever been during the first five hundred years of modernization. We should be relying upon the methods of education rather than upon military conquest, colonial intrusion, revolutionary subversion, authoritarian compulsion, economic exploitation, religious conversion, power politics, or any of the other means by which the advanced nations of the West—or the East—have tried to modernize the less advanced nations of the world. . . .

To repeat, we should be trying to strengthen the educational potential of the nations of the world so that they can achieve for themselves a unified and sturdy nationhood, a satisfying modernity, a genuine freedom, and a viable civilization.[4]

But that is only half the promise. At one and the same time an internationalized Western education must be promoting not only national and cultural diversity but also a loyalty to the welfare of the world itself. Barbara Ward and René Dubos posed the challenge to the United Nations Conference on the Human Environment:

> . . . to devise patterns of collective behavior compatible with the continued flowering of civilizations.
>
> It is deliberately that, in the last paragraph, we have used the word *civilizations* in the plural. Just as individual human beings differ in their life and aspirations, so do social groups. . . . There are possibilities within the human environment for many different kinds of surroundings and ways of life. . . . of developing the distinctive genius of each place, each social group, and each person—in other words of cultivating individuality. . . . The emotional attachment to our prized diversity need not interfere with our attempts to develop the global state of mind which will generate a rational loyalty to the planet as a whole. As we enter the global phase of human evolution it becomes obvious that each man has two countries, his own and the planet Earth.[5]
>
> . . . From family to clan, from clan to nation, from nation to federation—such enlargements of allegiance have occurred without wiping out the earlier loves. Today, in human society, we can perhaps hope to survive in all our prized diversity provided we can achieve an ultimate loyalty to our single, beautiful, and vulnerable planet Earth.[6]

Helping to achieve these dual loyalties is the fundamental role that the education of the West must now play and the promise it must keep for the future.

[4] Butts, op. cit., pp. 44-45.

[5] Barbara Ward and René Dubos, *Only One Earth; the Care and Maintenance of a Small Planet*, Norton, New York, 1972, p. xviii.

[6] Ibid., p. 220.

BIBLIOGRAPHICAL NOTES

In the notes that follow I have not listed all the sources I have used in this book nor have I compiled a reference bibliography for the research scholar. Instead, I have tried to provide a handy guide to recent books in English (many of which have been published or reissued in paperback since 1960) that are readable, available, and related to the major themes of traditional and modern civilization building. I have therefore not included much of value to the history of education in older, monographic, periodical, unpublished, or textbook sources. I have, however, concentrated on works of serious scholarship which are based upon primary source materials, which range across the social sciences, humanities, history, and education, and which stress the general ideas that lead to seasoned judgments of interpretation and policy.

PREFACE

Revisionism in Historical Writing   Several volumes that point to the need for reinterpretation in history are: Werner Cahnman and Alvin Boskoff (eds.), *Sociology and History: Theory and Research,* Free Press, New York, 1964; John Higham et al., *History,* Prentice-Hall, Englewood Cliffs, N.J., 1965; John Higham (ed.), *The Reconstruction of American History,* Harper Torchbooks, New York, 1962; and Edward N. Saveth (ed.), *American History and the Social Sciences,* Free Press, New York, 1964. Unfortunately, these volumes pay little or no attention to the history of education. One symposium that does is "Historical Studies Today," *Daedalus,* vol. 100, no. 1, Winter, 1971. In this publication John E. Talbott deals with the history of education.

The case for revisionism in the history of American education was set forth in the early 1960s: by Bernard Bailyn in his *Education in the Forming of American Society,* University of North Carolina Press, Chapel Hill, 1960; in a series of articles on education and American history in *Harvard Educational Review,* vol. 31, Spring, 1961; by Lawrence A. Cremin, *The Wonderful World of Ellwood Patterson Cubberley: An Essay on the Historiography of American Education,* Bureau of Publications, Teachers College, New York, 1965; and by William W. Brickman, "Revisionism and the Study of the History of Education," *History of Education Quarterly,* vol. 4, no. 4, pp. 209-233, December 1964.

The scholarly revisionists argued that the writing of educational history had been too narrowly professional and institutional, too parochial, too anachronistic, and too evangelistic in its approach. Predictably, the revisionists themselves were soon to be revised by a more radical approach. See, for example, Michael B. Katz, *Class, Bureaucracy, and the Schools: The Illusion of Educational Change in America,* Praeger, New York, 1971 and Colin Greer, *The Great School Legend; a Revisionist Interpretation of American Public Education,* Basic Books, New York, 1972. Still more radical were those critics who found organized education itself a socially and personally injurious institution. Among these were: Ivan Illich, *Deschooling Society,* Harper & Row, New York, 1970; Paulo Freire, *Pedagogy of the Oppressed,* Herder and Herder, New York,

1970; and Everett Reimer, *School Is Dead: Alternatives in Education*, Doubleday, Garden City, N.Y., 1971. In any case, neither the scholarly revisionists nor the radical revisionists stressed the international elements that I believe are most demanding of reinterpretation in the history of education—the world situation following World War II, the crises in modern civilization, the need for comparative study of the interconnected civilizations of the world, and an awareness of the major directions of worldwide social change toward modernization.

The Modernization Process   The most important single volume on the modernization process in historical perspective is C. E. Black, *The Dynamics of Modernization; a Study in Comparative History*, Harper & Row, New York, 1966. It contains a useful and selective guide to the rapidly expanding bibliography on this subject. The importance of this subject is indicated by the 2,500 items listed in John Brode, *The Process of Modernization; an Annotated Bibliography on the Sociocultural Aspects of Development*, Harvard University Press, Cambridge, Mass., 1969. In addition to Black, I have found the most useful books on modernization to be: Gabriel A. Almond and James S. Coleman (eds.), *The Politics of the Developing Areas*, Princeton University Press, Princeton, N.J., 1960; Gabriel A. Almond and G. Bingham Powell, Jr., *Comparative Politics; a Developmental Approach*, Little, Brown, Boston, 1966; Clifford Geertz (ed.), *Old Societies and New States; the Quest for Modernity in Asia and Africa*, Free Press, New York, 1963; Samuel P. Huntington, *Political Order in Changing Societies*, Yale University Press, New Haven, Conn., 1968; Guy Hunter, *Modernizing Peasant Societies; a Comparative Study in Asia and Africa*, Oxford University Press, New York, 1969; Daniel Lerner, *The Passing of Traditional Society: Modernizing the Middle East*, Free Press, New York, 1958; Marion Levy, Jr., *Modernization and the Structure of Societies*, 2 vols., Princeton University Press, Princeton, N.J., 1966; Robert A. Nisbet, *Social Change and History; Aspects of the Western Theory of Development*, Oxford University Press, New York, 1969; Talcott Parsons, *The Systems of Modern Societies*, Prentice-Hall, Englewood Cliffs, N.J., 1971; Lucian W. Pye, *Politics, Personality, and Nation-Building: Burma's Search for Identity*, Yale University Press, New Haven, Conn., 1962; Dankwart Rustow, *A World of Nations: The Dynamics of Modern Politics*, Brookings Institution, Washington, D.C., 1967; Edward A. Shils, *Political Development in the New States*, Mouton, The Hague, 1965; Myron Weiner (ed.), *Modernization: The Dynamics of Growth*, Basic Books, New York, 1966; and Kalmen H. Silvert (ed.), *Expectant Peoples; Nationalism and Development*, Random House, New York, 1963.

Comparative History   As Black's book reveals, study of the modernization process has stimulated attention to comparative history. Significant comparative studies have recently been made of such basic institutions or social processes as feudalism, bureaucracy, urbanization, population, elites, slavery, imperialism, and colonialism. Examples of these are listed at appropriate places in the following text. Ways in which American history can be put into a worldwide context are suggested in C. Vann Woodward (ed.), *The Comparative Approach to American History*, Basic Books, New York, 1968. Several periodicals provide a continuing source for pursuing comparative history themes. I have found the most useful to be: *Comparative Studies in Society and History*, published by the Cambridge University Press; the *Journal of Interdisciplinary History*, published by the Massachusetts Institute of Technology Press; *World Politics*, published by the Center for International Studies, Princeton University; the

History of Education Quarterly, published by the History of Education Society in cooperation with the School of Education, New York University; and the *Comparative Education Review*, published by the Comparative and International Education Society and the University of Wisconsin.

World History The trend toward using world history to redress the limitations of American-centered or European-centered history accelerated markedly in the 1960s. A landmark of interpretative writing, synthesis, and generalization in this genre is William H. McNeill, *The Rise of the West; a History of the Human Community*, University of Chicago Press, Chicago, 1963. Another outstanding example is R. R. Palmer and Joel Colton, *A History of the Modern World*, Knopf, New York, which had gone through four revisions by 1971. These two single-volume histories, along with C. E. Black, *The Dynamics of Modernization*, cited above, might well be used together to provide the basic world context from which to view the history of the education of the West. Pinpointed upon particular problems, but vast in their worldwide compass are such studies as: Lewis Mumford, *The City in History, Its Origins, Its Transformations, and Its Prospects*, Harcourt, Brace & World, New York, 1961; and D. V. Glass and D. E. C. Eversley (eds.), *Population in History; Essays in Historical Demography*, E. Arnold, London, 1965.

Anthologies of Readings in the History of Education Collections of readings pertaining to the history of education have experienced a recent burst of interest. Some of these collections deal primarily with Western education: Paul Nash (ed.), *Models of Man, Explorations in the Western Educational Tradition*, Wiley, New York, 1968; Frederick M. Binder (ed.), *Education in the History of Western Civilization: Selected Readings*, Macmillan, New York, 1970; D. W. Sylvester (ed.), *Educational Documents, 800-1816*, Barnes & Noble, New York, 1970. Two older collections have been reissued: Robert Ulich (ed.), *Three Thousand Years of Educational Wisdom: Selections from Great Documents*, 2d ed., Harvard University Press, Cambridge, Mass., 1971, and Robert R. Rusk, *The Doctrines of the Great Educators*, 3d ed., St. Martin's, New York, 1965. The Burgess Publishing Co., Minneapolis, Minn., has published several such volumes, including: Donna R. Barnes (ed.), *For Court, Manor, and Church: Education in Medieval Europe*, 1971; John Hardin Best (ed.), *The Revolution of Reason and Nature: Education in the Eighteenth Century* (in preparation); J. J. Chambliss (ed.), *Enlightenment and Social Progress: Education in the Nineteenth Century*, 1971; J. J. Chambliss (ed.), *Nobility, Tragedy, and Naturalism; Education in Ancient Greece*, 1971.

Recent collections that focus upon the history of American education are: John Hardin Best and Robert T. Sidwell (eds.), *The American Legacy of Learning; Readings in the History of Education*, Lippincott, Philadelphia, 1967; Carl H. Gross and Charles C. Chandler (eds.), *The History of American Education Through Readings*, Heath, Boston, 1964; Richard Hofstadter and Wilson Smith (eds.), *American Higher Education; a Documentary History*, 2 vols., University of Chicago Press, Chicago, 1961; S. Alexander Rippa (ed.), *Educational Ideas in America; a Documentary History*, McKay, New York, 1969; David B. Tyack (ed.), *Turning Points in American Educational History*, Blaisdell, Waltham, Mass., 1967; and Gerald Gutek (ed.), *An Historical Introduction to American Education*, Crowell, New York, 1970.

Republished Materials   Especially useful for their up-to-date, interpretive essays are the paper *Classics in Education* edited by Lawrence A. Cremin and published by the Teachers College Press, New York. These are listed at relevant points in the notes that follow. Cremin also acted as advisory editor for two series of books republished in 1970 and 1971 by Arno Press, a company of The New York Times. Entitled *American Education, Its Men, Ideas, and Institutions,* these 161 volumes collectively represent much of the earlier scholarship upon which the history of American education has rested. Two volumes with a unique international flair deal with foreign views of education. One of these books portrays the Europeans attitudes about American education and vice versa during the nineteenth century: Stewart E. Fraser and William W. Brickman (eds.), *A History of International and Comparative Education; Nineteenth Century Documents,* Scott, Foresman, Glenview, Ill., 1968. The other volume deals with foreign views of American education in the twentieth century: Stewart E. Fraser (ed.), *American Education in Foreign Perspectives; Twentieth Century Essays,* Wiley, New York, 1969.

Recent General Volumes on the History of Western Education   Two volumes that contain essays principally by a younger generation of educational historians, and that are devoted to a historical treatment of education in the West are: Paul Nash, Andreas M. Kazamias, and Henry J. Perkinson (eds.), *The Educated Man; Studies in the History of Educational Thought,* Wiley, New York, 1965; and Paul Nash (ed.), *History and Education; the Educational Uses of the Past,* Random House, New York, 1970. The latter includes British as well as American authors.

In general, there has been a revival of publishing interest in the history of Western education in recent years. See the discerning and critical "Review Essay, In Search of Structure and Significance," *Educational Studies; a Journal of Book Reviews in the Foundations of Education,* vol. 2, nos. 3 and 4, pp. 55-59, Fall-Winter, 1971. Among the more useful of the recent single-volume histories are: Edward J. Power, *Main Currents in the History of Education,* rev. ed., McGraw-Hill, New York, 1970; Gerald L. Gutek, *A History of the Western Educational Experience,* Random House, New York, 1972; and Christopher J. Lucas, *Our Western Educational Heritage,* Macmillan, New York, 1972. A three-volume *History of Western Education* is being written by James Bowen; the first volume is entitled *The Ancient World,* St. Martin's, New York, 1972.

In the review essay cited above Christopher Lucas says "there is always a pedagogical need to pull things together, to organize and present the material as a reasonably coherent whole. This requirement is especially acute in the history of education." It is to meet such a need that this book has stressed "organizing structure" and "interpretive scheme" based upon "sophisticated historiographical canons."

CHAPTER I.
A CONCEPTUAL FRAMEWORK FOR STUDYING EDUCATION IN HISTORY

Theory of History   For a comparison of recent studies of cyclical theories and evolutionary theories of grand design in history, see: Frank E. Manuel, *Shapes of Philosophical History,* Stanford University Press, Stanford, Calif., 1965; Werner J. Cahnman and Alvin Boskoff (eds.), *Sociology and History: Theory and Research,* Free Press, New York, 1964; Robert A. Nisbet, *The Sociological Tradition,* Basic Books, New York, 1967; and Marvin Harris, *The Rise of Anthropological Theory: A History of*

Theories of Culture, Thomas Y. Crowell, New York, 1968. For a variety of approaches to history as descriptive narration, see: John Higham et al. (eds.), *History,* Prentice-Hall, Englewood Cliffs, N.J., 1965; Edward N. Saveth (ed.), *American History and the Social Sciences,* Free Press, New York, 1964; and Trygve Tholfsen, *Historical Thinking,* Harper & Row, New York, 1967.

The Civilization-Building Process For the newer empirical foundations of the civilization-building process as formulated by archaeologists, anthropologists, and sociologists, see: Werner J. Cahnman, "The Rise of Civilization as a Paradigm of Social Change," in Werner J. Cahnman and Alvin Boskoff (eds.), *Sociology and History: Theory and Research,* Free Press, New York, 1964, pp. 537-559; Robert McC. Adams, *The Evolution of Urban Society; Early Mesopotamia and Prehispanic Mexico,* Aldine, Chicago, 1966; Robert J. Braidwood and Gordon R. Willey (eds.), *Courses Toward Urban Life: Archaeological Considerations of Some Cultural Alternates,* Aldine, Chicago, 1962; V. Gordon Childe, *What Happened in History,* Penguin, Baltimore, 1961; V. Gordon Childe, *Man Makes Himself,* Mentor, New York, 1955; Grahame Clark, *World Prehistory; an Outline,* 2d ed., Cambridge University Press, London, 1969; Glyn E. Daniel, *The Three Ages; an Essay in Archaeological Method,* Cambridge University Press, London, 1963; E. E. Evans-Pritchard, *Anthropology and History,* Manchester University Press, Manchester, England, 1961; Morton Fried, *The Evolution of Political Society; an Essay in Political Anthropology,* Random House, New York, 1967; A. L. Kroeber, *An Anthropologist Looks at History,* University of California Press, Berkeley and Los Angeles, 1963; Alexander Marshack, *The Roots of Civilization; the Cognitive Beginnings of Man's First Art, Symbol and Notation,* McGraw-Hill, New York, 1972; Talcott Parsons, *Societies; Evolutionary and Comparative Perspectives,* Prentice-Hall, Englewood Cliffs, N.J., 1966; Stuart Piggott (ed.), *The Dawn of Civilization,* McGraw-Hill, New York, 1961; Robert Redfield, *The Primitive World and Its Transformation,* Cornell University Press, Ithaca, N.Y., 1953; Margaret Redfield (ed.), *Human Nature and the Study of Society; the Papers of Robert Redfield,* University of Chicago Press, Chicago, 1962, vol. 1; Darcy Ribiero, *The Civilizational Process,* The Smithsonian Institution, Washington, D.C., 1968; Julian H. Steward, *Theory of Culture Change; the Methodology of Multilinear Evolution,* University of Illinois Press, Urbana, Ill., 1963; and Colin Renfrew, *The Emergence of Civilisation; the Cyclades and the Aegean in the Third Millenium B.C.,* Methuen, London, 1972.

Historians who approach civilization building with more attention to intellectual or religious ingredients than is common among empirically minded social scientists are: Rushton Coulbourn, *The Origins of Civilized Societies,* Princeton University Press, Princeton, N.J., 1959; Carroll Quigley, *The Evolution of Civilizations; an Introduction to Historical Analysis,* Macmillan, New York, 1961; Lewis Mumford, *The Transformations of Man,* Collier Books, New York, 1962; Jacquetta Hawkes and Sir Leonard Woolley, *Prehistory and the Beginnings of Civilization,* Harper & Row, New York, 1963; and D. C. Somervell's abridgement of Arnold J. Toynbee, *A Study of History,* 2 vols., Oxford University Press, New York, 1947.

CHAPTER II.
MANKIND'S PASSAGE TO CIVILIZATION—AND TO SCHOOL
(3500 B.C.-500 B.C.)

Many of the references cited for the civilization-building process in Chapter 1 deal with the origins of civilization in Mesopotamia and Egypt, particularly Adams, Childe,

Piggott, and Hawkes and Woolley. I know of no book devoted entirely to education for either civilization.

Mesopotamian Civilization   For Mesopotamia the most readable general interpretations bearing on education are Samuel Noah Kramer, *The Sumerians: Their History, Culture, and Character,* University of Chicago Press, Chicago, 1963 and A. Leo Oppenheim, *Ancient Mesopotamia; Portrait of a Dead Civilization,* University of Chicago Press, Chicago, 1964. Somewhat older but still seminal works are: Henri Frankfort, *The Birth of Civilization in the Middle East,* Anchor, New York, 1956; Robert J. Braidwood, *The Near East and the Foundations of Civilization,* University of Oregon Press, Eugene, Ore., 1952; and Carl H. Kroeling and Robert McC. Adams (eds.), *The City Invincible: A Symposium on Urbanization and Cultural Development in the Ancient Near East,* University of Chicago Press, Chicago, 1958.

Origins of Writing   Two extremely useful books for the origins of writing and literacy are I. J. Gelb, *A Study of Writing,* University of Chicago Press, Chicago 1952 (Phoenix edition, 1963) and Jack Goody (ed.), *Literacy in Traditional Societies,* Cambridge University Press, London, 1968. A recent work that illuminates the earliest literary uses to which writing was put is William H. McNeill and Jean W. Sedlar (eds.), *Readings in World History,* vol. 1, *The Origins of Civilization,* and vol. 2, *The Ancient Near East,* Oxford University Press, New York, 1968.

Egyptian Civilization   John A. Wilson, *The Culture of Ancient Egypt,* University of Chicago Press, Chicago, 1961 (Phoenix edition, 1965), does for the Egyptians what Kramer does for the Sumerians. Insights into the nature of Egyptian education can also be obtained by perusal of James B. Pritchard (ed.), *Ancient Near Eastern Texts Relating to the Old Testament,* 3d. rev. ed. Princeton University Press, Princeton, N.J., 1969 and Adolf Erman, *The Literature of the Ancient Egyptians; Poems, Narratives, and Manuals of Instruction, from the Third and Second Millenia, B.C.,* translated by Aylward M. Blackman, Methuen, London, 1927.

Indian Civilization   Useful single volumes about Indian history are: A. L. Basham, *The Wonder That Was India; a Survey of the Culture of the Indian Sub-continent Before the Coming of the Muslims,* Grove Press, New York, 1959; H. G. Rawlinson, *India: A Short Cultural History,* Praeger, New York, 1965; and R. C. Majumdar et al., *An Advanced History of India,* rev. ed., Macmillan, London, 1965. R. K. Mookerji, *Ancient Indian Education: Brahmanical and Buddhist,* Macmillan, London, 1947 is a voluminous portrayal of education as contained in Vedic, Sutra, and Buddhist literature. It therefore has little chronology. Some attention is given to chronology in A. S. Altekar, *Education in Ancient India,* 3d ed. Nand Kishore, Benares, India, 1948. Collections of Indian literature are contained in William Theodore de Bary (ed.), *Sources of Indian Tradition,* 2 vols., Columbia University Press, New York, 1958 and in William H. McNeill and Jean Sedlar (eds.), *Classical India,* Oxford University Press, New York, 1969.

Chinese Civilization   The best general history of early China in its bearings on education is Edwin O. Reischauer and John K. Fairbank, *A History of East Asian Civilization,* vol. 1., *East Asia: The Great Tradition,* Houghton Mifflin, Boston, 1965. Useful one-volume standbys are: L. Carrington Goodrich, *A Short History of the Chinese People,* 3d ed., Harper & Row, New York, 1959; C. P. Fitzgerald, *China: a*

Short Cultural History, Praeger, New York, 1953; Derk Bodde, *China's Cultural Tradition,* Rinehart, 1959; and John K. Fairbank (ed.), *Chinese Thought and Institutions,* University of Chicago Press, Chicago, 1957. William Theodore de Bary (ed.), *Sources of Chinese Tradition,* 2 vols., Columbia University Press, New York, 1960 and William H. McNeill and Jean Sedlar (eds.), *Classical China,* Oxford University Press, New York, 1970 make available some of the Chinese literary classics which formed the basis of school curriculum and examination. Joseph Needham's massive multivolume study of *Science and Civilization in China,* Cambridge University Press, London, 1954-1971 gives quite a different picture of Chinese intellectual development. I know of no book on Chinese education that combines these two traditions. Howard S. Galt, *A History of Chinese Educational Institutions to the End of Five Dynasties (960 A.D.),* Probsthain, London, 1951 gives considerable descriptive material from the classical literature but little chronology or development of themes.

CHAPTER III.
GREEK CIVILIZATION: WELLSPRING OF WESTERN EDUCATION
(800 B.C.-300 B.C.)

Aegean Civilization (1900 B.C.-1100 B.C.) Two fascinating summaries of the Aegean civilization are Leonard R. Palmer, *Mycenaeans and Minoans,* Knopf, New York, 1961 and John Chadwick, *The Decipherment of Linear B,* Cambridge University Press, London, 1958. A revisionist view, stressing local change as the key to innovation, is Colin Renfrew, *The Emergence of Civilisation,* Methuen, London, 1972.

Greek Civilization Two recent estimates stress Greek political development: Herbert Muller, *Freedom in the Ancient World,* Harper, New York, 1961 and Victor Ehrenburg, *The Greek State,* Norton, New York, 1960. Two older views stress Greek cultural genius: Edith Hamilton, *The Greek Way,* Mentor, New York, 1948 and H. D Kitto, *The Greeks,* Penguin Books Ltd., Harmondsworth, Middlesex, 1951.

Greek Education The two most useful general studies of Greek education are H. I. Marrou, *A History of Education in Antiquity,* Mentor, New York, 1964 and Frederick A.G. Beck, *Greek Education, 450-350 B.C.,* Methuen, London, 1964. The two most penetrating special studies are Donald L. Clark, *Rhetoric in Greco-Roman Education,* Columbia University Press, New York, 1957 and R. R. Bolgar, *The Classical Heritage and Its Beneficiaries,* Harper Torchbooks, New York, 1964. Two older studies are worthwhile. They are Kenneth J. Freeman, *Schools of Hellas,* 3d ed., St. Martin's, New York, 1932, reprinted by Teachers College Press, New York, 1969 and Werner Jaeger, *Paideia: The Ideals of Greek Culture,* 3 vols., Oxford University Press, New York, 1943-1945, if one can wade through the ponderous depth and length. By contrast, William A. Smith, *Ancient Education,* Philosophical Library, New York, 1955 and William Barclay, *Educational Ideals in the Ancient World,* Collins, London, 1959 are simpler but textbookish. Thomas Woody, *Life and Education in Early Societies,* Macmillan, New York, 1949 concentrates on physical education in the broadest setting. Good complements are the studies of the Greek language and literacy contained in Jack Goody (ed.), *Literacy in Traditional Societies,* Cambridge University Press, London, 1968 and I. J. Gelb, *A Study of Writing,* University of Chicago Press, Chicago, 1963.

If one is interested in Greek thought on education, one should read Plato's *Republic* and Aristotle's *Politics* and *Ethics* and then compare them with such recent commentaries as those by: James L. Jarrett (ed.), *The Educational Theories of the Sophists*, Teachers College Press, New York, 1969; Robert McClintock's foreword to Richard Lewis Nettleship, *The Theory of Education in the Republic of Plato*, Teachers College Press, New York, 1968; Paul Nash et al. (eds.), *The Educated Man; Studies in the History of Educational Thought*, Wiley, New York, 1968; Paul Nash, *Models of Man; Explorations in the Western Educational Tradition*, Wiley, New York, 1968; and J. J. Chambliss (ed.), *Nobility, Tragedy, and Naturalism; Education in Ancient Greece*, Burgess, Minneapolis, Minn., 1971.

CHAPTER IV.
THE DISPERSION OF HELLENISTIC EDUCATION
IN THE GRAECO-ROMAN WORLD (300 B.C.-1500 A.D.)

Hellenization of the East   For the dispersion of Hellenistic education to the Middle East, an excellent combination is: Moses Hadas, *Hellenistic Culture; Fusion and Diffusion*, Columbia University Press, New York, 1959; H. I. Marrou, *A History of Education in Antiquity*, Mentor, New York, 1964; and R. R. Bolgar, *The Classical Heritage*, Harper Torchbooks, New York, 1964.

Hellenization of the West   For the contextual background of the dispersion of Hellenistic education to Rome and on to the Latin West, see: Frederick B. Artz, *The Mind of the Middle Ages: An Historical Survey, A.D. 200-1500*, Knopf, New York, 1952; H. O. Taylor, *The Mediaeval Mind*, 2 vols., Harvard University Press, Cambridge, Mass., 1949; E. K. Rand, *Founders of the Middle Ages*, 2d ed., Harvard University Press, Cambridge, Mass., 1929; Edith Hamilton, *The Roman Way*, Norton, New York, 1932; Jerome Carcopino, *Daily Life in Ancient Rome*, Penguin Books Ltd., Harmondsworth, Middlesex, 1961; Lynn T. White (ed.), *The Transformation of the Roman World: Gibbon's Problem after Two Centuries*, University of California Press, Berkeley and Los Angeles, 1965; and Herbert Muller, *Freedom in the Ancient World*, Harper, New York, 1961.

Roman Education   The three best recent interpretations of Roman education have already been mentioned: Marrou, Bolgar, and Donald L. Clark, *Rhetoric in Graeco-Roman Education*, Columbia University Press, New York, 1957. The best older interpretation is now easily available in Aubrey Gwynn, *Roman Education from Cicero to Quintilian*, Teachers College Press, New York, 1966. For the early Roman Empire period the principal original sources are to be found in Cicero's *De Oratore*, 2 vols., Harvard University Press, Cambridge, Mass., 1959-1960 and Quintilian's *Institutio Oratoria*, Harvard University Press, Cambridge, Mass., 1921. W. H. Smail, *Quintilian on Education*, Oxford University Press, New York, 1938 has been reissued by Teachers College, New York, 1966, while a reissue of books 1 and 2 is available in James J. Murphy (ed.), *Quintilian, On the Early Education of the Citizen-Orator; Institutio Oratoria*, Library of Liberal Arts, Bobbs-Merrill, Indianapolis, Ind., 1965. Nothing has yet quite taken the place of the 1906 dissertation by Paul Abelson, *The Seven Liberal Arts; a Study in Mediaeval Culture*, Russell and Russell, New York, 1965 or the translations of the perennial medieval textbooks by Wayland J. Chase, *The Ars*

Minor of Donatus, University of Wisconsin Press, Madison, 1926 and *The Distichs of Cato,* University of Wisconsin Press, Madison, 1922.

Patristic Education For the patristic age Frederick B. Artz is very useful, and on education there is a new study by Eugene Kevane, *Augustine the Educator; a Study in the Fundamentals of Christian Formation,* Newman, Westminster, Md., 1964 to supplement Pierre J. Marique, *History of Christian Education,* Fordham University Press, New York, 1924.

Byzantine Education Western views of Byzantine Hellenism range from contempt through indifference to enthusiasm. Balanced views are contained in Artz and Muller. In addition to Bolgar there are chapters on Byzantine education in: N. H. Baynes and H. St. L. B. Moss (eds.), *Byzantium: An Introduction to East Roman Civilization,* Clarendon Press, Oxford, 1948; Steven Runciman, *Byzantine Civilization,* Meridian, New York, 1956; and J. M. Hussey, *The Byzantine World,* Harper & Row, New York, 1957. The analysis by Ernest Barker, *Social and Political Thought in Byzantium,* Clarendon Press, Oxford, 1957 has important bearings on education. Two studies are almost unreservedly glowing and laudatory. They are Charles Diehl, *Byzantium: Greatness and Decline,* Rutgers University Press, New Brunswick, N.J., 1957 and Jack Lindsay, *Byzantium into Europe,* Bodley Head, London, 1952.

CHAPTER V.
THE FORMATIVE PERIOD OF WESTERN EDUCATION
(500 A.D.-1400 A.D.)

European Middle Ages The towering interpretations of the intellectual history of the Middle Ages bearing on education have been: H. O. Taylor, *The Mediaeval Mind,* 2 vols., 4th ed., Harvard University Press, Cambridge, Mass., 1949; C. H. Haskins, *The Renaissance of the Twelfth Century,* Meridian Books, Cleveland, Ohio, 1959; and E. K. Rand, *Founders of the Middle Ages,* Harvard University Press, Cambridge, Mass., 1929. All of these books are still very useful for the context they give to the history of Western education, especially if compared with more recent studies like: Frederick B. Artz, *The Mind of the Middle Ages; an Historical Survey: A.D. 200-1500,* Knopf, New York, 1953; Sidney Painter, *Medieval Society,* Cornell University Press, Ithaca, N.Y., 1951; Rushton Coulborn (ed.), *Feudalism in History,* Princeton University Press, Princeton, N.J., 1956; and John W. Baldwin, *The Scholastic Culture of the Middle Ages, 1000-1300,* Heath, Boston, 1971.

For social and economic developments in the Middle Ages, the foundations for later modernization, the "Pirenne thesis" contained in Henri Pirenne, *Medieval Cities; Their Origins and the Revival of Trade,* Princeton University Press, Princeton, N.J., 1925 needs to be supplemented by such revisionist studies as Alfred E. Havighurst, *The Pirenne Thesis: Analysis, Criticism, and Revision,* Heath, Boston, 1958.

Islam For the educational bearings of Islam in medieval times see: H. A. R. Gibb, *Mohammedanism: An Historical Survey,* Oxford University Press, New York, 1959; Bernard Lewis, *The Arabs in History,* Harper Torchbooks, New York, 1960; Gustav E. Grunebaum (ed.), *Islam: Essays in the Nature and Growth of a Cultural Tradition,* Barnes & Noble, New York, 1961; and Bayard Dodge, *Muslim Education in Medieval Times,* Middle East Institute, Washington, D.C., 1962.

Medieval Education   The premier analysis of medieval European education is R. R. Bolgar, *The Classical Heritage and Its Beneficiaries from the Carolingian Age to the End of the Renaissance*, Harper Torchbooks, New York, 1964. It is required reading for understanding the emergent forms of Western schooling. The socialization process in medieval England is treated in Joan Simon, *The Social Origins of English Education*, Routledge, London, 1970 (Humanities Press, New York, 1971). The perennial textbooks used to teach Latin from Roman to modern times are translated by Wayland J. Chase, *The Ars Minor of Donatus*, University of Wisconsin Press, Madison, 1926, and *The Distichs of Cato*, University of Wisconsin Press, Madison, 1922.

The significance of medieval schools of court and cathedral is treated generally by Haskins in *The Renaissance of the Twelfth Century*, cited above, and by Paul Abelson, *The Seven Liberal Arts*, Russell and Russell, New York, 1965. These schools come to life in the recent studies of the people who were involved in them: Eleanor S. Duchett, *Alcuin, Friend of Charlemagne; His World and His Work*, Macmillan, New York, 1951; S. E. Easton, *Roger Bacon and His Search for a Universal Science*, Oxford University Press, New York, 1952; and Daniel D. McGarry (ed.), *John of Salisbury's Metalogician; a Twelfth Century Defense of the Verbal Arts of the Trivium*, University of California Press, Berkeley, 1962. Helen Waddell's novel, *Peter Abelard*, Holt, New York, 1933, stresses personalities more than ideas but is still intriguing.

University Education   On the rise of the universities the massive standard study is, of course, Hastings Rashdall, *Universities of Europe in the Middle Ages*, new ed., Oxford University Press, New York, 1936, while the older (1928) but shorter and more sprightly study is Charles Homer Haskins, *The Rise of Universities*, Henry Holt and Co., New York, 1928 (reprinted by Cornell University Press, Ithaca, N.Y., 1965). Three standard but more specialized studies are: Lynn Thorndike, *University Records and Life in the Middle Ages*, Columbia University Press, New York, 1944; Pearl Kibre, *The Nations in the Medieval Universities*, Medieval Academy of America, Boston, 1948; and Mary H. Mayer, *The Philosophy of Teaching of St. Thomas Aquinas*, Bruce, Milwaukee, Wis., 1929. Three newer studies on similar themes are: Helene Wieruszowski, *The Medieval University: Masters, Students, Learning*, Van Nostrand, Princeton, N.J., 1966; A. L. Gabriel, *Garlandia: Studies in the History of the Mediaeval University*, Medieval Institute, University of Notre Dame, Indiana and Frankfort am Main, 1969; and Gordon Leff, *Paris and Oxford Universities in the Thirteenth and Fourteenth Centuries*, Wiley, New York, 1968.

CHAPTER VI.
THE FLORESCENCE OF THE WESTERN EDUCATIONAL TRADITION—
WITH INTIMATIONS OF MODERNITY (1400 A.D.-1700 A.D.)

The Onset of Modernity   For various germinal and influential views of the intimations of modernity in Europe, see such classic works as: R. H. Tawney, *Religion and the Rise of Capitalism; a Historical Study*, Harcourt, Brace, New York, 1926; Max Weber, *The Protestant Ethic and the Spirit of Capitalism*, Scribner, New York, 1958; and Preserved Smith, *A History of Modern Culture*, vol. 1, *The Reformation*, Holt, New York, 1930. More recent studies that range over the whole context of the fifteenth- to seventeenth-century period include: Franklin Le Van Baumer (ed.), *Main Currents of Western Thought*, 3d ed., Knopf, 1970; Herbert J. Muller, *Freedom in the*

Western World; From the Dark Ages to the Rise of Democracy, Harper & Row, New York, 1963; and R. R. Palmer and Joel Colton, *A History of the Modern World,* 4th ed., Knopf, New York, 1971.

New views of the political side of modernity are contained in: C. E. Black, *The Dynamics of Modernization; a Study in Comparative History,* Harper & Row, New York, 1966; Robert Forster and Jack P. Greene (eds.), *Preconditions of Revolution in Early Modern Europe,* Johns Hopkins Press, Baltimore, Md., 1970; and Christopher Hill, *The Century of Revolution, 1603-1714,* T. Nelson, Edinburgh, 1961 (reprinted 1962).

The spirited controversy over the role of social classes in early modernization, especially the urban middle classes vis-à-vis the landed gentry in England, is detailed in J. H. Hexter, *Reappraisals in History; New Views on Society and History in Early Modern Europe,* Harper Torchbooks, New York, 1963 and in Lawrence Stone's massive *The Crisis of the Aristocracy, 1558-1641,* Oxford University Press, London, 1965.

The Expansion of Europe The discovery of the world overseas by Europe in the early modern period is discussed in a great many works. I recommend particularly: Palmer and Colton, cited above; William H. McNeill, *The Rise of the West; a History of the Human Community,* University of Chicago Press, Chicago, 1963; Donald F. Lach, *Asia in the Making of Europe,* vol. 1, *The Century of Discovery,* books 1 and 2, University of Chicago Press, Chicago, 1965; and Louis Hartz (ed.), *The Founding of New Societies; Studies in the History of the United States, Latin America, South Africa, Canada, and Australia,* Harcourt, Brace & World, New York, 1964. For the worst side of European expansion see David Brian Davis, *The Problem of Slavery in Western Culture,* Cornell University Press, Ithaca, N.Y., 1966.

The Scientific Revolution Perhaps even more vast is the literature on the scientific revolution as an aspect of early modernity. Especially readable or pertinent for education are the following: Herbert Butterfield, *The Origins of Modern Science, 1300-1800,* Macmillan, New York, 1951; Alfred R. Hall, *The Scientific Revolution, 1500-1800: The Formation of the Modern Scientific Attitude,* Longmans, London, 1954; Marie Boas, *The Scientific Renaissance, 1450-1630,* Harper, New York, 1962; Alfred R. Hall and Marie Boas Hall, *A Brief History of Western Science,* New American Library, New York, 1964; Christopher Hill, *The Intellectual Origins of the English Revolution,* Clarendon Press, Oxford, 1965; Richard Foster Jones, *Ancients and Moderns; a Study of the Rise of the Scientific Movement in Seventeenth Century England,* University of California Press, Berkeley and Los Angeles, 1965; Paolo Rossi, *Francis Bacon from Magic to Science,* University of Chicago Press, Chicago, 1968; and Melvin Kranzberg and Carroll W. Pursell, Jr. (eds.), *Technology in Western Civilization,* vol. 1, *The Emergence of Modern Industrial Society, Earliest Times to 1900,* Oxford University Press, New York, 1967.

Realism and Education The importance of the scientific revolution for realistic studies in education are treated largely in terms of people and their influence. For Ramus and Ramism see Walter J. Ong, *Ramus, Method, and the Decay of Dialogue,* Harvard University Press, Cambridge, Mass., 1958 and Neal W. Gilbert, *Renaissance Concepts of Method,* Columbia University Press, New York, 1960. For Comenius see *John Amos Comenius on Education,* with an introduction by Jean Piaget, Teachers

College Press, New York, 1967 and John Edward Sadler, *J. A. Comenius and the Concept of Universal Education,* Barnes & Noble, New York, 1966.

Humanism and Education   For general analyses of Renaissance humanism and education I recommend especially: R. R. Bolgar, *The Classical Heritage and Its Beneficiaries from the Carolingian Age to the End of the Renaissance,* Harper Torchbooks, New York, 1964; Paul Oskar Kristeller, *Renaissance Thought, the Classic, Scholastic, and Humanist Strains,* Harper Torchbooks, New York, 1961; and Fritz Caspari, *Humanism and the Social Order in Tudor England.* The humanist educators are dealt with in several recent publications: Craig R. Thompson (ed.), *The Colloquies of Erasmus,* University of Chicago Press, Chicago, 1965; William Harrison Woodward, *Desiderius Erasmus Concerning the Aim and Method of Education,* with an introduction by Craig R. Thompson, Teachers College Press, New York, 1964; William Harrison Woodward, *Studies in Education During the Age of the Renaissance, 1400-1600,* with a foreword by Lawrence Stone, Teachers College Press, New York, 1967; William Harrison Woodward, *Vittorino Da Feltre and Other Humanist Educators,* with a foreword by Eugene F. Rice, Jr., Teachers College Press, New York, 1963; and Marian Leona Tobriner (ed.), *Vives' Introduction to Wisdom: A Renaissance Textbook,* Teachers College Press, New York, 1968.

The Reformation and Education   For religious, political, and intellectual aspects of the Protestant Reformation see: Roland H. Bainton, *The Reformation of the Sixteenth Century,* Beacon Press, Boston, 1952; E. Harris Harbison, *The Christian Scholar in the Age of the Reformation,* Scribner, New York, 1955; Harold J. Grimm, *The Reformation Era,* Macmillan, New York, 1954; A. G. Dickens, *The English Reformation,* Schocken Books, New York, 1964; James Kelsey McConica, *English Humanists and Reformation Politics under Henry VIII and Edward VI,* Clarendon Press, Oxford, 1965; Charles H. George and Katherine George, *The Protestant Mind of the English Reformation, 1570-1640,* Princeton University Press, Princeton, N.J., 1961; and John F. H. New, *Anglican and Puritan: The Basis of Their Opposition, 1558-1640,* Stanford University Press, Stanford, Calif., 1964.

For the educational views of Puritan reformers see: G. H. Turnbull, *Hartlib, Dury, and Comenius,* University Press of Liverpool, Liverpool, 1947; Charles Webster (ed.), *Samuel Hartlib and the Advancement of Learning,* Cambridge University Press, London, 1970; and Richard L. Greaves, *The Puritan Revolution and Educational Thought; Background for Reform,* Rutgers University Press, New Brunswick, N.J., 1969.

CHAPTER VII.
THE DISPERSION OF LATIN-CATHOLIC EDUCATION
(1400 A.D.-1700 A.D.)

Education in Catholic Europe   For discussions of Catholic education in Latin Europe see not only R. R. Bolgar, *The Classical Heritage,* Harper Torchbooks, New York, 1964 for the dominant school tradition, but also Philippe Aries, *Centuries of Childhood, a Social History of Family Life,* Knopf, New York, 1962 for the family context of schooling, especially in France. An older study is H. C. Barnard, *The French Tradition in Education,* Cambridge University Press, New York, 1922. Descriptions of the two most influential Catholic teaching orders that grew out of the Reformation are contained in: Robert Schwickerath, *Jesuit Education; Its History and Principles*, Herder, St. Louis, 1904; Edward A. Fitzpatrick (ed.), *St. Ignatius and the Ratio Studiorum*, McGraw-Hill, New York, 1933; Allan P. Farrell, *The Jesuit Code of Liberal Education; Development and Scope of the Ratio Studiorum*, Bruce, Milwaukee, Wis., 1938; W. J. Battersby, *De La Salle, A Pioneer of Modern Education*, Longmans, London, 1949; and Edward A. Fitzpatrick, *La Salle; Patron of All Teachers*, Bruce, Milwaukee, Wis., 1951. These works will provide a picture of the education that Latin peoples transplanted in the sixteenth and seventeenth centuries.

The Latinizing Mission Overseas The Portuguese thrust to the East is well documented in Donald F. Lach, *Asia in the Making of Europe*, vol. 1, *The Century of Discovery*, University of Chicago Press, Chicago, 1965. The Spanish intrusion to the West far overshadows that of Portugal, up to 1700; some of the most illuminating studies of this occurrence are: Charles Gibson, *Spain in America*, Harper Torchbooks, New York, 1966; Charles Wagley, *The Latin American Tradition*, Columbia University Press, New York, 1968; Charles Wagley, *An Introduction to Brazil*, Columbia University Press, New York, 1963; Helen Miller Bailey and Abraham P. Nasatir, *Latin America: The Development of Its Civilization*, Prentice-Hall, Englewood Cliffs, N.J., 1960; German Arciniegas, *Latin America: A Cultural History*, Knopf, New York, 1967; and Lewis Hanke, *The Spanish Struggle for Justice in the Conquest of America*, University of Pennsylvania Press, Philadelphia, 1959.

Pre-Columbian Civilization in the Americas For background on American Indian civilization and education before the arrival of the Spanish, the following are useful: G. C. Valliant, *The Aztecs of Mexico*, Penguin Books Ltd., Harmondsworth, Middlesex, 1950; Miguel Leon-Portilla, *Aztec Thought and Culture; a Study of the Ancient Nahuatl Mind*, University of Oklahoma Press, Norman, Okla., 1963; Fray Diego Duran, *The Aztecs: The History of the Indians of New Spain*, Orion Press, New York, 1964; J. Alden Mason, *The Ancient Civilization of Peru*, Penguin Books Ltd., Harmondsworth, Middlesex, 1957; S. G. Morley, *The Ancient Maya*, Stanford University Press, Stanford, Calif., 1956; Gordon R. Willey, *An Introduction to American Archaeology*, vol. 1, *North and Middle America*, Prentice-Hall, Englewood Cliffs, N.J., 1966; and Alvin M. Josephy, Jr., *The Indian Heritage of America*, Knopf, New York, 1968.

Spanish Education in America For books about the Latin educational traditions that were transplanted to the Americas, see: Pius Joseph Barth, *Franciscan Education and the Social Order in Spanish North America, 1501-1821*, University of Chicago Press, Chicago, 1945; Jerome V. Jacobsen, *Educational Foundations of the Jesuits in Sixteenth Century New Spain*, University of California Press, Berkeley, 1938; John Tate Lanning, *Academic Culture in the Spanish Colonies*, Oxford University Press, New York, 1940; Luis Martin, *The Intellectual Conquest of Peru; the Jesuit College of San Pablo, 1568-1767*, Fordham University Press, New York, 1968; Robert Ricard, *The Spiritual Conquest of Mexico; an Essay on the Apostolate and Evangelizing Methods of the Mendicant Orders in New Spain, 1523-1572*, translated by L. B. Simpson, University of California Press, Berkeley and Los Angeles, 1966; and Antoine Tibesor, *Franciscan Beginnings in Colonial Peru*, Academy of Franciscan History, Washington, D.C., 1953.

Spanish Education in the Philippines For descriptions of the transit of Spanish education to the Philippines see· Encarnacion Alzona, *A History of Education in the*

Philippines, 1565-1730, University of Philippines Press, Manila, 1932; Horacio de la Costa, S.J., *The Jesuits in the Philippines, 1581-1768,* Harvard University Press, Cambridge, Mass., 1961; and John L. Phelan, *The Hispanization of the Philippines; Spanish Aims and Filipino Responses, 1565-1700,* University of Wisconsin Press, Madison, Wis., 1959.

French Education in Canada   For discussions of French education in Canada see Charles E. Phillips, *The Development of Education in Canada,* Ryerson, Toronto, 1957 and J. Donald Wilson, Robert M. Stamp, and Louis-Philippe Audet (eds.), *Canadian Education: A History,* Prentice-Hall, Scarborough, Ontario, 1970.

CHAPTER VIII.
THE DISPERSION OF ANGLO-PROTESTANT EDUCATION
(1400 A.D.-1700 A.D.)

Protestant Education in Northern Europe   Because of the eventual influence of Anglo-American education upon the rest of the world Chapter 8 concentrates on England and its American colonies. However, a glimpse of Germany and the Lowlands may be had through: Frederick Eby (ed.), *Early Protestant Educators,* McGraw-Hill, New York, 1931; Albert Hyma, *The Brethren of the Common Life,* Erdmans, Grand Rapids, Mich., 1950; Friedrich Paulsen, *German Education, Past and Present,* Scribner, New York, 1912; C. L. Robbins, *Teachers in Germany in the Sixteenth Century,* Bureau of Publications, Teachers College, New York, 1912; and, for the influence of printing, Walter J. Ong, *The Presence of the Word,* Yale University Press, New Haven, Conn., 1967.

Education in Renaissance and Reformation England   For several decades the writing about the history of education in England during the Renaissance and Reformation proceeded on an established way. A. F. Leach had set the tone in his *English Schools at the Reformation,* Constable, Westminster, 1896 followed by such studies as: Norman Wood, *The Reformation and English Education,* Routledge, London, 1931; T. W. Baldwin, *William Shakspere's Small Latine and Less Greek,* 2 vols., University of Illinois Press, Urbana, 1944; Donald L. Clark, *John Milton at St. Paul's School; a Study of Ancient Rhetoric in English Renaissance Education,* Columbia University Press, New York, 1948; and Clara P. McMahon, *Education in Fifteenth Century England,* Johns Hopkins Press, Baltimore, Md., 1947.

Then in the 1950s and 1960s English education of the sixteenth and seventeenth centuries became the object of active revisionism. Principal participants have been: J. H. Hexter, "The Education of the Aristocracy in the Renaissance," *The Journal of Modern History,* vol. 22, pp. 1-20, 1950; W. K. Jordan, *Philanthropy in England, 1480-1660,* G. Allen, London, 1959; Mark H. Curtis, *Oxford and Cambridge in Transition, 1558-1642,* Clarendon Press, Oxford, 1959; Lawrence Stone, "The Educational Revolution in England, 1560-1640," *Past and Present,* no. 23, pp. 41-80, July 1964; Kenneth Charlton, *Education in Renaissance England,* Routledge, London, 1965; and Joan Simon, *Education and Society in Tudor England,* Cambridge University Press, London, 1966.

Somewhat more specialized studies have been made by: A. C. F. Beales, *Education Under Penalty: English Catholic Education from the Reformation to the Fall of James II, 1547-1689,* Althone Press, London, 1963; Harris Francis Fletcher, *The*

Intellectual Development of John Milton, 2 vols., University of Illinois Press, Urbana, 1956-1961; and Lawrence Stone, "Literacy and Education in England, 1640-1900," *Past and Present,* no. 42, February 1969.

A particularly fascinating model for comparative historical study is Marius B. Jansen and Lawrence Stone, "Education and Modernization in Japan and England," in *Comparative Studies in Society and History,* vol. 9, no. 2, pp. 208-232, January 1967.

In addition to the discussions of higher education in Curtis, Simon, Charlton, and Stone, see H. C. Porter, *Reformation and Reaction in Tudor Cambridge,* Cambridge University Press, London, 1950 and Hugh Kearney, *Scholars and Gentlemen; Universities and Society in Pre-Industrial Britain, 1500-1700,* Cornell University Press, Ithaca, N.Y., 1970.

Education in Seventeenth-Century Anglo-America The indispensable book for the history of education in colonial Anglo-America is the discerning and elegant volume by Lawrence A. Cremin, *American Education: The Colonial Experience, 1607-1783,* Harper & Row, New York, 1970. It deals not only with schools and colleges but also with the educational influence of family, church, and community.

In addition to Cremin there are several specialized studies of seventeenth-century colonial American education of lasting value: Robert F. Seybolt, *The Public Schools of Colonial Boston, 1635-1775,* Harvard University Press, Cambridge, Mass., 1935; Marcus W. Jernegan, *Laboring and Dependent Classes in Colonial America, 1607-1783,* University of Chicago Press, Chicago, 1931 (reprinted by Ungar, New York, 1960); Samuel Eliot Morison, *The Founding of Harvard College,* Harvard University Press, Cambridge, Mass., 1935; and Samuel Eliot Morison, *Harvard College in the Seventeenth Century,* 2 vols., Harvard University Press, Cambridge, Mass., 1936. For general histories of American higher education that include the seventeenth century see the bibliographical notes for Chapter 12.

American Society and Thought Elaboration of the social and intellectual context of the transplantation of English education to America will be found in such older but germinal studies as: Edward Eggleston, *The Transit of Civilization from England to America in the Seventeenth Century,* Appleton, New York, 1900 (reprinted by Beacon Press, Boston, 1959); Samuel Eliot Morison, *The Intellectual Life of Colonial New England,* New York University Press, New York, 1936 (reprinted by Cornell University Press, Ithaca, N.Y., 1960); Carl Bridenbaugh, *Cities in the Wilderness: The First Century of Urban Life in America, 1625-1724,* Ronald, New York, 1938; Perry Miller, *The New England Mind, The Seventeenth Century,* Macmillan, New York, 1939 (reprinted by Beacon Press, Boston, 1961); and Richard B. Morris, *Government and Labor in Early America,* Columbia University Press, New York, 1946. Study of these books should be followed by a reading of such newer interpretations as: Louis B. Wright, *The Cultural Life of the American Colonies, 1607-1763,* Harper & Row, New York, 1957; Daniel J. Boorstin, *The Americans: The Colonial Experience,* Random House, New York, 1964; James Morton Smith (ed.), *Seventeenth Century America; Essays in Colonial History,* University of North Carolina Press, Chapel Hill, N.C., 1959; Bernard Bailyn, *Education in the Forming of American Society,* University of North Carolina Press, Chapel Hill, N.C., 1960; Richard M. Gummere, *The American Colonial Mind and the Classical Tradition; Essays in Comparative Culture,* Harvard University Press, Cambridge, Mass., 1963; and Carl Bridenbaugh, *Vexed and Troubled Englishmen, 1590-1642,* Oxford University Press, New York, 1968.

Europeans and American Indians Early contacts between whites and American Indians can be followed in several recent studies: Harold Driver, *The Indians of North America,* University of Chicago Press, Chicago, 1961; William N. Fenton, *American Indian and White Relations to 1830; Needs and Opportunities for Study,* University of North Carolina Press, Chapel Hill, N.C., 1957; Alden F. Vaughn, *New England Frontier: Puritans and Indians, 1620-1675,* Little, Brown, Boston, 1965; and William Kellaway, *The New England Company, 1649-1776: Missionary Society to the American Indians,* Barnes & Noble, New York, 1961. See also pp. 591-592, 594-595.

Whites and Blacks For early contacts between whites and blacks see: John Hope Franklin, *From Slavery to Freedom, a History of Negro Americans,* 3d ed., Vintage Books, New York, 1969; David Brian Davis, *The Problem of Slavery in Western Culture,* Cornell University Press, Ithaca, N.Y., 1966; and Winthrop D. Jordan, *White Over Black; American Attitudes Toward the Negro, 1550-1812,* University of North Carolina Press, Chapel Hill, N.C., 1968 (Pelican, 1969). See also pp. 591, 594-595.

CHAPTER IX.
THE TRANSMUTATION TO MODERNITY
(1700 A.D.-THE PRESENT)

The totality of the phenomena attendant upon the growth of modernity in Western civilization is well portrayed in William H. McNeill, *The Rise of the West; A History of the Human Community,* University of Chicago Press, Chicago, 1963 and in R. R. Palmer and Joel Colton, *A History of the Modern World,* 4th ed., Knopf, New York, 1971.

The Nation-State Of particular interest to the rise of the nation-state as discussed herein are: C. E. Black, *The Dynamics of Modernization; A Study in Comparative History,* Harper & Row, New York, 1966; Robert Anchor, *Germany Confronts Modernization: German Culture and Society, 1790-1890,* Heath, Boston, 1972; C. E. Black (ed.), *The Transformation of Russian Society: Aspects of Social Change since 1861,* Harvard University Press, Cambridge, Mass., 1969; and Seymour Martin Lipset, *The First New Nation; The United States in Historical and Comparative Perspective,* Basic Books, New York, 1963.

Religion, Secularism, and Enlightenment For the study of the interplay of established religion and secular enlightenment several classic treatments are valuable: Preserved Smith, *A History of Modern Culture,* vol. 2, *The Enlightenment,* Holt, New York, 1930; A. N. Whitehead, *Science and the Modern World,* Macmillan, New York, 1967; and Carl Becker, *The Heavenly City of the Eighteenth Century Philosophers,* Yale University Press, New Haven, Conn., 1932. A notable new study is that by Peter Gay, *The Enlightenment: An Interpretation,* vol. 1, *The Rise of Modern Paganism,* Knopf, New York, 1966 and vol. 2, *The Science of Freedom,* Knopf, New York, 1969. For widely divergent interpretations, see Robert A. Nisbet, *The Sociological Tradition,* Basic Books, New York, 1966 and J. D. Bernal, *Science in History,* vol. 2, *The Scientific and Industrial Revolution,* Massachusetts Institute of Technology Press, Cambridge, Mass., 1971. The problem of religious freedom is central in R. R. Palmer, *Catholics and Unbelievers in Eighteenth Century France,* Princeton University Press, Princeton, N.J., 1939 and R. Freeman Butts, *The American Tradition in Religion and Education,* Beacon Press, Boston, 1950.

The Democratic Revolution   The democratic revolution as a general phenomenon of Western civilization is treated superbly in Robert R. Palmer, *The Age of the Democratic Revolution; A Political History of Europe and America, 1760-1800*, 2 vols., Princeton University Press, Princeton, N.J., 1959-1965. The transaction of ideas across the Atlantic is also treated in: Caroline Robbins, *The Eighteenth Century Commonwealthman: Studies in the Transmission, Development, and Circumstances of English Liberal Thought from the Restoration of Charles II Until the War with the Thirteen Colonies,* Harvard University Press, Cambridge, Mass., 1961; Carl Bridenbaugh, *Mitre and Sceptre: Transatlantic Faiths, Ideas, Personalities, and Politics, 1689-1775,* Oxford University Press, New York, 1962; and Bernard Bailyn, *The Ideological Origins of the American Revolution,* Harvard University Press, Cambridge, Mass., 1967. Two widely divergent and provocative views of political stability and revolution are contained in Samuel P. Huntington, *Political Order in Changing Societies,* Yale University Press, New Haven, Conn., 1968 and Barrington Moore, *Social Origins of Dictatorship and Democracy; Land and Peasant in the Making of the Modern World,* Beacon Press, Boston, 1966.

Industrialization and Urbanization   Industrial urbanism is treated in: Lewis Mumford, *The City in History, Its Origins, Its Transformations, and Its Prospects,* Harcourt, Brace & World, New York, 1961; Gideon Sjoberg, *The Preindustrial City, Past and Present,* Free Press, New York, 1960; Leonard Reissman, *The Urban Process; Cities in Industrial Societies,* Free Press, New York, 1964; T. S. Ashton, *The Industrial Revolution, 1760-1830,* rev. ed., Oxford University Press, London, 1964; David S. Landes, *The Unbound Prometheus; Technological Change and Industrial Development in Western Europe from 1750 to the Present,* Cambridge University Press, New York, 1969; and Melvin Kranzberg and Carroll W. Pursell, Jr. (eds.), *Technology in Western Civilization,* Oxford University Press, New York, 1967, vol. 1.

   Urbanism in America is treated in Carl Bridenbaugh, *Cities in Revolt; Urban Life in America, 1743-1776,* Knopf, New York, 1955 and Richard C. Wade, *The Urban Frontier, 1790-1830,* Harvard University Press, Cambridge, Mass., 1959. For convenient compilations of source materials and essays on urban history, see: Alexander B. Callow, Jr. (ed.), *American Urban History; an Interpretive Reader with Commentaries,* Oxford University Press, New York, 1969; Charles N. Glaab (ed.), *The American City; a Documentary History,* Dorsey, Homewood, Ill., 1963; and Kenneth T. Jackson and Stanley K. Schultz (eds.), *Cities in American History,* Knopf, New York, 1972. For a brief synthesis of this subject, see Charles N. Glaab and A. Theodore Brown, *A History of Urban America,* Macmillan, New York, 1967.

Literacy and Modernity   For historical studies of literacy, see: Jack Goody (ed.), *Literacy in Traditional Societies,* Cambridge University Press, London, 1968; C. Arnold Anderson and Mary Jean Bowman, *Education and Economic Development,* Aldine, Chicago, 1965; and Carlo M. Cipolla, *Literacy and Development in the West,* Penguin, Baltimore, Md., 1969.

CHAPTER X.
EDUCATION IN THE MODERNIZING STATES OF EUROPE
(1700 A.D.-1860s A.D.)

Education in Britain   The most penetrating general histories of English education for this period are Brian Simon, *Studies in the History of Education, 1780-1870,* Lawrence and Wishart, London, 1960 and H. C. Barnard, *A History of Education from 1760*, 2d ed., University of London Press, London, 1961.

Studies that focus on different types of schools include: T. W. Bamford, *The Rise of the Public Schools; a Study of Boys' Public Boarding Schools in England and Wales from 1837 to the Present Day*, Nelson, London, 1967; M. G. Jones, *The Charity School Movement; a Study of Eighteenth Century Puritanism in Action*, Cambridge University Press, London, 1938 (reprinted by Archon Books, Hamden, Conn., 1964); W. A. L. Vincent, *The Grammar Schools: Their Continuing Tradition, 1660-1714*, J. Murray, London, 1969; H. McLachlan, *English Education under the Test Acts, Being the History of the Non-Conformist Academies, 1662-1820*, Manchester University Press, Manchester, England, 1931; and J. W. Ashley Smith, *The Birth of Modern Education: The Contribution of the Dissenting Academies, 1660-1800*, Independence Press, London, 1954.

Studies of English theorizing on education include: F. A. Cavenagh (ed.), *James and John Stuart Mill on Education*, Cambridge University Press, New York, 1931; Peter Gay (ed.), *John Locke on Education*, Bureau of Publications, Teachers College, New York, 1964; Francis W. Garforth (ed.), *John Locke's Of the Conduct of the Understanding*, Teachers College Press, New York, 1966; James L. Axtell, *The Educational Writings of John Locke*, Cambridge University Press, London, 1968; and John F. C. Harrison (ed.), *Utopianism and Education; Robert Owen and the Owenites*, Teachers College Press, New York, 1968.

Education in France   For the history of education in France see: Frederick B. Artz, *The Development of Technical Education in France, 1500-1850*, Massachusetts Institute of Technology Press, Cambridge, Mass., 1966; H. C. Barnard, *Education and the French Revolution*, Cambridge University Press, London, 1969; Robert Vignery, *The French Revolution and the Schools: Educational Policies of the Mountain, 1792-1794*, State Historical Society of Wisconsin, Madison, 1965; François de la Fontainerie (ed.), *French Liberalism and Education in the Eighteenth Century*, McGraw-Hill, New York, 1932; William Boyd, *The Émile of Jean Jacques Rousseau: Selections*, Bureau of Publications, Teachers College, New York, 1962; and John W. Padberg, *Colleges in Controversy; the Jesuit Schools in France from Revival to Suppression, 1815-1880*, Harvard University Press, Cambridge, Mass., 1969.

German Education   For education in German-speaking lands see: Nicholas Hans, *New Trends in Education in the Eighteenth Century*, Routledge, London, 1951; W. J. Battersby, *History of the Institute of the Brothers of the Christian Schools*, 2 vols, Woldegrave, London, 1960-1963; Friederick Paulsen, *German Universities and University Study*, Scribner, New York, 1906; Gerald Lee Gutek, *Pestalozzi and Education*, Random House, New York, 1968; and Michael R. Heafford, *Pestalozzi: His Thought and Its Relevance Today*, Methuen, London, 1967.

Russian Education   The tortuous awakening of Russia to Western education is treated in: Nicholas Hans, *History of Russian Educational Policy, 1701-1917*, King, Russell & Russell, London, 1931 (reprinted by Russell & Russell, New York, 1964); Nicholas Hans, *The Russian Tradition in Education*, Routledge, London, 1963; William H. E. Johnson, *Russia's Educational Heritage*, Carnegie Press, Pittsburgh, Pa., 1950 (reissued by Octagon Books, New York, 1969); and Patrick L. Alston, *Education and the State in Tsarist Russia*, Stanford University Press, Stanford, Calif., 1969.

Italy and Spain Although Italy and Spain are not specifically treated in this book, influential modernizing movements are represented by: Elio Gianturco (ed.), *Giovanni Battista Vico On the Study Methods of Our Time*, Library of Liberal Arts, Indianapolis, Ind., 1965; George M. Addy, *The Enlightenment in the University of Salamanca*, Duke University Press, Durham, N.C., 1966; and Robert McClintock, *Man and His Circumstances: Ortega as Educator*, Teachers College Press, New York, 1971.

CHAPTER XI.
PERSISTENT ISSUES IN MODERN EUROPEAN EDUCATION
(1860s A.D.-THE PRESENT)

Comparative Studies There is, of course, a vast literature on the development of education in the various countries of Europe since 1850. I have selected a few older, as well as some recent, studies that deal with more than one country in a comparative fashion: George Z. F. Bereday (ed.), *Charles E. Merriam's The Making of Citizens; a Comparative Study of Methods of Civic Training*, University of Chicago Press, Chicago, 1931 (reprinted by Teachers College Press, New York, 1968); Abraham Flexner, *Universities, English, German, American*, Oxford University Press, New York, 1930 (reprinted by Teachers College Press, New York, 1967); Raymond Poignant, *Education and Development in Western Europe, the United States, and the U.S.S.R., a Comparative Study*, Teachers College Press, New York, 1969; A. Stafford Clayton, *Religion and Schooling: a Comparative Study*, Blaisdell, Waltham, Mass., 1969; Ursula K. Springer, *Recent Curriculum Developments in France, West Germany, and Italy*, Teachers College Press, New York, 1969; Edmund J. King, *Education and Development in Western Europe*, Addison-Wesley, Reading, Mass., 1969; George Z. F. Bereday, *Towards Mass University: U.S.A., U.S.S.R., and Japan*, Organization for Economic Cooperation and Development, Paris, 1972; Paul Nash (ed.), *History and Education; The Educational Uses of the Past*, Random House, New York, 1970; a special issue, "Ten Years of European Educational Reform, 1956-1966," *Comparative Education Review*, vol. 11, no. 3, October 1967; A. D. C. Peterson, *A Hundred Years of Education; a Comparative Study of Educational Patterns in Western Europe and the United States*, Collier Books, New York, 1962; and Eric Bockstael and Otto Feinstein, *Higher Education in the European Community*, Heath, Boston, 1970.

Education in Britain Interesting comparisons in attitudes concerning the history of education in England can be gained by linking such older studies as those by J. W. Adamson, *English Education, 1789-1902*, Cambridge University Press, London (reprinted 1965) and S. J. Curtis, *History of Education in Great Britain*, University Tutorial Press, London, 1948, 5th ed., University Tutorial Press, London, 1963 (reprinted by Greenwood Press, Westport, Conn., 1971) with such newer studies as those by Brian Simon, *Studies in the History of Education, 1780-1870*, Lawrence and Wishart, London, 1960 and *Education and the Labour Movement, 1870-1920*, Lawrence and Wishart, London, 1965. Particular aspects are treated in: W. A. G. Armytage, *The American Influence on English Education*, Routledge, London, 1967; David Wardle, *English Popular Education, 1780-1970*, Cambridge University Press, London, 1970; Andreas M. Kazamias, *Politics, Society, and Secondary Education in England*, University of Pennsylvania Press, Philadelphia, 1966; John Wakeford, *The Cloistered Elite; a Sociological Analysis of the English Public Boarding School*, Praeger, New

York, 1969; Ian Weinberg, *The English Public Schools; The Sociology of Elite Education*, Atherton, New York, 1967; Sheldon Rothblatt, *The Revolution of the Dons: Cambridge and Society in Victorian England*, Basic Books, New York, 1968; James Murphy, *Church, State and Schools in Britain, 1800-1970*, Routledge, London, 1971; Marjorie Cruikshank, *Church and State in English Education; 1870 to the Present Day*, St. Martin's, New York, 1963; John Roach, *Public Examinations in England, 1850-1900*, Cambridge University Press, London, 1971; A. S. Bishop, *The Rise of a Central Authority for English Education*, Cambridge University Press, London, 1971; and J. F. C. Harrison, *Learning and Living, 1790-1960, a Study in the History of the English Adult Education Movement*, Routledge, London, 1961. Comparison between the ideas of two giant contemporaries can be gained from Andreas M. Kazamias (ed.), *Hebert Spencer on Education*, Teachers College Press, New York, 1966 and John Henry Cardinal Newman, *The Idea of a University*, Doubleday, New York, 1959.

Education in France   The most penetrating recent study of French education is John E. Talbott, *The Politics of Educational Reform in France, 1918-1940*, Princeton University Press, Princeton, N.J., 1969. Other perspectives on the relation of politics and education can be gained from: Carleton J. H. Hayes, *France, a Nation of Patriots*, Columbia University Press, New York, 1930; Donald W. Miles, *Recent Reforms in French Secondary Education*, Bureau of Publications, Teachers College, New York, 1953; and John W. Padberg, *Colleges in Controversy: the Jesuit Schools in France from Revival to Suppression, 1815-1880*, Harvard University Press, Cambridge, Mass., 1969.

Education in Germany   Fascinating differences of outlook on German education are to be found in comparing such pre-Nazi studies as those by Thomas Alexander and Beryl Parker, *The New Education in the German Republic*, John Day, New York, 1929 and Abraham Flexner, *Universities, English, German, American*, Oxford University Press, New York, 1930 (reprinted by Teachers College Press, New York, 1967) with post-Nazi studies of education as: Isaac L. Kandel, *The Making of Nazis*, Bureau of Publications, Teachers College, New York, 1935; Frederick Lilge, *The Abuse of Learning: the Failure of the German University*, Macmillan, New York, 1948; Fritz Ringer, *The Decline of the German Mandarins: the German Academic Community, 1890-1933*, Harvard University Press, Cambridge, Mass., 1969; and R. N. Samuel and R. Hinton Thomas, *Education and Society in Modern Germany*, Routledge, London, 1949.

Education in Russia   For information on Russian education in addition to the titles on p. 586 see: Jaan Pennar, Ivan I. Bakalo, and George Z. F. Bereday, *Modernization and Diversity in Soviet Education, with Special Reference to Nationality Groups*, Praeger, New York, 1971; George S. Counts, *The Challenge of Soviet Education*, McGraw-Hill, New York, 1957; George Z. F. Bereday and Jaan Pennar (eds.), *The Politics of Soviet Education*, Praeger, New York, 1960; George Z. F. Bereday, William W. Brickman, and Gerald H. Read (eds.), *The Changing Soviet School*, Houghton Mifflin, Boston, 1960; Seymour M. Rosen, *Education and Modernization in the USSR*, Addison-Wesley, Reading, Mass., 1971; Alexander Vucinich, *Science in Russian Culture, 1861-1917*, Stanford University Press, Stanford, Calif., 1970; Loren R. Graham, *Science and Philosophy in the Soviet Union*, Knopf, New York, 1972; William K.

Medlin, *Education and Development in Central Asia,* E. J. Brill, Leiden, The Nether-
lands, 1971; Nigel Grant, *Soviet Education,* Penguin, Baltimore, Md., 1964; and
Nicholas DeWitt, *Education and Professional Employment in the U.S.S.R.,* National
Science Foundation, Washington, D.C., 1961.

CHAPTER XII.
THE MODERNIZING MOMENTUM OF AMERICAN EDUCATION
(1700 A.D.-1860s A.D.)

General Studies of American Education   The best general volume on American
education in the eighteenth century is Lawrence A. Cremin, *American Education: The
Colonial Experience, 1607-1783,* Harper & Row, New York, 1970; his second volume
will deal with the United States in the nineteenth century (to 1876). There is a
wealth of reading on the development of the American public school: A. O. Hansen,
Liberalism and American Education in the Eighteenth Century, Macmillan, New York,
1926 is brought up to date by Frederick Rudolph (ed.), *Essays on Education in the
Early Republic,* Harvard University Press, Cambridge, Mass., 1965; and Rush Welter
(ed.), *American Writings on Popular Education; the Nineteenth Century,* Bobbs-
Merrill, Indianapolis, Ind., 1971.

Society and Education   The context of early nineteenth-century education is vividly
portrayed by: Rush Welter, *Popular Education and Democratic Thought in America,*
Columbia University Press, New York, 1962; Alice Tyler, *Freedom's Ferment; Phases
of American Social History from the Colonial Period to the Outbreak of the Civil War,*
Harper Torchbooks, New York, 1962; and Maxine Greene, *The Public School and the
Private Vision; a Search for America in Education and Literature,* Random House,
New York, 1965.

For recent studies of women, the family, childhood, and youth, see: "The
History of the Family," *The Journal of Interdisciplinary History,* vol. 2, no. 2,
Autumn, 1971; Robert H. Bremmer (ed.), *Children and Youth in America, a Docu-
mentary History,* 3 vols., Harvard University Press, Cambridge, Mass., 1970-71; and
Oscar Handlin and Mary Handlin, *Facing Life: Youth and the Family in American
History,* Little, Brown, Boston, 1971.

The role of the public school is stressed in: Lawrence A. Cremin, *The American
Common School; an Historic Concept,* Bureau of Publications, Teachers College, New
York, 1961; Michael B. Katz, *The Irony of Early School Reform; Educational
Innovation in Mid-Nineteenth Century Massachusetts,* Harvard University Press, Cam-
bridge, Mass., 1968; Lawrence A. Cremin (ed.), *The Republic and the School; Horace
Mann on the Education of Free Men,* Bureau of Publications, Teachers College, New
York, 1957; Gordon C. Lee (ed.), *Crusade Against Ignorance; Thomas Jefferson on
Education,* Bureau of Publications, Teachers College, New York, 1961; and Roy J.
Honeywell (ed.), *The Educational Work of Thomas Jefferson,* Harvard University
Press, Cambridge, Mass., 1931.

Religion and Public Education   The critical role of religion in the struggle for public
education is dealt with by: R. Freeman Butts, *The American Tradition in Religion
and Education,* Beacon Press, Boston, 1950; Robert M. Healey, *Jefferson on Religion
in Public Education,* Yale University Press, New Haven, Conn., 1962; Herbert M.

Kliebard (ed.), *Religion and Education in America: A Documentary History*, International Textbook, Scranton, Pa., 1969; and Vincent Lannie, *Public Money and Parochial Education*, Case Western Reserve University Press, Cleveland, Ohio, 1968.

Secondary Education   The challenge to the classical tradition by the practical trend in secondary education can be traced in: Robert Middlekauf, *Ancients and Axioms; Secondary Education in Eighteenth Century New England*, Yale University Press, New Haven, Conn., 1963; Theodore Sizer (ed.), *The Age of the Academies*, Teachers College Press, New York, 1964; Harriet Webster Marr, *Old New England Academies Before 1826*, Comet Press, New York, 1959; Thomas Woody (ed.), *Educational Views of Benjamin Franklin*, McGraw-Hill, New York, 1931; John Hardin Best, *Benjamin Franklin on Education*, Teachers College Press, New York, 1962; Robert F. Seybolt, *The Evening School in Colonial America*, University of Illinois Press, Urbana, 1925; Robert F. Seybolt, *Source Studies in American Colonial Education: The Private School*, University of Illinois Press, Urbana, 1925; and Robert F. Seybolt, *The Private Schools of Colonial Boston*, Harvard University Press, Cambridge, Mass., 1935; Thomas Woody, *A History of Women's Education in the United States*, 2 vols., Science Press, New York, 1929 (reprinted by Octagon Books, New York, 1966); and Frank Tracy Carlton, *Economic Influences upon Educational Progress in the United States, 1820-1850*, Teachers College Press, New York, 1965.

Higher Education   The struggles over popularization and professionalization of higher education are treated in: Donald G. Tewksbury, *The Founding of American Colleges and Universities Before the Civil War*, Teachers College Press, New York, 1932, (reissued by Arno Press, New York, 1969); R. Freeman Butts, *The College Charts its Course*, McGraw-Hill, New York, 1939 (reissued by Arno Press, New York, 1972); Douglas M. Sloan, *The Scottish Enlightenment and the American College Ideal*, Teachers College Press, New York, 1971; Theodore R. Crane (ed.), *The Colleges and the Public, 1787-1862*, Teachers College Press, New York, 1963; David B. Tyack, *George Ticknor and the Boston Brahmins*, Harvard University Press, Cambridge, Mass., 1967; Frederick Rudolph, *The American College and University; a History*, Vintage Books, New York, 1965; John S. Brubacher and Willis Rudy, *Higher Education in Transition; a History of American Colleges and Universities*, rev. ed., Harper & Row, New York, 1968; Richard Hofstadter, *The Development of Academic Freedom in the United States; The Age of the College*, Columbia University Press, New York, 1964; Richard Hofstadter and Wilson Smith (eds.), *American Higher Education; a Documentary History*, University of Chicago Press, Chicago, 1961, vol. 1; and Merle E. Borrowman (ed.), *Teacher Education in America; a Documentary History*, Teachers College Press, New York, 1965.

Typical School Books   Insights into pedagogy can be obtained from: Mitford M. Mathews, *Teaching to Read: Historically Considered*, University of Chicago Press, Chicago, 1966; Paul Leicester Ford, *The New England Primer*, Teachers College Press, New York, 1962; *Noah Webster's American Spelling Book*, Teachers College Press, New York, 1962; and *McGuffey's Fifth Eclectic Reader, 1879 Edition*, New American Library, New York, 1962.

CHAPTER XIII.
THE AMERICAN FAITH IN MASSIVE EDUCATIONAL ENDEAVOR
(1860s A.D.-THE PRESENT)

General Interpretations   For an overall picture of American education from the Civil War to the mid-1950s, see R. Freeman Butts and Lawrence A. Cremin, *A History of Education in American Culture*, Holt, New York, 1953. The definitive work, when it is finished, will be the third volume of Lawrence A. Cremin, *American Education*, Harper & Row. Meanwhile, differing views on the popularization of American education are given in: Lawrence A. Cremin, *The Genius of American Education*, University of Pittsburgh Press, Pittsburgh, Pa., 1965; Henry J. Perkinson, *The Imperfect Panacea; American Faith in Education, 1865-1965*, Random House, New York, 1968; Michael B. Katz (ed.), *School Reform: Past and Present*, Little, Brown, Boston, 1971; and S. Alexander Rippa, *Education in a Free Society, An American History*, 2d. ed., McKay, New York, 1971.

Education of Women   Among the educationally disadvantaged groups in America women were among the first to gain the attention of historians, but much more work needs to be done. Among the useful works thus far are: Thomas Woody, *A History of Women's Education in the United States*, Science Press, 1929, vol. 2 (reprinted by Octagon Books, New York, 1966); Louise Boas, *Women's Education Begins; the Rise of the Women's Colleges*, Wheaton College Press, Newton, Mass., 1935; and Mable Newcomer, *A Century of Higher Education for American Women*, Harper & Row, New York, 1959.

Education of Blacks   General histories of Negro education have been relatively few. They include: Horace Mann Bond, *The Education of the Negro in the American Social Order*, Prentice-Hall, Englewood Cliffs, N.J., 1934 (reissued by Octagon Press, New York, 1966); D. O. W. Holmes, *The Evolution of the Negro College*, Bureau of Publications, Teachers College, New York, 1934; Henry Allen Bullock *A History of Negro Education in the South: From 1619 to the Present*, Harvard University Press, Cambridge, Mass., 1967; Louis R. Harlan, *Separate and Unequal; Public School Campaigns and Racism in the Southern Seaboard States, 1901-1915*, Atheneum, New York, 1968. The outpouring during the 1960s of publications about black history has not particularly stressed the history of education, but rather the history of literary expression. A very useful comparative study is Carl N. Degler, *Neither Black Nor White; Slavery and Race Relations in Brazil and the United States*, Macmillan, New York, 1971. Two volumes that deal especially with the integration-separation problem are Harold Cruse, *The Crisis of the Negro Intellectual*, Morrow, New York, 1967 and John H. Bracey, Jr. et al. (eds.), *Black Nationalism in America*, Bobbs-Merrill, Indianapolis, Ind., 1970.

Education of American Indians   General histories of American Indian education are even fewer than those about black education. Although the specialized literature is vast, it needs organization and interpretation such as that by Brewton Perry, *The Education of American Indians; a Survey of the Literature*, prepared for the Special Subcommittee on Indian Education of the Committee on Labor and Public Welfare, U.S. Senate, Government Printing Office, Washington, D.C., 1969. A good overall historical account which contains a good deal of information on education is William T. Hogan, *American Indians*, University of Chicago Press, Chicago, 1961. An important, somewhat more specialized, study that bears heavily on education is Hazel W. Hertzberg, *The Search for an Indian Identity; Modern Pan-Indian Movements*, Syracuse University Press, Syracuse, N.Y., 1971. Nineteenth-century attitudes of the founder of Carlisle Indian School can be viewed in Richard Henry Pratt, *Battlefield and Classroom: Four Decades with the American Indian, 1867-1904*, Yale University Press, New Haven, Conn., 1964.

Education of Spanish-Speaking Americans   General histories of Mexican-American education are the scarcest of those for any of the major minority groups. Beginnings were made by George I. Sanchez, *Concerning Segregation of Spanish Speaking Children in the Public Schools*, University of Texas Press, Austin, 1951 and Herschel T. Manuel, *Spanish Speaking Children of the Southwest; Their Education and the Public Welfare*, University of Texas Press, Austin, 1965. An important ideological framework is provided by Stan Steiner, *La Raza; the Mexican Americans*, Harper Colophon, New York, 1969. A useful historical framework for viewing education is given in Wayne Moquin et al. (eds.), *A Documentary History of the Mexican Americans*, Praeger, New York, 1971.

American Educational Thought   The ideology of traditional versus modern views of American educators can be traced in Merle Curti, *The Social Ideas of American Educators*, Littlefield, Adams, Totowa, N.J., 1966 and, especially for the humanists and intellectualists, R. Freeman Butts, *The College Charts Its Course*, McGraw-Hill, New York, 1939 (reissued by Arno Press, New York, 1972). The writings of key individuals and recent commentaries on them are dealt with in: Martin S. Dworkin (ed.), *William T. Harris on Education*, Teachers College Press, New York, forthcoming; Charles Strickland and Charles Burgess (eds.), *Health, Growth, and Heredity; G. Stanley Hall on Natural Education*, Teachers College Press, New York, 1965; Edward A. Krug (ed.), *Charles W. Eliot on Popular Education*, Teachers College Press, New York, 1961; Geraldine M. Joncich (ed.), *Psychology and the Science of Education; Selected Writings of Edward L. Thorndike*, Teachers College Press, New York, 1962.

Progressive Education   The modernization of educational programs, especially with the ideological and organizational underpinnings of progressive education, is treated comprehensively and discerningly in Lawrence A. Cremin, *The Transformation of the School; Progressivism in American Education, 1876-1957*, Knopf, New York, 1961; and, on more specific topics within a similar framework, is: Jack K. Campbell, *Colonel Francis W. Parker, the Children's Crusader*, Teachers College Press, New York, 1968; Sol Cohen, *Progressives and Urban School Reform; the Public Education Association of New York City, 1895-1954*, Teachers College Press, New York, 1964; and Patricia Albjerg Graham, *Progressive Education: From Arcady to Academe, a History of the Progressive Education Association*, Teachers College Press, New York, 1967.

Secondary and Higher Education   Among the many general historical studies of secondary, technical, higher, and professional education, the following are particularly useful for the modernization theme: Edward A. Krug, *The Shaping of the American High School*, Harper & Row, New York, 1964; Bernice M. Fisher, *Industrial Education: American Ideals and Institutions*, University of Wisconsin Press, Madison, 1967;

Frederick Rudolph, *The American College and University, a History,* Knopf, New York, 1962; Laurence R. Veysey, *The Emergence of the American University,* University of Chicago Press, Chicago, 1965; Walter Metzger, *The Development of Academic Freedom in the United States; The Age of the University,* Columbia University Press, New York, 1964; John S. Brubacher and Willis Rudy, *Higher Education in Transition; a History of American Colleges and Universities, 1636-1968,* rev. ed., Harper & Row, New York, 1968; Bernard Berelson, *Graduate Education in the United States,* McGraw-Hill, New York, 1960; Merle E. Borrowman (ed.), *Teacher Education in America; a Documentary History,* Teachers College Press, New York, 1965; and Merle E. Borrowman, *The Liberal and the Technical in Teacher Education; a Historical Survey of American Thought,* Teachers College Press, New York, 1956.

Contemporary sociological studies that call into question America's historic faith in popular education as a means for achieving social and economic equality are assayed in Frederick Mosteller and and Daniel Patrick Moynihan (eds.), *On Equality of Educational Opportunity,* Random House, New York, 1972 and Christopher Jencks et al., *Inequality: A Reassessment of the Effect of Family and Schooling in America,* Basic Books, New York, 1972.

CHAPTER XIV.
EDUCATION IN THE "CIVILIZING MISSION" OF THE WEST
(1700 A.D.-1860s A.D.)

The Transplantation of Western Education in European-oriented Overseas Societies
Discussions of the dispersion of Western education through the transplantation of essentially European societies to various parts of the world may be found in: Charles E. Phillips, *The Development of Education in Canada,* The Ryerson Press, Toronto, 1957; J. Donald Wilson et al. (eds.), *Canadian Education: A History,* Prentice-Hall, Scarborough, Ontario, 1970; A. G. Austin, *Australian Education, 1788-1900; Church, State, and Public Education in Colonial Australia,* Pitman, Melbourne, 1961; R. Freeman Butts, *Assumptions Underlying Australian Education,* Bureau of Publications, Teachers College, New York, 1955; John L. Ewing, *Origins of the New Zealand Primary School Curriculum, 1840-1878,* New Zealand Council for Educational Research, Wellington, 1960; Charles Henry Schutter, *The Development of Education in Argentina, Chile, and Uruguay,* University of Chicago, Department of Education, Chicago, 1943; Robert J. Havighurst and J. Roberto Moreira, *Society and Education in Brazil,* University of Pittsburgh Press, Pittsburgh, Pa., 1965; Shirley C. Gordon, *A Century of West Indian Education,* Longmans, London, 1963; and Juan J. Osuna, *A History of Education in Puerto Rico,* Editorial de la Universidad de Puerto Rico, Rio Piedras, 1949.

Western Education and Defensive Modernization of Non-European Societies Examples of the uses of education in defensive modernization may be found in: Herbert Passin, *Society and Education in Japan,* Teachers College Press, New York, 1965; Marius B. Jansen and Lawrence Stone, "Education and Modernization in Japan and England," *Comparative Studies in Society and History,* vol. 9, pp. 208-232, January 1967; R. P. Dore, *Education in Tokugawa Japan,* University of California Press, Berkeley and Los Angeles, 1965; R. P. Dore, "Education," in Robert E. Ward and Dankwart A. Rustow (eds.), *Political Modernization in Japan and Turkey,* Princeton University Press, Princeton, N.J., 1964, pp. 176-204; Ronald S. Anderson, *Japan:*

Three Epochs of Modern Education, U.S. Government Printing Office, Washington, D.C., 1959; Knight Biggerstaff, *The Earliest Modern Government Schools in China,* Cornell University Press, Ithaca, N.Y., 1961; Chang-tu Hu (ed.), *Chinese Education under Communism,* Bureau of Publications, Teachers College, New York, 1962; Stewart Fraser (ed.), *Chinese Communist Education; Records of the First Decade,* Vanderbilt University Press, Nashville, Tenn., 1965; Y. C. Wang, *Chinese Intellectuals and the West, 1872-1949,* University of North Carolina Press, Chapel Hill, 1966; Andreas M. Kazamias, *Education and the Quest for Modernity in Turkey,* University of Chicago Press, Chicago, 1966; David K. Wyatt, *The Politics of Reform in Thailand; Education in the Reign of King Chulalongkorn,* Yale University Press, New Haven, Conn., 1969; Vartan Gregorian, *The Emergence of Modern Afghanistan; Politics of Reform and Modernization 1880-1946,* Stanford University Press, Stanford, Calif., 1969; Robert L. Hess, *Ethiopia: The Modernization of Autocracy,* Cornell University Press, Ithaca, N.Y., 1970; Charles C. Cumberland, *Mexico, the Struggle for Modernity,* Oxford University Press, New York, 1968; George C. Booth, *Mexico's School Made Society,* Stanford University Press, Stanford, Calif., 1941; George I. Sanchez, *Mexico: A Revolution by Education,* Viking, New York, 1936; George F. Kneller, *The Education of the Mexican Nation,* Columbia University Press, New York, 1951; Charles Nash Myers, *Education and National Development in Mexico,* Industrial Relations Section, Department of Economics, Princeton University, Princeton, N.J., 1965; Richard R. Fagen, *The Transformation of Political Culture in Cuba,* Stanford University Press, Stanford, Calif., 1969; and William W. Brickman (ed.), *John Dewey, Impressions of Soviet Russia and the Revolutionary World—Mexico, China, Turkey,* Bureau of Publications, Teachers College, New York, 1964.

Education and the Civilizing Mission   I know of no single comprehensive study of the civilizing mission as a worldwide educational force. It is a particularly fertile field for historical research. Inevitably it must be linked with Christian missionizing on one side and Western imperialism on the other. Particularly useful studies are D. K. Fieldhouse, *The Colonial Empires; a Comparative Survey from the Eighteenth Century,* Delacorte Press, and Philip D. Curtin, *The Image of Africa; British Ideas and Action, 1780-1850,* University of Wisconsin Press, Madison, 1964. An especially germinal study that links the two forces with education is Charles H. Lyons, *"To Wash an Aethiop White": British Ideas about Black African Educability, 1530-1960,* Teachers College Press, New York, 1973. The story of the British educational mission in various parts of the world is contained in Brian Holmes (ed.), *Educational Policy and the Mission Schools; Case Studies from the British Empire,* Routledge, London, 1967. A special case is personalized in Jonathan Spence, *To Change China; Western Advisers in China, 1620-1960,* Little, Brown, Boston, 1969. The worldwide spread of Anglican missions is detailed in Henry P. Thompson, *Into All Lands: The History of the Society for the Propagation of the Gospel in Foreign Parts, 1701-1950,* Society for Promoting Christian Knowledge, London, 1951 and in Hans Cnattingius, *Bishops and Societies: A Study of Anglican Colonial and Missionary Expansion, 1698-1850,* Society for Promoting Christian Knowledge, London, 1952.

Educating Africans in Africa   Civilizing the black African through education in his homeland is illustrated not only in Lyons, but also in: D. L. Summer, *Education in*

Sierra Leone, Government of Sierra Leone, Freetown, 1963; J. F. Ade Ajayi, *Christian Missions in Nigeria, 1841-1891; The Making of a New Elite,* Northwestern University Press, Evanston, Ill., 1965; Harris W. Mobley, *The Ghanaians' Image of the Missionary; an Analysis of the Published Critiques of Christian Missionaries by Ghanaians,* Brill, Leiden, Netherlands, 1970; the early chapters in Philip J. Foster, *Education and Social Change in Ghana,* University of Chicago Press, Chicago, 1965; David B. Abernethy, *The Political Dilemma of Popular Education; an African* [Nigerian] *Case,* Stanford University Press, Stanford, Calif., 1969; and Philip D. Curtin (ed.), *Africa and the West; Intellectual Responses to European Culture,* University of Wisconsin Press, Madison, 1972.

Educating Indians in India   The early British educational effort in India is described in: Bruce McCully, *English Education and the Origins of Indian Nationalism,* Columbia University Press, New York, 1940, (reprinted by Peter Smith, Gloucester, Mass., 1966); Syed Nurullah and J. P. Naik, *A Students' History of Education in India (1800-1965),* rev. ed., Macmillan, Bombay, 1971; Eric Ashby and Mary Anderson, *Universities, British, Indian, African; a Study in the Ecology of Higher Education,* Harvard University Press, Cambridge, Mass., 1966; and S. N. Mukerji, *The History of Education in India, Modern Period,* 5th ed., Acharya Book Depot, Baroda, 1966.

Educating Africans in America   For the civilizing as well as the uncivilized treatment of black Africans in the Americas see David Brion Davis, *The Problem of Slavery in Western Culture,* Cornell University Press, Ithaca, N.Y., 1966 and Winthrop Jordan, *White over Black, American Attitudes toward the Negro, 1550-1812,* University of North Carolina Press, Chapel Hill, 1968. For slavery in North America see Kenneth H. Stampp, *The Peculiar Institution: Slavery in the Ante-Bellum South,* Vintage, New York, 1956 and Stanley Elkins, *Slavery, a Problem in American Institutional and Intellectual Life,* University of Chicago Press, Chicago, 1959. For the education of Negro slaves and freedmen, see: Marcus W. Jernegan, *Laboring and Dependent Classes in Colonial America, 1607-1783,* University of Chicago Press, Chicago, 1931; Carter G. Woodson, *The Education of the Negro Prior to 1861: A History of the Education of the Colored People of the United States from the Beginning of Slavery to the Civil War,* Arno Press, New York, 1968; and Henry Allen Bullock, *A History of Negro Education in the South from 1619 to the Present,* Harvard University Press, Cambridge, Mass., 1967.

Educating Indians in America   The attempts to "civilize" the American Indian through education have not yet received full-scale treatment in published form. A useful essay and bibliography, including missions and education, is contained in William N. Fenton, *American Indian and White Relations to 1830; Needs and Opportunities for Study,* Russell and Russell, New York, 1957. For a general study that does not deal particularly with education see Roy Harvey Pearce, *The Savages of America: A Study of the Indian and the Idea of Civilization,* Johns Hopkins University Press, Baltimore, Md., 1965. For a specialized study that does deal with education, see John Calam, *Parsons and Pedagogues: The S.P.G. Adventure in American Education,* Columbia University Press, New York, 1971.

CHAPTER XV.
EDUCATION AND WESTERN IMPERIALISM
(1860s A.D.-THE PRESENT)

The Ideology and Practice of Imperialism   For important post-Marxist-Leninist analyses of imperialism, see such illuminating essays as those by: Richard Koebner and Helmut Dan Schmidt, *Imperialism: The Story and Significance of a Political Word, 1840-1960,* Cambridge University Press, London, 1965; A. P. Thornton, *Doctrines of Imperialism,* Wiley, New York, 1965; George Lichtheim, *Imperialism,* Praeger, New York, 1971; and Philip D. Curtin (ed.), *Imperialism,* Harper & Row, New York, 1971. For studies that range over several areas of the world see: D. K. Fieldhouse, *The Colonial Empires; a Comparative Study from the Eighteenth Century,* Delacorte Press, New York, 1967; Stewart C. Easton, *The Rise and Fall of Western Colonialism; a Historical Survey from the Early Nineteenth Century to the Present,* Praeger, New York, 1964; and Albert Memmi, *The Colonizer and the Colonized,* Beacon Press, Boston, 1965.

For studies of imperialism in specific parts of the world see: *Colonialism in Africa,* vol. 1, *The History and Politics of Colonialism, 1870-1914,* vol. 2, *The History and Politics of Colonialism, 1914-1960,* L. H. Gann and Peter Duignan (eds.), and vol. 3, *Profiles of Change: African Society and Colonial Rule,* Victor Turner (ed.), Cambridge University Press, London, 1969; Ronald Robinson et al., *Africa and the Victorians; the Climax of Imperialism,* Anchor Books, Garden City, N.Y., 1968; Christine Bolt, *Victorian Attitudes to Race,* Routledge, London, 1971; John K. Fairbank, Edwin O. Reischauer, and Albert M. Craig, *A History of East Asian Civilization,* vol. 2, *The Modern Transformation,* Houghton Mifflin, Boston, 1965; Edward Allworth, *Central Asia: A Century of Russian Rule,* Columbia University Press, New York, 1967; David Healy, *United States Expansionism: The Imperialist Urge in the 1890's,* University of Wisconsin Press, Madison, 1970; E. Berkeley Tompkins, *Anti-Imperialism in the United States, the Great Debate, 1890-1920,* University of Pennsylvania Press, Philadelphia, 1970; and Gordon K. Lewis, *Puerto Rico: Freedom and Power in the Caribbean,* Harper & Row, New York, 1968.

The Retreat from Imperialism and the Decolonization of Education   The decline of imperialism is stressed in: C. E. Black, *The Dynamics of Modernization; a Study in Comparative History,* Harper & Row, New York, 1966; Rupert Emerson, *From Empire to Nation; the Rise to Self-Assertion of Asian and African Peoples,* Beacon Press, Boston, 1960; Hans Kohn, *The Age of Nationalism; the First Era of Global History,* Harper Torchbooks, New York, 1962; Gunnar Myrdal, *Asian Drama; an Inquiry into the Poverty of Nations,* 3 vols., Random House, New York, 1968; Fritz Fanon, *A Dying Colonialism,* Grove, New York, 1965; Richard B. Morris, *The Emerging Nations and the American Revolution,* Harper & Row, New York, 1970; David C. Gordon, *Self-Determination and History in the Third World,* Princeton University Press, Princeton, N.J., 1971; Guy Hunter, *Modernizing Peasant Societies; a Comparative Study in Asia and Africa,* Oxford University Press, New York, 1969; Henry Wells, *The Modernization of Puerto Rico; a Political Study of Changing Values and Institutions,* Harvard University Press, Cambridge, Mass., 1969; and "Decolonization and Education," *Comparative Education Review,* vol. 15, no. 3, pp. 276-316, October 1971.

Western Education and Modernization in the New Nations Books that deal with education in a number of newly independent countries aspiring to modernization include the following: Don Adams and Robert M. Bjork, *Education in Developing Areas,* McKay, New York, 1969; James S. Coleman (ed.), *Education and Political Development,* Princeton University Press, Princeton, N.J., 1965; C. Arnold Anderson and Mary Jean Bowman (eds.), *Education and Economic Development,* Aldine, Chicago, 1965; Peter Hackett (ed.), *Problems of Educational Development and Modernization in Asia,* University of Virginia, Charlottesville, 1972; Frederick Harbison and Charles A. Myers, *Education, Manpower, and Economic Growth; Strategies of Human Resource Development,* McGraw-Hill, New York, 1964; Frederick Harbison and Charles A. Myers (eds.), *Manpower and Education: Country Studies in Economic Development,* McGraw-Hill, New York, 1965; David C. Gordon, *The Passing of French Algeria,* Oxford University Press, London, 1966; John Hanson and Cole S. Brembeck (eds.), *Education and the Development of Nations,* Holt, New York, 1966; Andreas Kazamias and Byron G. Massialas, *Tradition and Change in Education; a Comparative Study,* Prentice-Hall, Englewood Cliffs, N.J., 1965; Don Adams, *Education and Modernization in Asia,* Addison-Wesley, Reading, Mass., 1970; Economic Commission for Latin America, *Education, Human Resources and Development in Latin America,* United Nations, New York, 1968; Andreas Kazamias and Erwin H. Epstein (eds.), *Schools in Transition; Essays in Comparative Education,* Allyn and Bacon, Boston, 1968; A. B. Shah (ed.), *Education, Scientific Policy, and Developing Societies,* Manaktalas, Bombay, 1967; I. N. Thut and Don Adams, *Educational Patterns in Contemporary Societies,* McGraw-Hill, New York, 1964; Kalil I. Gezi (ed.), *Education in Comparative and International Perspective,* Holt, New York, 1971; Don Adams (ed.), *Education in National Development,* McKay, New York, 1971; and a special issue with an annotated bibliography on "Colonialism and Education," *Comparative Education Review,* vol. 15, no. 2, June 1971.

There is a vast literature on the role of education in foreign aid programs and technical assistance to developing nations. For a beginning see: Merle Curti and Kendall Birr, *Prelude to Point Four; American Technical Missions Overseas, 1838-1938,* University of Wisconsin Press, Madison, 1954; Harlan Cleveland, Gerard J. Mangone, and John Clarke Adams, *The Overseas Americans,* McGraw-Hill, New York, 1960; Edward H. Weidner, *The World Role of Universities,* McGraw-Hill, New York, 1962; R. Freeman Butts, *American Education in International Development,* Harper & Row, New York, 1963; William Y. Elliott (ed.), *Education and Training in the Developing Countries; the Role of U.S. Foreign Aid,* Praeger, New York, 1966; David G. Scanlon and James J. Shields (eds.), *Problems and Prospects in International Education,* Teachers College Press, New York, 1968; and Harold G. Shane (ed.), *The United States and International Education,* Sixty-eighth Yearbook of the National Society for the Study of Education, University of Chicago Press, Chicago, 1969.

Education in Southern Asia Recent studies dealing with the subcontinent are: Susanne and Lloyd Rudolph (eds.), *Education and Politics in India,* Harvard University Press, Cambridge, Mass., 1972; S. S. Dikshit, *Nationalism and Indian Education,* Sterling Publishers, Delhi, 1966; Philip G. Altbach (ed.), *Turmoil and Transition: Higher Education and Student Politics in India,* Basic Books, New York, 1969; Edward Shils, "The Indian Academic," *Minerva,* vol. 7, pp. 345-372, Spring 1969; A. B. Shah (ed.), *The Great Debate; Language Controversy and University Education,* Lalvani Publishing

House, Bombay, 1968; Percival Spear, *India, Pakistan, and the West,* 4th ed., Oxford University Press, New York, 1967; Anil Seal, *The Emergence of Indian Nationalism; Competition and Collaboration in the Later Nineteenth Century,* Cambridge University Press, London, 1968; John A. Laska, *Planning and Educational Development in India,* Teachers College Press, New York, 1968; K. L. Shrimali, *The Prospects for Democracy in India,* Southern Illinois University Press, Carbondale, 1970; Adam Curle, *Planning for Education in Pakistan,* Harvard University Press, Cambridge, Mass., 1966; Edward Shils, *The Intellectual Between Tradition and Modernity: The Indian Situation,* Mouton, The Hague, 1961; and Eric Ashby and Mary Anderson, *Universities, British, Indian, and African; a Study in the Ecology of Higher Education,* Harvard University Press, Cambridge, Mass., 1966.

Education in Africa   Recent studies that concentrate on Africa are: David G. Scanlon (ed.), *Traditions in African Education,* Bureau of Publications, Teachers College, New York, 1964; David G. Scanlon (ed.), *Church, State, and Education in Africa,* Teachers College Press, New York, 1966; Eric Ashby, *African Universities and Western Tradition,* Harvard University Press, Cambridge, Mass., 1964; A. Babs Fafunwa, *A History of Nigerian Higher Education,* Macmillan, Lagos, Nigeria, 1971; L. J. Lewis, *Education and Political Independence in Africa,* Nelson, Edinburgh, 1962; John Wilson, *Education and Changing West African Culture,* Bureau of Publications, Teachers College, New York, 1963; John Cameron, *The Development of Education in East Africa,* Teachers College Press, New York, 1970; Remi Clignet and Philip J. Foster, *The Fortunate Few; a Study of Secondary Schools and Students in the Ivory Coast,* Northwestern University Press, Evanston, Ill., 1966; Philip J. Foster, *Education and Social Change in Ghana,* University of Chicago Press, Chicago, 1965; David B. Abernethy, *The Political Dilemma of Popular Education; an African Case,* Stanford University Press, Stanford, Calif., 1969; Mohammed Omer Beshir, *Educational Development in the Sudan, 1898-1956,* Oxford University Press, New York, 1970; Abdou Moumoni, *Education in Africa,* Praeger, New York, 1968; Kenneth James King, *Pan-Africanism and Education; a Study of Race, Philanthropy and Education in the Southern States of America and East Africa,* Clarendon Press, Oxford, 1971; and Vincent M. Battle and Charles H. Lyons (eds.), *Essays in the History of African Education,* Teachers College Press, New York, 1970. The last book in this list is particularly significant to me. It represents research studies undertaken by young American scholars in the course of their doctoral candidacies. The future of the writing of educational history is in exceptionally good hands.

EPILOGUE:
THE PROMISE OF THE EDUCATION OF THE WEST

For a sample of studies that view the future with varying degrees of optimism or pessimism, see: Herman Kahn and Anthony J. Wiener, *The Year 2000: A Framework for Speculation on the Next Thirty-Three Years,* Macmillan, New York, 1967; Kenneth E. Boulding, *The Meaning of the 20th Century; The Great Transition,* Colophon Books, New York, 1964; Peter F. Drucker, *Landmarks of Tomorrow; a Report on the New "Post-Modern" World,* Colophon Books, New York, 1965; Amitai Etzioni, *The Active Society; a Theory of Societal and Political Processes,* Free Press, New York,

1968; John K. Galbraith, *The New Industrial State*, Houghton Mifflin, Boston, 1967; K. J. Holsti, *International Politics; a Framework for Analysis*, Prentice-Hall, Englewood Cliffs, N.J., 1967; Robert C. Angell, "The Growth of Trans-National Participation," *Journal of Social Issues*, vol. 23, pp. 108-129, 1967; Zbigniew Brzezinski, *Between Two Ages: America's Role in the Technetonic Age*, Viking, New York, 1970; and Daniel Bell, "Toward the Year 2000: Work in Progress," *Daedalus*, vol. 96, no. 3, Proceedings of the American Academy of Arts and Sciences, Summer, 1967.

Some observers believe that the future of civilization requires a rational approach to development on a worldwide scale. For elaboration of this view see Lester B. Pearson et al., *Partners in Development; Report of the Commission on International Development*, Praeger, New York, 1969; Barbara Ward, J. D. Runnalls, and Lenore d'Anjou (eds.), *The Widening Gap: Development in the 1970's*, Columbia University Press, New York, 1971; Edgar Faure et al., *Learning to Be; the World of Education Today and Tomorrow*, UNESCO, Paris and Harrap, London, 1972; and Barbara Ward and René Dubos, *Only One Earth; the Care and Maintenance of a Small Planet*, Norton, New York, 1972. Other observers believe that continuing stress on growth and development will destroy civilization. For discussion of this view see: Donella H. Meadows, Dennis L. Meadows, Jorgen Randers, and William W. Behrens III, *The Limits to Growth; a Report for the Club of Rome's Project on the Predicament of Mankind*, Universe Books, New York, 1972; Barry Commoner, *The Closing Circle*, Knopf, New York, 1971; and a special issue, "A Blueprint for Survival," *The Ecologist*, vol. 2, no. 1, pp. 1-44, January 1972. A more relaxed and optimistic note is struck by John Maddox, *The Doomsday Syndrome*, Macmillan, London, 1972.

AUTHOR INDEX

INDEX

Abbott, Jacob (1803-1879), 422, 423
Abelard, Peter (1079-1142), 155, 168, 169, 172, 174, 176, 202
Aberdeen, University of, 257, 346, 394, 420
Abitur, 362, 386
Abolitionism, 490, 492-493, 499, 500, 501, 509, 513
Academic freedom, 348, 355, 359, 379, 386, 388
Academies, 322, 344, 411, 414-418, 430, 476
   of Florence, 197
   Franklin's, 412, 416, 417
   of Geneva, 257
   of Plato, 99-101, 109
   of Science in Paris, 197, 419
   of Sciences in St. Petersburg, 365
   (*See also* Dissenters' Academies)
Acclahuasi, 239
Accountability, 397
Achievement-oriented pedagogy, 54, 59-65, 71-72, 238, 300, 302, 320, 327-328, 336, 345, 356, 358, 369, 371, 385, 386, 392, 394-401, 425-433, 444, 456, 468, 472-479, 556-561, 568
Achimota school, 541
Adams, John (1735-1826), 303, 407, 426
Adaptation, policy of, 532-535, 547, 548
Adult education, 247, 274, 311, 314, 375, 380, 389, 394, 431-432
Aegean civilization, 7, 30, 36, 48, 49, 54, 60, 63, 65, 73-77
Aesop (*c.* 620-560 B.C.), 88, 222, 255, 259, 289
Afghanistan, 11, 484, 555
Africa:
   East, 10, 20, 535
   North, 87, 137, 147, 149, 173, 520
   West, 490, 495, 499, 500, 508, 527, 533-535, 551
African Company of Merchants, 495
African Institution (1807), 500
Afro-Americans, 249, 276, 279, 317, 509-515
   (*See also* Blacks, Negroes)
Agricola, Rodolphus (1443-1485), 205, 255, 261, 263

Agriculture:
   development of, 10, 24-25, 132, 157, 318, 330, 546
   teaching of, 46, 59, 111, 132-133, 153, 216, 247, 252, 272, 278, 350, 354, 360, 368, 386, 389, 414, 416, 421, 424, 438, 464, 476, 478, 497, 499, 514, 523, 533, 546-548, 553-555
Akkadian language, 44-51, 74
Akkadians, 38, 44, 45, 50, 51, 517
Alabama, University of, 459
Albertus Magnus (1193?-1280), 173
Albuquerque, Alfonso de (1453-1515), 229
Albuquerque, Bishop Joao de, 230
Alcalá de Henares, University of, 245, 249
Alcuin (735-804), 149-151, 155
Aldheim, Saint (*c.* 640-709), 149
Alexander the Great (356-323 B.C.), 73, 91, 100, 104, 105, 114, 134
Alexander I of Russia (1777-1825), 365-366
Alexander II of Russia (1818-1881), 378, 379
Alexander III of Russia (1845-1894), 379
Alexander VI, Pope (1431?-1503), 228, 243
Alexander of Hales (d. 1245), 173
Alexandria, 104, 105, 109, 111, 112, 123, 131, 132, 147
Alfred the Great (849-899), 151
Algebra, teaching of, 46, 148
Alphabetic writing, 40-41, 48-51, 61, 83-84
Alsted, Johann Heinrich (1588-1638), 290
Ambrose, Saint (340?-397), 135
American Board of Commissioners for Foreign Missions (1810), 490
American Indian Chicago Conference, 465
American Institute of Instruction (1830), 431
American Missionary Association, 514
American Missionary Society, 453
American Philosophical Society, 405
Amerindian languages, 222, 227, 230, 244, 246-250, 278
Amerindians, 233-238, 240-250, 278, 444, 450, 467, 486, 489
   (*See also* Indians, American)
Amherst College, 422
Amish, 450